Commander, Troop "F"; Major Bradley G. Hibbard, Troop Commander, Troop "C"; Major Albert A. Simon, Division of Field Ser-vices, Community Policing; Major John A. Burns, Executive office, Division of Investigative Services Major John DiFava, Troop Commander Troop "H"; Major Robert J. Mullin, Bureau of Professional Standards. This is the Command Staff that will lead the Massachusetts State Police into the 21st century.

ENFORCEMENT ODYSSEY

The Massachusetts State Police

A History

TURNER PUBLISHING COMPANY
Paducah, Kentucky

TURNER PUBLISHING COMPANY

Publishers of America's History
412 Broadway•P.O. Box 3101
Paducah, Kentucky 42002-3101
(502) 443-0121

Publishing Consultant: Keith Steele
Project Coordinator: John Mark Jackson
Designer: David Hurst

Library of Congress Catalog No. 97-61567
ISBN: 1-56311-388-0
Second Printing 1999
Third Printing 2000
LIMITED EDITION
Printed in the U.S.A.

Photo below: General Headquarters, Boston, August, 1926 The State Police Equestrian Team. L to R kneeling: Pat. Richard Cotter, Cpl. James Ryan, Cpl. Harold McGinness, Pat. P. A. Whelan. Standing: Pat. J. J. Powers, 1st Sgt. James Hughes, Pat. John McLaughlin, Capt. Charles Beaupre (civ. clothes), Howard Read, Pat. Hollis Beattie, Pat. Geo Thompson, Dr. Edward T. Ryan (civ. clothes), Pat. Desmond Fitzgerald, Sgt. John Reardon and Pat. Andrew Tuney, Commissioner. Alfred E. Foote (seated, civ. clothes) holds trophy team won for mounted cavalry and infantry drills at the 1926 Philadelphia Sesqui-Centennial. Horses from 1921 until 1933 were a mainstay of state police field operations as well as ceremonial assignments.

CONTENTS

PUBLISHER'S MESSAGE

It has been a privilege to work with the author, William F. Powers, on this historic volume devoted to the remarkable history of the Massachusetts State Police. The author's dedicated effort has produced an outstanding new tribute to the Massachusetts State Police.

Our sincere appreciation goes to both the author and his wife, Lois, who shared our enthusiasm for this much needed commemorative volume. Special thanks also goes to the current Massachusetts State Police Department, the former Massachusetts State Troopers Association (FMSTA), the State Police Association of Massachusetts (SPAM), and to Major (Ret.) Johnny Hughes of the Maryland State Police who helped introduce the author to Turner Publishing.

In keeping with our commitment to preserve America's history, we are honored to add *"Enforcement Odyssey - The Massachusetts State Police"* to our list of law enforcement titles. This volume joins ranks with *"To Serve and Protect"* (National Law Enforcement Officers Memorial), *"Oklahoma Justice"*, (Oklahoma City Police), *"Baltimore City Police"*, *"Former Special Agents of the FBI"*, Utah Highway Patrol, *"Orange County (FL) Sheriff's Department"*, *"Forgotten Heroes - Police Officers Slain in Dade County, Florida"*, and hundreds of other county and military titles nationwide.

Turner Publishing salutes those who choose to serve their state and their country even though their lives are put at risk. We now proudly present to the current and former personnel of the Massachusetts State Police, this commemorative volume, *"Enforcement Odyssey."*

Keith Steele, Publishing Consultant
Turner Publishing Company

Dave Turner, President
Turner Publishing Company

PREFACE

With *Enforcement Odyssey*, former trooper William F. Powers completes his trilogy on the founding, evolution and modernization of the Massachusetts State Police. Inspired by his department's fascinating history, he began this three-decade project with 1965's *One Hundred Year Vigil*. That volume marked the centennial of the 1865 founding of the Massachusetts State Constabulary, the nation's first statewide enforcement agency. Building on that base, the author in 1979 wrote *French and Electric Blue*. *French* was focused by the 1921 beginnings of the State Police Patrol, the famed uniformed troopers, tracing their remarkable enforcement journey through six defining decades. Now, almost twenty years after that volume, Powers completes the enforcement trilogy with this insightful retrospective largely inspired by the 75th anniversary in 1996 of the Commonwealth's widely admired state force.

Odyssey builds on the historical developments described in the earlier volumes. This is especially true of *French and Electric Blue*. *French* has been out of print since 1981. Surprisingly, however, reader interest in that volume has increased with the passing years. Moreover, the prospective audience is much, much larger today than when *French* was published in June, 1979, almost 20 years ago.

Hundreds of current state police officers have never seen the prior volumes. Many have never heard of them. Time's passage will do that. For those reasons, and to preserve the historical record, the core chapters of *French*, spanning the state force's first six decades, are preserved in this work.

But much that is new brightens *Odyssey's* pages. Historical images are frozen in time and place by some 250 new photographs. Each has been placed in its original historical context, with precise personnel identifications and informative annotations. Earlier readers will appreciate that another 250 photographs from the prior volumes are preserved in the pictorial appendix. These will be, for readers old and new, visual reminders of time's inexorable effect on men and the institutions they create to rationalize a society's ongoing evolution.

Odyssey proceeds with a pictorial representation of the department's last 20 years, featuring the social and institutional currents that helped shape the contemporary organization. The enduring images necessarily review the celebratory events in 1996 commemorating the 75th anniversary of the 1921 founding of the rural, uniformed force.

The reader will find interesting the precise listing of the 73 Recruit Training Troops that have graduated from the Massachusetts State Police Academy since 1921. With measured poignancy, *Odyssey* also reminds us of law enforcement's inherent dangers by memorializing each officer killed in the line of duty during the past 75 years.

This final volume in the historical trilogy appropriately begins with *The Millennium Visible*. An essay penned in the 20th Century's final hours, *Millennium* is energized by the promise of those chosen to confront the limitless possibilities of the Third Epoch as law enforcement officers. Such an essay seems a fitting introduction to an enforcement odyssey largely influenced by time's relentless effect on men and the enforcement organizations they build in response to the ever-evolving challenges inherent in the human condition.

State Police General Headquarters, Boston, 1963. As a lieutenant, the author was public affairs director for the Massachusetts State Police and adjunct instructor at the State Police Academy.

ABOUT THE AUTHOR

William F. Powers in 1949 graduated from the Massachusetts State Police Academy following World War II naval service in the Asiatic-Pacific Campaign. First posted to Troop C Holden, he later served at several field barracks throughout southeastern Massachusetts.

The author in 1957 graduated from Northwestern University's famed Traffic Institute as a Kemper Fellow. Assigned to General Headquarters in Boston, he served in the Traffic Bureau, directed statewide public affairs activities, was an adjunct instructor at the state police academy in Framingham, rose to the captain's rank.

Governor Francis W. Sargent in 1969 appointed the former trooper as Massachusetts' Commissioner of Public Safety and head of the Massachusetts State Police. The appointment marked the first time since the 1921 founding of the state police that a uniformed officer had been elevated directly to the department's top office.

Following a 1971 appointment as the U. S. Justice Department's New England Regional Administrator for the Law Enforcement Assistance Administration, Powers in 1977 was the founding director of the federal National Public Safety Officers' Benefits Program (PSOB) in Washington D. C. As national director of PSOB until his 1994 retirement, the former trooper authorized approximately $300 million in death benefits for some 3,500 families of police officers and firefighters killed in the line of duty throughout the nation.

Powers in 1963 was the first police officer to matriculate in Boston University's College of Communication. In 1968, as a state police captain, he earned that school's bachelor of science, magna cum laude. Selected as a U. S. Justice Department Graduate Fellow, he later received the master of public administration from the John Jay College of Criminal Justice, and in 1982 was awarded the doctorate in public administration by Nova-Southeastern University's Washington, D. C., Public Policy Center. In 1988, he was selected as a Distinguished Alumnus by Boston University's College of Communication, and in 1994 received the same honor from Fall River's B. M. C. Durfee High School.

The author in 1954 married Lois V. Grover of Swansea in Fall River's Church of the Sacred Heart. Three sons and two daughters were born of their marriage. Mrs. Powers is a 1952 graduate of the Truesdale Hospital School of Nursing, and in 1978 earned the bachelor of arts from Boston's Emmanuel College. The family home is in Leesburg, Virginia.

AUTHOR'S FOREWORD

Enforcement Odyssey completes my efforts to help preserve the history of the Massachusetts State Police. I began this project more than three decades ago, with 1965's One Hundred Year Vigil. That modest beginning marked the centennial of the 1865 founding of the Massachusetts State Constabulary, the nation's first statewide enforcement agency. Building on that effort, in 1979 I wrote *French and Electric Blue*. French was inspired by the 1921 founding of the State Police Patrol, the famed uniformed troopers, tracing their remarkable enforcement journey through six defining decades. Twenty years after that volume, Odyssey completes my efforts to leave a historical record of one of the nation's most admired enforcement organizations.

Odyssey builds on the historical developments described in French and Electric Blue. French has been out of print since 1981. Surprisingly, however, reader interest in that volume has increased with the passing years. Moreover, the prospective audience is much, much larger today than when French was published in 1979, almost 20 years ago.

Hundreds of current state police officers have never seen the prior volumes. Many have never heard of them. Time's passage will do that. For those reasons, and to preserve the historical record, the core chapters of French, spanning the state force's first six decades, are the foundation of this work.

But much that is new brightens *Odyssey's* pages. Historical images are frozen in time and place by some 250 new photographs. Each has been placed in its original historical context, with precise personnel identifications and informative annotations. Earlier readers will appreciate that another 250 photographs from the prior volumes are preserved in the pictorial appendix. These will be, for readers old and new, visual reminders of time's inexorable effect on men and the institutions they create to rationalize a society's ongoing evolution.

Odyssey proceeds with a pictorial representation of the department's last 20 years, featuring the social and institutional currents that helped shape the contemporary organization. The enduring images necessarily review the celebratory events in 1996 commemorating the 75th anniversary of the 1921 founding of the rural, uniformed force.

I believe the reader will find informative the precise listings of the 73 Recruit Training Troops that have graduated from the Massachusetts State Police Academy since 1921. With measured poignancy *Odyssey* also reminds us of law enforcement's inherent dangers by memorializing each officer killed in the line of duty during the lengthening enforcement journey.

Following a prologue, I have begun this volume with The Millennium Visible. An essay penned in the 20th Century's final hours, Millennium was energized by the promise of those chosen to confront the limitless possibilities of the Third Epoch as law enforcement officers. Such an essay seems a fitting way to begin an odyssey largely influenced by time's relentless effect on the enforcement organizations men build in response to the challenges inherent in the human condition.

Acknowledgments

There is no way here to give credit to all those who made this volume possible. One shortly would exhaust the time, space and energy that effort would require. Needless to say, scores of people provided their remembrances of events long since past. Others loaned their treasured photographs, sharing the historical images that bring alive key junctures in the enforcement journey. In a word, this volume itself represents the end result of the willingness by so many people to see a complex project through to its completion. One hopes that this volume's publication will sufficiently reward those who made that outcome possible with their ready support.

Westwood, Massachusetts, August 1969. The Powers family. Left to right, Bill 13, the author, Caroline 4, Chris 8, Lois, Beth Ann 10. A third son, Kevin, was born a week after this photo was taken. Governor Francis W. Sargent that day had announced Captain Powers' appointment as state Commissioner of Public Safety and head of the Massachusetts State Police.

Inevitably, there are several key people without whom this effort would have long since foundered. These are the special few who made Odyssey a reality.

One begins with Troopers Robert H. Leverone and Robert S. Muto. Each wrote to me early on urging a sequel to French and Electric Blue. My initial reaction to avoid such a formidable task dissolved in the presence of their enthusiasm. Moreover, they pitched in with both their time and talents. Those are considerable. Each pinned an essay which brightens these pages, preserving first person accounts of key organizational junctures. Needless to say, they will always have my gratitude for their important contributions.

Right at the center of things as well were Lieutenant Edward J. Montague and Sergeant Barbara J. Bennett. These were the two "generalists" who coordinated the multiple research initiatives essential to this entire undertaking. Both were there for me from beginning to end. I couldn't have done it without them, and I shall always appreciate their timely responses no matter the difficulty of my request.

There often is a "first among equals." With the fact of Odyssey's publication, that individual necessarily must be Trooper John F. Crane. A member of 1993's 71st Recruit Troop, Crane early on volunteered to help in any way he could. Sensing the sincerity of his offer, I gave him the most challenging assignment: identify the photographs that would tell the story of the 1980's and 1990's decades, the modern era of the state force. The task included certifying precise information for each picture: date, location, careful identification of each person in a photo, and informative annotations that would bring the pictures alive. Having done a fair number of these over the years, I knew what a complex challenge I had set for the young enforcement officer.

Trooper Crane responded with an effort that far exceeded my expectations. In a relatively short period of time he identified, captioned and annotated almost 100 historical images for the most recent two decades of the enforcement journey. I am certain the reader will appreciate, as I do, the personal commitment and skills that made such a professional effort possible. Put differently, without Trooper John F. Crane, Enforcement Odyssey would have fallen short of whatever contributions it makes to the remarkable historical record of the state force.

Mr. Mark C. Ide provided a number of the photographs that Trooper Crane identified for this volume. A professional photo journalist, Ide has had a long association with the state force, capturing graphic operational photos of recruits somehow weathering the academy experience. Mark Ide's skills were crucial to the development of this volume. For his professional contributions, he richly deserves our enduring gratitude.

Finally, I want to thank two special people for somehow getting me to this point: Nancy Beachley and my wife Lois. Nancy's computer skills and sunny disposition were key ingredients in this entire effort. Enforcement Odyssey would not have seen the light of day without Nancy Beachley. She was right there at all the critical junctures, her skills and quiet encouragement more than once saving the day. For all that, and especially for her friendship, I'll always be grateful that a fateful meeting on a Maryland farm brought Nancy Beachley into the history of the Massachusetts State Police and its fascinating enforcement journey. That was a lucky day.

I was lucky, too, that my wife Lois once again was at my side each step of the way. Believe me, I couldn't have done it without her. It simply would not have happened.

In 1979 I wrote: "I want to thank my wife, Lois, for her tireless efforts on this book. The work was truly a family affair. Her editorial skills were essential. Her typing of the manuscript a demanding task. Her encouragement the steadying force at difficult, complex junctures." It is difficult to top that, but I want to try. But for Lois, this work, at this time, never would have gotten off the ground, would have bogged down in fretful anxiety if it had, and, with certainty, would have found its way onto the expanding list of things to be done in the presence of shortened time horizons and receding energy levels.

That brings me to a final personal note. Rather than ponder over the choice of a profound, memorable message, I am persuaded that what I had written in this space for French two decades ago is more relevant now than it was back then:
"... It is hoped that this work enables others to sense the importance of the past for an understanding of the present. That would be a large reward. Moreover, it would help compensate for once having had the privilege of wearing the distinctive French and electric blue.

While time has dimmed the focus of that immensely rewarding experience, it shall remain always the most closely held of personal remembrances."
W. F. P.
Leesburg, Virginia
Winter, 1998

Senate Chamber, State Capitol, September 25, 1969. The author with his family immediately before being sworn as State Police Commissioner by Governor Francis W. Sargent. Left to right, standing, Beth Ann, Bill, and Chris. Seated, the author's wife Lois, and his late parents Mr. and Mrs. Francis M. Powers.

When Time who steals your years away
Shall Steal your pleasures too
Then memories of the past will stay
And half your joys renew
Moore

PROLOGUE

This book's predecessor volume *French and Electric Blue* was published in 1979 with a colorful program at the Massachusetts State Police Academy in Framingham. Sergeant (Ret.) Theodore J. Stavredes and Major (Ret.) Francis T. Burke made that important historical juncture possible. Their contributions were essential. It could not have been done without them.

That earlier volume noted that "Stavredes and several others in 1949 founded the Former Massachusetts State Troopers Association. In 1954, he began the (Former Trooper's) Newsletter, a monthly communication to members where he authored brief accounts of events long since lost to time's effect upon men and their institutions." Those remembrances were critical. They were the fulcrum from which French progressed through six decades of public service. In a word, there would not have been a state police history called French and Electric Blue without Sergeant (Ret.) Theodore J. Stavredes.

Similarly, former Major Francis T. Burke made critical contributions to the 1979 volume. His administrative skills ensured that essential marketing, production and distribution activities were executed precisely and in timely fashion. Without him, neither French nor this subsequent work would have seen the light of day. Those are the facts. That is the historical record.

Ted Stavredes and Fran Burke are gone now. They are not here for *Odyssey*. One feels diminished, less confident without their presence. Each would surely have been in the forefront of this new work. That awareness sustained this effort. More, it led one through the difficulties of undertaking again to trace the lengthening history of the state force they served throughout their adult lives. Their biographies helped inspire this history. Their lifelong commitments energize its pages.

Former Massachusetts State Troopers

Ted Stavredes in 1949 founded the Former Troopers Association. He was the driving force. Former Troopers George D. Rapport and James P. Green joined him in the historic effort. Counseled by Judge William McGiveny of Attleboro, they filed articles of incorporation on December 8, 1949. With them were Thomas J. McGuiness, Augustine L. Murphy, Charles J. O'Connor and Michael J. Sullivan. Stavredes was elected president, Rapport the secretary and Green the treasurer. The Former Troopers Association was thus founded. They were the first . Many would follow in their pioneering footsteps.

Meetings were held annually in the formative years. As noted, Stavredes in 1954 began a monthly newsletter. That communication focused the growing organization, providing the timely information that energizes and sustains all such undertakings.

Early on, the Former Troopers increased their efforts in support of the statewide force in which they had all served. Several examples highlight these early activities:

• In 1957, the Formers Troopers commissioned the "Outstanding Police Service Award." It is presented at the organization's annual business-dinner meeting to uniformed personnel honored for exemplary enforcement accomplishments.
• The James E. Hughes memorial trophy. Named in memory of the one- time academy commandant and expert marksman, the award goes to the top shooter in the New England Police Revolver matches.
• The State Police Memorial. Located at Framingham's General Headquarters, the granite memorial in the early sixties was dedicated to those troopers "who have completed their last patrol." Among those enshrined during the 1997 Memorial Program was Leo F. Stankard, the last survivor of 1921's First Recruit Troop.

The Former Troopers in the mid-1950's joined Commissioner Otis M. Whitney in organizing the State Police Auxiliary. The 1953 Worcester Tornado and a riot the next year at the Concord Reformatory had convinced Whitney that such a backup force was a must. The vast enforcement experience of the Former Troopers was the answer. Action followed.

Sixty five retired troopers on April 16, 1955 were sworn into the State Police Auxiliary. Two were women, Mora E. (Terry) Schomer and Mary S. Ramsdell. Ramsdell in 1930 had become the nation's first state policewoman. Each auxiliary member must first have served a full enlistment in the uniformed force, and received an honorable discharge. With Commissioner Whitney presiding, Major John C. Blake administered the oath of office. Captain Theodore H. Stronach was the first commanding officer. Uniforms were issued, and during the New Year's holiday the backup force served its first duty tour.

Through the years the State Police Auxiliary trained regularly. The force backed up regular traffic patrols during major holidays, and, in uniform, participated in recruit troop graduations. There, the former troopers pinned state police badges on the graduating recruits as they began enforcement careers in their distinctive two-tone blue uniforms. That was always a poignant ceremony. Age and youth. Old and new. Achievement and promise. Endings and beginnings.

Pinning the badge on a new trooper had symbolized the enduring pride former troopers have always felt for once having worn the French and electric blue. Over time, hundreds have kept that pride intact as members of the Former Massachusetts State Troopers. Space prevents one's inclination to list the hundreds of current members. But it seems important in this volume to recognize those who have served as president since the 1949 founding, now almost five decades ago:

Theodore J. Stavredes	Stanley W. Jackson
Lorance P. Salmonsen	Arthur F. Kerrigan
Augustine L. Murphy	Joseph J. Regan
Howard H. Dacey	Edward G. Byron
Theodore H. Stronach	Francis V. Foley
George D. Rapport	Edward T. Aucoin
Herbert J. Stingel	James F. Cummings
Richard F. Cleary	Ralph C. Splaine
James J. Foley	Joseph A. Kelley

Richard J. Barry is the current president. By any measure, Dick Barry's active leadership has energized the Former Troopers organization. Membership is up substantially, attendance at fraternal activities has increased, and public support for the current state force is demonstratively stronger.

Leadership initiatives were especially evident during 1996's 75th anniversary of the 1921 founding of the uniformed "state police patrol." For example, President Barry and Lt. Colonel Ronald J. Guilmette co-chaired a 75th Anniversary Banquet on October 5 in Boston's World Trade Center. Hundreds enjoyed a gala evening held in what was once Commonwealth Pier, site of state police headquarters in the mid-1930's. Earlier, on September 24th, the Boston Red Sox helped celebrate state police night at Fenway Park by defeating the Baltimore Orioles, and on October 13th the New England Patriots had fallen short against the Washington Redskins on state police night at Foxboro Stadium. Hundreds of current and former state police personnel and their families attended these anniversary events. They heard Trooper Dan Clark sing the national anthem, and watched with admiration as the state police drill team went through its paces. Thousands of the Bay State's citizens applauded with admiration as well.

President Barry's productive tenure has not been authored in isolation. Rather, a strong leadership team has developed expanding public activities. First among equals in this regard have been James J. Foley and Stanley W. Jackson, secretary and treasurer respectively of the former troopers' organization. Both joined the state police in 1947 following World War II overseas service. Each has served as president of the Former Troopers, and now, five decades after donning the French and electric blue, each provides wise counsel in the formulation of policies and programs designed to achieve the organization's enhanced public service goals.

Foley, especially, has long since earned his place in the state police historical mosaic. Accepting in 1985 the daunting challenge of developing, editing and publishing the Former Troopers' monthly Newsletter, he has made remarkable improvements in the authoritative, widely-read communications bulletin. Words fall short in describing the pleasure it regularly provides for former troopers, their families and several hundred additional readers. In short, it is the heartbeat of the veteran troopers' organization, the fulcrum for its expanding public service initiatives. That is not a small accomplishment. But it is only Foley's latest.

The reader will find elsewhere in this volume a fuller account of Trooper James J. Foley's earlier contributions, especially his 1950's efforts to liberalize the restrictive working conditions of field troopers. The work was high risk, even career threatening. An authoritarian organization in that era did not shrink from blunting such efforts. Yet Foley persisted, and he and a small cadre of equally courageous colleagues generated a liberalizing impulse that yet energizes the Massachusetts State Police in the modern era. That is not a small legacy to leave.

Of necessity, the Former Troopers' leadership team of Dick Barry, Jim Foley and Stan Jackson have had strong, active support from their Board of Directors, each of whom served long uniformed careers in the state force:

Charles W. Coe	Thomas R. Mulloney
Nicholas L. DeCola	Francis K. Mahoney
Francis V. Foley	Paul F. Matthews
Charles W. Gilligan	Michael J. Noone
William P. Lennon	Albert Sabanski

Foley necessarily had worked closely in his time with the Bay State's political leadership and key policy officials. It seems important at this juncture, therefore, to recognize the few chosen to provide executive guidance to the Massachusetts State Police since the 1921 founding of the "State Police Patrol":

The Governors

State Police Forces long have been dubbed the "Governor's Police Department." And for good reason. Massachusetts Governor John A. Andrew in 1865 recognized that his office was virtually helpless in the presence of local resistance to newly enacted state criminal statutes that lacked public support. Thus, the Massachusetts State Constabulary was created on May 16 of that year, the nation's first statewide enforcement agency. Similarly, Pennsylvania's Governor Pennypecker in 1905 signed the law founding the nation's first uniformed state police department. Its mandate: contain the violence of the Keystone State's coal strikes. Moreover, it is likely not a coincidence that here in the Bay State Governor Channing H. Cox in 1921 signed the law authorizing a State Police "Uniformed Branch" within months of the infamous Boston "Police Strike."

It is appropriate, therefore, that Odyssey introduce at this juncture the Commonwealth's chief executives who, through the years, have observed with measured satisfaction the admirable public safety achievements of "their" statewide force.

•	•	•	•

Calvin Coolidge	1919-1921
Channing H. Cox	1921-1925
Alvan T. Fuller	1925-1929
Frank G. Allen	1929-1931
Joseph B. Ely	1931-1935
James M. Curley	1935-1937
Charles F. Hurley	1937-1939
Leverett Saltonstall	1939-1945
Maurice J. Tobin	1945-1947
Robert F. Bradford	1947-1949
Paul A. Dever	1949-1953
Christian A. Herter	1953-1957
Foster Furcolo	1957-1961
John A. Volpe	1961-1963
Endicott Peabody	1963-1965
John A. Volpe	1965-1969
Francis W. Sargent	1969-1975
Michael S. Dukakis	1975-1979
Edward J. King	1979-1983
Michael S. Dukakis	1983-1991
William F. Weld	1991- 1997
Argeo Paul Cellucci	1997 -

The Public Safety Secretaries

The Legislature in 1971 created the Executive Office of Public Safety. The office assumed administrative supervision of the Department of Public Safety and of the State Police. Those appointed to the state's senior criminal justice post since the 1971 modernization have brought much professional achievement to their exacting duties. Kathleen M. O'Toole in 1994 was appointed secretary of the Executive Office of Public Safety while serving as a lieutenant colonel in the state police. Her predecessors:

Richard L. McLaughlin	1971-1975
Charles V. Barry	1975-1979
George A. Luciano	1979-1983
Charles V. Barry	1983-1990
James B. Roche	1991
Thomas C. Rapone	1991-1994

The Public Safety Commissioners

General Alfred E. Foote in 1921 was the first public safety commissioner and commanding officer of the Massachusetts State Police. This office for 70 years was the highly visible leadership post of the statewide force. Governor William F. Weld in 1992 signed legislation creating the newly consolidated Department of State Police, with a top executive office of superintendent. Colonel Charles F. Henderson served in that leadership post for four years, and in 1996 was succeeded by the current superintendent, Colonel Reed V. Hillman. The following preceded Colonels Henderson and Hillman in one of the nation's most admired criminal justice leadership posts:

Alfred E. Foote	1921-1933
Daniel A. Needham	1933-1934
Paul G. Kirk	1934-1937
Eugene M. McSweeney	1937-1942
John F. Stokes	1942-1950
Daniel I. Murphy	1950-1953
Otis M. Whitney	1953-1959
J. Henri Goguen	1959-1961
Frank S. Giles	1961-1964
Robert W. MacDonald	1964
Richard R. Caples	1964-1965
Leo L. Laughlin	1965-1969
William F. Powers	1969-1971
John F. Kehoe, Jr.	1971-1978
Dennis M. Condon	1978-1980
Frank J. Trabucco	1980-1987
William McCabe	1987-1992

Of note in this context is the remarkable career of former Deputy Commissioner Edward F. Kelly. Kelly in 1949 graduated from the State Police Academy, rising to the senior commissioned ranks in a long career in the uniformed force. Appointed deputy commissioner in 1979, he served as acting commissioner for extended periods in 1980, 1986 and 1992. He was the last to occupy the commissioner's office prior to the July 1, 1992 establishment of the new office of superintendent.

• • •

From the May 16, 1865 founding of the Massachusetts State Constabulary to the December 1, 1919 creation of the Department of Public Safety, the following officials led the statewide force:

General King	Joseph E. Shaw
Edward M. Jones	Jophanus H. Whitney
Luther Stephenson, Jr.	George C. Neal
Rufus R. Wade	John H. Plunkett

At Century's End

Leadership of the Massachusetts State Police and its predecessor organizations always has been a complex administrative challenge. Never more so, however, than in the 20th Century's fast-dwindling, final days.

In the early years, the state force was highly authoritarian, isolated administratively, insulated in the extreme. One's duty tour, really one's life, began and ended at a rural, remote "barracks" where "...the senior man spoke only to the corporal, and the corporal spoke only to God." It was a system for the times. And times were hard.

Today's state force in almost every way is the polar opposite of its antecedents. This was not by choice. Rather it has been imposed by the cultural, political and professional impulses of a dynamic social environment on the cusp of the Third Millennium.

Current personnel surely must marvel at the personal hardships and deprivations imposed in 1921 on the early enforcement pioneers by an impersonal, largely faceless system. Alternatively, those first troopers would be hopelessly intimidated, frozen in awe, in the presence of contemporary technology and the dizzying pace of change that it imparts.

Nowhere have the ever-evolving challenges been greater than in the leadership positions. Where once there was a remote bureaucracy harnessed by authoritarian control largely shielded from public oversight, there are now multiple spheres of influence, articulate centers of oversight, and an expanding communications technology that may well exceed the grasp of even those who make believe they understand it all.

Throughout the state force's lengthening history each of its leaders has been confronted with the sensitive cultural nuances, internal dynamics and outside influences unique to a particular era, specific to a point in time. Each of the administrators recognized in these pages knew first hand the difficulties of leading a statewide enforcement agency in full view of the public it serves, especially in the modern era of ubiquitous communications technology.

Each also knew, however, the special feeling of having led one of the nation's premier law enforcement agencies. Only a relatively few have shared that unique experience. One doubts that any among them would have preferred a different public service honor.

All of it, taken together, has been a remarkable organizational journey. The following pages turn to the task of telling the story of that fascinating enforcement odyssey.

State Capital, Boston, 1998. Front to back: Governor Paul Cellucci, Secretary Executive Office of Public Safety Kathleen M. O'Toole, State Police Superintendent Colonel Reed V. Hillman. Theirs is the singular honor of leading the Massachusetts State Police in its enforcement odyssey on the cusp of the third millennium.

General Headquarters, Boston, 1951. Left to Right: James P. Green, Judge William McGiveny, Theodore J. Stavredes, Commissioner Daniel I. Murphy, George D. Rapport. Stavredes, Green and Rapport on December 8, 1949 founded the Former Massachusetts State Troopers. Judge McGivney assisted. Stavredes was the first president, Rapport the secretary, and Green the first treasurer. Stavredes and Murphy were classmates in 1934's 26th Recruit Troop which trained under canvas in West Bridgewater.

Shrewsbury, 1950. First annual dinner meeting of the Former Troopers Association. Left to Right: (seated) Commissioner Daniel I. Murphy and Mary S. Ramsdell. Left to Right: (standing) Charles J. O'Connor, Theodore J. Stavredes, Augustine L. Murphy, George D. Rapport. The first annual meeting was held at the "Moors." Ramsdell in 1930 was the nation's first state policewoman. She served throughout the Great Depression and World War II, retiring in 1950.

State Police Academy, Framingham, 1955. Left to Right: Theodore J. Stavredes, Hollis C. "Sam" Beattie, Commissioner Otis M. Whitney, Captain Theodore J. Stronach. Beattie first enlisted in the state police in 1926 with the 15th Recruit Troop, in this photo became a member of the State Police Auxiliary. Whitney authorized the auxiliary force following the 1953 Worcester Tornado and the 1954 Concord Reformatory riots. Stronach was the auxiliary's first commanding officer at its April 16, 1955 founding.

General Headquarters, Boston, 1959. Left to Right: Commissioner J. Henry Goguien, Formers Troopers' President and Secretary respectively, Howard H. Dacey and Theodore J. Stavredes. Dacey in 1931 graduated from the State Police Academy with the 24th Recruit Troop, served in the barracks' system throughout the state, was long active in the Former Troopers' organization. Stavredes devoted almost 40 years to the founding, development and fulfillment of the Former Massachusetts State Troopers Association.

State Capitol, Boston, 1955. Left to Right: Commissioner Otis M. Whitney, Governor Christian A. Herter, Trooper James J. Foley. Whitney's tenure, 1953-1959, marked a historical juncture wherein the uniformed force was invited into the political and policy processes, openly, for the first time. Foley, representing the rank and file, was a committed pioneer in a high risk "adventure." His efforts, and those of his supportive colleagues, opened the way to the legislative and policy initiatives that, over time, guided the state police organization into the modern era. A past president of the Former Massachusetts State Troopers, he authors the timely communications bulletins that yet sustain that organization's vitality 50 years after his enlistment in the Massachusetts State Police in 1947.

Academy, Framingham, 1961. Left to Right: George D. Rapport, Lt. Colonel John C. Blake, Theodore J. Stavredes. This was the May 31, 1961, unveiling of the state police memorial, donated by the Former Troopers' Association. Blake and Stavredes were classmates in 1934's "Golden Class" that trained under canvas in West Bridgewater. Rapport and Stavredes on December 8, 1949, helped found the Former Troopers' Association. Stavredes in 1954 started the Former Troopers Newsletter which is now sent to more than 1,100 readers. Following his state police career, he served some 30 years as an official in the Boston Municipal Court System, lived out his retirement years at his seaside home in Winthrop.

South Barre, 1968. Left to Right: (seated) Francis T. Burke, Albert England, Jr., William J. Owen. Left to Right: (standing) Robert F. Lynch, Ralph E. Johnson, Pompee P. Valenti. This was England's retirement dinner. All graduated with 1948's 33rd Recruit Training Troop. Burke, long responsible for state police budgets and capital acquisition planning, was the driving force in the 1971 construction and dedication of a modern state police academy in Framingham and the abolition of the "live in" barracks system that same year. He retired in 1973 at the major's rank, served for 23 years in key administrative posts in the U. S. Justice Department until his November, 1996, death.

Framingham, Annual Memorial Service, May 30, 1974. Left to Right: George A. Pollard '28, James P. Green '27, Daniel L. Jacobs '29, Joseph P. McEnaney '38, John F. Lally '27, Ernest J. Ryan '25, Joseph W. Doyle '28, Herbert J. Stingel '22, Hollis C. Beattie '26, Henry F. Meyers '36, Timothy F. Moran '41, Thomas P. Davy '36, Theodore J. Stavredes '34, William F. Powers '49, Clarence J. Ferrari. Ferrari for more than 40 years handled key support and supply functions at Framingham's "supply depot." All the others served in the uniformed force. Following his early 1960' retirement, Moran authored a distinguished career as an educator. Director of law enforcement programs at Northeastern University, he was a leading member of the pioneering cadre that professionalized criminal justice studies in the United States.

State Police Academy, Framingham, Annual Memorial Service, 1972. Former Troopers' President Stanley W. Jackson pays tribute to those "..who have completed their last patrol." Jackson during World War II authored a distinguished military record in the skies over Hitler's Fortress Europe, joined the state police with 1947's 31st Recruit Troop, later was a mainstay on the academy staff, in 1997 continued 50 years of service as treasurer of the Former Troopers and a lifetime commitment to the equitable administration of the Commonwealth's criminal justice statutes and services.

General Headquarters, Boston, 1991. Frances J. Mahoney (seated, center) on July 31, 1991, completed more than 44 years of service in the Department of Public Safety, for much of that time as executive assistant to the state police executive officer. Many of them gathered for this photo at her retirement fete, (seated, with Ms. Mahoney) Commissioner William McCabe, Colonel (Ret.) Julian Zuk, (standing) Left to Right: Colonels (Ret.) Frank J. Trabucco, Edward J. Kelly, Colonel Charles F. Henderson, Colonels (Ret.) Paul Lambalot, Robert D. Murgia, John R. Moriarty, James T. Canty. Fran Mahoney for years ensured key administrative skills for occupants of the top post in the state's uniformed force.

Ken's Restaurant, Framingham, September 20, 1997. Left to Right: (seated) Joseph J. Regan, Melville R. Anderson, William J. Hansbury, Bohdan W. Boluch, Byron E. Blake, Leo J. Martin. Left to Right: (standing) Manuel S. White, Jr., William F. Gross, Gerald F. Burns, Laurence Thodal, James J. Foley. Precisely 50 years after their graduation in 1947 from the academy as the 32nd Recruit Troop, these were the World War II Emergency Temporary State Police Officers. Assigned to barracks' duty without training, they rose to the challenge. As field veterans, they later passed entrance exams and academy requirements, provided senior leadership in the sixties and seventies. With 38 other colleagues, their service now long past, was a critical link in the enforcement odyssey. Much is owed to these few, most of whom had survived long overseas service during World War II.

Ken's Restaurant, Framingham, September 20, 1997. Left to Right: (seated) Stanley E. Bower, Edward T. Aucoin, Stanley W. Jackson, Francis V. Foley, Frank J. Barbaro, Hector J. Cote, Raymond T. Alzapiedi. Left to Right: (standing) James V. Molloy, Edward H. Dargan, John R. Moriarty, George E. Wall, John M. Keeley, Charles W. Eager, John D. Butler, James P. Bowler, Edward M. Dunn. In 1947, they and their colleagues were the 31st Recruit Troop, the first academy class after the World War II years. This is a remarkable, historic photo, made during the 50th anniversary reunion of their academy graduation. These 16 at the reunion represented the 50 recruits who, in 1947, arrived at the Framingham academy eager for service in French and electric blue. Coming of age in the Great Depression, coupled with World War II service, promised productive public service careers in the state force. They did not disappoint.

World Trade Center, Boston, 75th Anniversary Banquet, October 5, 1996. Left to Right: Richard J. Barry and James J. Foley, President and Secretary, respectively, of the Former Massachusetts State Troopers Association (FMSTA), Troopers Eugene O'Neill and Mark F. Blanchard, Lt. Colonel Ronald J. Guilmette. FMSTA honored O'Neill and Blanchard with its prestigious "Trooper of the Year" award. Barry and Guilmette co-chaired the 75th anniversary gala, held on the site of Commonwealth Pier, in the late 1930's the general headquarters location of the state force.

Framingham, October, 1986. Left to Right: Trooper Stephen F. Byron, Lieutenant (Ret.) Edward G. Byron, Trooper Robert J. Byron, Maine State Police. The senior Byron in 1948 enlisted in the state force, served for almost three decades in field and staff assignments. His son Stephen graduated from the Framingham academy with 1974's 58th Recruit Troop, while son Robert was a 1986 graduate of the Maine State Police Academy. The Commonwealth's ranks long have been strengthened by a family tradition of public service.

Former Trooper's Annual Banquet, Marlboro, October 21, 1995. Left to Right: Former Troopers' President Richard J. Barry, Mrs. Ann Chicoine, Trooper Shawn T. Chicoine, Colonel Charles F. Henderson. The Former Troopers presented Chicoine with its Trooper Alje M. Savela memorial award. Trooper Chicoine's dogged investigative work led to the arrest of the fleeing felon who had shot and killed Trooper Mark S. Charbonnier on September 2, 1994 in Kingston.

Harvard University, Cambridge, January 9, 1961. Left to Right: President-elect John F. Kennedy, Trooper Richard J. Barry, Professor Arthur Schlesinger, Jr. Kennedy on November 8, 1960 had been elected to the nation's highest office, visited his Alma Mater, selected Schlesinger as a senior advisor. Barry in 1956 graduated from the state police academy with the 40th Recruit Troop, served in several field troops, went on to executive responsibilities in corporate security. A long time member of the Former Massachusetts Troopers' Association, he has provided strong leadership for that organization during several terms as its president.

Marlboro, October 25, 1997. Left to Right: Former Troopers' President Richard J. Barry, Trooper Francis P. Hughes, Colonel Reed V. Hillman, state police superintendent, Trooper Efrain Montanez. Former Troopers' Association honored Troopers Hughes and Montanez with the Alje M. Savela trooper of the year award for heroic enforcement actions at the risk of their own lives. Savela in 1951 was shot and killed in Troop C, Barre.

15

Annual Memorial Service, State Police Academy, Framingham, June 6, 1993. Colonel Charles F. Henderson and Former Troopers' President Richard J. Barry. Henderson in 1968 enlisted with the 50th Recruit Troop, rose through the ranks in field and staff commands, in 1992 became the first uniformed colonel and superintendent in the July 1, 1992 consolidation of state enforcement agencies, retired in 1996 after nearly three decades of service.

General Headquarters, Framingham, June 8, 1997. Annual Memorial Service and Family Day. Left to Right: Lieutenant Edward J. Montague, Colonel Reed V. Hillman, Mrs. Joan Irving, Richard J. Barry and Paul F. Matthews, President, and Vice President respectively of Former Troopers' Association. Mrs. Irving made donation to the state police museum in memory of her husband William H. Irving, Jr., of 1953's 37th Recruit Training Troop. Montague, State Police Museum Curator, played a key role in the publication of Enforcement Odyssey.

Marlboro, October 25, 1997. Board of Directors, Former Massachusetts State Troopers, Annual Business Meeting. Left to Right: (front) President Richard J. Barry '56, Treasurer Stanley W. Jackson '47, Board Members Michael J. Noone '57, Charles W. Gilligan '53, William P. Lennon '64, (back) Board Members Francis V. Foley '47, Albert Sabanski '51, Nicholas L. DeCola '59, Vice President Paul F. Matthews '59, Board Members Francis R. Mahoney '54, Charles W. Coe '56, Secretary James J. Foley '46. Missing from photo, Thomas R. Mulloney '56.
The Board of Directors each October implements operational and policy initiatives designed to support the public safety activities of the state police organization in which they all once served.

World Trade Center, Boston, October 5, 1996. Left to Right: Troopers Eugene O'Neill and Mark F. Blanchard. O'Neill and Blanchard at the department's 75th anniversary banquet received the "Trooper of the Year" award from the Former Troopers' Association. The award memorializes Trooper Alje M. Savela who was killed in the line of duty in 1951. O'Neill and Blanchard arrested two armed robbery suspects following a high speed chase and exchange of gunfire.

Former Troopers Annual Business Meeting, Marlboro, October, 1991. This was Leo F. Stankard, then the sole survivor of the 1921's's First Recruit Troop. Stankard died at 100 in 1996, just days after the 75th anniversary of the 1921 founding of the state force he helped to launch in the aftermath of World War I.

THE MILLENNIUM VISIBLE
An Introductory Essay

Those are large words. But they fall short of the reality. The Millennium is visible. More, its approach seemingly quickens as one contemplates the challenge of writing an opening essay about an enforcement odyssey now on the cusp of the 21st Century. So much is out there. So much has happened. Choices, difficult choices, must be made. It is not easy.

To begin, one visualizes an "historical overview." Composed of three distinct eras, it spans the years from 1921 through the 1996 75th anniversary. In reality, these are three "mini histories," each 25 years long: from the 1921 founding until 1946, from 1946 until 1971, and from 1971 until the present.

Each era was unique. Each witnessed significant organizational change. All were profoundly affected by the social and cultural dynamics of the larger society. The latter, especially, is a fascinating perspective of how and why an enforcement odyssey carves out its historical journey. Clearly, it receives much prompting along the way.

BEGINNINGS
1921-1946

The automobile in 1921 created the uniformed "State Police Patrol". There were other factors, but the new mobility changed how people lived, - and how criminals operated. Trips were reduced from days to hours. Population centers were more closely linked. Mobility expanded steadily. Local law enforcement's reach was weakened. A statewide enforcement capability was the solution. The environment thus spawned the organization.

This volume's early pages describe in detail the 1921 founding and the first cadres of uniformed troopers. It is worth repeating here that these enforcement pioneers embodied an idea more than an enforcement organization. An idea whose time has come is a powerful force, but it is also fragile. It requires commitment and constancy, - over time. Those first troopers supplied both. And then some. Today's modern enforcement organization endures as their legacy. That is a large accomplishment.

Two profound forces shaped the first 25 years, The Great Depression and World War II. The 1920's had witnessed much turnover in the uniformed force as the organization struggled with its identity. By the end of the first decade, however, structural and staffing stability took hold as the enforcement odyssey found its footing. But more ominous threats were about to descend on the organization, the state and the nation.

Some things can be read and understood. One gets the feeling. But others, the truly transformational, must have been lived. The 1930's Great Depression was such an experience. With it, a pall of social and personal gloom descended upon a nation fearful for its future. The state force did not escape. Organizational expansion and personnel improvements were not ascendant in the presence of fears for the Federal Republic's survival, especially for its democratic institutions.

The 1930's Great Depression immobilized the nation. That is putting it mildly. Fear drove out hope. Personnel of the state force did not complain. With unemployment approaching 25%, they, at least, had jobs. But what a job it was.

The complement of the force during that decade hovered around 250. The duty week remained well over 100 hours. Most troopers traveled long distances to their duty post, - usually by bus. It was not a job, certainly not a profession, but a lifestyle. The organization, with its rigidity and authoritarian principles, was ascendant. The Great Depression had effectively muffled individual aspirations and the natural tendency to improve the working conditions of a maturing enforcement agency.

One example of the depression's direct effect on the state force was seen in the 25th Recruit Troop which began training in Framingham on August 15, 1933. Twenty-four recruits trained in that class. To put it mildly, they were the select few. They had been appointed to the academy from 7,000 applicants! Moreover, a substantial number of the fledglings held baccalaureates. Some had advanced degrees, a startling anomaly that reflected the Great Depression's impact on the professional classes. It was not the best of times. Not by a long shot.

Still, there at the depression's nadir, an enduring tradition was created when on November 4, 1933, the 25th Recruit Training Troop graduated in their brand new French and Electric Blue uniforms. That evening, in Boston's Commonwealth Armory, the 24 recruit troopers were the first academy graduates to wear the distinctive and distinguished two-tone blue colors that, as these words are written, yet instantly identify one of the nations' premier enforcement organizations. That is not an inconsequential legacy to author in the depths of this country's most fearsome domestic era.

Scholars yet argue about why and when the Great Depression ended. President Franklin D. Roosevelt's New Deal had begun to replace fear with hope. Clearly, his administration's bold legislative initiatives were beginning to turn things around. But it was the December 7, 1941, Japanese strike at Pearl Harbor that galvanized the latent patriotism of the American people. A dispirited population, weary from the depression's long siege, almost overnight transformed itself into the "Arsenal of Democracy." The Great Depression ended right then and there. Japan would pay dearly for its historic miscalculation.

World War II froze the Massachusetts State Police in place. For example, there was one recruit troop during the world conflict. Seventeen recruits graduated from the academy on February 24, 1942, just weeks after Pearl Harbor. There was no graduation ceremony. Diplomas were not officially awarded until after the war's close. Things were spare.

Scores of troopers enlisted in the armed forces. Others were drafted, even though law enforcement officers in some cases were granted deferments. Applicants were hired right off the street as temporary "N.O.W.'s," Night Office Watch. Their job was to cover the barracks' desk from 10 p.m. until 8 a.m. It was not the best of times.

Coupled with the Great Depression, the World War II years created a two-decade holding action in the state force. Put differently, salary and staffing levels were capped by the constraints imposed by the organizational environment. One observes how the phenomenon recurs throughout the long history of the Massachusetts State Police. Organizations are constantly influenced by their social and economic surroundings. They strive to remain consonant with the changes imparted by the environment in which they operate. Failure to do this creates conflict. When a law enforcement agency is involved, it is not a pretty sight. Conflict never is.

That was not a serious problem for the state force from 1921 through 1946, the first 25 years. The Great Depression and World War II imposed their influences with vengeance. Individuals and organizations were equally affected. Two values, powerful motivators each, were ascendant, - security and survival. In their presence, organizational growth and enhancement did not lead the policy agenda. First things are always first.

When the Enola Gay on August 6, 1945, dropped an atom bomb on Hiroshima, World War II effectively ended. Days later, the United States accepted Japan's unconditional surrender aboard the U. S. Missouri in Tokyo Bay. The world's bloodiest struggle was over. The human and material losses, more than 50 years later, are yet being calculated. That assessment, sadly, must continue to accommodate newly "discovered" atrocities in the waning days of the world's darkest century.

In retrospect, one perceives that the 1921 - 1946 era could accurately be described as a time of survival, both for the organization and for the individual. But with that survival, much was accomplished. The experiment with a uniformed, statewide enforcement agency was settled. Uniformed troopers, quartered in barracks, finely trained and highly mobile, had earned the respect of the citizens they served. This was particularly true in the state's rural areas where those enforcement pioneers had strengthened their limited numbers with the skills and values of the local folk. They could hardly have known that their enforcement techniques would reemerge these many years later as the nation's police agencies implemented a 90's innovation dubbed "Community Policing."

PASSAGES—1946-1971

A depleted state force in 1945 began recruiting applicants without examination. These were the "E.T.S.P.O.'s," the Emergency Temporary State Police Officers. Hired right off the street, they were given uniforms and assigned to a "senior man" for several months. No examination. No training. "Boots," in the classic meaning of that word.

But the "E.T.S.P.O.'s" did a job. They delivered under circumstances that broke some of their numbers. Additional temporary personnel joined the force in 1946. All were World War II veterans. Meantime, regular troopers were returning from the world conflict. They, with the "E.T.S.P.O.'s," got the agency through the war's immediate aftermath. There was even a promise of new cruisers. With statewide examinations posted for trooper applicants, the state force was about to enter a new, 25-year era. It is doubtful that anyone then could have imagined what their organization would look like after the dynamics of those years had run their course. The organization's environment was destined for much change in that quarter century. With periodic spates of conflict, the state force's structure, staffing, and policies kept pace. The result, in retrospect, was a remarkable organizational transformation.

Several hundred World War II veterans graduated from the state police academy in the years immediately following the global conflict. Among them were many of the "E.T.S.P.O.'s." They had survived their temporary trials, passed the examination, and graduated from the academy. No one deserved the two-tone blue more than they did.

The post-war enlistees were a remarkable source. Born in the aftermath of World War I, they grew up during the Great Depression, fought World War II. In short, they were old for their

years. Confident yet restrained, they would provide the leadership that moved the state force toward policies designed to loosen the authoritarian impulses that long had been ascendant.

Such openings began in the fifties' decade. A new administration quietly encouraged initiatives that resulted in modest reductions in the duty week, equally modest salary increases, and upgrading and expansion of staff and field ranks. Taken as a whole, these initiatives created a liberalizing impulse within the organization. Words written here fail adequately to convey the feeling. But the feeling was there.

The fifties' initiatives could not have anticipated the turbulence wrought by the 1960's in the larger society. "Camelot," the Kennedy Administration, in November, 1963 ended tragically in Dallas. Reverend Martin Luther King and Senator Robert F. Kennedy in 1968 were murdered only weeks apart. Center cities burned across the country. Violent riots erupted as the Vietnam War split the nation. The Kerner Commission concluded that the country was dividing into two spheres, one black and one white. Uncertainty was ascendant. The national anxiety was palpable.

The Massachusetts State Police was directly impacted by the societal dynamics. The state force was fully committed to riots in Harvard Yard and Harvard Square, and to massive anti-war demonstrations on Boston Common and at the State Capitol.

The state police massively deployed in Harvard Yard? The 1921 founders would not have believed it. This was urban policing up close and confrontational. With the clarity that hindsight provides, the 1968 - 1969 Harvard demonstrations are seen as an organizational passage. Where once the rural force was symbolized by a solitary trooper on horseback or astride his motorcycle, now, in response to societal dynamics, troopers in riot gear were drawn into urban unrest. That was new. And it was different. There would not be a turning back. New policing imperatives slowly were taking hold. The odyssey was taking a turn.

Notably, Senator Barry Goldwater in the 1964 presidential campaign had elevated crime to the national political agenda. Predictably, President Johnson responded with the President's Crime Commission. The commission shortly published several volumes of recommendations, some of them quite radical. Moreover, the Office of Law Enforcement Assistance (O.L.E.A.) was established in the U. S. Department of Justice. Its mandate: put several hundred million dollars into the state and local criminal justice system to reduce crime and strengthen professional operations. Thirty-five years and several billion dollars later that historic commitment continues apace in the Federal Bureau of Justice Assistance.

In between, there was the ill-fated Law Enforcement Assistance Administration (L.E.A.A.) and its centerpiece, the Law Enforcement Education Program (L.E.E.P.). L. E. A. A.'s rocket-like early years ended in political flameout when state and local police, with federal funds, assembled an inventory of "law enforcement" equipment that rivaled the armada that had secured Normandy's beaches in 1944.

L.E.E.P. was another story entirely. Federal funding of post-secondary education for the nation's police officers succeeded beyond anyone's fondest hopes. That story has not yet been told. In a word, it is this: the L. E. E. P. initiative opened up the nation's police agencies. For the first time, police officers and those they are paid to protect interacted in a neutral, non-threatening atmosphere. New understandings emerged. Old, unfounded perspectives dissolved. Make no mistake, an historic, healthy transformation was energized and continues apace. Its value for some of the Federal Republic's founding principles cannot be overestimated.

On the individual level, the result was more clearly discernable. An example makes the point. The federal government in 1968 offered competitive graduate fellowships to state and local police, with full tuition and a generous stipend. The host department would pay the officer's salary. The central requirement: applicants had to have a bachelor's degree.

The uniformed branch complement at that time was approximately 900. Only two of the officers held the required baccalaureate. Only two out of 900 were eligible for the graduate fellowships. This was not an anomaly. Rather, it was the norm. And it certainly wasn't a negative. It's simply the way it was. The nation's police officers had always come from the working class. The majority were first and second generation Americans. A college education was not then a priority for families only then emerging from the struggle with inherent barriers to upward social mobility.

Things have changed. The changes have been dramatic. Today's Massachusetts State Police may well be a leading example. The modern organization is staffed by men and women with exceptional educational credentials. Advanced and professional degrees abound. Academy recruits have all completed some college work. Many hold the baccalaureate. And they are only beginning their enforcement odyssey.

The police educational story is a clear illustration of how the organizational environment has imposed its dynamics on the state force. There are many others, not as compelling, perhaps more subtle, but clear examples none-the-less. Time and space limit an exposition of all of them, but brief commentary seems merited in this context:

The Promotional Statute
A promotional statute for uniformed personnel was authorized in 1965. Before that, promotions were based on subjective criteria, never a healthy experience for an enforcement organization. The new law was largely energized by reform impulses from outside the department.

Personnel Practices
The sixties decade witnessed gradual, but steady loosening of traditional personnel constraints. These ranged from such mundane, (but really important at the time), changes as summer uniforms, to modest reductions in the duty week. These improvements, long advocated on the inside of the organization, were measurably advanced by visible pressures from the outside such as the picketing of Boston's general headquarters by state police families.

State Police Association of Massachusetts (S.P.A.M.)
SPAM's historic roots, its own odyssey, are fully described elsewhere. Its 1968 founding seems not to have been a coincidence. Police unions were on the rise. Unions, however, were not in the state police tradition. But traditions are not static. They must adjust, stay in tune with emerging changes in the larger society. Modern personnel likely take SPAM for granted, as though it were always there. But it wasn't there until the organizational environment generated political and institutional attitudes supportive of such a radical undertaking. The idea's time had arrived.

Thus, as the state force in the late 1960's neared its fiftieth anniversary, a modernizing impulse was gathering both pace and direction. How the enforcement odyssey unfolded from 1971 through 1996 focuses this essay's following pages.

MODERNIZATION
1971-1996
The modern era had most likely begun in 1969 when Governor Francis W. Sargent appointed a career, uniformed officer as head of the Massachusetts State Police. It was a first. Never since the 1921 founding, 50 years past, had a career trooper been selected directly from the uniformed ranks for the state's top enforcement post. That historic appointment, in retrospect, is seen as a particularly appropriate fulcrum for the modernization impulse that yet energizes the state force even while these words are being written.

The odyssey at that juncture, however, faced its most formidable challenge: the "live-in" barracks' system. Uniformed troopers were still working an 84-hour duty week. Other people worked 40 hours. Clearly, the state force had slipped behind the societal curve. A system that had served so well in its time had outlived the social and economic forces that had created it.

Major surgery was the answer. It came quickly. Everyone, it seemed, had been waiting for the department to lead the effort to resolve its priority organizational issue. When in 1970 the state force provided that leadership, the executive and legislative support was total, and enthusiastic. That September, Governor Sargent signed legislation abolishing the live-in barracks' system. Effective May 1, 1971, a trooper's duty week was reduced from 84 to 40 hours, precisely 50 years after the May, 1921, founding. There would be no looking back.

The historical importance of the barracks' abolition cannot be overstated. Overnight, the organizational culture, traditions and operations entered a new era. To be sure, much was lost in the transformation. No question about that. The shared experiences imposed by a disciplined, spare system had created an esprit de corps and camaraderie that for fifty years provided the Commonwealth's citizens with public safety services second to none. The live-in barracks' life, and all that it represented, will always be at the center of state police lore. The enforcement odyssey would have long since ended save for that remarkable concept of policing and the personnel who energized its five decades of public service.

Meantime, the federal government's infusion of several billion dollars into state and local justice systems had begun to make a measurable impact. The Law Enforcement Assistance Administration (L.E.A.A.), roundly criticized by its adversaries, is yet to receive the credit it is due for the modernization impulses its programs brought to the American police service. Few remember what it did. A whole range of professional opportunities, skills and services, now taken for granted, did not exist prior to L. E. A. A. Current enforcement personnel, at least many of them, assume that these things were always there. But they weren't. Not by a long shot.

Earlier discussion, for example, focused on the Law Enforcement Education Program (L. E. E. P). L. E. E. P. in the 1970's was L. E. A. A.'s flagship program. For the first time in history, police officers got the opportunity to attend college. With the 1971 barracks' abolition, troopers joined the thousands of officers striving to get a college degree with federal financial support. When pay incentives for educational achievements were added, a dramatic transformation in the level of education among law enforcement personnel was underway. Make no mistake. The L. E. E. P. program marks a transforming juncture in the state force's odyssey. In a word, federal funding for police education opened up the American law enforcement community. Moreover, it created a criminal justice educational system, almost overnight. By any measure, the police educational breakthrough has been a truly remarkable achievement. It is not a coincidence that many similar initiatives were launched during the past quarter century. The federal money has pushed law enforcement in new directions, creating a professional momentum that was unknown just a few years ago.

That momentum, and its results, are especially observable in the state force itself. Nowhere has a modernization ethic taken hold more firmly. Professional goals, standards, plans and practices are pervasive. Uniformed personnel are even more impressive. One need only to observe their professional demeanor to appreciate the personal credentials and commitments that have earned them the distinctive two-tone blue. They are proud to wear that uniform. They are proud of themselves. More, they are proud of the organization that offers them personal satisfactions and professional opportunities that were beyond the wildest dreams of their predecessors in French and Electric Blue. They know they are privileged to serve in the modern era, a time that has witnessed steady acceleration in the pace and direction of the enforcement odyssey.

That focus sharpened in the early 1990's. The Weld Administration's strong support for state police modernization initiatives was crucial, - and productive. Recasting the policy of the prior state administration for a prison facility in the foothills of the Berkshires, planners committed the Commonwealth and its state force to a new training and educational complex in New Braintree. Actually, the sprawling facilities already existed, having been constructed in the mid-1960's by a religious community. A major renovation program was launched, and in 1992 the 70th Recruit Troop began training at New Braintree. With that notable historical transition, the conversion of the Framingham training academy to a modern general headquarters complex became a priority.

Meantime, a consolidation of state enforcement agencies, a proposal long debated, finally came to pass. The result was a new Department of State Police that on July 1, 1992, was expanded dramatically by legislation authorizing state police authority and status for enforcement personnel in the Metropolitan District Commission, the Registry of Motor Vehicles and the Capitol Police. The enormous complexity and historical impact of the consolidation leaves one breathless. Its importance, now and in future years, cannot be overstated. Only time's passage will provide the experience and perspective accurately to assess the public policy benefits, or lack thereof, of such profound organizational change.

Clearly, the state force and its odyssey once again had been dramatically affected by the ideas and forces ascendant in the organizational environment. Not unlike the 1921 founding, barracks' abolition and other historical initiatives, a long-developing idea had been energized by a coalition of seemingly divergent interests.

The consolidation added to the urgency of transforming the Framingham training complex into a modern administrative headquarters. In the public mind, Framingham long had been seen as the state force's nerve center. It represented the visible organization, the sprawling complex on busy Route 9, the Worcester Turnpike, with the academy flanked by supply and maintenance operations as well as Troop A headquarters. Few realized that,

since World War II, the organization's leadership and technical services had been housed at 1010 Commonwealth Avenue on the Boston-Brookline line. They called it general headquarters, and for fifty years it was. But the former greeting card factory, with its industrial elevators, was not an especially inspirational edifice. Nevertheless, the building was witness to the most significant junctures in the enforcement odyssey. And, with its demise as general headquarters, itself became a notable historical image in the organizational mosaic.

That mosaic in October, 1994, was measurably enhanced with the dedication of the new general headquarters complex at Framingham. The buildings, first dedicated on May 29, 1971, as a modern training academy, had been dramatically transformed by the multi-million dollar modernization program. For the first time in its history, the state force occupied an administrative and technical headquarters the equal of the nation's best. Much credit is due those who helped plan and execute the dramatic transformation. Their contributions will endure long after they depart their chosen careers in French and electric blue.

In retrospect, the 1971 - 1996 era looms large. While there were difficult times, much that was positive has come to pass. Principal, perhaps, has been the observable strengthening of the department's *professional ethos*. Grounded in the personal skills and values of uniformed personnel, it is energized by the organization's superior capacities and its commitment to public service goals. That is a huge achievement.

A state police organization competently providing the public services for which it exists earns the public trust and support crucial to its mission. That *is* a huge achievement. For a statewide enforcement agency, the equitable and timely provision of its public safety services must always be ascendant in the presence of multiple competing interests. That must be the enduring and visible constant no matter the inexorable changes that a new century will impose on the enforcement odyssey and the dedicated professionals chosen to make that journey.

The Future Visible
More than 16,000 young men and women on February 7, 1998, began their quest for a law enforcement career by taking the department's entrance examination. More than words can convey on this page, their youthful aspirations affirm the strength of public support state police personnel have earned during the nearly eight decades of public service.

These young people are the future visible. The best and brightest will emerge from among their ranks during a disciplined, demanding selection process. Those select few will be appointed to one of the nation's finest law enforcement academies. There, in bucolic New Braintree, they will internalize the values and skills essential to a professional enforcement career in a new century. When at graduation they wear *French and Electric Blue*, they will have earned the honor of carrying those distinctive colors deep into the 21st century. There, they will be guardians of one of the most respected law enforcement legacies in the nation, a remarkable public safety ledger authored by those who have preceded them in a lengthening enforcement odyssey.

How that fascinating journey began, its antecedents and beginnings, unfolds in the pages and images that follow.

Chapter One

ANTECEDENTS AND BEGINNINGS

Philosopher Santayana was not especially thinking of the Massachusetts State Police when he wrote those words. Yet it is a profound observation, one that provides a theme for beginning a history of the nation's first statewide law enforcement agency. How does one begin? It is not easy. What is the starting point? That critical juncture is elusive. The years have obscured precise, relevant documentation. Memories have lost their sharpness. The picture cannot be focused as clearly as one would prefer.

That, perhaps, is why we have undertaken this effort. The hope is that we shall catch a glimpse of one of the most admired records of public service as exists in the nation's history of law enforcement. It can only be a glimpse. More should not be expected. Ten volumes could not document the personal stories and the organizational events that, together, provide the history of the Massachusetts State Police. We must settle for something less then; a snapshot, rather than a rich portrait. The intent is that the fleeting glimpse will fairly represent the decades of public service provided by a privileged few.

This essentially, is the story of the Uniformed Branch of the Massachusetts State Police. The "State Police Patrol," as it was first called, was founded in 1921. This new, statewide enforcement agency was patterned after a policing concept first introduced in Pennsylvania. That experience exerted a strong influence on what was done here. For that reason, we shall examine that relationship later in more detail. Long before that, however, other events unfolded that would be directly related to the current state police organization. Review of those "antecedents and beginnings" is essential to this undertaking.

It seems unnecessary to note, beyond this mention, that English concepts of law enforcement were brought early to the Massachusetts Bay Colony. While Magna Carta becomes more remote with each passing year, its doctrines laid down in 1215, exert continuing influence on modern enforcement practices. Similarly, England's "hue and cry," "Watch and Ward," sheriff and constable remain conceptually imbedded in late 20th Century enforcement agencies.

These legacies are first observed when local policing is examined in Massachusetts. A Boston Town Meeting, in 1636, authorized a citizen Watch and Ward. William Cheseborough was the first Constable, supervising a force of young men who served without pay. The Boston Watch as it was called, was reorganized by the state legislature in 1786 adding substantially to its policing duties. By 1801, the Watch consisted of 16 Constables assisted by 20 Watchmen. Charles Bulfinch, the noted architect, served as the first Inspector of Police for the capital city. Watchman Jonathan Houghton in 1825 became the first Bay State policeman killed in the line of duty. One John Holland hanged for the infamous deed.

Meantime, Sir Robert Peel had become Home Secretary in England. Beginning his tenure in 1822, he argued that London needed an organized police department. The industrial revolution was creating teeming urban centers, and, with them, dramatic increases in criminal activity. The traditional citizen enforcement protection was ill suited for the new challenge. Peel worked for seven years to develop public support for his idea. His efforts were finally rewarded.

Parliament enacted Peel's legislative proposal in 1829. Entitled the "Metropolitan Police Bill," it founded the modern police organizational model. The bill established a uniformed patrol of 1,000 officers. These were the "bobbies," named after the Home Secretary. Peel's original concepts of organization and operations still endure. He is thus conceded to be the father of modern law enforcement. Influenced by the Peelian reforms, Boston disbanded its Night Watch on May 26, 1854. From that action, the forerunner of the city's current department emerged. A chief of police was appointed. He commanded 250 officers. The city was divided into seven police districts, and, in addition, the harbor was patrolled.

Boston's first chief was one Robert Taylor. His salary was $1800 per year. Patrolmen received two dollars a day. Officers were first issued pistols in 1863, partly in response to the widespread disorder created by conscription for Civil War duty. A captain of detectives had been appointed in 1860, and technical services emerged to support investigative activities. A "Rogue's Gallery" was instituted in 1861, and, later, the department's Mounted Patrol was established to cover the developing Back Bay. The Boston experience was shortly repeated in other urban centers. Policing of center cities expanded rapidly, spurred, as in England, by the social consequences of the industrial revolution.

But another kind of law enforcement problem remained. The state legislature was enacting laws to deal with the issues of the day. Among these was prohibition, a towering political question argued emotionally by the "wets" and "drys." Laws were passed prohibiting the manufacture and sale of alcoholic beverages. These were state laws, unpopular in some areas. That created a question. Who would enforce an unpopular state statute at the local level? The answer, unfortunately, was abundantly clear. No one would.

STATE CONSTABULARY

The historical stage was thus set for the creation of a statewide force to police prohibition compliance, as well as related illegal activities. This important juncture is seen clearly in retrospect; the passage of over one hundred years ensures that clarity. Then, however, the final, bloody chapter of the young nation's tragic internal conflict was closing. The South lay in ruin, crushed in spirit if not in pride. The people of Massachusetts did not rejoice. They, with all the rest, mourned for the flower of American youth.

In that poignant setting, Governor John A. Andrew on May 16, 1865, signed the law creating the State Constabulary. This legislative act to "establish a State Police Force" founded the nation's first statewide enforcement agency. It was an obscure event, little recognized by a people yet grieving for their war dead.

The first headquarters for this new concept in law enforcement was at 50 Bromfield Street, Boston. The Chief Constable directed the statewide activities of his deputies from here. These men had been invested with all the common law and statutory powers of sheriffs. They also exercised all the authority given to police and watchmen by existing state and local laws.

The first leader of the state police was a General King. His title was probably earned during the Civil War. Command experience would be essential in leading a new statewide force. King's successor had the honor of first reporting on the activities of the state police department. Chief Constable Edward M. Jones wrote of the impact of the new force on the Commonwealth's criminal element. He told the governor that he had named three of his men state detectives. Could he have realized that he had established a police title which would gain stature through more than one hundred years of public trust? It is not likely.

The department in 1867 was increased to 131. It moved swiftly against the illegal manufacture and sale of intoxicating beverages, creating an uproar among the liquor interests. People were being arrested for violations formerly committed with impunity. Political campaigns were contested on the prohibition question, and, for some, the state police was the principal target. One of the results in 1868 was a reduction of the force to 64 officers. Nevertheless, Chief Constable Jones was able to report one fact that must have pleased the taxpayers. He wrote that the state police had caused a much larger sum to be paid into the state treasury than it had cost the Commonwealth to sustain its statewide enforcement agency.

In 1869, headquarters was moved to 24 Pemberton Square, Boston. The law required the chief of the force to maintain his office in the capital city. During the same year, illegal liquor shops were dealt a crippling blow. The force brought 6,808 prosecutions for liquor offenses. The reaction was swift, and intense. Officers of the department were publicly scorned. Local officials testified for defendants throughout the state. Threats were made to abolish the organization. Some intended to do just that.

One of the results was a budget cut. The Chief Constable complained bitterly to Governor William Claflin, warning that legislative blows were seriously affecting the capability of the organization as a police force. His words went unheeded. Within a year, the General Court abolished the original force. A new constabulary of seventy men was placed under the control of a board composed of three police commissioners.

In spite of this harassment, the state force continued to do its job. Eloquent speeches, both attacking and defending the force, echoed in the General Court. The talk failed to hide the real issue from public view. The state police was the only force that could, and did, enforce restrictions on the manufacture, sale and use of intoxicating spirits, and related crimes spawned by that illicit activity.

William Gaston was elected governor in 1875. He had recommended the repeal of prohibition. True to his campaign pledge, Gaston devoted practically his entire inaugural address to this controversial subject. His words are still considered the best argument ever delivered against prohibition by a Massachusetts governor. The legislature responded with enactment of a liquor license statute during that session. An era had ended in Massachusetts. The necessity for a statewide enforcement agency for the principal purpose of smashing illegal liquor interests died with the prohibition law.

STATE DETECTIVE FORCE

The governor's signature on February 13, 1875 ended the ten

year life of the State Constabulary. There was no skip in the organizational heartbeat as the same law gave birth to the State Detective Force. Luther Stephenson Jr. was the state's first chief detective. Although the law authorized the appointment of thirty detectives, only fifteen were enlisted during the first year. After posting a bond of five thousand dollars, each detective was granted statewide police powers. The force was charged with aiding the attorney general and the district attorneys in procuring evidence for the detection of crime and the pursuit of criminals. The governor could also command the assistance of the detectives in suppressing riots and preserving the public peace.

The duties of the force in 1876 were greatly expanded. State detectives began inspecting public buildings and factories throughout the Commonwealth. Especially concerned with accident prevention, they ensured that adequate fire escapes were provided. The force also enforced all laws pertaining to child labor, and regulations limiting working hours. Chief Detective Stephenson wrote that the textile industry was hiring mill hands at a tender age. Detectives had found 63 children under ten working at the looms. These conditions later sparked labor strikes directly involving the new statewide enforcement agency.

The winds of change, however, were still blowing. Special interests were troubled by a statewide enforcement agency. The General Court of 1879 responded by closing the four year history of the detective force. The flame of continuity flickered low. It did not go out.

DISTRICT POLICE

The Massachusetts State Police would be known for the next forty years as the District Police. The force was created by the same legislation that abolished the state detectives, but the new organization was just a shadow of that agency. Authorized to enlist sixteen men, the appropriation limited the statewide complement to nine.

It is difficult to believe that a force of this size could accomplish much. Still, it had an impact in certain areas of public activity. For example, laws restricting child labor were being openly violated. Families needed the wages, little as they were, and local officials were reluctant to act. The District Police attacked this particularly sensitive problem wherever it was found. Their efforts were slowly rewarded. Public attitudes gradually shifted on this complex social issue.

The department early in its existence received a severe test. Fall River was in the throes of a textile strike. Workers roamed the streets. Chaos existed in some sections. Lawlessness seemed the order of the day. The entire force was ordered into the teeming mill city on the banks of the Taunton River. The effect of this presence was described by Mayor Crawford E. Lindsey. He wrote Chief Rufus E. Wade:

> No matter how good a local force of police a place may have, I am convinced that officers wearing the state authority have a moral influence in any community far superior to the best local police, whenever any general tendency to violate the law or create a disturbance exists. I have had some opportunity to see the working of the state police in its various forms in this city, and I do not hesitate to say that twice as many men, known to and knowing almost every person in the city, could not be as effective in preserving public order as the force under your direction.

Lindsay's words were prophetic. This was the era of rapid industrial development. The lofty dream of pure capitalism was punctured by the thrust of monopolies. It was the age of the railroad tycoon and the textile baron. The industrial machine was ravenous. Its principal resource was people, hired hands to work long hours under the worst conditions.

The problem was acute in Massachusetts. Great textile centers were springing up in the Merrimack and Taunton River Valleys. Mills were making the cotton goods demanded by an expanding population. The granite giants, however, posed a serious threat to the workers, and to the healthy development of the state. Mere children toiled within their thick walls. Many could not read nor write. They were committed to a life at the looms. The future held no promise.

District Police officers were assigned an important role during these critical years. Most efforts were directed toward the enforcement of minimum educational requirements for every child worker. The legislature was enacting laws to prevent the use of child labor. By the mid 1880's children under fourteen were required to attend school at least twenty weeks a year. The statute found scant support with working class parents, and local enforcement officials were reluctant to apply the new laws. They were familiar with local conditions and knew the need for money. Thus, the circumstances which had created the State Constabulary in 1865 were being repeated. Unpopular laws were not being enforced at the city and town level. The District Police would carry out its responsibilities with vigor.

Four men were added to the force in 1885. They were the first to be appointed after a civil service examination. Formerly, officers had been appointed by the governor following examinations conducted by a superior court justice. This civil service system of detective selection endured even though the organization changed substantially through the years.

Rufus R. Wade continued as Chief of the District Police throughout the 1880's. He described working conditions found by his officers when they inspected buildings and factories throughout the state. In one place children were working a ten hour shift for sixteen cents a day. All were under nine years old. Chief Wade told the governor of the perils created by these conditions. His eloquent words were a positive force for social improvement. He was especially concerned with the waste of human lives, warning the chief executive of the consequences:

Why should Massachusetts concern itself about factory children? Because she cannot afford to neglect them. The human machine will bear only so much strain. Speed is gained at the expense of power. There are broader interests than those of individual gain; grave perils, whose proportions are yearly becoming greater, impend over our land.

A vast immigration is pouring into our seaports and distributing itself within our borders; the capacity to absorb this immense addition to our population is not unlimited. If we can reach their children by our common-school system we have nothing to fear; no substitute for this will answer. Unsectarian education in the common English branches, made compulsory upon all parents, is a measure not of expediency merely, but of absolute safety for the nation.

No class of children—native or foreign, white or black, rich or poor should be cut off from their rights to the primary elements of education in our public schools. The perils of ignorance and vice among children should be guarded against.

The State must either train the young in knowledge and virtue, or enlarge and multiply its penal institutions.

A change was made in the organization of the statewide force in 1888. The legislature, acting on Chief Wade's recommendations, created two separate departments within the force. One section would be known as the detective department. This group, consisting of ten men, was assigned to investigate crime and prosecute criminals throughout the Commonwealth. The second department, numbering eleven, was named the division of inspections.

Broader responsibilities had made these changes necessary. New tasks were being delegated to the force each year. A detective, burdened with the complex problems of his office, could not be expected to cope with rapidly expanding building codes and work laws. Nor could a building inspector be asked to comprehend the growing body of law vital to an effective statewide enforcement effort. The Chief of the District Police supervised both departments. His was the ultimate accountability for the direction of the force and its expanding responsibilities.

This new organizational structure would endure for the lifetime of the District Police. It would later serve as a model for the 1919 Constitutional Convention in designing the Department of Public Safety. By the close of the nineteenth century, officers of the detective division had earned an outstanding reputation. In cooperation with local police and the district attorneys, they had solved some of that era's major crimes. Examples of that enforcement work served as professional criteria for those who aspired to public service.

RUFUS R. WADE

Rufus R. Wade had led the District Police since its 1879 founding. Writing to Governor W. Murray Crane, he reviewed two decades of duty by the force:

> In regard to the character and extent of the duties devolved by the statutes upon the District Police, it may be said that, in the twenty years since this force was established, its numbers have increased from nine officers to forty-nine. During the first year of its existence to the District Police were entrusted the enforcement of the laws in relation to the hours of labor, the employment of children and the inspection of factories and public buildings.
>
> It was evident then, and still more as the experience of years is showing, that the efficiency of such a force requires something more to sustain it than its badge of authority or the commission of the Commonwealth. Public confidence is accorded when it is believed that the officers of the law are men of integrity, and perform their duties without fear or favor.

Chief Wade extended those responsibilities in 1900 to coastal waters. Steamers from New York and Rhode Island had been invading Buzzard's Bay in search of menhaden, a fish which produced an excellent oil. These raiders, under cover of darkness, were taking thousands of pounds of menhaden in violation of the law. To prevent these violations, officers patrolled Cape Cod waters in the *Lexington*. Built in 1898, the steamer and her police crew were the scourge of illegal poachers. She cruised constantly between April and October, while steam was kept up during the winter in order that the vessel could be used on an hour's notice.

The District Police in 1902 added a third division. Charged with all the responsibilities formerly discharged by the state fire marshal, the division had a unique structure. Staffed by officers from the detective division, it functioned under the direction of a deputy chief. These men, because of their statewide police powers, exercised broad investigative authority. They could arrest and prosecute individuals who violated existing statutes, while, at the same time, enforcing fire prevention regulations. The 1904 legislature, however abolished the new division, assigning its work to the detective department.

An important chapter in the history of the Massachusetts State Police ended with the death of Chief Rufus R. Wade on February 10, 1904. With him died an unique era of dedicated leadership. For twenty-five years he had spoken out on the social and moral issues of his time, not limiting himself to the problems of his office. Many of his recommendations are found in today's law books. His words, after all these years, still shine with eloquent expression and extraordinary vision. Joseph E. Shaw became Chief of the District Police when Wade died. Writing to Governor John L. Bates he said:

> We have received the sad news of the death of our superior officer, Chief Rufus R. Wade, who passed away after a long and painful illness, during which time he exhibited the fortitude and patience which characterized his whole life. Mr Wade was appointed chief of the department by his Excellency William Claflin, in 1879. His sterling character, his strict attention to, and faithful performance of, all the duties connected with his office, his kind and sympathetic nature and patriotic instincts, endeared him to everyone who knew him.
>
> In the administration of the affairs of his office he was a strict disciplinarian, but always kind in his manner, and sympathetic and patient with all his subordinates; never under the most trying circumstances, losing his self-possession, but always maintaining a calm and dignified presence, which won for him the respect of all with whom he came in contact.
>
> He was typical New Englander, an excellent citizen and a true Christian. His death was a great loss to the Commonwealth whom he had served so long and so well. His funeral was attended by the entire department.

The early nineteen hundreds were far from routine for law enforcement. The carrying of concealed weapons had become a serious problem. On one occasion, detectives were called to the scene of a disturbance in a town near Boston. A dispute had arisen between a contractor and some of his men. The workers had seized their employer, holding him prisoner while insisting that their demands be met. State detectives, assisted by local officers, broke up the melee and arrested the offenders. The detectives found approximately one hundred stilettos and other weapons in a search of the prisoners. This, and similar incidents, caused Chief Joseph E. Shaw to demand laws regulating the carrying of concealed weapons.

In the meantime, state officers had never been authorized to carry badges and weapons. They had enforced the laws of the Commonwealth for almost fifty years on the strength of their individual integrity and the public reputation of their organization. The General Court responded to this issue, and to the widespread danger of concealed weapons. The 1906 legislature enacted a law prohibiting the unlicensed carrying of a loaded pistol or revolver. The statute also outlawed stilettos, daggers, dirk-knives and the like, imposing jail sentences on offenders. Two years later, state detectives were authorized to carry a badge, revolver, club, and handcuffs. The lawmakers attached an emergency preamble to the law making it immediately effective. The state force thus had completed almost a half-century of service before its officers were legally permitted to wear a distinctive shield signifying an office of high public trust.

UNIFORMED STATE FORCES

While Massachusetts was arming its officers for the first time, a more significant development occurred in Pennsylvania. The state's governor had discovered what had been experienced here years earlier; state laws often were unenforced when publicly opposed on the local level. Governor Pennypecker's frustration, however, resulted in public policy action. He decided to created a *uniformed* statewide force. It was a radical idea. But its time had arrived.

The 1905 Pennsylvania Legislature responded by enacting a law which founded the nation's first uniformed state police organization. The Keystone State in 1905 thus set in motion an enforcement idea that has since resulted in the establishment of state police or state highway patrols in every state except Hawaii.

The Pennsylvania state force was structured after the military model. Substantially decentralized, it had, on the other hand, a strong general headquarters operation. A system of troop headquarters and substations ensured uniform implementation of policies. These units were placed strategically in all sections of the state, somewhat as a military organization deploys its field forces. This new enforcement agency, therefore, was a clear departure from all predecessor police organizations in this country. While it could not have been sensed at the time, Pennsylvania was destined to be the basic model for the many statewide enforcement agencies that were to follow.

While enforcement of the law in rural areas was the principal rationale for organizing the force, other duties soon evolved. One of these, preserving order in widespread coal mine strikes, was to create a legal precedent. Opposition mounted quickly in each state that subsequently considered such an enforcement agency. The charge was that the state police, as in Pennsylvania, would be used as "strike breakers." The fear was not easily overcome. Later review will demonstrate that specific prohibitions were placed in the Massachusetts statute to prevent use of the uniformed force in labor strife, except under precisely defined conditions.

Nevertheless, motivated by the Pennsylvania experience, other eastern states enacted statutes to create statewide law enforcement departments. The first of these were founded between 1905 and 1919. New York, for example, authorized its statewide force in 1917 after a bitter legislative battle. For many years the Empire State boasted of having the largest state enforcement organization in the nation, yielding that honor to California only in recent years.

The state police idea also took root in the mid-west. Michigan organized a temporary force in 1917, rather as an emergency measure during World War I. That agency was given permanent authorization in 1919, later developing into one of the most respected departments in the country. West Virginia in 1919 organized a new department of public safety. A state police force was structured within that administrative agency.

New Jersey in 1921 would authorize a uniformed state police department, as would neighboring Rhode Island in 1925. Actually, much of the thrust for Rhode Island's force came from the Massachusetts experience. But that is a bit premature. Important events were yet to intervene here.

Not least of these was World War I. Verdun had become a household word in America as France and England struggled to stop the Kaiser's legions. The Allies were heartened as President Wilson in 1917 committed the nation's might to their cause. Flames from the "War That Would End All Wars" had reached most of the western nations. Men later to serve in the state police, were among those who saw war service. Many served with distinction on the high seas and in the trenches in France.

Special security measures had been put into effect in the Commonwealth. The governor was authorized to appoint special state police officers, and, in 1918, forty-four temporary officers were sworn to augment the detective force near army camps and naval bases. Some were assigned to guard duty at particularly sensitive service installations. Meantime, the American Doughboy had helped to turn the tide in Europe. Four years of bloodshed were ending. A weary nation rejoiced at the news of the armistice. It was November 11, 1918.

John H. Plunkett was then serving as the last chief of the District Police. His final report on November 30, 1919 emphasized to Governor Calvin Coolidge the necessity for a statewide force: "First, there must be officers versed in the detection and prosecution of crime committed in the smaller communities of the State, where it is financially impossible to maintain a competent force; and secondly, there should be, under some authority of law, a force of sufficient size to be of service to the Governor in assisting him in the enforcement of law, where local authority is unwilling or incapable of doing so."

Deputy Chief George C. Neal was the last supervisor of the detective department in the district police organization. In his final report Neal noted that the detectives consisted of himself, one chief fire inspector, one captain, who commanded the steamer *Lexington,* and twenty-six men, fifteen detectives and eleven fire inspectors. He concluded by describing the role the detective department had played in the Boston police strike: "There were twenty-three officers from this branch of the Force detailed to assist the Boston police authorities in enforcing the law and preserving order on the night that so many of the police force of the said city went on a strike, and from the reports of their services on the occasion I am sure they deserve much credit for the conscientious and fearless manner in which the duty was performed."

Deputy Neal assured Governor Coolidge that the detective department was in sound condition. He especially praised the morale and discipline of the force. After reporting further on administrative matters, Neal signed his report. His signature officially closed that particular chapter of public service by the state detective force.

Chief Plunkett had referred to the "act of consolidation." He was in fact talking about a broad reorganization of the Bay State's executive branch of government. These recommendations resulted from a Constitutional Convention which had streamlined the state's administrative services. Much of the focus had settled on the area of public safety. Following extensive deliberation, conferees had recommended abolition of the District Police, ending that organization's forty year record of public service officially on November 30, 1919.

DEPARTMENT OF PUBLIC SAFETY

Chapter 350 of the General Acts of 1919 transferred the duties of the District Police to a new Department of Public Safety. The leadership position was changed from "Chief of the District Police," to "Commissioner of Public Safety":

The Department of Public Safety shall be under the supervision and controls of a commissioner, to be known as the Commissioner of Public Safety, who shall be appointed by the Governor, with the advise and consent of the Governor's Council. The first appointment shall be for the term of one, two, three, four or five years, as the Governor may determine. Thereafter, the Governor shall appoint the Commissioner for the term of five years, shall fill any vacancy for the unexpired term and may, with the consent of the Council, remove the Commissioner. The Commissioner shall receive such annual salary, not exceeding five thousand dollars, as the Governor and Council may determine.

The statute specified the commissioner's authorities, noting that he would be both the executive and administrative head of the department. The occupant would be charged with the administration and enforcement of all laws, rules and regulations assigned to the new statewide agency. In addition, there would be the responsibility for directing all inspections and investigations, except those expressly reserved by statute to several administrative boards also incorporated into the new public safety structure.

The department was organized into three divisions. One was the state police. The commissioner was expressly instructed to administer that function under his own immediate supervision. That legislative specification would endure through the years, ensuring a strong administrative relationship between the Commissioner's office and state police operations.

A division of inspections was created under the authority of a director to be known as the chief of inspections. Finally a division of fire prevention would function under the administrative control of the state fire marshal. The governor was to appoint the chief inspector and the state fire marshal. Both appointments required confirmation by the Governor's Council. Salaries could not exceed five thousand dollars. The commissioner was directed to organize the state police division to include the functions formerly handled by the detective and fire inspection departments of the District Police. Moreover, he was assigned all the powers and duties formerly reserved to the chief of the District Police.

Governor Coolidge on December 1, 1919 appointed Alfred E. Foote as the state's first Commissioner of Public Safety. Former District Police Chief John H. Plunkett was named head of the inspections division, and George C. Neal became State Fire Marshal. William H. Proctor was honored with the first captaincy of state police in the new public safety department.

A number of appointments were made during the first year's operations. While several of the appointees were to enjoy commendable careers in the public service, two in particular are worthy of mention. John F. Stokes on October 4, 1920 began duty in the state police division. Earlier, on February 15, Sadie J. Graham commenced her duties in the division of fire prevention.

Stokes was destined to carve out an admirable record for criminal investigations. He would, in addition, complete his long tenure in the department by serving during the 1940's in the commissioner's post. Miss Graham was to serve in a variety of responsible positions throughout the department. In the 1950's she would cap her career as confidential assistant to Commissioner Otis M. Whitney.

A Rural Statewide Force

In the years immediately following World War I the automobile had impacted dramatically upon the national consciousness. People were able to take a "Sunday ride," often a distance measured formerly by a lifetime of travel. One sensed that something profoundly important was happening. Yet, in retrospect, most could not have imagined that social customs centuries in the making would be substantially altered in short decades.

The new mobility had profound implications for law enforcement. Criminal could strike, and, within minutes, be several miles from the crime scene. Rural areas suddenly became crime targets. Essentially, there was no organized police capability outside the center cities. The Bay State's small towns had relied on traditional policing concepts dating from the colonial experience. Now, almost overnight, values were threatened that had endured since the Republic's founding. The impact aroused the rural electorate, concerned for the first time with social problems once reserved to the state's industrial areas.

The problem was not entirely that of controlling criminals. There was a leisure dimension to it, a very serious one. People were literally killing themselves in the new automobiles. Death on the highway became one of the state's most challenging public issues. The Commonwealth had led the way in enacting statues for the licensing of drivers, and the inspection of vehicles. A growing body of law was designed to ensure safe driving.

But there was a problem. Who would enforce such regulations in and between the small towns dotting the state's landscape? It was the same question as that asked in 1865 about state laws to control illicit liquor activities. The answer also was the same. No one would. The stage thus was set for an idea whose time had come. A uniformed police force was needed to patrol the state's rural areas.

The legislature in May of 1920 enacted a resolve for an investigation of the "desirability of establishing a rural statewide force." A commission was created. Governor Coolidge and the legislature named its members. The Commissioner of Pubiic Safety and the State Adjutant General were assigned to lead deliberations. General Alfred E. Foote, then in the commissioner's post but six months, was thus destined to play a critical role in the historic proceedings about to commence.

The commission met throughout 1920. Members analyzed the essential problems. Systematic supervision of automobiles in sparsely settled areas seemed the priority. Equally important was the necessity of providing police protection to the Bay State's far flung rural hamlets. Always near the consciousness of commission members was the specter of the newly mobile criminal. His growing portfolio of crimes had to be stopped. The ominous trend had to be reversed.

The commission in January 1921 submitted its final report to the legislature. This historic work remains a critical juncture in state police history. Members reviewed what had been done in other eastern states, notably Pennsylvania in 1905, and New York in 1917. Each had founded a uniformed statewide force. The report specifically noted that:

It has become increasingly apparent, not only to the residents of the rural and suburban districts of the Commonwealth, but to the close observers of police conditions, that there is immediate need of a greater degree of police protection in the sparsely settled districts of the state.

The professional criminal and the occasional offender have kept pace with the changes incident to our civilization and have adapted their methods to the conditions that surround them, with the result that the rural districts of the state are no longer remote from the activities of the criminal who in times past operated almost wholly in the larger cities.

The development of the use of the automobile by the criminally inclined element of our population has greatly extended their sphere of operations. Because of the advantage offered by the means of swift transportation, crimes that are planned in the large cities may now be executed in distant towns, and the offence being committed, flight accomplished with excellent chances of avoiding detection and apprehension. The bandit type of hold-up man, the safe-blower, the poultry thief, the garden despoiler, the automobile thief and the like, are now able to come from distant points, carry out their designs and leave the scene of the crime without detection.

The unlawful use of the automobile has thus developed a condition that can only be coped with successfully by a motorized patrol of the state highways carried out by an efficient force of men specifically trained for the purpose.

By the work of such a patrol force, the traffic in stolen automobiles would be greatly reduced and the detection and apprehension of those who have hitherto taken advantage of inadequate police protection, be rendered more certain.

Among the desirable results to be obtained by the establishment of such a force are the uniform enforcement of the laws in the different sections of the state; the cooperation with local authorities wherein the administration of the patrol force or any of its units should be conducted so as to secure effective liaison without infringing on the jurisdiction of cities and towns where organized police departments are maintained. The cooperation thus effected would particularly facilitate the work of the police departments of towns by affording them the assistance of an organization with a wider range of operations and resource.

The patrol of the state highways by a trained motorized force would be incalculable value in protecting pedestrians, law abiding motorists and the users of horse-drawn vehicles from intoxicated and reckless drivers, and in preventing the alarming number of fatal accidents now occurring. This patrol would be constantly available for general police work and the expenditure for its maintenance would be justified. It would become insurance against the various undesirable conditions that now exist.

Commission members then underlined a concern that would result in traditional state police duties:

> The annual county and agricultural fairs attract a vast amount of automobile traffic and are productive of conditions which require extensive police protection in the localities where the fairs are held. The handling of the automobile traffic at the fairs and on the highways could be effectively performed by a state patrol force, and the congestion and danger attendant on gatherings of this kind be practically eliminated.

> The character of police patrol which we consider it advisable to create is a specially organized and highly trained body, acting under state supervision and constantly employed in the prevention of crime, the apprehension of criminals, and the protection of life and property generally throughout the state and especially in the rural and sparsely settled districts. This force should be organized on a semi-military basis for the purpose of discipline, training and administration; and should be distributed over the state in small groups for patrol duty, but capable of being quickly mobilized in to larger units in an emergency.

The commission closed its report with precise recommendations for legislative action. Members visualized a highly trained, mobile organization assigned strategically throughout the state. Motorcycles were recommended as the principal means of transportation. Horses would play a critical role. There would be enough animals to mount half the new force for training purposes, and later, for use on difficult winter patrols.

A Uniformed Branch

The commission's report referred to the force as a "uniformed branch." The new organization would be placed in the Department of Public Safety, itself just more than a year old. More specifically, commission members specified that the uniformed force be located in the state police division. The action preserved the direct line of continuity between the 1865 founding of the State Constabulary and the events then about to unfold in the spring of 1921.

The recommendations of Commissioner Foote and his colleagues received swift legislative action. A bill containing the commission's principal proposals moved in timely fashion through both houses of the General Court. Final legislative enactment was completed by late May. The historic bill required only the governor's signature to become law.

Governor Channing H. Cox on May 27, 1921 signed the legislation. The Massachusetts State Police Patrol had been founded. The statute became effective on August 27, authorizing the enlistment of fifty men. That cadre would carry a heavy burden. Theirs would be the responsibility for translating an idea into the reality of a statewide, uniformed force. Public support would be critical. It would not come easily. The performance of those selected would determine the outcome of this state's experiment with a uniformed, state police organization.

Personal biography and public policy often intersect at a crucial juncture. That fact of history often is critical to the success of a new enterprise. In retrospect, one can perceive how that phenomenon operated here. It merits brief review.

Commissioner Alfred E. Foote on December 1, 1919 had been appointed head of the new Public Safety Department. Named as chairman of the commission to examine rural crime problems, he participated actively in framing legislative recommendations. A key specification was that the new uniformed force be placed in the state police division of the Department of Public Safety. Foote was the agency's administrative head.

Perhaps as important, the commissioner had earned the military title of general. He had commanded infantry during World War I, serving with the 104th Division in France. General Foote thus was ably prepared to provide requisite leadership in recruiting the new force. Moreover, he could turn for help to those who had served under him in the American Expeditionary Force. The performance of his immediate subordinates would be critical. Organizing, equipping and training the first contingent of "State Troopers" would prove a formidable challenge.

George A. Parker rivaled Foote in military experience. He had served on the Mexican border under Colonel John J. Pershing. It was a campaign designed to destroy the legendary Pancho Villa, thereby ending the border raids then taking a heavy toll of life and property. Cavalry had provided the principal military thrust in border fighting. That experience would prove invaluable to Parker in his new responsibilities. George Parker also had served under General Foote in France. That association now caused Foote to turn to him for assistance. Time would not be on their side. The first decisions on personnel would be critical. An untested public policy would ride on the personal qualities of those selected.

A number of those who would be chosen had served with Foote and Parker in the 104th Infantry Division. All had some type of military experience. Strength of character would be essential. These men were to be organized on a "semi-military basis for the purpose of discipline, training and administration."

That was the charge. It was a formidable challenge. There would be a public accounting of the outcome.

THE ROARING TWENTIES

Boston, 1921. General Alfred E. Foote. Foote during World War I served in France, on December 1, 1919, became the state's first commissioner of public safety, chaired the 1920 commission that recommended a rural, uniformed force, and in 1921 was the first commanding officer of the State Police Patrol. He served in that post until 1933, longer than any of his distinguished successors.

Springfield, Indian Motorcycle Factory, 1921. Left to Right: Thomas J. McConnell, Instructor Charles Armstrong, William F. Fitzmaurice (in sidecar), Richard H. Mooney, Charles T. Beaupre, Joseph A Fouche. Beaupre in 1925 was promoted to captain and executive officer, then the top rank in the uniformed branch. He succeeded George A. Parker who had helped to launch the 1921 experiment with a uniformed, statewide force.

Chapter Two

THE STATE POLICE PATROL

The French poet and novelist was dead 35 years when the idea of a statewide, uniformed enforcement agency was formalized by statute. But Hugo had been right. In fact, history had proven the wisdom of his perceptive observation long before he uttered the memorable words. Nothing in the human experience *is* more certain of ultimate vindication than an idea whose time has come. An idea, though, begins as an image in the mind's eye. It is a fragile thing, and it is elusive. Whether it will take form and substance is the formidable challenge of those confronted with the risks that always attend a new and untested enterprise.

Forty young men on September 1, 1921 stood at attention on the State House steps. The Capitol's historic gold dome glistened brightly on sunlit Beacon Hill. On signal, each raised his right hand as Secretary of State Frederick Cook carefully articulated the oath of office. As the men repeated his words, they became members of the State Police Patrol. It was a proud moment. Excitement was in the air. They were the first. None had gone before.

Governor Channing H. Cox presided at the historic ceremony. He and Commissioner Alfred E. Foote must have been extremely gratified as they congratulated the "First Class." The two had completed successfully the first, critical phase in transforming a law enforcement concept into an operational reality. George A. Parker was equally pleased. Now he was Captain Parker, the State Police Patrol's first executive officer. His responsibilities were substantial. He was prepared. The men would soon know the personal challenge of meeting the exacting standards of their new leader.

Those standards began immediately. The men were marched to the Boston and Worcester Transportation Depot in downtown Boston. They boarded the trolley for Framingham Center. It was a rather long trip. The sense of distance was reduced by the conversations that soon began, generated by the unspoken awareness of sharing a new adventure. Shortly before dusk they arrived at Framingham Center. The training site was another three miles.

The "Poor Farm" loomed large at the side of Southboro Road. It was not noted for modern facilities. The day's second march had dulled any lingering expectations that the new enterprise might be attended by the best in contemporary tastes, whether for housing or in personal equipment. Reality slowly took hold as firmly as the first night's darkness.

The Poor Farm became the operations nerve center of the State Police Patrol. It would serve both as a troop headquarters and as the training school. The men mustered at dawn the next day behind the rambling buildings. Their horses were quartered in a large barn. Within several days, new motorcycles arrived. The "bikes," with the horses, would be the sole means of transportation for the duration of training.

Ten additional men shortly joined the training troop. They had been sworn as provisional state patrol officers some weeks earlier, and had been guarding President Warren G. Harding while he vacationed on Cape Cod. Such assignments were repeated occasionally while the group was in training. For example, two of the recruits were assigned to an investigation in New Bedford. Even though the Whaling City was some seventy miles from the training site, they used motorcycles for the trip. Nevertheless, such assignments, and the storytelling they generated, strengthened the group's resolve to complete successfully the rigorous training requirements.

Surplus army uniforms were the official clothing issue. Few of the recruits enjoyed a complete, matched uniform. Some had light shirts, while others wore darker shades. Puttees, destined to become a revered tradition, were a particular problem. A few of the trainees were blessed with leather "putts," while their more unfortunate colleagues suffered with canvas ones. A comparison with "Coxey's Army" would not have been severe. But this army knew where it was going.

Inevitably, special talents emerged. Several of the recruits were expert mechanics and that talent now paid off. Twelve abandoned World War I army ambulances were "requisitioned." The vehicles were completely stripped. In their place appeared six newly overhauled touring cars; the first cruisers of the State Police Patrol.

Intensive training continued throughout the fall of 1921. Demanding physical requirements were exceeded only by the necessity to comprehend an enormous amount of information essential to enforcement of the Commonwealth's statutes. Officers of the detective branch made important contributions. Their field experience was invaluable, and they enjoyed the credibility of an admired record in the complex field of law enforcement. As the weeks wore on, the confidence of the recruits grew. They knew they were making it.

Finally, the 1921 recruit troop, the "First Class," mustered on the training field for graduation exercises. It was mid-November. Shadows lengthened even as the men went through a performance designed to demonstrate newly acquired skills. State dignitaries, enforcement officials, families and friends were impressed and encouraged. The tough training had paid off. This was a disciplined, coherent body of men. A unique array of individuals were now one in spirit, if not in fact.

The ceremonies were shortly over. The work began. Captain Parker wasted no time. In an exercise that would become a tradition, he read the assignments for the new graduates. Anticipation was in the air as the executive officer went down the roster. Some of the men had never even visited sections of the state where shortly they would be enforcing the law. In truth, some of the recruits had not heard of the towns they would patrol. This was especially so for those assigned to B Troop Headquarters in Northampton. Half of the new graduates were assigned there. The others would begin their state police careers as members of A Troop, Framingham.

ASSIGNMENT: THE BERKSHIRES

Captain Parker charted five widely separated routes for those going to B Troop. The trip began early the next morning, on horseback, riding in pairs. The longest route was estimated at five days hard riding, while the shortest would require three days travel. The controlling factor was the endurance of the horses, a consideration not accorded the riders. Each mounted officer carried a carefully drawn map pinpointing the rural hamlets on his assigned course of travel.

Patrolmen, that was their official title, Williams and O'Neil rode a route north of the center line. They would have four days of steady riding. Patrolman MacMillan and Holleran were assigned the northernmost route, at least five days of hard riding to B Troop Headquarters.

That first public venture by the State Police Patrol created several legendary stories, each destined to become more fascinating, and humorous, with the passing years. MacMillan and Holleran had stopped at a small, sleepy village at the end of the third day. They were greeted by an empty building marked "Town Hall." It was boarded up. Encouraged by a dim light from the inside, they approached a nearby house.

Their knock brought a tentative opening to the front door. Blinking at them in amazement was a local farmer, heir to years of peaceful living without interruptions from "outsiders." Looking for all the world like World War I "Doughboys," MacMillan and Holleran proudly announced that they were officers of the new State Police Patrol. Could they and their horses board for the night? As the door slammed shut, the noise emphasized that many citizens had not even heard of the new police organization.

Things changed for the better as the riders assembled in Northampton on Thanksgiving Day, 1921. The town fathers, local dignitaries and many of "Hamp's" citizens greeted them warmly. That greeting, and the turkey dinner that followed, began a relationship that would endure. B Troop Headquarters would remain for years the administrative nerve center for state police operations in the Bay State's four western counties.

Lieutenant George E. Burke was the first B Troop commander. Charles T. Beaupre was assigned as first sergeant. Corporal Thomas H. O'Neil first wore the distinctive chevrons which signified that rank. Nineteen patrolmen completed the roster. Thus, a total complement of 22 first staffed B Troop Headquarters.

The headquarters operation was established in the state armory on King Street. A small room in one corner of the military structure served as the first administrative office. The men were also quartered there. Space, to put it mildly, was at a premium. The horses fared better. They were kept at a stable about five minutes walk from the armory. There was one "troop cruiser." It was enshrined under close supervision inside the armory, flanked by the troop motorcycles.

What could have been the inspiration for this unique enterprise in policing? It was not salary. The men had been paid $50.00 per month while in the training school. The level of "remuneration" rose to $75.00 per month following graduation. Finally, the organization's salary schedule, after six months, was prescribed by the famous "Rule 16":

Rank	Salary Per Year
Captain	$2,500.00
First Lieutenant	$2,000.00
Second Lieutenant	$1,800.00
First Sergeant	$1,500.00
Supply Sergeant	$1,450.00
Corporal	$1,300.00
Farrier	$1,260.00
Mechanic	$1,260.00
Patrolman	$1,200.00

The "Farrier" was actually the "horse-shoer," a critical responsibility in a police operation so heavily dependent upon horses. This was especially so during the first winter in B Troop. Most patrols were mounted. Typically, a patrol would last five days, usually beginning on Monday morning.

One of these found Patrolman Harold B. Williams crossing the Connecticut River, turning north at Amherst, and resting the first night in New Salem. The next day's ride covered towns later flooded to create the Quabin Reservoir. Then, on through Pelham, with a return to Amherst by darkness for a night's sleep. Following a different patrol route the next morning, Williams slept the third night in New Salem. By the fourth evening he and his horse were back in Amherst. The fifth and final patrol day followed a different route in returning to troop headquarters in Northampton.

Weekends were largely committed to barracks duty. Personal gear was checked and polished, horses were groomed, and reports were written, reviewed and carefully filed. In addition, there were many "housekeeping" chores assigned, just to keep everyone "turned to." Leisure time would have to wait.

Grooming the horses presented problems. Many of the animals previously had not enjoyed such careful attention. Most had been borrowed and they came from a wide variety of owners. Several had been donated by wealthy horse fanciers. Most however, had earned their keep on the front end of a farm plow. A bargain had been struck in order to get the horses for the training school and the first patrols. The state force would groom and care for them during the long winter, thus returning superbly conditioned animals in the spring. The owners, in turn, "donated" the trusty steeds.

The deal had a lighter side. Because of the great variation in the quality of the horse flesh, there was friendly but firm competition to ride certain of the animals while studiously avoiding others. One such outcome found Patrolman Duncan MacMillan ceremoniously astride a purebred animal worth some $1500, while his partner, Patrolman Joseph E. Holleran, suffered the antics of a balky steed unable to bring $30.00 at an auction.

The five-day patrols were assigned for three consecutive weeks, followed by one week of barracks duty. The men had to pay for their food and lodging for one month. Then, with a silent prayer, each would submit his expenses hoping for reimbursement within a few months. There was no "padding." There wasn't room for it. A night's lodging and food, for horse and rider, averaged about $1.00. There was, however, small print in that contract. The state police patrolman was required to help with chores while boarding overnight. Predictably, stories that grew out of that experience enshrined several of the "First Class" as legends of the state force.

A unique patrol technique was the distribution to farmers of black cards. They were eight by ten inches and had big letters "S.P.P.," for State Police Patrol. The cards were placed conspicuously in a front window to signal the need for police service. The system was patterned on one used by city dwellers to summon the "ice man" and his horse and wagon to replenish the natural coolant in the family "ice box." Through experience, the "ice man" would know whether a "ten cent piece" or, perhaps, a "fifteen cent piece" of the refrigerant was required.

Stories abound about the use of the cards. Time has enhanced most. Following a blizzard, for example, Patrolman Williams and his mount plowed a path to an isolated farmhouse with the "S.P.P." card prominently displayed. Did the officer have a two-cent stamp? He did. Could he mail the letter? He would. This was later followed by an order for a corset to be purchased in Northampton, delivered subsequently by regular patrol!

Innovation was the watchword. There were no precedents. This void included the problem of uniforms, especially missing parts. Regular issue was forest green. If an officer desired matched breeches, he bought them. The first rainstorm was a bit of an embarrassment; there were no raincoats. Gloves were considered a luxury item. They too were purchased by the men. The well dressed state patrolman, therefore, owned his own breeches, raincoat and gloves. The state owned the rest. It is not an overstatement to say that, during that era, the ownership included all but a tiny fraction of his private life.

WHY THEY SERVED

In reality, the first uniformed, state officers did not have a job. They embraced a lifestyle. Duty tours were not measured in hours or days, but in weeks. Originally, leave, or "time off" as it soon became known, was limited to forty-eight hours per month. Time off could be cancelled on a moment's notice. It often was. This system in practice soon evolved to "one in fifteen," a 24 hour day off following duty on fourteen consecutive days and nights.

What kind of men would make such a commitment, in a statewide force introducing a yet radical concept in policing? What had lured them? What kept them going? Why didn't they walk away? Who were their loved ones? Why didn't *they* demand that these husbands and fathers return to their homes, frequently many, many miles away?

Answers could not have come easily for them, nor do they now. Glib explanations have been attempted. But those offering simplistic reasoning did not, themselves, live the early experience. What, then, was the answer, the *real* reason? It remains illusive. Years afterwards, a woman who had been a state police wife committed her feelings to paper. She remains anonymous. But the deeply felt thoughts she authored preserved the poignancy of that long lost time of severe personal sacrifice:

> I married a state trooper. Boy, I had courage. His salary was fifty dollars a month for the first three months, and when he graduated his pay went to $75.00 for the next three months.
>
> The day his class graduated, I couldn't afford to take a day off from my job to watch him receive that famous diploma. My heart would have been broken, anyway, for our home was in Boston . . . and when they read off the travel orders . . . he was sent, of all places, to "B" Troop. A little farther west and he would have been in the New York State Police.
>
> One day off in ten. That was bad enough, but in those days the words "travel time" were a big joke. He spent half the night getting to Boston, and he always left the night before his day off ended to be back to the barracks in time the next

morning. Very few troopers owned automobiles, and travel was by the the well-known "Greyhound". We hardly saw each other.

Came the end of the six months' probationary period and "we" went to $100 a month . . . . with $5 taken out for retirement. I wonder how we ever lived on $95 a month. Food was cheap, however, and I recall going shopping on Saturday night with five dollars and coming out with two big paper bags full of groceries.

Then came our first baby. We were so happy, but we also learned that our baby had added greatly to our expenses. Doctors' bills had to be paid. The hospital wanted their money in advance, and in the state police there was no way to supplement the small salary, so we just learned to stuff our pride in our pockets and live on what we had. Waiting for the annual step rate increase was all we lived for. Eventually things got better. We got back some of the pay cut we had suffered, so I decided I could afford to move to "B" Troop, with my baby, so that we could see daddy on a night off.

The big bogey man hit us . . . TRANSFERS . . . the only thing that could scare a state trooper. Maybe it was because of the mean way they used to do it. Orders came out on the teletype, effective at midnight. No time to say good-bye to any friends in the territory, no time to do anything but pack his foot locker and be on his way. All over the state other troopers would be doing the same thing.

Many a night I sat alone in the living room wondering what dangers my man might be facing, even at that moment. Every time I heard the words "State Police" on the radio I would nearly break an arm trying to turn up the volume. I wondered when some trooper got hurt, who he was . . . what troop he was in . . did he have a family? I guess I wasn't as tough as I pretended to be.

Several years went by and our faith was finally rewarded. One big, big day he called me to tell me that he had just been promoted to corporal. I was so happy. The title didn't mean a thing to me and I didn't gloat over his promotion, for I knew there would be troopers' wives who would be disappointed that their husbands didn't get "made." I had already figured out how much more money we would get, for we were expecting our second baby and we would need money. But time marches on. It is unbelievable how fast the years go by when you are on the state police. The children were now going to school and that took more money. I learned to sew and make dresses for the girls because I had to save money. Came the day when he was "made" sergeant. What a thrill that was. Financially, we were sitting on top of the world.

Finally came the day when he left the state

police. That really took courage. You just don't give the best years of your life to an outfit and then walk out. You cannot forget.

We look back over the years now. We owe a lot to the state police. It helped us when we needed help the most. It taught us many things, for which we are grateful. It gave us an education that no college could provide and we appreciate it. The children are all grown up now and married, and we are alone again. All we have left are memories . . . all pleasant ones, for life is too short to recall any but the pleasant ones. Whenever you think of the word "courage" think of me . . . for I had courage . . . I married a state trooper.

What can be added? Very little. These first troopers were a unique breed. They had rough edges, but they were courteous. They were physical but they felt deeply about protecting the underdog. They would listen, but they would fight. Some were unlettered, but they all understood people, especially the rural folk who became their staunchest supporters.

The years have taken their toll of these men and what they did. But their accomplishments are secured for posterity by the fact of the current state police organization. They served at a unique, historical moment. Their selflessness and courage gave life to an idea whose time had come.

They were the first. Every trooper, since privileged to serve, owes a lasting debt of gratitude to these law enforcement pioneers. They were the Class of 1921. The "First Class." That honor shall always remain reserved to them alone:

• • •

THE FIRST RECRUIT TROOP

September 1, 1921

Barber, Alfred W.	Howland, John P.	O'Neil, Thomas H.
Barrett, Edward J.	Jason, Justin F.	Ontus, George F.
Beaupre, Charles T.	Kelley, Edward P.	Parker, George A.
Brown, George E.	Kimball, Roy E.	Russell, Harold G.
Burke, George E.	Lenhart, Ernest J.	Sardina, Anthony
Carey, John Francis, Jr.	Lundberg, Frederick W.	Scott, Bertrand G.F.
Cole, Frederick R.	MacMillan, Duncan	Sheeran, James H.
Collins, James J.	Mahoney, James P.	Sheerin, William J.
Cote, George H.	Manning, Axel A.	Skinner, George D.
Dasey, Albert W.	Marsh, Irving L.	Soderberg, Gustaf A.
Fitzmaurice, William F.	McCarthy, Charles B.	Stankard, Leo F.
Fouche, Joseph A.	McConnell, Thomas J.	Stowell, Eugene E.
Glaras, Nicholas	McNamee, George E.	Sullivan, William J.
Gully, Edward J.	Mooney, Richard H., Jr.	Thom, Walter A.
Hackett, William J.	O'Connor, Joseph E.	Whittemore, Howard M.
Hayes, George E., Jr.	O'Donnell, John J.	Williams, Harold B.
Holleran, Joseph M.		

Chapter 461 of the Acts of 1921 had authorized the first appointments to the State Police Patrol. The Pennsylvania "strike breaking" experience had caused fears, especially in organized labor, that the force would be used here for similar purposes. The legislature disarmed that threat by defining precisely when the agency could be mobilized: "Said force shall not be used or called upon for service in any industrial dispute, unless *actual violence* has occurred therein, and then only by *order of the Governor* or the person acting in his place.

The opponents of the force were not yet finished. The General Court enacted Chapter 331 of the Acts of 1922, authorizing ninety additional men for the agency. A petition was filed with the Secretary of State to block the appointments and force the issue to a general referendum. The petition's sponsors were vocal. They worked hard to get the required number of signatures. By then, however, the State Police Patrol had earned a growing number of strong supporters. The referendum petition failed to get the required support, and, on July 25, 1922, the force was authorized to enlist ninety new recruits.

Meantime, preparations for selection of personnel and training had gone ahead. There was thus no time lost in getting the second recruit class, the Class of 1922, ready for field service. Some of the new patrolmen repeated the long trek to "Hamp," headquarters for B Troop. Several of the new arrivals helped to staff B Troop's first substation in East Lee. The barracks was actually a barn behind the home of Judge Bossidy of the Lee Court. Horses were quartered on the first floor. Naturally, the men lived in the loft. "B-1," Lee's designation, was first staffed by Corporal H.M. Whittemore, and Patrolmen Stankard, Mooney, McGady and Stingel.

For several, the stay was short. Increased patrol coverage was a priority. New, strategic barracks locations were established. Thus, Whittemore and Stingel on November 14, 1922 were transferred to the new C Troop Headquarters in Paxton, just north and west of Worcester.

TROOP D ESTABLISHED

Commissioner Alfred E. Foote, meantime, had received a petition requesting a barracks in Plymouth County. This was shortly accomplished. The first state police operations were set up on Main Street in South Scituate, now part of Norwell. The barracks was located next to the post office, adjacent to the community's general store. Quarters consisted of a single, open room. There was no toilet, nor was there running water. A saving feature was the presence of yet another "Poor Farm," directly across the street. The men swallowed hard. Prides does not go down easily. But necessity prevailed. The state police complement shortly trooped across the street to share the "Poore Farm's" running water and toilets with its unfortunate, but better supplied, residents.

Norwell originally was a substation under A Troop, Framingham. Lieutenant Charles T. Beaupre was A Troop commander. Worcester's George E. Brown, a corporal, was Norwell's first supervisor. Herbert J. Stingel followed Brown. Along with several patrolmen, five horses completed the original complement. The animals were stabled behind the "Blue Bowl Tea Room." Following early morning chores, the men sat down to hearty breakfasts prepared by Mrs. Phipps. She charged fifty cents for making breakfast for five officers, whether or not all were present.

A new barracks was opened in Norwell in 1923. It was luxurious by comparison. There were four bedrooms, a kitchen and an office. Mrs. Phipps' first "blue plate" special must have carried the day. She was hired by the state for sixty dollars per month. Canned goods were purchased in large lots. The corporal supervised local shopping for meat, fish and fresh vegetables. The early operation center featured a pot bellied coal stove, and, a welcome innovation, an electric pump for the well. The men knew they had arrived, when, a bit later, the benevolent Commonwealth installed a bath tub!

Norwell's original "area" was formidable. Patrols, motorcycles or horses, began at Hull on Boston's outer harbor. The patrol route meandered south, through Plymouth, to the Sagamore Bridge, then a wooden span across the newly opened Cape Cod Canal. The men would turn east at the canal, patrol the seaside communities bordering Buzzards Bay, and pass through the teeming industrial centers of New Bedford and Fall River. That arduous journey completed, the route then took them north through Middleboro, Bridgewater and the "shoe city," Brockton. Finally, after several days, they would return to Norwell.

That return signalled the chance for some rest and leisure time, after a myriad of "in house" duties were completed. But, poignantly, in retrospect, they could not go home. That happy event, as in B Troop, came only once, for 24 hours, following fifteen days and nights of duty. It could not have been an easy time. But, then, one's personal life was not especially important when measured against the organization's public mandate.

By late 1923, the four original troops of the State Police Patrol had been established. After Northampton and Framingham, C Troop Headquarters in September 1922 had been set up on route 122 in the old Paxton Inn. The early experience with Norwell as an A Troop substation evolved to the first D Troop Headquarters operation in Middleboro, not far from the sprawling "State Farm" in Bridgewater. Each troop developed an organizational structure, strategically located. For example, Westminster was the first C Troop substation, followed by an outpost in Petersham. These were shortly followed by Brookfield and Oxford.

Troop C headquarters moved in 1923 from Paxton to neighboring Holden. The Westminster barracks was later shifted to Lunenburg, then to North Leominster. Petersham's operations were transferred to Athol, and a new Brookfield building replaced the old, rented quarters. Oxford subsequently was shifted to Grafton following completion of route 140, the then modern artery linking Worcester with Cape Cod.

A barracks in Barnstable, on Cape Cod, had functioned originally with Norwell as A Troop substations. Each became in 1923 part of the new D Troop. The Barnstable barracks was located in the county court house. Some of the "D-2" originals like Ed Gully, Jim Mahoney and "Fats" Stoli ate at the nearby Nickerson home. Mrs. Nickerson, like Mrs. Phipps, her colleague across Cape Cod Bay at Norwell, and their counterparts throughout the state, saved many a gloomy day with a piping hot "homecooked" meal. They were among the first "cooks" who themselves became legends in the early years of the state patrol experience.

The authorized strength of the force was steadily increasing. Training classes were in session yearly. The first "in service" courses had begun in B Troop. Initial sessions were, in fact, called "B Troop Day." Training was conducted at Leeds, a section of Northampton then serving as B Troop headquarters. Operations had moved there from the original armory site.

Lieutenant William J. Sheeran supervised the first B Troop refreshers in 1924. Among those attending were: Francis J. O'Connell, Jack Powers, George F. Alexander, Warner F. Eaton, Ralph E. Small, Martin J. Beattie, Louis J. Perachi, Thomas Mitchell, John J. Donahue, and Llewelyn A. Lowther. For Lowther, the first "B Troop Day" at Leeds would be one of his final duty tours. On September 20, 1924 he became the first uniformed state police officer to lose his life in the line of duty. Patrolman Lowther was killed when his motorcycle left the road on a bad curve in Adams. His tragic death was a shock to the yet young enforcement organization. The two wheelers, unfortunately, were destined to

take a heavy toll in death and injuries during the years they would serve as the principal transportation of the statewide force.

By the mid-1920s, the authorized personnel complement stood at 140. The organizational structure of the force had developed rapidly. General Headquarters remained in the State House, in Boston. Troop A was headquartered in Framingham, with substations in Reading, Concord and Rowley. Troop B Headquarters in Northampton commanded barracks in Lee, Shelburne Falls, Agawam and Chesire. Troop C had moved from Paxton to Holden, with outposts in Westminster, Oxford, Brookfield and Bolton. Middleboro housed D Troop Headquarters. Barracks were strategically located in Norwell, Barnstable and Freetown. Officers were also stationed on the islands of Martha's Vineyard and Nantucket.

"BRICKBOTTOM"

If the "Roaring Twenties" would be remembered for anything, it would be as the heyday of "Prohibition." Congress on January 29, 1919 enacted the Volstead Act, the nation's "Noble Experiment." Massachusetts subsequently ratified the eighteenth amendment, and enforcement began here on December 5, 1924. The "bootlegging" era had dawned. The state force would be deeply involved.

Commissioner Alfred E. Foote had remained in office. He summarized the force's activities in a report to the governor, especially the enforcement of prohibition.

> Added to the already extensive duties of the state police has been the enforcement of prohibition, a matter of wide-spread operation, oftentimes in out-of-the-way places, chosen because of their quiet, isolated locations, in order to divert suspicion and not to attract attention. This duty has caused our uniformed branch of the state police to be doubly vigilant and to greatly extend the patroling of roads and highways which would ordinarily not need such close observation.
> No road today is too obscure or rough to prevent the operators of bootleg cars to use them. Night and day the movement of these goods is attempted and our limited force is compelled to be alert and on duty to a far greater extent than any other police force in the Commonwealth.
> Our efforts in connection with prohibition enforcement have met with marked success and a number of cases have been outstanding. The so-called 'Brickbottom' raid of last spring at Somerville is, perhaps, the one best known to the public at large because of the wide publicity given to it in the newspapers. It was carefully planned and well executed and there is no doubt but that it had a good effect in the entire vicinity for some time afterward. However, though this particular affair was heralded far and near, it was nothing new in the almost every day operation of our State Police. Day after day the members of this division, both detectives and patrolmen, are busy with the problems confronting them.

"Brickbottom" indeed was a spectacular raid. Over one hundred officers had been brought secretly into Commonwealth Armory for the massive strike. Commissioner Foote, Captain

Beaupre and District Attorney Arthur K. Reading of Middlesex County had huddled all afternoon on final details. Raiding parties moved out about 9:30 p.m., traveling in fifteen Reo trucks to the sections of Somerville and Cambridge known locally as "Brickbottom."

Thirty-eight separate locations were hit. Each was a success. Over one hundred were arrested. Huge quantities of illegal spirts were seized. A problem developed when the court house cellar quickly filled up with seized containers. Five gallon cans were piled high at the rear of the building. The next day, a Sunday, a hot sun broiled the alcoholic contents, splitting some of the cans. Throughout that day, the odor of "booze" wafted through East Cambridge, proof of the "bootlegger's" skills, and the high quality of the illicit spirits.

Grand Jury indictments were handed down against those arrested, and some received jail sentences. Forfeiture proceedings were held, and the alcoholic beverages were ordered destroyed, under "heavy guard." The "Brickbottom" raids would become the operations model for hundreds of similar thrusts during the prohibition era. The raids helped immeasurably to establish the credentials of the state force as an enforcement organization free of localized restrictions.

The raids had required close communications. This was still a difficult task, but unique systems had evolved that ensured maximum performance. As an example, General Headquarters would telephone a priority message from Boston to troop headquarters in Framingham and Middleboro. Framingham would immediately call C Troop Headquarters in Holden, with a rapid relay from there to B Headquarters in Northampton. Each troop headquarters would then alert each of its substations.

Troop substations would quickly notify "call stations" by phone. "Call stations" were gas stations and stores on roads regularly covered by patrols. They, in turn, would place the "S.P.P." card in their windows to notify a passing patrol of the waiting message. Some gas stations had roof lights. These would be illuminated when a trooper was needed. The system worked remarkably well, and, usually, a message could be sent across the state in minutes. In reality, it was a more sophisticated version of the basic "S.P.P." card system devised by the first Northampton mounted patrols in 1921.

THE "PROTECTOR"

Meantime, other capabilities were developing. The *Protector* had been commissioned on October 4, 1924 as the third state police patrol vessel, following the *Lexington* and the *Lotus*. The *Lotus* was actually a small launch. She had remained in the service during the *Lexington's* tenure, used principally for shallow water duties. The *Protector* had been designed at ninety feet. Funds, however, fell short, and she came off the ways 68 feet bow to stern. The patrol craft drew nine feet of water, cruised at nine knots, and had a "one-pounder" fore and aft. The Massachusetts State Seal, prominently displayed in her wheelhouse, proclaimed her authority to enforce the Bay State's laws.

Lieutenant Clifton W. Kendall was the only skipper the *Protector* ever had. He captained the craft from her 1924 launching until she retired from active service in 1933. Kendall, a former Navy man, headed a crew of five civilians. Uniformed officers were assigned aboard for special details. There were many such duties. In one year alone, 63 vessels were boarded for inspection purposes,

and 319 oil spills were investigated. Each winter the sturdy craft broke ice in the Charles River Basin, not far from her berth at Pier One in East Boston.

The *Protector's* relatively slow speed, nine knots, prevented direct action against speedy "rum runners." But there were other, more glamorous duties. On one assignment, she and her proud crew escorted His Majesty's Ship *Scarborough* on 1929 visits to New Bedford and Boston. The *Protector* was the last of the state police vessels, phased out of service in 1933. Lieutenant Kendall later donated the craft's official name plate to the state force. It remains displayed at the state police academy, a reminder of a unique public safety service performed in the now distant past.

During this period, an "Auto Squad" had been organized under the direction of Detective Lieutenant Silas Smith. Assigned in the mid-1920s to the special unit were J.J. Dacy, Everett I. Flanders, Joseph C. Crescio and John F. Dempsey. The select group was extremely active. Investigations were mounted against auto theft, including serious crimes committed with the stolen vehicles.

One unique case found Crescio and Dempsey in downtown Boston. The pair was looking for a particularly active Canadian who had been confounding enforcement authorities with his illicit activities. Suddenly, the two stopped, staring in disbelief. There, right in front of them, was the long wanted suspect, casually strolling with his dog, all the while tapping the sidewalk with a prized cane. A swift apprehension was quickly followed by trial and conviction. The formerly elusive target received three to five years.

Crescio, some time later, had occasion to visit the Norfolk Prison Colony. Presently, a prisoner casually approached. As their eyes met, the state officer immediately recognized his old adversary, the Canadian auto thief. Following nervous amenities, the prisoner thanked Crescio for arresting him, and, especially, for helping him to get to Norfolk. There he had received quality medical attention for several ailments he had been neglecting on the "outside." He offered that, as soon as his enforced stay ended, he would return to Canada, there to share his new sense of stability with his loved ones. The chance meeting ended as abruptly as it had begun. A profound thanks was again offered by a man deprived of his freedom. It was a towering irony, one reserved on occasion for those charged with enforcement of criminal statutes.

Meantime, a well defined staff section continued to develop. Most likely it was not planned but, rather, was a response to critical needs. Thus, in 1925, Patrolman Julius W. Toelken and Walter Tompkins were assigned to start the "photo bureau" with fifty dollars. That sum bought all the necessary equipment for this forerunner of what would become a highly technical support operation.

About the same time, Lieutenant Harold B. Williams helped to set up the traffic bureau. Auto accidents were analyzed for cause, and enforcement bulletins were issued to focus traffic enforcement activities. Similarly, there was need to coordinate the administration of support materials. Horses, motorcycles, uniforms, personal equipment; all had to be accounted for. These critical activities were centered in a headquarters supply bureau. Sergeant Warner F. Eaton was the first supervisor. Supply administration was destined to grow in complexity with the expanding organization.

THE TRICK RIDERS

The 1920 study commission had cited policing of the state's many fairs as a principal responsibility of the recommended uniformed force. This duty began early. By the mid-1920s members of the state patrol were a fixture at these annual events. One of the largest was the "Eastern States Exposition," in reality, the "Springfield Fair." One of the finest state fairs in the nation, the exposition annually drew large throngs.

The state force quickly had developed expertise in trick motorcycle riding and horsemanship. Special units were formed to provide demonstrations of the complex skills the men had mastered. The 1925 Springfield Fair featured a special state patrol motorcycle drill team under the direction of Sergeant Herbert J. Stingel. Team members were: Corporal R. Terpstra, Corporal J. Ryan, and Patrolmen J. Concannon, F. Lambert, T. Greer, T. Anderson, W. White, D. McIsaac and G. Rapport. The intricate motorcycle drills were a big hit wherever the unit performed. This type of public presentation played a key role in the rapid development of citizen support for the state force.

A number of the "fair" assignments were in the southeastern section of the state. These festive events were annually held in Norwell, Marshfield and Brockton. It appears that the state patrol's trick horse riding unit first went through its paces in these D Troop locations. By 1926 the men had gained a considerable reputation for their skills.

The riding team was in great demand. Appearances were made throughout the state. A berth on the team was a prized assignment. But it wasn't all glamour. The riding feats performed by man and horse required long hours of training. Yet, volunteers eagerly sought the assignment. Among them were: Sergeant Al Dasey, Andy Tuney, Hollis "Sam" Beattie, Joe Crowley, John Avedian, Desmond Fitzgerald, Pat Whalen, Al Dodge, Jim Ryan, John Reardon, Tom Norton, Charles Morrison, Ted Fitzgerald, Arnie Olsson, Herb Stingel and Bill Shimkus.

Some of these men performed at the 1926 Philadelphia Sesqui-Centennial. The team captured top honors from a host of other state forces. A feature of the centennial activities was a dress parade, led by three Bay State troopers: John Reardon carried the national colors, James P. Ryan held the state flag, and Thomas P. Norton posted the distinctive colors of the state force. The trick riding tream was active throughout the remainder of the decade. Membership was a select assignment. The mounted unit, however, slowly gave way to changing modes in transportation. The team was to be disbanded in the early 1930s, shortly before the 1933 termination of mounted patrols.

The twenties witnessed one of the most famous cases in the history of American jurisprudence. "Sacco and Vanzetti" became household words during the decade. Their trial at Dedham Court House aroused passionate protests throughout the world. State police officers had been deeply involved in all aspects of the case from the night the tragic murder led, ultimately, to the investigation, arrest, conviction, and execution of the Italian immigrants.

The Dedham Superior Court trial held the world's attention. Detectives and uniformed state officers provided security throughout the emotion packed proceedings. Inside the court house the drama unfolded daily. It peaked when Charles J. Van Amburgh, the state police ballistics expert, testified. Van Amburgh calmly explained the defendant's gun fired the death bullet. While a great deal of controversy has since attended this case, Van Amburgh's scientific conclusions stand uncontroverted after more than seven decades.

Sacco and Vanzetti's final hours passed slowly, but inexorably. A special detail was quartered in the state armory on Commonwealth Avenue in Boston, not far from "Charlestown," the ancient, brooding state prison. These men had the responsibility to maintain order as the execution hour approached. On August 22, 1927 uniformed state officers were posted around the massive gray structure that housed the state's final sanction, the electric chair. Others were stationed inside, at key sites. Detectives who had literally lived the Sacco Vanzetti case from its beginning, were now also involved in the final, poignant act of the decade long human drama.

Days earlier, the 1927 recruit class had graduated from the training school in Commonwealth Armory. Some of the new officers were assigned guard posts, a duty that, for them, would not again be approached in emotion throughout the remainder of their police careers. The recruits, joined by seasoned veterans, took up stations atop hay sheds adjacent to the death building. Lieutenant James E. Hughes commanded the unit, assisted by Sergeant William V. Shimkus. Some of their men were: D.A. Murphy, J. Higgins, R. Chamberlain, T. "Red" Norton, M. Manning, W. Delay, V. Carpenter, T. Burke, G. Conn, T. Johnson, N. Altieri, M. Hayden and F. McGady.

As darkness slowly turned to light, the state exacted the supreme legal sanction. Sacco and Vanzetti were dead. But the controversy surrounding their fate was destined to live on. For the state force, "Sacco and Vanzetti" would symbolize an era more than a trial, a time of passage from an untested, rural force to a widely respected law enforcement organization.

B TROOP FLOODS

The State Police Patrol's principal strengths were *versatility* and *mobility*. City and town lines presented no barriers. Personnel were mobilized when they were needed, where they were needed. Only a semi-military organization could do this, staffed by men who would accept severe hardships, and be willing to sacrifice personal values for organizational goals. They, and they enforcement agency they served, were, in reality, a product of the times.

It was the only way a small force could respond to the disasters that, inevitably, struck without warning. Just two months after the electrocution of Sacco and Vanzetti, B Troop suddenly faced its first, major test. It began without notice. News media on November 1, 1927, reported a tropical storm off the Atlantic coast. Veering inland, it struck Vermont. Three days and nights of heavy rain followed. Meandering streams turned to raging torrents. The Winooski and White Rivers claimed scores of lives. Property damage was over fifty million, and 105 perished in the raging flood waters. It was a warning. But there was no time.

Suddenly, in North Adams, Main Street was under three feet of yellow, angry water. The Housatonic left four hundred homeless in Pittsfield. East Lee, Chester, Middlefield and Huntington were hard hit. To the east, the mighty Connecticut was eleven feet above normal at Holyoke. Just south, the river cut a new, one mile wide bed, leaving six thousand homeless in Agawam. A disaster was happening; the great B Troop Floods of 1927.

Becket was a typical B Troop community. But the residents of the sleepy, serene hamlet would live a night of terror on November 4. An earthen dam generated the water power for the Ballou family wood-working mill. As the torrential rains continued, the mill's dam weakened. Becket lay below, defenseless. Mr. Ballou and Fred Crochiere fought their way to the top of the dam. One look was enough. A disaster was impending. The two headed to the

McCormack home, site of the local telephone exchange. As they gasped out their warning, McCormack telephoned subscribers, setting in motion a chain reaction. Neighbors were startled from their sleep, but lives were on the line. McCormack stayed at the switchboard. Ballou and Crochiere raced through the town blasting the horn on their Paige touring car.

Suddenly, with a frightening roar, the Ballou Dam collapsed. A wall of water roared through the blackness. The first wave was 25 feet high, 150 yards wide. Nothing in its path was spared. Thirty-one homes were lost. The town's post office and silk mill were destroyed. Miraculously, only one life was lost.

The morning sun revealed the true dimension of what had happened. Becket lay devastated. Corporal Marty Joyce at Lee dispatched Patrolman Charles Boakes to the ravaged hamlet. He was the first to get through. Boakes was stunned by what he saw. He knew Becket for the typical beautiful B Troop town that it was. Now, hardly believing his eyes, he moved quickly into action. Rescue and repair efforts followed swiftly. They would continue for weeks. Boakes teamed up with Larry Kidney and Mr. McCormack to rig a telephone hookup. Kidney's son, Bill, would join the state force in 1938. That morning, though, his efforts quickly got emergency messages on the repaired telephone lines. Additional help began to arrive in the stricken community.

Within hours, about twenty men from the state force were there. Headquarters was established in an inn that had survived the raging waters. Some of those on the scene had just completed the Sacco and Vanzetti detail. Joining Boakes were: J. Dempsey, L. Bond, M. Joyce, M. Sullivan, W. Eaton, V. White, H. Dineen, P. Whalen, J. Horgan, J.P. Sullivan, W. Shimkus and J. Ryan. In addition, Harold Craig was sent into Becket to coordinate support activities. Craig for years would handle administrative matters at B Troop Headquarters in Northampton.

The men remained in Becket assisting with medical treatment and helping to restore essential services. The B Troop Flood of 1927 was the first natural disaster they had faced. That experience would be repeated as the force developed expertise as the state's primary response to unexpected, life-threatening crises, whatever their location or nature.

Time passed. For men and events, it must. The flood waters had receded, and, for a time, the emotion attending the Sacco and Vanzetti ordeal had lessened. Governor Al Smith of New York had lost his 1928 bid for the presidency. Herbert Hoover was in the White House, and there was a "chicken in every pot." That briefly popular phrase was mocked as the stock market crashed in 1929. Fortunes were lost overnight. Lives were destroyed. But life itself went on.

AT DECADES END

Commissioner of Public Safety Alfred E. Foote led the enforcement organization as the decade closed. His had been a unique tenure. From the study commission in 1920, through the first, halting steps in 1921, to the accomplishments of the decade, his imprint was unmistakeable. Captain George A. Parker, Foote's first executive officer, had seen the fledgling police agency through its early challenges. His successor, Captain Charles T. Beaupre, now commanded the uniformed force.

General Headquarters remained in the State Capitol. Troop headquarters were located in Framingham, Northampton, Holden and Middleboro. Substations were strategically related to these headquarters operations in each section of the state. Support services had developed steadily.

Two hundred thirty men were in the uniformed branch, and some 220 motorcycles were assigned throughout the Commonwealth. Horses had provided almost the sole means of mobililty during the first winters. Now, after ten years of yeoman service, the faithful steeds numbered but sixty. "Cruisers" had steadily increased; there were now fifty "touring cars." Eleven sedans were restricted, rather zealously, for use by the "brass."

"Time off" still resembled service in the military. While minor variations had evolved, the official schedule remained "one in fifteen." Officers would work fourteen days and nights consecutively. A day off then followed. Upon return, they repeated the duty tour.

Salaries had not changed essentially since 1921. Recruits received $50 per month. During the first three months in the field, the "boots" jumped to $75 each month. Following six months of service the salary topped out at $100 per month. Longevity increases over the years brought incremental steps to a maximum patrolman's salary of $1,550 per year.

Life on the State Police Patrol was not easy. But neither was life generally. The nation and its people were about to enter the most threatening years in the history of the Federal Republic. The "Great Depression" had not yet arrived, but it was impending. Butter was 25 cents per pound. Cigarettes, those prized possessions, sold at two packs for 25 cents. A weekly shopping basket, topped off with the Sunday roast, might cost five or six dollars. It was a different time, a different era. Its demands and seemingly meager rewards cannot fairly be judged with the powerful advantage of hindsight.

Such an experience must have been lived. Nothing else can substitute. That understanding is reserved, therefore, to those who served in the "Roaring Twenties."

• • •

The following officers were killed in the line of duty during the 1920s:

Llewellyn A. Lowther: Died September 20, 1924 in a motorcycle accident in Adams.

George L. Prentiss: Died October 1, 1927 in a motorcycle accident in Cheshire.

John E. Higgins: Died April 14, 1928 in a motorcycle accident in Southboro.

The following personnel were among those appointed to the Detective Branch during the 1920s:

Proctor, William H.	Horrigan, Edward P.	McCarthy, Edward J.
Barrett, Michael J.	Keating, Arthur E.	Grady, James J.
Bligh, Thomas E.	Kirlin, Frederick M.	Hale, Frank G.
Bradford, Ernest S.	Manning, David J.	Loomis, James L.
Brouillard, Albert L.	Molt, Robert E.	Martin, William H.
Clemmey, Francis W.	Murray, William F.	Murtagh, Edward H.
Daly, Joseph V.	O'Neil, Edward P.	Nelligan, Maurice P.
Ferrari, Joseph L.	Sherlock, Edward J.	Reardon, John E.
Fleming, Michael F.	Stokes, John F.	Trainor, James A.
Griffin, Richard J.	Taylor, Ira C.	Whittemore, Howard M.

• • •

The following were appointed to the Massachusetts State Police Academy during the 1920s:

THE FIRST RECRUIT TROOP
September 1, 1921

Barber, Alfred W.
Barrett, Edward J.
Beaupre, Charles T.
Brown, George E.
Burke, George E.
Carey, John Francis, Jr.
Cole, Frederick R.
Collins, James J.
Cote, George H.
Dasey, Albert W.
Fitzmaurice, William F.
Fouche, Joseph A.
Glaras, Nicholas
Gully, Edward J.
Hackett, William J.
Hayes, George E. Jr.,
Holleran, Joseph M.

Howland, John P.
Jason, Justin F.
Kelley, Edward P.
Kimball, Roy E.
Lenhart, Ernest J.
Lundberg, Frederick W.
MacMillan, Duncan
Mahoney, James P.
Manning, Axel A.
Marsh, Irving L.
McCarthy, Charles B.
McConnell, Thomas J.
McNamee, George E.
Mooney, Richard H. Jr.,
O'Connor, Joseph E.
O'Donnell, John J.

O'Neil, Thomas H.
Ontus, George F.
Parker, George A.
Russell, Harold G.
Sardina, Anthony
Scott, Bertrand G.F.
Sheeran, James H.
Sherrin, William J.
Skinner, George D.
Soderberg, Gustaf A.
Stankard, Leo F.
Stowell, Eugene E.
Sullivan, William J.
Thom, Walter A.
Whittemore, Howard M.
Williams, Harold B.

SECOND RECRUIT TROOP
January 3, 1922

Burrows, Charles A.
Cooley, Charles B.
Leary, John F.
Majeskey, Edward J.

Ryan, Joseph C.
Sullivan, Daniel F.
Tompkins, Walter L.

Matz, Henry
Toelken, Julius W.
Long, Thomas R.

THIRD RECRUIT TROOP
July 26, 1922

Barrett, Francis E.
Burke, Joseph P.
Cook, Raymond R.
McGady, Francis J.
Rich, Earle G.
Sistare, Reginald W.
Stingel, Herbert J.
Annis, Kenneth G.
Beattie, Martin J.
Ducey, Patrick W.
Hall, Roy H.
Helquist, Carl A.
Jobert, Charles A.
Keefe, Arthur A.

Morrisch, Charles F.
Thomson, Albert G.
Wittenberger, Harold E.
Brown, James T.
Callahan, Carl L.
Delory, Joseph S.
Hughes, James E.
Kell, James V.
Krukowski, Joseph J.
LeBlanc, Oliver W.
Legge, Wesley I.
McGonologne, John J.
Moyes, Gilbert H.

Powers, Bertram A.
Rogerson, John J.
Ryan, James P.
Severance, George A.
Sherman, Ralph C.
Streeter, Edwin W.
Trainor, James A.
Breau, Aaron C.
Danehy, Eugene M.
Howard, Samuel P.
Foster, John T.
Terpstra, Richard F.
Russell, Walter C., Jr.

FOURTH RECRUIT TROOP
December 18, 1922

Goodnough, Henry E.
Cassidy, Thomas A.
DeCoste, James P.
Fiske, George F.
Hogan, John A.
Legasey, Edward
Manning, Francis
McCleery, James J.
Murphy, Daniel A.
Redding, Stuart P.
Sargent, Edmund H.
Butters, Albert E.
Cassidy, Francis E.
Collins, George B.

Cullen, Henry P.
Dacey, Jeremiah J.
Farrington, Edward H.
Hersum, Harry W.
Larkin, Edward A.
MacFarlane, Harold A.
Malone, George L.
Mann, Douglas E.
Martin, William H.
Matson, Waine O.
Murphy, Frederick G.
McLaughlin, John F.
Peterson, Theodore G.
Puzzo, William J.

Russo, Vincent F.
Smith, Arthur E.
Sullivan, James H.
Sullivan, John N.
Woodcock, Charles E.
Murphy, John J.
Chamblis, Tommie G.
Mitchell, Thomas H.
Flood, John H.
Wise, Oliver J.
Dean, Edward L.
Dearborn, Russell P.
Lowther, Llewellyn A.
Plett, Henry A.

FIFTH RECRUIT TROOP
April 2, 1923

Allen, Joseph F.
Atwood, Arthur L.
Brooks, George W.
Cassidy, Frank J.
Charpenter, Clyde T.
Cressy, Nelson F.
Daniels, Clifton A.

Morrison, Kenneth
Murphy, Joseph F.
Niles, Frank L.
Snyder, Israel
Wheeler, Raymond F.
White, Walter R.
Burns, Melville A.

Driscoll, Denis T.
Connelly, Patrick J.
Dirocco, John J.
Eaton, Warner F.
Jones, Loon W.
Lundberg, Eric O.
O'Connell, Francis J.

Sullivan, Thomas J.
Varnam, Leon W.
Bowditch, Edward A.
Colleran, William J.
Connelly, John M.
Dodge, George A.
Holt, Charles L.
Kendall, Clifton W.
Mathisson, Arthur E.
McConnell, Anthony J.

Clark, Lawrence H.
Drohan, Martin P.
Hoyt, Walter R.
McNeill, Francis D.
Sullivan, John P.
Yess, Thomas
Sullivan, Charles H.
Canavan, Edward J.
Hannan, Thomas F.
Delano, Richard W.

Shimkus, William V.
Landers, John R.
Anderson, George J.
Burke, Joseph A.
Fortin, Alfred J.
Mutz, Alfred W.
Moody, Edwin D.
Cotter, William H., Jr.
Griffin, Daniel F.

SIXTH RECRUIT TROOP
July 2, 1923

Carroll, John A.
Hennessey, Thomas M.
Martin, Wellington W.

Reid, Eugene G.
Spencer John
Walton, Charles L.

White, James F.
LaPrade, Harvey G.
Flanders, Everett I.

SEVENTH RECRUIT TROOP
September 28, 1923

Bond, Lewis E.
Crescio, Joseph C.
Dempsey, John F.
Dodge, Charles S.
Greenough, Walter J.

Pengilly, Elmo C.
Regan, John P.
Small, Ralph E.
Tynan, Charles J.
Alexander, George F.

Higgins, William A.
Preston, Lyman B.
Riley, Melville S.
Roberts, Thomas C.

EIGHTH RECRUIT TROOP
January 9, 1924

Anderson, Thomas D.
Butler, Patrick H.
Conant, Walter W.
Donahue, John J.
Koloski, Peter
McConnell, Charles D.
McKeon, William J.
McMurray, Walter J.
Townsend, Richard K.

Veator, Vincent J.
Burke, John R.
Fitzgerald, Desmond A.
Fitzpatrick, Chester G.
Flaherty, Joseph H.
MacIsaac, Daniel V.
McInnis, Wallace B.
Perachi, Louis J.
Reardon, John E.

Henderson, John H.
Meissner, Alfred A.
Gallivan, John T.
McGarry, Frank D.
McGuinness, Thomas J.
Bradley, William B.
Knox, George T.
Pelletier, Gideon J.

NINTH RECRUIT TROOP
June 9, 1924

Bregnard, Emile F. Jr.,
Ganley, John H.
Nelson, Warren E.
Rhodes, Robert S. F.

Rapport, George D.
Brown, Norman H.
Canavan, Thomas A.
McGinnis, Harold J.

Sheehan, Frederick J.
Whalen, Patrick A.
Clink, Richard A., Jr.
Tuney, Andrew J.

TENTH RECRUIT TROOP
September 22, 1924

Derosier, Alfred L.
Matthes, Sumner D.
McDonnell, Francis M.
Pelletier, Hector J.

Powers, John J.
Read, Howard C.
Barnicle, John F.
Edmonds, Frederick J.

Murphy, William D.
Quinlan, Joseph
Downey, Edmund V.

ELEVENTH RECRUIT TROOP
December 31, 1924

Avery, Harry L.
Borden, Andrew A.
Cotter, Richard, Jr.
Fratus, Joseph

Moran, Joseph F.
Morden, Parker C.
O'Brien, Ralph
Pinksham, William C.

Smith, George A.
Thompson, George H.
Moreau, Everett R.
Pratt, William H.

TWELFTH RECRUIT TROOP
April 28, 1925

Bartolotte, Sebastian
Ellis, William, Jr.
Foisy, Maurice J.
Galvin, Jeremiah G.

Horgan, John F.
Joyce, Martin W.
Lathan, Leo J.
Metcalf, Charles G.H.

Morse, Frank L.
Tinskey, John H.
Todd, Horace G.

THIRTEENTH RECRUIT TROOP

July 30, 1925

Thompkins, Ezra P.
Greer, Frederick M.
Higgins, George P.
Lambert, Frank
Lavoie, Albert J.

Noonan, Michael J.
Norton, Thomas P.
Graham, Howard X.
Concannon, William L.
Crowley, Joseph G.

Fitzgerald, Edward L.
Bergstron, Roy F.
Sanborn, Frank K.
Truther, Ernest J.

FOURTEENTH RECRUIT TROOP

November 2, 1925

Baron, Frank L.
Dineen, Harold B.
Johnson, John E.
Wesley, Orville L.
Sheehan, John, Jr.
Fitzpatrick, Walter J.

Gosselin, Arthur J.
Murphy, Edward V.
O'Brien, Abner F.
Aleckno, Rudolph C.
Armstrong, William T.

Arnold, Charles P.
Mulreany, John F.
Klein, Walter J., Jr.
Ryan, Ernest J.
Boakes, Charles R.

FIFTEENTH RECRUIT TROOP

February 1, 1926

Beattie, Hollis E.
Canavan, Cornelius P.
Covell, John J.
Farmer, Bernard G.

Hall, Everett J.
King, Harold C.
Vinsky, Joseph J.
Zeigler, Francis H.

Berry, Wilfred
McBane, James M.
Foley, William E.

SIXTEENTH RECRUIT TROOP

October 18, 1926

Phillips, John M.
Green, Frank S.
Hornby, Donald L.
Ferrari, Robert L.
Bruyn, James S.

Byrne, Andrew J.
Prentiss, George L.
Richardson, Arthur E.
Johnson, Theodore W.
McPhee, George F.

O'Brien, John G.
Delaney, Harold A.
Dunn, John J., Jr.
Jones, Robert G.

SEVENTEENTH RECRUIT TROOP

June 2, 1927

Andrews, William A.
Shea, Michael J.
Burke, Thomas E.
Cleary, Leo
Conn, George J.
Salmonsen, Lorance P.
Thomas, Carl H.
Manning, Michael
Avedian, John S.
Carpenter, Homides
Gioyoso, Richard
Riley, George H.
Almond, Emmett P.
Altieri, Antonio N.
Blustine, William
Canavan, John J.
Chamberlain, Roland N.

Clauretie, David B.
Daley, Martin J.
Delay, William H.
Donovan, Robert P.
Drake, Chester L.
Dwyer, Frank A., Jr.
Fay, John L.
Finn, James J.
Flynn, Timothy L.
Ford, Arthur V.
Ford, Francis W.
Fredette, George E.
Green, James P.
Hayden, Myron H.
Higgins, John E.
Hurley, John J.
Lally, John F.

Laskey, Ronan J.
Mahoney, Timothy J.
Moriarity, John F.
Murphy, Augustine L.
Norton, Thomas M.
Phillips, Joseph E.
Shea, Arthur J.
Shore, Arnold G.
Smith, William
Sullivan, Michael J.
Taugher, James P.
Taylor, Henry H.
Thornton, Charles W.
Watkins, LeRoy A.
White, Victor W.
Wright, William C.
Hennigan, John W.

EIGHTEENTH RECRUIT TROOP

September 6, 1927

Foley, Raymond L.
Eliason, Henry W.
Hazelton, Thomas E.
Lyons, James L.
Carter, George H.

Phillimore, Frederick D.
Powers, John A.
Davey, Charles E.
Dumont, Talbot T.
Lewis, Michael J.

Mercer, William A.
O'Connor, Charles J.
Ridge, Patrick F.
Byrne, Francis J.

NINETEENTH RECRUIT TROOP

April 2, 1928

Bowler, John J.
Burdette, Waldo H.
Cleary, Richard F.
Cozzens, Charles C.
Culkin, Edward

Finn, John J.
Gorman, Thomas J.
Lynch, Walter F.
McColgan, Edward A.
Sidney, Norman S.

Smith, Charles L.
Voyer, Clement L.
Winn, James A.
Miller, George F.

TWENTIETH RECRUIT TROOP

September 4, 1928

Blanchard, Reginald J.
Blanck, Frederick H.
Chisholm, William A.T.
Collins, John W.
Conroy, James F.
Dineen, Joseph A.
Donovan, John J.
Doran, James W., Jr.
Doring, George F.
Doyle, Joseph W.
Fitzgerald, Theodore E.
Fleming, William B.
Furze, Charles F.
Hannon, Joseph P.
Keating, Joseph A.
Kelley, William H.
Kramer, George W.
MaGuire, Andrew T.
Martin, Leonard N.

Maturo, John A.
McCarthy, Charles J.
McDonald, Walter R.
Moran, Raymond J.
Murphy, Daniel J.
Nelson, William E.
Pollard, George A.
Roche, George F.
Ryan, Frederick J.
Ryan, Leo H.
Scannell, Michael D.
Sheehan, Albert J.
Sirois, Wilfred
Skillings, Stanley S.
Spurr, George E.
Storme, Leo V.
Vierra, Francis
Berglund, Herbert S.
Burke, Walter A.

Camara, Manuel
Cooke, Arthur
Deady, Philip W.
Garm, Joseph D.
Galvin, John F.
Geist, Frank W.
Grealis, George E.
Higginson, Thomas J.
Keegan, Charles J., Jr.
McDonald, Michael J.
Mellen, Joseph M.
Murphy, Joseph V.
Nardone, John
Poguse, Hollis
Smith, Harry C.
Sullivan, Cornelius T.
Thompson, Robert E.
Hayes, Albert T.
Ryan, William F.

TWENTY-FIRST RECRUIT TROOP

October 17, 1929

Taylor, John F.
VanAmburgh, John F.
Bardsley, Howard, Jr.
Barker, George C.
Brady, William J.
Bruno, Arthur H.
Burke, Walter P.

Codding, Frederick F.
DePelteau, Edward A.
Halstrom, Reginald F.
Hourihan, Joseph F.
Jacobs, Daniel L.
LaCaire, Anthony S.

Langsette, Gorden L.
McGinley, Edward L.
Murphy, Joseph G.
Nolan, John H.
Stevenson, Robert T.
Sullivan, Simon C.

Springfield, Indian Motorcycle Factory, 1921. Recruit Patrolman Joseph A. Fouche won the honor of riding this beauty from Springfield to Framingham's "Poor Farm" for the November, 1921 graduation of the First Recruit Troop. He later supervised both motorcycle and mounted trick riding teams.

Northampton, Troop B Headquarters, National Guard Armory, 1922. Left to Right: Patrolmen Harold Williams and Leo F. Stankard. Williams, Stankard and their colleagues in November 1921 rode their horses for five days from Framingham to establish Troop B Headquarters. Stankard died at 100 in November, 1996, the last survivor of the historic cadre that in 1921 had launched the Massachusetts experiment with a uniformed, statewide enforcement agency.

Troop A Framingham, The Poor Farm, 1922. Site of the first training "academy," it doubled as Troop A headquarters in the early months. Left to Right: George A. Cote, Edward J. Barrett, Richard H. Mooney, Jr. All three were in 1921's First Recruit Troop, and were posted to Troop A Framingham on their first field assignments. Note ammunition bandoleers on riders, and holstered rifles on horses' left sides.

The "Poor Farm," Framingham, 1921. Members of the First Recruit Training Troop. They and their colleagues transformed an idea into the reality of a rural, uniformed, "State Police Patrol". Though individual names in this historic photo have been lost to time's inexorable effect on men and their institutions, the fact of today's superior enforcement organization is the enduring legacy of their personal sacrifices and professional commitments.

State Capitol Boston, September 1, 1921. The swearing in of the First Recruit Troop of the State Police Patrol. Governor Channing H. Cox, center, straw hat in hand. Commissioner Alfred E. Foote, next to governor. Captain George A. Parker, behind Foote. William F. Fitzmaurice, uniformed man extreme left. Thomas J. McConnell, uniformed man right. Secretary of State, Frederick Cook, extreme right. Center, two rows behind governor, Leo F. Stankard. Stankard, until November, 1996, was the only survivor in the historic photograph. This caption was rewritten to note his symbolic passing that month, precisely 75 years after the November, 1921, graduation of the First Recruit Troop. He was 100.

Springfield, Indian Motorcycle Factory, 1923. Left to Right: Albert W. Dacey, James V. Kell, Francis Manning. They rode the "iron horses" to Worcester County, the site of the first Troop C Headquarters in Paxton.

East Lee Barracks, 1922. Left to Right: Corporal Joseph A. Fouche and Patrolman Francis J. McGady. Fouche in November, 1921, graduated from the state police academy with the First Recruit Troop, in 1922 was corporal and commanding officer of the Troop B substation in East Lee.

Wrentham Barracks, 1929. Left to Right: W. Ratigan, J. Ruddy, R. Chamberlain, G. Roche. Note the handsome, leather jackets and fur collars worn by Ratigan, Rudy and Roche, - a great favorite of uniformed personnel until the early 1930's. Almost since the 1921 founding of the State Police Patrol, uniformed personnel were quartered in Wrentham. That ended with a mid-1950's barracks in Foxboro.

Paxton, Troop C Headquarters, 1924. William J. Colleran, Edward J. Canavan. Colleran and Canavan were classmates in 1923's Fifth Recruit Troop, helped to establish the first state police presence that year just north and west of Worcester at Troop C Headquarters in bucolic Paxton.

Troop A, Ashland, 1926. Left to Right: J. Mosconi, D. MacIsaac, J. Sullivan, J. Horgan, T. Mitchell, Sergeant C. Callahan, Captain C. Beaupre, (civilian, front, unidentified). State Police raids on illegal "booze" operations like this one were commonplace during the 1920's while America's "Noble Experiment" to abolish alcohol foundered on the human instinct to find periodic escape from life's daily realities.

Middleboro, Troop D Headquarters, 1924. Left to Right: Lieutenant T. McConnel, J. Ryan, H. McGuinnis, E. Canavan, W. Cotter, J. Sullivan. Troop D headquarters were later located at West Bridgewater, the State Farm in Bridgewater and in 1956 at the present site on Route 28 in Middleboro.

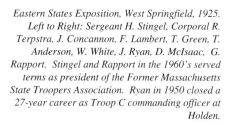

Eastern States Exposition, West Springfield, 1925. Left to Right: Sergeant H. Stingel, Corporal R. Terpstra, J. Concannon, F. Lambert, T. Green, T. Anderson, W. White, J. Ryan, D. McIsaac, G. Rapport. Stingel and Rapport in the 1960's served terms as president of the Former Massachusetts State Troopers Association. Ryan in 1950 closed a 27-year career as Troop C commanding officer at Holden.

State Prison, Charlestown, 1927. The Sacco and Vanzetti electrocution detail. Left to Right: D. Murphy, J. Higgins, R. Chamberlain, T. Norton, M. Manning, J. Hughes, W. Delay, V. Carpenter, T. Burke, G. Conn, T. Johnson, W. Shimkus, N. Altieri, M. Hayden, F. McGady. The August 22nd execution inside Charlestown's foreboding walls was the final act in a case that yet intrigues criminal justice scholars around the world.

Troop D, Freetown, 1928. Trooper Gus Murphy setting out on the New Bedford "Water Works" patrol. Such assignments usually lasted three or four days, with overnight stays at remote farmhouses, - or by sharing accommodations with resident livestock.

Salem, 1926. Left to Right: Sergeant C. Jobert, Lieutenant H. Williams, Sergeant J. Sullivan. They were in charge of a uniformed detail for the 1926 Salem Tercentenary. Williams in 1921 had made the arduous horseback trip from the Framingham academy to establish Troop B at Northampton.

Agawam Barracks, 1924. Left to Right: L. Lowther, M. Beattie, A. Morrison, W. Mattson, Corporal J. Fouche. Llewelyn A. Lowther later that year was killed in a motorcycle accident in Adams, the first line of duty death in the State Police Patrol. He had enlisted with 1922's 4th Recruit Troop. Motorcycles exacted a tragic toll in the early decades.

Eastern States Exposition, West Springfield, 1929. Left to Right: J. O'Brien, J. McLaughlin, J. O'Kane, D. McIsaac, T. Hazelton, C. Smith, J. Ryan, S. Matthes, Corporal G. Fiske, N. Sidney, Sergeant C. Jobert. Sidney served into the late 1950's, concluding his career as Troop D commander at Bridgewater, and captain and division inspector at Boston's general headquarters. He lived out his retirement years in Norwell until his 1979 death.

Springfield, Indian Motorcycle Factory, 1928. Right to Left: Sergeant W. Shimkus, F. Lambert, H. Dineen, A. O'Brien, J. O'Brien, A. Richardson, J. Ryan, G. Prentise, J. Donahue, J. Barnicle, S. Watson, troop mechanic. New motorcycle deliveries were major events. Sadly, the two-wheelers in the early years exacted a heavy toll of death and injury.

Framingham, Troop A Headquarters, circa 1925. Left to Right: Sergeant Oliver LeBlanc, Sergeant John Sullivan, Corporal Louis Perachi, Patrolman Arthur Ford, Patrolman Duncan McMillan. McMillan was in 1921's First Recruit Troop, was assigned to Troop B at the Northampton Armory, rode five days on horseback to help establish that first western outpost.

Wrentham Barracks, 1927. Left to Right: M. Daley, S. Matthes, Corporal T. McGuinnes. Wrentham for years was a Troop A substation at several locations in that community. Daley served into the early 1950's, saw much service as a senior sergeant at Troop C Headquarters in Holden

Reading Barracks, 1927. Left to Right: Sergeant Oliver LeBlanc, Ernest J. Ryan, Cornelius P. Canavan. Ryan enlisted with 1925's 14th Recruit Troop, was active in the Former Massachusetts State Troopers Association, lived into the mid-1990's.

Barnstable Barracks, 1929. Left to Right: J. Dempsey, J. Crowley, Corporal D. Murphy. Jack Dempsey in the 1930's won promotion to detective lieutenant, served over four decades in the Cape Cod area, knew President John F. Kennedy as boy and man, became a state police legend in his own time, lived out his years on Cape Cod.

Barnstable Barracks, 1929. Left to Right: J. Daily, C. Furze, W. Wiano ("Mess Boy"), Corporal J. Dempsey, C. McGonagle, W. Burke, W. Armstrong. Furze was a Fall River native, enlisted in 1928, rose to the captain's rank prior to his 1950's retirement. His last field command was at Troop D headquarters in Bridgewater.

Agawam Barracks, 1929. Left to Right: J. Couto, G. Pollard, W. McDonald, G. Grealis, Sergeant J. Barnicle. Barnicle in 1924 trained with the 10th Recruit Troop, served throughout the state in a 25-year career in Forest Green and French and Electric Blue.

Troop D, Hanover Fire Works explosion, 1927. Left to Right: C. Keegan, J. Horgan, Corporal G. Rapport. John F. Horgan later won the Carnegie Medal for Heroism for his lifesaving response when the steamer Robert E. Lee, with several hundred passengers aboard, foundered on Manomet's treacherous shoals during the winter of 1928.

Troop C, Lunenburg, 1928. Left to Right: J. Hannon, R. Jones, J. DeCoste, J. Phillips. The forest green uniforms in 1933 gave way to the new French and electric blue that at century's close remain the distinctive colors of the Commonwealth's state force.

THE THIRTIES
Coming of Age

*Academy, Commonwealth Armory, Boston, 1930.
Left to Right: Herbert H. Tickle and Lawrence W. Irving. Tickle saw
extensive service in the field troops, completed his career in 1956 as a
lieutenant at Troop D, Bridgewater, lived out his retirement years in
Somerset.*

*Troop B Northampton, 1930. Left to Right: G. Carter, A. Meissner, Sergeant E. Majesky, G. Grealis, Corporal W. White, J. Fay. Majesky on January 3, 1922,
enlisted with the 2nd Recruit Training Troop. He served throughout the "Roaring Twenties" and into the 1930's in Troops B and C, helped in 1923 to establish
the first Troop C headquarters in Paxton.*

*"The only thing we have to
fear is fear itself."*
Franklin Delano Roosevelt

Chapter Three

COMING OF AGE: THE SECOND DECADE

President Roosevelt uttered those words in 1933. They applied, however, in 1930. The Great Depression's full impact had not yet set in. But signs were everywhere. Paper fortunes were eroding daily. "High flyers" were coming back to earth. Panic was impending. Fear, *was* in the air.

The State Police Patrol had done an able enforcement job in the 1920s. The record is clear on that. The solid achievement had been forged from makeshift facilities. All the early barracks were temporary. Most were rented quarters of one kind or another. From the day they set foot in the Northampton Armory in 1921, "B" troopers had made do in a variety of shelters that could hardly qualify as police operation center. The first Lee barracks, remember, was a barn and stable area behind the local judge's home.

The other troops had faced similar problems. One thinks of that first Norwell "barracks," with an outhouse and running water only available at the "Poor Farm." Men stationed at Barnstable had fared better. The county courthouse, buttressed by Mrs. Nickerson's home cooking, was a marked improvement. The problem of poor facilities was, in retrospect, a natural one. The organization did not begin with modern, fully equipped quarters. Those, like everything else, had to be earned.

Thus it was of no small importance when Commissioner Foote announced early in 1930 that new facilities would be constructed in Holden, Brookfield, and Grafton· Holden was to cost $50,000, Grafton and Brookfield $25,000 each. A special town meeting in Grafton on August 4 of that year had voted to buy a parcel of land specifically for construction of the new state patrol facility. But an unwelcome event intervened. On the night of November 24 a fire broke out in the old Grafton barracks, then the Maxwell house on South Street. Patrolmen John Avedian, Ted Stronach and Al Sheehan, just in from the late patrol, smelled smoke coming from upstairs. Within moments, the bathroom was ablaze. Local firefighters responded swiftly, but not fast enough to salvage the sleeping quarters. Damage was estimated at $3,000. The men were out of a home, but, fortunately, no one was injured.

The barracks operation was shifted to a nearby hotel. It was a first class operations center. The Commonwealth footed the bill, and, as might be expected, the men quickly adapted to their new surroundings. Their stay was short lived. The new Grafton barracks was officially dedicated a few days later. "C-2," Grafton's designation, was located on state route 140, the principal artery between Worcester and Cape Cod. Holden was officially opened as C Troop headquarters on December 20, 1930. An impressive building, it was the first of the new facilities designed especially as a troop operations center. Strategically located on route 122A, it was destined to serve as C Troop headquarters for many years.

Brookfield was dedicated a week later, on December 27. Commissioner Foote and Captain Beaupre officiated at the ceremonies. The general public was invited to inspect the new facility. Corporal Joseph J. Vinskey, and Patrolmen George A. Pollard,

George F. Doring, John F. Taylor, Daniel J. Murphy and Arthur H. Bruno handled the visitors. But not for long. They were soon on regular patrols as, within a few hours, the new building was fully operational. Holden, Grafton and Brookfield in 1930 were the first of the modern, red brick barracks facilities constructed for the State Police Patrol. The building program continued throughout the decade. New barracks were erected in each of the four troops. Locations followed the strategic patterns first established in the twenties. New roads, however, were shifting major traffic routes. This caused periodic changes in substation locations, as optimum patrol coverage remained the priority enforcement consideration.

One such example was the B Troop substation at Shelburne Falls. Originally, the men were quartered on the second floor of the town hall. The first move was to a portable facility on Maple Street. The next relocation came just in time, on February 4, 1934. The temperature was twelve degrees *below zero* in the *bedroom*. The men made that move in record time, to the rambling, white house perched near the mountain top on the Greenfield road. Finally, on August 2, 1935, "B-2" was located in a brand new, red brick building. The men, reluctantly, refused a local farmer's offer to provide "cider" for the ceremonies which officially dedicated the modern enforcement facility.

THE NATION'S FIRST

The force in 1930 had established a first in the nation's state enforcement agencies. In February two women were enlisted. Notices had been posted, and 26 women had applied for the positions. Following background investigations, a review board had screened the applicants for educational credentials, aptitude and related work experience.

Mary B. Ramsdell and Lotta H.Caldwell emerged from that process as the leading candidates for the State Police Patrol. One stumbling block remained. There would have to be successful completion of the training school requirements. Ramsdell and Caldwell thus began the three months grind taking essentially the same training subects as the men. A couple of concessions were made. They did not have to ride the horses, and, at 6:00 a.m., they were excused from completing several laps around the track. Other than that, they plunged into all of the school's requirements. Foremost among these was the criminal law. Here they were advantaged in having Lieutenant Mike Barrett as an instructor. Barrett brought enormous experience and tact to his work. Beyond that, the veteran had a way with words. Many a recruit was left in awe of the "captain's" knowledge of law and criminal investigations. Needless to say, the two women did some of their best work in the sessions dealing with Barrett's subjects.

By June, all requirements had been met and the women took their oaths as the first state policewomen in the country. Then came the first assignment, a statewide tour in company with Commissioner Foote and Captain Beaupre. They met many of the "troops," paving the way for the radical idea they represented. There were some tense moments as the recruits were presented as "state policewomen." Some wondered aloud about what they could possibly accomplish. It was a new idea, and, as with all emerging notions, it would take time for acceptance slowly to take hold. Lotta Caldwell was assigned to Troops A and D. Mary Ramsdell drew Troops B and C. Each was to cover one half of the Commonwealth! There were no patterns to follow. Each was a trail blazer. That makes a big difference. Their mere presence signified a daring new concept in state policing. Their obligation was to prove its worth.

Years of faithful service followed. They *did* justify the confidence placed in them. Lotta Caldwell retired from injuries suffered at Salisbury Beach in the Great New England Hurricane of 1938. Mary Ramsdell served two decades before retiring in 1950. She would later receive a special commendation at the centennial banquet in October 1965. Her acceptance speech was easily the highlight of the evening's festivities. These two left a career path brightly illuminated, one that was later followed by a number of women in the statewide enforcement agency.

Telephones, and, later, one way radios, had been the communication throughout the twenties. But technology was improving. A "Page Telephone Typewriter" circuit was first used on July 1, 1931. The communications center was located in the State Capitol. The new circuit had direct ties to troop headquarters at Framingham, Northampton, Holden and Middleboro. This was a giant step in rapid enforcement communications. Messages now moved in minutes throughout the Commonwealth, where, formerly, hours might have been required.

Everything, however, would not go so smoothly. The "Depression" was creating new social currents. Emotions ran strongly. A "hunger march" began in Clinton. It was said that the marchers were "Reds," communist inspired. No matter, it fell to the State Police Patrol to ensure tranquility in the Worcester County community. Commissioner Foote, Captain Beaupre, Lieutenant William V. Shimkus, Sergeant Edward J. Canavan and ten patrolmen teamed with the Clinton police to keep the march orderly, and to preserve public order.

Sad things happened too. Patrolman Charles F. McGonagle of the Monson barracks was killed on August 2, 1932. McGonagle skidded off the road on his motorcycle in East Longmeadow, receiving fatal injuries. Motorcycles had been the transportation backbone of the force from the beginning. But they took a fearsome toll. "Bikes" were killers. A man's biggest mistake was to believe he had mastered the two wheeler. That was bad. It was, too often, the beginning of a tragedy. The State Police Patrol would continue for years to use motorcycles heavily. The "bike" always would be a serious threat to its rider. Through the years a heavy toll was exacted in crippling injuries, and, too often, in sudden death.

Transfers, a euphemism for "shakeups," occurred with regular frequency. These moves usually involved patrolmen. Routine transfers were expected. The novelty had long since worn off. Thus, it came as something of a surprise when a big "shake up" hit the commissioned and non-commissioned ranks. In one such move, practically every such officer was affected. Some went a long distance, closeness of one's home was never a positive factor. Predictably, headquarters issued a press release explaining the sudden moves. With disarming simplicity, the statement noted that "the transfers were for the good of the service, would be future policy, and would be repeated." Brevity was the soul of the 1930s administration.

BARRACKS LIFE

The 1930s organization reflected the times. Things were spare. Discipline and conformance were ascendant. Lieutenant was the top troop rank. The rating of first sergeant was first authorized on April 6, 1933. Substations were then commanded by corporals. Next in authority was the "senior man." This was the veteran patrolman, an officer with wide experience, not yet promoted into the non-commissioned ranks.

A barracks was a tight ship. It may not be possible now to sense what that meant; what it required in personal commitment from the men. An expression then in popular currency may help to explain. A patrolman, particularly a "boot," getting up courage to speak to a supervisor, would be cautioned by a wiser head that "the senior man spoke only to Jesus, and the corporal spoke only to God." If such timely advice paralleled that also given to those wishing to converse with the Cabots and Lodges, it was because the studied aloofness was not dissimilar.

The onset of the "Great Depression" had deadened a natural thrust for change. Conservative attitudes look deep root in the nation. Private lives and public institutions were similarly affected. The commitment to bear any burden to keep one's livelihood became a powerful force. This was clearly evident in the state force. Although some years had passed, leisure time, "time off" from the organization, had improved only slightly. By the early thirties, a patrolman still had but one day off in ten. This meant that he worked a duty tour of ten consecutive days and nights before being "granted" a day off. Meantime, the concept of a "night pass" had been started. This pass was on every fifth night, and consisted of approximately fourteen hours.

To fully comprehend these demands, it is necessary to observe how they affected an individual. Most men were stationed a long way from home. This was departmental policy. Thus, when a recruit graduated from training school he was assigned to a distant barracks. This meant, for example, that a Boston resident, and there were many, would be first stationed in B Troop, Northampton. The distance often would be over one hundred miles. From that first assignment, the recruit would mature to a seasoned veteran as he "worked his way back" to his home troop.

Typically, the new officer was a young man born and raised in greater Boston. Following graduation from the training school, his first assignment might be to the B Troop substation in Shelburne Falls, well over a hundred miles from the capital city. Once there, the fledgling patrolman would work the first five day tour looking forward to the cherished "night pass." But there was a problem. The "boot" had to put in eight hours on the fifth or final day of the duty tour. Consequently, by the time he finished his patrol, completed reports, and took care of other incidentals, it would be near five or six o'clock. His upcoming night off was brief, scheduled to end at eight the following morning. How could the aspiring patrolman then travel from rural Shelburne Falls to the sprawling urban center of Boston in the allotted time? It was, after all, nearly 120 miles. The roads were not the best, especially west of Worcester during the winter months. The answer was, painfully, he did not go home.

FRENCH AND ELECTRIC BLUE

One of those intangibles was pride in wearing the uniform of the state force. This may seem trite, even incomprehensible to some. But it was an important factor, one not taken lightly by those who had been privileged since 1921 to have worn the forest green colors. There was recognition in that uniform. It stood for something. Its wearer was respected. He was a special breed. By the early thirties, the organization commanded substantial respect. Each man shared this. It was important. And it was zealously guarded.

Thus it was a matter of great importance when, after twelve years, uniform colors were officially changed in June of 1933. The first year had seen the men dressed principally in World War I leftovers. In 1922, the forest greens had been introduced. There had never been a "complete" uniform, as the men purchased special items required to combat cold or wet conditions. Now there would be new, attractive uniforms. The colors were "French and electric" blue. The "two tone" blue would become a symbol of the organization, providing instant recognition for its members.

One item of apparel already long since discarded had been the red ties. Yes, *red* ties. These had been worn in the early twenties, and, with white shirts, had resulted, occasionally, in unwelcome comments. Such remarks, in turn, led quickly to an "appropriate" response by the offended officer. Thereafter, such derogatory observations were observed to diminish. One did not seek in the early twenties an encounter with members of the state force, especially a misunderstanding caused by something as delicate as neckwear color.

Something new, however, drives out something old. So it was with the acquisition of "French and electric" blue. A revered garment fell by the wayside. It was the long leather jacket, a mainstay of the force since its founding. The heavy black coats had been life savers on bitter cold nights, especially on winter motorcycle patrols. Now they gave way to the two tone "reefers." The new garments were attractive. But they did not win the men over easily. For a long time there remained a yearning for the heated comfort of the traditional leather jackets.

The new uniforms were instantly recognizable. People knew the "staties" immediately when they spotted the distinctive colors. On occasion, however, the men didn't exactly arrive in full gear, at least not those who conducted undercover investigations as a prelude to a "raid." One of the biggest illicit activities in the early thirties was "cock fighting." These bloody frays pitted roosters against one another, fitted with special spurs, often in a fight to the death. Large sums were wagered. It was a betting contest for city slickers, but most often held in a rural area.

C Troop was the locale for one of the largest such raids ever held. Word had been received that a cock flight would be held in Millville, at the Duffy farm. Cars had been steadily arriving. The crowd was building. Attendees grew anxious as fight time neared. Aficionados of the "sport" were a special breed. For them, nothing equalled the emotional high provided by the fighting birds. The situation was rapidly assessed. Troop substations were stripped as troopers arrived at C headquarters in Holden. They were briefed and divided into teams. Shortly, they were going over the back roads to the Blackstone Valley town. The raiders were led by Sergeant John F. McLaughlin, Sergeant Ed Canavan and Corporal Joe Phillips. The following were among those who rounded out the raiding party: Patrolmen John Avedian, George Pollard, Joe Noone, Bob Mitchell, Andy Golden, Usha Malkasian, Jim Coniff, Jim Concannon, Jim Cronin, Barney McCabe, Joe Mellen, Jim Leary, and Frank Hennigan.

On signal, without warning, the state raiders swept into the fight scene. Pandemonium reigned. Men and birds scrambled for safety. A few might have made it; it is not easy to make an accurate head count in such a bizarre scenario. It was over in moments. The promoter and 51 "sports" fans were under arrest. Seventy-four game cocks were seized along with the two "rinks" used for the fights. Next morning, the entrepreneur paid a fifty dollar fine, while his customers were assessed ten each. One had avoided the court appearance when it was discovered that he was blind! The fighting cocks did not fare any better than their avid backers. Seventy-four of the birds had been seized. Their fate? The court ordered them killed, dressed and delivered to needy area families.

THE GENERAL LEAVES

Meantime, the years were slipping silently by. Alfred E. Foote had been the state's first commissioner of public safety, appointed in 1919. He had chaired the commission that had first recommended a "uniformed branch." The selection, training and appointments of the "First Class" had taken place under his leadership. Foote had seen the State Police Patrol carry a new idea to old places, and to succeed, often against heavy odds.

The "General" had witnessed first hand the trials of the twenties, and, yes, the organization's coming of age with "Brickbottom," the B Troop Floods, Sacco and Vanzetti, and the hundreds of little, but important things his men did to prove their worth and the utility of the state force. Now, his tenure was ending. Leave-taking was at hand. It is never an easy time. But for General Foote it was especially difficult. The state force, in many ways, had been "his" organization. He was, till then, its only leader. Others would follow, but he was the first. That distinction would remain reserved, his alone, no matter how the decades would dim the accomplishments of the early years.

Daniel A. Needham was appointed in 1933 as commissioner of public safety, succeeding Foote. During the same period, James P. Mahoney, a member of the 1921 class, was named captain and executive officer of the uniformed branch. Captain Mahoney filled the sensitive command post vacated upon the retirement of Captain Charles T. Beaupre, also a member of the first recruit troop. Beaupre had held the highest ranking uniformed position since the mid-twenties, having succeeded the original executive officer, Captain George A. Parker, on September 9, 1925. The first three executive officers thus had been recruit colleagues in the "First Class."

Commissioner Needham, like his predecessor, was an experienced military man. He retained his service rank of brigadier general while serving in the commissioner's post. He, too, was frequently addressed as "General." His World War I duty had included command of the Twenty-Sixth "Yankee" Division's Fifty-First Artillery.

On the national level the Roosevelt presidency had begun to take hold. Briefly away from Washington, the president was spending several days in central Massachusetts. A Roosevelt son, John, was graduating from Groton School. The president arrived in Worcester by train, and, escorted by a state police detail, motored to Groton. The state force used both motorcycles and cruisers to ensure presidential security. All went well. The men on the detail received accolades for the job they did, at times under trying conditions. Such escorts were to become a tradition on presidential visits. The nation's chief executives who followed FDR on trips to the Bay State also would benefit from the expertise in security the force had developed. This would especially be so, when, years later, a native son would make the "Kennedy Compound" and Hyannisport synonymous with the nation's highest office.

Roosevelt was destined to serve more than twelve years. None, however, would prove more difficult than the beginning of his record tenure. The early and mid-thirties had to be lived to be understood. Such experiences cannot be communicated. Words fall short. They can create the picture, but they cannot convey the feeling. The effect was seen dramatically in the state force. Applicants numbered in the thousands for the few available positions. The 1933 recruit training class had 23 members. When they took their oath of office on November 4, they represented the seven thousand who had taken the original qualifying examination! Their graduation, coincident with the "bottom" of the Great Depression, brought the authorized complement to 270.

The 1933 training troop had the unique distinction of being the first to wear the new, two-tone blue uniforms for graduation ceremonies. Commissioner Needham, Captain Mahoney and Lieutenant Hughes, the school commandant, also sported the new colors at the Commonwealth Armory exercises. Additionally, as commissioned officers, they wore the famed English riding boots complete with elegant, highly polished spurs.

Spurs long had been standard equipment. Now, however, they would become largely ceremonial trappings, reminders of nostalgic times past. Horses had been a mainstay of the force. As 1933 ended, however, only one, or, depending upon which account may be correct, two horses would remain. "Teddy" was one of the survivors left to ring down the curtain on a distinguished service record. The handsome animal had shared 1933 summer service with Corporal "Dusty" Rhodes, and Patrolmen Charles "Bunny" Furze, Donat LaCasse, Stan Skillings and George Conn at the Concord Barracks near Lake Walden.

Vying with "Teddy" for honors as the last to serve was "Ginger." "Ginger's" last patrol was a symbolic trip from Shelburne Falls to Northampton troops headquarters. Patrolman Richard A. Hiller was in the saddle. The last mounted patrol signalled the passing of a romantic tradition in the Berkshires. Hiller turned "Ginger" over to officials from the Belchertown State School. If such a faithful companion could no longer remain with the state force, she was permitted at least to continue in state service.

MILLEN-FABER

While 1933 witnessed the last of the mounted patrols, the year also ushered in new developments directly involving the agency. Jobs were scarce. Money was tight. Men take risks when under severe economic pressures. Radical ideas, and, on occasion, fearsome actions gain ascendancy. Normalizing constraints weaken. Violence is sometimes used to gain ends. It is a social pattern that, periodically, tends to repeat. Only the causes change.

In the mid-thirties the cause was jobs, money, and the things money buys. Some turned to crime. Among them was the notorious Millen-Faber gang. Their crime spree had culminated in the brutal slaying of two Needham police officers. Irving Millen, his brother Murten, and Abraham Faber would not easily be captured, convicted and executed for their infamous crime. It was a complex, demanding investigation.

State detectives worked around the clock with local authorities to crack the case. Newspaper stories daily informed an alarmed public on new developments. Destined to emerge from the welter of media accounts was a detective team, "Stokes and Ferrari," the epitome of the esoteric profession. Stokes would be named that year as captain of detectives. He would later be commissioner. Now,

however, he, Ferrari and their colleagues had their hands full with the Millens and Abe Faber.

Lieutenant Joseph L. Ferrari had sharpened his investigative skills during long years of state service. He, like Stokes, had become a member of the detective division about the time the public safety department was founded in 1919. Moreover, he was the first in a line of Ferraris. A son, Robert, served in the uniformed branch, rising to the rank of captain during his career. Clarence, a second son, would spend more than forty years in key support positions in the state force, closing his service as chief quartermaster. By then, Clarence's son, Thomas E. Ferrari, had become the third generation of Ferraris to serve in the statewide force.

Stokes and Ferrari had a lot of talented assistance with the Millen-Faber investigation. One who played a key role was Joseph C. Crescio. Crescio would one day become Captain of State Police Detectives. But that was in the future. When the Millen-Faber gang struck he was a member of the auto squad. His skills soon came into play.

The Millen-Faber story remains one of the most fascinating of crime dramas. The Millens and Abe Faber were really not products of their time. They were not poverty stricken, nor were they untutored. They were intelligent offspring of hard working parents, members of solid families. They enjoyed superior educational opportunities. But something had gone wrong. For obscure reasons, made more so by time's passage, they embarked upon a bizarre plot to accumulate a lot of money, other people's money. In record time. Such schemes are doomed before they begin. Yet when they are planned, the excitement created by images of large sums of money drives out rational thought. Incredible scenarios become, in the beholder's eye, workable plans. Paradoxically, in this one, the state police would be the first victims.

The Millens and Faber on January 25, 1934 went to an auto show in Mechanics Building on Boston's Huntington Avenue. They were fascinated by a state police gun exhibit, which also featured the latest in police communications. They could hardly conceal their excitement. The enforcement equipment melded perfectly with their plan for a series of robberies. A machine gun on display got special attention. It was a must. The lethal weapon would complete their small arsenal.

That same night, the Millen-Faber gang broke into Mechanics Building. They used a car already hunted throughout the state, a bandit vehicle used in Fitchburg and Lynn robberies that had ended in violent killings. The heist went easily. A couple of guards were overpowered. The gang grabbed the guns and ammunition, taking special care to seize the machine gun. A Boston police cruiser pulled up moments after the daring break. It was too late. Within minutes the bandit trio was inside the Millen's Roxbury home. The stolen firearms were carefully concealed. That done, they waited a few days for the furor over the stolen state police weapons to subside. But they didn't wait long.

Within days, the Millens and Faber were driving through Needham enroute to casing a Wellesley bank. Ever alert for a target, they were fascinated by the attractive location of the Needham Trust Company building. It was a sitting duck. The gang did not think about it very long. Several days later, on February 2, they went into the bank, the stolen machine gun the centerpiece of formidable weaponry. It was over in minutes. No one had been hurt. But trouble loomed outside. The alarm had gone off.

Needham Patrolman Forbes McLeod approached just as the Millens and Faber came running out. He didn't have a chance. Abe

Faber gunned him down with a burst from the stolen tommy gun. Startled by the sudden turn of events, they forced two bank employees at gun point to ride on the running board of the bandit car. It was a wild scene. The car careened down Needham's main street; Patrolman Frank Haddock jumped into the middle of the street, poised to stop the getaway. He never had a chance. Murton Millen, driving with one hand, triggered a burst from the machine gun. Haddock fell, mortally wounded.

Two heroic police officers were dead. A manhunt was mounted that made all prior murder investigations pale by comparison. The Millen brothers and Abe Farber were clever. But this time they had made a fatal mistake by murdering the two Needham officers. The entire investigative capability of the state force was thrown into a relentless search for the perpetrators of the dastardly Needham crimes. Early frustrations mounted. Leads petered out. It was as though phantoms had struck, fled and disappeared, their trail obscured by a welter of conflicting reports in each new edition of the newspapers. That was the way it seemed, out front. Behind the scenes, state and local police were beginning to piece together the scattered parts of the tragic puzzle. A dramatic break suddenly occurred. Predictably, it was not sensed when it happened.

A Packard sedan was found in Norwood, burned almost beyond identification. But there were tell tale signs! Investigators suspected that it was the murder car. A check of the vehicle's serial number with the Boston Police revealed that it had been stolen. Painstaking examination uncovered the fact that the powerful auto had been repaired six months earlier in a Commonwealth Avenue garage. Several investigators pursued these leads. The Auto Squad's Crescio, with the garage man in tow, went to Norwood. They went over the Packard with a finetooth comb. A battery cell in the burned vehicle had been replaced. Crescio took it to the laboratory at headquarters. Photos were made and further examinations were conducted.

Meantime, the press was covering every breaking detail. Pictures of the suspect battery were featured in early editions. That brought a call next day from a Roxbury battery shop. A weak cell had been replaced there. Records listed the Millens as having brought the battery in. The loop was closing. The battery, the Roxbury repair shop, the stolen car record, the discovery and identification of the burned Packard, each link, connected, led back to the brutal Needham slayings. Headlines identified the Millens as prime suspects. Alerted, they fled. The trail led to New York, to a hotel in Manhattan where the Millens were suspected of hiding out.

Meantime, Acting Captain Michael Barrett, and Lieutenants Michael Fleming and Joe Ferrari had picked up Faber and daily were questioning him about the string of vicious crimes. Faber adopted a helpful posture. Yes, he was a friend of the Millens, but, no, he couldn't provide critical insights. As the ring tightened, Faber's attitude shifted to one of self preservation. Ferrari, especially, was making telling inroads into the seeming self-assured manner early adopted by Faber. Lieutenant Ferrari's technique of showing his hand a bit at a time had its calculated effect. Aware now that the investigators knew a good deal more than they had told him, Faber made his move for leniency. He took Ferrari to a Dorchester house, and, as the veteran of the state force looked on in amazement, Faber motioned to the garage. Ferrari peered through the windows. He knew immediately the end was in sight. Shortly reinforced by detectives and uniformed troopers, Ferrari opened the garage door. There, stacked carefully, lay the stolen weapons, including the state police guns. It was an impressive arsenal. Included were pistols,

tear-gas bombs, dynamite, a gas mask, and an array of ammunition. The deadly crime scheme was unravelling fast.

Detectives quickened the pace. Lieutenant John F. Stokes was already in New York. With Manhattan investigators, he had staked out the lobby of the Lincoln Hotel. Stokes was not taking chances. He had with him a "finger man," a friend of the Millens who would make the positive identification. It came swiftly. Unnoticed, Irving Millen had strolled into the lobby, picked up a newspaper and was scanning it casually while relaxing in a finely upholstered chair. Stokes spotted him, but was a bit uncertain. The veteran's foresight now paid off as the "finger man" confirmed his suspicions. It was indeed Irving Millen, one of the Bay State's two most notorious criminals.

Lieutenant Stokes and the New York detectives quickly overcame Millen's short but violent attempt to escape capture. The scene was shortly repeated when Murton Millen and his wife Norma walked in. The sound of gun fire erupted in the lobby. It ended as quickly as it began. The Millens were under arrest. Irving's wife was charged as an accessory. She had driven them back from Norwood on the night the murder car was burned.

Back in Boston, Acting Captain Barrett, and detectives Ferrari and Fleming were tying up that end. Abe Faber was placed under arrest and booked as the third member of a vicious criminal conspiracy whose popular name the "Millen-Faber" gang, was destined to join "Sacco and Vanzetti" as symbolic, emotional events of that era. Incredibly, however, the Millen-Faber story would have an even more dramatic epilogue. The gang had held up Lynn's Paramount Theatre on January 2, 1934. One C. Fred Sumner had been fatally shot during the robbery. But, through a chain of mystifying circumstances, two Boston taxi drivers had been arrested for the murder. Following indictments, the two went on trial in Essex Superior Court. The state put eleven eyewitnesses on the stand. Nine identified the taxi drivers, Clement Molway and Louis Berrett, as the gunmen. The eye witness testimony was the clincher. Guilty findings, and, beyond, the electric chair, were a foregone conclusion.

There was, however, one unsettling fact. Captain Charles J. Van Amburgh, the state police ballistics expert, had testified that the Lynn death bullet was identical to one fired in a Fitchburg robbery-murder. Now fate and hard work intervened. Detective Lieutenant Richard Griffin, assigned to District Attorney Hugh Craig's office, had kept close tabs on the Millen-Faber investigation. He was aware that the Millens had been captured in New York. More importantly, he was privy to Faber's expanding confession to Lieutenant Ferrari and others. Just as the Molway-Berrett trial neared its predicted end, Faber confessed that he and the Millens had killed Sumner in the Paramount Theatre robbery!

Lieutenant Griffin immediately briefed District Attorney Craig on the startling turn of events. The Molway-Berrett trial was suspended. Reopened on February 27, in the evening, the defendants, still shackled, were led into the courtroom. Craig addressed the court, slowly unfolding the bizarre revelations. The prisoners in the dock were, in fact, unwitting victims of a crime they had not committed, one for which, till that moment, they seemed doomed to pay the state's supreme penalty in Charlestown's electric chair.

When the Essex County District Attorney finished, the silence was towering. Nine *eye witnesses* had made positive identifications of the defendants. How could nine people who witnessed a crime be mistaken? One or two, perhaps, but not that many people could be wrong. Yet, they had been. It was not a moment for finger pointing.

The jury was polled, and, in time honored tradition asked, "What say you, Mr. Foreman and gentleman of the jury, is the defendant Louis Berrett guilty or not guilty?" The sound for a moment hung heavily, replaced shortly by the foreman's words, "not guilty." The same procedure within moments also made Clement Molway a free man.

In a classic example of supreme irony, Molway and Berrett later would attend sessions of the Millen-Faber trial in Norfolk Superior Court. The ugly details of the gang's crime spree unfolded in Dedham Court House, scene in the prior decade of the Sacco-Vanzetti drama. Crowds daily attended the trial, some for a glimpse of the famous defendants arriving or leaving the granite court building. Uniformed troopers ensured security outside the court house. Inside, District Attorney Edmund R. Dewing led state detectives through key testimony. The thoroughness of the combined state-local investigation was an insurmountable obstacle for defense tactics. The weight of the Commonwealth's evidence crushed any lingering hopes harbored by the Millens or their crime partner, Abe Faber.

In an anti-climatic ending, the Millens and Faber were convicted of their crimes, quickly receiving the state's ultimate sanction. Their electrocutions were carried out behind Charlestown's foreboding walls. Another chapter had closed in the history of the state force. Like Sacco and Vanzetti, Millen-Faber would mark an era, a distinct period of time, rather than a particular criminal trial. And, associated with that era, enduring in its own way, would be the legends created by "Stokes and Ferrari." They, as a renowned detective team, had set symbolic standards. These professional yardsticks would endure, indeed grow, beyond the time of their own careers in the nation's first statewide enforcement agency.

LABOR UNREST

While the Millens and Abe Faber represented a 1930s criminal type, a second phenomenon took place. This was a broad-based social response to the grinding economic pressures. Workers were long docile. Unions were taking hold. Management was fighting a rear guard, losing battle. The stakes were high. This had special significance in the Bay State's teeming textile centers. Unrest erupted in Lowell and Lawrence on the banks of the mighty Merrimack. Violence broke out in the "Spindle City," Fall River, where, years earlier, Mayor Crawford Lindsey had commended the District Police for containing similar threats to public order. Now, however, for the first time, these disorders would confront the uniformed branch.

The 1921 statute prohibited the use of the state force in an industrial dispute unless violence had occurred, and then only on order of the governor. That order was swift in coming as violence erupted in Southbridge, Dudley, West Warren and Ludlow. Non-strikers had attempted to cross picket lines. Some were badly beaten. Their homes were damaged. Reacting, Governor Joseph B. Ely on December 22, 1934 ordered the state force into the stricken communities. A harsh reception awaited the first uniformed arrivals. The men were called "strike breakers," and worse.

The legacy of the use of the Pennsylvania State Police in that state's coal mine strikes loomed in the background. The setting was tense as forty uniformed men moved into the fire station on Elm Street in Southbridge. In nearby Webster additional officers were headquartered in the municipal banquet hall. Just west, in Ludlow, the "staties" were billeted in that town's community building. All

time off was cancelled. No one went home, under any circumstances. The men were there for the duration, whatever time would be required to ensure public order in the stricken communities.

Outside agitators infiltrated the striker's ranks. While troopers were escorting workers through a side street, a melee erupted. Rocks flew. Screams split the air. Clubs and fists made thumping sounds on soft flesh. People were getting hurt. Blood was flowing. The state force moved quickly, seizing key leaders and agitators. The howling mob turned on the men in blue. Cruiser windshields and windows were smashed. The force took injuries as attempts were made to free those under arrest. The mob chanted for their release, but to no avail. Leaderless, they dispersed, and, slowly, order returned.

The men who performed that duty had not welcomed it. But they did not shrink from the extra demands. These were substantial. Those ordered into Ludlow had lived in the community building. Little things were appreciated. A large gymnasium got heavy use. There were nice, clean showers. In such times a hot shower is a treasured commodity, soothing frayed nerve ends rubbed raw on the picket lines.

Preparing for a shift change, each man made certain that essential gear was in top condition. Then followed a disciplined march, in double file, to the town's sole eating place. Meals were eaten in three sittings. Each was allowed 75 cents per meal. Spare eaters could keep the change, with unwritten guidelines that the money could be used to buy cigarettes. Popular brands sold two packs for 25 cents, and, before long, a couple of the more enterprising among them had opened a "small stores" operation back at the community building. Innovation long had been the mother of necessity. Several of that maxim's most devout advocates also wore the two-tone blue during the 1930s industrial disorders.

THE GOLDEN CLASS

Those times would pass. Lingering tensions eased as the organization moved on to new duties. Some of these, ironically, would closely resemble the industrial disruptions. But only in the nature of their violence. There would be new issues; global questions of war and peace and threats of destruction, a consequence of man's expanding quest for technological answers to aggressive strains in the human condition. Even while responding to such emergencies the organization continued to evolve. Recruits were in training yearly. Many of those demanding "training troops" had been conducted in Framingham. Several other classes had gone through their paces in Boston's Commonwealth Armory. The huge facility was especially suited to vigorous courses in horsemanship and motorcycle riding, standard features of that era's training sessions.

Meantime, field locations continued to change with enforcement needs. One of the more significant of these had been the 1932 shift of D Troop headquarters from Middleboro to West Bridgewater. The new site straddled route 28, the main route to Cape Cod where it crossed route 106. Nearby, the 1934 training troop established its campsite. Forty-five strong, the class settled into nine squad tents. They would live "under canvas" for the duration of training. A much larger tent served as the mess hall, and, when it rained, as the classroom. More often, classes were held outdoors with the recruits grouped around the instructor, hanging on every story that hinted at what they might face *if* they could handle the rigorous demands.

Training responsibilities had always attracted some of the

organization's best men. The 1934 troop was no exception. Lieutenant Jim Hughes was commandant, a post he had held for a number of years. Corporal Joe Philips put the would be troopers through their athletic paces, while Patrolman John Collins, with cavalry service behind him, taught the nuances of superior horsemanship. This, even though mounted patrols would not survive the year. Lieutenant Mike Barrett taught criminal law and investigations. He held the recruits spellbound with accounts of criminals that unfolded with an ease that sprung from being completely at peace with one's responsibilities. "Captain Mike," his informal but preferred title, would lecture while seated in a folding chair on the parade grounds. While a lesser being would have been intimidated by such ambience, he relished it. With eager listeners grouped around, he would adroitly mix a recitation of statues with "yarns" from his long police career. It was a style for the times.

The 1934 training troop was to become the "Golden Class," a sobriquet largely attributable to one of its members, Theodore J. Stavredes. Stavredes has since imprinted firmly in organizational lore that rather dramatic description of a group that, in actuality, was substantially intimidated even while they toasted their impending graduation. The long awaited event finally occurred on August 28. Commissioner Daniel A. Needham presided, ably assisted by his executive officer, Captain James P. Mahoney. The recruits went through their paces, demonstrating newly acquired skills for visiting dignitaries, families and friends. Then, in what had become a tradition, Captain Mahoney posted the field assignments. Strange sounding names rent the air. Some of the city boys in the "Golden Class" had second thoughts about their new careers. Feelings were eased, however, by the knowing glances of the veteran instructors, who, themselves, had survived the same ritual not so long before.

Each training troop has its special uniqueness, a character which rises from individuals who together have overcome a difficult challenge. Something has been shared. It is not easily explained. It is more a *feeling* than an observable fact or event. This has been true in the training troops before and since that of 1934. It will be so in the future. In each class there are individuals who, more than others, will be remembered as a consequence of the career paths that unfolded with passing years. On occasion, this results from personal initiative. More frequently, unplanned events intervene creating opportunities not contemplated. The "Golden Class" experienced a full measure of these phenomena as the years lengthened from that August day in West Bridgewater.

One of its members, Daniel I. Murphy, would enjoy a notable career in the state force. Service in the uniformed branch would be followed by an appointment as a detective lieutenant. That duty would culminate in 1950 with "D.I." being named commissioner of public safety, the organization's highest post. Colonel Murphy would later serve as director of the agency's subversive activities division, and, finally, as captain of state police detectives before concluding almost four decades of public service in 1971.

While presiding at the graduation of the 1934 training troop, Commissioner Needham was attending his last official function. Within a month, on September 25, 1934, Governor Joseph B. Ely appointed Paul G. Kirk to the commissioner's post. Captain Mahoney stayed on as executive officer of the uniformed branch. Patrolman John C. Blake of the 1934 class would, in the summer of 1935, draw a coveted assignment. Coveted, that is, if one were single and didn't mind a long stint away from home. Assuming that were acceptable, and it was to a "boot," then Salisbury Beach's cooling breezes could be enjoyed, while on salary. The "Beach" was a summer substation

in Troop A. The popular resort area was jammed each season with sun seekers, and the local police required assistance.

Patrolman Blake shared that 1935 summer with another young man, a "civilian." He was Alexander Woick, known to several generations of uniformed personnel as "Albie." Albie in 1929 had become one of those youngsters known affectionately as "mess punks." These towheads provided every conceivable service in a barracks. Their specialty, of course, was topping the regular cook with gastronomic delights. Alexander "Albie" Woick would serve more than four decades, with special assignments at the recruit training schools. Albie's long tenure, moreover, would be officially recognized in 1971 when he would be among the first recipients of the agency's highest civilian award, the Massachusetts State Police Medal for Meritorious Service.

Blake and Woick had some experienced company at the "Beach." Senior Patrolman Charles "Bunny" Furze, far from his native Fall River, was in command. Rounding out the complement were Patrolmen Bill Killen, Arthur McCabe and Arthur Chaisson. The Salisbury summer station was destined to provide fascinating lore, enlarged whenever veterans of the state force gather.

THE BEY MANHUNT

Another memorable event took place that summer, but at the opposite end of the state. It began in Connecticut. A drifter had been surprised stealing milk by a constable. What happened remains obscure. Gun fire suddenly erupted in the milk shed. The constable lay mortally wounded as his murderer fled the blood spattered scene. The Connecticut State Police mounted a week long search, without success. This was no ordinary fugitive. He was John Bey, an acknowledged outdoors expert, a man who could live off the land for weeks on end. Bey's name would become synonymous with a criminal manhunt. The die was cast when a week after the killing in Connecticut, rifles and revolvers were stolen in a break in Hadley. Bey had a brother living in that B Troop community. Every available man was committed to Bey's capture. He was armed and an expert shot. Risks ran high on both sides.

The day following the Hadley break, Patrolman Ed Sivik and a Connecticut trooper spotted Bey on a back road. Before they could get out of the cruiser rifle shots rang out. One round went through the windshield, while the second shot creased the horn button. Bey escaped. News of the near miss increased mounting tensions. Three weeks passed as, incredibly, Bey eluded the biggest manhunt ever mounted by the state force.

The fugitive's trail led through several communities. Bloodhounds pressed the search. At one point they missed Bey by minutes. Shortly, he was spotted by Patrolmen "Jake" Daley and "Okie" O'Connel. They opened fire, but, again, Bey escaped, apparently unharmed. But time was running out. He was soon cornered on Mountain Street in Northampton, not far from B Headquarters. The area was sealed off. Two of those caught up in the final hours of the drama were Patrolman George Grady and a Connecticut trooper named Herr. Patrolling near the LaCourse farm on Mountain Street, they were approached by a youngster. He blurted out a tingling message; an armed man had walked into the nearby milk shed demanding a pitcher of milk.

Grady and Herr faced a tough decision. They had Bey trapped. But radios were still just one way. The men could receive calls but they couldn't summon help. Without hesitation they acted decisively, bursting with drawn guns into the milk shed. The scene staggered them. Inside, five men recoiled in shock as they faced menacing enforcement rifles. Which was John Bey? The irony of their dilemma was lost on Bey as he slowly raised his hands thereby answering the unasked question. Transferred swiftly to troop headquarters, he confessed to the August 31 murder of Connecticut Constable DiCarli.

Bey's September 25 capture ended the state's longest manhunt. The grueling enforcement drama closed as cruiser radios crackled with the dramatic words: "All cruisers on the John Bey manhunt return to Northampton." and, following an interminable pause,— "he has been captured." Bey got life for the DiCarli murder. He spent the rest of his time in prison, dying there in the 1970s with much less fanfare than that which had accompanied his dramatic capture years before.

By the mid thirties the Boston Athletic Association Marathon had become *the* event in the world of long distance racing. Names like DeMarr, Pawson, "Tarzan" Brown and Kelly had become established in the 26-mile, 285-yard grind from Hopkinton to Boston. It was the supreme test for the amateur. No money could be won; only the glory of proving something to one's self, and, of course, to the thousands who annually lined the fame route over Newton's "heartbreak hill" to the capital city. By then, the state force handled such "special events" with professional expertise. The special detail brought in troopers from various sections of the state. Motorcycles were used almost exclusively. The two wheelers alone had the requisite maneuverability that was essential once the starting gun fired promptly at 12 noon in Hopkinton Center.

The 1936 Patriot's Day race was held under trying conditions. It was unseasonably cold. Runners wore overcoats at the starting line, waiting for the gun. Lieutenant John McLaughlin that year headed up the state police detail. His men wore heavy winter reefers even though the calendar read April 19. Among those astride the two-tone blue "bikes" that day were Patrolmen Charley Collins, Donat LaCasse, Carl Thomas and Sumner Mathes. Predictably, the riders arrived at the Exeter Street finish line in better condition than the runners. The uniformed escorts nevertheless shared in the race's only reward, the traditional bowl of "B.A.A." beef stew.

The 1936 Floods

The previous month had seen B Troop devastated by floods reminiscent of the 1928 catastrophe that had struck the four western counties. On March 11 Northampton received reports of a rising Connecticut River. Ice in the Vermont and New Hampshire streams feeding the beautiful Connecticut was melting. Torrential rains fell on March 18. Hope was fading. Meandering streams were fast becoming angry torrents of yellow water, threatening life and property in the normally peaceful communities bordering the fertile valley. The signs were ominous as the state force galvanized for action with a statewide alert. Accounts of such disasters fall short of the actual experience. Still, a trooper's eye witness report conveys how it was that morning when, suddenly, major sections of B Troop were isolated by what is now remembered with nostalgia as "The Great Floods of 1936."

> Chief Engineer Tom Bean of the Western Electric Company had flashed a final, sudden warning to Northampton headquarters, "Evacuate all of the Connecticut Valley immediately." The word was relayed to every police officer, sheriff and constable who could be reached. Everyone was to be evacuated from all river lowlands. A disaster was impending. Lives were on the line.
> Night patrols had watched the Connecticut and Deerfield rivers through the blackness, straining for sounds of the "ice going out." I had never heard or seen such a thing. I pulled out of the barracks at 5 a.m., heading for the cement bridge in Charlemont. I looked at the Deerfield River below, even then threatening to overflow its banks. Suddenly, I was startled by a strange noise. It sounded like a clap of thunder rolling through the hills. Looking up the river, I was startled by the sight. The ice, two feet thick, was "breaking up," moving as though guided by a giant hand. I jumped into the cruiser and headed for the barracks. We called Bean at Turners Falls Dam, reporting that the ice was going out of the Deerfield.
> By late that morning most of the winter's thick ice had broken up. B Troop's rivers were threatening death and destruction. The Shelburne Falls barracks became the center for emergency operations. The first two days we got no sleep. The next few days were not much better, with about four hours of sleep out of each twenty-four.
> Civilian Conservation Corps, "C.C.C." camps dotted western Massachusetts, having salvaged thousands of young men from the Great Depression. They were mobilized along with another depression era group from the Public Works Administration, the legendary "W.P.A." With enforcement officers, these volunteers performed yeoman service as the floods battered a score of Berkshire communities. In one rescue alone, members of the Warwick "C.C.C." camps saved eighteen men, women and children where the Connecticut had inundated Northfield Farms. Huge ice flows had threatened sudden death.
> You get hardened to trouble and misery on the state police, but this small group of homeless people kind of twisted my heart. They had lost all of their worldly possessions. They had no idea where their next meal would come from. The unshaved and tired farmers were grim, but they held their chins high. Charles Tenney was one of the farmers hardest hit, losing 347 prized cattle, a life time of hard work and savings. Still, when I found him, he was making sandwiches for the "C.C.C." boys.
> Weeks later we heard of many acts of heroism along the river in Deerfield, Amherst, Northampton, and Springfield. Many stories never came to light, heroic services by our own State Police, the Coast Guard, local police and constables, "W.P.A." workers, and, yes, the city boys of the "C.C.C." camps. We heard later that even the governor and the commissioner had been in the B Troop floods. James Michael Curley and Commissioner Paul G. Kirk had inspected rescue operations in the Connecticut valley towns punished severely by the raging flood waters. By March 23, the Connecticut River had returned to normal. Health problems were

enormous. Wells were shut down. Medicine, housing, clothing and food supplies were brought in for weeks.

Finally, after 21 days and nights we were given a great big night off. We later got back the days we lost, but we never did get the night off and we didn't care because everyone agreed they were for a good cause.

Today all of the scars of that great catastrophe have been erased and the Connecticut River Valley is once again the beautiful country that it used to be. If you are riding out that way, look for the signs posted along the main highways marking the flood crest. When you stare in amazement, stop and think of the job done by the troopers and local officers who lived through that flood. And remember the courage of the farmers who lost everything they had to the "Great Flood" of 1936, and then, somehow, made a heroic comeback in the fertile Connecticut valley.

Nineteen thirty-six was also the year of the "academicians." The Depression had taken a heavy toll of professional jobs in the nation's private sector. A college education in the mid-thirties was not the fabled economic ticket that it would become following the Second World War.

When state police recruiters that year added up their applicants, they had several thousand. Many were young men who, in other circumstances, might not have sought a police career. But things were not ordinary. They were very tight. It is easy, after all, to reduce one's ambitions when the paramount issues are food, shelter and clothing, usually in that order.

The Twenty-Seventh Recruit Troop began training on August 18. The group had to deal with the usual requirements. And a new hurdle or two. Each training class has to complete something that its predecessors hadn't faced. Survivors of such rugged training inevitably insist that the next class take what they handled, and a bit more. The curriculum and physical requirements by 1936 were well developed. Much experience had been gained since that first enterprise at the "Poor Farm." Nevertheless, the 1936 class passed muster with flying colors. And well they might have. Ten held college degrees including the following: one Doctor of Philosophy; one Master of Arts; one Bachelor of Philosophy; four Bachelor of Arts; two Bachelors of Science; and one Mechanical Engineer.

There was some irony in that. Educational credentials would one day become requisite to top advancement in the nation's enforcement community. But only after the 1960's "crime in the streets" became a national political issue, followed by a congressional response that pumped tens of millions into law enforcement education. Between the two, the "Great Depression: and "crime in the streets," there would be a hiatus when educational criteria would not be especially perceived as positive yardsticks in recruit selection, or in career advancement.

A New General Headquarters

Paul G. Kirk presided at the graduation of that Twenty-Seventh Training Troop. He had been commissioner since September 1934, having been reappointed by Governor James Michael Curley. A Curley aide at the time was Trooper Arthur T. O'Leary of the 1933 training class. O'Leary would, following World War II, become

commandant of the training program, and, after service as a troop commander, rise to major and adjutant.

The pressing administrative issues of the late thirties were those of pensions and medical protection. Commissioner Kirk exerted vigorous leadership in response to these critical personnel questions. There had never been a real insurance program. The men on their own had protected their loved ones. On one hundred dollars per month, with five dollars deducted for annuity payments, precious little could be done. State police personnel were in a high risk job with almost no protection. An added problem was that of meager compensation for men seriously injured on duty. Moreover, the pension died with the man. A widow was left to shift for herself if she lost the breadwinner. The situation had not been contrived but, rather, was a reflection of the national times. It was, in fact, that vacuum that allowed President Roosevelt to launch most of the social programs he called the "New Deal."

Kirk's efforts paid dividends. Regulations were promulgated to strengthen both medical insurance and death benefits. Public dialogue on the issues highlighted the inadequacy of the pension system. The department moved to correct the situation, with legislation designed to make permanent the badly needed personnel policies. While these would take several years to become law, they were begun during Commissioner Kirk's tenure.

The "boy commissioner," as Kirk was sometimes called, focused on another pressing matter. He had been startled in 1934 to find his "general headquarters" in the basement of the State Capitol. The view from the summit of Beacon Hill was breathtaking, but one could hardly enjoy the vista from the bowels of that historic structure. Kirk was not alone. Each of his predecessors since 1921 directed the statewide force from there. Moreover, the capital building also quartered administrative operations and technical services. The detective branch under Captain John F. Stokes also suffered silently in the cramped surroundings.

Commissioner Kirk broke the silence in private talks with Governor James Michael Curley. He convinced the chief executive that the prestigious state force needed, indeed was entitled to, much more professional quarters. Curley concurred. Within weeks a move was made to Commonwealth Pier in South Boston. A large area was cleared, and paneling provided the offices requisite to the headquarters operation of the Commonwealth's Public Safety Department.

There were some deficiencies at the pier. The commissioner knew that civilian employees would have difficulty getting public transportation to the new location. He was not ecstatic either with the proximity of the state's fishing fleet, and its concomitant odors. But, in the end, the choice had been easy. He had traded the converted coal bins in the depths of the state house for much more adequate space in one of the Commonwealth's finest buildings. Kirk, years later, would remember that move with a solid feeling of accomplishment.

And his accomplishments were destined to be many. On December 16, 1937 he became Associate Justice Kirk of the Superior Court, appointed to the bench by Governor Charles F. Hurley. Justice Kirk served on the Commonwealth's trial court for 23 years, with time out for military service as a colonel in World War II. The distinguished jurist's exemplary service on the Superior Court was rewarded in December of 1960 with his appointment by Governor Foster Furcolo to the Supreme Judicial Court, the state's highest tribunal. He served in that august institution for a decade, retiring on December 31, 1970. He never forgot, however, that once, years earlier, he had occupied the commissioner's post at a critical juncture in the force's history. He thus returned occasionally through the years to participate in activities of his old enforcement organization.

THE GREAT NEW ENGLAND HURRICANE

Nineteen thirty-eight would provide a severe test of the emergency capabilities of the state police force. Its much heralded mobility would enable an almost instant response as central Massachusetts' rivers suddenly began topping their banks on the night of September 20. A score of communities in the Blackstone River Valley were evacuated. As the emergency escalated, the state force went into action. Men from throughout the state were ordered into the stricken area. The lessons of 1928 and 1936 had been hard earned. The first hours were the most threatening.

Emergency operations were directed from C Troop headquarters in Holden. Incoming reports were screened, and police and fire units dispatched by priority need. Pouring rain continued throughout the night of September 20. Cloudbursts greeted the first streaks of light the next morning, but operations went well. By noon, the threat to life in Worcester County had subsided. It had also rained hard for 24 hours in the eastern and southeastern sections of the state. Still, at noon on the 21st, there was no undue alarm. But an enormous storm was even then moving into the southern reaches of the Connecticut River and Rhode Island's Narragansett Bay. It was a ferocious tropical hurricane, the grand daddy of them all. But, somehow, the killer storm pounced on southeastern Massachusetts with almost no advanced warning.

Whatever alarm might have forewarned those living along the Bay State's coast line was largely ignored. Time has provided partial answers. The word "hurricane" was something then associated with tropical islands, far away places. None had occurred here during the twentieth century. There was thus no experience to galvanize into action the summer communities stretching from Point Judith, Rhode Island, north and east to A Troop's summer station at Salisbury Beach. The stage was thereby set for man's greatest foe in life threatening situations, that of being caught unaware; the crippling element of surprise.

The recruit troop of 1938 had begun training at Framingham on September 8. Tents provided the shelter. Now, on the 21st, the canvas sagged from the steady pelting of the downpour. But another, even more threatening portent began to worry the fledgling troopers. As the wind whipped through the tents, each realized that these were not usual autumn gusts. At mid-afternoon, A Troop's towering radio antenna snapped with a piercing crack, plunging into the nearby muddy field. Something unusual, out of the ordinary, was happening.

The same kind of thing, very suddenly, began to happen throughout the eastern and southeastern sections of the state. Few realized the extent of the storm's ferocity until trees began falling on houses, automobiles, and, tragically in several instances, on people. At that point it sunk in. This was not really a "storm." It was, rather, the most devastating natural disaster in the state's history. Indeed it *was* a tropical storm, one that had travelled some 1,500 miles from the Caribbean, and, now, it was thrusting an enormous tidal wave ahead of it. It was the "Great New England Hurricane." But on September 21 the storm's fury so isolated its victims that no one really knew what was happening beyond an immediate locale. The devastation would not fully be comprehended for weeks.

For the 1938 recruits it meant immediate action. The training site was a quagmire. The trainees had no uniforms, no equipment, no badges, and no police authority. But it was not a moment for formalities. The entire state force had been mobilized. Time off was cancelled, and off duty men were called in. In such circumstances, uniforms and authorities are not important. Willing hands and staying power are the priorities. Thus, the recruits, with thirteen days service under their belts, found themselves posted on key traffic posts in A Troop. Wires were down. Trees blocked major arteries. It was a tough first assignment. Uniforms were "simple." Most wore khaki pants, "tee" shirts and raincoats. But, with senior patrolmen, they did a vital job. Such circumstances would not be repeated during the remainder of their careers in the state force.

The storm finally began to abate late in the day. Only then were there reports of what had happened along the coast. Several hundred people were killed. Thousands of homes, summer cottages and mansions alike, had been smashed to shreds by the tidal wave that rode into the bays and rivers on a flood tide. The hurricane's power had been awesome. Small craft were sunk at their berths or driven inland, some beached a half mile from normal high water. In Fall River, the "Phoenix" had been torn from her moorings at the Shell Oil docks on the Taunton River. The twelve thousand ton ocean going tanker was driven aground on the Somerset shore, far inland. She remained there for a year or more while a channel was dredged to get her back to sea.

The recruits next morning were loaded into trucks and transported to Buzzard's Bay. It was devastated. Looting had begun. They were paired for twelve-hour patrols with senior patrolmen who had arrived from throughout the state. Fairhaven barracks served as the operations center. The recruits and regular officers were quartered in town halls in Marion, Mattapoisett, Bourne and other nearby communities. Some stayed in the area for several weeks, until rescue operations returned a degree of normalcy to the usually idyllic shoreline hamlets.

The emergency duty was not without its lighter moments. Boats were used to patrol the shoreline. On one trip recruit Eugene "Lobster" Sullivan got lost, raising concern for his safety. Other incidents eased the gravity of the emergency assignments. These, when they happen, are serious. But, somehow, with time's gentle way of coloring things past, they take on a more humorous dimension. In that way, the mind's eye is provided with a fond remembrance of what was, in reality, a difficult time.

That's the way many of the 1938 class remember their introduction to the state force. Not all completed the recruit training. Some stayed for a few years. Most completed over two decades of public service before retiring from the uniformed force. Some are gone. But they were all caught up together in perhaps the most unusual drama to intrude on the normally prosaic recruit training school. It was not unusual, then, for the Twenty-Eighth Recruit Training Troop to be immortalized as the "hurricane class."

PENSION IMPROVEMENTS

Eugene M. McSweeney had been Commissioner of Public Safety since December 1937. McSweeney for two years pursued the reform policies first initiated by Commissioner Kirk. The proposals were defeated in the General Court in 1937 and 1938. Nineteen thirty-nine, however, brought success and much strengthened pension system. Governor Leverett Saltonstall promptly signed the measure, making it law. The new statute mandated retirement from the uniformed branch at 50, provided the officer had completed twenty years service. On the other hand, if a man completed twenty years, say, at age 46, he was required to remain in service until age fifty. The pension was set at one half the last year's salary. The law, which became effective on December 1, also provided for disability retirement. This covered serious line of duty injuries and illnesses. An additional feature ensured a widow's pension of one thousand dollars yearly, with another two hundred dollars for each surviving child.

The new pension system was contributory. Monthly deductions of five percent were made on salaries up to two thousand, six hundred dollars. Retirement at fifty was now mandatory. Thirty was set as the maximum age for first enlistment. This was modified after World War II for veterans of that conflict. A group insurance plan also was approved in 1939. Personnel could purchase one thousand dollars worth of life insurance payable at death for any cause. Dues were 85 cents monthly. Ninety percent of the men joined. Earlier, a committee appointed by McSweeney had discovered that 75 percent of the state force carried *no* insurance.

The thirties closed on a strongly structured, ably staffed statewide enforcement agency. McSweeney was commissioner. His executive secretary was Timothy C. Murphy. General Headquarters remained at Commonwealth Pier in South Boston. The state force was structured basically in two separate units, detectives and uniformed officers or, officially, the detective and uniformed branches.

Captain John F. Stokes, of "Stokes and Ferrari" fame was chief of detectives. He had under his command twenty detectives and five detective inspectors, one of whom was Joseph L. Ferrari. These men staffed the district attorneys throughout the state, with a backup force at Commonwealth Pier. Additionally, the following uniformed officers were assigned to detectives: Sergeant Robert L. Ferrari, Corporal James A. Winn, Corporal George S. Pollard, and Patrolmen James F. Conniff, George E. Grady, James C. Leary and Arnold W. Olsson.

Captain James P. Mahoney was, as he had been since 1933, executive officer of the uniformed branch. Edward J. Gully was lieutenant and adjutant. Gully that year had graduated from the Traffic Institute at Northwestern University in Evanston, Illinois, the first of a number of officers to attend the famed school. Lieutenant William F. Shimkus served as division inspector.

The field troops of the uniformed branch had stabilized at four. Lieutenant John P. Sullivan commanded A Troop headquarters in Framingham. John F. Barnicle filled the key post of first sergeant. A Troop covered the counties of Essex, Middlesex and Norfolk. The following officers commanded A Troop substations:

Corporal Arthur V. Ford	Andover
Corporal Richard F. Cleary	Topsfield
Corporal Robert S.F. "Dusty" Rhodes	Concord
Corporal Arthur T. O'Leary	Wrentham

Substation A-5, Salisbury Beach, was opened only during the summer months.

B Troop was still headquartered in Northampton. The troop patrolled the counties of Berkshire, Franklin, Hampden and Hampshire. Lieutenant John F. McLaughlin was troop commander, assisted by First Sergeant Warner F. Eaton. "Hamp," as B-H was called, included the following substations and supervisors:

Corporal Michael J. Sullivan	Lee
Corporal Charles F. Furze	Shelburne Falls
Corporal James M. Lyons	Monson
Corporal Louis J. Perachi	Pittsfield
Corporal Frank Lambert	Russell

Holden since 1923 had been C Troop headquarters. The C-H territory included all Worcester County and the northwestern portion of Middlesex. Lieutenant James E. Hughes, long commandant of the training academy, was troop "C.O." Edward J. Majesky was firs sergeant.

C Troop substations and commanders included:

Corporal Charles J. O'Connor	Athol
Corporal Robert G. Jones	Grafton
Corporal Harry C. Smith	Brookfield
Corporal Theodore H. Stronach	Lunenburg

D Troop headquarters had shifted to Bridgewater, on the site of the "State Farm." The troop commander was Lieutenant George H. Thompson. Second in command was First Sergeant Edward J. Canavan.

Bridgewater had six substations, four directed by corporals, and two supervised by sergeants:

Corporal Henry W. Eliason	Norwell
Corporal Norman S. Sidney	Yarmouth
Corporal Edward L. McGinley	Fairhaven
Corporal John W. Collins	Rehoboth
Sergeant Antonio N. Attieri	Oak Bluffs
Sergeant Harvey G. LaPrade	Nantucket

By 1939 the state force had a clearly identifiable staff section in general headquarters. There was a unique split, however, in its organization and "chain of command." Structured under the detective branch were the following supervisors of technical and forensic services:

Supervisor Roscoe G. Hill	Bureau of Criminal Identification
Special Officer Sergeant Julius W. Toelken	Bureau of Photography
Lieutenant Joseph T. Walker	Chemical Laboratory
Expert Assistant Charles J. Van Amburgh	Ballistics Laboratory
Medicolegal Consultant Robert P. Phipps	Handwriting and Questioned Documents Laboratory

On the other hand, two staff functions had evolved in the uniformed branch. Each reported to Lieutenant Gully who was also adjutant:

Lieutenant John A. Carroll	Bureau of Supplies
Lieutenant Martin W. Joyce	Bureau of Police Communications

It is not the purpose of this work to evaluate, but, simply, to report the evolution of the state force. Yet one is struck by the seeming ambiguity of organizational and command relationships that, by 1939, had taken firm root in the general headquarters structure. The dichotomy startles. Some staff functions reported to the chief of detectives. Others reported to the uniformed lieutenant and adjutant.

In retrospect, one perceives that these staffing anomalies were rooted in history. The detectives rose from the State Constabulary, District Police, and 1919 founding of the Department of Public Safety, emerging as a "division" of State Police in the new agency. The 1921 statute placed the uniformed "branch" in the existing

State Police division. Some technical support services predated the uniformed branch.They remained under the detectives. Others evolved after 1921. Some were placed under the detective operation, while at least two were structured in the uniformed branch.

Compounding the problem has been the variable use of words to describe the organizational relationships, especially the investigatory function. This activity in annual reports, studies, internal communications and public accounts has been referred to, at a minimum, as "detective division," — "detective bureau," — "detectives," — "division of detectives," — "detective branch," — "state detectives," and more. The 1939 annual report, for example, uses the terminology "Detective Bureau." Yet, the same document identifies four staff "Bureaus" under the overall Detective "Bureau."

Interested observers would for years grapple with the policy and operational complexities generated by these historical ambiguities. It is, therefore, with substantial timidity that one observes in retrospect that the 1939 enforcement structure might more easily be understood as follows:

• The Commissioner of Public Safety
• The department contained three *divisions;* State Police, Fire Prevention and Inspections (buildings, boilers, etc.)
• The state police *division* had two *branches*: the detective branch, and the uniformed branch.
• The detective branch had a *line* operation, detectives assigned to the district attorneys and general headquarters, and a *staff* operation, specialists who supervised headquarters staff functions.
• The uniformed branch also had a *line* and *staff* structure. The four field troops made up the *line,* and the two headquarters functions, supply and police communications, were the *staff* activities.
• The two *branches* operated with substantial independence of each other. In 1939 Captain John F. Stokes was "Chief of Detectives," commander of the detective branch. Captain James P. Mahoney was "Executive Officer," commander of the uniformed branch. Each reported *directly* in the "chain of command," to Commissioner McSweeney.

The 1939 budget for the Department of Public Safety was approximately $1,600.000 dollars. Of this, the state police expended approximately $1,200,000 dollars. A special appropriation of $16,000 dollars covered the extra costs incurred in the September, 1939 hurricane.

The following officers were killed in the line of duty during the 1930s:

Charles A. Better: Died September 28, 1930, as the result of a motorcycle accident in Topsfield.

Charles F. McGonagle: Died August 2, 1932, as the result of a motorcycle accident in East Longmeadow.

Earl W. Tobin: Died March 30, 1934, as the result of a motorcycle accident in Marion.

Joseph W. Kelly: Died July 23, 1938, as the result of a motorcycle vehicle accident in Plymouth.

• • •

The following were among those appointed to the Detective Branch during the 1930s:

Cotter, Richard N.	Dempsey, John F.	Murphy, Daniel A.
Cresco, Joseph C.	Foley, Raymond L.	Puzzo, William J.
Delay, William H.	Johnson, Theodore W.	Sullivan, John N.

The following were appointed to the Massachusetts State Police Academy during the 1930s:

TWENTY-SECOND RECRUIT TROOP

February 3, 1930

Allen, Adrian C.	Fraser, Joseph P.	Murphy, George
Barboza, Augustine J.	Golden, Anthony J.	Nadolski, Walter J.
Barrett, Jeremiah A.	Gormley, Leo J.	Olsson, Arnold W.
Better, Charles A.	Hamilton, Herbert	O'Neill, James H.
Breare, Joseph	Hanson, Victor H.	Ratigan, William A.
Burpee, Marshall T.	Harris, Frederick W.	Ruddy, James J.
Chaisson, Arthur F.	Hiller, Richard A.	Seery, Marous H.
Coutu, Jean D.	Howe, Karl T.	Sidney, John W.
Daily, James F.	Larkin, Thomas A.F.	Smith, Donald D.
Desmond, Arthur D.	Lloyd, Thomas L.	Stanley, Joseph H.
Edwards, George C.	Luppold, John J.	Stronoch, Theodore H.
Faron, William B.	McGonagle, Charles F.	Tarvers, Anthony P.
Fielding, George J.		

TWENTY-THIRD RECRUIT TROOP

April 18, 1930

Caldwell, Lotta H.	McCarthy, Robert E.	Nichols, Oliver F.
Irving, Lawrence W.	McDonnell, Walter J.	Ramsdell, Mary S.
Killen, William B.	Mitchell, Robert J.	Tickle, Herbert H.
Mallett, Warren E.		

TWENTY-FOURTH RECRUIT TROOP

June 1, 1931

Artenstein, Isadore	Garvin, Milton J.	Murphy, Robert J.
Barrett, William J.	Hanigan, Francis O.	Nelson, Victor
Brown, Harold	Hennigan, Francis W.	Noone, Joseph M.
Brown, John T.	Horan, Bernard D.	Peters, Theodore W.
Caggiano, John T.	Joyce, Arthur R.	Queena, Racci
Cassidy, Henry C.	Kukkula, Edward E.	Redding, Michael J.
Comfort, Francis C.	LaCasse, Donat A.	Regan, Francis S.
Cronin, James E.	Laitinen, Albert V.	Regan, Joseph L.
Dacey, Howard H.	Leary, James E.	Reinstein, Arthur J.
Davison, Harry C.	Malkasian, Usha	Shea, Wilbur A.
Deviney, George A.	McCabe, Arthur E.	Smith, Robert B.
Donahue, Joseph P.	McCarthy, Michael W.	Snow, John P.
Dumas, Leo J.	Morse, Carroll B.	Sullivan, Thomas F.
Fitzgerald, Joseph M.	Munro, Ansel D.	VanAmburgh, Charles P.
Fitzgerald, Thomas T.	Murphy, D. Francis	Walden, Leo H.

TWENTY-FIFTH RECRUIT TROOP

August 15, 1933

Collins, Daniel J.	Moore, Melvin W.	Ralls, George A.
Concannon, James L.	Niziolek, Edward	Randlett, E. Prescott
Conniff, James F.	O'Leary, Arthur T.	Savage, Roland M.
Grady, George E.	Orth, Gilbert P.	Seales, Harold E.
Hall, Ralph M.	Peabody, Ernest W.	Thompson, E. Barton, Jr.
Hayes, James H.	Peloquin, Harold J.	Thorsell, Ernest A.
Howarth, James H.	Peltier, Norman A.	Tobin, Earl W.
Hurley, Joseph B.	Qualters, Thomas J.	Tullock, Donald P.

TWENTY-SIXTH RECRUIT TROOP-"THE GOLDEN CLASS"

May 28, 1934

Ashe, James P.G.	Gavin, Edward H.	Menard, Rene E.
Bailey, Kenneth W.	Goslin, Albert E.	Milosh, Stephen W.
Bean, Leward L.	Grant, James V.	Murphy, Daniel I.
Blake, John C., Jr.	Guiffrida, Domenico D.	Riley, Leo F.
Bourbeau, Robert F.	Haley, Joseph D.	Ryan, William H.
Bradshaw, Ellis B.	Haughey, Edward J.	Sivik, Edward
Brennan, James T.	Hunt, Burton D.	Slattery, John J., Jr.
Callanan, William A.	Jewell, Robert H.	Stavredes, Theodore J.*
Carney, John J.	Killen, George E.	Sullivan, Frederick F.
Cashman, John J.	King, Leonard J.	Sullivan, John J.
Collins, Charles J.	Kingston, Francis A.	Sullivan, William J.
Dorsey, John H.	Lindstrom, Edgar T.	Tague, John J. Jr.
Eidt, Edward W.	Martin, James J.	Townsend, Robert
Feeney, Edmond J.	Martin, Stephen D.	Wallace, Joseph E.
Frost, Wendell E.	Mawn, Ernest M.	Wersocki, Stephen S.

*State Police Historian and, in 1949, founder and first president of the Former Massachusetts State Troopers Association.

Commonwealth Armory, Boston, 1930. Karl T. Howe practicing for the state police trick riding team. Howe for years was a standout in that famed equestrian group, graduated in 1930 from the state police academy with the 22nd Recruit Troop.

TWENTY-SEVENTH RECRUIT TROOP

August 18, 1936

Blockel, Arthur J.	MacLean, John D.R.	Shimkus, Theodore J.
Brothers, Francis A.	McCarthy, John F., Jr.	Storkweather, Edw. M.
Davy, Thomas P.	McGrath, Bernard H.	Sughrue, Daniel F.
Fallon, John H.	McLean, John E.	Sullivan, Daniel G.
Fiedler, Richard B.	McManus, Joseph E.	Sullivan, Edward J.
Hales, Herbert A.	Moran, James F.	Tonis, Richard
Janulis, Adolph A.	Myers, Henry F.	Treacy, Michael F.
Kelly, Joseph W.	Noone, Francis W.	Tulis, John
Leary, William F.	Russell, Augustine D.	Uzdavinis, Joseph P.
Mabardy, Mitchell A.	Sanders, Alfred J.	Walker, Joseph T.
Mack, William J.		

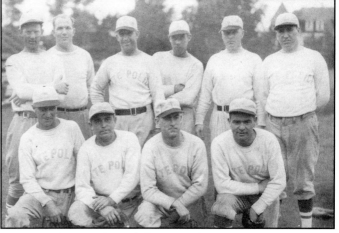

Troop C, Grafton Barracks Baseball Team, 1936. Left to Right (front): J. Avedian, E. Jones (civ.), G. Fiske, J. Luppold. (rear) J. Concannon, J. Phillips, J. Cronin, P. Gadaire (civ.), V. Nelson, J. McLaughlin. The Grafton Barracks in 1997 remained a Troop C substation on Route 140, a faithful sentinel on the 'Cape' road since the early 1930's.

TWENTY-EIGHTH RECRUIT TROOP

September 8, 1938

Arntz, Irwin W.	Halloran, Francis T.	McQueen, Cyril P.
Balkus, B. William	Hanley, Patrick L.	Mee, John
Boakes, William R.	Harding, William J. Jr.	O'Brien, Walter C.
Bowen, Walter F.	Horne, Henry K.	O'Keefe, Francis D.
Brady, Roger M.	Kelly, John J.	Power, Vincent L.
Brosnahan, Edward F.	Kidney, William F.	Powers, John B.
Brown, Kenneth T.	Knightly, William T.	Riley, John J.
Buckley, John H.	Lane, Joseph M.	Roth, Charles E. Jr.
Cairns, Robert H.	Lawrence, Winston J.	Shields, William F.
Carroll, Joseph D.	Lordan, John T.	Sienkiewicz, William J.
Daley, Leo S.	Lynch, James H.	Sullivan, J. Eugene
Driscoll, Joseph J.	Lynch, Joseph M.	Swanson, Gustave R.
Egan, Francis D.	Mackaj, Frank	Sweeney, Frank P., Jr.
Flanagan, William J.	Mahoney, William E.	Wojtkowski, Mieczslaw S.
Fowler, Bruce K.	McCauley, Peter A.	Zuk, Julian
Gibbons, Edward A.	McEnaney, Joseph P.	

BELOW, *State Police Trick Riding Team, 1930. Left to Right: Sergeant A. Burns, J. Collins, T. Norton, t. Fitzgerald, W. Nadolski, A. Olsson, T. Haselton, H. Beattie, R. Hiller (with American flag), K. Howe (with state flag), Lieutenant J. Hughes. Olsson in 1942 topped the detective lieutenant examination, went on to a distinguished legal career, in 1997 remained active in the Former Troopers' Association until his death that year.*

Troop B, Springfield Fair, 1931. Corporal George D. Rapport. Rapport in 1949 was a founder of the Former Massachusetts State Troopers Association, served as its president, for years was an active supporter of association activities.

Troop D, Rehoboth, 1932. Edward L. McGinley trained with 1929's 21st Recruit Troop, saw field and staff service throughout the state, in 1952 became major and executive officer, served in the top uniformed post until his 1956 retirement.

Troop A, Concord, 1933. Hollis E. "Sam" Beattie trained with 1926's 15th Recruit Troop. An expert horseman, he was a key member of the trick riding team, participating in equestrian events throughout the eastern United States. Beattie served until the mid-1950's, and in retirement helped train a new state police mounted drill team.

Trick Riding Team, 1931. Left to Right: A. Tuney, H. Beattie, J. Crowley, J. Avedian, D. Fitzgerald, P. Whelan, A. Dodge, Sergeant A. Dasey (front). Dasey was a member of 1921's First Recruit Troop, was for years a coach and member of the trick riding team. "Sam" Beattie became a legend in his own time, the master of "creative" solutions to administrative constraints.

Troop C, Brookfield Barracks, 1932. Left to Right: A. Golden, T. Lloyd, C. Smith, D. Jacobs, L. Latham, W. McDonnell, R. Foley. Andy Golden trained with 1930's 22nd Recruit Troop, in 1996 attended the 75th Anniversary Gala at Boston's World Trade Center.

Commonwealth Armory, Boston, November 4, 1933. Graduation of the 25th Recruit Training Troop. Left to Right: Captain James. P. Mahoney, Lieutenant James E. Hughes-Academy Commandant, Commissioner Daniel E. Needham, Patrolman James H. Hayes. Hayes in 1938 became the first superintendent of the New Hampshire State Police, served for a number of years in senior justice positions in New Hampshire. The Granite State's law enforcement complex in Concord is the James H. Hayes Public Safety Center.

Lunenburg barracks, 1932. Left to Right: (front) H. Dacey, Corporal J. Donahue, (rear) T. Fitzgerald, H. Hamilton, A. Bruno, T. Norton, L. Gormley. Fitzgerald and Norton during the 1930's were key members of the department's trick riding and horsemanship teams. Dacey later was president of the Former Troopers' Association.

Troop B, Shelburne Falls Barracks, 1933. Left to Right: A. Munro, J. Coutu, D. Hiller, D. Murphy, W. Mallett. Hiller in 1933 rode "Ginger" from Shelburne Falls to Northampton, turning his mount over to officials from the Belchertown State School. That ride reportedly was the last state police mounted patrol.

Topsfield Barracks, 1933. Left to Right: (front) J. Brown, D. Jacobs, J. Donovan, Corporal H. Stingle, C. Thomas, W. Faron, F. Byrne. (rear) R. Bergstrom, H. Berglund. Stingle in 1922 trained with the 3rd Recruit Troop, served later as president of the Former Troopers' Association. Herb Berglund became chief of police in Easton. Topsfield, formerly a private residence, was popularly known as "Nangle's House" and had a key Route 1 location.

Troop B, Monson Barracks, 1933. Left to Right: Corporal F. Lambert, L. Irving, T. Peters, L. Walden. The troopers on this long ago day were sporting the recently issued French and electric blue uniforms, still the salient distinguishing characteristic of state police personnel and equipment. Lambert wears the corporal's chevrons, the rank of a barrack's commander until the 1950's.

Troop D, Rehoboth Barracks, Between Taunton, Mass. and Providence, R.I., 1933. Rehoboth was phased out in 1971. The first barracks in this area during the 1920's had been on Milford Road in Swansea. In 1997 it is a private home, obscure in the anonymity imposed by time's passage.

Willimansett, Connecticut, 1933. Left to Right: (front) V. Nelson, J. Leary, J. Cronin, R. Mitchell, R. McCarthy, W. McDonald, (rear) A. Desmond, J. Maturo, G. Murphy, J. Avedian, A. Meissner. This search detail tracked down the killer of a guard at the Springfield, Mass., House of Correction. James E. "Jim" Cronin was a champion prize fighter in his youth, trained with 1931's 24th Recruit Troop, long served in central and western Massachusetts until the mid-1950's, lived out his retirement years on Cape Cod.

General Headquarters, Boston, 1933. State Police Pistol Team. Left to Right: Captain C. Van Amburgh, N. Sidney, J. Crescio, T. Johnson, Lieutenant J. Hughes, Commissioner Daniel A. Needham. Van Amburgh's crucial ballistics testimony in the sensational 1920's Sacco and Vanzetti trial remains uncontroverted 70 years after their executions at Charlestown State Prison. Joe Crescio went on to become Captain of State Police Detectives in a 40 - year enforcement career.

Troop A, Salisbury Beach Barracks, Summer, 1935. Left to Right: (seated) Arthur E. McCabe, Charles F. Furze, Arthur F. Chaisson. Left to Right (rear): John C. Blake, Alexander Woick, William B. Killen. Salisbury Beach for decades was a summer state police outpost. Woick was one of the barracks' "mess boys," became a legend during his long years of service, in 1971 received the State Police Medal for Meritorious Service. Furze was the "senior patrolman" and barracks commander.

Cheshire Barracks, 1933. Left to Right: Corporal L. Perachi, F. Regan, M. Redding, (civilian unknown), J. Coutu, M. Sullivan. Cheshire in the early years was a Troop B substation, was phased out in the 1930's accelerated construction program of the first red brick "barracks" buildings.

Troop D, Bridgewater, circa 1935. Left to Right: James F. Daily, James V. Grant. Grant in 1934 trained with the famed "Golden Class" in West Bridgewater, closed his career in the late 1950's as captain and commanding officer of Troop D, Middleboro. His widow, Lillian, in 1997 continued to do yeoman's work for the Former Troopers' Association.

State Police Academy, Framingham, 1933. Left to Right: G. Grady, E. Thompson, M. Moore, E. Tobin, J. Concannon. As recruits they were garbed in the traditional forest green, but on November 4, 1933 were the first to graduate in the spanking new French and electric blue. Tobin in 1934 was killed in a tragic motorcycle accident in Marion.

Topsfield Barracks, 1938. Left to Right: William J. Sullivan, Corporal Arthur T. O'Leary, Theodore J. Stavredes. Sullivan on March 31, 1956, welcomed his son Richard J. Sullivan into the uniformed ranks with the graduation of the 39th Recruit Training Troop. They were the first father and son to serve together in the uniformed branch of the Massachusetts State Police.

Academy, Framingham, 1938. Left to Right: Recruits J. Sullivan, F. Mackaj, R. Brady. Members of 1938's 28th Recruit Training Troop, they lost their tents and equipment to the Great New England Hurricane of September 21, 1938. A hearty academy breakfast launched an intensive 16 hour day.

Framingham State Police Academy, circa 1939. Francis J. McVey, Sr. "Specky" McVey in the 1930's began as a state police "mess boy," was for years a barrack's cook, saw his son Francis Jr. graduate from the academy with 1966's 47th Recruit Troop, in 1971 received the state police medal for meritorious service. McVey Sr. was a state police original, a legend in his own time until his mid-1990's death.

Framingham, 27th Recruit Troop, 1936. Left to Right (front): J. Tulis, A. Blockell, F. Noone, E. Sullivan, J. McCarthy, J. McLean, J. Moran, M. Treacy, (middle) F. Brothers, D. Sughrue, T. Shimkus, H. Myers, W. Leary, R. Tonis, E. Starkweather, D. Sullivan, A. Russell (rear) A. Janulis, J. MacLean, T. Davy, B. McGrath, M. Mabardy, H. Hales, J. Fallon, H. Wentzell, R. Fielder, W. Mack, J. Davinus. Dick Tonis during World War II authored a distinguished combat record in the Asiatic-Pacific Campaign. Herb Hales in 1952 died at 41 while he was sergeant in charge of the South Yarmouth Barracks.

Framingham, State Police Academy, 1938. Left to Right: H. Delaney, Corporal J. Collins, Lieutenant J. Hughes, academy commandant. Tents were standard academy housing until the 1949 arrival of Quonsett Huts, a World War II mainstay. Hughes was a long time academy commander, a superb horseman, one of the nation's finest marksmen.

Troop D, Brockton Fair, 1935. Left to Right: Sergeant J. P. Sullivan, P. Tulloch, F. Kingston, E. Lindstrom, J. Ruddy, A. O'Brien, J. Sidney. Sullivan in 1949-1950 was captain and executive officer, the force's highest rank. Lindstrom served many years on Nantucket Island. Tulloch became sheriff of Barnstable County.

State Capitol, Boston, July 1930. Reception for President Herbert C. Hoover during the Bay State's tercentenary celebration. In front: Detective Captain Thomas E. Bligh. First row, from left: Frank G. Hale, David J. Manning, Silas Smith (behind Manning), Joseph L. Ferrari, William F. Murray, Edward J. McCarthy, Albert L. Brouillard, John G. Stokes.
Middle from left: Edward J. Sherlock, Michael F. Fleming, Ernest S. Bradford, Edward P. O'Neil, Theodore W. Johnson, Harry L. Avery.
Rear row, from left: Francis W. Clemmey, Edward J. Canavan, John A. Carroll, Harold A. Delaney, Harold B. Williams, Richard K. Townsend, Joseph C. Crescio. Johnson, Avery, Canavan, Carroll, Delaney, Williams, Townsend and Crescio were from the uniformed branch. The others were detective lieutenants under Captain Bligh. John A. Carroll in 1933 was the first to wear the new French and electric blue uniform. He modeled the distinctive colors for Governor Joseph B. Ely and Commissioner Alfred E. Foote.

BELOW, *Academy, Framingham, 1938. 28th Recruit Troop. (front): Walter F. Bowen, (rear left to right): Joseph Lally, Peter A. McCauley, William J. Sienkiewicz, Joseph P. McEnaney, Joseph M. Lane, Steven S. Wersoski, Francis D. Egan. Bowen and McEnaney served into the 1960's as commissioned officers. Tents were the focus of academy life from the 1921 founding until the 1949 arrival of "Quonsett Huts," a technological breakthrough from World War II.*

THE FORTIES
The War Years

Troop C, Holden, 1948. Left to Right: Troopers Alje M. Savela and Thomas D. Rourke. Savela on August 31, 1951 was gunned down on Route 122 in Barre, a bucolic town in the patrol area of Troop C's Athol Barracks. His family in June, 1979, accepted the posthumous award of the department's newly authorized State Police Medal of Honor. Trooper Savela's killer, it is believed, was later executed in Florida for a murder committed in that state.

Troop C. Shirley Barracks, 1948. Left to Right: Steven Obartuck, Edward G. Conrad, Alfred A. Hewitt, John A. Winn. The Shirley Barracks was part of a "reform school" for boys, some of whom served as barracks' "mess boys." Trooper Alfred A. Hewitt on January 4, 1950 was killed on patrol in a tragic motor vehicle accident on Route 1 in Saugus.

Chapter Four

THE WORLD WAR II YEARS

Nineteen thirty-eight had been the year of the "Great New England Hurricane." Abroad, however, the year had witnessed a different kind of event, one that portended ominous consequences for large numbers of the world's population. Neville Chamberlain had returned to Great Britain from his meeting in Munich proclaiming "peace in our time." Chamberlain's umbrella became a symbol of futile appeasement when, shortly, Nazi panzer divisions crushed several of Germany's defenseless neighbors. A new word, "blitzkreig," was coined. It meant death and destruction. In record time.

Adolph Hitler had boasted of the "Third Reich." It would endure, he said, for a thousand years. Nearby nations were not then in a position to challenge his frightening rhetoric. Not, at least, those on the same continent. But just across the narrow water known as the English Channel there was such a country, a nation that had already endured for nearly a millennium.

Moreover, there was in that island nation a leader who could match the German Fuhrer's charisma, and his power with the spoken word. His mother was an American. But his stout heart rose from the centuries of civility that yet marked the British experience. He was, of course, Sir Winston Churchill. Churchill was born in the Nineteenth Century, the Victorian Age, but he was a contemporary man, ahead of his time, such was his foresight. Destiny had decreed his rise to power in 1940, the hour of his beloved island nation's greatest peril. As prime minister he would, for the first time in the history of warfare, it would later be said, "take the English language and send it into battle."

The British prime minister also had something else in mind. That rested on his close personal relationship with the American president, Franklin Delano Roosevelt. Soon, the headlines would announce to an anxious nation Roosevelt's policy of "lend lease." Britain would allow this country to use Bermuda as a naval supply base, in return for a score of World War I destroyers. It was at the time perceived as a bargain. History seems to instruct that it was carefully conceived, a segment of a grander design that would save Britain through the force of this nation's arms and materials. Whatever the historical truth, it brought Europe's war ever nearer to these shores as the decade of the nineteen forties began.

At home, the nation's sports fans marveled at the skills of a "colored" heavyweight. He was Joseph Louis Barrows, son of an Alabama sharecropper who had joined the migrant stream north to find a job in Detroit. The young heavyweight, in the mid-thirties, had won the crown from James J. Braddock, the "Cinderella Man" from the Jersey docks. That sixth round win in Chicago's Comiskey Park, had won him the sobriquet "the Brown Bomber."

He would need all of the power the name implied right after beating Braddock. For, shortly before, he had suffered a humiliating defeat at the hands of the powerful German, Max Schmeling. The fight took on something of a test between Nazi Germany and this country. Louis did not disappoint the nation or its rabid fight fans. He stopped Schmeling in one round, punishing him so severely that the German spent several days in the hospital. Louis's performance in that classic encounter signalled that he would rule the world's heavyweights for a long time. In the end, some fifteen years later, it was time rather than an opponent that finally defeated a man who, in that era, could be introduced publicly as both the "Brown Bomber," and as "being a credit to his race."

Meantime, the Bay State's entries in the world of professional baseball were having problems. The Boston "Braves," lately the "Bees," were in the National League. Their home field was hard by the state police training school in Commonwealth Armory. Now the site of Boston University's west campus and athletic complex, "Braves Field" had no pennant banners competing with the ubiquitous pigeons during those years. Casey Stengel, later of Yankees fame, was the manager. His tenure here was such that a Boston writer commended publicly a taxi driver whose vehicle had struck the "professor," breaking his leg.

A mile down Commonwealth Avenue lay Kenmore Square, and, just beyond, Fenway Park's famous left field screen. Fenway had been the home park for a number of years for Boston's entry in the American League, the "Red Sox." The Sox had fallen on hard times. The immortal Babe Ruth and others had been sold off in the twenties to finance the owner's theatre investments. Then, in the early thirties, Tom Yawkey had tried to purchase an instant pennant by buying a young Joe Cronin from the Washington Senators, and "Lefty" Grove and Jimmy Foxx from Connie Mack's Philadelphia Athletics.

Yawkey's quick infusion of large chunks of his personal fortune, however, did not get a championship for pennant hungry Bostonians. And for one principal reason. There was a club in the league the Red Sox could not beat, the hated "Yankees" of New York. The New Yorkers had brought up a young Californian in the mid-thirties, and, by 1940, he was perhaps the most skilled and graceful center fielder in the history of the game. He was, of course, Joe DiMaggio, the "Yankee Clipper." He was loved in New York and hated in Boston. But he was always respected; both for his skills and leadership on the field, and for his class off the field.

Boston, too, had a young Californian in its outfield. Theodore Samuel Williams had come off the sandlots of his native San Diego with perhaps the greatest natural swing in the game's history. But he came with a lot more. Baseball writers struggled to describe it, finally settling for the word "color," a term universally understood by sports' buffs. Whatever it was, the "Splendid Splinter" had it. Even then, in an uncertain and threatening 1940, one sensed that the gangling young athlete who refused to wear a tie would dominate Boston's sports' scene for years. He was not to disappoint.

Williams patrolled Fenway's right field his first couple of seasons. Roger "Doc" Cramer was in center field and Joe Vosmik guarded the left field wall. Manager Cronin directed the club from shortstop, anchoring an infield of Jim Tabor at third, Bobby Doerr at second, and the memorable "Double X," Jimmy Foxx, at first base. "Lefty" Grove was the ace of the staff, soon to notch his three hundredth major league win. The Red Sox had talent, plenty of it. But they were eternally destined to finish behind DiMaggio, Kellar,

Dickey, Selkirk, Henrich, Ruffing and the rest of the Yankees who intimidated other clubs in the "House That Ruth Built," hard by the banks of the Harlem River. The Yankees' spell would last through the mid-forties, finally giving way to a Sox pennant in the post-war year of 1946.

Nineteen forty in some ways had an air of normalcy about it. But that was on the surface. There was a pervasive sense that something ominous was impending. There were no dramatic peaks, no electric announcements. But, rather, there was a felling that the nation's involvement in the mushrooming world conflict was inevitable. No one seemed in control. It was a time of enormous national uncertainty, of personal anxiety.

Leverett Saltonstall in 1940 had been reelected governor of the Commonwealth.Saltonstall's place in state police history had been assured by his strong support for the 1939 pension reforms. The state force began the forties with seasoned leadership. John F. Stokes, then beginning his third decade of service, was captain of the detective branch. Captain James P. Mahoney was rounding out his seventh year as executive officer of the uniformed branch. A member of the 1921 training troop, Mahoney in a sense personified the founding, development and coming of age of the uniformed statewide force. His career had paralleled the structural development of the organization.

MARY "K."

There had not been a recruit training troop in 1939. Nor was there one in 1940. The first year of the new decade did, however, bring an important addition to the roster of the state force. *She* was Mary P. Kirkpatrick. Enlisted on October 21, 1940, "Mary K.," an affectionate title she would later earn, was the first state police-woman to join the force since Mary Ramsdell and Lotta Caldwell had trained with the 1930 recruit troop.

Kirkpatrick's appointment filled the vacancy caused by Lotta Caldwell's retirement from injuries she sustained at Salisbury Beach during the September 1938 hurricane. There was no recruit troop in 1940 for her to join for the rugged training requirements. But the leadership had something else in mind, just as difficult, and, in some ways, providing quicker insights into the workings of the department. State Policewoman Kirkpatrick was to spend the first eight weeks in general headquarters at Commonwealth Pier. She had the distant advantage there of studying first hand the structural features of the organization, as well as quickly becoming familiar with available technical capabilities. In addition, veteran detectives and patrol members tutored the "rookie" on the legal esoterics that would be essential to discharge of her responsibilities.

Those mandates would be both complex and comprehensive. Mary Ramsdell had been handling the entire state since Lotta Caldwell's retirement. Now, with Kirkpatrick's appointment, the veteran would get a breather. She would cover one half of the Commonwealth from B Troop headquarters in Northampton, while Kirkpatrick handled everything east of Worcester, while based at Framingham. This arrangement would continue throughout the 1940s. It didn't make any difference whether it was a lost child, or, on occasion, a brutal slaying. When the skills and insights of these dedicated specialists were required, the job was done. The clock and the calendar played no roles during that era. Investigations were conducted when they were required, and for as long as it took to achieve a resolution.

"Time off," as in the uniformed force, was a sometime thing. The commitment was total. It is not to repeat unnecessarily to emphasize that such service was not employment, not a job. It was a lifestyle. Duty obligations came first, last and always. Personal plans automatically were deferred to work responsibilities. There was no other choice. That is the way it was. That was the way it had been for two decades.

Policewomen Ramsdel and Kirkpatrick would see their organization through the 1940s. Additional policewomen would join the ranks in 1949. That year would also bring Mrs. Kirkpatrick her first promotion, to the rank of sergeant. Later she would join Ramsdell in having established a first in the nation's state police departments. Where Ramsdell and Lotta Caldwell had been the nation's first state policewomen, Sergeant Kirkpatrick on April 23, 1954 would become the first commissioned state policewoman in the nation with her promotion to the rank of lieutenant.

Nor did the lieutenant's bar cap her career of public trust. Additional honors would come following twenty years with the state force. Governor John A. Volpe would, on August 2, 1961, honor Lieutenant Kirkpatrick and, indeed, the state police, by appointing her a member of the Massachusetts Parole Commission. Commissioner Kirkpatrick would serve in that sensitive public post for more than eleven years, closing, in 1972, three decades of public service.

DECEMBER 7, 1941

The recruit class of 1941 would be the last formal training troop for six years. There was some irony in the fact that they reported to Framingham's World War I "muster" grounds to begin the arduous ordeal that promised, at its end, a career in law enforcement. There was irony too, most likely unnoticed, in that the state force had now completed two decades of public service.

That made it different for these recruits. They were not there to demonstrate the value of a new concept. That had been accomplished. Their challenge, rather, was to live up to the enviable public record carved out by those who had gone before. A tradition had been firmly established. Their principal task was to strengthen the public record which, by then, was cherished by those across the state privileged to wear the "French and electric blue." It was no less a burden of accountability than that discharged by the men who first assembled at the "Poor Farm" exactly two decades earlier to launch the Commonwealth's experiment in policing.

While the 29th recruit training troop would be the last to undergo regular requirements until 1947, a great deal would happen during those six short years. Lives would be disrupted. Poignant partings would be redeemed with happy reunions, sometimes. Others were destined to be permanent. Europe's storm clouds had hovered over this nation's peacetime "normalcy" with ominous portents. Yet, when the fire storm broke, the war flames erupted on a distant, Pacific shore. Human experience can be shared in the telling. But it cannot really be felt. That is reserved for those who lived the historic moment. Time stands still at those momentous junctures. Those present absorb a vivid picture which steadfastly resists life's later intrusions.

December 7, 1941 was such a moment. Time stopped that Sunday for the nation, and for its people. Most had not heard of the distant naval base with the romantic name of Pearl Harbor. They would not in their lifetimes forget when they first heard it, and what they and their loved ones were doing at the moment an unbelieving nation heard the news of the devastating Japanese strike against America's Pacific Fleet.

President Franklin Delano Roosevelt next day addressed the Congress. It was the age of radio. The famous voice was strong as "FDR" asked for a declaration of war against the Japanese Empire. One hung on every word, sensing that individual lives would not again be quite the same. Roosevelt had been, from the beginning of his presidential tenure, an aggressive leader. The Japanese had now provided the provocation that would enable a full flowering of those abilities.

Experiences since that day that "will live in infamy" have clouded a distinguishing feature of World war II. The conflict was a "popular" war. The nation had been attacked without warning. Losses at Pearl Harbor had been enormous. Japanese planes crippled the Pacific Fleet, laying bare the sea lanes to the West Coast. The attack overnight galvanized a latent spirit of nationalism. Hundreds of thousands of young men volunteered for war duty within hours of the sneak air attack. There was no agonizing evaluation of the nation's role. Values cherished for two hundred years were threatened. The threat had to be repulsed.

Actually, there had been a military buildup prior to Pearl Harbor. Units of the Massachusetts National Guard had been federalized and placed on active duty. A number of men were called up from the state force. Lieutenant and Adjutant Ed Gully became Major Gully of the U.S. Army, joined by Bill Callanan who assumed his service rank of captain. Former Commissioner Paul G. Kirk, then a justice of the Supreme Court, became, once again, Colonel Kirk.

Even as Pearl Harbor had exploded in flames, Marty Joyce returned to the service as a communications officer in the Hawaiian Islands. State Fire Marshal George Mansfield became Lieutenant Mansfield of the U.S. Navy. Departmental Secretary Tim Murphy joined the fleet as a lieutenant commander. Tom Mitchell's law degree was key to a unit he set up in the naval intelligence services. Predictably, he turned to colleagues on the state force to staff his operation, enlisting, among others, Cy Sullivan, Bob Mitchell, George Edwards, Mal Malkasian, Eddie Sullivan, Dan Sullivan and Ollie Nichols. Trooper Steve Martin commanded a Fort Devens military police outfit as Captain Steve Martin.

Two members of the 1934 "Golden Class" were in the first wave to report for active duty. Steve Wersoski donned his navy chief's blues, and Steve Milosh again wore the silver bar of an army lieutenant. Although the 1941 class had barely completed recruit training, a number of its members changed uniforms. Among the first was Timothy F. Moran who wore the distinctive shield on the right sleeve of his blues, confirming that he was a member of the Coast Guard, already shifted from the Treasury Department to the Navy under war powers.

These, and many more, had either enlisted or had been called up from reserve units. Those actions in most cases were expected. But an aura of uncertainty hung over an additional question, one of prime importance to the state force and its law enforcement capabilities. Would members of the state police be drafted? No one really knew. Rumors raised more questions than they answered. Draft boards had been set up. Every male who was reasonably fit had to register. Most of the complement of the state force were men in the prime draft years. It was a time of substantial uncertainty.

An answer came suddenly. It removed all doubt. Trooper Eddie Gibbons got his "greetings" from the president, passed requisite tests, and was inducted. He was reportedly the first to be drafted. It came as a shock. Because a large number of men had enlisted and many had been called up from reserve units, assump-

tions had been made that the state police officers would be deferred. The Gibbons induction shattered that illusion. Men who were prime targets sought to bring their enforcement experience into play with specific duty assignments, rather than waiting for the tap on the shoulder that now loomed certain.

Meantime, administrative actions brought some relief. Nineteen men were selected as military substitutes. They had taken the same examination as the 1941 class. Two didn't even make it to the supply depot for outfitting. Bill Hansbury and Dave McCarthy had to don military uniforms without getting a chance to wear the two-tone blue. The remaining seventeen reported to Framingham for uniforms and orientation. Two weeks of classes followed at Commonwealth Pier. Then, on March 9, 1942 the men took their oaths and reported to the barracks hardest hit by service call ups. In a final bit of irony, several of these men soon made the mandatory switch from state to federal service.

The Class of 1942 did not undergo regular recruit training. Nor did they, until late in 1948. Interestingly, after more than six years, the men reported to the training school at Framingham for their "recruit" instruction. The intervening years had taken their toll. Of the original nineteen "military substitutes," only nine remained. Finally, on December 17, 1948, the men received the prized diploma which certified that, somewhat belatedly, each had "satisfactorily completed the prescribed course of study and training in criminal procedure and police science at the state police Recruit Training School, Framingham."

NIGHT OFFICE WATCH

Soon after the uniformed military substitutes had reported for duty in 1942, the administration made another move. Twenty-two men were hired right off the street to man the desks at substations throughout the state. These replacement were essentially civilian. It was not intended that they be used for field enforcement duties, but, rather, to handle desk duties in order to free up regular officers for patrol. Their responsibilities were generally those of a permanent night watch, the infamous "N.O.W." The men reported each night at 10 p.m., put on uniform shirts and slacks, and covered the desk until 8 a.m. No formal training was provided. There was not time for such amenities. Instruction was "on the job." It was not an ideal situation, but such measures provided some relief in what rapidly was becoming a desperate situation.

The famous "N.O.W." or, more formally, Night Office Watch, had evolved from arrangements made in the early twenties. There had not been such an official assignment during the first couple of years. The reason was simple enough. Each barracks had just several men, the largest having no more than five. One of the patrolmen, often the one who had finished the evening's patrol earliest, handled night desk duties. It was not an elaborate setup, but it worked. The officer simply slept by the telephone in full uniform.

It appears that the night office watch officially did not begin until around 1928. Rumor had it that some illicit spirits had disappeared during the dead of night from one of the barracks. The usual investigation followed. Little, predictably, was turned up. One point did emerge. The night desk officer had been an unusually sound sleeper. Further rumor had it that the culprit was a corporal. But, then, the story may well have been planted. Corporals, even then, led a hazardous experience. Two stripers for years were in an administrative twilight zone, the post dubbed by management analysts as "first line supervisor."

In any event, the night office watch was formalized in the late 1920s. From the beginning, it was a tough and demanding job. Rewards were few. Problems could be substantial. The hours alone were enough to wear down even the most dedicated of uniformed personnel. While practices differed among the troops, a number of stations assigned the night office watch for ten consecutive nights. Days were spent on duty in the barracks. There were motorcycles to wash and personal gear to polish. It was, in reality, an around-the-clock tour of duty.

Typically, a man got the desk duty coming in from a day off. That meant he would arrive from home, often a bus trip of a hundred miles, at 8 a.m. He would need several hours sleep that day to begin the night's grinding desk tour at ten. However, that is not the way the Commonwealth, and, especially, the state force, worked in those days. There had to be a certain number of duty hours each day. For that reason, an officer reporting from a day off at 8 a.m., had to do six hours of patrol that first day. Then, taking the night office watch at 10 p.m., he would put in two more hours till midnight. The magic number was thus met. Six hours of patrol and two hours on the desk completed the eight hours. But, that was just the beginning. All that midnight meant was the reporting of the prior day's activities to troop headquarters. That done, the "N.O.W." faced an unknown. Would it be a quiet night? One never dared to predict.

The late patrols would be coming in at three or four a.m. There was coffee to be made, and "kitchen" talk. Those kitchen conversations in the wee hours provided the most reliable information one could get, both about the area's criminal activities, and, indeed, the "inside" information that was always one step ahead of headquarters pronouncements. Variations of the night office watch developed through the years. The duty hours were adapted to the slowly evolving time off system. But it remained a punishing exercise in survival. The men, predictably, always found answers. One was to sleep in the "guard room," after the night's prescribed duties were completed. Each barracks had a large oak table, usually reserved for report writing, and, frequently, hotly contested card games. A pillow, blanket and a little courage brought some needed rest in the hours just before dawn.

As long as everything went well, there was studied unawareness by the "brass." If it didn't, well, hadn't the "N.O.W." known about the regulation that prohibited sleeping on duty? It was high risk. But the odds were good, and few were deterred by the hypothetical imperatives that ran for many pages in the rules and regulations.

PATROLMAN CHARLES J. COLLINS

One who had done many a night watch was Patrolman Charles J. Collins. Collins in 1934 had trained with the "Golden Class." Like most, his early service had been at barracks a long way from home. But, like the others, he endured the drawbacks because he liked law enforcement work.

Beyond that, he was proud to be a state police officer, proud of being able to wear the two-tone blue. That feeling made up for the shortcomings, the inconveniences.

By 1942 Collins was a seasoned veteran. Stationed in Troop A, he had just completed a special assignment in the office of Governor Charles Hurley. That had been prestigious duty. It was an honor to be assigned to the governor, and Patrolman Collins had been quietly pleased with his selection. There had also been another important

achievement. Collins had passed the detective lieutenant's examination. That was a major break in his career, he had looked forward anxiously to the appointment. To top off his good fortune, he was back in Troop A, stationed at the Topsfield Barracks. That was important. It meant that he and his wife could share more time together in their Beverly home. Things couldn't have been better for Patrolman Collins.

Yet, one is not allowed to know at what hour, in what place, fate will disrupt even the most meticulously arranged plans. Collins had every reason to look forward eagerly to a spring night's patrol out of "A-2." He had done many of them. And, in his quiet and unassuming way, Collins could handle himself, no matter the problems that might crop up.

There was no reason to suspect on May 19, 1942 that the night's duties would be anything but ordinary. Topsfield's ringing phone early that evening suddenly changed the routine into one of the saddest nights in the history of the state force. Years later, Richard F. Cleary wrote a poignant remembrance of that fateful night. Cleary had joined the State Police Patrol in 1928, and was the corporal in charge of Topsfield. Cleary knew Collins as well as anyone. It wasn't easy for him, even after time had softened the memory of the tragedy, to remember, as he put it, that Charley Collins was a great guy:

Officer Richard Kneeland of Georgetown had picked up one Edward Rogers to give him a lift home. Much to Kneeland's surprise, Rogers whipped out a gun and ordered Kneeland to stop the car. Rogers got out of the car and disappeared. It was later learned that he stopped another man at the point of a gun, and was driven to his home in Byfield. Once inside his home, Rogers gathered all five members of his family into the living room where he made them sit in chairs forming a semi-circle. None dared defy him, none dared to even say a word. They sat in silence.

A short time later, Charley Collins, George Edwards and Chief Louis Holt of the Georgetown P.D., following Rogers' trail of kidnappings, arrived at the family home in Byfield. The only light in the huge farmhouse came from the middle room of the first floor, probably the living or dining room. The three officers surveyed the scene and made their plans. The chief was to try and enter by a side door, Charley was to try the front door and George was to try the rear door. All three were to try and enter without any nose and were to try and reach the dining room, where they hoped to surprise Rogers.

Charley found the front door unlocked and tiptoed into the darkened front room and worked his way slowly towards the lighted room. Not a sound came from that room and much to Charley's surprise, when he peeked through the draperies, he saw three men and three women sitting in a semi-circle. The chief had found the side door locked and went back to the front door to find Charley. In the meantime George went through the woodshed which was attached to the rear of the house. He searched the woodshed, but no Rogers. Then he tiptoed up three wooden steps to the kitchen door. He put out his flashlight and slowly opened the door, his gun in his right hand. The kitchen was pitch black except for a small patch of light that came under the dining room door. George heard voices and stopped in his tracks. It was Charley talking and he was asking which man was Edward Rogers. Neither Charley nor George knew Rogers. Suddenly three revolver shots in rapid succession rang out. The door to the dining room swung open. A form stood there silhouetted against the bright lights behind it. Suddenly two flashes of light, one from each hand of the unknown form, and two thuds in the door frame beside George.

George knew then it was not Charley who was shooting. He brought his own gun up to his hip, fired three shots in rapid succession. George knew that all three had hit their target. The man spun sideways and then turned and started running towards him. As he staggered towards George his two guns spit flame. Two shots went past George. He remembers saying, "Thank God" as both shots thudded into the wall behind him. The man was half way across the kitchen now. George fired again, his fourth, fifth and sixth shots. George numbly knew that his shots had landed as the man staggered and shuddered but still he came on. He fired two more shots. They landed in the wall and then as he reached George, whose gun was now empty, his body quivered. George stepped aside and the man fell down the woodshed stairs, dead.

George made sure he was dead, wiped the sweat off his brow, and then dashed into the dining room. Charley was on the floor and the chief was trying to stop the blood that was coming through his blouse. George felt for a heart beat. There was a faint one, very faint. Then, in one of the wildest rides ever, George drove Charley to the Anna Jacques Hospital in Newburyport, ten miles away. The best of doctors answered our emergency call. Nothing was spared by the hospital. The day nurses stayed through the night with the hope that they might be of some help. Police officers and even civilians, some of whom did not even know Charley, called in offering their blood for transfusions. Charley regained consciousness. He even told the doctors what had happened, how Rogers had been sitting with his arms folded, hiding two guns.

Our hopes ran high, but Charley lapsed into unconsciousness. The good doctors worked hard all that night trying to keep the weak spark of life alive. But in the early hours of the morning, that spark fluttered out. A brave trooper was dead. On May 22nd Charley was laid to rest in the beautiful Saint Mary's Cemetery in Salem. I kept my eyes on Charley's brother, the Reverend Michael Collins, to give me strength. He seemed to have more strength and courage than all of us that day.

There were no card games in Topsfield for a long time. There was no laughter either. Today there hangs in the guard room a swell picture of Charley Collins, sitting on a bike. He seems to be smiling as he looks upon us. That is the way he would want us to remember him. Not as the bravest trooper I ever knew, but as the nicest. A man with a heart of gold. Yes sir, Charley Collins was a great guy.

The uniformed branch turned out in record numbers for the wake and funeral service. In addition, representatives of a score of police departments paid their last respects to the young enforcement officer. Many others also came. These were the people who had known the private Charley Collins, those who loved and respected him for the humaneness that characterized his tragically shortened life. Later, there would be official recognition from a grateful Commonwealth. Governor Leverett Saltonstall and members of the Governor's Council, in State House ceremonies, awarded citations to Patrolman George Edwards, and, posthumously, to Patrolman Charles J. Collins. Reverend Michael Collins accepted the honors for his later brother. The ceremony closed the public part of the poignant events that saddened the entire state force in that long ago springtime.

PROMOTIONAL EXAMINATIONS

Not long before his untimely death, Collins had taken the examination for detective lieutenant. That post for many years was considered the premier enforcement position in the Commonwealth. Uniformed personnel studied long and hard to crack the detective ranks. Competition was fierce. It was a civil service test, open also to qualified applicants from local departments across the state. Uniformed branch personnel had a distinct disadvantage. The barracks life was not conducive to preparation for a tough examination. The demand on one's time left little opportunity for the systematic commitment essential to success in such a highly competitive situation. Members of the uniformed state force thus had to overcome extra obstacles to have a realistic chance at the prized appointments.

There was, therefore, a good deal of rejoicing in the far flung barracks system when the results of the 1942 detective lieutenant examination were announced. More than a thousand had taken the comprehensive battery of tests. Most were local enforcement officers who were primed for the effort by months of concentrated study. Nevertheless, men from the uniformed branch captured 64 of the 172 passing grades, truly an impressive performance. Moreover, one of them, Arnold W. Olsson, topped the list. Given the nature of the competition, Olsson's effort was a once in a lifetime achievement. He had covered a lot of ground since the days when he was a star performer on the department's trick riding team. Olsson and a number of his uniformed colleagues later were sworn in as lieutenants in the detective branch of the state police. Several subsequently rose to prominent leadership positions in the senior branch of the state force.

The 1942 detective lieutenant examination was big, a major

event. But there was another test that year, that if not as large, was more unique. It was rooted in the 1939 legislation that mandated retirement from the uniformed branch at age fifty. Captain James P. Mahoney had served since 1933 in the top uniformed post, only the third executive officer in over two decades. Now, however, his service would end on his fiftieth birthday, February 3, 1942.

Shortly before, another major change had occurred when Eugene M. McSweeney completed his tenure as commissioner of public safety. McSweeney had served in the department's highest post for over four years. His leadership efforts with the major pension and insurance reforms in 1939 remain as lasting achievements, permanently appreciated by a grateful organization.

Captain of Detectives John F. Stokes was named acting commissioner when McSweeney left. He and Governor Saltonstall determined that a competitive examination should be held to fill the post of captain and executive officer. Lieutenant Clifton W. Kendall was appointed acting executive officer while preparations for the comprehensive tests were made. This would be a first in the uniformed state force. Examinations had never before been used. All prior promotions had been based upon performance factors and leadership potential. It was subjective, but, from the beginning, had been clearly specified in the official manual of the uniformed branch. The pertinent sections from the 1922 rules and regulations directed that:

(a) All commissioned officers of the Patrol shall be appointed by the Commissioner upon such conditions as he may fix and determine. All officers so appointed must have been enlisted by the same procedure as that prescribed for other members of the Patrol.

(b) Non-commissioned officers shall be appointed from the patrolmen of the Patrol by the Commissioner upon recommendation of the troop commander to whose troop such appointee is attached, after approval by the executive officer.

(c) Patrolmen may be appointed to the ratings of horseshoer, saddler or mechanic by the troop commander.

The 1942 test thus was the first competitive examination for promotion ever held in the uniformed branch. Indeed, it turned out to be the only such test until a December 1965 statute mandated comprehensive promotional examinations for all ranks. Boston English High School was the site for the written section of the tests. These had been prepared by former Commissioner Needham, the first executive officer, Captain George A. Parker, and a justice of the superior court. The examination was scheduled for February 27, and arrangements were made for supervision to be handled by the state board of bar examiners. Commissioner Stokes announced that all lieutenants, sergeants and corporals were eligible to try for the top uniformed post. Forty-two men applied amid an air of anxiety and expectation. Rumors spread, naming the favorites. These continued to expand as the examination hour approached.

Finally, the tenseness gave way on the day of the examinations. Divided into two groups, the men were given two hours to analyze and answer a comprehensive test on criminal law. Following lunch, the applicants faced another two-hour inquiry on the rules and regulations. It was, by all accounts, a difficult test. No one had an easy time. A great deal of speculation filled the following days. Commissioner Stokes did not relieve the pressure on April 4 when he announced that twelve officers had passed the written examination. No names were given, just the identification numbers that had been assigned.

That was a small challenge for the informal communication system. Within a couple of days the men had pieced it all together

and, as subsequently confirmed, identified correctly those who had passed: Bill Shimkus, George Thompson, Mike Noonan, John (J.P.) Sullivan, Everett Flanders, Ted Stronach, Tony LaCaire, B.B. Ratigan, Ted Stavredes, John Maturo, George Pollard, and John W. Collins. The select group included three lieutenants, one sergeant and eight corporals. The twelve reported on April 9, to general headquarters at Commonwealth Pier for oral interviews. A three man board conducted the interviews. Next day a final list was established and Lieutenant Shimkus topped it.

Governor Saltonstall appointed yet another board, Commissioner Stokes, former Captain James P. Mahoney, and Attorney General Robert Bushnell, to review the grades and qualifications of the finalists. This board chose William V. Shimkus and, on April 16, 1942, he was elevated to the top uniformed post of captain and executive officer. The other finalists shortly received promotions based on their success with the sole examinations held in the uniformed branch since the 1921 founding. In subsequent years, selections were again made against criteria established in the uniformed force's rules and regulations. This would remain constant until the first mandated examination took place in May, 1967.

TRYING TIMES

The World War II years were difficult ones for those who, for one reason or another, were forced to stay behind. Some of the men were older, over two decades had passed since the enlistments in the early twenties. Others had big families, and, therefore, were exempted from military service. By 1944 the force was extremely thin. There had been no uniformed replacements after the seventeen military substitutes were sworn in 1942.

During the same time, however, new duties were added. Military convoys were constantly crossing the state. Patrols had to provide requisite escorts. This was especially critical when large shipments of explosives moved from cargo ships in Boston to the large military installations that had been established. There were several of these huge bases. Some were training sites, while others served as staging areas for troops going to the European Theatre. One of these was right in the center of Troop D, near Taunton. Known as Camp Myles Standish, it was the last stop for thousands of American soldiers who would spearhead the 1944 assault on the Normandy beaches.

Patrols were long and arduous throughout the war years. Cruisers were run down. There were no replacements. The nation's industrial might was committed to the war effort; police cruisers were not a high priority. Moreover, it was all but impossible to get gasoline for private cars. Fuel was sorely needed on the numerous battle fronts. State police vehicles had the top half of their headlight lenses painted black. This reduced projected shore light, a special hazard for American tankers carrying fuel into the Bay State's ports. German submarines earlier had sunk several within sight of land. Their technique was to sight the tankers against the background of light from shore. Silhouetted, the slow vessels were easy prey for German "Wolf Packs."

The war had not gone well in the early forties. Pearl Harbor had taken a heavy toll. In Europe, Hitler's divisions had overrun large areas of the continent. Only the channel, and the Royal Air Force, had saved Great Britain. By the end of 1943, however, the flow of the war began to shift. German troops had been stopped at Leningrad's gates, hurled back by Russia's troops and bitter winter.

Great naval battles had been fought in the Pacific. American industrial might slowly turned the tide by constructing one of history's greatest naval forces. Tiny Pacific atolls became household names as American troops made Japanese forces pay severely for islands taken in the war's early months.

On June 6, 1944, the greatest armada in history crossed the English Channel and landed Allied troops on Normandy's beaches. The massive assault, was, in retrospect, the beginning of the end for the Axis powers. Germany later would attempt desperate measures to rescue victory from impending defeat. But the die had been cast. Superior Allied air and sea power supported the ground troops that cut quickly into the industrial heartland of Hitler's Third Reich. Russian troops meantime had broken through German defenses in the east. It was then only a question of time. The death and destruction was unnecessarily prolonged as Hitler, under siege in a Berlin bunker, died in the war's final hours.

The long war was coming to a close. But there was a national mourning as President Franklin Delano Roosevelt died suddenly in Warm Springs, Georgia. "FDR" had led the nation for over twelve years, through the Great Depression, and the darkest days of World War II. Now, at victory's hour, he was gone. In his place was a plain man from Independence, Missouri. He was hardly known to the American people, even though their Vice President. He was Harry S. Truman and he would soon prove that he had the resolve required in the nation's highest office.

Events moved swiftly. With Germany's surrender, the Japanese Empire stood alone. The February, 1945, capture of Iwo Jima in one of the Pacific's bloodiest battles, signalled the end of the ill advised adventure upon which Japan had embarked on December 7, 1941. After Iwo, American forces cut swiftly through the southwest Pacific. By summer, the Japanese homeland itself faced an impending invasion.

Meantime, in iron clad secrecy, American scientists had split the atom. Man had devised history's most devastating weapon. President Truman faced a momentous decision. He never hesitated. American planes on August 6, 1945 dropped an atom bomb on Hiroshima. Within days, a second "A Bomb" burst over Nagasaki. The effect was total. Thousands died in the fiery, radioactive blast. A new weapon had been added to man's destructive arsenal, one, for the first time, capable of destroying life on the planet. The Japanese leadership debated, but not for long. Within hours, the unconditional surrender of Japan's military forces was accepted.

World War II officially ended on the USS *Missouri*, anchored in Tokyo Bay. There, on September 2, 1945, General Douglas MacArthur accepted the surrender of the Japanese Imperial Forces. The war was over. It had exacted a terrifying global toll.

THE "ETSPO's"

At war's end, the state force awaited the return of its officers. But the years had taken their tolls. By later summer of 1945, there were over one hundred vacancies in the uniformed branch's authorized complement. New men were needed desperately, right away. There was not even time for regular training. Officers were enlisted, sworn and assigned directly to barracks on a priority need basis.

The new personnel were called Emergency Temporary State Police Officers, "ETSPO's." These were men who had earned early discharges because of long war service, time overseas, age, and related factors. One "ETSPO" was Harold W. Brewster. Brewster in the Navy since the late 1930s, had earned the necessary discharge points, and had returned to his Randolph home in late summer, 1945. He was the type of young veteran the state force needed until time permitted a return to regular recruiting practices, and the long and arduous training requirements.

Years later, Brewster described the experience of becoming an "ETSPO," a transition from his Randolph living room to a state police assignment within a matter of hours:

I was one of the first to be discharged after World war II under the high-point system used at the time by the Navy. It was based on time in service, time served overseas in battle zones, etc. I arrived home in September, 1945. Police Chief Pat McDonnell who always worked closely with the troopers, came by the house to see me and welcome me home. He told me that the state police was desperately in need of men and were interested in honorably discharged servicemen with good war records for on-the-job training as temporary troopers pending the time when exams could be held.

This of course would have to be a few years hence to allow for regular troopers to return to the job from the armed forces, at which time the manpower situation would be reassessed. It was made crystal clear that, come exam time, the ETSPO's would have to qualify along with the new applicants and would be given no extra consideration.

I met with Sergeant Tom Norton of Troop D headquarters in Bridgewater. We went to 1010 (general headquarters) where I was interviewed by Captain Shimkus, and made out an application. The following day Sergeant Norton transported me to Framingham Supply Depot where "Clarry" Ferrari outfitted me.

Next, I was sent to Bridgewater and assigned to Patrolman Bernie H. McGrath for training. I guess the state police figured that servicemen were the best bets as ETSPO's because we had already received military training, and could be trained in police techniques in the field by experienced troopers. After about four months of working with Patrolman McGrath, I was turned out alone. Desk duty training resulted in one or two night office watches per week.

During the next two years or so, I was stationed at Bridgewater, Norwell and Rehoboth. Our uniform was the same as the regulars except for the badge. Badges were the same shape and size, except that the number was on the bottom and was all silver plate. Then came the 1946 statewide exams. As I recall, there were some 1500 applicants and some 250 passed. Many ETSPO's who had a year or more on the job flunked out. From the eligibility list, they selected fifty men for immediate training, keeping the ETSPO's on duty until the first class graduated. When they finished their training and joined the troops, ETSPO's who passed became the second Class of 1947. Out of fifty, forty-one survived the training school.

Many ETSPO's came and went long before exams were held. Many left of their own volition. Others were let go, being unable to adapt. And that's the way it was to have been an Emergency Temporary State Police Officer, 'ETSPO,' in the years immediately following World War II.

Patrolman Harold Brewster later saw service in Troop C. In the early 1950s he enlisted in the Fort Lauderdale, Florida Police Department. His background in the state force proved a solid asset, as over the years, he advanced to the commissioned ranks of that department. Much of that service was in the development of innovative law enforcement programs, as Fort Lauderdale's population expanded dramatically in the fifties and sixties. Brewster also lectured on law enforcement topics throughout Broward County, completing almost three decades of public service prior to his retirement in the mid-1970s. He died in 1990 at his Ocala, Florida home.

In describing his ETSPO experiences, Brewster referred to the 1946 examination, noting that some 1500 applicants had applied. Time had, understandably, made difficult a precise remembrance of that event. In fact, the statewide tests were held in January, 1947, when 3,467 young men applied. Of these, 1,171 took the written examination, with 673 passing. Physicals then reduced the eligibles to 346. Three hundred and forty of these took the oral tests, and 251 were certified for appointment to the training academy.

There were two recruit troops in 1947. The initial class began training on June 16. It was the first formal session of the academy since the 1941 recruit troop. Nevertheless, training requirements were as demanding as always. The balance between tough physical requirements and challenging intellectual criteria had, if anything, become more sharply honed over the years. This group, though, had one important asset going. Each was a service veteran, accustomed to rigid discipline and less than optimum living conditions.

The June, 1947 training class was the Thirty-First Recruit Troop. And, like the thirty that went before, they were well prepared for enforcement duties by graduation day. Ceremonies were impressive. Commissioner John F. Stokes confirmed their appointments as patrolmen in the uniformed branch. That done, Captain and Executive Officer William V. Shimkus made the traditional assignments to the field troops. Like their predecessors, the fledgling officers winced at the strange sounding names of the far flung barracks. The uneasiness passed quickly. Thoughts turned instead to the opportunities ahead. Each had eagerly sought the appointment, the chance to become a state police officer. Now, they had made it. The academy was behind them. They would be enforcing the law throughout the Commonwealth. It was a sobering thought, one that had confronted new "staties" for more than a quarter of a century.

For two of the recruits, tragedy, without warning, would end their enforcement careers. Patrolman Alfred A. Hewitt on January 4, 1950 was killed on Route One in Saugus. His classmate, Alje M. Savela, was shot and killed on August 31, 1951 in Barre. One member of that training troop would later occupy the highest post in the uniformed branch. John R. Moriarty on July 24, 1972 capped his career with a promotion to lieutenant colonel and executive officer, a rank he held until, after 27 years of service, he retired in 1974.

The Thirty-Second Recruit Troop began training on September 9. This was the "second class" of 1947, composed entirely of the Emergency Temporary State Police Officers who had passed the January examinations. These men could hardly be classified as "boots." Some had been sworn as early as 1945, about the same time as Patrolman Brewster. There were distinct advantages to prior service. There also were, as it turned out, some disadvantages.

Foremost among these was the very fact of prior field duty. Some, apparently, perceived themselves not as recruits, but, rather, as seasoned officers. This had implications for the the acceptance of discipline, the center of the recruit's academy's severe constraints. The use of "demerits" was the core of the system. When a recruit violated an academy standard, a mark was assessed against him. A specified number of these brought discharge. "Demerits" proved a particular irritant to the ETSPO's. In frustration, several tore down the demerit board. A swift investigation followed, and, unfortunately, several were discharged.

Those who remained acquitted the "ETSPO Class" of 1947 in superior fashion. Many were to serve the state force for more than a quarter of a century. Several assumed leadership positions as troop and headquarters commanders. They had accepted difficult and demanding tasks without training. They had passed all regular, qualifying tests, even though, by that time, many were experienced officers. The academy had been the final hurdle, a difficult one under any circumstances. Most dealt successfully with all of these constraints, affirming the confidence placed in them during one of the most difficult periods in the history of the state force. These were the "ESTPO's":

THIRTY-SECOND RECRUIT TROOP-THE "ETSPO'S"

September 9, 1947

Anderson, Melville R.	Cordery, Henry C.	Murphy Vincent F.
Ashworth, Phillip M.	Downey, John F.	Obartuck, Steven
Barry, Francis X.	Foley, James J.	O'Brien, Edward F.
Benoit, John W., Jr.	Gross, William F.	O'Brien, Howard J.
Blake, Byron E.	Hall, Martin B.	Peterson, Paul A.
Bogdanchuk, Walter	Hansbury, William J.	Prendergast, Edward M.
Boluch, Bohdan W.	Harrington, Charles W.	Regan, Joseph J.
Breton, Francis J.	Hickey, Francis J.	Robinson, Joseph A.
Brewster, Harold W.	Kane, William F.	Rys, Stanley W.
Brown, Milo F., Jr.	Keeley, Thomas H.	Spafford, Norman A.
Burns, Gerald F.	Kerrigan, Arthur F.	Stanley, James W.
Callahan, William E.	Leary, John F.	Strout, George H.
Cannon, Robert T.	LaShoto, Walter D.	Thodal, Lawrence
Cantelmo, Peter	Martin, Leo J.	Vallon, Casimir M.
Canty, George D.	McCarthy, David L.	Walsh, Patrick, J.P.
Carey, Edward F.	McNair, William E.	White, Manuel S., Jr.
Conrad, Edward G.		

These men had no sooner returned to the field than preparations began for additional recruit training. The war years had created over one hundred vacancies in the authorized complement. Moreover, those who had enlisted in the twenties were now in their late forties. The age factor had taken on a new meaning.

Chapter 720 of the Acts of 1945 had changed the impact of the 1939 pension law. The 1939 reform measure had made retirement mandatory at age fifty with twenty years of service, *whichever last occurred.* This meant, for example, that a man enlisting at 21 had to remain 29 years, until he became fifty. The 1945 law made retirement optional after twenty years in the uniformed branch. In other words, an officer enlisting at 21 could, after twenty years, retire at 41. This had a dramatic impact on retirements.

The net effect was to create vacancies with regularity. The state force required an ongoing training program in the post war years. The first class of 1948 thus began training on April 7, 1948. These men had taken the same January 1947 examination as the two 1947 recruit troops. In addition, this group ended a tradition. They were the last class at Framingham to train under canvas. New facilities had been constructed on the site of the World War I muster field, and subsequent recruit troops slept, ate and attended classes in "Quonset Huts" rather than in army tents.

There was another interesting thing about this class. Although they sought service in a rural police organization, they were, for the most part, products of the state's urban centers. This phenomenon had long been a paradox. Yet, when thought through, most of the recruits would have to have come from the population centers. The thought persists, however, that the public perceived an enforcement agency staffed by men from rural areas. There has always been, in effect, a self-fulfilling prophecy at work. Many did become residents of the bucolic towns they first patrolled. And, as time passed, newer members of the state force simply assumed that they, the older men, had *always* lived there.

There has tended to be, therefore, some misperception of where most members of the state force originated. Observation of the first class of 1948 provides some interesting insights. While one recruit troop can hardly be presented as representative, the feeling persists that review of most others would yield a similar result. This is who they were and where they lived:

THIRTY-THIRD TRAINING TROOP

APRIL 7, 1948

Burke, Francis T., East Walpole	Lynch, Robert F., Charlestown
DaPaola, Raymond F., Fall River	Budukiewicz, John V., Dorchester
Haggerty, Charles W., Jr, Winchester	Desrusseaux, Wilfred P., Fall River
Rourke, Thomas D., Brookline	Murphy, John F., Cambridge
Whitcomb, Edward E., Winthrop	Ritchie, Arthur J., Waltham
Uzdawinis, Bronius M., Norwood	Owen, William J., Worcester
Haber, Joseph E., South Hadley Falls	St. Michel, Walter F., Marlboro
Valente, Pompee P., Somerville	Cummings, James F., South Boston
Hunt, William H., Brookline	Fredericksen, Walter A., Mattapan
Murgia, Robert D., Lawrence	Murphy, Edward F., Fall River
Forbush, William H., Brockton	Burns, Donald J., Worcester
Denommee, Laurier, J., Lowell	Rollins, Charles J., Everett
Kulik, John J., Maynard	Cabral, Alfred, Fall River
Furze, Charles W., Fall River	Peers, Robert, Malden
Bienkowski, Henry W., Dorchester	McDermott, James A., Randolph
Viel, Lawrence L., Worcester	McGuire, Raymond M., Fall River
Haranas, Peter R., Framingham	Johnson, Ralph E., Palmer
Ramsey, Harold W., Worcester	Rammel, Robert H., Plainville
Munighan, Thomas F., Everett	Chase, Courtland E., Swampscott
Lordan, George W., Jamaica Plain	Fuller, Wayland S., Edgartown
Murphy, Peter J. Jr., Somerville	Peterson, Thomas H., Arlington
Byron, Edward G., Waltham	Humphrey, Melvin R., Peabody
Nickerson, George W., Waltham	Underhill, William H., Fall River
England, Albert Jr., Worcester	Porter, James S. Revere
Fralin, Arthur G., Jamaica Plain	Dunn, Owen F., Fall River

Review affirms that a substantial majority of the recruits were from the state's urban centers. Many, in fact, settled in rural parts of the Commonwealth. Quite a few became residents of the beautiful Berkshire towns that dot the four western counties. They thus became year round residents rather than urban commuters to the rural Troop B barracks locations.

This recruit class was the last of the post-war trainees to receive veteran's "benefits." The 1947 training troops had also received the federal stipend. This is how it worked. The recruits received a salary of $1,500 per year. After taxes, the take home pay was $102.47 per month. This qualified each recruit for a monthly V.A. benefit of $45. A July 1, 1948 pay increase raised starting salaries to $2,580 annually. This brought the recruits' salaries up to a level where the federal subsidy was terminated. At the same time, a new statute required a $30 per month deduction for "maintenance," room and board at the barracks. The net result, paradoxically, was a put *cut* of a little over a dollar per month!

Still, that first 1948 recruit class was destined to fill several leadership posts by the late 1960s. For example, Robert D. Murgia would become in February 1967 lieutenant colonel and executive officer. A classmate, William J. Owen, would influence hundreds

of state police recruits as a long time member of the academy staff. Thomas H. Peterson, another of this recruit group, would, in 1970, be the first recipient of the uniformed branch's medal of honor for his part in the capture of a convicted felon who had shot and killed a Boston policeman during a bank robbery.

A second 1948 class began training on July 6. They too had taken the January 1947 qualifying class. Thus in two years over two hundred had been appointed to the academy as recruit trainees. The effect was to exhaust the pool of eligible applicants and create a need for new statewide examinations. In addition, an important leadership change had taken place. Captain and Executive Officer William V. Shimkus had completed almost 25 years in the uniformed branch by late 1947, and five since his appointment as executive officer on April 15, 1942. Shimkus concluded his state police career on December 31, 1947. He was succeeded by Captain John P. "J.P." Sullivan. Shimkus and Sullivan had trained together with the fifth recruit troop in 1923. Now, in the twilight of long enforcement careers, they exchanged congratulations in a brief headquarters ceremony.

An equally significant leadership shift had also occurred in the detective branch. Captain Joseph L. Ferrari, of "Stokes and Ferrari" fame, had completed a long and productive career in the state force, serving as chief of detectives under his old partner, Commissioner John F. Stokes. After more than two decades, the famous detective partnership ended with Ferrari's retirement. Captain Ferrari was gone. But his career left a legacy that would keep his memory bright long after his departure. It would serve, time's passage has demonstrated, as a yardstick for evaluating the investigative skills of those who followed.

Ferrari's successor needed no introduction. Joseph C. Crescio was the first captain of detectives to have begun service in the uniformed branch. Crescio had trained with the Seventh Troop in September, 1923. Following field assignments, he joined the original auto squad in the mid-twenties. His work on the Millen-Faber case set the stage for service in the detective branch. Captain Crescio had risen to the detective branch's top post with almost a quarter century's experience to sustain him. He would serve as chief of detectives until the early 1960s.

THE FORTIES CLOSE

The state force had recruited and trained some two hundred men during 1947 and 1948, providing sorely needed relief. By winter 1949, however, the pool of eligible applicants had been exhausted. Another recruit class was planned, and statewide examinations were held on April 9. Approximately 1,245 applied, with 1,064 actually taking the comprehensive written tests. There was a high mortality rate that year, as only a final 202 successfully met the exacting criteria.

Fifty of these young men became the Thirty-Fifth Recruit Troop. The group on September 19 reported to Framingham, eager, as hundreds before them, to merit appointment as state police officers. The new quonset huts were freshly painted, and, for the first time, there was a macadam "company street." The era of horses, tents and dusty parade grounds was fast fading into the mosaic of the state's force's three decades of history.

That 1949 class thus went through its paces on the same World War I muster field where, eleven years earlier, the 1938 recruit troop had lost its tents to the Great New England Hurricane. Each recruit class has a special event, a happening of some kind, which marks its passage through the disciplined rituals of "boot" training.

For the '49 class, it may have been the daily trips to Babson College's beautiful swimming pool for water safety classes. The ultra-modern facility that year echoed with the demanding instructions of Frank "Dutch" Holland of the American Red Cross, and Joe Rogers from the University of Massachusetts. Countless numbers of volunteers like Holland and Rogers for years freely gave of their time and skills to ensure the best in police training. The two also helped with boat safety and the rescue and dragging instructions held that year at nearby Lake Cochituate.

Holland and Rogers for years were fixtures at the academy. But, even for them, there had been an entirely new training challenge earlier that year. Five recruits had reported, eager to meet the academy's demanding requirements. There was, however, a difference. Certain adjustments would be required because the academy's hallowed halls echoed with the unfamiliar sounds of *women* recruits.

Where Mary Ramsdell and Lotta Caldwell in 1930, and Mary Kirkpatrick in 1940, had received individualized training courses, this was the first time women had been required to complete a structured training curriculum prior to field assignments. It was a unique milestone in the department's history, and, looking back, one who was there remembered how it was to be a "boot," and a woman, in the final year of the forties decade:

On August 3, 1949, five women were appointed to the uniformed division of the Massachusetts State Police by Commissioner John F. Stokes. The appointees were: Mora E. Terry, Hull; Mary E. Sullivan, Fall River; Florence R. McBride, Cambridge; Patricia Coleman, West Roxbury; and Kathryn G. Mead, Belmont. At the same time, Mary F. Kirkpatrick of Framingham who had been a member of the state police for ten years, was promoted to the grade of sergeant, and given supervision over the new women officers.

It was the first time that a group of women was appointed and assigned to the State Police Training School for instruction in criminal law, police science and procedure, rules and regulations, use of firearms, first aid, juvenile delinquency, police relations and scientific aids in crime detection. We had previously passed a written oral examination. On completion of training, Patricia Coleman was assigned to Troop A, Mora E. Terry to Troop B, Kathryn G. Mead to Troop C, Mary E. Sullivan to Troop D and Florence R. McBride to Headquarters. Subsequently, S.O. (Special Officer) McBride was transferred to A and B Troops, and S.O. Mead was at various times assigned to each of the four troops.

Our work was principally investigation of juvenile crimes and law infractions by women. However, we were used in investigations of all types of crime and were involved in virtually everything except patrol and traffic violations. We never wore uniforms, and were accompanied on all investigations by either a trooper or a state detective. Each woman was assigned an unmarked cruiser equipped with police radio, and we were on twenty-four call, seven days a week. We usually had Saturday afternoon and Sunday off, but we were subject to call during time off and always had to leave word where we could be reached. In addition to regular duty, we also were required to accept speaking engagements all over the Commonwealth.

It was exciting, challenging and very demanding work. The long hours and obligation to be on twenty-four hour call even on days off, precluded any type of social life, and, as a result, all but one of the five appointees resigned after a few years. S.O. Coleman married Trooper Daniel Desmond and resigned on June 30, 1951. S.O. Terry was married and resigned on June 30, 1951. S.O. McBride resigned on August 8, 1953, and resumed teaching school in Cambridge. S.O. Mead resigned on April 16, 1955 to accept an appointment as probation officer at Suffolk Superior Court, Boston. S.O. Sullivan married Trooper Robert Coveney and remained on duty until her May 14, 1971 retirement.

GRADUATION DAY

December 7, 1949 marked the eighth anniversary of the infamous Pearl Harbor attack. The date was circled on the calendar of the class of 1949. Not in their case, however, because of the historic anniversary, but, rather, because it was graduation day; a mere 24 hours that , for weeks, threatened never to arrive. The ceremony was a modest one, held in the academy's sole classroom. Commissioner John F. Stokes presided. And, as before, the executive officer, Captain John P. Sullivan posted the recruits to their field troops.

Troop commanders attended the graduation. They wanted a preview, a first look at the "boots" they would shortly command. One veteran "C.O." was Lieutenant James P. Ryan. He congratulated five of the fledgling officers. They would be his men, assigned to Troop C, Holden. Graduation over, the brand new C Troopers loaded a 1937 Buick with their gear. Each was in full uniform. They were on their own, sworn state police officers. But there was one problem. No one in the Buick knew how to get to Holden. Some forty miles west of Framingham, one finally said it out loud. They were, he thought, probably lost.

There was a solution. Steady resolve would be required, more than they would ever need in their enforcement careers. Shortly, the big Buick rolled to a stop at a roadside diner. Once inside, the five ordered coffee. A few minutes seemed like an eternity under the puzzled gazes of the diner's regulars. Still, the question had to be asked: would the counterman provide directions to the state police barracks in Holden? The moment hung heavily. Words were not required; the scene spoke for itself. How could they track law breakers if they couldn't find the barracks? The gentle tones of the response signalled understanding of their plight. Every job has its first day. None escapes the anxious entrance into a new and complex world of unknowns. It was a sobering lesson. There was much to be learned in the passage from a civilian to a seasoned state police officer.

Lieutenant Ryan that evening welcomed the new C Troopers. It was, for them, the beginning of state police careers. Ryan, a member of the 1922 recruit class, was completing his long public service, a career that had spanned the organization's first three decades. Theirs would extend well into the 1970s. Their combined service records would bridge the first fifty years of the birth, development and fulfillment of the Massachusetts State Police.

Nineteen forty-nine would also be the final year of Commissioner John F. Stokes' tenure. Stokes had been appointed in 1920, rising to captain of detectives prior to his 1942 appointment to the commissioner's post. The enforcement veteran had seen it all, from the 1921 founding of the State Police Patrol, to the post war years that began steady expansion of the structure and complement of the uniformed branch.

In the final month of the 1940s Captain John P. "J.P." Sullivan was executive officer of the uniformed force. Captain Joseph C. Crescio was chief of the detective branch. They were headquartered at 1010 Commonwealth Avenue in Boston. Four field troops were located in Framingham, Northampton, Holden and Bridgewater. The academy was permanently based in Framingham. Lieutenant Arthur T. O'Leary was commandant there, assisted by Sergeant John C. Blake. Patrolmen Walter F. Bowen and Joseph M. Lynch rounded out the staff.

Lieutenant Ryan, one of the four troop commanders, ran Troop C, Holden. First Sergeant John Collins was second-in-command. Rounding out the C-H supervisory staff were Sergeants Frank Hennigan, Jim Cronin, Jake Daley and Fred Sullivan. The patrolmen assigned to Holden were Andy Golden, Dennis O'Keefe, Steve Obartuck, Walter LaShoto, Harold Brewster, Marty Hall and Paul Kane. Policewoman Kay Mead completed the sworn complement, handling special assignments throughout Worcester County.

TIME OFF AND SALARY

Personnel policies had evolved slowly. Leave had improved to one day off in seven. The new schedule actually was approved during World War II, but implementation had been suspended until war's end. A day off consisted of 39 hours. The "night pass" had increased from fifteen to 24 hours. A duty tour in 1949 thus appeared as follows:

Monday, 8 a.m.   —report for duty
Wednesday, 3 p.m.—start night pass
Thursday, 3 p.m.   —report for duty
Saturday, 5 p.m.   —start day off
Monday, 8 a.m.   —report for duty

The total time off per week was 63 hours. The remainder, 105 hours, was committed to patrol, investigations, barracks duties, and, finally, to much needed rest. The system had evolved, in three decades, from one in fifteen, to one in ten, to one in seven. The traditional barracks concept remained central to statewide operations. The men *lived* in the state police, and, when authorized, travelled substantial distances to enjoy limited time with family and friends.

Within the 105 hour work week there was a rigid schedule of duties. While variances existed among the field troops, a typical week's duty would approximate the following:

Mon.	8 a.m.	report for duty
	8 a.m. - 6 p.m.	barrack's duties, report writing, wash cruisers and motorcycles, leisure time
	7 p.m.	begin assigned patrol.
Tues.	3 a.m.	return to barracks from patrol
	9 a.m.	court appearance if an arrest were made during the prior patrol. No compensation (time or fees) for court appearance.
	1 p.m.	begin assigned patrol
	5 p.m.	return to barracks for evening meal
	7 p.m.	begin assigned patrol
Wed.	3 a.m.	return to barracks from patrol.

Again, if an arrest were made during the prior twelve hours of patrol a court appearance would be required at 9 a.m. No fees of any kind, under any circumstances, were permitted. If no court appearance was required, the duty schedule would be completed as follows:

	10 a.m.	begin assigned patrol
	12 Noon	lunch in barracks
	12:30 p.m.	begin assigned patrol
	2:30 p.m.	return to barracks from patrol
	3:00 p.m.	begin 24 hour night pass
Thur.	3 p.m.	return to barracks from 24 hour night pass.

Essentially, the same duty schedule would then begin again. At the completion of the second cycle a day off started, thus the "one in seven." One notes a full duty schedule on the day the night pass began, and on the day the pass ended. It was, in effect, a precise 24 hour period away from the barracks. Importantly, full availability was ensured on each of the days straddled by the 24 hour period.

The traditional barracks system compensated for the limited number of state police officers. Even after thirty years the authorized complement was only 336 in the uniformed branch.

The 1920s, the Great Depression and World War II had not been conducive to substantial increases in the statewide force. Salaries had not fared much better. By 1949 the famous "rule sixteen" proclaimed the following remuneration for the Bay State's uniformed enforcement agency.

Rank	Minimum	Maximum (6 years)
Captain and Executive Officer	5,460	6,660
Lieutenant and Adjutant	4,980	6,180
Lieutenant & Division Inspector	4,980	6,180
Lieutenant (troop commander)	4,620	5,820
First Sergeant	3,660	4,560
Sergeant	3,540	4,440
Policewoman	3,420	4,020
Corporal	3,360	3,960
Patrolman	3,120	3,720
Recruit Trainee	3,120	3,720

The foregoing, even in retrospect, must be carefully evaluated. The Great Depression had been devastating. Salary was not the problem, but, rather, was there a job? Employment, any kind of work, was a precious commodity. In those circumstances, a state police officer was both respected and envied. Hours were irrelevant. Income, while always a consideration, was not a crucial factor. The overriding question, the ever present, very real concern was, did the breadwinner have a job?

Security, that was the overpowering factor. The state police organization was a symbol of that essential value. Why else would thousands vie for a job that offered iron discipline and a military style existence? By adding the total disruption of the war years, one gains comprehension of the national pressures that profoundly affected the state force during its first thirty years.

The immediate post war era signalled the beginning of an expansion destined to accelerate throughout the fifties and sixties. Much of the requisite leadership would emerge from the seven recruit classes that trained during the forties. More than three hundred men had enlisted between January 1, 1940 and December 31, 1949. There were, in addition, six women who joined the state force during the decade. Lieutenant Colonel Winthrop E. Doty, from the 1949 class, would retire in late spring, 1978. His separation would be symbolic. He would be the last to leave the uniformed force of all those who had begun their state police careers during the 1940s.

They are gone now, but, like their predecessors, they served well and faithfully in their time.

• • •

The following officers were killed in the line of duty during the 1940s:

Albert T. Hayes: Died February 9, 1940 in an automobile accident in Holyoke.

Charles J. Collins: Shot and killed May 19, 1942 in Byfield.

• • •

The following were among those appointed to the Detective Branch during the 1940s:

Olsson, Arnold	O'Leary, Cornelius J.	Shay, Edward W., Jr.
Trodden, Andrew T.	Mead, Sylvester A.	Hogan, John W.
Butler, John N.	Peloquin, Harold J.	Fried, Charles S.
Sullivan, Jeremiah J.	Gahm, Joseph D.	Wells, William F.
Deady, Philip W.	Winn, James A.	Carney, John J.
Conniff, James F.	Crowley, Cornelius J.	Keane, Timothy F.
McCarthy, Gerald F.	Falkland, Alfred J.	Simmons, Joseph E.
LaCaire, Anthony S.	Fleming, Francis F.	Shimkus, Daniel A.
Monsour, John A.	Young, John J.	Murphy, David B.
Murphy, Daniel I.	Maher, Raymond F.	Driscoll, Joseph J.
Walsh, William J.	Leary, James E.	Killen, George E.
Burke, Thomas E.	McCauley, Peter A.	Cahalane, John A.
Cullinane, Michael J.	Murphy, Timothy A.	Harnois, George F.
Feeney, Edmond J.	Kelleher, Joseph E.	Kelley, Edward B.
O'Connor, Michael		

The following were appointed to the Massachusetts State Police Academy during the 1940s:

TWENTY-NINTH RECRUIT TROOP

September 12, 1941

Anton, Peter	Griffin, Raymond F.	O'Neill, Joseph P.
Benson, Thurston I.	Griffith, Francis F., Jr.	Perry, Philip P.
Carns, Arthur P., Jr.	Gumbleton, John F.	Pires, Anthony T., Jr.
Cleary, James H.	King, Harold F.	Quinlan, John J.
Conlon, John J.	Larson, Carl H.	Quinn, Paul F.
Connelly, William G.	Loughlin, John J.	Sadler, John F.
Cretecos, James A.	Maloney, Francis W.	Sarmuk, Chester A.
Cronin, William F.	McGrail, John E.	Shea, Dennis F.
Czarn, Edward M.J.	McKinnon, Raymond	Sherburne, Richard A.
Driscoll, Daniel F., Jr.	Moran, Timothy F.	Zuk, Peter
Evangelos, James	Murphy, Patrick T.	Murphy, Thomas D.
Gaffney, James G.	Norton, John J.	Rooney, Edward J.
Gaudry, Charles A.	O'Leary, Arthur W.	Murphy, Jeremiah G.
Grady, William F.		

THIRTIETH RECRUIT TROOP

February 24, 1942

Costello, Thomas P.	Kelley, William J.	O'Connell, Douglas R.
Finan, Thomas H.	LaFrenniere, Wendell	Quill, Joseph T.
Glavin, Francis A.	McCarthy, Francis J.	Stavredes, James J.
Green, Mathew J.	Mercer, Harry	Tabaroni, Robert F.
Hobbs, Walter H.	Moynihan, Francis J.	Yankunis, Peter
Jacknauh, John J.	Murphy, Paul T.	

THIRTY-FIRST RECRUIT TROOP

June 16, 1947

Alzapiedi, Raymond T.	Eager, Charles W.	Morgan, James H., Jr.
Armitage, Martin T., Jr.	Fitzgibbon, James J.	O'Neal, John T., Jr.
Aucoin, Edward T.	Flanagan, Ambrose J.	Paquette, Harvey J., Jr.
Barbaro, Frank J.	Foley, Francis V.	Rudy, Michael J.
Besanko, Richard W.	Gosselin, Richard A.	Rusczyk, Chester M.
Bower, Stanley E.	Haley, Robert G.	Savela, Alje M.
Butler, John D.	Herrick, James P.	Somerset, John E.
Bowler, James P.	Hewitt, Alfred A.	Sullivan, Joseph W.
Byrne, Thomas L.	Hyde, John J.	Wall, George E.
Cole, James R.	Ilg, Reynold A.	Wall, John
Collins, Alvin B.	Jackson, Stanley W.	Winn, John A.
Cooney, Basil H.	Kelly, Daniel T.	Andrick, Stephen P.
Cooney, Joseph J.	Leccese, Thomas J.	Cleaves, Kevin J.
Dargan, Edward H.	Marshall, James H.	Cote, Hector J.
Desmond, Daniel J.	Matowitz, Walter S.	Keeley, John M.
Donahue, James N.	Mikalauskas, George A.	Moriarty, John R.
Dunn, Edward M.	Molloy, James V.	

THIRTY-SECOND RECRUIT TROOP-THE " ETSPO'S"

September 9, 1947

Anderson, Melville R.	Cordery, Henry C.	Murphy, Vincent F.
Ashworth, Philip M.	Downey, John F.	Obartuck, Steven
Barry, Francis X.	Foley, James J.	O'Brien, Edward F.
Benoit, John W., Jr.	Gross, William F.	O'Brien, Howard J.
Blake, Byron E.	Hall, Martin B.	Peterson, Paul A.
Bogdanchuk, Walter	Hansbury, William J.	Prendergast, Edward M.
Boluch, Bohdan W.	Harrington, Charles W.	Regan, Joseph J.
Breton, Francis J.	Hickey, Francis J.	Robinson, Joseph A.
Brewster, Harold W.	Kane, William F.	Rys, Stanley W.
Brown, Milo F., Jr.	Keeley, Thomas H.	Spafford, Norman A.
Burns, Gerald F.	Kerrigan, Arthur F.	Stanley, James W.
Callahan, William E.	Leary, John F.	Strout, George H.
Cannon, Robert T.	LaShoto, Walter D.	Thodal, Laurence
Cantelmo, Peter	Martin, Leo J.	Vallon, Casimir M.
Canty, George D.	McCarthy, David L.	Walsh, Patrick J.P.
Carey, Edward F.	McNair, William E.	White, Manuel S., Jr.
Conrad, Edward G.		

THIRTY-THIRD RECRUIT TROOP

April 7, 1948

Burke, Francis T.	Murphy, Edward F.	Lordan, George W.
Haggerty, Charles W., Jr.	Rollins, Charles J.	Byron, Edward G.
Whitcomb, Edward J.	Peers, Robert	England, Albert Jr.
Haber, Joseph E.	McGuire, Raymond M.	Lynch, Robert F.
Hunt, William A.	Rammel, Robert H.	Desruisseaux, Wilfred P.
Forbush, William H.	Fuller, Wayland S.	Ritchie, Arthur J.
Kulik, John J.	Humphrey, Melvin R.	St. Michel, Walter F.
Bienkowski, Henry W.	Porter, James S.	Fredericksen, Walter A.
Haranas, Peter R.	DePaola, Raymond F.	Burns, Donald J.
Munighan, Thomas F.	Rourke, Thomas D.	Cabral, Alfred
Murphy, Peter J., Jr.	Uzdawinis, Bronius M.	McDermott, James A.
Nickerson, George W.	Valente, Pompee P.	Johnson, Ralph E.
Fralin, Arthur G.	Murgia, Robert D.	Chase, Courtland E.
Budukiewicz, John V.	Denommee, Laurier J.	Peterson, Thomas H.
Murphy, John F.	Furze, Charles W.	Underhill, William H.
Owen, William J.	Viel, Lawrence L.	Dunn, Owen F.
Cummings, James F.	Ramsey, Harold W.	

THIRTY-FOURTH RECRUIT TROOP

July 6, 1948

Douglas, Bruce
Herzog, Robert E.
Bushek, Paul D.
Hammond, John J.
O'Connor, John J.
Kelley, Joseph A.
Bergeron, Richard W.
Collins, John F.
Linhares, Matthew F.
Dzenis, Walter
Sullivan, Michael D.
O'Brien, Daniel F.
Parady, Harold J.
Kret, Raymond W.

Flaherty, Martin F.
Harvey, William J.
Kornachuk, Walter M.
Flaherty, John L., Jr.
Splaine, Ralph C.
LeBrun, Arthur F.
Murphy, John J.
Pastuch, Joseph P.
Baker, James A.
Bowse, George F.
Tessier, Alfred V.
Henault, Noel E.
Gates, Henry D.
Bentley, Robert

Meier, William T.
Bowles, Donald L.
Green, Sidney I.
Boutiette, Francis E.
Martins, Arthur F.
Konderwicz, William
Szablinski, Victor S.
Whitney, Alfred T.
Mortimer, Phillip
Cotton, Charles E.
Hemple, Carl H.S.
Kane, Paul F.
McBride, James P.

THIRTY-FIFTH RECRUIT TROOP

September 19, 1949

Shea, Edward F.
Doty, Winthrop E., Jr
Morgan, Herbert R., Jr
Ready, William F., Jr.
McDonough, John A.
Sullivan, Daniel F.
White, Walter R., Jr
Duggan, Cornelius J.
Flynn, John F.
Spofford, Richard C.
Herbst, Joseph R.
Kelly, Edward F.
Killoran, James L.
Lyons, William W.
Powers, William F.
Driscoll, Walter R.
Stanley, Russell F.

John Cooney
Mahoney, John J.
Hacking, George B.
Boles, John J., Jr.
Courtney, John D., Jr.
Faherty, Michael E.
Koutrouba, William X.
Murphy, Martin A.
Doyle, Joseph C.
Hibbert, Thomas
Regan, John J.
Shea, John N.
Brown, Ralph V.
Clark, Merle L., Jr.
Foley, Maurice D.
Hall, Harold J., Jr.
Houchin, Leroy S.
Flannery, Robert E.

Donald Walsh
Fountain, Robert J.
O'Connell, John D.
Burns, John J.
Jacobson, Carl A.
Garvey, William D.
Callahan, Donald D.
Trainor, Thomas T.
Leonard, John E.
Carney, Leo J.
Carr, Thomas E., Jr.
Wisnioski, Stanley W., Jr.
Thompson, Lawrence J.
Ryan, Joseph A.
Cotter, William J.
Jasinski, Stanley J.
Furtado, Daniel
Houghton, George F.

Troop B, Shelburne Falls, 1941. Left to Right: (seated) Lawrence W. Irving, Corporal Charles F. Furze, Francis Vierra, (standing) Frederick F. Sullivan, Michael S. Wojtkowski, ("Mess Boy", front, unidentified, - but a barracks' savior). Corporal was a powerful rank in the early barracks' years, the commanding officer and final arbiter. Furze, a Fall River native, enlisted in 1928, retired in the late 1950's as a captain. "Mess Boys" for five decades were essential to support activities in the "live-in" barracks' system.

State Capitol, Boston, 1944. Left to Right: Commissioner John F. Stokes, Governor Leverett Saltonstall, William T. Knightly, Arthur F. Chaisson. Knightly and Chaisson were commended for their painstaking investigative work in solving the Salem murder of Rose LaCombe. Chaisson enlisted with 1930's 22nd Recruit Troop, long served at the Topsfield Barracks, earned wide respect for his enforcement skills during extended service in North Shore area barracks.

General Headquarters, Commonwealth Pier, Boston, 1941. Left to Right: Theodore J. Stavredes, Walter C. O'Brien, Julian Zuk, Lieutenant James E. Hughes, Alfred J. Sanders, Commissioner Eugene M. McSweeney, Theodore H. Stronach, Hollis E. Beattie, Martin J. Daley, Wilfred Sirois, George F. Alexander, Donat A. LaCasse. The state police pistol team distinguished itself in matches throughout the east. The Commonwealth Pier headquarters site on October 5, 1996 was the location of the Massachusetts State Police 75th anniversary gala. The historic waterfront building is now the World Trade Center.

Troop D, Plymouth, 1946. Left to Right: James J. Martin, Chester A. Sarmuk, William F. Grady. They were investigating the Hubert Miller murder case in Plymouth. Sarmuk and Grady trained with 1941's 29th Recruit Troop. Grady in the 1960's retired as captain and A Troop commander, was for years general manager of Wonderland Race Track in Revere.

Troop D, Marshfield Fair, 1946. Left to Right: Corporal Norman S. Sidney, Richard Tonis, Robert Louker, William McGarry, Joseph J. Regan, Peter Yankunus. The 1920 commission report, and the 1921 founding legislation, committed the uniformed branch to "fair details" each summer across the state. Regan in 1946 was an "E.T.S.P.O.," served over two decades in several troops, later was president of the Former Troopers' Association.

State Police Academy, Framingham, 1947. Left to Right: Lieutenant Francis J. O'Connell, Lieutenant George F. Alexander, Captain and Executive Officer William V. Shimkus, Lieutenant Michael J. Noonan, Sergeant John F. Barnicle, Lieutenant Timothy L. Flynn. All of these veteran officers in 1947 were in the final years of enforcement careers begun in the first decade of the uniformed force. Note that the commissioned officers wear the traditional "Sam Brown" belt over the right shoulder, while Sergeant Barnicle's is over the left.

State Police Academy, Framingham, 1947. Left to Right: Sergeant John W. Collins, William J. Sienkiewicz, Walter F. Bowen, Sergeant Edward L. McGinley. Bowen trained with 1938's 28th Recruit Troop, was long a top flight academy instructor, rose to the major's rank as the department's civil defense officer, in 1997 remained an active participant in the activities of the Former Troopers Association.

Troop A, Lake Cochituate, Framingham, 1947. Left to Right: "Dutch" Holland, Sergeant J. Barnicle, Sergeant J. Collins, J. Rogers, Sergeant W. Sienkiewicz, Lieutenant E. Flanders. They were the state police academy's water safety instructors. Holland and Rogers were water safety professionals who, for years, volunteered their time and expertise for state police recruit training.

Suffolk Downs Race Track, East Boston, 1947. Left to Right: V. Murphy, W. Bowen, J. Regan, Dr. Bradley, State Police Chemist J. McHugh, J. Regan, S. Obartuck, J. O'Neill, J. Tague. "Race Track" assignments, a traditional duty of the department ensured the integrity of saliva and urine specimens from winning horses. John McHugh and his colleagues for years provided timely forensic science skills for the statewide force.

State Police Academy, Framingham, 1947. Trooper George H. Strout receiving diploma, (seated) William F. Gross and Joseph J. Regan, (returning to seat) Melville R. Anderson. Staff Instructor Walter F. Bowen, standing right. Gross rose to the commissioned rank, in the early 1970's commanded the Criminal Information Bureau, later became chief of police in Stoughton. Members of this class were the World War II "E.T.S.P.O.'s."

Academy, Framingham, 1947. Left to Right: Henry C. Cordery, Robert T. Cannon, William F. Gross, William R. Finch, James J. Foley, Lawrence Thodol, Paul A. Peterson, (demonstrating front) Byron E. Blake, Sergeant Wilfred Sirois. This was the second class of 1947, the Emergency Temporary State Police Officers, the "E.T.S.P.O.'s." Blake rose to the lieutenant's rank, directing field activities in Troop D Middleboro. He has spent his retirement years on Martha's Vineyard Island. Sirois long was one of the nation's crack pistol shots.

State Police Academy, Framingham, 1947. Left to Right: Alje M. Savela, Edward M. Dunn, Michael J. Rudy, Lieutenant Everett L. Flanders, Governor Robert F. Bradford, Former Commissioner Paul G. Kirk, Commissioner John F. Stokes, Captain William V. Shimkus, Staff Instructor Walter F. Bowen. Savela, Dunn and Rudy were in the 31st Recruit Troop, the first training class since the 1941 beginning of World War II. Commissioner Kirk had served from 1934 to 1937 in the top departmental post, was appointed in 1937 to the state's Superior Court, and in 1960 was elevated to the Massachusetts Supreme Judicial Court. He lived out his retirement years on Cape Cod.

Troop A, Framingham, 1947. Left to Right: Lieutenant Francis J. O'Connell, Lieutenant Michael J. Noonan. O'Connell trained with the 5th Recruit Troop in 1923. Noonan in 1925 enlisted with the 13th Recruit Class, served in all field troops, completed his career in the early 1950's as captain and division inspector at Boston's General Headquarters.

State Police Academy, Framingham, 1947. Left to Right: Henry C. Cordery, Edward F. Carey, Milo F. Brown, Jr., Peter Cantelmo, Harold W. Brewster, John W. Benoit, Jr., Melville R. Anderson. This was the class first appointed as temporary officers, "E.T.S.P.O.'s," at the close of World War II. Trooper Melville R. Anderson rose through the ranks to become captain and commanding officer of Troop B, Northampton, retired in 1971 as a major in charge of field services, went on to a distinguished career in corporate security.

Troop C, West Boylston, 1948. Left to Right: Edward G. Conrad, Byron E. Blake, Martin B. Hall, Sergeant Martin J. Daley, Francis D. O'Keefe, James J. Martin, Sr. They had just conducted a gaming raid at the Wachusett Country Club. O'Keefe in 1938 had trained with the 28th Recruit Troop, retired in the early 1960's as a lieutenant, was noted for a fine singing voice as well as his enforcement prowess, lived out his retirement years in his native Worcester County.

Troop B, Northampton, 1940. These "two-tone blue" cruisers during the late 1930's and early 1940's were the backbone of the state police fleet. Because World War II halted the manufacture of "civilian" commodities, cruisers of this vintage had to survive the ravages of time and use until the war's end.

Troop C Headquarters, Holden, 1940. Left to Right: Corporal H. Smith, R. Jones, C. O'Connor, T. Stronach. Holden in 1930 was the first building constructed specifically as a troop headquarters. Then strategically located on Route 122A just north of Worcester, it narrowly missed destruction during the great Worcester Tornado of June, 1953. The photo depicts the repair facility to the rear of the main barracks' building.

State Police Pistol Team, 1948. Left to Right: Herbert H. Tickle, Alfred J. Sanders, George E. Grady, Richard Tonis, Richard A. Sherbourne, Walter C. O'Brien. Tickle enlisted in 1930, was a Fall River native, retired in 1956 as a lieutenant at Troop D, Bridgewater. Tonis, a much-decorated World War II marine, in 1997 was living in Brewster on Cape Code 60 years after his 1936 state police enlistment.

Troop D Headquarters, Bridgewater, 1949. Located on the sprawling state farm and prison, this facility served as troop headquarters until the 1956 opening of the current barracks on Route 28 in Middleboro. At Bridgewater, the nearby "villa" served as the troopers' sleeping quarters during a 100 hour duty week.

Troop D, South Yarmouth Barracks, 1948. Left to Right: (front) Charles M. Harrington, Walter S. Matowicz, Corporal Richard Tonis, station commander, Francis A. Glavin, Harold F. Ellis, (rear) William R. Finch, Charles W. Eager, John D. Butler, James H. Cleary. Ellis and Glavin enlisted in 1942 with the 30th Recruit Troop, the only recruit class during World War II. Butler for years was a detective lieutenant and respected investigator. Harrington in the early 1970's retired as captain and Troop D commander.

Troop B, Monson, 1948. Left to Right: Cyril P. McQueen and Arthur D. Desmond. Desmond in 1930 enlisted with the 22nd Recruit Troop, served for most of his long career in Western Massachusetts field barracks. McQueen in the early 1960's completed his service as captain and Troop B commanding officer.

Academy, Framingham, December 7, 1949. Left to Right: Lieutenant Arthur T. O'Leary, Commissioner John F. Stokes, Trooper Cornelius J. Duggan, Staff Instructor Walter F. Bowen (behind Duggan), seated left Captain Michael J. Noonan, Captain John P. Sullivan (behind O'Leary). This was the graduation of the 35th Recruit Troop. O'Leary had enlisted in 1933, was academy commandant for several years, retired in the early 1960's as major and adjutant.

Troop C, Holden, 1949. Left to Right: Troopers William F. Powers and Harold W. Brewster. Brewster saw lengthy naval service in World War II's Asiatic-Pacific Campaign, in 1946 enlisted in the State Police, later served for 25 years with the Fort Lauderdale, Florida, Police Department, died in 1990 at his home near Ocala, Florida.

State Police Academy, Framingham, 1949. Left to Right: Lieutenant Arthur T. O'Leary, Commissioner John F. Stokes, Staff Instructor Walter F. Bowen, (seated left) Lieutenant George E. Grady, Lieutenant Michael J. Noonan, (accepting diploma) Recruit Thomas T. Trainor. This was the 35th Recruit Troop which graduated on December 7, 1949. One of its members, Daniel Furtado, was killed in a motorcycle crash on his first duty tour.

Troop B, Ashfield, 1949. Left to Right: Detective Lieutenant Timothy A. Murphy, Sergeant John W. Collins, James V. Molloy, Edward M. Prendergast. They were investigating the Walter Leseur murder case in Ashfield. Prendergast was a World War II "E.T.S.P.O.," served throughout the state, retired in the 1960's as a captain and troop commander.

State Police Academy, Framingham, 1949. Left to Right: Staff Instructor Joseph M. Lynch, Recruit John N. Shea. Shea graduated with 1949's 35th Recruit Troop. Lynch in 1957 was the first troop commander of the newly opened Massachusetts Turnpike. He was himself a recruit in Framingham with the "Hurricane Class" of 1938, and in 1997 was a member of the Former Troopers' Association.

Troop D, South Yarmouth Barracks, 1948. Left to Right: Troopers James H. Cleary, Charles M. Harrington, Charles W. Eager, Walter S. Matowicz, Corporal Richard Tonis, Troopers Francis A. Glavin, Harold F. Ellis, John D. Butler, William R. Finch. Ellis was a native Cape Codder, rose to the captain and division inspector's post in the mid-1960's, enjoyed a Cape Cod retirement until his 1996 death. Tonis in the 75th anniversary year was enjoying retirement in Brewster, in one of the Cape's oldest homes.

Troop A, Wrentham Barracks, 1942. Left to Right: Troopers Carl M. Larson, Joseph T. Quill, Corporal Arthur T. O'Leary, Troopers Thomas P. Davy, Robert F. Bourbeau. Note the height differentials! Larson and Bourbeau were in the 6'5" range! O'Leary and Davy in the late 1940's served together at the state police academy, O'Leary as commandant and Davy as adjunct traffic law instructor. Davy later as a lieutenant was director of the General Headquarters Traffic Bureau, retiring in the early 1960's as captain and commander of Troop D at Middleboro.

Troop B, Russell, 1949. Subject of a thousand yarns made more colorful by the passing years, this was "Fort Apache," home to troopers for several decades during the bygone era of the "live in" barracks system. "Fort Apache" in 1961 was replaced by a modern facility, but its presence in state police lore is secure.

State Police Academy, Framingham, 1949. Left to Right: Lieutenant Arthur T. O'Leary, Lieutenant Timothy L. Flynn, Lieutenant Michael J. Noonan, Lieutenant Francis J. O'Connell, Captain John P. Sullivan, Lieutenant James P. Ryan, Commissioner John F. Stokes, Secretary of State Edward J. Cronin, (standing right) Trooper Walter F. Bowen, (seated rear) Lieutenant John A. Maturo. The group was assembled for the graduation of the 35th Recruit Troop. O'Leary was academy commandant, retired in early 1960's as major and adjutant. Captain Sullivan, the force's top uniformed officer, had enlisted in 1923 with the 5th Recruit Troop.

THE FIFTIES
A Decade In Transition

Troop A, Suffolk Downs, East Boston, 1950. Left to Right: Maurice D. Foley, Edward F. Kelly, Walter R. Driscoll. The three were classmates in 1949's 35th recruit troop. Kelly in 1977 retired as a lieutenant colonel, was appointed deputy public safety commissioner in 1979, served on several critical occasions as state police commissioner, retired in the 1992 phaseout of the state department of public safety.

Troop A, Suffolk Downs, East Boston, 1950. Left to Right: (front) Maurice D. Foley, James P. Herrick, Edward F. Kelly, Robert T. Cannon, Henry W. Bienkowski, (rear) Walter D. LaShoto, Martin A. Murphy, Sergeant Simon C. Sullivan, Walter R. Driscoll, John W. Benoit. Murphy enlisted in 1949, long served on the academy staff, closed his career in the 1970's as captain in charge of the detective division, died at 50 in 1977.

"There is nothing more difficult to take in hand, more perilous to conduct, or more uncertain in its success, than to take the lead in the introduction of a new order of things."
Nicolo Machiavelli

Chapter Five

A DECADE IN TRANSITION

The 1950s would bridge two distinct eras, a decade of growth and substantial change in the state police. This perception rises in retrospect. It is clear now, after the fact. The experience of that decade provides a comprehensive record of the steady evolution of the organization, its structure, staffing and enforcement capabilities. One doubts, however, that the decade's impending impact was sensed as the fifties began.

The uniformed branch was beginning its fourth decade of public service. Much had transpired since 1921. In many ways, however, administrative policies and operational procedures had remained remarkably stable. The underlying philosophy which provided the impetus for the founding of the State Police Patrol was essentially intact. It was still a semi-military organization; highly mobile, capable of swift enforcement strikes.

The original concept was rooted in a barracks system designed to provide a strong police presence in rural areas, and on the highway system between urban centers. While barracks' locations had shifted with enforcement needs, the basic system remained intact. Demands on personnel remained heavy. The notion of a "life style" rather than an occupation was still central to service in the state force. One's commitment in time, energy and purpose was focused on the job's demands rather than on personal and social obligations. In actuality, there had been but modest change in time off and salaries during the first thirty years.

The reasons for the seemingly slow pace of improvement were not, however, entirely within the statewide agency. The force was but a single unit in a large and complex array of public and private institutions. Almost without exception, all had experienced only marginal positive change during the era marked by the Great Depression and World War II. Indeed, a representative number of such organizations had been weakened by the enormous economic and social pressures of those years. Such phenomena occurred throughout national life, and at the state and local levels of government as well.

The 1950s thus were ordained to open an era of historical departure from the values that had sustained nation, state, and, indeed, family and personal life styles. There was, in that sense, a pervasive social evolution getting underway. The result would be the dramatic changes of the sixties and seventies, which yet continue unabated. The state police, as a single institution in a galaxy of social groupings, could not have avoided the impending organizational dynamics even if, as seems unlikely, there was clear awareness of what was beginning to occur as the decade began.

In fact, the fifties began with poignant impact. Patrolman Alfred A. Hewitt on January 4, was killed on route one in Saugus in a tragic motor vehicle accident. Hewitt had been a member of the first post-war academy class. There, and in barracks' assignments, he had earned the respect both of his colleagues and the public he so ably served. Patrolman Hewitt was stationed at "A-2" the Topsfield barracks, when his untimely death ended a promising law enforcement career. Veterans of the state force were reminded of

Charley Collins' death eight years earlier. Collins too had begun his final duty tour from Topsfield.

A LONG CAREER CLOSES

In March of 1950 a remarkable law enforcement career ended as John F. Stokes closed his tenure as commissioner of public safety. His initial appointment to the detective branch had come in 1920, just a few months after the December 1, 1919 authorization of the department of public safety, and a year before the May, 1921 statute founding the uniformed branch.

Stokes' public service had been unique. He was the first state public safety commissioner to have been appointed from state police ranks. His 1920 enlistment in the detective branch began his involvement in the major events of the first three decades, including the Sacco-Vanzetti and Millen-Faber cases. Those were the notorious cases, the ones that captured the headlines. But there were scores of others, the tough, demanding investigations for which he was uniquely suited by temperament and skill.

His career in the detective branch had culminated with appointment to captain and chief of detectives. It is not to overstate to say that being chief of the detective branch of the Massachusetts State Police was then one of the most prestigious enforcement positions in the nation's police service. His 1942 elevation to the commissioner's post was the first time a state police officer had reached the high office. Stokes' eight year tenure as commissioner spanned two distinct periods in the force's history. The first was the difficult World War II years. Then, at war's end, the rebuilding years which saw, from 1947 to 1949, over 250 men enlisted, trained and assigned to the field troops.

In a way, Stokes was the epitome of those who served in the twenties and thirties. Their values and personal commitment were essential in the closely structured, highly disciplined organization. Many had been born in the last years of the nineteenth century. By the late forties and early fifties these men were closing long enforcement careers. Stokes in many ways represented that dedicated cadre. Now, in the first months of the second half of the twentieth century, his long and distinguished career came to its end. In a symbolic way, that departure ended an era. The department had established its credentials as a professional, statewide law enforcement agency. Adaptation to society's evolving problems and demands would be the principal challenge in the time ahead.

Daniel I. Murphy was appointed commissioner of public safety by Governor Paul A. Dever on August 20, 1950. Murphy especially honored the uniformed force with his ascension to the state's top enforcement post. He was, after all, one of their own, a member of the Twenty-Sixth Training Troop, the "Golden Class" of 1934.

Commissioner Murphy had served in the uniformed branch until January, 1943, rising to the sergeant's rank. He was one of the uniformed officers who did such a remarkable job with the 1942 examination for appointment to the commissioned ranks of the detective branch. His service as a detective lieutenant throughout the forties had included some of the most complex criminal investigations of the decade. Murphy was thus ably prepared by extensive experience in both the uniformed field force and the detective branch for the complex responsibilities of the commissioner's office.

When Murphy was sworn as commissioner by Governor Paul A. Dever, he joined General Foote and John F. Stokes in authoring a first in state police history. The 1921 statute had directed the commissioner specifically to exercise direction of the state police division. Foote, therefore, was the first commander of the uniformed force. Stokes was the first promoted to the commissioner's post from the state police division. He was thus the first *career* officer so elevated. Commissioner Murphy's appointment added another unique dimension. He was the first appointed to that high office after having begun his career in the uniformed branch. "D.I." remains, therefore, the only one to have served as commissioner following duty in both detective and uniformed branches of the state police.

Commissioner Murphy's tenure marked the first years in a substantial expansion of the uniformed force. This steady evolution would include changes in organization structure, ranks, staffing and operational procedures. The first significant change came in the leadership of the uniformed branch. Captain and Executive Officer John P. Sullivan closed more than 27 years of public service on August 1, 1950. He had enlisted with the Fifth Training Troop on March 16, 1923, served in all ranks, in all troops, in all sections of the state. Following his January, 1948 appointment to the top uniformed post, Sullivan had provided the operational leadership for Commissioner Stokes' policies to rebuild enforcement capabilities weakened during World War II.

Captain Sullivan had been in the vanguard of those who proved the validity of a uniformed, statewide police force. His nearly thirty years of public trust had embraced the significant junctures in the rise and fulfillment of his organization. Following Sullivan's retirement, Commissioner Murphy made his first major appointment, that of Lieutenant George F. Alexander to captain and executive officer. Alexander was just completing 27 years in uniform, a member of the October, 1923, Seventh Training Troop.

Alexander also had wide, diversified experience. For example, in 1924 he had participated in the first in-service training ever held, appropriately dubbed "B Troop Day," and conducted at Leeds, then Troop B Headquarters. A long time member of the pistol team, he was one of the best pistol shots in New England. As late as 1949, Captain Alexander had demonstrated his expert marksmanship for members of the Thirty-Fifth Recruit Troop then in training in Framingham. The new executive officer, by any measure, was ably prepared as he assumed his exacting leadership duties.

In writing of an organization's history one resists the inclination to dwell exclusively on leadership figures and major events. It is not easy. Even personal remembrances focus on major events; manhunts, floods, prison riots. These are symbolic happenings, the actions that gained recognition and public support for the state police organization. They are remembered vividly. Time's passage seems even to have made details clearer, and, at times, more heroic than they actually were.

TROOPER DANIEL FURTADO

Behind it all, always, have been the human stories. There are thousands of them. Most are lost, gone with the individual who lived the personal experience. Most will never be told. But they happened. And, often, tragedy was the only witness. That must not be the fate of a now dim, obscure event that happened in October, 1950. There was no forewarning as two troopers headed their motorcycles that day for the Holden barracks. Their patrol was over. Thoughts were of time off. They would relish the hard earned leisure hours.

The patrol itself had been significant. It was the *first duty tour* for Patrolman Daniel Furtado. Furtado was a New Bedford boy. His family had a bakery business in the "Whaling City." As a teenager, he often had delivered bread to the North Dartmouth barracks. That experience made a lasting impression on him. He longed one day to become a trooper. That was his goal. Young Furtado never wavered in his ambition to wear the distinctive colors of the state force.

Furtado's quiet persistence paid off. He successfully passed all of the qualifying tests in the spring of 1949, and was appointed to the training academy that September. The shy kid, slight of build, his sight strengthened with glasses, was now a member of the Thirty-Fifth Training Troop. For him, the academy's demanding requirements were especially difficult. He put everything he had into the effort to reach the cherished goal. He desperately wanted the uniform and badge of the state police.

On December 7, 1949 Dan Furtado graduated from the academy and took his oath of office. One impediment remained. There were not enough vacancies in the uniformed force to accommodate all the new officers. A reserve list was established. Furtado was one of 24 placed in the backup status. It was a disappointment. He had hoped for an immediate troop assignment. That setback behind him, he returned to New Bedford to wait out his assignment to active duty.

Winter, spring, and summer of 1950 moved slowly. Finally, the call came. He was to report to Framingham for uniforms and equipment, and then to Troop C Headquarters at Holden for duty. He was elated. His proud family shared his joy as he left for his first assignment as a state police officer. The happy moment was spared the fact that they would never seem him alive again.

Patrolman Daniel Furtado was killed on his first assignment with the state force. With Patrolman Paul F. Kane he was completing his first duty tour when tragedy struck without warning on October 8, 1950. Kane and Furtado had finished their motorcycle patrol and were headed for the Holden barracks. Suddenly, without warning, Furtado's motorcycle went off the road, striking a tree. The young officer was killed instantly. His death shocked and saddened the state force. He had waited years to wear the state police uniform. He had worn it for three days.

His New Bedford funeral remains one of the most poignant of memories. Patrolman Daniel Furtado was laid to rest in the uniform he cherished. His name and service record occupy but brief lines in the voluminous reports and records of the uniformed branch. But that is not important. Dan Furtado's moment in the French and electric blue shines steadily in the proud annals of the organization he loved. The brightness is not diminished by its brevity. Yet, poignancy will always attend the memory of a trooper taken suddenly at the age of 23.

A CHANGING ORGANIZATION

Nineteen fifty-one brought several basic changes in the structure and ranks of the uniformed branch. The top uniformed post for thirty years had been captain and executive officer. The commissioner of public safety, directed by the 1921 statute specifically to administer the state police division, held the rank of colonel. The adjutant, division inspector and supply officer, all general headquarters assignments, were lieutenants. Troop commanders were also lieutenants, assisted by a first sergeant. "Buck" sergeants rounded out the troop headquarters staffing. Corporals, long the supervisory backbone of the agency, commanded substations, supported by the ranking patrolman or "senior man."

Commissioner Murphy proposed to upgrade ranks and strengthen supervisory capabilities. His plan was approved by Governor Paul A. Dever, and became effective on March 5, 1951:

- Executive officer, from captain to major.
- Adjutant, division inspector, and supply officer, from lieutenant to captain
- Troop commander, from lieutenant to captain.
- Troop first sergeant to lieutenant.
- Troop headquarters sergeants to sergeant (senior grade).
- Corporal to sergeant (junior grade).
- Senior patrolman to corporal.

Murphy had also proposed pay increases, and, when Governor Dever signed the new "Rule 16," the salary scale was increased on March 5, 1951 as follows:

Rank	Minimum	Maximum
Major and executive officer	5,460	6,960
Captain and adjutant	5,040	6,240
Captain and division inspector	5,040	6,240
Captain and supply officer	5,040	6,240
Captain	4,680	5,880
Lieutenant	3,660	4,560
Sergeant (senior grade)	3,540	4,440
Policewoman	3,420	4,320
Sergeant (junior grade)	3,360	4,260
Corporal	3,240	3,840
Patrolman	3,120	3,720
Trainee (recruit)	3,120	

There was a second pay boost on July 1. The increase averaged several hundred dollars per year. For example, maximum salary for the major and executive officer went from $6,960 to $7,320. A patrolman's maximum was raised from $3,720 to $4,080. Those increases seem modest by current standards. But at the time, they were welcomed with enthusiasm. Two pay raises in one year was a major breakthrough, one made possible in large measure by the close relationship with Governor Dever enjoyed by Commissioner Murphy.

There were six "steps" between the minimum and maximum salaries. A patrolman, for example, would receive $3,720 per year upon graduation from the academy. After completing a year, he received a raise of $60. The $60 boost was repeated each year until, after six years, the maximum of $4,080 was reached. An additional salary feature related to the "live in" system. The "room and board" was valued at $360 per year. That money was not received; one's room and food were valued at that figure. Men assigned to general headquarters enjoyed a much shorter work week. There was no barracks system, no "room and board."

These personnel, therefore, did not receive the food and lodging valued at $360 per year. In lieu of that support, each received a $30 monthly check. In effect, "G.H.Q." staffers, at all ranks, enjoyed salaries $360 per year higher than those in the field troops. That additional money, and the substantially shorter work week, made an assignment in general headquarters highly desirable throughout the life of the traditional barracks system.

Governor Dever had also signed a bill creating a statutory training program for local police officer. This was chapter 335 of the Acts of 1951, and it made such training compulsory. The proposal had become law with the strong, coordinated support of Commissioner Murphy and the state Chiefs of Police Association. The first local class had begun on February 5 at the state police academy in Framingham. Forty-two officers represented as many of the Commonwealth's cities and towns. The course was demanding. The men met the same essential requirements as state police recruits. They remained at the training academy throughout the week, with a brief weekend pass the only break in the rigid structure and discipline.

From the beginning, the local training program was an acknowledged success. Those who graduated, and their families, took special pride in the accomplishment of meeting the exacting standards of the state force. Later, the program would be expanded to a network of regional training schools, conducted usually in local police departments. But the honor of having graduated from the state police program would grow in stature. Diplomas soon graced the walls in many of the state's local police departments. The men who handled the rigors of the program were proud of their achievements. The framed graduation certificate was proof that they had completed successfully a course molded from three decades of superior training experiences administered by the statewide enforcement agency.

Meantime, the Thirty-Sixth Recruit Troop entered the academy late in 1951. Forty-six men were appointed to that class. They had passed the April 1949 examination, and had remained in a reserve pool of applicants. The class would not graduate until February 8, 1952, and, even then, would return for motorcycle drills cancelled by winter snows. Captain John C. Blake commanded that training troop, his first. He was ably assisted by Sergeant (senior grade) Joseph M. Lynch, and Patrolman Stanley W. Jackson. Guest lecturers had always added lustre to regular academy staff. That year was no exception. Among those who addressed the aspiring officers were: Captain and Adjutant Edward L. McGinley, Captain of Detectives Joseph C. Crescio, Captain and Supply Officer John A. Maturo, Lieutenants Thomas P. Davy and Joseph P. McEnaney, and Sergeant James A. Cretecos. Cretecos was freshly returned from the famed Traffic Institute of Northwestern University in Evanston, Illinois. He had studied there as a Kemper Fellow, a distinct honor won in national competition.

The improvement in salary and rank had bolstered the morale of uniformed branch members. Such positive change had come slowly during the first three decades. The post-war training classes had brought several hundred young men into the organization. They experienced the severe personal restrictions that yet marked the organization. Most were service veterans. They understood the need for discipline, and the requirements that ensured statewide mobility with a limited complement of officers.

One had seen in the persistence of Patrolman Daniel Furtado an example of the enthusiastic willingness to give up the comforts of "civilian" employment to take the oath of office as a state police officer. There have been many attempts to rationalize why men chose to follow a career which promised increased hours, often a salary reduction, and severe restrictions on any semblance of a normal family life. It has never been satisfactorily explained.

There have been many men like Furtado, hundreds of them. Most have moved through their careers without fanfare, doing the job, making the contributions that, in total, have authored one of the most admired of law enforcement records. A few gained fame for their skills or, perhaps, their courage, when lives were on the line. Fate has often dictated such circumstance. Most critical enforcement action occur swiftly, without warning. Some have brought tragedy. It did not come with advanced fanfare, allowing time for rational choice. Rather it struck suddenly, leaving victim, loved ones, and colleagues in despair.

TROOPER ALJE M. SAVELA

Those had been the poignant circumstances of young Furtado's sudden death. There had been others, too many, during the early years. But that did not spare the men and families of the state force one of their saddest ordeals in the late summer of 1951. August 31 had been a routine day in the far-flung barracks system. The usual amount of activity had transpired, nothing out of the ordinary. Evening patrols had begun. There was no hint of the gloom that would shortly envelop the entire state enforcement agency.

First reports crackled over cruiser radios. For some reason, the rapid burst of alerts was heard clearly across the state. That was unusual. The radio system was still limited by geography. But that night, a trooper on route 28 at the Middleboro rotary heard every chilling word. A state police officer had been shot. His name was flashed over the air. The young officer hoped fervently the report was wrong. He knew the reported victim, had worked with him the year before in Troop C, Worcester County. Tense moments followed. A series of terse messages punctured the air. First reports had been wrong. The trooper named in the first flashes was okay. Rising hopes, however, were quickly dashed. There had in fact been a shooting.

A trooper had been hit, killed instantly. Alje M. Savela had been murdered, felled by multiple shots from a nine millimeter automatic pistol. Stationed at C-1, the Athol barracks, he had been patrolling route 122, just west of Barre Center. He had stopped a car. He did that often. For some reason, his suspicions had been aroused. Savela had returned to his cruiser, apparently to use the radio. His message was never received.

Patrolman Alje Savela had enlisted on June 16, 1947, a member of the Thirty-First Training troop. His early service been in Troop A, Framingham. A transfer to his native Worcester County, Troop C, had been a pleasant surprise. An October 1950 marriage had followed. His career and private life melded with bright promise for the future.

The promise ended that mild summer evening. Decades have eased the memory of that night for those privileged to have known Alje M. Savela, the state police officer, and the man. In many ways he typified those who enlisted following World War II. Mature, disciplined, thoughtful, sensitive beyond his years, he had been profoundly affected, like so many of his colleagues, by the social, economic and emotional impacts of the Great Depression, and the Second World War.

The total capability of the state force was committed to the investigation of his brutal murder. Commissioner Daniel I. Murphy personally directed the massive effort. Detectives and troopers worked around the clock as days lengthened into weeks in the all out effort. Local departments responded fully, without qualification. The Federal Bureau of Investigation committed its vast resources to the closely coordinated, massive probe.

Time has since worked its way, the years have softened the perception of a deeply emotional tragedy. The investigation ultimately focused on a single suspect. Later, justice intervened in a series of events, each a link in a solid chain that led, ultimately, to Florida's foreboding state prison at Raiford. There, years after the Savela murder, his killer, it is believed, paid with his life for yet other homicides committed in that state.

Alje Savela and Daniel Furtado had not known one another. Yet, each had a fierce desire to be a state police officer. Fulfillment of that goal brought both, finally, to Troop C, in the foothills of the Berkshires. Each died in uniform, not ten months nor thirty miles apart. Each possessed the personal attributes that have always sustained the state police organization, no matter the challenges or the difficulties of a particular hour. Each left a path, brightly illuminated, to sustain and inspire those not fortunate enough to have been touched by their tragically shortened lives.

As it must, though, organizational life went on. The Thirty-Sixth Recruit Troop graduated on February 7, 1952. Snow had prevented the full motorcycle program. For that reason, the group, now "veterans," returned in Spring 1952 for drill on the two wheelers. They found, as the "ETSPO's" had in 1947, that it was tough to handle requisite discipline after service in the field. Nevertheless, each did what was required. They had not yet completed six months, and, under the rules and regulations, were still liable to discharge without a hearing.

One member of the class did not return to Framingham that spring. He was James J. Murphy. Murphy in February had been assigned to the Andover barracks. He worked out of that substation for several weeks, learning slowly the complex responsibilities which seem so massive to the newcomer. The young officer had done well in the academy, and he had continued that able performance in the field. Here again, fate intervened. Without warning, while on a regular duty tour, Murphy, at age 28 suffered a severe coronary thrombosis.

His life hung in the balance for days. While his classmates returned to Framingham, he slowly battled back from the attack's devastating effects. The sudden illness, unfortunately, prevented his return to duty, and, with great reluctance on his part, his career in the uniformed branch was closed, almost before it began. He subsequently moved on to a productive personal and professional life. But his first love was the state police, and he regretted, as did those familiar with his enormous desire to serve, the loss of the opportunity to have pursued his chosen career in the two-tone blue.

Meanwhile, a leadership change occurred in the late summer of 1952. Timothy L. Flynn on August 16 retired from the uniformed branch, completing more than 25 years of service. Flynn had enjoyed steady promotions through the years, and, in addition, had become the second executive officer to assume the rank of major. That change had come in the March, 1951 overhaul of the rules and regulations, rank structure and salaries, and had resulted in George F. Alexander's promotion from captain to major while holding the executive officer's post.

Edward L. McGinley succeeded Flynn. McGinley had trained with the Twenty-First Recruit Troop in 1929, and had served in a wide variety of troop and headquarters posts. He would continue as executive officer for almost four years. That tenure would witness the ongoing expansion of the organization's structure and complement.

Both Flynn and McGinley had been appointed by Commissioner Daniel I. Murphy. Now, as 1953 began, "D.I." was preparing to close the segment of his career that had carried him to the summit of the Commonwealth's law enforcement community. Officially, he left the commissioner's office on March 5, 1953. Without missing a day's duty, however, he became commanding officer of the newly created Division of Subversive Activities, a unit placed by the General Court within the Department of Public Safety. Murphy would later return to the detective branch, there to continue a career of public service that ultimately would span more than 37 years.

C TROOPS BLACK DAY

A new commissioner was not appointed until late June. Meantime, a natural disaster struck the Bay State. For sheer intensity and power, it remains the most frightening storm to have ever hit New England. No serious warning had alerted the men stationed at the Holden barracks as they prepared for the evening meal. It was June 9, 1953. Not a special day when it began. But, by nightfall, it would be etched permanently in the annals of the state force.

Just before 5 p.m., a black funnel descended into the Petersham Forest, northwest of Worcester. As the noise increased, the frightening sound was intensified by lightning flashes playing at the funnel's edges. Mature trees suddenly began swirling in the air. No one named it at that moment. There wasn't time. But the massive, cone shaped storm would be remembered as the "Worcester Tornado." Years have softened the tragic aftermath of the tornado as it cut a wide swath through Petersham, Barre, Rutland, Boylston, Holden, Worcester, Shrewsbury and the Fayville section of Southboro. After leaving the ground there, the storm dropped for a final time in Wrentham, some 25 miles further east.

Miraculously, Troop C headquarters at Holden was spared. The tornado passed within mere yards of the large brick facility. Just south, along route 122A, homes were smashed to shreds. People were killed instantly. Moments later, the Great Brook Housing project in Worcester caught the brunt of the storm's fury. Neat rows of houses were laid waste. Panic added to the devastation. No one knew what was happening, at the time it happened. Rumors began. Reports had it that the tornado would turn, regain its strength, and double back through its original route. Ominous black clouds pressed close to the ground. An eerie silence moved into the storm's vacuum.

The state police committed its total resources to Worcester County. Time off was cancelled. Only a desk officer was left in each barracks. Eighty-five people had been killed. Several thousand were injured. Hundred had lost their homes. Medical facilities were taxed beyond capacity. Federal, state and local agencies performed heroically. Troopers from all sections of the state were in the area within hours. They remained there, guarding life and property, for a number of days.

One of those sent to Troop C that evening, would, years later, attempt to share the awe that overcame the first arrivals. There was nothing in the officer's experience with which to compare it. He noticed the trees first. Big trees. Strong trees. Many had been sheared off eight or ten feet from the ground, like so many stalks of celery. Yes, he remembered, that's what it reminded him of; stalks of celery that had been twisted in order to break them.

Curiously, that was the vivid recollection, trees that resembled shredded stalks of celery.

Other tragic sights remained in the mind's eye. One especially was poignant. It was that of a young mother with enough of herself left to report how her infant was torn from her arms, sucked into the storm's center, and lifeless, dropped several hundred feet away. Such accounts, the officer remembered, had not been uncommon. He remembered the irony, when as it often does after a natural disaster, the sun next day shone so brilliantly. For him, that too had made a lasting impression. All around, there was desolation and death. Yet warm and sunny days followed, as though mocking man's efforts to understand and control nature's unlimited force.

The June 9, 1953 Worcester Tornado thus took its place with, among others, the 1928 and 1936 B Troop Floods, the Great Hurricane of 1938, and other natural phenomena that had severely tested the state force's capability to respond to disasters that wrought widespread devastation and death. On the record, on each occasion, the response added to a distinguished ledger of public service.

The reputation for such service had, that same year, attracted a large pool of applicants for enlistment in the uniformed branch. Moreover, it brought a new commissioner. Governor Christian A. Herter on June 30, 1953 appointed Otis M. Whitney to administer the public safety department and its division of state police. Whitney already had a distinguished record of public service. He particularly had enjoyed wide experience in the military, with many years of command responsibility. That part of his prior public career was especially suitable to the semi-military structure of the uniformed branch.

Whitney had also been actively involved in the state's political life, serving in elective offices for a number of years. His most recent post had been as a member of the Governor's Council. General Whitney, that was his preferred title, would remain for an extended tenure, some six years. That time frame would mark accelerated expansion of state police staffing and enforcement capabilities.

One of Whitney's first official acts was the appointment of 48 candidates to the Thirty-Seventh Training Troop. The recruits trained throughout the summer, graduating from the academy on October 23. Following a traditional commencement, the new officers, like all those before them, were posted to field stations throughout the state. Selectivity runs the risk of leaving people and events out. Such omissions are not intended when noting that several members of the class were to enjoy notable careers in public service. Charles W. Gilligan, for example, would one day serve as lieutenant colonel, discharging major responsibilities in the historic role of the state force in the court ordered integration of Boston schools. John F. Regan, Jr., following distinguished service in uniform, would go on to an equally productive tenure in the detective branch, serving as its first major following a 1970s reorganization. John L. Barry, Jr., "Larry" Barry, would later earn the distinct honor of being named "Trooper of the Year" by the Former Massachusetts State Troopers Association. James V. Oteri, along with ascension to high command rank, was destined to become president of the state police Association of Massachusetts.

George A. Luciano was also in the thirty-seventh troop. His career would be distinguished by a 1960s assignment as executive state police aide to Governor John A. Volpe. That relationship aided productive legislative years for the statewide enforcement agency. Later, following command of Troop D Middleboro, Luciano would be appointed Superintendent of the Bureau of State Buildings, a post that brought responsibility for the security and maintenance of the Commonwealth's far flung facilities including the Capitol and the imposing structures popularly known as "government center." Finally, in January, 1979, Governor Edward J. King would name the former trooper as Secretary of the Executive Office of Public Safety.

The Thirty-Seventh Recruit Troop would enjoy, with the rest of the uniformed branch, a pay increase. "Rule 16," the salary yardstick, was upgraded on March 15, 1954. Commissioner Whitney's proposal for the increase had been promptly endorsed by Governor Herter. Each rank received a modest boost. For example, the major and executive officer went to a maximum of $8,380, while captain and troop commander received $6,600, after the required six years. The corporal's scale was increased to a range from $3,660 to $4,260. This was, for some reason, only $120 a year more than a patrolman's top pay of $4,140.

"TROOPERS" AFTER 33 YEARS

This particular Rule 16, that of March 15, 1954, was the first time the rank of "trooper" was officially used. For 33 years "troopers" had been known as "patrolmen." That was the official rank. The public had long since settled for "trooper." It was a rank made famous in the cavalry and it gave rise to images of rugged individualism. But for years rosters and reports had contained the designation patrolman, or, for short, "Pat." No one really liked it. Almost without exception, uniformed personnel thought of themselves as "troopers." The men introduced themselves, or one another, in that fashion. Nevertheless, it was not until 1954 that "trooper" was used officially to identify the officers serving in that grade.

That year also brought an additional 46 new troopers. Following an extensive selection progress, they trained during the late summer and early fall. This was the thirty-eighth class to complete academy requirements. Graduation ceremonies were held on October 30, and the new officers were immediately posted to the four field troops.

This particular training class had nearly repeated the experience of the 1938 recruits in having been assigned to emergency hurricane duty. Hurricanes were, by then, named after the fairer sex. The 1954 storm was "Carol," but she was no lady. "Carol" on August 31 followed a route similar to the 1938 storm. The "eye," or center, moved up Narragansett Bay with its most powerful gusts to the east, driving a flood tide. Once again there was widespread damage, most of it in the Buzzards Bay and Cape Cod shore communities.

This time, however, there had been ample advance warnings. Experience had taught a hard lesson. Troop D was mobilized in an hour. Sergeant John F. Downey at the Rehoboth barracks committed his entire complement to the Ocean Grove section of Swansea. Damage was heavy there. Summer homes were swept away, some from the same foundations left from the 1938 storm. No lives were lost in Ocean Grove, a sprawling resort area. But, strangely, a rumor circulated about a drowning. Worse, the report had it that a trooper had been lost.

Several anxious hours passed. It is not easy to kill an erroneous report, especially if there is some truth to it. And, in this case, there was basis for the fears. A trooper *had* lost his life, swept away by the flood tide while trying to rescue others trapped by the high water. The facts slowly emerged. While Rehoboth troopers were mounting rescue efforts in Ocean Grove, the Rhode Island State Police had been totally committed on the other side of Narragansett Bay. The Ocean State had been struck a devastating blow by "Carol." Downtown Providence was under thirteen feet of water. Property loss rose to $200,000,000. Some 3,500 automobiles were destroyed by the tidal wave. Over 2,000 fishing boats and pleasure crafts were sunk or damaged.

A number of these boats had been moored in East Matunuck, near famed Point Judith. The tidal wave had rushed with unexpected speed into the scores of inlets, trapping residents. It was there that the basis for the rumor at Ocean Grove had occurred. Rhode Island Trooper Daniel L. O'Brien had been drowned at East Matunuck by the angry brown waters of the tidal wave. As it had in this state, too often, sadness settled over that enforcement agency. One of its own had been killed in the line of duty. Suddenly, without warning, a promising career had ended abruptly.

The Rhode Island State Police Distinguished Service Ribbon was awarded posthumously to O'Brien. The citation struggled to explain the tragic loss of a young life, " . . . For heroism displayed at the cost of his life while in the performance of duty and engaged in the rescue of persons endangered by the raging sea overflow caused by Hurricane Carol in East Matunuck on August 31, 1954. His supreme sacrifice will always stand to those who follow in the service, as testimony of a dauntless spirit dedicated to his oath of office and brave beyond the call of duty in the acceptance and discharge of an incident of his calling presenting insurmountable difficulties and having fatal consequences."

Several men at Rehoboth had met O'Brien, much of D-4's area bordered the Ocean State. There was a common bond, a shared sense of pride in serving as state police officers. His heroic death, therefore, is set down here lest it be forgotten that Trooper Daniel L. O'Brien of the Rhode Island State Police was lost in the line of duty during an August 31, 1954 hurricane called "Carol."

STAFFING CHANGES

Nineteen fifty-four had witnessed additional changes in the staffing of the uniformed force. Commissioner Whitney had proposed a new headquarters rank, and restructuring of supervision at troop headquarters and substation levels. Governor Christian A. Herter approved the recommendations, and the changes had become effective on March 15.

A new position, that of captain and civil defense officer was created. This reflected a growing national concern that a nuclear war might erupt between this country and its World War II ally, the Soviet Union. The threat was real. There was an emotional reaction. Newspapers featured pictures of people constructing backyard bomb shelters. Firms offered bargains if several shelters were built at the same time. One photograph showed an armed man standing at the door to his underground bunker. He had vowed to shoot anyone trying to survive a nuclear blast by using the limited rations he had stored. Fear created by the "Cold War" daily surfaced in a variety of bizarre "protective" actions taken by anxious citizens.

The state took steps to preserve requisite government functions should the dreaded strike occur. One result was the construction of Civil Defense Headquarters in Framingham, adjacent to Troop A Headquarters. An underground facility, it would ensure the continuity of governmental functions. Large quantities of food and supplies were stored in the massive bunker. Life could go on for weeks without the necessity of leaving the facility.

In retrospect, one is reminded of Hitler's last days in the Berlin bunker, and the siege mentality that reduced the German capital to dust. One could have probably survived a nuclear holocaust underground, with enough provisions to outlast the radiation fallout. But what sight would greet the survivor when he emerged? That question eventually shifted efforts to prevention of nuclear weapons in the first instance. It is an enterprise that yet remains at the center of this nation's policies in what, as Wendell Wilkie had predicted, has become "one world."

Captain and Civilian Defense Officer thus was a key post in the mid-fifties. The responsible officer also coordinated the duties of the state police Auxiliary. Staffed by members of the Former Massachusetts State Troopers, the Auxiliary did yeoman work on holidays, and as a backup force during enforcement emergencies. Because of the contributions the Former Troopers made, the organization was discussed more fully in the prologue of this volume.

Commissioner Whitney had been especially concerned about adequate supervision in substations. Interested observers knew that level of the organization to be the most critical of the entire administrative structure. For that reason, ranks were strengthened there, and at the troop headquarters level as well. The new designations upgraded the post of sergeant (senior grade) to staff sergeant. These were the men who, during a duty tour, actually ran a troop operation. Thus, as of March 15, 1954, a troop headquarters was staffed by a captain, lieutenant, and, usually, five staff sergeants.

Substation staffing was substantially changed. The rank of sergeant (junior grade) was elevated to sergeant. Formerly, there had been one corporal in each barracks. The new structure called for two. Some 25 *new* ranks were created. That now seems like a routine move. It was not. The change represented an earlier chance at advancement. The 1954 changes created openings, and, over time, hundreds have aspired to supervisory ranks that did not exist until March, 1954.

The mid-fifties also began increased use of technical ranks. The ratings had been part of official staffing for years, but they had seen limited use. These posts were usually related to technical assignments in general headquarters such as photography and ballistics. Such functions began to expand in the middle years of the decade, and, of necessity, additional men were assigned to "GHQ." These were considered choice assignments. Several things came with such a transfer. First, there would be for the officer a dramatic reduction in duty hours. The field troops were working over one hundred hours per week. The barracks system had not changed significantly during the first four decades. Additionally, a GHQ post usually meant a promotion. The wait for the coveted stripes was not so long there as in the troops.

A headquarters assignment accomplished another important objective. An officer could "jump over" a rank with his first promotion. GHQ staffing did not include the corporal rank. If the first promotion occurred in general headquarters it would usually be to special officer sergeant. This was the rough equivalent of the troop rank of sergeant, the individual responsible for a substation. The headquarters promotion ladder then went to technical sergeant. In salary, this rank was approximately equal to the field rank of staff sergeant.

This created some tensions. There was a sense that such a system was unfair to the men in the troops. They carried the major share of the organization's duties, while, at the same time, their personal lives were severely restricted by duty requirements. Headquarters promotions often went to younger men. Such an officer could aspire to a technical post requiring special skills. Seniority was much more critical in the field troops. One advanced pretty much in accordance with the amount of time served. It was a powerful factor. Many conversations related to one's "time on the job." Rosters, special assignments, reports; all were prepared with careful attention to a listing of names by seniority.

There was, then, organizational tension between the field troops and general headquarters. Such strains exist in most public and corporate structures. Troops may be called regions or territories, but tensions usually exist between the administrative headquarters and "the line," the people doing the work that represents the essence of the organization and the reason for its existence. In the state force, the GHQ-Troop dichotomy had always been there. It vanished with the early 1970s abolition of the barracks system.

CHERRY HILL

In an emergency, however, GHQ personnel were often among the first arrivals. This was especially so when rapid mobilization was necessary in the greater metropolitan areas of Boston. One such incident was famed "Cherry Hill," the maximum security section of the aged Charlestown State Prison.

It was bitter cold at 1:30 a.m. on January 18, 1955 when four long-term convicts made a desperate move for freedom. Blocked, they seized five guards at gun point. The four desperados were not new to Charlestown. Crime had been a lifestyle, their names associated with some of the Bay State's most vicious criminal acts. It was a formidable convict roster: Theodore "Teddy" Green, the ringleader, Walter Balben, "Fritz" Swensen and Joseph Flaherty. Thwarted and trapped, but armed and dangerous, they dug in, prepared to negotiate for the best deal they could extract from their hopeless situation.

Prison officials attempted to end the uprising quickly. It was not in the cards. Lives were on the line. Green and his comrades wanted commitments for their hostages. For openers, Green demanded a get-away car. Refused, he resorted to a constantly changing agenda as demands ranged from outright freedom to better conditions and improved parole opportunities. It was a standoff. Both sides dug in for the long, tension filled hours destined to follow.

Commissioner Whitney, Major McGinley and Detective Captain Joseph C. Crescio had been alerted early. Now they took a more active role, conferring with prison supervisors and other enforcement officials. Teddy Green, late on the first day, threatened to kill a hostage if demands were not met. That prompted a decision to bring in the state police. By 11 p.m., heavily armed troopers had "Cherry Hill" sealed off. There was no way out. The rebels, at some point, would have to settle inside the walls.

Next morning, an Army tank appeared outside the prison. The steel monster completed the picture of an armed camp. Charlestown resembled more a military battleground than a prison facility. But the point had been made. The dramatic show of force accelerated negotiations. Shortly, the convicts requested that a citizen committee be formed. Composed of prominent public figures and clergy, the group began intensive, ongoing discussions with the rebels. Patrick J. "Sonny" McDonough, a member of the Governor's

Council, served as spokesman. But, importantly, each committee member played a crucial role in the life saving talks.

State police officials were kept closely informed. Men were brought in from throughout the state. Years later, they would remember those January days and nights in Charlestown more for the bitter cold than the personal danger, more for the long, monotonous waiting than for the tenseness of the anticipated action which, with good fortune, never came. Finally, on Friday, January 21, the citizens committee negotiated an agreement with Green, Balben, Swensen, and Flaherty. The four turned over their guns as the hostages were released, shaken but uninjured. Troopers moved in quickly, and, with prison personnel, placed the rebels in secure cells. The "Cherry Hill" uprising was over. It had lasted 85 hours, the second longest prison riot in the nation's history.

It is not important really to identify specifically the men who weathered the danger and harsh temperatures on Charlestown's walls. Each has his own memories of the tensions and public controversy that attended the unfolding drama. There was irony too, when a Suffolk County Grand Jury ordered a sweeping investigation by Attorney General George Fingold of the state's prison system. Members of that Grand Jury were publicly commended for their work by the presiding Superior Court Justice. His remarks were widely quoted by news media. He was Associate Justice Paul G. Kirk, the same Paul Kirk who had served, two decades earlier, as commissioner of the state police. It was a fitting conclusion to an eventful juncture in the history of the nation's first statewide law enforcement agency.

A SUMMER VACATION

Meantime, more prosiac things were happening. For uniformed personnel, however, they were important. One such change came in Summer, 1955. Troopers *for the first time* were allowed a vacation during the summer season. In retrospect, it seems hardly worth mentioning. In fact, when announced, it was a major breakthrough. For 35 years officers had been required to select vacations during the late fall, winter and early spring. It was one of the little isolated restrictions that, taken together, demanded a major share of one's personal life to sustain the organization's vaunted statewide capability.

Hundreds of such obscure events and actions meld in the history of an evolving institution. Most go untold. They often involve poignant examples of life's difficulties. One such mid-fifties incident found Trooper John M. Keeley and another officer doing the late patrol out of D-4, the Rehoboth barracks. Keeley's eye picked up a figure walking along route 44 in Dighton. It was near 3 a.m. The man had a white cloth wrapped around his hands. The individual's answers left no doubt that he was ill, in need of medical help.

Once arrived at the barracks, the officers were startled when the man insisted that, at one time, he too had worn the two-tone blue. It seemed incredible. Could it be true? Keeley checked with headquarters authorities. It was so. The individual had in fact served in the uniformed branch, had become ill, and had left the service. It was a sad moment, the kind one never forgets. Arrangements were quickly made for appropriate medical assistance. Subsequent inquiries confirmed that the former trooper was back in his home community, receiving medical attention, and, once again, leading a reasonably normal life. Trooper Keeley would later rise to the

rank of major, responsible for the management of sophisticated communications' systems. But those accomplishments would never erase the vivid memory of one of the most unusual experiences he encountered in more than 25 years as a state police officer.

Nineteen fifty-six brought a key series of events. In January, Commissioner Whitney was reappointed by Governor Christian A. Herter. Whitney had completed almost three years in the commissioner's post, and, as a seasoned administrator, would guide the organization through the late fifties.

Something else happened that January. It received a lot more press notice. Just hours before the statute of limitations was to expire, a Grand Jury handed down eleven indictments in the famous "Brink's" Case. It was a dramatic stroke. Federal statutes had expired three years earlier. But, at the eleventh hour, just before the state limitations expired, the infamous gang was rounded up. All, that is, except one. He was Joseph J. "Specks" O'Keefe. "Specky" had been in on the record haul on the night of January 17, 1950. Cheated out of his share of loot, he had informed authorities how the daring crime had been carried out, and, more importantly, he had named those who, with him, had executed the daring heist.

Following the indictments, the gang was lodged in Boston's Charles Street Jail. The old fortress had not before seen the likes of that class of criminal. Special precautions had to be taken. The state police were brought in to handle security. For one of the assigned troopers, it created a special irony. Six years earlier, on January 17, 1950, the robbery night, he had been on the late patrol out of the Holden barracks when word of the Brink's robbery flashed across the state. He remembered the confusion in the early hours. No one seemed certain of what had happened. Details were sketchy. The young trooper sensed a big robbery had been pulled off, but there were no specifics. As the hours ticked off, the enormity of the Brink's heist became clear.

State police patrols remained posted throughout the night, covering key road junctions. In fact, the Brink's gang had fled only a couple of miles, to the home of one of its members. There they had counted the enormous loot, and made a pact. Failure to follow through on the night's plan, later caused O'Keefe to confess. He named those who had cheated him of his share of the loot. The young officer did not know those things as he spent all that night in Northboro Center, checking every car on the "Old Post Road," the principal artery to New York. Only when he read newspaper accounts, would he realize that "Brink's" had been the largest armed robbery ever executed.

Years had passed. New public events moved memories of Brinks off center stage. Then came the dramatic indictments. Shortly, the same officer found himself on the tier of the Charles Street jail, guarding the Brink's gang! With other troopers, he had the duty for weeks while the defendants waited for their famous trial. The shift was usually from 4 p.m. until 12 midnight. Before long, the officer felt he had known the notorious group a long time. Each had a fascinating way of protesting his innocence.

State police personnel remained at the Suffolk County Jail throughout the spring of 1956. Troopers commuted daily from both A and D Troops. The uniformed branch had been in many prisons over the years, but, almost always, with riot gear. This had been the first extended stay, and for good reason. Members of the Brink's gang were not petty thieves. Each had long lived outside the law. Those careers, however, ended abruptly on October 6, 1956. The trial jury came in with guilty verdicts. Each defendant received a long sentence at Walpole, the new state prison.

One final bit of iron remained. It was played out several years later at Walpole. The same trooper who had been involved in the January 17, 1950 all night vigil and the 1956 guard duty at Charles Street Jail, was escorting visitors through Walpole's maximum security wing. Brink's had faded from public view. But the link of irony persisted. As the state officer was about to enter the maximum security building, he noticed a prisoner puttering in a flower bed. It was a serene setting. Sun, flowers, a warm breeze; it couldn't have been more tranquil. The figure bending over the flowerbed, however, had not, on January 17, 1950, been so passive. He was Michael V. Geagan. Geagan on the robbery night had held a gun on a lot of people. He had done that often in a long criminal career. Yet there he was, years later, tending his flowers.

A fleet meeting of the eyes confirmed that they had known each other on the tier at Charles Street. No words were spoken. But each acknowledged the other's presence. The Brink's "vision" would not again recur. It had proved a somewhat disconcerting presence for well over a decade of the state officer's enforcement career.

A STATE POLICE FIRST

The Thirty-Ninth Recruit Troop graduated from the academy on March 31, 1956. Graduation ceremonies were impressive. There was, in addition, a first in the department's history. As Trooper Richard J. Sullivan took his enforcement oath, he joined his dad, Lieutenant Bill Sullivan, in the uniformed branch. They were the first father and son to serve at the same time. Bill Sullivan had graduated from the academy with the "Golden Class" of 1934. He beamed with pride as he pinned the coveted shield on his son. The elder Sullivan did not live long after that memorable day. But his fondest wish had been fulfilled as his son joined him on the state force.

Meantime, a building program as underway. For years, Troop D had desperately needed a new headquarters building. Early in 1956, a new facility was dedicated in Middleboro. It had been a long wait, but it had been worth it. The new building was an impressive structure, located on route 28, the then principal route to Cape Cod. Commissioner Whitney presided at the colorful dedication ceremonies. Present in spirit were several former Troop D commanders, like Robert L. Ferrari and Norman S. Sidney. Each had labored long and hard on the construction project.

Troop D Headquarters had for many years been quartered on Bridgewater's "State Farm." The buildings had once been a women's prison. Key administrative buildings were separated from the sleeping quarters. The latter were in a dull, gray building aptly dubbed the "Villa." Officers slept in the "Villa," immediately across the street from the State Farm's many prisoners. It was, to put it mildly, an uneasy setting. One's imagination had to be kept in tight check. Eerie sounds, on occasion in the dead of night, would float over the walls. Yet, Bridgewater's "farm" served many years as the administrative nerve center for state police operations throughout southeastern Massachusetts.

Samuel M. Range was one of the first officers assigned to the new Middleboro headquarters. Trooper Range graduated from the academy with the Fortieth Training Troop in August of 1956. His service in the uniformed branch marked a milestone in the state force's history. He was the first African American to wear the two-tone blue. A number of blacks have enlisted since then, but Range was the first of his race to complete academy requirements and be sworn as a state trooper. His historic tenure proved brief. He left

shortly to accept a position in the judicial branch of the criminal justice system.

The year ended with further expansion of patrol capabilities. A new barracks was opened in Lynnfield, at the junctions of routes one and 128. Traffic volumes were increasing dramatically as construction of a modern interstate highway system got underway in earnest. The Lynnfield facility was not newly constructed, but, rather, had once served as a private residence.

The first complement of fourteen men was assigned on December 15, 1956. They were under the command of Sergeant John R. Moriarty, a Winthrop resident. Moriarty had trained with the first class of 1947. He would later become executive officer of the uniformed branch. In December, 1956, however, Sergeant Moriarty's mission was to establish Lynnfield as a key operations center for traffic enforcement. He and his men did exactly that. And they accomplished it more swiftly than the policy planners had thought possible.

Lynnfield was no sooner operating, than another new barracks was opened in Troop A. This one was at Foxboro. A brand new building, the handsome structure was dedicated on February 12, 1957. It replaced Wrentham, an aging, wooden facility on route 140. There had been a state police presence in that section of the state almost since the organization's founding. "A-4" had long served as home for those who patrolled route one, the principal connector between the Bay State's capital city and its sister capital to the south, Providence, Rhode Island.

Lasting relationships developed there and throughout the barracks system, the home away from home. As time passed, men who patrolled together followed individual career paths. On occasion, through, events would bring former patrol partners back into a duty relationship, one not contemplated in the earlier assignment. The old Wrentham barracks seemed especially marked for such unexpected outcomes. For example, Corporal Arthur T. O'Leary during the forties commanded A-4. Among those stationed there were John C. Blake, Carl M. Larson and Joseph P. McEnaney. Blake later became the lieutenant colonel and executive officer. His old corporal, Arthur "A.T." O'Leary, about the same time, was promoted to major and adjutant. Following O'Leary's early 1960's retirement, Larson was promoted to the adjutant's post. The three thus followed separate career paths, but, subsequently, served together at general headquarters in the organization's top administrative positions.

McEnaney, meantime, had succeeded O'Leary as public relations officer. This post emerged fully during the mid-fifties given Commissioner Whitney's policy of increased public exposure for agency activities. Captain McEnaney would handle news media during several dramatic events in the late fifties, including a serious Walpole riot, and the famous Coyle Brothers manhunt in Middleboro. The latter remains one of the best examples of public reporting on a critical enforcement operation. McEnaney and his staff remained at the search scene around the clock. Their efforts were largely responsible for the tremendously favorable publicity the uniformed branch received during that historic manhunt.

The Massachusetts Turnpike on May 15, 1957 was opened from route 128 in Weston to the New York state line. The toll road was a major breakthrough. A trip that once took a day could now be made in two hours. A high speed era had arrived and, with it, a new challenge for those charged with enforcing the state's traffic laws. The Turnpike Authority judged the state police best suited for the unique responsibilities. Their early confidence has since been fully justified.

Captain Joseph M. Lynch first commanded the Pike's enforcement personnel. It was a complex assignment. Lynch was responsible for planning the entire enforcement operation, including required staffing and equipment. He had begun the task a year earlier, working in Boston's Little Building on Boylston Street. Lynch was a seasoned officer. In 1947 he handled some of the first assignments at Logan International Airport. There was then no regular complement at the air facility. Rather, personnel from nearby Troop A were assigned specific patrols. Lynch remembered years later how he would meet the men at a specific location to assign patrol orders. He particularly remembered several troopers who shuttled between Logan and regular duty stations. One was Robert G. Haley, later to spend many years at the Nantucket substation. Two others were C Troopers at heart; Martin T. Armatage and his partner Alje M. Savella, victim subsequently of the tragic shooting in Barre.

The new turnpike had three substations; Southboro, Charlton and Westfield. Thirteen men were assigned to each. Lieutenant Joseph P. O'Neill was second in command, and Trooper Michael E. Faherty handled administrative details, especially traffic enforcement. The men slept on cots. It was a demanding assignment. Their performance would be judged critically. More than four decades have confirmed the professional quality of their response to a new and complex enforcement responsibility.

Meantime, 62 new troopers joined the ranks on September 28, 1957. They were the Forty-First Recruit Troop, and they had trained throughout the summer. Governor Foster Furcolo welcomed them into the uniformed branch, and Secretary of State Edward J. Cronin administered their oath of office. Major John C. Blake posted the fledgling officers to field assignments in, as always, the high point of the graduation ceremonies.

The Former Massachusetts State Troopers that day awarded their "Outstanding Police Service Award" for the first time. The honor would go each year to an officer who had brought credit to the organization, as well as to himself. The first recipient was Corporal John J. Regan, originally an "ETSPO," and a member of the 1949 class. Commissioner Whitney assisted the governor in making the presentation, noting the presence of many members of the Former Troopers Association. A number of the "old timers" that day wore the uniform of the state police Auxiliary, and, later, pinned badges on the new troopers. The former troopers were getting a bit older. Almost forty years had fled since the first 1921 enlistments. Earlier that year James E. Hughes had passed away. Hughes trained with the 1922 class, had served in Troops C and D, was best remembered by the men who had undergone "boot" training while he commanded the academy.

Hughes had been an expert marksman. He had helped the pistol teams garner honors throughout the East. Later that year Commissioner Whitney accepted the James E. Hughes Memorial Trophy from the former troopers organization. It was to be awarded to the officer scoring highest in the New England Police Revolver League's annual matches. Captain of Detectives Joseph C. Crescio and Detective Lieutenant Theodore W. Johnson made the presentation. Each had served in the uniformed branch with Lieutenant Hughes, and had been on several championship pistol teams with him.

TOP CAREER RANK

During Hughes days in the uniformed branch, the executive officer's rank had been captain. It had been that way from the 1921

appointment of Captain George A. Parker, until George F. Alexander was designated the first major by Commissioner Daniel I. Murphy in 1951. Timothy L. Flynn and Edward L. McGinley subsequently served in that rank, and John C. Blake completed two years as a major and executive officer.

Commissioner Whitney in 1958 proposed a restructuring of top uniformed ranks. Governor Furcolo approved the staffing plan, and, on July 1, Blake became the uniformed branch's first lieutenant colonel and executive officer. The promotion capped a long career for Blake dating to the 1934 "Golden Class," including extended stints as an academy instructor and commandant, and as a troop commander.

Captain Arthur T. O'Leary at the same time was promoted to major, the new designation for the adjutant's post. Rounding out the headquarters command staff was Captain and Division Inspector Norman S. Sidney. Sidney had long served in field assignments, especially in the southeastern section of the state where he had been Troop D commander at Bridgewater's "State Farm." Years later he would reflect on his relatively short stay at GHQ, noting that, in his career, he had found the "troops" the most satisfying duty in almost three decades of public service. A salary increase also became effective on July 1. The lieutenant colonel's post was boosted to a maximum of $9,826. Major O'Leary had come a long way from his 1933 salary of $50 per month as a recruit trainee. As adjutant, he now received a maximum in the major's grade of $8,684. Each uniformed rank received a relative increase. A trooper's salary was raised to $4,043 upon graduation from the academy, with boosts to $5,213 after six years of service. Trainees were paid $3,770, or just over $300 per month.

One of Lieutenant Colonel Blake's first duties was a pleasant one. He and Commissioner Whitney on July 28 assisted Former Trooper's President Howard Dacey in making the presentation of that organization's second annual outstanding police service award. The recipients were Troopers Charles W. Gilligan and Mario E. Indorato. The two were cited for their handling of a complex and dangerous investigation which resulted in the apprehension of those responsible for the crimes that had been committed.

Major O'Leary shortly supervised a public function, but, for him, it was replete with poignant memories. Former Governor James Michael Curley died in late 1958. The legendary Curley's body laid in state in the Capitol's Hall of Flags for two days and nights. A large detail of troopers was assigned. Curley had been a father figure to many in the capital city, especially those who had known poverty during the Great Depression. The outpouring of affection would have been savored by a man who had come from among them.

Major O'Leary commanded a large uniformed detail. He had been assigned to Governor Curley as a young trooper. For O'Leary, that mid-thirties duty had begun a lifelong friendship with the legendary orator and members of his family. Troopers posted in the Hall of Flags observed the closeness of that relationship throughout the impressive tribute. Most had not served under Curley. They understood, though, that he, in his time, had made timely contributions to the state force. One who clearly recalled these events as he paid last respects, was the Superior Court's Associate Justice, Paul G. Kirk. As commissioner, in that very building, Kirk and James Michael Curley had arranged the relocation of general headquarters from the Capitol to Commonwealth Pier in South Boston.

WALPOLE

On March 7, 1959 six Walpole State Prison inmates attempted an escape. The modern "correctional institution" had replaced ancient Charlestown, scene of the January 1955 "Cherry Hill" uprising. The new setting did not change things. Prisons are prisons, even if called by another name. Men there are deprived of freedom. Society has inflicted that punishment for violation of its laws. It is a severe sanction, intended to punish while, at the same time, deterring others from committing similar crimes.

Efforts to make prisons a place to be "rehabilitated" have failed. There is conflict between deprivation of freedom and renewal of more disciplined personal values. Prison punishes. One is not enlightened there. Theories of prisoner rehabilitation have been among the most disappointing and costly concepts attempted in this nation's efforts to achieve the fair and equitable administration of criminal justice.

The Walpole convicts seized six guards, the warden and the prison chaplain. Threatening their hostages with violent death, they bartered, as at Charlestown, for their freedom. It was a tense setting. At one point the hostages were soaked with gasoline. A lighted match would have brought the state its most frightful tragedy. Moments seemed like hours as negotiations dragged on, moving inexorably toward a climax.

Troopers had been brought in during the first hours. Heavily armed, they had taken up key positions inside the mammoth facility. The action was centered in the metal shop. The rebels had barricaded themselves and their hostages in fortress fashion. It was a standoff. Demands and, especially, threats, escalated. Each was rejected. The situation was desperate. The convicts could not win. But, and they threatened it, they could take life. It was a trump card, one that must always be respected in such confrontations.

At Walpole, the card was never played. Troopers and prison guards stormed the rebel stronghold. It was a swift, overpowering assault. Caught unaware, the convicts were seized. The hostages were released without serious injury. A desperate situation had been salvaged by the courage and skills of the assault force.

Scarcely six weeks later, a riot erupted at the Concord Reformatory. Sergeant John Kulik got the first report at the Concord barracks. He flashed word to Framingham. A full alert went into effect. Captain Bill Mack, the troop commander, ordered all personnel into the A-3 area. Dick Tonis, Dick Sherburne and Bill Grady loaded riot gear and heavy weapons at the supply depot. Within minutes, the equipment was moving over the road to Concord to be issued to some sixty troopers already assembled. They were buttressed by local officers from Concord and surrounding communities.

Acting Commissioner Clayton L. Havey and Colonel John C. Blake, quickly on the scene, assumed command. They were joined by Captain Joseph C. Crescio, chief of detectives. The three conferred with prison officials. As at Walpole, it was a critical situation. Charles "Bull" Martin had a gun. He appeared to be leading the uprising. The convicts were holding fifteen hostages. Some of the rebels had been transferred from Walpole following the riot there.

Again, demands were made. Superintendent Edward Grennan rejected them outright, instead threatening a massive assault. Following further assessments, Colonel Balke ordered a tear gas barrage. Forced out of the high security block, the rioters retreated to the third floor where they were cornered by a squad of troopers

and quickly subdued. The hostages were rescued without injury. The second major prison uprising in a few weeks had ended without concessions, and, fortunately without serious injury to hostages or the scores of law enforcement officers who had diffused a potentially explosive escape attempt.

A SOLID RECORD

Commissioner Whitney in special orders commended the men who had brought order out of chaos at the prison. This was his last official act as head of the agency he had led since 1953. Whitney in early May resigned to accept appointment by Governor Furcolo as commissioner of the state's department of insurance.

Much had taken place during the six years tenure of Otis M. Whitney. Some of the more significant changes have been reported. It is not possible, however, to illuminate all that transpires in the course of an administration. Moreover, others have played key roles in upgrading personnel policies, equipment, and related organizational capabilities. A volume ten times this size could not record the contributions of those who ensured progress in a particular time span, improvements during a specific era.

One such example was the increase in the uniformed branch's authorized strength. In the late forties and early fifties, there were 336 uniformed officers. That figure had remained constant for an extended period of time. Commissioner Whitney changed that, getting periodic increases that resulted, by 1959, in a uniformed complement of 512. Salaries had been substantially upgraded. By the close of the fifties' decade, a trooper drew a starting salary of $4,394, with increases to $5,564 per year. The lieutenant colonel and executive officer's pay was increased to a maximum of $10,738 annually, a major breakthrough at the time.

Summer vacations were allowed in 1955 for the first time. The next year had witnessed improved time off with a schedule popularly called "two in eight." In effect, the night pass was abolished, and, in its place, a second day off was allowed. The new schedule worked in the following manner:

- Monday: report for duty at 8 a.m.
- Wednesday: begin day off at 5 p.m.
- Thursday: regular day off.
- Friday: report for duty at 8 a.m.
- Monday: regular day off.

This represented a major breakthrough. The men still lived in barracks. That system remained the backbone of the statewide operation. But two days off in eight, each of 39 hours duration, was light years removed from "one in fifteen," "one in ten," and, even, the "one in seven" that marked a dramatic improvement at the end of World War II. The decade of the nineteen fifties had also brought a number of significant changes in uniforms and equipment. New boots replaced the two piece leg wear, puttees and shoes. A new style uniform hat was introduced, and, additionally, "quick draw" holsters and gun belts were issued.

Commissioner Otis M. Whitney left a solid record of improved personnel policies. It is doubtful if any commissioner enjoyed the military traditions as he did. Troopers were startled when, on occasion, they saw Whitney and his aide, Sergeant Stanley W. Wisnioski, Jr., ride up to a barracks on motorcycles, in full uniform.

Perhaps others had done it too, but not with the same elan as General Whitney.

Whitney left to serve as commissioner of the state department of insurance, and, in the early 1960s, was appointed to the bench by Governor John A. Volpe. Even then, however, much of him remained in the state police. This seemed the case, when, at the ceremony marking his elevation to presiding justice of the Concord District Court, state officers attended in the same French and Electric Blue he had once worn with relish as the state's public safety commissioner.

THE COYLE BROTHERS

Following Whitney's departure, Governor Foster Furcolo appointed J. Henry Goguen of Leominster to the commissioner's post. Goguen had by then completed a substantial amount of public service. He had been a member of the state House of Representatives, and, in addition, had served as United States Marshal. Earlier, following the death of Edward J. Cronin, he had served as interim Secretary of State.

Goguen's experience was almost immediately called into play by one of the most dramatic manhunts in the history of the state force. It was June 15, 1959, a typical spring day in the southeastern section of the state, the gateway to Cape Cod. The tranquility did not last. Two young men walked into a liquor store in Middleboro on the "Cape Way," route 28. They minced no words. With drawn guns, they demanded receipts from the manager. It was over in a moment. Only a wild shot had punctured the morning stillness.

A frantic telephone call brought state and local police to the holdup scene. Events moved with unexpected swiftness. Trooper Daniel F. Sullivan of the Middleboro barracks and Patrolman Daniel Guertin of the local department spotted the wanted vehicle just off route 28, partially hidden in a sandy lane. Cautious, they approached the car slowly. A hail of bullets erupted from the vehicle. Sullivan and Guertin returned the fire, driving the suspects from the car and into the heavily wooded area.

A quick check of the bandit car brought an incredible discovery. Cowering in the trunk was a third man. He gasped out an amazing story, one that was shortly verified. The fugitive pair had kidnapped him in Philadelphia, holding him for ten days while driving throughout the northeast. He had recognized his captors during his long ordeal. They were not ordinary law breakers, but, rather, the notorious brothers, John and William Coyle of Philadelphia.

The Coyles were suspects in countless armed robberies, sought by the Federal Bureau of Investigation as well as a number of state and local enforcement agencies. They had shot and killed a Philadelphia policeman who had surprised them stealing a bottle of milk! The route 28 shootout triggered one of the most dramatic manhunts in the state's history. One hundred and twenty-five troopers were committed to the capture of the fugitive brothers. Every enforcement agency in southeastern Massachusetts joined the massive search effort. Federal authorities actively participated in planning, and helped coordinate search actions. Meantime, the Philadelphia Police Department offered a $5,000. reward for John and William Coyle; dead or alive.

The massive enforcement effort centered in a five mile square area, snake infested and swarming with mosquitos. The tense operations dragged on for two days and two nights. Many believed

that the Coyles had slipped through the net; they had often avoided capture. Troopers were unconvinced. It was an eerie scene, especially during the long hours of darkness. Middleboro's woods and swamps were not the best places to spend the night tracking two known killers. One's imagination had to be kept in check. Flights of fancy had no place in such a tense enforcement situation. Reality was tough enough.

There was tremendous media coverage. Search activities caught the imagination of the public as periodic bulletins sustained the drama. Captain Joseph P. McEnaney, Lieutenant Daneil F. Driscoll and Sergeant George A. Luciano handled the difficult press assignment flawlessly. It was a critical responsibility in an enforcement emergency of that magnitude.

Without warning, the end came on the third morning. The desperate killers had been spotted by an alert citizen. Officers responded to the scene within minutes, surrounding the exhausted pair in a thick wood. Troopers Paul Keating and John LaCasse confronted the Coyles first. Shots were exchanged. The fire fight continued for several minutes. Then, suddenly, it was quiet as the heavy gunfire ended abruptly.

William Coyle lay mortally wounded in the damp grass. His brother John surrendered meekly. Several troopers took him into custody. Among those who had joined LaCasse and Keating in the final moments were Sergeant Martin A. Murphy, and Troopers Paul Conway, John J. Powers, Donald H. Gould, Francis Kane, Leonard von Flatern, Sanford Brodsky, Ralph Olszewski, John McDonald and Robert Enos. More than a hundred other officers had help bring the Coyles to bay. Many had been in the deep Middleboro woods for over two days and two nights.

John Coyle the next morning was brought to a Middleboro funeral home to identify his brother's body. It was a curious scene. The elder Coyle was calm, showing special interest only in his brother's fatal bullet wounds. When Captain John J. Kelly asked him if the body were that of his brother, Coyle nodded his confirmation. It was an odd ending to an enforcement drama of the first order.

The brothers were returned to their native city, William for burial and John later to be convicted of the Philadelphia's officer's murder. The Coyles were gone. But the story of their wild escapade, and the fatal gunfight, would endure in the annals of the state force. Indeed a special irony had attended the Coyle Brothers manhunt. It was, in many ways, reminiscent of the famous 1935 John Bey search in Northampton. Bey, too, had killed a law officer who caught him stealing milk. Like the Coyles, he had eluded capture for several days, and was captured by Patrolman George E. Grady and a Connecticut trooper, hiding, of all places, in a milk shed.

Several days later, Governor Foster Furcolo in an impressive Hall of Flags ceremony presented a citation to the state police. Accepting the honor on behalf of the personnel who had earned it were Commissioner Goguen, Colonel Blake, Major O'Leary and Detective Lieutenant Michael J. Cullinane. The citation noted the decisive actions taken at Walpole, Concord and Middleboro, all in a span of just several weeks. It had been, by any measure, one of the most remarkable, sustained performances in the history of the statewide enforcement agency.

AT DECADES END

The last official ceremony of the nineteen fifties was the December 12, 1959 Commonwealth Armory graduation of the

Forty-Second Recruit Training Troop. It was an impressive performance, attended by approximately three thousand relatives, friends and spectators. There were several notable events during the graduation. Commissioner J. Henry Goguen presented the "Trooper of the Year" award, sponsored by the Former Massachusetts State Troopers, to Trooper Richard J. Clemens of the Pittsfield barracks. Former Lieutenant Clifton W. Kendall who had skippered the "Protector" throughout the patrol boat's police tenure, presented her handsome name plate to the department for display in a planned museum.

The most significant moment in the program was, as always, a personal one. Accepting his oath of office that day was Trooper James J. Martin. His dad would have been proud beyond words. The elder Martin had been in the 1934 class, and had shortly before completed his own state police career. He was not in the armory that night to see young Jim sworn as a law officer in his old organization. But others were present who knew the significance of the moment. One was the new trooper's mother; the old trooper's widow. For those in attendance who understood, it was a fleeting glimpse at the strong foundation of continuity that had sustained four decades of public trust to the Commonwealth's citizen.

The fifties thus ended as a beginning for the 45 members of the December 1959 recruit class. They joined the following officers who had entered the academy during that decade. Quite a number of these one time "boots" were up front when the "Worcester Tornado," "Hurricane Carol," "Cherry Hill," "Walpole," "Concord" and the "Coyle Brothers," marked the 1950s as particularly notable decade for the men who, always with pride, wore the French and Electric Blue.

* * *

The following officers were killed in the line of duty during the nineteen fifties:

Alfred A. Hewitt: Died January 4, 1950 in a motor vehicle accident in Saugus.
Daniel Furtado: Died October 8, 1950 in a motorcycle accident in West Boylston.
Alje M. Savela: Shot and killed on August 31, 1951 in Barre.
Wallace E. Mathews: Died April 23, 1953 in a motorcycle accident in Russell.

The following were among those appointed to the Detective Branch during the 1950's:

Roy, Ramond G.	Joyce, Frank J.	Ahern, Joseph E.
Cass, Richard J.	Schofield, Edward J.	

* * *

The following were appointed to the Massachusetts State Police Academy during the 1950s.

THIRTY-SIXTH RECRUIT TROOP

February 7, 1952

Tonell, Edward P.	Ashworth, Philip M.	Perch, Burton G.
Smith, Edward J.	Morrison, William	Bellevue, Thomas H.
Sweeney, Charles J.	Crowley, Richard E.	Maurais, Kenneth C.
Teahan, Edward J.	Jagodowski, Joseph S.	Gavin, David W., Jr.

Renaux, Albert F.	Sullivan, Walter M.	Marden, Charles H.
McNulty, Leo F.	Smith, Robert J.	Farrell, John M.
LaPoint, John J.	Harlow, Robert N.	Ray, Joseph S. Jr.
Latsey, Peter A.	MacDonald, Donald H.	Longval, Armand J., Jr.
Murphy, James J.	Donohue, John C. Jr.	Scarth, Sidney J.
Pendergast, David J.	Gustavis, Robert J.	Coffey, Joseph L.
Danilchuk, David	Nolan, John E.	Bolduc, Robert A.
Joyce, John J.	Nasuti, Ralph R.	Heffernan, Myles F. Jr.
Logan, Earle N.	Sousa, Americo J.	Ashe, John D.
Mathews, Wallace E.	Sabanski, Albert	Crowley, Gerald P.

THIRTY-SEVENTH RECRUIT TROOP

October 23, 1953

Halloran, James E. Jr.	Meagher, John	O'Brien, John F.
Keough, Robert J.	Robertson, George R.	Irving, William H., Jr.
Majesky, Carl M.	Nightingale, Roy N.	Higgins, Edward J. Jr.
Gearin, William F.	Lally, Thomas J.	Haraden, Edward A.
Mathewson, Chester A.	Fitzgerald, John F.	Leary, Francis G.
Cady, Robert E.	Clemens, Richard J., Jr.	O'Neill, Richard D.
Birmingham, Robert J.	Birkbeck, Donald E.	Blanchard, Robert W.
Leary, John S.	Murphy, Francis J., Jr.	Jefferson, Wallace L.
Gilligan, Charles W.	Luciano, George A.	Kennedy, Edward F. Jr.
Boyd, Harry D.	Lightbody, Raymond	Dunne, James P.
Wallace, Rodney	Keeler, Robert A.	McQuade, Donald J.
Carter, Lawrence	Finan, Ernest T. Jr.	Clemens, John B.
Dauphinee, Richard E.	Murphy, Eugene L.	Gillis, Edward A.
Regan, John F., Jr.	Sharkey, James H.	Coveney, Robert S.
Cummings, Robert J.	Abbate, Francis	Quinlan, Arthur W., Jr.
Barry, John L., Jr.	Oteri, James V.	Brennan, Richard H.

THIRTY-EIGHTH RECRUIT TROOP

October 28, 1954

McDonough, Robert J.	O'Brien, Paul F.	Brown, Thomas J.
Cummings, William F.	Kapinos, Theodore A.	Procaccini, Joseph M.
Dzikiewicz, Eugene H.	Chase, Arthur E.	Spafford, Herbert M., Jr.
MacCormack, Edward R.	Carlstrom, Francis R.	Brisbois, Richard G.
White, John J.	Musante, David B., Jr.	Nielsen, John A.
Trefry, Harvey W.	LaCasse, John L.	Cassell, George F. Jr.
Mitchell, Paul C.	Essigman, Karl P.	Brenton, Donald L.
Rizzo, Mario A.	Brodsky, Sanford I.	Souza, Edmund J.
Walsh, Basil B.	Lima, James J. Jr.	Cornish, Ralph E.
Sullivan, Francis L.	Suneson, Norman O.	Masuret, Robert R.
Desilets, Joseph M.	Driscoll, Daniel M.	Lawlor, Robert E.
Robinson, Enoch H.	Gaffney, Kevin J.	Morrison, Arthur W., Jr.
Reddish, Harold J.	Pettingill, Robert A.	Fountaine, Russell P.
Arena, Dominick J.	Mahoney, Francis R.	Vuilleumier, George H. Jr.
Burns, Thomas E. Jr.	Grave, Adriano L,. Jr.	Bosse, Robert E.
Hart, Edward D.		

THIRTY-NINTH RECRUIT TROOP

March 31, 1956

Jowett, Arthur	Vets, Carl J.	Carew, Lawrence F. Jr.
Sullivan, Richard J.	Zullas, Robert J.	Mulloney, Thomas R.
Harding, Lawrence W.	Alben, Albert C.	Woodward, Robert C.
Turcotte, Arthur L.	Coe, Charles W. Jr.	Keating, Paul E.
Demyer, Clarence W.	Morton, Paul E.	Fitzgerald, Robert J.
Driscoll, John H.	Hall, George H.	Daniel, William L.
Cabral, Frank, Jr.	Butler, Thomas P.	Wills, Robert
Kennedy, John F.	Trabucco, Frank J.	Murphy, George J.
Blouin, Aime J., Jr.	Egnet, Daniel E .	Dahill, Robert E.
Walsh, Milton C.	Jennings, Richard B.	Henley, Frederick A.
Kimball, George A., Jr.	Willis, Bruce A.	O'Brien, John W.
McNally, Edwin A.	Martin, Gilbert W.	Murphy, Paul H., Jr.
O'Brien, Daniel J.	McEachern, John A. Jr.	Indorato, Mario E.
Ober, Arthur T.	McGuire, Ralph A.	Stewart, William J.
McDonough, John A.	Bellevue, Richard J.	

FORTIETH RECRUIT TROOP

August 10, 1956

Barry, Richard J.	Cederquist, Carl G.	Mackey, John J.
Quelle, Arthur V.	Welcome, Alfred J. Jr.	Blago, Alfred W.
Patterson, Robert W.	Russo, Robert J.	Kerwin, William R.
Nawn, Paul F.	Baliunas, John I.	Ciocci, Dino G.
Cadoret, Eugene A.	Kelley, Edwin F.	Orszulak, Louis R.
Cain, Thomas J. Jr.	Nelson, George V.	VonFlatern, Leonard F. Jr.
Carew, Kenneth J.	Carr, William T.	O'Donnell, John J.
Morris, John E.	Waterhouse, William H., Jr.	Gould, Donald H.
White, Joseph H.	Nagle, Joseph C.	Topulos, Timothy W.
Charles, John F.	Erdeski, John M.	Grinham, John L., Jr.
Bavaro, Vito J.	Mahoney, John D.	Greim, Walter E.
Hunt, Edward O.	Graves, Raymond H., Jr.	Khoury, Douglas J.
Ethier, Raymond G.	Pratt, Marvin J.	Donahue, Robert B.
Walwer, Donald D.	Johnson, Clifford E., Jr.	Range, Samuel M.*
Kennett, James T.	Reardon, Francis J.	Delaney, Daniel L., Jr.
Schofield, Kenneth	Campbell, Leslie E.	Murray, Raymond P.
Conway, Paul V.	Sibley, Roy F.	Bradford, David L.
O'Donovan, John R., Jr.		

First African American academy graduate and trooper.

FORTY-FIRST RECRUIT TROOP

October 1, 1957

Sullivan, Edward J.	Noone, Michael J.	Warner, William E.
Olzewski, Ralph	Cogan, James J.	Bullock, William M., Jr.
Smith, Robert A.	Gilmore, Kenneth E.	Long, Francis R.
Goldberg, Gene S.	Carreiro, Antonio	Gradie, Joseph V., Jr.
Finn, Thomas A.	Canty, James T.	Zilewicz, John A.
Montgomery, John M.	Caggiano, Vincent J.	Jones, Donald E.

Gaylord, Jonathan	Donovan, James R., III	Dolan, George R.
Crocker, Donald D.	Byrne, Joseph N., Jr.	Powers, Richard J.
Doran, Joseph F.	Allward, Karol B.	Wheeler, Clifford H., Jr.
Heck, Robert O.	D'Alessandro, Hugo R.	Winn, Robert B.
Taylor, Clifford J.	Paine, Stanley E.	Schumaker, Lawrence F., Jr.
Beloff, Paul M.	Rheaume, Alphonse T.	Mahoney, Charles P.
Delforno, Domenic R.	Perenick, Charles H.	Driscoll, Joseph M.
Jurczyk, Edward H.	Trainor, Robert J.	Geary, Richard J.
Kane, Francis P.	Warner, Allen G.	Mayo, Robert S.
Scott, Henry C.	Powers, John J., Jr.	Sedgwick, Richard H.
Scales, George R.	Hardcastle, Joseph F.	Kane, Robert D.
Johnson, Barry W.	Enos, Robert A.	Norman, Donald R.
Mason, David K.	Goss, Kenneth B.	Hallice, Chester E. Jr.
Lucas, Robert P.	Jarrett, William C.	Mulligan, Edward J., Jr.
Loynd, Richard N.	Olson, Richard B.	

FORTY-SECOND RECRUIT TROOP

December 12, 1959

Crosby, William E., Jr.	Port, James G.	Gunnery, Edgar T.
Hunt, Robert E.	Cronin, John J., Jr.	Doheny, Joseph M., Jr.
Shea, George J.	McCormick, James M.	Batts, Richard M.
Rodrigue, Donald R.	Baril, Ronald J. Mallett,	George F.
Caron, Bertrand A.	Whitten, Louville B., Jr.	Martin, James J.
Matthews, Paul F.	Letendre, Robert P.	Cloran, William M.
Malloy, William P.	Angeli, Robert F.	Dateo, Robert G.
Schneiderhan, Richard J.	Raposa, Raymond	Robichaud, Richard L.
Hall, Robert I.	Shea, George R., Jr.	Noonan, Thomas J.
Malatesta, Paul E.	Ryan, Robert M.	DeCola, Nicholas L.
O'Neil, Francis J.	Mathews, Donald R.	Gillespie, William J.
Boutelle, Wesley R.	Kane, Walter J., Jr.	Hupfer, Karl W.
Lounsbury, Francis G.	Mahoney, Edward A.	Danehey, John F.
Martin, Paul A.	Foley, Francis P.	Sarnie, Richard W.
Linehan, Cornelius J., Jr.	Scott, Norman S.	Reilly, Philip J., Jr.

General Headquarters, Boston, 1950. Left to Right: Mora E. Terry, Mary E. Sullivan, Elinor P. Coleman, Mary P. Kirkpatrick, Florence R. McBride, Mary S. Ramsdell, Kathryn G. Mead. This was the weekly meeting of state policewomen. Ramsdell, with Lotta H. Caldwell, in 1930 was the nation's first female state police officer. She retired one month after this photo was taken.

State Capitol, Boston, 1950. Left to Right: (front) Lieutenants George E. Grady and Arthur T. O'Leary, Commissioner John F. Stokes, Captain and Executive Officer John P. Sullivan, Lieutenant Michael J. Noonan (rear) Lieutenants James P. Ryan, Timothy L. Flynn, Francis J. O'Connell. Sullivan enlisted in 1923, served in all field troops during the Great Depression and World War II, retired from the top uniformed post shortly after this photo was taken. Note that the others wear two gold stripes. In 1950, two gold stripes signified the lieutenant's rank.

General Headquarters, Boston. 1952. Major Edward L. McGinley, executive officer, Massachusetts State Police. McGinley in 1929 graduated from the academy with the 21st Recruit Troop. He served in the top uniformed post for four years, following more than two decades in a variety of field and staff assignments.

Troop B, Lee Barracks, 1952. Left to Right: Lawrence Thodal, Richard A. Gosselin, Burton G. Perch, Corporal Michael J. Redding, Robert J. Smith, William D. Garvey, John E. Leonard, Edward M. Dunn. Garvey and Leonard were academy classmates in 1949's 35th Recruit Troop, saw more than two decades of field service in central and western Massachusetts barracks' outposts during the demanding era of the 100-hour duty week. Corporal Redding was rounding out a state police career begun on June 1, 1931 with the 24th Recruit Troop.

Troop D, Rehoboth Barracks, 1952. Left to Right: Troopers Arthur D. Ritchie and William F. Powers. Photo was taken on Route 6 in Seekonk, not 1/4 mile from the Rhode Island line. Route 6 for 50 years was the principal route linking the U. S. East Coast to Cape Cod. Ritchie in 1948 graduated from the State Police Academy with the 33rd Recruit Training Troop, long served as a field trooper in all sections of the state.

Troop A, Framingham, 1952. Left to Right: John W. Benoit, Walter F. St. Michael, Raymond F. DePaola, Henry C. Cordery, Peter A. Latsey. Cordery was a World War II Emergency Temporary State Police Office (E.T.S.P.O.), served more than two decades in the field barracks' system, lived out his retirement years in Florida.

RIGHT, *State Police Academy, Framingham, 1953. Reverend James E. Dunford and Commissioner Otis M. Whitney. Father Dunford in the 1930's appears to have been the first official state police chaplain. He befriended hundreds of troopers for more than three decades, especially during their trying days as academy recruits. Like Whitney, he had a military background and relished wearing the distinctive French and electric blue.*

FAR RIGHT, *Troop A, Framingham, 1953. (on motorcycle) Commissioner Otis M. Whitney with Sergeant Thomas D. Murphy. Newly in the commissioner's office, Whitney quickly mastered the two wheelers, using them often to tour the state in full uniform during his 1953-1959 tenure. Murphy retired in 1967 as lieutenant colonel and executive officer of the uniformed force.*

General Headquarters, Boston, 1954. Left to Right: Commissioner Otis M. Whitney, Martin P. Luthy, Trooper Arthur G. Fralin, Major Edward L. McGinley. Vice President of Luberman's Mutual Casualty Insurance Company, Luthy presented Kemper Fellowship won by Fralin for year's study at Northwestern University's famed Traffic Institute. Fralin later taught at the academy, directed the State Police Traffic Bureau, rose to the captain's rank, retired in 1968 to Tucson, Arizona.

Troop A, Angle Tree Gun Club, Attleboro, 1956. Left to Right: Raymond W. Kret, Noel E. Henault, Richard A. Gosselin, Corporal Lawrence Thodal, Edward R. MacCormack, Lieutenant William T. Knightly, Sergeant George F. Houghton, Commissioner Otis M. Whitney, Walter S. Matowicz. Corporal Thodal accepted winning trophy for Troop B, Northampton, in the annual inter-troop revolver matches. Trooper Kret was a Fall River native, served in key administrative posts as a commissioned officer, was a crack pistol shot and long time participant in revolver matches throughout the state.

Troop A, Ayer District Court, 1955. Left to Right: Edward G. Byron, Peter Zuk, Joseph M. Procaccini, Ralph C. Splaine, Judge Williams, Commissioner Otis M. Whitney, Stanley W. Wisnioski, Sidney J. Scarth, Corporal Stanley W. Jackson. Jackson returned from World War II's air war over Europe, joined the state police in 1947, in the early 1950's was on the academy staff, served as president of the Former Troopers' Association, in 1997 continues his five decades of service as Treasurer of the Former Troopers Association.

Troop A, Angle Tree Pistol Range, 1956. Left to Right: John W. White, William D. Garvey, Corporal Lawrence L. Thodal, Leonard F. VonFlatern, Jr., Deputy Commissioner Clayton L. Havey, John D. O'Connell. This was the crack pistol team from Troop B Headquarters at Northampton, consistent victors in the 1950's of the statewide, inter-troop revolver matches.

Troop B, Pittsfield Barracks, 1957. Left to Right: Troopers Dino G. Ciocci and Richard J. Clemens. Ciocci went on to a distinguished career in both field and staff posts. He was especially expert in the complex area of forensic photography. Clemens gained fame as the subject of one of Norman Rockwell's best loved paintings, "The Runaway."

State Police Academy Staff, Framingham, 1957. Left to Right: Sergeant Robert F. Lynch, T/Sergeant Raymond T. Alzapedi, Commissioner Otis M. Whitney, Captain James A. Cretecos, T/Sergeant William J. Owen, Corporal Robert E. Herzog. Cretecos trained with 1941's 29th Recruit Troop, graduated in 1954 as a Kemper Fellow from Northwestern University's famed Traffic Institute, was captain and Troop D commander at his early 1960's retirement.

Troop D Headquarters, Middleboro, 1956. Trooper Joseph P. Pastuch with vintage "two tone" blue cruiser. Pastuch trained with 1948's 34th Recruit Troop, long served in barracks throughout southeastern Massachusetts. The Middleboro Barracks in 1956 replaced Bridgewater's "State Farm" as D Troop Headquarters.

Troop D Headquarters, Middleboro, 1957. Left to Right: (front) Joseph P. Pastuch, Donald D. Callahan, Robert Bentley, George B. Hacking, Mario A. Rizzo, (rear) Captain Thomas P. Davy, Grayce V. Johnson, Mary E. Coveney, Major John J. Kelly, Staff Sergeant Thomas P. Costello. John J. Kelly joined the state police with 1938's "Hurricane Class," for years was stationed at D Troop barracks, rose to the major's rank prior to his early 1960's retirement, died during 1996's 75th anniversary year.

State Police Academy, Framingham, 1957. Left to Right: Captain Carl M. Larson, Captain Francis T. Halloran, Captain Cyril P. McQueen, Major Arthur T. O'Leary, Colonel John C. Blake, Governor Foster Furcolo, Commissioner Otis M. Whitney, Secretary of State Edward Cronin, Chaplain James E. Dunford, Captain William J. Mack, Captain William F. Kidney. Occasion was the graduation of 1957's 41st Recruit Troop. Halloran, McQueen and Kidney survived their own recruit indoctrination with 1938's "Hurricane Class." General Whitney from 1953 to 1959 was the state's commissioner of public safety and state police head.

Troop A, Framingham, circa 1957. Bloodhounds Lieutenant Sid and Sadie. The famous trackers were for decades an integral part of state police search and rescue operations. Dedicated handlers, here Trooper Reynold A. Ilg, made career sacrifices to ensure the integrity of the Bloodhound program. Ilg lived to see his son earn the privilege of wearing the French and electric blue.

Boston, 1957. Left to Right (front) Sergeant Timothy F. Moran, Commissioner Otis M. Whitney, Sergeant James J. Foley, (rear) Trooper Noel E. Henault, Trooper Raymond F. DePaola, Sergeant John D. Butler, Corporal Joseph J. Cooney, Corporal James F. Cummings. This group, especially Foley, ran substantial career risks to launch early legislative initiatives. As commissioner, Whitney opened the door for their historic efforts. Moran long was public affairs officer, carved out a second career as a distinguished educator at Northeastern University.

General Headquarters, Boston, 1958. Commissioner Otis M. Whitney, and Trooper Richard J. Clemens, Jr. Clemens enlisted in the state police with 1953's 37th Recruit Troop. He has been accorded enduring fame as the subject for the state trooper in one of Norman Rockwell's most admired paintings, "The Runaway." The famed artist lived out his senior years in Troop B's West Stockbridge, long Clemens' "home troop" during a distinguished state police career.

General Headquarters, Boston, Christmas, 1957. Left to Right: Lieutenant Byron E. Blake, Sergeant George A. Luciano, Sergeant Edward F. Kelly, Lieutenant William F. Leary, Sergeant Wiliam J. Harvey, Lt. Colonel John C. Blake, Major Arthur T. O'Leary, Captain Gustave R. Swanson. They were wrapping Christmas gifts for the benefit of the "Jimmy Fund" and its youthful cancer patients, a favorite charity of Colonel Blake's longtime friend, Red Sox slugger Ted Williams.

South Boston, St. Patrick's Day, 1958. Commissioner Otis M. Whitney and Chaplain James E. Dunford lead uniformed parade detail, (out front) Lieutenant William J. Owen. (color guard) Left to Right: John F. Kennedy, George A. Kimball, Edward R. Ardini, Robert T. Russo. Kennedy enlisted with 1956's 39th Recruit Troop, was state police academy commandant in the late 1970's, retired as a major in charge of administrative services, in 1997 was in federal service as a senior manager in the National Highway Traffic Safety Administration.

State Police Academy, Framingham, 1959. Left to Right: Eleanor G. Dalton, Grayce V. Johnson, Beverly R. Ellis, Mary T. Connolly, Evelyn S. Kenney, Mary E. Coveney. Coveney enlisted in 1949, was promoted in 1970 to staff sergeant, was honorably discharged in 1972. Johnson served from 1956 until 1976, retiring as a lieutenant.

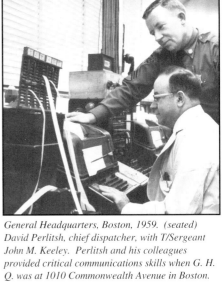

General Headquarters, Boston, 1959. (seated) David Perlitsh, chief dispatcher, with T/Sergeant John M. Keeley. Perlitsh and his colleagues provided critical communications skills when G. H. Q. was at 1010 Commonwealth Avenue in Boston. Keeley served into the 1970's, retired as a major, forged a second enforcement career in the U. S. Department of Justice.

Troop B, Russell Barracks, 1959. Left to Right: Commissioner Henry J. Goguen, Governor Foster Furcolo, Sergeant James V. Malloy, Lieutenant Melville R. Anderson, Captain Cyril P. McQueen, Former Commissioner Otis M. Whitney, Major Arthur T. O'Leary. The new Russell Barracks replaced "Fort Apache," site of a hundred enduring "barracks' stories," real and imagined. O'Leary had enlisted in 1933 at the nadir of the Great Depression, rose to the major's rank at his early 1960's retirement.

Troop A, Concord Reformatory, 1959. Left to Right: Joseph A. Kelley, Edward G. Byron, Edward F. Kelly. Swift state police action blunted many prison uprisings through the years. Both Kelley and Byron served as president of the Former Troopers Association after retirement.

Troop C, Athol Barracks, 1958. Left to Right: Alfred Welcome, George F. Bowse, Corporal Paul F. Kane, Captain William J. Mack, Sergeant Richard W. Besanko, Corporal Phillip Mortimer. Kane enlisted with 1948's 34th Recruit Troop, was cited in Troop C for outstanding investigative work, served in several Troops in a long career, is active in the Former Troopers' Association.

Troop D Headquarters, Middleboro, 1959. Mrs. Nellie C. Grimshaw began in 1942 as a barracks' chief cook at the "State Farm" in Bridgewater, fed several generations of troopers, retired May 1, 1971, the day the "live in" barracks' system ended. She and her devoted colleagues across the state for 50 years were the heart and soul of barracks' life.

Troop A, Framingham, 1959. Left to Right: T/ Sergeant William F. Powers, Trooper Karl P. Essigman. Radar was in its infancy as a law enforcement tool, developed later in tandem with chemical testing for intoxication. Essigman had a distinguished military career, later earned his law degree, enjoyed a second criminal justice career as a trial attorney.

Troop F, Logan International Airport, Boston, 1959. Left to Right: Stanley W. Jackson, Robert E. Dahill, Lieutenant Robert F. Bourbeau, Cuban Revolutionary Fidel Castro, Captain James A. Cretecos, Alvin B. Collins, Sergeant Walter S. Matowicz, Robert J. Birmingham. Castro had just swept into Havana from the Sierra Madre to seize power from a bankrupt Batista Regime. He was hailed as a conquering hero, but that afternoon killed democracy's promise for his island nation with a tutorial on Communism's virtues delivered at Harvard University.

Troop D, South Yarmouth Barrack, 1959. Left to Right: Sergeant Charles W. Eager, Lawrence Carter, Arthur V. Quelle, Robert A. Boldue, Thomas R. Mulloney, John A. McEachern, Jr., (on motorcycle) Corporal Daniel F. O'Brien. Mulloney in 1971 played a key role in the State Police Association of Massachusetts's (S.P.A.M.) support for abolition of the live-in barracks' system. Subsequently, he retired at the lieutenant colonel's rank.

State Police Academy, Framingham, 1959. Right to Left: Robert S. Coveney, Basil B. Walsh, Winthrop E. Doty, Jr., Earle N. Logan, William H. Irving, Jr., (out front) Lieutenant William J. Owen. These were field troopers attending a required, in-service seminar. Doty enlisted in the state police in 1949, rose to the lieutenant colonel's rank, in 1978 was the last uniformed officer to retire from those who joined the state force immediately after World War II.

Boston College, Chestnut Hill, 1959. Left to Right: (front) T/Sergeant Robert F. Lynch, Captain James A. Cretecos, Commissioner J. Henry Goguen, Wendell Coltin, Lieutenant William J. Owen. Personnel on this occasion had attended a traffic law enforcement seminar at Boston College. Coltin long reported on state police activities for area news media. Lynch enlisted in 1948, served in several field troops, was for years a key academy staffer.

THE SIXTIES
New Mandates

Logan Airport, Boston, 1960. Left to Right: Lt. Colonel John C. Blake, President-elect John F. Kennedy, Trooper Robert J. Fitzgerald (behind the president), Trooper Leo J. Carney (center rear), Sergeant George A. Luciano (far right). Kennedy's presidency was an exhilarating time for the state police. He was a native son, a boy on Cape Cod, and their president like none before or since that golden time called "Camelot."

South Yarmouth Barracks, 1960. Sergeant Charles W. Eager and Corporal Joseph J. Regan. Eager enlisted in 1947, served 11 years at South Yarmouth, rose to the captain's rank and command of the Traffic Bureau. In that post, he led efforts for federal funding in 1969 that launched the State Police Air Wing. Subsequently, Captain Eager directed the planning and legislative program that on May 1, 1971, abolished the live-in barracks' system, reduced from 84 to 40 a trooper's duty week, and launched a pay-incentive educational program. In retirement on Cape Cod, he has held a variety of key elective and volunteer offices.

"... Ask not what your country can do for
you — ask what you can do for your country
... knowing that here on earth God's work
must truly be our own."
President John F. Kennedy
January 20, 1961

Chapter Six

NEW MANDATES

It would be another year before John F. Kennedy delivered those memorable words in his inaugural address. Before then, in the first year of the sixties' decade, a series of events would affect the evolution of the state police as an enforcement organization.

That is the way history unfolds. There is, in effect, a melding of two parallel streams. One is broad, organizational development. Here are seen the significant junctures; Sacco and Vanzetti, the Millens and Abe Faber, the John Bey manhunt, "Cherry Hill,"Concord, Walpole, the Coyle Brothers, to name a few. The second historical stream is personal. It is that of individual lives. These tend to be more obscure, but no less important. Without the individual act, the personal sacrifice, there would not be an organizational history, with its founding, growth and fulfillment.

In retrospect, one perceives a number of points where an individual seemed to affect a specific, critical phase in the state force's development. Thus, at the beginning, the prior experiences of General Foote and Captain Parker made possible the recruitment and training of the first men to join the state patrol. Others no doubt could have handled such a challenge. But those two were uniquely qualified for that particular responsibility, at that specific point in the force's history.

These, then, have been the visible junctures. Those that have, for one reason or another, been recorded by news media or in official reports. But what of the rest? What of the contributions made by the hundreds who have worn the distinctive colors of the nation's first statewide enforcement agency? Were their contributions less critical for their lack of public documentation? The answer, of course, is obvious. Each made a specific contribution to an admired public record. Most go unrecorded. A hundred volumes could not report on the countless individual acts, most known only to those who performed the duty.

The Former Troopers Association had those officers in mind when, on May 14, 1960, they sponsored the first annual memorial service. The idea had been discussed among Commissioner Goguen, Colonel Blake, Major O'Leary, Detective Captain Crescio and the Former Troopers Association. All were enthusiastic, and an impressive ceremony was held on the academy drill field in Framingham. Father James E. Dunford and Reverend Ernest A. Thorsell conducted the services. Father Dunford had been a spiritual advisor to the state force since the mid-thirties, while Reverend Thorsell, uniquely, had been a member of the 1933 recruit training class.

For one family, that first service was especially poignant. George W. Lordan had died suddenly on January 2, 1960, at the Holden barracks. Later that same year, on October 21, James H. Marshall would die after a struggle with a prisoner at the Shelburne Falls barracks. Both Lordon and Marshall were World War II

veterans. They had been among the large number of men who enlisted between 1946 and 1949, strengthening a personnel complement seriously weakened during the war years.

Another career would close that year, but on a happier note, Major Arthur T. O'Leary had completed 27 years in the uniformed ranks, a member of the 1933 "college" class that trained in the Great Depression's darkest hours. That group had been the first to wear two-tone blue for their graduation. O'Leary would be especially remembered for the meticulous appearance of his uniform and equipment.

Boston's Statler Hilton on September 18 was the scene of the retirement banquet. Predictably, it took on the appearance of a state police reunion. Seated at the head table were such figures from the past as former Commissioners Daniel E. Needham and Otis M. Whitney. Also on the dais were Commissioner Goguen, Captain and former Commissioner D.I. Murphy, Captain Crescio, Lieutenant Jack Dempsey and Reverend Ernest A. Thorsell, O'Leary's 1933 classmate.

Later that month, a new state police motion picture was premiered. Entitled "Dedicated To You," its initial showing was held in the finely appointed Dolley Madison Room in Boston's John Hancock Building. "Dedicated" was a sequel to "A Chosen Career," a film depicting the rigors of the recruit training program. The new picture subsequently would be enjoyed by thousands of Bay State citizens, most of whom enjoyed the graphic portrayal of enforcement actions, including the 1959 capture of the Coyle Brothers. These scenes were enacted under the guidance of Lieutenant Timothy F. Moran and Sergeant George A. Luciano. The two worked closely with Acorn Films to create a "low budget," high quality motion picture.

A feature of the evening was the presentation of citations to officers who had completed twenty years of service. It was an impressive ceremony. Accepting the twenty year awards from Commissioner Goguen were: Lieutenant Colonel Blake, Captains Bowen, Kelly, Sullivan, Lynch, Mack, McQueen, and Zuk. Also honored were Lieutenant Sanders, Leary, Sienkiewicz, Lane, O'Brien, and Power. Also a recipient of the unique citation was Sergeant Robert H. Cairns, like several of the others, a member of the 1938 training class.

Some of "Dedicated's" scenes had been shot during the training of the Forty-Third Recruit Troop. They had been at Framingham throughout the summer of 1960. Finally, in time honored tradition, the recruits took their oaths during an October 7 graduation ceremony in Boston's Commonwealth Armory. Commissioner J. Henry Goguen welcomed the 35 new officers into the uniformed branch. Following a display of newly acquired skills, Lieutenant Colonel Blake posted the fledgling troopers to their field assignments.

A NATIVE SON

Meanwhile, political interest was at high pitch both in the state and nation. Senator Joseph Ward was the Democratic nominee for governor. His opponent, not especially well known, was John A. Volpe. Volpe was a former high federal official, and had previously served as State Commissioner of Public Works. He would prove to be a tireless campaigner, defeating Ward for the governorship in the November, 1960 election. As governor, Volpe was to play a major role in state police affairs for the entire decade.

There was high interest that year in the presidential race. A native son, John Fitzgerald Kennedy, had become the first Catholic with a serious chance to occupy the nation's highest office. His primary victory over Senator Hubert H. Humphrey in West Virginia had silenced skeptics and excited believers.

Senator Kennedy, although young in the fall of 1960, was a seasoned political veteran. More pertinent, he and his family long had been admirers of the state police. The Kennedy summer home was located in Hyannisport, on Cape Cod. There, for years, troopers had met the Kennedys as they enjoyed those golden summers on Nantucket Sound. There was a special friend, Detective Lieutenant John F. Dempsey. Dempsey was close to the Kennedy family. Their relationship had matured over many, many years.

John F. Kennedy captured the imagination of the country during the 1960 democratic primary contests. His popularity soared during the televised convention in Los Angeles. One can still visualize a young Edward M. "Ted" Kennedy rejoicing among the Wyoming delegation as that state sealed the nomination with its votes. Immediately following Los Angeles, Kennedy returned to the Bay State. A huge throng greeted him at the American Airlines hangar at Logan Airport. That day's scene would be repeated many times during his presidency as he returned to Hyannisport for the physical and intellectual rest that he found there on the shore of Nantucket Sound.

As president, John F. Kennedy would be especially revered by the men of the state police. Wherever he went in his home state, they were there. Whether it was an arrival at Logan Airport or guard duty on the dock at Hyannisport, the two-tone blue was conspicuous. It was an honor, no question about that. For years, they had escorted presidents, but they were from other states. Now, there was a native son. He was special. State police officers did not hide their pride when honored with an assignment that brought them into close contact with *their* president. Memories of those assignments would remain vivid, surviving the harshness of subsequent events in Dallas that ended a remarkable presidency, tragically shortened to one thousand days.

When Kennedy was inaugurated president on January 20, 1961, it was, by any measure, a New England event. Richard Cardinal Cushing, long a personal friend, delivered the Invocation. Robert Frost read a special poem, distracted, as was the vast audience, by wind and bright sunlight playing about the podium. It was an historic occasion, the beginning of a brief era when Kennedy challenged Americans to ask what they could do for their country, rather than what their country might do for them. The inaugural parade was a long one. State police honor guards from many of the nation's statewide enforcements agencies added much color. They looked good. None, however, looked better than those smartly uniformed in the French and electric blue. None was prouder either.

The newly sworn chief executive was observed to smile, nodding recognition, as the men from his home state swept by the reviewing stand, the Bay State's colors standing stiffly against the January air. Many others from the state force were there that memorable day. Among them all, however, none was as thrilled, and nostalgic, as Detective Lieutenant Dempsey. He had seen the man as boy. Now he was president. It was difficult to grasp. But Dempsey relished every moment, much as he would enjoy each day of the thousand that marked the remarkable administration.

"... THEIR LAST PATROL"

Lieutenant Dempsey and many of his colleagues were to attend another impressive ceremony a couple of months later. It was the May 13 dedication of the State Police Memorial on the academy grounds. The program had almost been postponed as Lieutenant Timothy Moran spent several frantic hours getting assurances that the handsome granite memorial would be delivered on time. Former troopers were much in evidence that day. The memorial was in memory of the men, as the plaque noted, "who had completed their last patrol . . ." The list was getting longer. It was then forty years since, not far from that field, the first contingent of the state patrol encamped at the "Poor Farm." A lot had happened. Many had served. Now, a crowd of several hundred gathered to dedicate a permanent memorial to those who had made certain that the state police idea would endure.

Father James E. Dunford gave the Invocation. Commissioner J. Henry Goguen welcomed those assembled. Goguen was assisted by Detective Lieutenant Anthony S. LaCaire. LaCaire had joined the uniformed branch in 1929, becoming in the early 1940's a lieutenant in the detective branch. His had been a thorough and varied law enforcement experience. In his assignment as executive aide to Commissioner Goguen, Lieutenant LaCaire provided valuable insights and sound counsel to the department's chief administrator.

During the program, Captain James A. Cretecos, long academy commandant, explained how the permanent memorial was conceived. The bronze plaque had been donated by the Former Troopers Association. The current organization had provided the handsome granite base. It was a fitting reminder that a lot of men had made key contributions over a long period of time.

The State Police Auxiliary, composed of former troopers, was very much in evidence. Representing the group on the podium were President George Rapport and Secretary Theodore J. Stavredes. A number of their colleagues were in uniform, helping with traffic details prior to participation in the program. They were under the supervision of Lieutenant James Evangelos, newly appointed to those responsibilities. George Rapport officially presented the plaque during the program. Trooper Donald R. Mathews spoke briefly in dedicating the granite base. His appearance was especially fitting. His brother, Trooper Wallace E. Mathews, had been killed in an April 1953 motorcycle accident in Russell.

The May memorial service would be one of Commissioner Goguen's final appearances. He had held the commissioner's post since early 1959, and had guided the agency into the first years of what would become the turbulent sixties. His tenure had not been especially long, but, nonetheless, he had relished the leadership assignment. Goguen was a public man. He had held a number of important assignments. While he would shortly leave the commissioner's office, he would remain actively involved in public affairs for a number of years.

Governor John A. Volpe early that summer appointed Frank S.

Giles of Methuen the state's new commissioner of public safety. Giles was no newcomer to the world of public administration. A police officer for nine years in his home town, he had entered the political arena by winning a seat in the state House of Representatives. Some fifteen years of service in that chamber had brought him to several leadership positions. Immediately prior to his appointment he was serving as minority leader for his party. In 1960, he had been a serious candidate for the state's highest office, the governorship.

Giles readily acknowledged that he had long desired to become the Commonwealth's public safety chief. His early law enforcement experience had fueled that ambition, and now it had happened. He did not waste time in making early administrative moves. In part, these were dictated by time's passage. Lieutenant Colonel John B. Blake, in the uniformed branch since 1934, announced his impending retirement. Blake had witnessed a lot of changes. From the 1934 training field at West Bridgewater, he had made about every possible stop in an enforcement career of 27 years, one that had spanned four different decades.

Commissioner Giles on August 13, 1961 named Carl M. Larson lieutenant colonel and executive officer. Larson had trained with the 1941 class, a veteran of two decades in the state force. He too had enjoyed wide, diversified experience. In fact, Larson and Blake had patrolled together years earlier out of the old Wrentham Barracks. One of his assignments had been a prestigious one; state police aide to Governor Christian A. Herter. Larson had also served as a troop commander prior to being named major and adjutant, at that time the second ranking post in the uniformed branch.

Moving up to the major's post the same day was John J. Kelly. Kelly had been serving as captain and division inspector. That job, in some ways, embraced thankless tasks. Yet, its responsibilities were crucial. The division inspector ensured the integrity of the state police organization. His was the duty, swiftly and firmly, to investigate any allegations of questionable conduct or actions by members of the uniformed force. It was not, never had been, a particularly attractive post. But it was a vital administrative obligation, one that required the long and varied enforcement experiences of a man like Kelly.

The new major had come out of the Boston suburbs, settled in Taunton, fallen hard for southeastern Massachusetts, especially Cape Cod. He was, at heart, a "D" trooper, happiest when he patrolled out of Rehoboth, commanded South Yarmouth, handled the desk duty at Bridgewater's Troop D headquarters. Kelly's promotion to major and adjutant was widely applauded. He was, in many ways, a "trooper's trooper," a man who had handled all manner of enforcement duties in his rise through the ranks to the leadership position he now held.

Joining him on the promotion list that day was Captain Julian Zuk. Zuk succeeded Kelly as division inspector. He had recently supervised the Auxiliary and numbered many former troopers among his friends. Zuk also had a good record in the state force, with experience in all of the supervisory and command responsibilities. Moreover, he was one of the best marksmen in the state police. A long time member of the pistol team, Captain Zuk had won more than 500 matches in competitive shooting.

Commissioner Giles did not hesitate either in appointing his personal aide. He was Frank J. Trabucco. Trabucco, a member of the 1956 class, would provide yeoman service in a taxing post. Those assignments always looked easy. They were, in fact, just the opposite. Commissioners did things at the last minute, often chang-

ing travel plans in mid-stream. Sergant Trabucco's new job was, as others before him had learned, not all that it was cracked up to be. But he enjoyed the challenge, and the prestige. It was not every day that an officer was chosen to support the man in the top leadership post. That experience for Trabucco would pay dividends when, in the mid-seventies, he would become colonel and deputy superintendent of the state police, and in 1980 be appointed to the commissioner's office.

FORTIETH ANNIVERSARY

Colonel Larson, Major Kelly, Captain Zuk and Sergeant Trabucco soon had a chance to enjoy the perquisites of office. The occasion was auspicious. The uniformed branch had completed four decades of public service. Commissioner Giles determined that the milestone should be suitably observed. He presented his ideas to Governor Volpe, and, predictably, received enthusiastic support from the state's chief executive. Volpe signed a proclamation designating the week of October 29, 1961 as "State Police Week." Giles had additional plans. He had given a formidable task to Lieutenant Timothy F. Moran and Trooper Edward R. MacCormack. Their charge: put together an anniversary banquet in a Boston hotel; make sure all living former commissioners are there; invite dignitaries who have played a role in the state force's history; be certain that many former and current troopers attend.

The banquet was held at Boston's Copley Plaza on November 1. Several hundred attended. And, as ordered, Moran and MacCormack produced. It was an impressive dais. The forty-year history of the uniformed branch was bridged in the persons of those at the head table including Governor Channing H. Cox, chief executive in 1921, the first commissioner, Alfred E. Foote, and Commissioners Daniel A. Needham, Paul G. Kirk, John F. Stokes, Daniel I. Murphy and Otis M. Whitney.

Governor John A. Volpe brought the greetings of all his predecessors. Each had given the state force requisite support during its first forty years. Of particular note was the presence of several men who made the first long march down Southboro road in September 1921. Quite a few were there including the first executive officer, Captain George A. Parker, and his successor, Captain Charles T. Beaupre. Also present were John J. O'Donnell, Joseph M. Holleran, Leo F. Stankard, Edward J. Barrett, Eugene F. Stowell and William F. Fitzmaurice. Their presence highlighted the link between old and new. Several hundred others also attended. Many were in leadership positions in the state's criminal justice system. Their presence was proof, not that it was needed, that the Massachusetts State Police had become a much admired law enforcement agency.

Not long after the fortieth anniversary banquet, hundreds of young men vied for appointment to the uniformed branch by taking the examinations held in early 1962. Following a comprehensive selection process, the Forty-Fourth Training Troop reported to Framingham in early spring. They faced an expanded curriculum. New enforcement duties each year required additional subjects. The time had long since passed when the academy could be opened for a training class, and then closed till the arrival of the next one. The first class of 1962 handled the added requirements well. The recruits graduated on July 7 in an impressive public ceremony.

Within weeks, another batch of eager aspirants reported for orientation prior to beginning formal training sessions. The first hours came as quite a shock for those who had not adequately prepared. The first order of business was an exhausting run on the academy track; no easy task when one is still garbed in civilian attire. The staff did not especially make things easier. Sharp commands punctured the air. These were brand new sounds to some of the recruits. A few, no doubt, wondered what they had gotten into. Romantic visions of the two-tone blue uniform fast gave way to survival efforts in the first few days at the academy.

As before, those who wanted the state police badly enough would survive. The goal was a powerful incentive, one that had sustained many of their predecessors when doubts pressed heavily from all sides. And it would sustain the Forty-Fifth Recruit Troop too, right through colorful graduation ceremonies on December 14, 1962. The exercises were held on Friday evening in Boston's Commonwealth Armory. Few among those taking their enforcement oaths that night knew that hundreds before them had trained in that very building. The floor of the huge structure had been converted to macadam, no longer suitable for the mounted drills that were once a feature of recruit training.

Some two thousand attended the graduation. Governor John A. Volpe inspected the recruit troop accompanied by Commissioner Giles and Deputy Commissioner Clayton L. Havey. Joining them in the symbolic act were Colonel Larson, Major Kelly and Captain and Division Inspector Julian Zuk. A second division inspector's post had been created, and Captain Thomas D. Murphy occupied that new position. Murphy had trained with the 1941 class, and was for several years commanding officer of the traffic bureau in general headquarters. Captain Murphy was in the armory that night, as were Captain and Civil Defense Officer Joseph M. Lynch and Staff Captain Francis T. Burke, the department's supply officer.

Troop commanders always attended recruit graduations. They wanted the first look at the men soon to serve in their commands. That evening was no exception. As Colonel Larson posted the new officers to field assignments, there was more than ordinary interests evident on the faces of Captain William F. Grady of Troop A, Framingham; Captain Walter C. O'Brien, Troop B Northampton; Captain John J. Hyde of Troop C Holden; Captain James J. Stavredes, Troop D Middleboro; and Captain Joseph M. Lane who commanded Troop E, the Massachusetts Turnpike.

A new ceremony had been introduced. The top academy graduate accepted command of the training troop from the staff, the final interaction between recruits and instructors. An academy staff is proud of the officers they have trained. They represent the best the staff could impart in a relatively short period of time. There was, then, a touch of nostalgia, when, at evening's end, the academy staff received the salute of the recruit troop as the now sworn officers made a final "pass in review" under the command of one of their own members. Accepting that final symbolic tribute were Lieutenant Stanley W. Wisnioski Jr., Staff Sergeant Robert F. Lynch, Sergeant Martin A. Murphy, Sergeant Charles W. Gilligan and Corporal Eugene H. Dzikiewicz. They had brought the recruit troop from unknowing civilians to a disciplined cadre of enforcement officers. The staff's job was done. Each felt the personal satisfaction that goes with completion of an important assignment.

For two veteran officers attending the December exercises, the event represented their last official assignment. Early in 1963, Captain William F. Grady closed a career begun with the 1941 recruit troop at Framingham. Grady had served in all types of assignments during 22 years of service, topping his career as commander of Troop A. Another member of the 1941 class also had doffed his uniform for the final time. He was Captain Timothy F.

Moran. Moran started his state police career at the Pittsfield barracks, worked his way back to the eastern part of the state, and finished up his service in the photography and public relations bureaus in general headquarters. His departure had been of special note. He had joined the faculty at Northeastern University, the first school to establish formal programs in law enforcement education.

Northeastern Professor Robert Sheehan had worked closely with state and local police to launch formal education for law enforcement officers. Sheehan had received timely assistance in the late fifties from Captain Cretecos, Lieutenant Owen and Sergeant Lynch of the academy staff. Captain Moran joined Sheehan's staff just as police education was getting underway. His contributions would help develop one of the nation's foremost criminal justice programs.

Joining Grady and Moran in an early 1963 move to a second career, was Major John J. Kelly. Kelly had been involved in a unique situation in the Volpe Administration's final hours. Governor Volpe had nominated him as Registrar of Motor Vehicles. Such a nomination, at that time, required confirmation by the Governor's Council. Kelly narrowly failed to get that body's confirming vote. With Major Kelly's departure, Commissioner Giles named Julian Zuk the new adjutant. Zuk had ben serving as the senior captain and division inspector. Captain Thomas D. Murphy moved up to that responsibility. Leadership positions thus continued to evolve, an eventuality imposed periodically by the statutory mandate that prohibited service in the uniformed branch after age fifty.

Other events of note transpired during the spring of 1963. Some were procedural. Others had substantial impact on the organization and its policies. For example, uniformed officers for the first time were issued metallic name plates. These were worn over the right breast pocket, and bore the officers' initials and last name. It seems now an insignificant happening. At the time, however, the idea met resistance. Many felt it an unnecessary "extra," not really needed. The name plate in time became accepted as an appropriate part of the uniform. The force had grown considerably since the days when each officer knew all the others. The total complement was close to six hundred, and the new "I.D.'s" were needed as much by the men as by the general public.

THE HUNDRED CLUB

Commissioner Giles had been concerned for some time about the families left behind when a public safety officer was killed in the line of duty. Aware of a new concept called the "100 Club," he sought inclusion of the state police in its benefits program. Preliminary inquiries led to formal negotiations, and, finally, to inclusion of the state force in the fiscal protections provided by the philanthropic organization. To finalize the agreement, Giles invited to his office Sheriff Howard Fitzpatrick and Mr. George Swartz. Fitzpatrick was sheriff of Middlesex County, and Swartz was a Boston insurance executive.

A group of Detroit businessmen had become seriously concerned for police and fire families when the breadwinner was suddenly killed. They knew there were death benefits, and pensions. But these did not provide the assistance required by a widow and children suddenly deprived of the family's income. The answer, they believed, was to make certain that such families would not be left wanting. Out of that concern had come the "100 Club." Each member donated $100 per year. Those funds would provide immediate benefits to those left behind by the sudden death of a public safety officer.

Fitzpatrick and Swarz, backed by area businessmen, had spearheaded the program in the Bay State. Their meeting with Commissioner Giles did not take that long. But it was an important one. When it was over, state police personnel were covered by the club's fiscal program. Those benefits, a number of times since, have eased the economic pressures of families who have lost a loved one.

Not long after that meeting, an enforcement operation almost created the need for the very protection assured by The Hundred Club, as it later became officially known. This was no ordinary police investigation, but, rather, one of the most dramatic enforcement strikes ever to have involved state police personnel.

The *Boston Globe's* June 24, 1963 editions headlined the story: "One Shot Dead in Police Ambush — Pal Critically Wounded at Towne Line House, Lynnfield." The words struggled to describe an explosive shootout. Investigators had learned that two thugs would take the Towne Line House, almost directly across route one from the Lynnfield barracks, right after the weekend's large cash receipts. The *Globe* reported the swift and deadly action that followed:

> One gunman was shot dead and a second critically wounded about 9:20 this morning by state troopers at the Towne Line House restaurant on Rte. 1, near Rte. 128, Lynnfield. The two masked men were shot down by State Police who had been staked out in the restaurant since receiving a tip two weeks ago that the place was to be held up. Police tentatively identified the dead gunman as Atwood "Ackie" White of Polk St., Charlestown, a former inmate of State Prison. Critically wounded and not expected to live is James A. "Barney" Johnson, ex-convict who celebrated his 41st birthday yesterday...

The *Globe* continued the fascinating details of a bold robbery attempt gone awry in the presence of state police weaponry:

> The gunmen were first spotted driving by the building by Boston Det. Edward J. Walsh of the Intelligence Bureau, who three weeks ago received a tip that White and Johnson were going to hold up the restaurant on Monday, after a good week-end business. It was estimated that $12,000 to $15,000 in receipts was in the building this morning. Walsh said the gunmen drove by the place five times before entering the driveway... The pair entered a door leading to the cellar and went up a flight of stairs into the kitchen.
> There Johnson, first to enter, pointed a .32 automatic at Lieutenant John Collins, State Police ballastician, who was posing as a chef. He told Collins 'this is a stickup.' At this point Collins hit the floor and State Police Captain John Moriarty, hiding in the kitchen, stepped out and said, 'Johnson, this is the state police. Drop your gun.' Johnson fired at Collins. The bullet hit a refrigerator and fragments hit Capt. Robert D. Murgia, commanding officer of Troop A, Framingham. The fragments struck Murgia over the left eye and pierced his straw hat.
> Both officers fired at Johnson, and he was hit. He followed White down the stairs where they were met by a volley of shots from Trooper Harold

Reddish. They staggered out to the driveway where more state troopers were waiting, several with sawed off shotguns. A blast from one of the shotguns hit White in the face and he fell, mortally wounded. Johnson was hit several times, and collapsed against the side of the building.

It was a wild and dangerous encounter. Trooper John Regan had been on lookout with Boston detective Walsh, and had relayed word to those posted inside. After White and Johnson had parked in the restaurant driveway, Trooper Robert Letendre had blocked their escape with his cruiser. A ring of armed troopers then snapped shut a trap that no one, not even two desperate gunmen, could hope to penetrate. Moriarty, Murgia, Collins, Regan, Reddish and Letendre were backed up by an impressive support force including: Lieutenant Peter Zuk, Detective Sergeant John D. Butler, Sergeant James H. Halloran, Corporal Donald D. Callahan, and Troopers Daniel L. Delaney, John R. O'Donovan, John P. Tobin, Eugene L. Murphy, Arthur W. Quinlan and Aime J. Blouin. Each played a critical role in blunting the daring efforts of White and Johnson to rob the famed eating establishment.

Deserving accolades were accorded the law officers who had risked their lives in discharge of a law enforcement responsibility. Commissioner Frank Giles commended them publicly. Governor Endicott Peabody presented each with a special citation on behalf of the Commonwealth's citizens. And, in a touch of irony, the men received a standing ovation the next night at a state police testimonial held at Caruso's restaurant, just minutes from the Towne Line House.

The occasion was a retirement tribute to Captain James J. Stavredes, commanding officer of Troop D, Middleboro. Warren Rockwell, long an avid supporter of the state police, was toastmaster. He spoke briefly of the job the men had done at great risk to their own lives, and joined the large crowd in a standing ovation for the officers, many of whom were present at the Stavredes' testimonial. It was a fitting tribute, one that emphasized the public's appreciation for one of the most dramatic examples of law enforcement capability ever demonstrated by members of the statewide enforcement agency.

The uniformed branch had a change in its top uniformed post on the first day of 1964. Lieutenant Colonel Carl M. Larson closed a 23 year career on that day. Major Julian Zuk succeeded Larson. The promotion capped Zuk's career which had begun with the "hurricane" class in 1938. Captain Thomas D. Murphy moved up to major and adjutant in the same promotional orders. Those were to be the final top level elevations made by Commissioner Giles. He was shortly to leave the commissioner's office, following almost three years in the complex administrative post. Giles had seen the organization through several key junctures, an era when strongly held military traditions were coming under increasing pressure from changes then accelerating in the larger society.

Foremost of these had been the assassination of President John F. Kennedy the prior November in Dallas. That poignant tragedy had left the state police, and, indeed, the world, in a state of unbelieving shock. It had been an especially hard blow for those in the state force who had developed a close personal relationship with that man of destiny. Several had helped to provide the comfort that comes from long time friendships when the Kennedy family returned to Hyannisport in the immediate aftermath of Dallas.

Events, inexorably, moved on. Governor Endicott Peabody on April 16, 1964 appointed Robert W. MacDonald of Sandwich as the state's public safety commissioner. MacDonald was a Boston native. He had graduated from its public schools, had served five years in the U.S. Air Force during World War II, and had later taken his law degree from Suffolk University.

Commissioner MacDonald was not well known to the men of the state force. He had, however, served in key public positions, first as Bourne town moderator, and, for several years, as assistant district attorney for the counties of Bristol, Barnstable, Dukes and Nantucket. Moreover, in 1960, he had made a bid for national office, losing a close race for the congressional seat from the Cape Cod district. That experience helped him to address the wide variety of issues that daily came to the commissioner's office.

An early one, fortunately, was not too difficult for the new commissioner. Longtime Chief of Detectives Joseph C. Crescio earlier had completed almost four decades in the state force. Crescio had been the first to head up the detective branch following uniformed service, begun in 1923. When the veteran closed his distinguished career, Detective Lieutenant Michael J. Cullinane had become captain and chief of the detective branch. That had been a popular appointment. Cullinane was a "policeman's policeman." Moreover, he was an immense human being, one of the finest men ever to have served in the department, and he did an outstanding job with a taxing accountability.

Following Cullinane's tenure, Commissioner MacDonald on May 10, 1964 named Captain Daniel I. Murphy supervisor of statewide detective operations. None was more prepared for a responsibility that had increased substantially in its scope since the days, ten decades earlier, when the original "State Constabulary" operated out of a small office on Bromfield Street in downtown Boston. Murphy had touched about every base in the organization, from recruit trooper in 1934, to the commissioner's post in the early fifties. He had organized and staffed a new division of subversive activities, and had run the sensitive operation throughout its early experiences. Now he assumed a major administrative post, one he would direct for the remainder of his four decades in the state force.

Commissioners traditionally had uniformed aides who worked with them, assisting with key administrative details. Commissioner MacDonald may have been the only one who appointed the first uniformed officer he met. MacDonald, new in office, had completed an evening Boston appointment without having transportation to his Cape Cod home. Captain Edward J. Teahan was with him. Teahan contacted a cruiser by radio. Arriving shortly was Trooper Richard N. Loynd. Within moments Commissioner MacDonald was enroute to his home.

During the trip, the fledgling commissioner observed that he did not yet have a uniformed officer assigned to him. Loynd made no response, certain that someone had been selected for the key post. That had long been the accepted practice. But MacDonald insisted, and, arriving at his residence, asked the trooper to pick him up the next day. That initial meeting culminated in Trooper Loynd's permanent assignment to the commissioner's office. Had Loynd not been on patrol that evening, in that area, they perhaps would never have met. As it turned out, he served Commissioner MacDonald ably throughout his tenure. That service brought Trooper Loynd his first promotion, and opened a career path that brought him eventually to the top ranks in the state force.

The men of the uniformed force were advantaged to have had Trooper Loynd working closely with the new commissioner. One of the administrative problems that persisted was that of "time off."

By the mid-sixties, the issue was a difficult one. The work week remained just under one hundred hours; a stark contrast with most other employment. Moreover, the question was receiving increased attention in the state legislature, and, predictably, in the far flung barracks' system.

Commissioner MacDonald shortly issued an order reducing the work week to 92 3/4 hours. This was accomplished by changing the return from a day off to noon rather than 8 a.m. The official hour for starting a day off remained 5 p.m. Troop commanders were authorized, and encouraged, to allow a trooper to begin his day off earlier if adequate coverage were available. This new system became effective on May 15, 1964, and constituted the so-called 92 hour week.

The following September 4, the department's patrol responsibilities were substantially increased with the opening of the nine mile in-town extension of the Massachusetts Turnpike. The new roadway was officially dedicated in exercises led by Governor Endicott Peabody and Richard Cardinal Cushing. The ceremonies were held at the Weston entrance to the new facility, and speakers paid tribute to the man most directly responsible for the modern throughway, the late William F. Callahan, formerly chairman of the Turnpike Authority. The chairman's widow had been too ill to attend. The previous day, however, in a sensitive gesture, the new chairman, John T. Driscoll, had driven her over the road and showed her the plaque placed in her husband's memory. The in-town extension, Driscoll pointed out, brought state police into the heart of Boston. It was a unique sight as troopers patrolled through the capital city, but one to which Bostonians soon became accustomed.

Captain Michael E. Faherty supervised a uniformed complement of 24 officers quartered in temporary facilities in West Newton. The additional personnel brought the Troop E complement to seventy, providing around-the-clock patrols of the 132 miles from the New York state line in West Stockbridge to downtown Boston. The following April, the headquarters operation moved to a new building at the Beacon Park interchange in the Allston section of the capital city. That move completed a phased transition that had begun when the Pike's first troopers slept at the interchanges in May of 1957.

THE CENTENNIAL YEAR

Shortly after the in-town pike dedication, Lieutenant Colonel Julian Zuk completed a state police career begun in 1938. Following Zuk's retirement, Commissioner MacDonald on November 1, 1964 named Thomas D. Murphy the new executive officer. Murphy, a member of the 1941 recruit class, thus assumed the uniformed branch's highest post. Moving up to major and adjutant was Captain Robert D. Murgia. Staff Captain and Division Inspector Harold Ellis completed the new general headquarters staffing alignment.

The final month of 1964 brought more changes as Commissioner MacDonald announced his intention to leave office. Without delay, Governor Peabody appointed Richard R. Caples as the state's new public safety head. Caples was a well known Boston lawyer and had served as an assistant attorney general. In addition, he had represented the Brighton section of Boston in the Massachusetts Senate where he had actively supported progressive criminal justice legislation. The Caples' tenure coincided with the centennial anniversary of the founding of the Massachusetts State Police. Although there had been many changes in form and function, there was in fact a direct line from the 1865 founding of the State Constabulary to the 1965 organization known as the Division of State Police in the state's Department of Public Safety.

Commissioner Caples set out to ensure that the centennial year would be one to remember. It proved to be all of that. The first of a series of public events was held on the academy grounds on May 22, 1965, conducted in conjunction with the annual memorial services. The ceremonies were attended by approximately two thousand, many of whom were former members of the uniformed branch. Following the traditional memorial program, the public was treated to a display of state police capabilities and equipment. Featured were the agency's latest rescue equipment, ambulance cruisers, radio equipped motorcycles, and, of course, the faithful Bloodhounds. It was the most colorful public exposition to that time, and its theme was to be repeated throughout the centennial year.

A feature of the day long activities was the awarding of a new service medal. Sergeant Edward R. MacCormack had done the design work. Men with ten, fifteen and twenty years of service received the recognition. Over sixty were honored on the parade field that day. First to step up for the coveted award was the academy staff. Included were: Lieutenant William J. Owen, and Sergeants Robert F. Lynch, Martin A. Murphy and Charles W. Gilligan. Officers who had earned the service awards and who were not present, received them at subsequent events held throughout 1965.

The week following the academy ceremonies witnessed a truly unique happening in Boston. On the evening of May 30, in Symphony Hall, Maestro Arthur Fiedler conducted the famed Boston Pops in a program entitled, "State Police Night at the Boston Pops." Several hundred state police officers, families and friends attended the musical tribute to the state force. Fiedler was also chairman of the Citizen's Centennial Commission. He joined that evening with Governor and Mrs. John A. Volpe and Commissioner Caples and his wife in welcoming the enthusiastic audience to the unique musical tribute to the state's law enforcement agency. It was a memorable evening.

State Police "Night at the Pops" was followed in August by "State Police Night at Fenway Park." The Red Sox hosted some two thousand present and former troopers, and their families. A uniformed honor guard opened pre-game ceremonies in recognition of the state force's ten decades of public service. And, in a first, Commissioner Caples presented the new Medal for Meritorious Service to John J. Kulik and John R. O'Donovan, Jr., of the uniformed branch. The two veterans had earned the distinctive recognition for enforcement actions taken at substantial risk to their own safety.

Richard R. Caples was succeeded as Commissioner of Public Safety on September 29, 1965 by Leo L. Laughlin of Winchester. The *Boston Globe* in covering the appointment reviewed Laughlin's credentials: "Laughlin, once mentioned prominently for in the Boston police commissioner's post, is a twenty-seven year veteran of the FBI. He joined the bureau in the Boston office shortly after taking his law degree at Catholic University, Washington, D.C., in 1935." The *Globe* focused on the new commissioner's enforcement experience, noting that his FBI service had seen him "assigned to fourteen cities across the country," including duty as agent-in-charge of the Boston office.

During his lengthy enforcement career, Laughlin had, in addition to Boston, worked in New York, Washington, Newark, Cincinnati, St. Paul, Baltimore and Providence. The Bureau had also tapped him for special assignments. One was to the Federal Surplus Property Administration where he set up that agency's compliance and control division. Immediately prior to his appointment by Governor John A. Volpe, Laughlin had owned a Boston management security consultant firm, after having served as vice president of Harrington and Richardson, a Worcester firearms manufacturing company.

Commissioner Laughlin was no sooner settled in his new post than it became his pleasant chore to finalize details for the department's centennial banquet. The program was held on the evening of October 23, 1965 in the Sheraton Boston hotel. Some eight hundred attended. Many were state police personnel and their families. They saw a long time state police friend, J. Gordon "Buck" MacKinnon, handle the toastmaster's duties with an expert's finely honed touch.

Governor John A. Volpe gave the principal address. He delivered a talk that made every state police officer in the room proud of his calling. The state's chief executives had always been close to the "Governor's Police Force," as the state force was sometimes called. None, however, had been more concerned than Volpe that personnel policies be improved in order to attract the best of the state's young men to a career in statewide law enforcement. The chief executive, then in his second tenure as governor, had been out of office in 1963 and 1964. He knew the organization, and he knew many of its officers. His executive leadership would prove a key factor in the salary and personnel increases which marked the remainder of the sixties.

The centennial banquet head table was impressive, a tribute to the department. For example, with Volpe that evening was his lieutenant governor, Elliot R. Richardson. Attorney General Edward W. Brooke joined the state's other constitutional officers on the dais. Many former commissioners were present. Each was introduced, including Daniel I. Murphy then serving as chief of the detective branch. Lieutenant Colonel Thomas D. Murphy and Major Robert D. Murgia represented the uniformed branch. A number of other governmental and law enforcement leaders completed an impressive testimonial of public appreciation to the country's first statewide law enforcement agency.

The centennial banquet properly recognized the total organization, all the men and women who had discharged ten decades of public trust. There were, however, the individual acts, the personal efforts well beyond regular duty requirements, which brought recognition to individuals who had risked their lives in discharge of public duty. Several such officers were recognized in general headquarters ceremonies later in 1965.

Commissioner Laughlin on that occasion presented the state police Medal of Merit to Sergeant Peter R. Haranas. Sergeant Haranas with other troopers, on November 29, 1964, in Carlisle, had surrounded a house barricaded by a mentally deranged individual. The heavily armed fugitive threatened to kill anyone who approached. Ignoring threats to his own safety, Haranas, with Troopers David Baker and Amadeo Imperiali, fired short range gas projectiles into the barricaded residence. The officers rushed in behind the fusilade and ended without further incident an extremely tense and dangerous situation. Their courageous efforts allowed the safe release of a woman and two children held captive by the gunman. Subsequent to the headquarters ceremony, Trooper Baker and Imperiali also received the Medal of Merit for their efforts in the dramatic rescue operation.

At about the same time, the "100 Club" honored two uniformed branch members at that organization's annual fall dinner in Boston's Statler Hilton Hotel. Trooper James T. McGuinness and Henry E. Sullivan of the Leominster barracks were cited for the capture of Ernest R. Robertson and Richard J. Tanguay in Westford. Robertson and Tanguay, parolees from the Billerica House of Correction, had been trapped inside a sports store in the early morning hours. Heavily armed, they were taken at gunpoint by McGuinness and Sullivan. In addition to suitably inscribed watches presented by the Hundred Club, the two troopers were commended in special orders, and each received two days off with pay.

Troopers McGuinness and Sullivan could not have known John F. Horgan. Horgan died about the same time they were accorded public recognition. There was irony in that, because he too had been, in his time, a genuine public hero. Horgan had won the famous Carnegie Medal for Heroism, and he had gained that coveted honor while wearing the distinctive uniform of the state force.

Horgan entered the state police with the class of 1925. He served many years in Troop D, and, in 1940, while a sergeant, passed the examination for the detective branch. Not long after he left the academy, however, he had nearly lost his life in a dramatic rescue operation.

The steamer *Robert E. Lee,* with 263 passengers aboard, had run aground at Manomet during a raging snowstorm in the winter of 1926. Horgan and a number of other troopers had rushed to the scene. The Coast Guard had been trying to reach the stricken vessel. Suddenly, one of the rescue boats capsized. Seven sailors were pitched into the frigid, angry sea. They would be dead in minutes. Horgan moved swiftly, and, with a civilian, got to them in time. All were brought safely ashore, and the rescue operation was completed without further incident.

Corporal John F. Horgan received one of the nation's highest honors, the Carnegie Medal for Heroism, for his selfless, life saving action that cold and snowy night off Manomet's rocky bluffs. His untimely death in the fall of 1965 linked his heroic efforts with those of Haranas, McGuinness and Sullivan almost four decades later. That link exemplified the public service commitment that had, since the beginning, identified members of the statewide enforcement agency.

A PROMOTION LAW

As 1965 closed, the General Court passed landmark legislation affecting every member of the uniformed branch. The bill created a competitive promotional system for all grades from corporal through staff captain. The ranks of lieutenant colonel and major were the only two exempted. The legislative proposal required that examinations be weighted among several factors including a written test, performance evaluation, seniority and oral interviews. This was no ordinary bill. It had profound ramifications for the manner in which officers would be promoted for years to come.

Governor John A. Volpe promptly signed the bill making it law. The state police thus had a new promotional system. The statute would become effective in March 1966. After that, each promotion up to the major's post would be earned through the specified competitive process. Members of the state force would, for the first time since 1942, vie with one another for the coveted promotion that meant so much to one's enforcement career.

It is important to record that substantial controversy preceded legislative enactment. The proposal represented a dramatic change, one especially traumatic to men who had already served for many years. There were strong efforts to block the bill in its long journey through the legislative process. But those backing the reform legislation were committed, strongly convinced that change was needed. Interestingly, a leading advocate of the promotional system was Representative Michael S. Dukakis. He would, one day, become the state's chief executive.

Additional impetus had come from the academic community. There, among other actively involved, Professor Robert Sheehan of Northeastern University was in the forefront, urging publicly and privately that the promotional law be passed. Sheehan had strong allies in the state police. Time has obscured the roles of most, but one who played a significant part in the bill's development and enactment was Corporal Eugene H. Dzikiewicz. Dzikiewicz, long a staffer at the academy, felt strongly that a competitive system was a priority personnel need. He worked long and hard to bring it to reality. When he left the state force to accept a position with Northwestern University's Traffic Institute, he must have felt the satisfaction of knowing that the risks he willingly accepted would benefit the many who would join the uniformed branch long after he had departed.

The promotional law became effective officially in March, 1966. Implementation of the statute presented a formidable administrative challenge. There were really no precedents, nothing to build on. Commissioner Laughlin promptly appointed a task force to spearhead the work. The makeup of the group changed a number of times, but those first assigned included Dzikiewicz and Lieutenant John F. Downey and William J. Owen. They would, with others, work on the project throughout the remainder of 1966 before the first examinations could actually be conducted. During that period, over one hundred promotional vacancies would develop within the uniformed branch.

Meantime, Commissioner Laughlin had moved in February of 1966 to reduce the duty week of the uniformed branch. The last change had been effected by the Commissioner MacDonald on May 15, 1964 when the total work week had been lowered to 92 3/4 hours. Laughlin's directive changed the return time from a day off to 3 p.m, rather than 12 noon. The new schedule also adjusted the starting time on a day off from 5 p.m. to 3 p.m. The net effect was to reduce each duty tour by five hours. Over a seven day period the reduction amounted to 8 3/4 hours, and a new work week of 84 hours. Additionally, troop commanders could allow personnel to begin time off immediately at the completion of a duty tour. This further lowered, on occasion, the weekly hours worked by an individual officer.

The "time off" question by the late sixties had emerged as a public issue. State police wives had formed an association, and, with increasing frequency, were publicly urging fundamental changes in the "time off" system. The movement was especially active in western sections of the state. As early as 1964, a group of wives had met with Commissioner MacDonald and Lieutenant Colonel Zuk to urge modification in the traditional barracks system.

The issue would persist. It was rooted in patrol and enforcement concepts that had served the state's citizens for over four decades. Only through the barracks system could so few have provided so much, for so long. There was no other way that the state police could have done its job during that era without the organization's basic, sustaining foundation; individual barracks located strategically throughout the state.

But the burden had always fallen heaviest on the individual, and his family. That responsibility had been willingly accepted during a time when substantial sacrifices were required throughout national life. As change began to accelerate in the sixties, constraints that had once been accepted without comment became more controversial. It was inevitable, in retrospect, that the structure and procedures of the organization would have to be adjusted to the dynamics then accelerating in the larger society. It was, it can now be seen, simply a matter of time before major changes would eventually come to pass.

That eventuality was hastened later in 1966 with the release of the Massachusetts Taxpayers Foundation's report. Mr. James E. Ellis was the principal author of the far reaching document. Ellis had trained at Michigan State, worked in the planning unit of the St. Louis Police Department, and authored a number of incisive studies on police management practices. Moreover, he lived on Cape Cod and knew well the statewide force and many of its personnel.

The Taxpayer's Report was released late in 1966. The work would prove historically important. A number of principal recommendations would, in time, be implemented. Some of these would have a profound effect on the structure, staffing and law enforcement operations of the state police, especially the uniformed branch. For example, the 1966 document recommended:

- establishment of a formal planning unit.
- a major reorganization of the leadership structure.
- establishment of five administrative bureaus, each to be commanded by a major.
- division of the field forces into two bureaus; western field operations and eastern field operations
- abolishment of the traditional barracks system, with the installations being used as operational command posts.

There were over twenty substantial recommendations in addition to those listed. One urged immediate construction of a new academy, while another supported establishment of an air wing. In fact, a number of the recommendations had already been under active development within the department. For example, Commissioner Laughlin and his predecessors had been trying for some time to convince the legislative leadership that a new academy was absolutely essential. Other of the report's proposals had also been pursued, and were receiving increased policy support.

The study was published at a particularly important juncture. Several of the proposals would have been outrageous if made a decade earlier. But time's passage had transformed radical concepts into feasible proposals. Almost all of the report's recommendations were destined to be implemented during the years that followed. The 1966 Taxpayers Foundation report, then, is perceived in retrospect to have played a key role in organization changes that took place in the years following its publication.

THE INDIVIDUAL

The study had addressed the total organization; it was a comprehensive document. As such, it had not focused on individuals. That had not been its purpose. But the individual officer remained the backbone of the statewide force. This had been true in the early years. It remained so in the late 1960s. Risks attend

descriptions of specific examples of superior law enforcement duty. Left out are scores of similar incidents which merit attention as well. Time, nor space, nor energies, could ever be available in such abundance as to permit the telling of every enforcement story that, in its time, commanded the attention of news media while adding further to the admired public record of the state police.

Now and then, however, an example seems appropriate to establish that such happenings were not uncommon. For example, on Wednesday night, April 27, 1966, Corporal John R. O'Donovan, with other officers, cornered a dangerous fugitive in Boston's Back Bay. Gunfire erupted. Within moments, the entire area was in an uproar. A volley of shots was exchanged in the crowded neighborhood.

The incident lasted only moments. But the cost was high. O'Donovan had been hit, rushed to Massachusetts General Hospital. The fugitive, one Myles Connor, had taken several police bullets and was in grave condition. Commissioner Laughlin, Colonel Murphy, Major Murgia and Captain D.I. Murphy joined the O'Donovan family at Massachusetts General. Word finally came that he would recover. A look of relief lit the faces of those who had rushed to O'Donovan's side. Connor, too, would recover, and stand trial for the Back Bay shooting. As it turned out, he had been in and out of scrapes before. Fate had marked O'Donovan as the one who, with others, would bring Connor to bay that spring night in the Bay State's capital city.

Corporal O'Donovan was an extremely active investigator during that particular era. Just months before the Connor shooting, he and Lieutenant John J. Kulik had trapped Vincent J. Flemmi in a surprise raid on a Brookline apartment. Flemmi, a vicious gunman, had been wanted for a string of serious crimes, including at least one incident of assault with intent to murder. Both Kulik and O'Donovan had been officially commended for their apprehension of Flemmi, and, in addition, each had received the state police Medal for Meritorious Service during the August, 1965, centennial ceremonies at Fenway Park.

There were other individual stories in the mid-sixties, but not all had happy endings. One marked an historic milestone in state police history. George A. Parker, the first executive officer, had died at 78. Forty-five years had fled since a young Captain Parker marched the "First Class" down Southboro Road to begin the State Police Patrol at Framingham's "Poor Farm." Parker had seen it all: the swearing in on the Capitol's steps that sunny day in September, 1921; the November graduation of the first recruit troop; the five day trek on horseback to establish Troop B headquarters in Northampton. Captain George A. Parker had accomplished much after he left the state force in 1925. But his heart and mind remained always in the organization he helped to found. This was never clearer than when he had reminisced for the last time with some of his old buddies on the occasion of the fortieth anniversary banquet in 1961.

Death that year claimed another influential veteran. He was James P. Ryan, from the very beginning a "trooper's trooper." A member of the 1922 recruit troop, he was for almost three decades involved in most of the significant events affecting the state force. Ryan's face stares out from scores of photographs depicting major milestones in the force's early history. He seemed to be everywhere, on every detail: the Springfield Fair; the Philadelphia Sesquicentennial; the Boston Marathon; the escorts of Wendell Willkie and other presidential aspirants. He made them all.

Lieutenant James P. Ryan's service spanned the first three

decades, from 1922 until late 1950. He represented, as an individual, the founding, growth and fulfillment of the state police idea. He was, clearly, of the "old school," a physical man. But he adjusted to changing times and evolving enforcement practices. He commanded Troop C Holden during 1950 in his last duty tour. That had been light years removed from 1922, the "Poor Farm," horse and tents. Now, some fifteen years following his retirement, he was gone. But his death, and his duty, are noted here lest it not be recorded somewhere that it was James P. Ryan, and hundreds like him, who gave so very much that others one day might wear the same uniform he wore with unabashed pride during the most fulfilling years of his life.

Many of those uniforms were in evidence on August 1, 1966 in the Senate Chamber. Governor John A. Volpe had reappointed Leo L. Laughlin for a five year term as commissioner. The Governor administered the oath of office in the presence of a large gathering, including family, friends and members of the state force. Laughlin had then completed almost a year in office. Now he was embarking on a full, five year tenure in the organization's top administrative post.

One of Commissioner Laughlin's first duties following the state house ceremony was a pleasant one. He would, as was customary, preside at the graduation of a recruit training troop. This was the 47th since 1921, and graduation day was set for Saturday, September 10, 1966. Fifty-one recruits had been looking toward that day since their arrival at the academy on June 1.

One among them was especially eager. He was Francis J. McVeigh, Jr. The name had not especially impressed those who had trained with young McVeigh. They, after all, could not have known his dad, Francis J. "Specky" McVeigh, Sr., a state police legend in his own time. McVeigh, Sr. in 1934 had met his first troopers as a "mess boy." "Mess boys" were lads who cooked and served meals in the barracks system. They were part of the state police "family" along with uniformed troopers, the cook, and the janitor. "Specky" McVeigh had literally grown up in the state police. For years he had prepared meals at the very academy where his son would take his oath as a member of the uniformed branch.

Members of the Forty-Seventh Recruit Troop that day gave an outstanding demonstration of their skills. Commissioner Laughlin formally reviewed the training class, assisted by Captain Stanley W. Visnioski, Jr., the academy commandant. Governor John A. Volpe praised the recruits, while alerting them to their public responsibilities. The most poignant moment, however, was when Trainee Francis J. McVeigh, Jr. became Trooper McVeigh. Pinning on his badge was his dad, known to legions of troopers simply as "Specky." Speck, wearing his best whites, knew a moment of great pride as he welcomed his son into the uniformed branch.

Young McVeigh's training troop had benefited from a pay raise while at the academy. The salary hike had become effective on July 1, 1966 and it increased a trooper's starting salary to $5,990, and the maximum to $7,581. The trooper's so called "job group" was also changed from eleven to twelve. The statutory shift brought another increase on November 27, bringing a trooper's maximum yearly salary to $8,034.

The salary schedule still noted "and M," meaning "and maintenance." This was the $360 annual value placed on barracks room and board. In fact, one could not have purchased the quality food and food service provided in a state police barracks for five times that amount. Men in general headquarters continued to receive an additional monthly check of thirty dollars in lieu of the maintenance

provision. They, however, went home after each duty shift. "GHQ" duty remained a very desirable assignment through the remainder of the sixties.

LEADERSHIP CHANGES

Lieutenant Colonel Thomas T. Murphy in February, 1967 completed 26 years of active duty, closing his career in the uniformed branch. Commissioner Laughlin shortly named Robert D. Murgia the new executive officer, and, in the same promotional order, elevated John R. Moriarty to the key post of major and adjutant. Colonel Murgia was then a nineteen year veteran, training with the April, 1948 recruit troop. In his early years he had served throughout Troop A, later doing a tour as a lieutenant in Troop C, Holden. Murgia had been promoted to captain in 1963, assuming the troop commander's post at Framingham. That was followed by his December 1964 promotion to major and adjutant, a position he held until assuming the highest career rank in the uniformed branch.

Major Moriarty early in 1947 enlisted with the first training class after World War II. His early assignments were in Troop D Bridgewater, followed by an extended tour in the western part of the state. Then followed field service throughout Troop A Framingham, including duty as the first commanding officer of the Lynnfield barracks when that installation opened. As a commissioned officer, Major Moriarty had been extremely active with the Special Service Unit, a general headquarters strike force. The strike group during the sixties was in the vanguard of the department's accelerated efforts against organized crime, gaming, drug operations and the like. Moriarty had performed yeoman service in that capacity, and, in 1965, he had been named commander of Troop F, Logan International Airport.

While Murgia and Moriarty assumed new duties, several men closed their careers. One was Lieutenant John J. Regan, originally a World War II "ETSPO," and, later, a member of the 1949 recruit troop. Regan commanded the Special Service Unit after Moriarty, and had carved out a superior record in all types of vice investigations. He especially became a scourge of smut peddlers, an activity picking up momentum in the late sixties. And Regan, as a corporal, had been the first recipient in 1957 of the Trooper of the Year award presented by the Former Troopers Association. Leaving at about the same time was William M. Cloran. Cloran had been on the leading edge of those seeking higher education while in the police service. Police education was just emerging and he had studied for the bachelor's degree at Boston College. He later earned his law degree, and, subsequently, became top administrative officer of the Supreme Judicial Court, a key post in the state's criminal justice system.

Separations were not always accompanied by pleasant memories. A few were tragic, sad beyond words. Such were the circumstances of Corporal Joseph J. Cooney's accidental death in a January, 1967 gun cleaning accident in general headquarters. Cooney was a twenty year veteran with a legion of friends. He fought the gunshot's effects for weeks, finally succumbing on March 7. More than fifty uniformed officers attended his Roslindale funeral. It was a final gesture of respect to a man who had spent two decades of his life in the uniform he wore to the grave.

Trooper Dominick J. Arena in that spring of 1967 also closed his career, following some thirteen years of service. Arena was an outgoing personality, known popularly as "Jim." He could not have imagined that he was soon to become an international celebrity.

After all, he had accepted a "quiet" post as police chief in Edgartown, on Martha's Vineyard Island.

That was in 1967. In July 1969, Chief Arena would be at the center of events in the aftermath of Senator Edward F. Kennedy's motor vehicle accident at Dyke Bridge on Chappaquiddick Island. Arena, the former trooper, looked out from television screens for weeks on end as the tragedy quickly became an international media event. His professional demeanor was such that the Boston Press Photographers later presented a special commendation to him, citing his handling of one of the most complex and sensitive enforcement responsibilities in the Bay State's history.

PROMOTIONS

Meantime, work had progressed on implementation of the new promotional system. All elevations through the rank of staff captain had been frozen since March 6, 1966, and, by spring 1967, there were about one hundred vacancies. Finally, in May 1967, written tests were ready. The examinations were scheduled for that month.

Several hundred men had studied hard, preparing for the written tests. They reported to Framingham State College on a Saturday morning. These were the first competitive tests since 1942, and, moreover, the first for all ranks in the history of the uniformed branch. Competition was keen. For example, ten captains were vying for a single vacancy at the rank of staff captain. Although there was substantial tension, the tests went off without a serious hitch. The new promotional system was a fact. It was, in many ways, a new era for the organization and its personnel.

There followed throughout that summer the remaining parts of the comprehensive examinations. Seniority was computed for each officer, and tedious performance evaluations had to be completed on every applicant. In addition, oral interview panels were appointed and each applicant appeared before such a board. Because of specific restrictions in the statute, this important section of the tests presented substantial administrative problems. For example, three majors from other state police organizations made up the interview board for the ten men contesting for the single vacancy in the staff captain rank. The entire process placed a severe administrative strain on the uniformed branch. But it was a critical activity, one made particularly sensitive because promotions had not been made at any rank in well over a year.

Finally, on November 1, 1967, a public promotional ceremony was held on the academy's parade field in Framingham. It was then almost two years since the promotional system, Chapter 785 of the Acts of 1965, had been signed into law. The long wait was over. Families and friends had gathered to witness the colorful ceremonies. Commissioner Laughlin presided, assisted by Lieutenant Colonel Murgia, Major Moriarty and Captain William J. Owen, the academy commandant.

There were 124 officers promoted that morning to the following ranks: one staff captain, two captains, thirteen lieutenants, 27 staff sergeants, 39 sergeants and 42 corporals. It was truly a unique occasion, one without precedent, and one, almost certainly, that would never occur again in quite the same way. In retrospect, November 1, 1967 marked an historical juncture wherein the traditional promotional process, then in use some 46 years, changed to a system of personnel evaluation and selection prescribed by statutory mandate.

SUMMER UNIFORMS

The long awaited promotions had been welcomed with enthusiasm. But an even greater reception had greeted another administrative move which had come, most appropriately, during the summer of 1967. The uniformed branch, for the first time in its history, had issued *summer uniforms*. Readers may wonder at the emphasis on such a routine happening. In fact, it was a breakthrough of the highest order. A trooper, his name is lost to time and events, had earlier been quoted as saying in response to a newspaper's inquiry: "the commissioner who gets summer uniforms will win a place in the department's history."

There were reasons for all the fanfare. For almost five decades personnel in the state force had *worn the same uniform* on the summer's *hottest day* as in the *coldest weather* mounted by a New England winter. It seems, now, incredible. But it was so. A trooper wore the same high boots (formerly high shoes and puttees), heavy woolen breeches, heavy woolen, long sleeved shirt, buttoned collar and tie, gun belt and cross strap, and finally, heavy cloth hat, all year round. There was no seasonal change. While summer vacations had arrived in 1955, it was twelve more years before the men in two-tone blue were able to don much cooler, lightweight uniforms to patrol the broiling roads of the Bay State's far flung highway system.

The new material retained additional colors. Importantly, however, a new shirt, with open neck and short sleeves, brought much relief. Slacks replaced the revered breeches and boots, and a new modified holster added further to an officer's comfort. In addition, straw campaign hats replaced the heavy, woolen variety that had warmed many a state police skull. In summary, new, lightweight uniforms made the summer of 1967 one that ranks right up there with the major evolutionary changes in the organization's history. Some may doubt the authenticity of that judgment. But numbered among such doubters will not be those hundreds of suffering souls who, on summer's hottest day, wore uniforms designed to protect against the harshness of winter's cruelest blows.

As the summer uniforms were phased in, two men who had long supported the change completed their service in the Department of Public Safety. One, Clayton L. Havey, had been deputy commissioner for some twelve years, having begun his tenure in 1955. Havey previously had served two terms in the House of Representatives, and for thirteen years had been a member of the Governor's Council. He had coordinated construction of a number of new barracks during the late fifties and early sixties. He would later return, in a symbolic appearance, for the September 26, 1969 ground breaking for the new State Police Academy.

Also retiring that summer was Detective Lieutenant Michael J. Cullinane, a "policeman's policeman," and, more importantly, a wonderful human being. Cullinane had begun his enforcement career in 1928 with the Metropolitan District Police, the "Mets." He then served thirteen years with the Boston Police, winning both the Department's Medal of Honor and the coveted Walter Scott Medal for Valor. In 1943 he was appointed a state police detective lieutenant, a post he filled with distinction for 25 years. Lieutenant Cullinane had been captain and acting chief of the detective branch following Captain Joseph C. Crescio's 1961 retirement. He served in that capacity until 1964, earning respect for his even handed management of a complex enforcement responsibility. But, always, he was more admired for his personal qualities, values that transcended his enforcement skills.

Detective Lieutenant Michael J. Cullinane was not, in his time, especially well known to uniformed troopers across the state. Nor could he have met most of those who followed him because he did not, after his departure, live for many years. But his personality and strong sense of ethics left an imprint on those privileged to have known him, and, importantly, upon the organization in which he served. That much, at least, merits the awareness of those who one day will serve in the same state force to which he committed the most productive years of his long enforcement career.

Nineteen sixty-eight would be remembered as the year of the state police academy. No less than four recruit troops went through their paces in Framingham during the twelve month span. The Forty-Ninth Recruit Troop had actually trained during the fall of 1967. Graduation was held in Commonwealth Armory on a Friday evening, January 12, 1968. Captain William J. Owen had returned to the academy as commandant, succeeding Captain Stanley W. Wisnioski, Jr., who had held that post for several years. Owen was supported by an able staff, each a specialist in one or more of the technical areas in an expanded curriculum. They were: Staff Sergeant William H. Irving, Staff Sergeant Robert J. Fitzgerald, Sergeant James V. Oteri, Corporal Thomas R. Mulloney, Corporal Frederick A. Henley, and Troopers Robert E. Hunt and John P. Tobin.

The staff led the recruit troop through a colorful graduation program. Commissioner Laughlin inspected the new officers, accompanied by a man later to play a central role in state police activities, Lieutenant Governor Francis W. Sargent. Lieutenant Colonel Murgia and Major Moriarty handled troop assignments, while Reverend John E. Hartigan and Reverend Frank A. Bauer, State Police Chaplains, conducted traditional prayer services. Secretary of State John F.X. Davoren administered the oath of office to the 57 graduates, and the fledgling officers received special awards from Frank B. Holland of the American Red Cross and Merrill E. Wright of the New England Police Revolver League.

Three days after the January 12 armory graduation, the Fiftieth Recruit Troop reported to the academy. These appointments had exhausted the applicant pool, and comprehensive tests for the uniformed branch were held on March 30, 1968. The written examinations were conducted in two locations. Some 827 candidates were certified at Boston College, while 284 took the same qualifying tests at the Springfield Armory. The total of 1,111 applicants compared favorably with the 915 who had taken entrance tests in 1967. Physical agility tests, background investigations and oral interviews for those who passed the written tests continued throughout that spring.

In the meantime, members of the Fiftieth Recruit Troop completed training requirements. Graduation was held on May 4, 1968 on the academy grounds. The 59 graduates were posted to field assignments, survivors of an original complement of 78 that had reported to the academy on January 15.

The new recruit pool enabled appointment of two additional training troops that year. The fifty-first class graduated on September 7, and the fifty-second the following December. A total of 230 men had completed academy requirements, and had been sworn into the uniformed branch between January and December of 1968. The academy staff had performed ably under extreme pressures, while, at the same time, ensuring that traditional disciplines and scholastic achievement were maintained.

The accelerated training resulted from an increase in the authorized strength of the uniformed force. The department's request for one hundred additional officers received Governor Volpe's strong support, and was endorsed by the legislature. Thus, by the end of 1968, there were 622 uniformed men in the state force. In addition, seventy were assigned to the Massachusetts Turnpike, while some forty more were stationed at Troop F, Logan International Airport. The overall uniformed complement, therefore, stood at 732 at year's end. The Turnpike and Port Authorities annually reimbursed the Commonwealth for personnel and equipment costs.

There was also a salary boost. The increase brought a trooper's starting salary to $7,389 per year. A six step schedule of increases raised the maximum pay to $9,074 annually. That represented, at the time, a major breakthrough. That top figure, not too many years earlier, had been well beyond the reach even of the highest ranks in the uniformed branch.

Nineteen sixty-eight also marked a particularly poignant juncture in state police history. Alfred E. Foote died that May at 86. Forty-seven years had passed since General Foote directed efforts to recruit, train, organize and assign the first members of the "State Police Patrol." Foote had seen the idea through to fruition, serving in the commissioner's post until 1933. Now, at the close of the department's fifth decade of public service, he was gone. His passing, and the earlier death of Captain George A. Parker, closed symbolically the era spanning the founding and fulfillment of the state's uniformed enforcement agency.

VOLPE LEAVES

In January of 1969 Governor John A. Volpe accepted appointment as Secretary of the United States Department of Transportation. Volpe had first won the governorship in 1960. Defeated by Governor Endicott Peabody in the 1962 election, he was out of office for two years. In a remarkable political comeback, he regained the governor's office and was again sworn to that high post in January, 1965. Governor Volpe had followed that achievement with yet another, winning in the 1966 election the first four year term in the Commonwealth's history.

Governor Volpe had been close to the state police, there was no doubt about that. He had strongly supported salary increases and improved personnel policies. Throughout his tenures, state police officers participated actively in gubernatorial policy discussions focused on law enforcement issues. As governor, John A. Volpe had enjoyed the ceremony of office. He especially relished official appearances accompanied by state officers wearing the French and electric blue. When he departed the Commonwealth for high national office in the winter of 1969, state police personnel sensed that they had enjoyed a special place with the man who had governed the Commonwealth for six years.

Lieutenant Governor Francis W. Sargent assumed the state's highest office upon Volpe's departure. Sargent had long served in state government, including tenures as an administrator in the Department of Natural Resources and in the Public Works Department. He was an "environmentalist" before the phrase was coined. Moreover, he cared deeply about clean land, sea and air prior to the headlong rush for dictionaries to grapple with a new-old word, "ecology." Sargent, in retrospect, is seen to have assumed office at one of those rare junctures wherein personal biography intersects with the evolution of an organization. As it turned out, his leadership would be the essential ingredient in major structural changes in the uniformed branch during his tenure as the state's chief executive.

Commissioner Laughlin on February 24, 1969 announced the appointment of Walter P. Parker as Deputy Commissioner of Public Safety. Parker, a native of Taunton, had been executive assistant to Attorney General Elliot L. Richardson, and was a policy advisor to Richardson when the latter served as lieutenant governor. Deputy Parker had solid credentials for the administrative post. He had captained a World War II armored division in the European Theatre, winning the Silver and Bronze Stars for gallantry in combat. Then had followed two decades in the Army Reserves, where he rose to the colonel's rank. The new deputy assumed several key responsibilities, including implementation of computer technology in the department's communications system. He would later play a central role in the efforts which resulted in major changes in the enforcement operations of the uniformed branch.

A Turbulent Time

Meantime, the Vietnam War had dragged on, claiming too many of the nation's youth. A national protest movement had steadily gained strength, drawing its sustenance from the same generation dying on the battlefields of the mysterious part of the globe once called French Indochina. The 1968 Democratic National Convention in Chicago had been seriously disrupted by radical protestors. Television coverage transfixed much of the nation as Chicago police tried to handle street disorders for which they had not been prepared. Television's exaggerated focus amplified the clashes. The result was not inspirational, and it signalled an extended period of confrontation between civil authorities and those bent on radical attacks against the nation and its institutions, especially centers of learning.

These seemed especially vulnerable, and Massachusetts long had been a seat of such educational institutions. Yet, one could not have predicted that the state police would meet one of its most difficult challenges in Harvard Yard, the symbolic center of one of the country's great universities. But the spring of 1969 did not lend itself to reliable predictions. And, on April 10, two hundred troopers joined local police in removing radical Students for a Democratic Society from Harvard's University Hall. The protestors had seized the building, demanding abolition of the Reserve Officer Training Corps Program, and, in addition, the resignation of Harvard President Nathan M. Pusey. Negotiations had failed. Reluctantly, President Pusey had requested police assistance.

The *Boston Herald Traveler* reported the sequence of events to yet unbelieving readers: "At 3:30 a.m, Commissioner Laughlin with Deputy Commissioner Walter P. Parker, Lieutenant Colonel Robert D. Murgia, head of the uniformed branch of the state police, and Major John R. Moriarty, led the two hundred State Troopers across the avenue to Commonwealth Armory, where additional riot protection equipment was obtained and all gear checked. Then busses and cruisers were boarded for the trip across Boston University Bridge to Cambridge and Harvard Square." The *Herald* story noted the close coordination between state and local police, "Leaders of the departments received specific instructions not to make any move . . . that could be implied as comprising a sneak attack. With helmets, gas masks, shields and batons, or other full riot protection gear, the police assembled outside Memorial Hall, with cruisers, patrol wagons and busses lined up on the street."

When a final negotiation with those who held University Hall collapsed, Cambridge Mayor Walter J. Sullivan warned student leaders that force would be used to retake the building. At about 5:00 a.m, state and local police units moved in and began clearing the sprawling facility. Before the action ended, 196 demonstrators had been arrested and 32 persons injured, including a number of police officers. Afterward, Commissioner Laughlin, according to the *Herald,* said he was heartsick "that we should have to come to this great seat of learning for something like this." Major John R. Moriarty defended tactical actions, noting that the state force had adhered to good police procedures.

Several days of student rallies followed those enforcement actions in Harvard Yard. Even more disruptive demonstrations would follow during the next several years. These were radicalized by elements who sought to tear down the nation's institutional arrangement without thinking, or worse, caring, how or what would replace them. It was an unsettling time. There were no easy answers. Harvard Yard had represented but one day in the long history of the state police. But its significance was important. Traditionally a rural force, the department was now discharging enforcement responsibilities in urban centers. That was a dramatic change, a departure from traditional duties.

There had always been a remoteness, a professional distance about the state police organization. City dwellers rarely saw a state trooper. The public perception was that of a trooper on horseback, or, later, on a motorcycle, patrolling a rural byway. It was a strong image. The distance strengthened a respectful deference, a perceived sense that a trooper acted decisively and impartially in maintenance of public order. It was a self-fulfilling prophecy. Because it was believed, it was so. And the long, consistent record of such enforcement accomplishments was a cherished value of the organization's personnel.

Now, however, the rapidly emerging social disorders were to present new and different problems. These disruptions required close contact with masses of people, on city streets, under provocative conditions. Traditional responses were no longer appropriate; police actions were evaluated almost instantly, in thousands of living rooms, in living color. A whole new enforcement era was emerging for the state force, and in retrospect, more rapidly than most realized.

April 1969 in Hard Yard portended an increased state police presence to ensure public order in urban communities. The melee at University Hall had signalled that historic change. The issues of the larger society were the determinant. The social dynamics would continue unabated, with important meaning for the state police and its public responsibilities as a law enforcement organization.

Change At The Top

On May 19, a month after Harvard yard, 64 recruits were appointed to the state police Academy. This was the Fifty-Third Training Troop, and its members would be the last to join the uniformed branch in the sixties. Not all of them made it. At the September 6 graduation, fifty would take the oath of office and be posted to initial field assignments. While the recruit troop trained throughout the summer of 1969, important policy changes had occurred. Commissioner Laughlin in July had accepted appointment as Executive Director of the Hundred Club of Massachusetts, the public spirited organization which had done so much for families of policemen and firefighters who died in the line of duty. Laughlin tendered his resignation to Governor Francis W. Sargent effective August 31.*

Leo L. Laughlin had been commissioner since his September 1965 appointment by Governor Volpe. That tenure, coupled with his long service in the Federal Bureau of Investigation, completed more than three decades in law enforcement. Those years were to prove a valuable asset in the management of the Hundred Club's critical support programs for the law enforcement and firefighting service.

Following Laughlin's announcement, the August 29, 1969, *Boston Evening Globe* reported: "State Police Captain, 41, New Public Safety Head." The story continued, "State Police Captain William F. Powers today was named commissioner of public safety by Governor Sargent." Powers had enlisted in the state force with the Thirty-Fifth Training Troop in 1949. During two decades he had served in Troops C, D and A, in that order. Then followed general headquarters assignments during the sixties, including duty in the traffic bureau, and an extended tour as public relations officer.

As the *Globe* noted, the new commissioner was a captain in the uniformed branch at the time of his appointment. He therefore joined former Commissioners Stokes and Murphy in authoring a first in the state force. Commissioner Stokes in 1942 had been the first appointed from the division of state police. Commissioner Murphy's 1950 appointment was the first of a man who had begun his career in the uniformed branch. Later, in 1943, Murphy had been appointed a detective lieutenant and was in the detective branch when appointed by Governor Dever to the department's top post. Powers thus became the first commissioner appointed directly from the ranks of the uniformed branch.

Governor Francis W. Sargent on September 25 administered the oath of office to the new public safety head. The ceremony was held in the Senate Chamber, witnessed by a representative gathering of family, friends and law enforcement officials. The sixties thus closed with a change in the top state police post. The organizational structure, however, had remained remarkably constant, with one major exception. A new troop had been added in the early part of the decade. It was designated Troop F, Logan International Airport. The troop's first commanding officer had been Captain Edward J. Teahan, later to rise to senior leadership posts in the uniformed branch.

At the end of the decade, Deputy Commissioner Walter P. Parker assisted with the department's administration. Lieutenant Colonel Robert D. Murgia continued as executive officer of the uniformed force, while John R. Moriarty served as major and adjutant. Staff Captains Edward P. Tonelli and Melville R. Anderson functioned in key roles as division inspectors. Staff Captain Francis T. Burke managed complex duties as supply officer, while Staff Captain John J. Hyde served as civil defense officer.

In the final months of the sixties, the field troops were commanded by a veteran corps of officers. Each had enlisted in the years immediately following World War II. They were posted as follows:

- Captain John F. Downey — Troop A, Framingham
- Captain Americo J. Sousa — Troop B, Northampton

Following Commissioner Laughlin's resignation Governor Sargent in August, 1969 named the writer public safety commissioner. Accounts of that tenure are paraphrased from public documents and news stories, or quoted directly from the cited source. Related items are presented in the third person.

- Captain Stanley W. Wisnioski, Jr. — Troop C, Holden
- Captain Edward F. Murphy — Troop D, Middleboro
- Captain Michael E. Faherty — Troop E, Mass. Turnpike
- Captain Robert E. Herzog— Troop F, Logan Airport.

Well over one hundred lieutenants and non-commissioned officers staffed general headquarters bureaus, and the more than thirty field barracks. Lieutenant Charles W. Gilligan headed up an academy staff that had trained several hundred recruits during the decade, over two hundred in 1968 alone. There had been in 1969 an increase of fifty positions in the uniformed branch, bringing the authorized complement to 672. There were, in addition, some 125 troopers stationed on the Massachusetts Turnpike and at Logan Airport. The uniformed state force, therefore, was near 800, a far cry from the original fifty who, almost five decades earlier, had set out to patrol the Commonwealth's rural hinterland.

Captain Daniel I. Murphy, then completing 35 years of service, commanded the detective branch. He supervised a force of lieutenant detectives in general headquarters, as well as those handling investigations for district attorneys in the state's fourteen counties.

Several hundred recruits had graduated from the state police academy between January 1, 1960 and December 31, 1969. In so doing, they embraced an enforcement tradition that, by decade's end, had been nearly a half century in the making.

These were those men. They aspired successfully to follow the revered traditions established by their predecessors, and, in so doing, earned the privilege of wearing the respected colors of the Commonwealth's law enforcement organization.

•   •   •

There were no personnel killed in the line of duty in the decade of the 1960s.

The following personnel were among those appointed to the Detective Branch during the 1960s:

Brown, Milo F.	Clarkson, Gordon S.	Veronneau, Raymond
Fay, Thomas J.	Flynn, Bernard J.	Zullas, Robert J.
Doyle, Leo J.	Regan, John F.	Castles, Thomas F., Jr.
Dullea, John J.	Geary, Edward F.	Romanski, Teddy C., J.
Cronin, William F.	Agnes, Peter W.	Asquino, Michael
Powers, George W., Jr.	Masuret, Robert R.	Dillon, John
McNulty, Leo F.	Hoban, Allan F.	O'Donovan, John R.
Butler, John D.	Coughlin, Richard C.	Clancy, Frederick G.
Ahern, Jeremiah E.	O'Connor, Francis T.	Gonyea, Arthur O.
Ambrogne, John R.	Nally, William C.	Hulme, John G.
Mahoney, Raymond G.	Daly, Albert J.	Foley, Martin E.
Walsh, Leo E.	White, William B.	Hunter, Edward F.
DeFuria, James F.	Byrne, Charles L.	Arnold, Joseph A.
Ricciardi, Emilio J.	Irving, William H.	Bergin, William G.
Evans, Thomas F.	Burns, John F.	Dwyer, Joseph L, Jr.
Murphy, Martin A.	Broderick, William G.	Duemling, Alfred
Melchionno, Richard J.	Fitzgibbon, James J.	Henley, Frederick A.
Dunn, John J.		

The following personnel were appointed to the Massachusetts State Police Academy during the 1960s:

FORTY-THIRD RECRUIT TROOP

October 7, 1960

Francouer, Robert T	Otenti, Charles Jr.	McKenna, James M.
Kozlowski, Charles J., Jr	Elliott, Richard J.	Riordan, John T.
Delle Chiale, Ronald J.	Finneran, James F.	Tobin, John P.

Branscombe, Edward J.
Sullivan, Robert G.
Lalone, Donald J.
Drewniak, Walter L., Jr.
Cox, Richard D.
Stone, Joseph A.
Nickerson, Leslie M.
Berube, Alvan G.
Lussier, Edward A., Jr.

Dacey, Howard W.
Viens, Joseph R.
Lewis, Richard D.
O'Shea, Richard H., Jr.
Pelkey, Donald L.
Balcom, William E.
Preziosi, Vincent R.
Lopez, Anthony A., Jr.
McCabe, William

Flaherty, John E., Jr.
Noone, Ronald L.
DiTomaso, David W.
Silverbrand, Harold A.
Grillo, Anthony J.
Tobin, Francis X.
King, Joseph A.
Connolly, Gerald J.

FORTY-FOURTH RECRUIT TROOP

July 7, 1962

Bavis, John J., Jr.
Goldman, Robert W.
Wasylow, Peter J.
McGrady. John F., Jr.
Giabbi, John W.
MacDonald, Richard C.
Sott, Donald L.
Fay, Lawrence P.
Rand, Clinton L, Jr.
Bernard, Norman H.
Flaherty, Thomas J.
Flynn, John J.
Celli, Richard P.

Derry, James O.
Fitzgerald, Thomas
Larkin, Paul F.
O'Connell, William M.
Whelan, Richard L.
MacDonald, Frederick B.
Gagne, Donald A.
Gorski, Barry W.
Heitman, Charles E.
Jorritsma, Donald R.
Copello, Francis A., Jr.
Ciulla, Joseph J.

Levings, Howard R.
Magliozzi, Robert P.
Mahoney, Paul B.
Gianquitto, James A.
Grudzinski, Robert G.
Harrington, James W.
Gilman, John W.
Goodale, Alton P.
Stillings, Carleton A.
Sullivan, James P.
Dooley, Raymond T.
Pariseau, Ronald N.

FORTY-FIFTH RECRUIT TROOP

December 14, 1962

McGovern, Frank E.
Sullivan, Henry C., Jr.
Whittier, Bruce V.M.
Ardini, Edward R.
Sweeney, William F.
McGuinness, James T.
Dunn, Robert E.
Towsey, John L., Jr.
Cahoon, Robert M.
Grant, William J.
Carlson, Robert M.
Thomas, Leonard J.
Bailey, Warren W.
Charette, Gerard O.
Frechette, Gilbert K.
Baran, Ronald J.

Sheehan, Bryan J.
Baker, David D.
Cassidy, Henry E.
Powell, David B.
Imperiali, Amadeo E.
Lambalot, Paul E.
Phelan, Vincent R.
Stevens, Henry J.
Tully, Gerald F.
McDonnell, Robert P.
O'Hara, Edward L.
Lowney, Daniel T.
Clark, William T.
Porrovecchio, Lewis W.
Kadra, Malcolm P.
Kelley, Eugene J.

Johnson, Joseph M.
Currie, Thomas J.
Ellis, Arnold W. Jr.
Moran, David W.
Sayers, Robert A.
Scott, Arthur J., Jr.
Shimkus, Michael J.
O'Brien, Paul E.
Sullivan, Jerold H.
Dumas, Richard C.
Garvin, William A.
Hunter, James R.
Headd, Martin J., Jr.
Hardcastle, Thomas F.
Gilbert, Carl V.

FORTY-SIXTH RECRUIT TROOP

June 26, 1964

Hanlon, John J., Jr.
Lenti, Constance L., Jr.
Campbell, Chester W. Jr.
Brown, Edward M., Jr.
Dolan, Peter F., Jr.
McDermott, Arthur L., Jr.
O'Neill, Patrick E.
Grazio, Hector J., Jr.
McDonald, Richard J.
Sedgwick, Bruce E.
Dunphy, Kenneth G.
Neary, Thomas E.
Colburn, James F.
Walsh, George R.
Birmingham, Paul J.
Lennon, William P.
Benson, Richard W.

Munroe, Robin C.
Bohnenberger, Frederick G.
Donoghue, Denis J., Jr.
Treadway, Robert L.
Walsh, Roderick K.
Goodrow, Raymond H., Jr.
Peabody, Kevin W.
Comtois, Robert R.
Mitchell, James E. Jr.
Marois, Paul J.
Lonergan, William M., Jr.
Brosnan, David J.
DiBartolomeo, Carmine A.
Tolos, Ernest G. Dunn,
Sullivan, Henry E.
Campbell, Alexander A., Jr.

McAuliffe, William P.
Wojciehowski, Walter C., Jr.
Howland, John C.
Doherty, Thomas K.
Bellanti, Ronald J.
Joyce, John P.
Naimovich, John Z.
O'Leary, Timothy F.
Hedlund, Paul O.
McKenna, Brian L.
Richards, George C. III
Thomas, Melvyn T.
Birch, Thomas L.
Thomas H., Jr.
DiNatale, Joseph J.
Norton, Michael Jr., Jr.

FORTY-SEVENTH RECRUIT TROOP

September 10, 1966

Beraudo, David C. A.
Mattioli, Eugene D. Jr.
Morse, Robert A.F., Jr.
Ward, Ronald B.
Brooks, William J.
Wheaton, Lloyd E., Jr.
Sorbera, John A.
Gilson, Robert W.
O'Connor, Thomas J. Jr.
Dunderdale, George W.
Roberts, Norman P., Jr.
Peterson, Everett J.
Paluch, Ferdinand
Baron, Norman G.
Hommel, Frank H., Jr.
Collins, Francis P.
Mattie, James A.

Salois, Eugene H. Jr.
Rudnicki, Richard P.
Taylor, Jeffrey W.
Dooling, Thomas M.
Carmody, Cornelius J.
Hiller, Richard P.
Hallice, James F.
Carroll, Maurice M.
Dean, Robert E.
Boyle, Thomas F.
Carchedi, Ralph
Worster, Galen J.
Buckley, Bruce L.
Latham, Charles B.
Spratt, James E.
O'Keefe, William J.
Gundersen, Lawrence J.

Kennedy, Thomas J.
Rembiszewski, Philip D.
Sartori, James C.
White, Donald S.
Conlon, Robert M.
Galloway, John
Anderson, Glenn B.
Roche, Michael J. Jr.
O'Donnell, John M.
Maroney, John T. Jr.
Murphy, Francis R.
David, Richard E.
Howe, William J.
Halloran, Robert B.
McVeigh, Francis J., Jr.
Blanchard, Vincent P.
Gumbleton, John F., Jr.

FORTY-EIGHTH RECRUIT TROOP

September 23, 1967

Harding, Herbert W.
Tervo, Robert L.
French, Paul R.
Pomerleau, Walter M.
Martin, John H.
Tammaro, Carmen V.
Brown, James F.
Vale, Manuel M.

Renaud, Louis A.
Shea, William J.
Bell, Robert A.
Deleva, Joseph A.
McDonough, John M.
Pilkington, John E.
Saccardo, Jospeh C.
Mann, William W.

Johnston, Frederick L., Jr.
Cassidy, Frederick E.
Butler, Walter J.
Skinner, Edward J.
Charest, Marc R.
Farrell, Thomas K.
Cauley, John M.

FORTY-NINTH RECRUIT TROOP

January 12, 1968

Patnode, Ernest H.
Kirby, Robert L.
Bruso, Edward N.
Britt, Gerard D.
Sheehan, Thomas F. Jr.
O'Keefe, Robert J.
McNulty, Thomas J. III
Dempsey, Edward W.
MacDonald, Jospeh H.
Prendable, Frederick J., Jr.
Morrissey, Robert D.
Walsh, Thomas J.
Stockwell, Richard S.
Connolly, Richard W., Jr.
Didick, Joseph D.
Coonan, David A.
Scotti, Arthur M.
Egan, Gary F.
Driscoll, Paul J.

Petersen, David C.
Zalgenis, Benjamin J., Jr.
Cronin, Edward J.
Cody, Donald C.
Brace, Nelson T.
Flynn, Daniel A., Jr.
Fitzgerald, Patrick D.
Stevens, Thomas E.
Sparda, Edward L.
MacDonald, Mark A.
Phair, Michael J.
DeRoche, Richard P.
MacDonald, Arthur
Marshall, James W.
Verock, Michael J.
Wakefield, Richard W.
Harding, Wayne P.
Hamilton, Walter J.
Fernandes, Robert A.

McComiskey, Michael A.
Thompson, Gerald S.
Sullivan, Edward L., Jr.
Savastano, Nicholas T.
Lee, Thomas F.
Risatti, Peter A.
White, Thomas R.
Zundell, Gerald L.
Smith, Bruce E.
Burns, Robert T.
Sutherland, William R.
White, George R., Jr.
DeAngelis, Edward B.
Nasuti, John P.
O'Rourke, John J., Jr.
Reidy, James D.
Werner, Henry F., Jr.
Primeau, David J.
Thompson, Paul J.

FIFTIETH RECRUIT TROOP

May 4, 1968

Newell, Barry F.
St. Germaine, Francis X., Jr.
Anderson, William S.
Henderson, Charles F.

Duke, William E.
Begin, Edward H.
Fitzgerald, Paul J.
Sheehy, Richard N.

Kelly, James P., III
Freeman, John P.
Hippler, Robert F.
Dupuis, Roland L., Jr.

Skroback, Edward S.
Schumaker, John B.
Lajoie, Bernard L.
McLaughlin, Charles A. Jr.
McCauley, Colin P.
Rickheit, Peter M.
Anderson, George W., Jr.
Monahan, Robert F.
Roche, James B., III
Harrington, Edward D. III
Matson, Peter A.
Corbett, Randall J.
Boudreau, Donald P.
MacDougal, Robert J.
Boardman, James S.
Brophy, Charles J.

Peterson, William J.
Long, Robert J.
McIsaac, Michael J.
McSweeney, Donald F.
Bell, Todd R.
Machado, Joseph E.
Tipping, Edward J.
Chamberland, Alan P.
Horn, Lawrence T.
Mason, Stoddard H.
Nosek, Stanley P.
Barnes, Sherwood J.
Morin, David R.
Leonard, James F.
Fay, Martin E.
Jacintho, Robert W.

Leffler, Anthony C.B.
Murphy, Robert
Ramos, Ronald J.
Bertulli, Dennis M.
Cabeceiras, Lawrence T.
Kurgan, Anthony M., Jr.
Ebert, John J.
Rich, Paul F.
Shaughnessy, John K.
Guerriero, Frederick T., Jr.
Botelho, Robert P.
Haley, Robert K.
Cloran, James P.
George, John C.
Ford, Thomas J., Jr.

FIFTY-FIRST RECRUIT TROOP

September 7, 1968

Lisano, William A.
Uminski, Ronald J.
Provencher, David A.
Silvia, Richard F.
Thompson, Alan H.
Windisch, George F.
Mace, John J.
Moschella, Kenneth
Zukowsky, Allan S.
Gardner, Dean J.
Bendonis, John R.
Stevens, Gale P.
Deyermond, William M.
Beaton, Roderick J.
Sproules, Richard J.
Lapriore, Natale L.
Flavin, Dennis J.
Ford, Ronald A.

Murray, James J., Jr.
Klekotka, Robert A.
Garrison, Roland L.
Exarhopoulos, Alexander J.
Abraham, William F.
Dondero, Richard W.
Gore, Richard D., Sr.
Duke, Francis T., Jr.
Chamberlain, Thomas E.
Downey, Richard E.
Kelley, Stephen E.
Norton, Joseph K., Jr.
Savage, Richard P.
Doyle, Michael L.
Hall, Herbert B., III
Erickson, Peter G.
Noberini, Werner S.
Tessicini, Peter T.

Brock, William E. Jr.
Battcock, James J.
Gomes, George L.
Martin, Richard E.
Wiles, Ronald E.
McDonald, James F.
Shea, Ralph F.
Zebrasky, Frederick W.
Fearing, William E., Jr.
Ameral, Harold E.
Johnson, Perley K., Jr.
Bruneau, Joseph T.
Roderigues, Charles A.
Pinkham, Richard D., II
Palmer, Kenneth R., Jr.
Kelly, Donald C.
Olearcek, Francis A.
Quinn, Peter T.

FIFTY-SECOND RECRUIT TROOP

December 9, 1968

Studley, R.H.
Doherty, G.P.
Long, R.A.
Lawson, W.H.
LaPrise, R.J.
Lane, J.C.
Baran, F.P.
Ledwith, W.E.
Smith, J.L., Sr.
DiCarlo, A.J.
Barber, J.A., Jr.
Cote, R.T.
Tribou, R.W.
Whelan, E.L.
Melanson, A.F.
Mazeikus, P.J.
Trapasso, P.A.
Scanlan, J.J.
Guilmet, T.P.
Ashman, L.S.

Bean, L.D.
Decouto, A.W., Jr.
Bradley, D.F.
Kaleta, W.J.
Corstange, W.H.
Rivet, A.R.
Neale, D.A.
Hunt, P.J.
Nardone, F.M.
Vincelette, R.E.
Maher, T.F., Jr.
Ryan, P.R.
Plummer, R., Jr.
Murphy, J.C.
Cedrone, L.P.
Arnold, M.R.
Curtin, J.J., Jr.
Good, J.F.
Stevens, E.R.
Iula, F., Jr.

Finnegan, W.T.
Woods, T.R.
Welch, W.F.
Gillis, C.W.
Whitehead, R.N.
Roche, W.F., Jr.
Wyatt, B.W.
Guilmette, R.J.
Hall, J.J.
Pizzo, A.A., Jr.
Orzechowski, J.P.
Colozzi, S.
Cahill, P.A.
Brunetta, J.J. Jr.
Roberts, F.J., Jr.
Tocchio, R.T.
Simon, J.M.
Crotty, F.C.
Giardino, J.W.
Russell, F.J., Jr.

FIFTY-THIRD RECRUIT TROOP

September 6, 1969

Moschella, Dennis B.
Stone, Kenneth W.
Marino, William R.
Mullen, Robert J.
Lombard, Brian H.
Brooks, Joseph L.
Redding, Lawrence L.
Wise, William A., Jr.
Foley, Michael M., Jr.
Shaughnessy, William M. Jr.
Morse, Frederick J.
Jajuga, James P.
Twomey, Daniel J.
Manning, Leon A.
Doyle, Paul J.
Anderson, Ralph L.
Burke, David J.

Doherty, Henry J., Jr.
Leary, Stephen C.
Perry, John D., Jr.
Micalizzi, Joseph J.
Chaisson, George E.
Ostiguy, Nelson N.
Monahan, John P.
Ardita, Francis R.
Petrie, Steven M.
McMahon, Brian P.
Mendes, Frank W. Jr.
Keeney, Kenneth R.
Ethier, Kenneth D.
Gerstel, Leo R.
Crawford, John H.
Cloutier, Michael H.
Appleton, Charles N. Jr.

Craig, Harry F.
Sheehan, James M.
Pilson, Dale S.
Kilpeck, Robert J.
Dockerty, David J.
McCarthy, Robert N.
Howe, Desmond A.
MacDonald, Charles A.
Harvey, Theodore E.
Gralinski, Michael E.
Gregory, Paul F.
Lavoie, Andre J.
Ferrari, Thomas E.
Cronin, William F., Jr.
Lemay, Denis J.
Devlin, Brain F.

Logan Airport, Boston, December, 1960. Left to Right: John Kenneth Galbraith, Lieutenant Robert E. Herzog, Trooper Robert J. Russo, President-elect John F. Kennedy, Jacqueline Bouvier Kennedy. Mrs. Kennedy is boarding the "Caroline," mainstay of the 1960 presidential campaign. Herzog enlisted in 1948, was captain and Logan's commanding officer prior to mid-1970's retirement.

Hyannis, Cape Cod, November 1960. Lieutenant Colonel John C. Blake escorts President-elect John F. Kennedy from National Guard Armory following election victory statement. Trooper Karl W. Hupfer in background. Kennedy's election energized the state and nation, launched "Camelot's" 1,000 days of soaring promise, ended with a national trauma permanently etched in the country's psyche.

Troop C Headquarters, Holden, 1960. Left to Right: (front) Policewoman Grayce V. O'Dell, Secretary Anne O'Malley, Cook Marie Hudson, (middle) Lieutenant Joseph M. Lane, S/Sergeant Robert D. Murgia, Trooper Joseph M. Desilets, (rear) Captain William J. Mack, S/Sgt. Martin T. Armatage, Jr. Holden in 1930 was first building constructed as a troop headquarters. The day of this photo, memorabilia, including the photo, was enclosed in a time capsule buried in a new entrance walkway.

Commonwealth Armory, Boston, 1960. Left to Right: (standing) Lt. Colonel John C. Blake, Commissioner J. Henry Goguen, Captain James A. Cretecos academy commandant, (seated) Left to Right: Captain William J. Mack, Captain Walter F. Bowen. Bowen enlisted in 1938, led countless recruits through their paces at the academy, retired as major and civil defense officer, in 1997 remained active in Former Troopers' Association.

Troop C, Route 9 Shrewsbury, 1960. Left to Right: T/Sgt. William F. Powers and Captain William J. Mack. Radar was in its infancy, and a "tuning fork" was used to calibrate its accuracy. Mack had enlisted in the state police in 1936, and was captain and Troop C commanding officer. He died shortly after his early 1960's retirement.

State Capitol, Boston, 1961. Left to Right: Lieutenant George A. Luciano, Trooper Richard N. Loynd, Commissioner Frank S. Giles, Major John J. Kelly, Lt. Colonel Carl M. Larson, Former Governor Channing H. Cox, (at desk) Governor John A. Volpe. Volpe signed proclamation commemorating the 40th anniversary of the 1921 founding of the uniformed "State Police Patrol." Governor Cox on May 27, 1921, signed legislation which launched the Bay State's experiment with a uniformed, statewide force.

Boston, September, 1960. Left to Right: (seated) Captain Julian Zuk, Captain William J. Mack, Captain John J. Kelly, Commissioner J. Henry Guguen, Lt. Colonel John C. Blake, Captain Walter F. Bowen, Captain Frederick F. Sullivan, Captain Joseph M. Lynch, (standing) Lt. Walter C. O'Brien, Lt. Vincent L. Power, Lt. Alfred J. Sanders, Lt. William F. Leary, Lt. William J. Sienkiewicz, Lt. Joseph M. Lane, Sergeant Robert H. Cairns. All were honored for 20 years' service at premier of state police film "Dedicated To You," screened in Dorothy Quincy Suite of John Hancock Hall in Boston.

Boston, 1961. First Lady Jacqueline Bouvier Kennedy dances with Governor John A. Volpe. Native sons of the Bay State, President Kennedy and Governor Volpe had just won the nation and state's top offices. It was a heady time, etched permanently in the collective memories of state police personnel who ensured security at the Kennedy Compound in Hyannisport on Cape Cod, and for most of the 1960's served under Governor Volpe's executive leadership.

Troop C, Brookfield Barracks, 1961. Left to Right: (front) B. Johnson, W. Greim, Corporal W. Morrison, Sergeant R. Alzapiedi, Corporal A. England, J. Hammond, (rear) T. Noonan, D. Walwer, J. Hardcastle, E. Branscombe. Alzapiedi in 1947 graduated with the first recruit troop after World War II, long served on the academy staff, was a senior commissioned officer in both field and staff posts, in retirement is a leading participant in Former Trooper Association activities.

Troop B, Pittsfield Barracks, 1961. Left to Right: Thomas A. Finn, George V. Nelson, John J. White, Corporal Edward J. Haughey, Normand McDonald, Corporal John N. Shea, Withrop E. Doty, Jr., Sergeant Stanley E. Bower, William J. Gillespie, Corporal William Konderwicz, Richard J. Clemens, Jr., James M. McCormack. Shea and Doty in 1949 graduated from the state police academy with the 35th Recruit Troop, served into the 1970's in the department's commissioned ranks. Note Troop B's beautiful Berkshire Mountains in background.

Commonwealth Armory, Boston, 1961. Left to Right: (standing, in uniform) Trooper Edward R. MacCormack, Trooper Edwin F. Kelley. (Seated, head table) Left to Right: Senator John O. Pastore R.I., Governor John A. Volpe (behind MacCormack), President John F. Kennedy, Richard Cardinal Cushing (behind Kelley), U. S. House Speaker John W. McCormack. Kennedy's "Camelot" lit up the Massachusetts Political scene for 1,000 days, ending abruptly with the Dallas Tragedy. Trooper MacCormack rose to senior commissioned posts, retired at the major's rank, authored a distinguished second career in the private sector.

Boston, Sheraton Plaza Hotel, 40th Anniversary Banquet, 1961. Left to Right: Former Commissioners Daniel I. Murphy, Daniel A. Needham, Alfred E. Foote, Former Governor Channing H. Cox, Governor John A. Volpe, Commissioner Frank S. Giles, Former Commissioners Paul G. Kirk, John F. Stokes, Otis M. Whitney. Governor Cox on May 27, 1921, signed authorizing legislation for uniformed, statewide force. Foote was first state police commissioner. In 1997, all in photo were deceased.

General Headquarters, Boston, 1961. Lieutenant Colonel John C. Blake. Blake trained in West Bridgewater with 1934's "Golden Class." He served in field barracks throughout the Great Depression and World War II, was an academy instructor in the late 1940's and early 1950's. A captain and troop commander, he moved up to major and adjutant in the late 1950's, and in 1961 retired as the first executive officer with the lieutenant colonel's rank. He lived out his retirement years on Martha's Vineyard and in St. Petersburg, Florida.

General Headquarters, Boston, 1961. (front) Captain William F. Leary, Captain Alfred J. Sanders, Commissioner J. Henry Goguen, Major Carl M. Larson, Captain Walter G. O'Brien, (rear) Lieutenant James Evangelos, Lieutenant Edward M. Prendergast, S/Sergeant James N. Donahue, S/Sergeant Raymond T. Alzapiedi, T/Sergeant Casimir N. Vallon, Sergeant Edward G. Conrad, Sergeant William E. Garvey, Lieutenant Robert E. Murgia, Lieutenant John J. Moriarty. Goguen presided at promotional ceremony for veteran officers. Larson, Moriarty and Murgia capped careers as lieutenant colonel and executive officer.

Memorial Service, Framingham, 1961. Major Carl M. Larson and Lt. Colonel John C. Blake place memorial wreath at monument. Captain James A. Cretecos at lectern, Lieutenant William J. Owen with color guard. Monument in 1961 was donated by Former Troopers' Association. Blake and Larson in early forties had been troopers together at the old Wrentham Barracks, each completed his career as lieutenant colonel and executive officer.

State Capitol, Boston, 1961. Left to Right: Lieutenant George A. Luciano, Commissioner Frank S. Giles, Trooper Richard N. Loynd, Major John J. Kelly, Former Governor Channing H. Cox, Lt. Colonel Carl M. Larson, Trooper William J. Stewart. Governor John A. Volpe signed proclamation commemorating 40th anniversary of May 27, 1921, signing by Governor Cox of legislation creating the "State Police Patrol."

State Police Academy, Framingham, 1961. Commissioner J. Henry Goguen, Former Commissioner Otis M. Whitney. (rear) Captain James A. Cretecos, academy commandant. Goguen and Whitney dedicated the new memorial to deceased troopers. Its inscription reads: "In memory of those state troopers who have completed their last patrol, - may they rest in peace in the company of God." Goguen, Whitney and Cretecos in 1997 themselves were memorialized by the monument's poignant words.

Memorial Service, Framingham, 1962. Left to Right: Governor John A. Volpe, Dep. Commissioner Clayton L. Havey, Lt. Colonel Carl M. Larson, Former Trooper's President Herbert J. Stingel. Stingel enlisted with 1922's 3rd Recruit Troop, saw long field and staff service, was active in early development of Former Troopers' Association.

State Capitol, Boston, 1962. Governor John A. Volpe with T/Sergeant George A. Luciano. A former federal highway administrator and state public works director, Volpe was first elected governor in 1960. Defeated in 1962, he returned in 1964, and in 1966 won the state's first four-year gubernatorial term. In 1969, he became the U. S. Secretary of Transportation, later serving several years as U. S. Ambassador to Italy, his ancestral home. Always a strong supporter of the state police and its personnel, he remained publicly active until his 1994 death.

Academy Staff, early - 1960's. Left to Right: T/ Sergeant Robert F. Lynch, Sergeant Charles W. Gilligan, Lieutenant Stanley W. Wisnioski, Sergeant Martin A. Murphy, Corporal Eugene H. Dzikiewicz. Murphy became a detective lieutenant when he left the academy, in 1971 was named captain and detective commander, with Dzikiewicz taught first criminal justice courses at St. Anselm's College in New Hampshire.

Troop D, Brockton, 1963. Left to Right: Troopers Frederick A. Henley, Richard J. Bellevue, George H. Hall, Rex Trailer, Lieutenant William F. Powers, Sergeant Edward R. MacCormack. Trailer, a popular TV personality, flew helicopter to deliver "Dedicated To You," a state police public information film screened that year in area theaters. Henley became captain and troop commander of Troop A, Framingham, later served as chief of police in North Conway, New Hampshire.

Boston, Christmas, 1962. Left to Right: Lt. William F. Powers, Attorney General Edward R. Brooke, Governor John A. Volpe, Commissioner Frank S. Giles, Trooper Armand J. Longval, Jr. Longval enlisted in 1952 with the 36th Recruit Troop. He served in several field troops, saw extended service in key supervisory posts at Troop F headquarters at Logan International Airport, is an active member of Former Troopers' Association.

Hall of Flags, State Capitol, Boston, 1962. Left to Right: Lieutenant Governor Edward McLaughlin, First Lady Mrs. John A. Volpe, Governor John A. Volpe, Commissioner Frank S. Giles, Lt. Colonel Carl M. Larson, Major John T. Kelly, Captain Julian Zuk, Captain Thomas D. Murphy, Captain William F. Leary, Captain Francis T. Burke, Captain William F. Grady. (rear) Lieutenant George A. Luciano. The governor's "hand shaking" detail was an annual ritual each year on Washington's birthday, February 22nd. Volpe was the state's governor during most of the 1960's decade.

State Police Academy, Framingham, 1964. Left to Right: Sergeant Edward R. MacCormack, Sergeant Richard N. Loynd, Lieutenant Edward J. Teahan, Richard L. McLaughlin. McLaughlin long was the state's registrar of motor vehicles, in 1971-1975 served as the state's first secretary of public safety. Building in rear was academy's "mess hall," site of thousands of recruit meals during some 40 years of service. Teahan later served in key senior command posts, retired at the lieutenant colonel's rank.

Logan Airport, Boston, 1963. This was October 20, 1963, one month before President Kennedy's assassination in Dallas. Left to Right: Captain Robert D. Murgia, Sergeant Edward G. Byron, Sergeant Stanley W. Jackson, the President, Corporal Edward F. Kelly. President Kennedy's presidency was an immense source of pride for state police officers, many of whom ensured the security of the family's Hyannisport "Compound."

Logan Airport, Boston, October, 1963. Left to Right: U. S. Representative Thomas P. O'Neill (back to camera), President John F. Kennedy, Lieutenant Edward J. Teahan, (behind O'Neill and Kennedy) Lieutenant Governor Francis X. Belotti, Treasurer John Driscoll, Governor Endicott Peabody. Teahan was state police executive aide to Governor Peabody, rose to the lieutenant colonel's rank prior to 1970's retirement. Photo taken the month before Dallas assassination. O'Neill later won the speaker's post in U. S. House of Representatives.

Troop B, Northampton, 1964. Left to Right: S/ Sergeant Thomas H. Keeley, Corporal Howard J. O'Brien, Lieutenant Melville R. Anderson, Trooper Leonard F. VonFlatern, Sergeant Edward M. Dunn. Anderson, Keeley and O'Brien began state police careers as World War II Emergency Temporary State Police Officers (E.T.S.P.O.'s). VonFlatern in 1959 played key role in shootout and capture in Middleboro of Philadelphia's notorious Coyle Brothers.

Grand Staircase, State Capitol, Boston, 1965. Left to Right: (front) Trooper George V. Nelson, Captain George A. Luciano, First Lady Mrs. John A. Volpe, Governor John A. Volpe, Commissioner Richard R. Caples, Trooper Lawrence Carter, Trooper Daniel L. Delaney, Jr., (second row) Captains Melville, R. Anderson, Stanley W. Wisnioski, Francis T. Burke, Edward F. Murphy, Major Robert D. Murgia, Lt. Colonel Thomas D. Murphy, Captains Harold Ellis and Edward P. Tonelli. (Immediately behind Wisnioski) Lieutenant James J. Foley who led early fight for substantial benefits for uniformed personnel and families, in 1997 was secretary of Former Troopers and editor of the organization's communication programs.

South Boston, 1967. Left to Right: T/ Sergeant Edward F. Kelly, Trooper William McCabe, Captain William F. Powers, Richard Cardinal Cushing, Captain Francis T. Burke, Trooper Thomas R. Mulloney. Cardinal Cushing that morning offered Mass at the annual state employee religious service. A South Boston native, he reveled in visits to his boyhood neighborhood. Kelly became the department's deputy commissioner, McCabe commissioner, Powers commissioner, Burke a major and Mulloney a lieutenant colonel.

Foster, Rhode Island, 1966. Left to Right: Lieutenant John F. Downey, Captain John F. Collins, Major Robert D. Murgia, Lieutenant Hector J. Cote, Captain William F. Powers, Lieutenant Charles W. Eager. Uniformed officers that day graduated from State Police Staff and Command College, a federally funded educational program at Rhode State Police Academy in Foster. Murgia represented administration at graduation program.

State Police Academy, Framingham, 1965. Left to Right: Corporal Thomas T. Trainor, Corporal James L. Killoran, S/Sgt. Francis V. Foley, Lieutenant Raymond T. Alzapiedi, Sergeant Richard W. Besanko, Sergeant Francis L. Sullivan, Trooper David J. Pendergast. Foley later served as president of the Former Troopers' Association and as an elected official in his native Marlboro. The detail was for day-long activities commemorating the centennial of the 1865 founding of the Massachusetts State Constabulary.

Troop A, Norwood Airport, 1969. Left to Right: Commissioner William F. Powers, Trooper-Pilot Bruce V. M. Whittier, Governor Francis W. Sargent. The October, 1969, delivery of the Bell Jet Ranger launched the State Police Air Wing. The federal National Highway Traffic Safety Administration funded the helicopter purchase, based on acquisition strategies developed by traffic bureau and air wing staff directed by Captain Charles W. Eager.

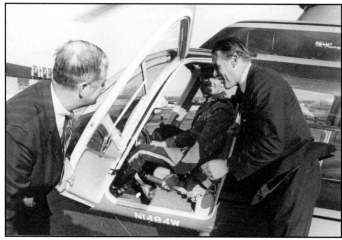

State Police Academy, Framingham, November 1, 1967. Left to Right: Troopers James H. Sharkey, Richard G. Brisbois, Arthur T. Ober, Roy N. Nightingale, Daniel M. Driscoll, Staff Sergeants Charles J. Rollins and Casimir M. Vallon. These officers were among 124 promoted that day as the result of the 1965 promotional statute, the first in the history of the uniformed force. All the troopers in the photograph were promoted to corporal, while Rollins and Vallon received the lieutenant's gold bar.

State Police Academy, Framingham, 1969. Left to Right: Irving P. Rochford, Commissioner William F. Powers, Captain Francis T. Burke. This was the September 26, 1969, ground breaking for the new state police academy. Rochford's company built the modern training complex. Burke led the planning and budget preparations for the academy, supervised the construction program, officiated at the academy's May 29, 1971 dedication. Following a dramatic modernization, the sprawling facilities in October, 1994, were dedicated as the new state police general headquarters.

Senate Chamber, State Capitol, September 25, 1969. Left to Right: Thomas R. Mulloney, Commissioner William F. Powers, Governor Francis W. Sergeant, James V. Oteri. Powers that day was sworn as first commissioner directly from uniformed ranks. Oteri was first president of State Police Association of Massachusetts, Mulloney was treasurer. This quartet led legislative and policy initiatives that in 1971 abolished live-in barracks' system, reduced trooper's duty week from 84 to 40 hours.

Statler Hilton Hotel, Boston, 1969. Left to Right: Trooper Paul M. Beloff, Deputy Commissioner Walter P. Parker, T/Sergeant John F. Kennedy. As deputy commissioner, Parker in 1970 supervised policy and legislative initiatives that abolished the live-in barracks' system and reduced from 84 to 40 a trooper's duty week. He had also authored a distinguished military career in World War II, and held senior state and federal posts in a long public service career.

THE SEVENTIES
Toward A New Era

Logan Airport, Boston, 1979. Left to Right: Commissioner Dennis M. Condon, Colonel Frank J. Trabucco, Public Safety Secretary George A. Luciano, Superintendent Lawrence Carpenter, Metropolitan District Commission Police. Pope John Paul II's historic 1979 visit to the United States began with the vast throngs that attended several Boston area religious and civic ceremonies. State police personnel ensured the Pontiff's security in adhering to a hectic schedule.

State Capitol, Boston, September, 1970. Left to Right: Trooper Kevin W. Peabody, Commissioner William F. Powers, Trooper Richard J. Powers, Trooper G. William Dunderdale, Sergeant James V. Oteri, Trooper John W. Giardino. This was a historic moment in the state force's historical journey. Governor Francis W. Sargent had just signed legislation abolishing the live-in barracks' system while reducing a trooper's duty week from 84 to 40 hours. Sergeant Oteri and Troopers Dunderdale and Powers were officers in the State Police Association of Mass. The Troopers' union teamed with state police leadership and the Sargent Administration to end five decades of spartan barracks' life for state police families.

"God gives all men all earth to love,
But, since our hearts are small,
Ordained for each one spot should prove
Beloved over all."
Rudyard Kipling

Chapter Seven

TOWARD A NEW ERA

Kipling said it for all who have held dear a special place. There is that fond remembrance of how it was, how things used to fit in a more orderly way. And with that mind's eye imagery, there is the yearning to go back, to rediscover the quiet center. But going back is almost always a disappointment. People have moved on. Old, comprehensible patterns have changed. It is the reason Thomas Wolfe penned his axiom, "you can never go home."

The state police organization had remained quite stable in structure, staffing and enforcement procedures well into the aftermath of World War II. The fifties, as seen, witnessed changes in rank structure, increases in salary and complement, and substantial modifications in uniforms, equipment and procedures. That decade, moreover, had portended accelerated change principally because the larger society was itself under the pressure of a rising technology. Where the automobile once had helped create the need for the uniformed branch, television, for example, was exerting its dramatic impact on both law enforcement problems and the nature of the police response.

Change in the larger society, and organizational adaptations to it, had continued apace throughout the 1960s. The clearest, if not the most popular, example was that of the State Police Wives Association. Such an organization would have been thought outlandish in earlier times. The twenties and thirties had not been suitable for such a provocative enterprise. Public utterances related to agency matters had not had a place in the tightly disciplined, mobile organization where, for years, the "senior" patrolman and the corporal represented the court of last resort for men quartered a hundred miles or more from their homes.

It can be seen, in retrospect, that the impetus for major changes in the state force had been building steadily since the close of World War II. Summer vacations had come in the 1950s, followed by summer uniforms in the sixties. The promotional statute in March, 1966 had ended overnight a subjective system of personnel evaluation used for the first 45 years. Thus, as the sixties closed and the seventies began, the stage was set for the substantive changes in organizational structure, staffing and enforcement policies then about to unfold.

If a symbolic event were needed, it was the groundbreaking for a modern state police academy. The September 28, 1969 *Boston Sunday Globe* informed its readers that, "the state police, Friday broke ground for a new $3 million training academy . . . The academy will provide training quarters for 116 men and a staff of 16. It will include a gymnasium, pool, firing range, classrooms and administrative offices. Completion is expected within 19 months."

The *Globe* was almost correct. Actually, $3 million 30 thousand had been appropriated for the new facility. The requisite budgetary and legislative processes had taken many years. As early as 1960, Deputy Commissioner Havey, Captain Francis T. Burke, Captain James A. Cretecos and Sergeant William J. Owen had

travelled to Hershey, Pennsylvania to inspect the state's modern training plant. Several commissioners had pursued academy funding aided by technical advisors in the department, and by key contacts on Beacon Hill.

Ground breaking for the new academy was, in summary, a product of the tireless efforts of a number of people over an extended period of time. The ceremony was held September 26 on Framingham's old muster grounds, site of a thousand stories from the more than two-score recruit classes that had trained in that place. Commissioner Powers was joined for groundbreaking by Deputy Commissioner Walter P. Parker, and former Deputy Clayton L. Havey. Staff Captain Francis T. Burke, he most represented the long years of endeavor, that day put a gold shovel in the brown earth flanked by Lieutenant Colonel Robert D. Murgia and Major John R. Moriarty.

While construction began on the new academy, the department's leadership established the following priority policy goals:
- abolishment of the "live in" aspect of the barracks system
- reorganization of the command and operational structure
- substantial reduction in the duty week
- a mobile patrol system, doubling the existing fleet.

Those policy goals were end products. An enormous amount of research, planning and administrative implementation would be required. To launch the effort, a research and planning unit was established under the general supervision of Deputy Commissioner Parker, with office space in the Saltonstall Building near the State Capitol. Captain Charles W. Eager was named commanding officer, with authority and accountability for operations. Assigned as his staff were:
- Detective Lieutenant Martin A. Murphy
- Staff Sergeant Edward R. McCormack
- Sergeant Robert C. Woodward
- Trooper Robert E. Dahill
- Mr. George K. Campbell
- Mrs. Mary O'Shea

Sergeant Woodward had been nominated for the key assignment by the State Police Association of Massachusetts, while Campbell was initially on loan from the Executive Office of Administration and Finance. In addition, Mr. James H. Ellis of the Massachusetts Taxpayers Foundation worked with the group as a technical consultant.

While the difficult planning work went forward, more prosaic activities transpired. One was the traditional "Governor's Reception," held each year on Washington's birthday in the State Capitol's beautiful Hall of Flags. Governors for years had received the general public there, shaking hands, while, at the same time, gauging the crowd size as an indicator of popularity. It was a yearly ritual, and, for the state police, an annual detail. Uniformed officers each year came to the State House from the Commonwealth's farthest reaches, adding to the color of the traditional ceremony.

Thousands would move briskly through the Hall of Flags, satisfied by a running hand shake with the state's chief executive. The final group, always, would be the state police; officers in dress uniforms and spurs, the men somewhat haggard after standing smartly on the hard marble floors for several hours. Traditionally, the governor would join his state police escort for a photograph on the grand staircase, a treasured keepsake earned by several hours on a formal, "spit and polish," detail.

The February 22, 1970 Hall of Flags detail was to be the last until 1979. The photograph taken that day was especially appropriate. Governor Sargent on February 1, had signed a new "Rule 16," the salary yardstick. The schedule raised a trooper's starting salary to $7,935.00 per year. Yearly steps increased the maximum, after six years, to $9,713.00 annually.

Members of the Fifty-Fourth Recruit Troop were among the first to benefit from the salary upgrading. They had begun training in January, 1970, and, in so doing, enjoyed another unique experience. Their entire recruit program was conducted at a military installation in Sudbury. That move was necessitated by the fact that the new academy was being constructed on the traditional Framingham training site.

The temporary dislocation did not slow academy activities. The staff had adjusted quickly, and, for the recruits, the location of their daily challenges was far less important than successful completion of demanding academy requirements. That ultimate accomplishment was in large measure due to the leadership of the academy commandant Lieutenant Charles W. Gilligan and his able staff:

• S/Sgt. Robert J. Fitzgerald	Troopers:
• S/Sgt. David J. Pendergast	• Robert E. Hunt
• S/St. James V. Oteri	• Robert E. Dunn
• Sgt. Thomas R. Mulloney	• Dennis J. Donoghue

The Fifty-Fourth Recruit Troop graduated on April 24 in a Friday evening ceremony in Commonwealth Armory. Following the Invocation by Father John E. Hartigan, Commissioner Powers, Deputy Commissioner Parker, Lieutenant Colonel Murgia, Major Moriarty and Lieutenant Gilligan inspected the recruit troop, much as those before them had done in that same building. The recruits that evening displayed their newly learned skills, except motorcycle riding. That requirement, after fifty years, had been phased out of the academy's curriculum.

Governor Francis W. Sargent delivered the principal address, urging adherence to the state force's traditional values, and its excellence in public service. For the new troopers, that service began when Lieutenant Colonel Murgia posted the 56 graduates to the six field troops. None present that evening could have known, veteran or recruit, that these would be the last state police recruits to report to the "live in" barracks system. Before another class could complete academy requirements, events would alter the traditional system, mainstay of the uniformed branch since its founding.

THE POLITICS OF CONFRONTATION

Within days of that graduation, some of the recruits faced a severe test in Cambridge's Harvard Square. Civil unrest had continued to worsen as opposition to the Vietnam War choked city streets across the nation. The issue was a divisive one. Friendships, even families, were disrupted as American casualties rose alarmingly in that distant, foreboding land. The Commonwealth was a hotbed of anti-war protest. Universities were especially vulnerable to radical action. Such institutions had always relied on rationality, and the reasoning process, to resolve conflict. Those concepts collapsed in the presence of unreasoning, physical confrontation.

Moreover, there was a dangerous element in the most peaceful of protest demonstrations. Without warning, radicals frequently turned an orderly gathering to their purposes. That would happen often in the spring and summer of 1970. The effect placed an enormous burden on civil authorities to preserve order in the face of riotous mobs bent on destruction for its own ends. There was, therefore, apprehension on May 8 when over 100,000 gathered on Boston Common to demand an end to the Vietnam War. Everything went reasonably well during the mass protest. Yet, the mere size of the crowd concerned law enforcement observers. The concern, it turned out, had been well placed. That evening proved one of the most trying in the long experience of the state police.

As the huge rally ended, several thousand people began streaming toward Cambridge. Slowly, imperceptibly at first, there began a rash of minor incidents. Car windows were broken along Massachusetts Avenue. Fires were set in refuse containers. This was "trashing," and it kindled the spark of violent, physical confrontation. By mid-evening, a full scale riot raged in the streets around Harvard Square.

The state police 150 man tactical unit was committed, with as many local police. In some ways, it was similar to the April, 1969 confrontation in Harvard Yard. But it was different in one important respect. In Harvard Yard there had been submission to authorities once the police moved in. The Harvard Square rioters, on the other hand, were far more violent. As state police units swept a street, they were attacked from above and behind. It was a violent, physical confrontation between police obligated to preserve social order, and young radicals who saw in those same civil forces the power of a national government unresponsive to demands to end the Vietnam War.

The melee of May 8 continued with sporadic outbursts through most of the night. It was 2:00 a.m. before state police units could be withdrawn. By then, more than one hundred rioters had been arrested. Some fifty were hospitalized. Over twenty police officers had been injured, including a number of troopers.

Meantime, similar protests were occurring throughout the nation. One in particular ended in tragedy. Four students on May 4 had been shot and killed at Ohio's Kent State University by National Guardsmen. Within hours, several students were killed in a similar confrontation at Jackson State College in Mississippi. The two incidents triggered even more mass gatherings, with a rising potential for violence, injuries, and additional deaths.

One of these found thousands of protestors massed outside the Massachusetts State Capitol. Speakers quickly raised the crowd to fever pitch. One could feel the tenseness in the air. State police tactical units were deployed inside the State House. Capitol police protected key legislative and executive areas, and Boston police were posted in surrounding streets. An event then occurred which caused much controversy. Governor Sargent, Lieutenant Governor Dwight and key staffers were in the governor's suite immediately above the speaker's platform. At one point in the protest, a speaker, looking up to the open window in the governor's office, requested that the national colors be lowered to half staff "in memory of the students who died at Kent State." Governor Sargent directed Lieutenant Governor Dwight to have the American flag lowered to half staff. The protestors subsequently dispersed peacefully.

The "flag incident" was widely reported, and, in the reporting, the reason for the governor's decision were hopelessly distorted. Some charged that the state's chief executive had ordered the flag lowered in some sort of "surrender" to the assembled protestors. That, in reality, had not been the case. The facts to this day remain disarming in their simplicity. Four young students had been killed protesting the continuation of the Vietnam War. During the massive State Capitol rally, a speaker requested that the flag be lowered to half staff "in memory of the students who died at Kent State." Governor Sargent had ordered the flag lowered for that reason. It was not a "surrender" as some claimed, but, rather, reasoned acknowledgement of the request's validity given the enormity of the Kent State tragedies.

The May, 1970, State Capitol demonstration would not be the last. Vietnam had given rise to a new phenomenon, the "politics of confrontation." The movement had already dissuaded a sitting president, Lyndon B. Johnson, from seeking his party's nomination for another term. That had been followed by the disorders at the 1968 Democratic National Convention in Chicago. And, not long after that, the melees had erupted in Harvard Yard, Harvard Square and on Boston's Beacon Hill. Mass protests challenged traditional law enforcement concepts, and, especially for the state force, ushered in an era of urban oriented police responsibilities. The late sixties and early seventies, therefore, mark a time when traditional state police duties were overtaken by the forces then reshaping the larger society. There would be no turning back.

Meantime, the annual memorial service was held near Troop A headquarters in Framingham. Construction of the new academy, then well underway, necessitated the temporary relocation of the traditional ceremony. Commissioner Powers welcomed some two hundred guests, and, with senior staff officers, reviewed uniformed color guards from each of the six troops, general headquarters and the academy. Major John R. Moriarty and Lieutenant (Ret.) James J. Foley of the Former Troopers Association placed floral wreaths at the memorial monument.

There were also two special ceremonies that day. In one, Sergeant John L. Barry received the "Trooper of the Year" award from the Former Massachusetts State Troopers. It was a richly deserved tribute to a veteran officer. The second award was more unique. Four civilian employees, with 160 years of combined service, were awarded the state police Medal for Meritorious Service. Deputy Commissioner Walter P. Parker made the presentations to four men who had become legends in their own time during long and faithful service to the uniformed branch: Alexander J. "Albie" Woick, Francis J. "Specky" McVeigh, Clarence J. "Clarry" Ferrari and Louis P. Berube. Each had carved out a distinctive career dating from the time of mounted patrols, one day off in fifteen, and unending extra duties that had made such employment a lifestyle rather than a job.

THE MEDAL OF VALOR

On September 23, 1970 Boston Patrolman Walter A. Schroeder was gunned down during a Brighton bank holdup, leaving nine children. His senseless killing triggered a massive manhunt for William M. "Lefty" Gilday and four accomplices. The group, a combination of Walpole parolees and female campus revolutionaries, had committed a series of crimes prior to the fatal $26,000.00 bank heist. Within hours, Robert Valeri and Stanley Bond were in custody. Two women, Susan E. Saxe and Katherine Power dropped from sight. Gilday led police on a series of high speed chases along the New Hampshire border, wounding a Haverhill officer in the process. The climax to the tension filled drama came on the day of Officer Schroeder's funeral.

Gilday was spotted on the Massachusetts Turnpike by Sergeant Thomas H. Peterson. Peterson's cruiser radio was dead. He commandered a turnpike maintenance truck, radio equipped, and trailed the fugitive to the Worcester exit. Alerted, state police cruisers converged on the felon's car in Worcester. Caught in traffic in a city square, Gilday made a desperate try for freedom. His move came too late.

Trooper Robert A. Long of the Grafton Barracks had blocked the escape route. Long and Peterson, with two Worcester officers, rushed Gilday's car, disarmed hiim and placed him under arrest. No one had been hurt. A dangerous fugitive, accused of murdering Officer Schroeder, was in custody. His reign of terror was over.

Later, Commissioner Powers presented Sergeant Peterson and Trooper Long with the State Police Medal of Valor. They were the first ever to receive the highest honor accorded by the state police to its officers. The general headquarters ceremony, attended by the families of the two men, brought deserved public recognition not to them alone, but, as always, to the enforcement organization in which they served.

Gilday, Valeri and Bond received long prison terms. Bond was subsequently killed by a self-made bomb at Walpole State Prison. Susan Saxe, years later, would be tried, convicted and sentenced for the Brighton tragedy. Katherine Power, decades later, was also finally sentenced for her role in one of the most senseless, poignant crimes in the state's history.

While day-to-day enforcement activities transpired, research and planning went forward on major policy initiatives. This effort was strengthened by close coordination between the department's administration and the State Police Association of Massachusetts (S.P.A.M.). Sergeant James V. Oteri was S.P.A.M.' president, backed by a slate of officers and a solid communications system in the field troops. Treasurer Thomas R. Mulloney worked closely with Oteri, conferring frequently with the department's leadership to ensure a united position in both the legislative and executive branches. Governor Francis W. Sargent provided public leadership for the major modifications proposed for the "live in" barracks system, and the structural reorganization of the uniformed branch. House Speaker Bartley and Senate President Donahue were strong allies. Acting Senate President Kevin B. Harrington augmented their support. A number of House and Senate members actively supported the state police legislative program as it moved through the maze of committee hearings and conferences.

Changing the barracks systems was an ambitious enterprise. Yet, the historic proposal advanced smoothly. There was, it was clear, one overriding reason; the time of the idea had come. The barracks concept had been essential to the statewide enforcement operation since 1921, and for decades thereafter. The system produced the men and the accomplishments that forged a distinguished public service record. Their numbers had been few, their achievements beyond anything that could fairly have been expected. But time had passed. Much had changed. It was a far different "outside" world, with evolving demands and needs. These inexorable pressures were reflected in the attitudes and lifestyles of the young men coming into the organization. They, and their families, saw beyond their organization to the changes then well underway in the nation's law enforcement community, and, indeed, in all of its principal institutions.

By mid-1970 only Massachusetts and Rhode Island required its state police officers to live in barracks. An era was ending. A system that served long and well was under rising pressures from all sides. Change would be planned from the inside, or, inevitably, it would be imposed from the outside. Those who knew the state force and its organizational history perceived this, understood its implication. As a consequence, legislative proposals to effectuate major policy and operational changes went forward with broad based support and dramatic swiftness in the winter and spring of 1970.

By late summer, the legislature had enacted several proposals dramatically affecting structure, staffing and operational policies. These were summarized in a September, 1970 bulletin from the State Police Association of Massachusetts to its membership throughout the uniformed branch. By then, the following legislative enactments had become law with Governor Francis W. Sargent's signature:

• A 40 hour work week. This reduced by more than half the official 84 hour duty week. The law was to become effective on May 1, 1971, ending the "live in" barracks system.

• A budget appropriation of $800,000 for 270 additional cruisers. This increase was necessary to implement the "cruiser per man" patrol coverage plan. An additional $270,000 was obtained from the Law Enforcement Assistance Administration for additional cruisers. Some of these were later assigned to the detective branch.

• A career incentive program. This provided salary increments based upon an officer's educational achievements. A major breakthrough, it had been only a distant possibility a year or two earlier.

• A court time statute. This provided payments to officers appearing for court proceedings during off duty time. For years, a trooper received neither a witness fee nor compensary time for court appearances, even if he were on a regular day off.

• A $100,000.00 appropriation for urgently needed civil disorders equipment. This funding was essential to the state force's critical role in responding to increased mass demonstrations throughout the state.

• A budget appropriation for four additional majors and a supervisor of policewomen. This allowed implementation of a major reorganization of the command structure of the state force.

The reduction of the duty week to 40 hours represented the first legislative change in required duty hours since the "two in eight" had become effective in 1954. The new system focused on one fairly simple change, but its impact was of major significance. A trooper, at the completion of a patrol, no longer would remain in the barracks. He would simply return to his home in a marked patrol cruiser. Following the off duty hours, he would report to the barracks to begin his next assignment. In effect, the duty week was reduced by cutting the hours formerly spent in a barracks between patrol assignments.

The new duty week was to begin on May 1, 1971, fifty years to the month from that distant time when the "State Police Patrol" had received legislative approval. The authorization for four new major's positions enabled a substantial realignment of the

department's command structure. The major and adjutant's office for years had been responsible for all general headquarters functions, including the academy. There was, in addition, an unclear chain of command between troops commanders and the adjutant's post. Field commanders, according to charts, reported directly to the lieutenant colonel and executive officer. That was the line of authority. But, in reality, the authority line often shifted to the major and adjutant, creating reporting ambiguities.

The new organizational structure clarified command relationships, and assigned specific accountability for clearly identified areas of responsibility. The October 28, 1970 *Boston Globe* reported on the changes with its story caption. "State Police Name Four Majors, Create Five Bureaus in Shakeup." Richard Connolly of the *Globe* wrote that "One of the most drastic reorganizations in the 105 year history of the Massachusetts State Police went into effect today with adoption of a new operational structure and the elevation of four staff captains to the rank of major designed to streamline the oldest statewide police force in the nation. Some of the changes were made through administrative orders signed by Governor Sargent and State Public Safety Commissioner William F. Powers during a State House ceremony." Promoted that day to fill the new majors' posts were Staff Captain Edward P. Tonelli and Melville R. Anderson, both of whom had served as division inspectors, Staff Captain Francis T. Burke, supply officer, and Staff Captain John Hyde, civil defense officer.

Major John R. Moriarty for several years had discharged the broad responsibilities of the adjutant's post. He assumed command of the Bureau of Investigative Services, directing all of the investigative capabilities of the uniformed branch. This seemed a natural assignment for Moriarty. He had been for years in the forefront of the department's efforts against organized crime, and had directed some of the era's most complex criminal investigations. Moreover, Moriarty had made important contributions to the reorganization initiatives. That the program succeeded was in large measure due to his tireless commitment to daily operational responsibilities, while, at the same time, providing requisite leadership for major policy initiatives.

There was also in 1970 an increase of 50 positions in the uniformed branch, bringing the authorized complement to 722. These personnel were augmented by over 100 officers patrolling the Massachusetts Turnpike and those providing police services at Logan International Airport. The 1970 personnel increase was followed shortly by two salary boosts. An uprgrading of "Rule 16," the pay standard, coupled with Chapter 116 Acts of 1971 made effective on December 27, 1970 the following salary scale:

Rank	Minimum	Maximum
Lt. Colonel	15,763	19,991
Major	14,214	18,098
Captain	12,071	15,311
Lieutenant	11,403	14,461
Staff Sergeant	10,813	13,637
Sergeant	10,111	12,810
Policewoman	10,111	12,810
Corporal	9,516	11,918
Trooper	8,938	11,138
Trainee	8,411	

That kind of remuneration was a long way from the $600 per year received by members of 1921's First Training Troop. But, then, the decade of the 1970's was equally distant from the economic values of the Post World I era. The nation and state had changed. So had the state force. Yet everything remains relative. In that sense, increased state police salaries mirrored the inflationary spiral then taking firm root at the center of the nation's principal policy concerns.

AN ERA CLOSES

The early months of 1971 marked the deaths of two men from the "First Class." Charles T. Beaupre had trained with the 1921 recruits, later serving in the first contingent of "B" Troopers in western Massachusetts. Beaupre had become in 1925 the second executive officer, succeeding Captain George A. Parker. He served in the top post until 1933, later taking an executive postion, one held for many years, at Revere's Wonderland Greyhound Track.

Captain Beaupre in 1933 had been followed in the executive officer's position by Captain James P. Mahoney. Mahoney also had made the long march down Southboro Road in September of 1921 to begin a career in the State Police Patrol, later serving nine years as captain and executive officer. His 1942 retirement had resulted in the open, competitive examination for that top command post. Now, five decades after their enlistments in the state force, Captain Beaupre and Mahoney had passed on. It was a reminder of time's inexorable toll upon men and events.

The two veterans could hardly have imagined a state police organization where personnel returned to their homes following a regular patrol. That kind of concept was foreign to their era, to their way of getting things done. Yet on May 1, 1971 that is what happened. The 1970 statute abolishing the "live in" barracks' system became effective that day. The historic change transpired with relative smoothness. There were procedural snags to be sure, and more than a touch of nostalgia. But there had been a great deal of preparation. Several hundred cruisers had been purchased, equipped and assigned. Duty schedules had been developed during endless planning sessions. Over 200 officers had been transferred. It had not been easy. But it had been done, on time.

Troopers for the first time travelled in marked cruisers between their barracks and homes. The impact of that day now is obscure. Several thousand personnel have since joined the department. They have only heard of how it was. The deeply felt pleasures of "barracks life" are reserved, therefore for those who served in a system that gave way to the changes that time imposes on men and their institutions.

Later, on May 29, the annual memorial service was held at Framingham. That ceremony was particularly well attended because the new academy was also dedicated that afternoon. One in attendance received special attention. He was Joseph L. Regan, a member of the 1931 recruit class. He had left in the late 1930s, pursuing an enforcement career in New Hampshire. In 1961 he had become Colonel Regan, commanding officer of the New Hampshire State Police. Regan, though, had always cherished memories of his service in the French and electric blue.

Colonel Regan was surprised that day when Commissioner Powers presented him with the trooper's badge he had earned four decades earlier. As Regan sought words to express his appreciation, the lesson of the moment's emotion was not lost on those in attendance. Here was a man who had reached the top in his profession, a state police colonel. Yet he was visibly moved by an event forty years past, the beginning of a distinguished career as a

"boot" in the Massachusetts State Police. The scene provided insights as to why men like Colonel Regan served in the state force, and why the organization had authored its much admired public service record.

The new academy was dedicated before a large crowd. Commissioner Powers, Deputy Commissioner Parker, Lieutenant Colonel Murgia, senior commissioned officers, and a host of distinguished guests were present. A large uniformed detail added color to the ceremonies. Featured was a mounted unit under the direction of the Captain Stanley W. Wisnioski, Jr., the first time horses had been used officially since the early thirties. Following the Invocation by Father John H. Hartigan, Lieutenant Governor Donald R. Dwight accepted the academy for the Commonwealth. Mr. Irving P. Rocheford, the general construction contractor, presented the ceremonial keys, and Mr. John A. Valtz represented the firm of Valtz and Kimberly, designers of the impressive structure.

A special moment in the program honored the one individual most responsible for the new academy. When Major Francis T. Burke stepped up to the podium to receive a gubernatorial citation, few present realized the importance of his contributions. For over a decade he had guided the academy project. Many others had helped during the long years of effort. But Burke had provided the continuity essential to a project of the academy's magnitude. His thoughts that day may have drifted back to the early 1960s, and that trip to the Pennsylvania State Police Academy with Deputy Commissioner Havey, Captain Cretecos and Lieutenant Owen. That had been a long time ago. Burke, more than the rest, knew what it had taken to get the new academy.

Following Benediction by Reverend Frank J. Bauer, hundreds toured the new installation. They were impressed. Every need had been considered for a modern, law enforcement training operation. The academy was yet another sign that the uniformed branch had covered much ground during its five decades. The new buildings stood symbolically on the very grounds where tents, and later Quonset Huts, had sheltered aspiring state police recruits. The men and the tents were gone, but not their tradition. Those values would remain important to the modern academy and the young men and women yet to train there.

The dedication ceremony was the final official appearance for Captain of Detectives Daniel I. Murphy. He retired the next month, closing an enforcement career that had spanned four decades. From 1934 recruit training at West Bridgewater, and a decade in the uniformed branch, he had gone on in the 1940s to extended duty as a detective lieutenant. The highpoint of his service was the 1950 appointment by Governor Paul A. Dever to a three year tenure as commissioner of public safety. Then had followed service as captain in charge of state police detectives. Murphy had served in five separate decades. As that service closed in June, 1971, he knew the satisfaction of having made significant personal contributions to his organization's public safety achievements.

With an irony that recurs in the state force, the retirement of former Commissioner Murphy enabled the promotion of another Murphy. A June 16 *Boston Globe* story noted that, "A former state trooper with 21 years in police work has been appointed acting head of Massachusetts State Detectives." The account continued, "Detective Lieutenant Martin a. Murphy, designated as acting captain by State Public Safety Commissioner William F. Powers, will be in charge of the 75 man force until a captain's examination is held later this year."

Captain Murphy had begun his career in the uniformed branch with the Thirty-Fifth Recruit Troop in September, 1949. Following graduation, he was assigned to several barracks in the central and eastern sections of the state. Murphy in 1966 had transferred to the detective branch, serving tours with the district attorneys for Essex and Hamden Counties. While in the uniformed branch, he also had been a member of the academy staff, especially noted for his erudite lectures. It was from that post, as a member of the academy's tactical field unit, that he had led the 1959 capture of John and Wililam Coyle in a Middleboro swamp.

Murphy later in 1971 was appointed permanent chief of detectives following competitive examinations. He brought to that highly sensitive post a unique combination of superior professional skills and strong personal ethics. Knowledgeable in the law, he applied this expertise with a sure sense of reasoned fairness. Those attributes promised superior leadership in his new and taxing post. The years that followed affirmed that perception, strengthening the public reputation of the detective branch as a premier investigative body.

The leadership change in the detective branch was followed shortly by major changes in the organization of the state's executive agencies. The legislature in 1969 had created a cabinet system in the executive branch. One result was the grouping of the Department of Public Safety, including its Division of State Police, the Registry of Motor Vehicles and other public safety units in a new Executive Secretariat of Public Safety. Another practical effect was to sever the direct authority line between the governor and the state police commissioner. That relationship had been an important one for five decades. The new configuration inevitably would lead to a different set of policy relationships, with implications for the authority and accountability of statewide public safety services.

Governor Sargent in July, 1971, named Richard E. McLaughlin the state's first secretary of public safety. McLaughlin, from a distinguished Bay State family, had enjoyed a long public service career. In the early 1960s, he had been on Governor Peabody's executive staff. Then had followed long service as Registrar of Motor Vehicles, a tenure distinguished by reappointments under Governors Volpe and Sargent.

McLaughlin staffed the secretariat to ensure experienced supervision of its complex responsibilities. Two key appointments were those of Edward P. Tonelli and Andrew M. O'Brien as assistant secretaries. Tonelli, a major in the uniformed branch, had enlisted in 1951 with the Thirty-Sixth Recruit Troop. O'Brien had served in key posts in the public safety department. An extended tenure as a communications dispatcher had led to several promotions to responsible administrative posts. The latter had included overseeing the department's budget preparation, as well as developing requests for state police personnel increases.

TROOPER ROBERT J. McDOUGAL

Meantime, a tragedy occurred which underlined the inherent dangers of being a state police officer. Trooper Robert J. McDougall on August 6 was killed by a tractor trailer unit on Route 20, the Worcester "cutoff." Once the principal route between Boston and New York, the road had witnessed countless such tragedies. Troopers had handled many of these over the years, part of the responsibility in every "routine" patrol. This time, however, it was one of their own, a realization that always exacted a heavy personal toll. Norwood's St. Catherine's church was crowded for Trooper

McDougall's funeral Mass. A uniformed detail paid its last respects to one who had served honorably in the French and electric blue.

Commissioner Powers, Deputy Commissioner Parker and senior commissioned officers attended Trooper McDougall's funeral. For Powers it was a poignant duty, one of his last as commissioner. He resigned effective August 31, 1971 to accept appointment as New England Regional Administrator of the Justice Department's Law Enforcement Assistance Administration. In that post he would be responsible for the allocation of some $50 million annually to criminal justice agencies in the six state region.

Governor Francis W. Sargent on September 1, 1971 appointed John F. Kehoe, Jr. the state's new public safety commissioner. Kehoe, a Dorchester native, had served 29 years in the Federal Bureau of Investigation following his 1941 graduation from Boston College. That career had carried him to Washington, D.C., Phoenix, New Orleans, New York, and finally, back to Boston. He served in the FBI's Boston office throughout the sixties, including an extended tour as supervisor of the organized crime section. The post brought him extensive knowledge of organized crime, especially in the New England region. That experience had proved invaluable in 1970 when he left the FBI to accept appointment as executive director of the New England Organized Crime Intelligence System (NEOCIS). NEOCIS functioned under the region's state police commissioners and attorneys general. Kehoe administered NEOCIS until he was appointed to the public safety post.

The new commissioner took his oath from Governor Sargent in the Chief Executive's office. Commissioner Powers attended, as did Secretary Richard E. McLaughlin. Many of Kehoe's former FBI colleagues witnessed the impressive ceremony. Kay Kehoe, the newly sworn commissioner's wife, was more than an interested spectator. She had rushed to Boston from the couple's South Shore home, barely arriving in time to witness her husband's confirmation as head of the statewide law enforcement agency.

Commissioner Kehoe's first public function was a rewarding experience. He presided on September 18 at the Framingham graduation of the Fifty-Fifth Recruit Troop. There was, as always, an impressive display of the recruits' skills; capabilities developed during the long weeks of training that summer. Each training troop fashions a unique image. This one was no exception. The class was the first to go through its training paces at the new academy. As training had progressed, the 63 neophytes benefitted from the much improved facilities housed in the modern structure. It was, to be sure, a long way from the tents, bikes and horses. But the demands and disciplines remained. And this group, like its predecessors, had proven equal to the constant, daily challenges.

The graduation ceremony followed a time honored sequence, with Governor Sargent, Secretary McLaughlin, Commissioner Kehoe and Deputy Commissioner Parker performing specific functions. Following demonstrations of newly developed skills, the trainees became troopers when Secretary of State John F.X. Davoren administered the oath of office. That done, tension mounted as Colonel Murgia and Major Moriarty made assignments to the field troops. By nightfall, the new state police officers were enroute to barracks across the state, a traditional trek for fledgling troopers. But this time there was a difference. These were the *first* academy graduates who would not be required *to live* in a barracks. The system had changed. They would never know, at least not first hand, the mixture of pleasure and frustration that accompanied that traditional lifestyle.

These "boots" would soon benefit from further adjustment in

the duty week. Early in 1972, Commissioner Kehoe issued guidelines for a new "4 and 2" time off schedule, providing two days off following four duty days. Moreover, officers were allowed to "bid" for various patrol shifts. Bids were governed by rank and seniority, except for corporals. They were restricted to evening and night duty. Nothing, it seemed, had changed for the "poor corporal." After fifty years he was still in the twilight zone, not quite management, but no longer one of the boys.

About the same time, the state police force launched a new concept for criminal investigations. It was called Crime Prevention and Control (CPAC), and reflected the interests of Commissioner Kehoe in major investigations. The first CPAC units were established at the Middleboro and South Yarmouth barracks. The former covered Plymouth County, while the latter handled Dukes and Nantucket.

The special strike teams ensured central coordination of enforcement strategies against major criminal activities, organized crime, narcotics and gaming. Each unit was staffed with seasoned investigators from both the uniformed force and detective branch. Planning had been closely coordinated with District Attorneys Phillip A. Rollins and Robert L. Anderson. The total commitment of the two county prosecutors was a key factor in the outstanding record of successful investigations subsequently chalked up by the unique CPAC teams.

While the CPAC concept was being implemented, 64 new trainees were undergoing the rigors of academy life. Their graduation day was April 29, 1972, with colorful ceremonies held against a backdrop of the sprawling, new training plant. Dignitaries crowded the reviewing platform, led by Governor Sargent and Commissioner Kehoe. The exercises were under the supervision of a new academy commandant, Captain Edward F. Kelly. Kelly had discharged a range of field and general headquarters duties prior to the academy assignment. His responsibility for the recruits had been shared by a seasoned staff including: S/Sgt. Robert J. Fitzgerald, S/Sgt. James V. Oteri, Sergeant Robert E. Hunt, and Corporals Joseph A. King and Paul F. Matthews. In addition, the following troopers had kept the training pace in high gear: Lawrence P. Fay, John W. Gilman, William J. Grant, Robert E. Dunn, Roderick K. Walsh, John A. Sorbera and Kenneth W. Moschella.

State Police Civilians

On May 27, the annual Memorial Service was held. A feature was the award of the State Police Medal for Meritorious Service to three civilian employees. The recipients were Gardner F. Bayley, a veteran of 32 years in radio maintenance, Raymond J. Mendes who had completed 34 years in support activities, and Julius J. Boronsky who, for four decades, had helped keep the state police fleet rolling. The three exemplified countless numbers of civilians who, without fanfare, had provided essential support services to the state force since its founding.

Lieutenant Colonel Murgia and Major Moriarty had participated in the awarding of the coveted honors. Within days, Murgia closed his 24 years of service, a career begun in the unsettled time following World War II. Commissioner Kehoe on July 24, 1972 promptly appointed Moriarty the new executive officer. Few had been as well prepared for the post's exacting responsibilities. His service had spanned four different decades, dating from the first 1947 training class. Throughout the fifties, he had served in just about every patrol and supervisory post in the field troops. That

background provided a solid foundation for the leadership he later provided for the department's concentrated efforts against major criminal activities, including organized crime, illicit drugs, gaming and related crimes. He had also played a primary role in the major legislative accomplishments in 1970.

Toward the end of 1972 there were increases in both the salary levels and authorized complement of the uniformed branch. The salary boost, effective December 31, was, in reality, retroactive. It was authorized by Chapter 426 of 1972. The increase brought the lieutenant colonel's salary to a maximum of $21,541 annually, with relative upgrading in all ranks. Troopers received $9,630 per year, reaching a $12,000 maximum after three, two-year enlistments. Recruits were upped to an annual rate of $9,061, or approximately $755 monthly, while in the academy. These salary levels were augmented for officers who accepted paid details, and for an increasing number then working toward academic degrees.

Along with the salary boost, there was an increase of 57 authorized positions in the uniformed force. This brought the complement to 789. In addition, there were 83 men in Troop E, the Massachusetts Turnpike, and 53 officers at Logan International Airport, designated Troop F. The total complement thus stood at 925. That figure focused the historic growth pattern of the uniformed branch. From the authorized fifty positions in 1921, there had been an increase to 336 by the early 1950s, not a substantial change during three decades. In the twenty years between 1952 and 1972, however, the authorized complement had risen by almost 600. This reflected the ever-increasing scope of statewide enforcement responsibilities, and the necessity of developing commensurate capabilities and staffing.

Meantime, individual stories continued to reduce large, impersonal numbers to the ever present human dimension. Nineteen seventy-three began that way, with the untimely death of Thomas H. Keeley. Keeley's story began like that of many other troopers, with a youngster's desire to join the state force. His dad, Dr. Thomas Keeley, for years had taken care of personnel stationed at the Monson Barracks. Troopers would often stop by the family home when ill, or more likely, just to visit. The good doctor never hesitated to come to the barracks if he were needed. He was one of those people, there have been many, who was especially close to the troopers in a barracks area.

Dr. Keeley would often have young Tom with him when he called at Monson. The youngster became a favorite of the troopers. He in turn developed a life long ambition to serve in the state police. That dream became a reality in 1947 when the younger Keeley enlisted in the uniformed branch. He served over two decades, most of that time in his native "B" Troop, the state's four western counties. Keeley's sudden death in early 1973 saddened the many troopers who had known him as a child, and, in his own time, as a member of the state force. It was yet another reminder that the organization's strengths had always been based on individual commitments to public service ideals.

A Troubled Prison System

Those commitments were tested that year as the state's penal system began to disintegrate in a tangle of conflicting philosophies. John O. Boone, a new corrections commissioner, had attempted reforms focused on rehabilitation. The system, if it would ever be ready for such innovation, was not ready then. Boone's policies ran headlong into two intractable groups with big stakes in the outcome; hard core prisoners, and a well organized guard force. The result was not reform but chaos, not improved prison conditions, but prisons that resembled more a dangerous no man's land than a correctional institute.

The inevitable result exploded on the front page of the March 16, 1973 *Boston Globe:* "Walpole Strike Grows, . . . State Police Called; Sargent in Plea." Over 150 prison guards had walked out of Walpole. Governor Sargent took a hard line. He told the guards they were "illegally on strike," and warned inmates to spurn the leadership of the hard core in the inmate population. The same day the state police tactical unit was ordered into Walpole. Troopers secured key control points inside the state's maximum security prison. Squads then moved into each cell block, putting prisoners back in their cells and restoring order and control. It was a swift, efficient operation.

Walpole for days reeked of tear gas. Acrid water covered the floors. Tensions hung heavily in the dank air. Control could only be maintained with force. Unrest ebbed and flowed inside the walls of the modern correctional facility, a complex proclaimed at its mid-fifties dedication as an inspiring departure from the sordid legends of Charlestown, its brooding, ancient predecessor.

Events climaxed several weeks later, and with dramatic swiftness. Governor Sargent relieved Commissioner Boone. He put Colonel John R. Moriarty in charge of Walpole. It was a sudden turn of events. A contingent of state police officers moved in with Moriarty, clamping tight security on the troubled institution. Prison operations slowly returned to normal, but the state police were destined to remain inside Walpole for a number of weeks. During that time, prisoners returned to work assignments. Medical care was improved. Educational programs were reinstituted. Vocational activities returned to normal. Taken together, these brought the troubled insititution some relative calm. Walpole once again was being directed by the authorities, rather than being on the edge of daily chaos as prison "heavies" contended for power positions in the inmate population.

That "inside" perspective was an enigma. But insights were later provided by Peter Remick, a Walpole inmate. His book, "In Constant Fear," provided a fascinating account of what really happened, and how the inmates reacted while troopers slowly forged order out of chaos. Remick wrote: "Colonel Moriarty, however, wasted no time in taking control. First all inmates were locked in their cells during a shakedown for contraband. A week after this, Moriarty began a 'controlled' lockup. He allowed inmates to shower, one at a time. When there was no trouble, Moriarty allowed an entire tier to shower and enjoy a few minutes of exercise. When there was still no trouble, he allowed an entire block out at a time. With a good many of the killers, gangsters, and troublemakers in Blocks Nine or Ten, most of the inmates went along with Colonel Moriarty."

The inmate-author provided revealing glimpses of the inner workings of a maximum security prison, especially its power structure: "On July 18, the gangsters sent word from Block Nine and Ten to the other inmates: 'You are going along with Moriarty too well. Cool it or else'." Remick pinpointed the reason for the threat, " . . . Moriarty was restoring order, and that threatened the power of the cons." Then followed a tour of the stricken facility by news media to document state police security procedures. The "heavies," according to Remick, sent a message to those appearing to cooperate, "If any inmates work they'll have their heads cut off when the state police leave."

Thus, behind the scenes, factions struggled for control of the brooding fortress. Effective security procedures, nevertheless, slowly but surely took hold. Authority was reestablished in the prison administration. The state police presence brought stability where formerly it was every man for himself. Such a no man's land had cost the life of Albert De Salvo, the self-confessed "Boston Strangler," one of a number of such victims behind Walpole's high walls.

The investigation of such vicious crimes also had been a state police responsibility, largely handled by detective branch personnel from the Norfolk County District Attorney's office. Lieutenant Detective William A. Miller particularly had been heavily involved. Miller later headed up a task force which presented comprehensive recommendations for correcting Walpole's principal administrative and operational problems.

Governor Sargent on September 4 relieved the state police of Walpole responsibilities. Thus ended some ten weeks of emergency duty, one of the finest performances in the state force's distinguished history. The governor that day appointed Frank Hall the new commissioner of the Department of Corrections. The authority transition went smoothly, without incident. The withdrawal of uniformed troopers was accomplished without fanfare, a contrast to their dramatic intervention in June. They had done their job. Personnel of the state force once again had added a bright chapter to a lengthening ledger of distinguished public service.

Many had contributed to the Walpole operation. It had been a difficult assignment, tough on the individual. Time off had been severely limited. Duty hours were long and tension filled. Troopers travelled long distances from regular patrol stations to the prison's remote location. Space does not permit the credit due each officer who ensured the success of such a hazardous mission. But they delivered, and then some.

The General Court later recognized all who served at Walpole by means of a rare public tribute to Lieutenant Colonel Moriarty. On September 20 he was honored in both the Senate and House of Representatives. Each body presented him with a resolution expressing the appreciation of the Commonwealth and its citizens for the grave responsibilities he and his men discharged at Walpole. It was a proud day for Moriarty, the highpoint of an enforcement career that had spanned more than a quarter of a century. He addressed each chamber, praising Commissioner Kehoe, and, especially, the men who had ensured success at Walpole with a total commitment of personal energies and enforcement skills.

About Colonel Moriarty's General Court honors, a law enforcement commentator wrote: "It was a wonderful tribute, not only to John Moriarty, but to his staff of officers and his detail of uniformed troopers. Some day historians will say that this was one of the greatest chapters in the history of the Massachusetts State Police." The intervening years have confirmed that insightful perception. It is recorded here to prevent time's passage from eroding the true achievements of those who served in Walpole during a major 1970s crisis in the state's penal system.

BOSTON

Within days of the state police withdrawal from Walpole, the force would embark on *the* most difficult, tension filled assignment in its fifty year existence. That mission resulted from deeply rooted social patterns struck down by the 1954 U.S. Supreme Court in *Brown vs. Board of Education.* That decision had declared equal but separate educational facilities in violation of constitutional safeguards. While early difficulties were in the South, *Brown's* impact moved inexorably toward the North's teeming urban centers. There, school populations were a function of where people lived, their neighborhoods. The result was city schools with either black or white enrollments in substantial conflict with the mandates of *Brown.*

The Commonwealth's capital city of Boston for several years was in the direct legal path of the Supreme Court decision. Administrative remedies during that period ultimately were judged inadequate. Actions, meantime, had begun in the federal court system. These resulted in the promulgation of a specific mandate by the Federal District Court. The Court's orders were designed to attain the goal of racial balance in Boston's schools. Implementation of the directives in a city of neighborhoods required massive transporation plans. "Busing" thus became a code word. It has often been said that "one picture is worth a thousand words." In this case, the opposite was true. One word, "bus," created a thousand different pictures. They were not pretty images.

Those perceptions hardened as Boston's schools opened in September, 1973. Violence soon erupted. School authorities were out of their element. Boston police had been prepared, but their numbers were not sufficient to ensure the twin essentials of a civilized society; individual liberty within a framework of social order. Policy conferences between city and state leaders were held daily, even as tensions rose. Suddenly, in early October, Governor Francis W. Sargent ordered state police units to augment Boston and Metropolitan District Police preserving order in an around affected schools.

Commissioner Kehoe, Colonel Moriarty and senior officers had anticipated such an order. Plans had been carefully formulated. Yet, this was not the usual kind of assignment, a question of law and law breakers. Rather, it was the nation's priority problem, one grounded in two hundred years of social and economic history. It would not yield to law enforcement alone, no matter how professional that essential effort might be.

Following Governor Sargent's directive, more than 150 troopers were sent into Boston. A majority of the men were stationed at South Boston High School, with small units posted at two junior highs. Thus had begun the most challenging responsibility in the state force's history. Each officer's personal skills, values and sense of fairness would be severely tested. The trial would not end in weeks or even months, but would persist without discernable time boundaries, the sort of open ended commitment that weakens the will of all but the most resolute. In those circumstances, the state force would author its most distinguished accomplishment, one that, in the end, received universal accolades from those familiar with the social ordeal of balancing the capital city's school population.

Lieutenant Colonel Moriarty had participated in the tense discussions that preceded the Boston assignment. He had seen the portents of the 1960s confirmed as the once rural enforcement agency became fully involved in far more difficult urban issues. In reality, the trend had been in that direction, slowly but inexorably, since Moriarty's 1947 enlistment. Now, several months after troopers first assembled in South Boston, Moriarty's career came to a close. His retirement was effective on February 19, 1974, the conclusion of 27 years of duty that had included service in most all sections of the state police organization.

Commissioner Kehoe shortly appointed Americo J. Sousa as the uniformed branch's new executive officer. Colonel Sousa had entered the academy with the Thirty-Sixth Recruit Troop in December of 1951. Sousa was from Western Massachusetts, the first from that section to attain the uniformed branch's top post. He had served extensively in both patrol and investigatory duties during the fifties. His rise through the non-commissioned ranks had led to the position he enjoyed most, commanding officer of Troop B Northampton, with supervision of uniformed personnel in the four western counties.

NEW RANKS AND STAFFING

Meantime plans had been completed for major changes in the staffing and ranks of the state police organization. Chapter 639 of the Acts of 1974 substantially changed rank structure and the functional grouping of enforcement resources. The statute authorized Governor Sargent and Commissioner Kehoe to alter organizational relationships rooted in history, even predating the uniformed branch's 1921 founding. These modifications became effective on September 9, 1974 when Sargent and Kehoe signed new administrative rules and regulations.

One immediate effect was the abolition of the distinction between the uniformed and detective branches of the state police. Uniformed officers had always been recruited, trained and enlisted as state police recruits. Detectives, on the other hand, often entered the state police after serving in municipal police departments. It was not the best of arrangements, and tensions had always existed even though close coordination on specific cases had had always resulted in outstanding accomplishments through the years.

The new law required that all officers be enlisted through a *unified recruitment process.* That was a major breakthrough. The agency would be strengthened as a statewide, law enforcement organization. The new organizational structure was aligned as follows:

- Office of the Commissioner and Superintendent
- Office of the Deputy Superintendent
- Office of Field Operations
- Office of Investigations and Intelligence Operations
- Office of Staff Operations

Commissioner Kehoe thus became state police superintendent as well as public safety chief. The deputy superintendent was assigned the rank of full colonel, the highest post in the career ranks. The remaining three officers were to be supervised by those holding the rank of lieutenant colonel. The effect was to unify the command structure. Where formerly the commanding officers of the uniformed and detective branches each reported directly to the commissioner, now only the deputy superintendent reported to him. The deputy in turn had authority and accountability for all subordinate units. The state police division for the first time was unified under a single office.

Commissioner Kehoe on December 28, 1974 named Americo J. Sousa the first deputy superintendent, promoting him to full colonel. Major Edward J. Teahan was elevated to lieutenant colonel assuming responsibilities for the Office of Field Operations. A pleasant irony attended those two promotions. Sousa and Teahan had been classmates in the Thirty-Sixth Recruit Troop. While their careers had followed divergent patterns, they had come full circle and were now responsible for the effective functioning of the newly designed organizational structure. At the same time, Captain James V. Oteri was promoted to the major's rank.

For Sousa, 1974 had been a good year. While his own promotions were welcome, another event may have caused even more rejoicing in family circles. The occasion had been the October 19 graduation of the Fifty-Eighth Recruit Troop. Another Sousa, Stephen J., was a member of the class. At the appropriate moment in the graduation ceremony, Trooper Sousa was posted to his first field assignment by the executive officer, Lieutenant Colonel Sousa. It was the first time a new trooper had received his first barracks' assignment from his dad.

There were that same day other seniors who were equally proud. In addition to young Sousa, five of his classmates were continuing a family tradition with their appointments to the uniformed force. The program's "Roster of Graduates" contained the following names, each had a familiar ring to it: Stephen F. Byron, James J. Fitzgibbon, Jr., Reynold A. Ilg, Jr., William F. Leary, Jr., and Thomas R. Leccese. Young Leary's dad had enlisted in 1936, while the other seniors had donned the French and electric blue fresh from World War II service. Each had since completed his enforcement career, but the tradition of duty in the two-tone blue would endure during the tenures of a new generation of troopers.

KEHOE REAPPOINTED

Governor Dukakis on January 21, 1975 reappointed John F. Kehoe, Jr. as public safety commissioner. Dukakis' decision was a vote of confidence in Kehoe, and in the administrative record of the prior three years. The appointment, under the 1969 "modernization" statute, was for four years, coterminous with that of the chief executive.

That same evening Commissioner Kehoe joined many others in a tribute to Captain Martin A. Murphy, commanding officer of the detective branch. Murphy was feted at a Framingham testimonial attended by over 600 in recognition of his outstanding law enforcement career. Twenty-five years earlier he had trained a short distance down route nine with the 1949 recruit class. Later, his uniformed service completed, he had served with distinction as a lieutenant detective. That tenure had culminated in his June 1971 appointment as captain and chief of state police detectives.

Martin A. Murphy had earned the respect of all who had been touched by his years as a state police officer. Certain words recurred when he and his service was discussed: "reasonable," "thoughtful," "fair," "able,"; these and other adjectives, however, fell short exactly of describing the personal qualities that had earned the respect of all privileged to have known him. Captain Murphy's years were destined to be limited, poignantly short. His death at fifty in 1977 would halt abruptly new achievements as a teacher and counsellor of young people pursuing careers in criminal justice.

Governor Dukakis at about the same time appointed Charles V. Barry to the cabinet position of secretary of public safety. Secretary Barry was a veteran member of the Boston Police Department, having risen through the ranks to deputy superintendent. Among other responsibilities, he had been heavily involved with the disorders caused in the capital city when busing began in the school system. He had worked closely in that capacity with state police units, an experience that would be beneficial in the secretary's office. Barry was joined in the public safety secretariat by Assistant Secretaries Arthur C. Cadigan, Jr., and Joseph D. Toppin.

One of Secretary Barry's first duties was at the February 28 Commonwealth Armory graduation of the Fifty-Ninth Recruit Troop. The ceremony was held on a Friday evening, attended by

some 3,000 spectators. There were 105 graduates, making it the largest recruit class to that point in time. There was, in addition, another distinctive first in this particular recruit troop. Two of the graduates were women. Not *policewomen,* but *uniformed officers.* Joan M. Farrell and Lorraine R. Ray thus became the first of their sex to wear the French and electric blue. It had been 45 years since Mary Ramsdell and Lotta Caldwell in 1930 had become the nation's first state policewomen. They had established a precedent in their time. Troopers Farrell and Ray would accept the same challenges in their era.

Family traditions were also strengthened at this graduation. Three sons followed their seniors into the uniformed force. One, Richard R. Bolduc, joined his dad Staff Sergeant Robert A. Bolduc, then still on active duty. His two classmates were James M. Cummings, son of retired Lieutenant James F. Cummings, and Peter J. Downey whose dad, after almost three decades of uniformed service, had retired as Major John F. Downey.

Commissioner Kehoe and Deputy Commissioner Lamson opened the graduation program, and, with Colonel Sousa and Lieutenant Colonel Teahan, inspected the training troop standing smartly at attention on the vast armory floor. Senior uniformed branch commanders were on the dais that evening. Participating in the exercises were: Major Edward F. Kelly, Major Frank J. Trabucco, Major George B. Hacking, Major Charles W. Gilligan and Major James V. Oteri. Gilligan and Oteri especially were familiar with the graduation ritual, each having completed an extended tour on the academy staff.

That staff had been expanded, a necessity with 105 green recruits aspiring to become state police officers. Captain Robert J. Fitzgerald was academy commandant, ably assisted by the following:

- Staff Sergeant Robert E. Hunt
- Sergeant Lawrence P. Fay
- Sergeant Paul F. Matthews
- Corporal Robert E. Dunn
- Corporal Philip J. Reilly
- Corporal John P. Tobin
- Corporal Frank E. McGovern

Handling day-to-day training activities were Troopers Sorbera, Moschella, Thompson, Ardita, Gordon, Redfern, Scofield and Donovan. As always, the academy staff had done its job. Proof was the readiness of the men and women they had trained at Framingham for sixteen long weeks. The transition from civilian to trooper once again had been accomplished, largely due to the commitment and skills of the officers who staffed the academy in the winter of 1975.

Several of the new troopers were in the uniformed detail at the annual memorial service on June 6 on the academy grounds. Herbert J. Stingel of the 1922 training class that year placed the memorial wreath for the Former State Troopers. Stingel's role was especially appropriate. He had joined the academy staff in 1925, exactly a half century earlier.

As 1975 closed, the state police role in Boston's school desegregation continued. It was, by any measure, the most taxing duty ever assigned to the department. Over 350 uniformed officers had been committed through most of 1975. Security responsibilities had expanded to South Boston High School, two junior high schools, and nine elementary schools. Duties included monitoring school activities, lunch rooms, gymnasiums, halls and points of access and egress. Bus routes received special attention. It was a total effort. Resources were strained. But the difficult duty ground on, always in close coordination with the Boston and Metropolitan District Commission Police Departments. They, from the beginning, had been at the center of a law enforcement operation unique in its legal, racial and cultural dimensions. Nothing quite like it had ever before occurred in the Commonwealth.

Major Charles W. Gilligan had directed much of the Boston field activity. State police units under his supervision had helped prevent bloodshed in clashes on South Boston's Carson Beach. Gilligan was especially suited for the demanding role. His long service at the academy, coupled with extensive duty in the Harvard Square riots and the Walpole uprisings, had provided valuable lessons for command responsibilities during the school desegregation crisis. On January 1, 1976 Commissioner Kehoe promoted Major Gilligan to the rank of lieutenant colonel, filling the opening caused when Lieutenant Colonel Edward J. Teahan retired. Major Frank J. Trabucco was also elevated to lieutenant colonel in the same order. Trabucco's promotion completed the staffing of senior command positions created by the 1974 reorganization statute.

The Boston school integration duties were a heavy burden on field personnel, the "troops." Since 1921, the assignment as a troop commander had been a prestigious, hard earned post. Lieutenants had commanded the four field troops until the early fifties. The rank was upgraded at that time to captain, and, later, Troops E and F were designated for the Massachusetts Turnpike and Logan International Airport. The troop commander's rank, however, had not changed. Rather, new organizational structures were created, that in their effect, subordinated the troop commander in a lengthening chain of command.

The Troop "C.O.," however, remained the authority figure in field operations. His was the responsibility to produce personnel and resources where and when they were needed. On time. Ready for any eventuality. Veteran state police officers were discharging that critical function in early 1976. Their careers represented a cross section of law enforcement experience not easily duplicated:

- Captain Frederick E. Henley Troop A, Framingham
- Captain Winthrop E. Doty, Troop B, Northampton
- Captain Bohdan W. Boulch, Troop C, Holden
- Captain Raymond M. McGuire Troop D, Middleboro
- Captain James L. Killoran, Troop E, Mass. Pike
- Captain John B. Clemens, Troop F, Logan Airport

For Captain McGuire, Troop D was familiar territory. A Fall River native, he had trained with the last class "under canvas" at Framingham in the spring of 1948. His early years had been spent in barracks throughout Troop D, with a stint at A-2 Andover in the mid-fifties. He had then served an extended tour as an investigator for the Bristol County District Attorney's Office.

In mid-1976 Captain McGuire was in a unique situation, along with a number of other officers. He was over age fifty. His earlier mandatory retirement at that age had been waived because of a court case testing the constitutionality of the mandatory retirement law. Lieutenant Colonel Robert D. Murgia had initiated the legal action in 1972. Several federal courts had heard the case. Conflicting decisions had resulted. Appeals eventually had brought the constitutional issue before the United States Supreme Court. Finally, the nation's highest tribunal on June 25, 1976 upheld the state police mandatory retirement law. The decision affirmed the 1939 statute which had resulted from Governor Leverett Saltonstall's initiative and the work of a legislative commission.

The Supreme Court's decision directly affected Captain McGuire and a number of others in the uniformed branch. Within days they had turned in their equipment at Framingham's Supply Depot, an abrupt end to their enforcement careers. Most of the men held high rank. The immediate effect was to open up some seventy promotions as the departures impacted the command and non-commissioned rank of the state force.

One who had served in those ranks for over four decades was Detective Lieutenant John J. Carney. His uniformed service had begun in 1934 with the much heralded "Golden Class." During the forties, Carney had left the state force for a tour with the Framingham Police Department. He returned in 1949, earning appointment as a lieutenant in the detective branch.

Ten new lieutenant detectives that fall had taken part of their training with the Thirty-Fifth Recruit Troop. These were police veterans, most of them in their late thirties. It was a rugged assignment, especially the swimming sessions held at Babson College in Wellesley. Carney had gone on from that experience to a distinguished state police career, much of it as the supervising state detective in the Worcester County District Attorney's Office.

Former Commissioner Daniel I. Murphy on May 24, 1976 led several hundred others in paying tribute to Lieutenant Carney as he closed his state career. Murphy and Carney had been training academy classmates in 1934, and, throughout their careers, had enjoyed a close personal relationship. Carney's May 24, testimonial was held at the Wachusett Country Club in Worcester County, the jurisdiction where he had made legions of friends, while, at the same time, earning a reputation as an able, professional law enforcement officer. The several hundred present that evening testified with their presence that his personal contributions, during 42 years of public trust, had contributed measurably to the documented achievements of the state force he served so long and so well.

TROOPER EDWARD A. MAHONEY

Detective Lieutenant John J. Carney had known Trooper Edward Andrew Mahoney. Mahoney had enlisted in the uniformed branch in 1959. On April 13, 1973, while he was patrolling the Massachusetts Turnpike, a report had crackled over the cruiser radio. There had been a crash. A car was in flames. The driver was trapped. Mahoney never hesitated. On the scene in moments, he had rushed into the thick smoke to get the occupant out. His own life had been on the line, but he had gotten the job done. Later, on June 30, 1973, he was honored during the graduation ceremonies of the Fifty-Seventh Recruit Troop. His family looked on proudly that day as Commissioner Kehoe awarded Mahoney the state police Medal for Meritorious Service for his selfless act of heroism.

Trooper Mahoney had saved another from fire. Tragically, he would lose his own life in a similar blaze. On November 21, 1976 he stopped a speeder on the Massachusetts Turnpike. Suddenly, a truck slammed into his cruiser. The police vehicle burst into flames. The hero trooper was trapped. Edward Andrew Mahoney left his widow Albertine and four children, the oldest eleven. They were strengthened by their faith, and their friends, in their time of need. The Mahoneys were assisted further with timely financial aid. First, former Commissioner Leo L. Laughlin, on behalf of The Hundred Club, provided immediate financial help. Laughlin represented the philanthropic organization in lifting the spectre of immediate economic hardship.

Later, $50,000.00 was awarded under the Public Safety Officers' Benefits Act of 1976, a federal program administered by the U.S. Justice Department. Former Commissioner Powers, then in Washington as that program's founding director, wrote to Commissioner Kehoe confirming the award:

"This letter constitutes official approval notification of the benefits claim which resulted from the death of Trooper Edward Andrew Mahoney of your department." After specifying procedures, the communication concluded by noting that "While such benefits can never replace the loss of a loved one, we hope the financial assistance will lessen the sudden economic burdens which often attend these tragic events," and, that " . . . it is, in a small way, a fitting memorial to the public service contributions . . . of Edward Andrew Mahoney of the Massachusetts State Police."

A PRESIDENTIAL VISIT

Nineteen seventy-seven began with an auspicious assignment for uniformed troopers. President Jimmy Carter on March 16 and 17 visited the Troop C community of Clinton. He was there to conduct a "town meeting," a forum where he answered questions and talked informally with local residents. The president was an overnight guest of a Clinton family, and he mingled freely during his two day stay.

Troopers coordinated closely with U.S. Secret Service personnel and Clinton police to ensure presidential security. It was a complex assignment, one that required constant vigilance no matter how informal the President's activities appeared to be. Such duty was not new. The state force was long on experience in guarding presidents. While the Carter visit did not create the excitement once so much a part of the Kennedy Hyannisport "Compound," it served as a reminder that the state police for years had been responsible for safeguarding the nation's chief executive on visits to the Bay State.

Days later, in Southeastern Massachusetts, uniformed personnel responded to a phenomenon then rapidly emerging in law enforcement. The New Bedford Police Department was confronted with a "job action." In reality it was strike. There had been little of that since the famous Boston walkout of 1919. On that occasion, state police detectives had been ordered into the capital city. In New Bedford, five decades later, the mayor requested state police assistance to preserve order. Troopers patrolled the Whaling City for four days, responding to 237 calls for police service, and ensuring public order for the duration of the "blue flu" attack. Such police walkouts were steadily increasing throughout the nation, as public employees used militant tactics earlier employed by the labor movement in its classic struggles with the country's industrial giants.

Near New Bedford is Fall River, the "Spindle City." There, in late spring, a testimonial dinner was held for three retired members of the uniformed branch: Captain Raymond M. McGuire, Lieutenant Bertrand A. Caron and Staff Sergeant John M. Farrell. Among the hundreds present was Dr. William Reed, headmaster at South Boston High School. He had won the admiration and respect of state police personnel with his tireless efforts to find peaceful solutions to the conflicts caused by busing in the capital city's school system.

Dr. Reed presented certificates of appreciation to the officers who had helped him shoulder the burdens of his office during that difficult time. The certificates bore the words "Amicus Scholar," friend of the school. Personnel of the state force had developed a deep respect for this man. In the most trying of circumstances, he had held fast to the values which brought him decades earlier to a calling where he sought to share knowledge with others. A commissioned officer who had worked closely with him during the worst of those times later wrote: "Dr. Reed was an educator and humanitarian. He was responsive to all parties, and completely loyal to South Boston High, its faculty, students and all others who were in need of him. He was truly a remarkable human being in a delicate situation. His feelings for the state police were warm and personal. His respect for each of us was admirable and friendly. Dr. Reed left a mark on each of us by his compassion and love for his students black or white. He will always be part of us, a friend of the state police."

The state police commitment in South Boston would end in November, 1977, after *more than three years.* There had never been an assignment of that duration, with an emotional intensity that divided neighborhoods, friends, even families. Hundreds served during those long months. Each performed in such a way as to ensure universal praise for the state force. A brief newspaper article on November 24, 1977 noted the phasing out of the state police from the Boston assignment. One commentator, a former trooper, added a fitting epilogue: "there was never a word of complaint about the men on the state police detail, in fact there have been many words of praise for the manner in which they handled themselves. Their work, in such an explosive atmosphere, under the most trying conditions, will go down as a proud and gallant page in our history." Those words are recorded here to ensure that, years from now, a public record will remain of state police service in Boston during one of the most agonizing eras in the city's storied history.

Hundreds had served in Boston. To identify individuals is selective, unfair to all the rest. Yet that risk must be taken in documenting leadership changes which mark significant junctures in the historical evolution of the state force. For example, Commissioner Kehoe on June 20, 1977 appointed Frank J. Trabucco as the new deputy superintendent of the Massachusetts State Police. Trabucco replaced Colonel Americo J. Souza in the top career post. Souza's appointment as colonel and deputy superintendent had been the first to the newly created office. That distinction, together with some 26 years of duty in the uniformed branch, provided a solid record of public service. Moreover, he remains the only executive officer in the department's history to have posted his son to his first barracks assignment.

Deputy Superintendent Frank J. Trabucco, like Souza, had been intimately involved in difficult policy discussions related to the Boston school assignments. By mid-1977, he had completed over two decades of service both in field and headquarters commands. That balanced experience would prove an asset as administrative issues grew more complex with each passing year. Once, in the distant past, the executive officer of the uniformed branch commanded by fiat. His word was law. Policy was what he said it was. That time was gone. In its place was an era marked by complex relationships between those in senior policy positions and the uniformed personnel across the state.

One area where those relationships had been handled smoothly was in the formation of a new mounted unit. The select group was a throwback to the twenties when a trooper and his horse symbolized the rugged image of the State Police Patrol. Trooper Hollis "Sam" Beattie beginning in 1926 had mounted many of those patrols. Moreover, he was a standout on the trick riding teams of the late twenties and the early thirties. It was natural, then, that the veteran Beattie would help drill the new unit, shaping their riding skills for a ceremony held on the grounds of the National Lancer's parade field in Framingham. Receiving their spurs under Lieutenant (Ret.) Beattie's critical eye were: Lieutenant Richard Olson, Sergeants Eugene J. Kelly, John W. Gilman and Richard C. MacDonald, Corporal John C. Howland, and Troopers Gale P. Stevens, Norman G. Baron, James M. Fell, Charles A. MacDonald, Richard D. Samelson and Richard Seibert.

The new mounted unit, as well as all state police personnel, was shortly affected by Chapter 797 of the Acts of 1977. The law provided that all future promotions to lieutenant in the detective branch come from the ranks of uniformed personnel. It was historic legislation. The statute ensured that all commissioned officers, uniformed or investigative, would henceforth come from the same recruit selection, training and promotional system.

STATE HOUSE VIGIL

But that was for the future. The overriding issue in 1977 was money, or, more accurately, the lack of it. In some ways, the salary dispute was similar to the barracks issue of a decade earlier. Then, in the late sixties, state police wives had picketed the headquarters building on Commonwealth Avenue. They had sought an end to the live-in barracks system, especially its 84 hour duty week. Their trooper-husbands had not joined that bold, precedent making public adventure. Institutional attitudes had not yet evolved sufficiently to have allowed such direct action. But in the late 1970s, the larger society was in the full throes of substantial change in attitudes, expectations, roles and behavior. No institution, especially a public one, could long remain independent of such historical pressures.

The salary issue in late 1977 thus culminated in actions that, while foreign to state police traditions, were consistent with contemporary standards. Over 500 troopers, wives and children in late December marched on the State Capitol demanding a pay raise. Such an increase was long overdue. Inflation had bloated prices dramatically. The dollar's value had shrunk. There had not been a salary increase since December 30, 1973. A trooper's starting pay had been set at $10,288.40, with a maximum of $12,755.60 after six years of service.

That income scale may have been adequate in 1973, but the intervening four years had sapped its purchasing power dramatically. Moreover, uniformed branch personnel were receiving less pay than most municipal departments, and substantially less than other statewide forces of comparable size and capability. In summary, salaries, in December, 1977, were as follows:

Rank	Minimum	Maximum
• Col., Deputy Superintendent	19,656.00	$25,022.40
• Lieutenant Colonel	18,038.80	22,874.80
• Major	16,263.00	20,724.60
• Captain	14,648.40	18,532.80
• Lieutenant	13,049.40	16,543.80
• Staff Sergeant	12,373.40	15,602.60
• Corporal	10,888.80	13,650.00
• Trooper	10,228.40	12,755.60
• Trainee	9,622.60	

The "Christmas March" on the State Capitol was aimed principally at Governor Michael S. Dukakis. That fact alone was a dramatic twist in the relationship between the statewide force and the Commonwealth's chief executive. Governors traditionally had been close to the state police. They were rarely seen in public without a uniformed state police officer close at hand. That closeness had been a treasured asset, a proud assignment. It was the reason that a commentator, years earlier, had dubbed the men in two-tone blues as the "Governor's Police Force." The events of December, 1977, signalled publicly that an unsettling adversarial relationship would mark the remainder of the Dukakis Administration.

That feeling was not evident at the January 30, 1978 premier of "Over One Hundred Years . . . New", a film about the state force. While the title was taken from the 1865 founding of the State Constabulary, the motion picture was centered on the contemporary law enforcement role. Several famous cases were featured, including the renowned 1959 Coyle Brothers manhunt in Middleboro.

Captain Harold J. Reddish and Corporal Paul M. Beloff did yeoman work in getting the film produced, landing such figures as John Wayne and Walter Cronkite for key roles. Uniformed officers handled most of the action roles, replaying a number of scenes that, not long before, had been dangerous enforcement encounters. The film followed earlier movies depicting various aspects of statewide public safety duty. The first, "A Chosen Career," had focused on the recruit training program. Then followed "Dedicated To You" and "When Help Is Needed." Each proved an effective medium for informing the public on the capabilities and enforcement activities of the state police organization.

THE WEEK THE STATE STOOD STILL

Commissioner Kehoe had been joined at Framingham's Monticello for the January 30 screening by a distinguished list of law enforcement officials. Exactly one week later the Monticello was completely isolated. But so was much of the state. The "Great Blizzard of 1978" had racked the entire area beginning at noon on Monday, February 6, and continuing with devastating effect until late Tuesday night. It is impossible now for words adequately to describe the enormity of that killer storm. It was, in effect, a "winter hurricane." Northeast winds drove a tidal wave of ice against the Bay State's North and South Shores. More than a score died. Property damage was in the millions. Devastation lay on all sides. Seaside summer homes were reduced to splintered, icy timbers by the awesome force of wind and water.

The "Blizzard of '78" took its first life quickly, early on Monday. A state highway worker was killed on route 128. By evening that highway was hopelessly blocked. Nothing moved. As the storm's fury rose, its magnitude became evident. It was a monumental natural disaster, one of the worst in the state's history. The blinding snow was estimated in feet rather than inches. By Tuesday, the white blanket had created an eerie scene, without signs of life. Snow plows were snow bound. Public safety efforts stalled. But they never stopped. Troopers braved the killer drifts to rescue people buried in cars. Individual acts went far beyond duty requirements. Most went unrecorded. But they remained permanently etched in the memories of those saved from the numbing clutches on the deadly elements.

Governor Dukakis early had proclaimed a state of emergency. All travel was banned. Army units joined the state's emergency crews in the monumental job of opening vital roadways. Meantime, forced out of their cars, people simply walked. In the process, they rediscovered one another. It was a brief return to a more placid time, before the automobile forever changed the pace and content of daily life. That fleeting sense of things and times past likely will remain imprinted in the mind's eye, crowding out the reality of the hardships left in the wake of the "Blizzard of '78."

By Friday, February 10, major highways had been opened. In the following days schools reopened. People went back to their jobs. A degree of normalcy returned. The state force had been on emergency status from the beginning. As in prior natural disasters, there was no way officially to record the individual acts that, in total, added a bright page in the public service ledger of the state police. The "Great Blizzard of 1978" thus ranks with the Troop B floods of 1928 and 1936, the Great New England Hurricane of 1938, the 1953 Worcester Tornado, and other natural disasters wherein personnel of the state force distinguished themselves with a public service performance found only in the best of law enforcement agencies.

Just days later, those same disciplines were demanded of 119 trainees who reported to Framingham as members of the Sixtieth Recruit Troop. Eight women answered the first roll call. In addition, thirteen of the male trainees represented racial minorities. The Sixtieth was the largest recruit class ever. Their training ordeal began on February 20. The planned graduation date of July 8 must have seemed remote that first morning as requirements fell heavily and often. As in every prior class, there were casualties during the first few days. By the time daily routines settled into a cogent pattern of required activities, only 85 of the original 119 recruits remained.

The loss of 34 trainees resulted in some adverse press reports. Several who had resigned charged that academy staff had subjected them to unnecessary pressures, measures inconsistent with the modern law enforcement role. That same feeling had existed in every recruit troop since the 1921 founding. It was a genuine reaction to the realities of training techniques designed to forge a cohesive unit from a group of strangers; a disciplined, self-reliant individual able to handle a crisis under stress.

The media stories caused some controversy. Doubts were created concerning the validity of the training program. The *Boston Herald,* not the originator of the February news accounts, dispatched writer Eleanor Roberts to the academy in April to do a follow-up story. Following her on-site analysis, Ms. Roberts wrote in part, "A lot of heat was generated when the class first started about the dropout rate of trainees in the current program." Continuing, the story noted: "They started with 119 recruits. Today, 85 are left. The other 34 dropped out for a variety of reasons — many finding the para-military training and discipline too difficult."

The *Herald* account focused on the rationale for the training techniques: "Parris Island it is not. But tough, demanding, rigid, — it is. How else could you turn out crack troopers who could quell a riot in Walpole State Prison or handle a bloody racial demonstration such as the Carson Beach melee in 1975." Captain John F. Kennedy, the Academy commandant, commented on a factor that was obscure but important: "We have only 13 veterans in this class. Most of the trainees had not been subjected to any military training prior to this. Understandably, they found it hard to accept. We have weeded-out those who felt it wasn't right for them or who didn't meet our standards." Kennedy pinpointed a particular aspect of the training he called "purposeful harassment." Amplifying, he noted that "It's very important because when they finish their training and get on the job they're going to get ethnic slurs hurled at them. They're going to have to take a lot of abuse. So, we train them to keep cool, to contain their anger."

The mortality rate in the Sixtieth Recruit Troop seemed high. In reality, it was not. A state police career had never provided physical or psychological comforts. In fact, in a relative comparison, pressures appeared to have eased somewhat. For example, the *Springfield Union* on September 7, 1924 had saluted the "State Police Patrol" on its third birthday. Of the original 1921 complement, however, only thirteen could return that public salute. Twenty-nine had doffed the forest green uniforms during the first three years! Similarly, the *Boston Traveler* on August 20, 1927, reported: "38 husky young men join the ranks of State Police following 10 weeks of high tension training." They had survived from a recruit class of 52. Over 25% of the original trainees had not made it!

The Sixtieth Recruit Troop, then, on balance, was not that different from its predecessors. What had changed, though, was the world around the state force, and its rigid training requirements. If further proof were needed, it had been in the appointment of eight women as trainees. That, in the not too distant past, would have been the butt of a hundred barracks' stories. While, by April, only one woman remained, her incisive comments to *Herald* reporter Roberts explained much. Kathleen M. Coletta of Quincy, described as "slim, attractive, intelligent," compared the academy to her past experiences: "It's very different from U. Mass, Amherst. Relaxed is the word for life on campus. At first I wondered if I could stand the strain and constant supervision — the yelling, the rigorous physical training. But I've adjusted now, though I still find the physical end very difficult." So did the 84 men. But they had a personal objective to be sworn as state police officers. The power of that incentive would sustain them through one of the most demanding recruit programs in the American Police Service.

Meantime, as Trainee Coletta doggedly pursued her trooper's badge, an era ended in the state force. State Policewoman Gloria T. Kennedy retired on May 5, 1978, the last of the women who had followed the traditions first established in 1930 by Mary S. Ramsdell and Lotta H. Caldwell. Her departure signalled the end of almost five decades of public trust discharged by women whose professional skills had been essential to the state enforcement role. Sally J. Raynes had enlisted with Kennedy on January 1, 1962. The two had joined Evelyn S. Kenney, Mary T. Connolly, Alice V. Bragdon, Gracye V. O'Dell, Margaret A. Sheehan, Eleanor G. Dalton, Ann H. Bagley and Mary E. Coveney on the state force. Coveney and her colleagues were joined in 1964 by A. Barbara Johnson. Her enlistment rounded out the roster of state policewomen who served in the fifties, sixties and seventies.

The years since the 1930 pioneering effort by Ramsdell and Caldwell had changed the state policewomen's role, but responsibilities remained substantial to the end. The most intractable demand was that of availability; one's time was never really one's own. One of the women, some years removed from her active 1960's service, recalled that duty requirements were not easily separated from "leisure time" "We were on call 24 hours a day, 7 days a week, and were *frequently* called in from time off to work. It was a necessary hardship to always report our whereabouts to someone, and it was not unusual to be paged over the loudspeaker of a department store to go investigate a cohabitation of a year's duration. It's also amusing to note (in 1979) that many of the crimes policewomen were called upon to investigate are no longer crimes at all."

The "P.W.'s," as they were called, are gone. But their record of public service remains, brightly illuminated in the annals of the state force. That ledger was authored by women who made substantial sacrifices in helping to establish the enviable reputation of their enforcement organization. They made that commitment for 48 years, through the Great Depression, the war years, and, finally, during a time when society's value system seemed ready to disintegrate in the pursuit of instant gratification. The achievements of that era will always be a source of pride for the special few who, with distinction, served as Massachusetts State Policewomen.

GRADUATION DAY

On July 8, in 90 degree heat, the Sixtieth Recruit Troop paraded onto Framingham's well trod field to receive their oath of office. The moment seemed light years removed from the day they had reported, unknowing, in the aftermath of the "Blizzard of '78." Now, though, their time had come. One sensed the pride each felt as the training troop "passed in review" under the practiced stare of senior officers, and the approving eyes of some 3,000 spectators.

Once in place, the recruit troop came to attention during the twentieth annual memorial service, held in conjunction with their graduation. Commissioner John F. Kehoe, Jr. and Colonel Frank J. Trabucco placed a wreath at the memorial on behalf of the state force. President Francis V. Foley of the Former Troopers Association did the same for his membership, many of whom were present. He was assisted by Sergeant (Ret.) Theodore J. Stavredes, secretary of the former troopers. Stavredes had not missed attending the poignant ceremony during the two decades since he helped inaugurate the annual event.

As the graduation ceremony began, few present realized it would be Commissioner's Kehoe's final public responsibility. He shortly announced his intention to leave, completing a tenure begun in 1971. Kehoe was joined on the review platform by Public Safety Secretary Charles V. Barry, and Deputy Commissioner Fred L. Lamson. Father John E. Hartigan opened the graduation activities. The state force's senior commissioned officers were present. They signalled with their presence that the fledgling troopers were beginning careers with revered traditions. Flanking Colonel Trabucco were Lieutenant Colonels James T. Canty, John R. O'Donovan and Robert R. Wills. In addition, the following majors, each a bureau commander, were present: John F. Regan, Clarence W. Demyer, George H. Hall, Richard N. Loynd, James E. Halloran, Jr., and John A. Nielsen.

The recruit troop awed the large crowd with demonstration of skills newly learned during the twenty weeks of rugged training. Several received special recognition for having excelled in key phases of the comprehensive training regime. Those honored for their outstanding performances were:

• Trooper Robert S. Muto, the honor graduate. He received the Captain William V. Shimkus Memorial Trophy. Named for the former executive officer, the award was presented by his nephew, Staff Sergeant Michael J. Shimkus.

• Trooper Kenneth E. Sullivan. He authored the highest academic average in the training class. Sullivan received a scholarship for study at Northeastern University presented by Captain (Ret.) Timothy F. Moran, Dean of the University's law enforcement program.

• Trooper Robert J. Maziarz. As a trainee, Maziarz fired a perfect range score of 360, a first in the academy's history. Staff Sergeant James J. Martin presented a trophy to Maziarz in memory

of his dad, James J. Martin of the "Golden Class" of 1934.

While the recruits deserved recognition for superior training performances, twelve veteran officers were honored for outstanding law enforcement achievements. Each was awarded the state police Medal for Meritorious Service, receiving, in addition, three days off:

• Trooper Thomas L. McLaughlin. McLaughlin on April 3, 1977 had rescued three people from a blazing wreck. He also received the coveted "Trooper of the Year" award from the Former Massachusetts State Trooper organization.

• Detective Lt. George W. Powers, Sergeant James T. McGuiness, Corporal William E. Duke and Trooper Thomas J. O'Connor: These men solved a triple murder in Easthampton, working intensively on their own time to resolve the tragic slayings.

• Detective Lt. John G. Hulme, Sergeant Eugene D. Mattioli, Jr., and Trooper R. White: Their dogged 22 month investigation ended with the arrest of two felons wanted in Connecticut and Rhode Island, as well as in the Bay State.

• Trooper Daniel J. Kavanaugh. Kavanaugh on September 13, 1977, arrested two felons for the armed robbery of a Worcester residence.

• Trooper Donald E. Shea. Trooper Shea apprehended the suspect in a November 13, 1977 rape and robbery in Framingham.

• Detective Lt. William G. Bergin. The detective veteran led an investigation which ended with the conviction of ten people; 25 bank robberies were solved in the process.

• Detective Lt. Milo F. Brown, Jr. Lieutenant Brown's extended probe of a December 13, 1976 murder in North Adams resulted in the murder conviction of two men.

The awards ceremony symbolized the strong traditions of the state force. While new troopers were entering the organization, veteran officers were officially recognized for personal achievements. There was symbolism, too, as Commissioner Kehoe presented graduation diplomas to the 84 newly sworn troopers, and Colonel Frank J. Trabucco posted them to the six field troops. The closing moments of the graduation exercises were tinged with a vague sense of loss, of final parting. The feeling was created by the "exchange of guidons," the transfer of the recruit troop to the ranks of the uniformed branch. The academy guidon was returned to the staff. It would be unfurled with the arrival of the next recruit troop.

For the academy staff the symbolic exchange of colors completed their responsibilities. Their jobs had been difficult. This staff had proven its mettle. One look at the disciplined recruit troop spoke volumes about the quality of the training imparted by the staff. The academy had always drawn men with talent and commitment. The solid performance of those who trained the 1978 recruit class measurably strengthened that tradition:

• Major John F. Kennedy Commandant	• Trooper Donald A. Cucinelli
	• Trooper John E. Murphy
• Lieutenant Phillip J. Reilley	• Trooper James A. Redfearn
• Staff Sergeant James J. Martin	• Trooper Daniel J. Donovan
• Sergeant Frank E. McGovern	• Trooper John W. Nulty
• Corporal Thomas J. McNulty	• Trooper Donald W. Woodson
• Trooper Allan H. Thompson	• Trooper Gerald Venezia
• Trooper Alex J. Exarhopolous	• Trooper John DiFava
• Trooper Francis R. Ardita	

Reverend Frank J. Bauer closed the graduation program. The academy staff was proud, satisfied with a job well done. Each knew that his professional commitment had helped to prepare new state police officers with the knowledge and skills essential to effective discharge of contemporary law enforcement responsibilities.

As the new troopers reported for their first duty, the passing of an old trooper saddened members and friends of the state force. Reverend Ernest A. Thorsell in 1933 had joined the uniformed branch. His training class had been the first to wear the new, two-tone blue uniforms for graduation. Thorsell had authored another first, a personal one. He was, at his enlistment, an ordained minister. Following some eleven years of active duty, he returned to that ministry, serving for an extended time at the Theodore Parker Church in West Roxbury. His July, 1978 death ended a unique career of public trust, one marked by the distinguishing feature of service to his fellow man.

A TENURE CLOSES

Commissioner Kehoe in August announced his intention to leave to accept a position as Director of Corporate Security for the Boston Edison Company. Kehoe had completed seven years in the commissioner's post, a substantial tenure for the state's top enforcement office. The Boston College graduate had begun his public career in 1941, thus completing almost four decades in law enforcement on the federal and state levels.

Kehoe had served during a difficult era. He had begun his tenure in September 1971, soon after the live-in barracks system had ended. That had not been an easy time. There was a new system to implement, one that broke from traditional practices. In addition, uniformed personnel were newly organized as an effective lobbying unit, one to be reckoned with on policy and administrative matters. In short, it was a time of substantial transition. The structured, set ways of the past had given way to changes generated by the dynamics of the larger society. The commissioner's office was not an easy post during the 1970's decade.

Each such tenure leaves its mark, often in the eye of the beholder. It depends upon one's perception of things. Thus, in one view, there emerges the consolidation of the state police organization as a single, unified enforcement structure. Generated by the 1974 authorizing legislation, this accomplishment looms as a significant historical achievement. The net effect was to create an enforcement organization wherein all personnel are selected, trained, assigned and promoted based upon statutory criteria and uniform management policies. Put differently, the changes ensured that all future members and leaders of the state police would begin their careers with appointments to the state police academy. Observers of the state force will appreciate the substantial operational implications of that change. Future personnel will probably view it as a footnote in history, one that also includes forest green uniforms, red ties, horses, "mess boys", and a live-in barracks system. That seems the fate of any "major" reform once time lends its dimension, proving, always, that the only constant *is* change.

Governor Michael S. Dukakis on August 30 named Dennis M. Condon Commissioner of Public Safety. The appointment capped Condon's long public service career, one begun in the post World War II years in his native Boston. Commissioner Condon had interrupted studies at Boston College for World War II service as a Navy lieutenant. Returning to Chesnut Hill, he took the Bachelor of Arts degree in 1947, going on to graduate work at Boston University. Then followed three years as a teacher in the Boston school system.

Condon in 1951 joined the Federal Bureau of Investigation.

Assignments followed in Washington, D.C., Philadelphia, New York City and Boston. He developed expertise during those tours in criminal investigations, especially bank robberies and organized crime. During his 26 year F.B.I. career, he received a number of commendations from the Attorney General and the Director of the F.B.I. Special Agent Condon, in addition, was cited in 1972 by the American Legion for superior contributions to the criminal justice field.

Following his 1977 retirement from the F.B.I., Condon was appointed to the Massachusetts Board of Appeals on Motor Vehicle Liability Policies and Bonds. He was discharging those responsibilities when selected by Governor Dukakis as the fifteenth public safety commissioner since the 1921 founding of the State Police Patrol.

Commissioner Condon on September 6 officially began his new duties. Within days, Edward J. King defeated Governor Michael S. Dukakis in the Democratic primary. It was, at the moment it happened, a startling upset, one deemed improbable by political pundits only weeks earlier. One searched modern history to find only one prior upset of such magnitude; the Francis X. Bellotti defeat of Governor Endicott Peabody in the 1964 primary. But Bellotti had been lieutenant governor, with a substantial following in the electorate. King's emergence as an outsider added lustre to his dramatic victory. Everyone, it seemed, had been taken by surprise with this unanticipated juncture in biography and history.

In the aftermath, however, answers emerged. The signs had been there. For the first time in its history, the state force had been publicly involved in a gubernatorial contest. Analysts had seriously underestimated the impact on the Dukakis Administration of the unrelenting public attacks mounted by state police personnel across the state. Pundits acknowledged, with hindsight, that the fulcrum of the startling upset had been the sustained, ubiquitous allegations made by the State Police Association of Massachusetts against their governor.

If one needed to be convinced that things had indeed changed in six decades, the King victory provided more than enough assurances. The 1921 founding of the State Police Patrol had created a rigidly structured, semi-military organization. Because communication and information were key to the exercise of authority, they were closely held by the leadership. It is not to overstate to say that, back then, a patrolman's world began and ended in his barracks, often many miles from home.

That system was right for its time. Without it, today's organization would not exist. Discipline was rigid. Personal latitude did not exist. This was especially true in terms of self-expression. One did not venture an opinion in the presence of the early established maxim that "the Senior Man spoke only to Jesus, and the Corporal spoke only to God." That principle guided *internal* opinions. *Public* expression on policy issues required no such inhibitors. The thought simply did not occur to those who served through the Post World War II years. And, if it had, the hypothetical imperatives were such to convince even the most courageous that the sanctions far outweighed the remote possibility of gaining the objective.

Thus, the inhibition against public expression on agency matters was deeply rooted in the state force's standards of conduct. A 1964 meeting between Commissioner Robert W. MacDonald and a committee of state police *wives* had portended subsequent events. The late sixties had then witnessed picketing by wives of General Headquarters in Boston. Finally, in what can now be seen as the inevitable outcome of a decade's long process, the State Police Association of Massachusetts was organized in late 1968.

Still, with all of that, the 1977 "Christmas March" on the State Capitol had immediately opened new vistas. Clearly it was a new era, one where traditional prerogatives gave away to the exigencies of the hour. Where "time off" and the barracks system had been the object of the 1960's demonstrations, salaries shrinking daily in the presence of an unrelenting inflationary spiral had proven the final straw, the fulcrum for public confrontations between a governor and his state police organization.

Edward J. King on November 7 followed his primary upset of Governor Dukakis by winning the chief executive's office over Francis W. Hatch, Jr. King's public service career had thus culminated in the state's highest elective post. His earlier leadership had been largely responsible for the modernization of Logan International Airport. The new governor had achieved that complex goal as executive director of the Massachusetts Port Authority. That tenure earned him a deserved reputation as a strong supporter of the state police. Troopers assigned to port facilities consistently enjoyed the superior personnel policies and enforcement equipment provided by port authority leadership.

There seems now not much doubt that state police support was crucial to Edward J. King's ascendancy to the Commonwealth's governorship. Election night photos highlighted the state police presence. Post-election analyses pinpointed the role played by the state force in the outcome. Thus, the uniformed branch had, in six decades, completed its public journey. In the beginning there was the remote State Police Patrol, known but to its members, families and the rural folk who quickly became staunch supporters. There was now a statewide enforcement agency fully involved with policy and political issues central to the discharge of the Commonwealth's public safety responsibilities to its citizens.

Governor-elect King on December 15 announced the appointment of George A. Luciano as Secretary of the Executive Office of Public Safety. At the same news conference, King confirmed the reappointment of Dennis M. Condon as public safety commissioner. That dual announcement established the state police leadership positions for the new Administration.

For Secretary Luciano, elevation to the cabinet post capped a quarter century in the state's criminal justice system. He had begun that career with the Thirty-Seventh Recruit Troop in 1953. Following graduation from the academy, assignments followed in Troop D, at the Rehoboth and Nantucket Barracks. In the late 1950's, the then Sergeant Luciano was transferred to General Headquarters, Boston, assigned to the Public Relations Bureau.

Governor John A. Volpe in 1961 selected Luciano as his state police aide. The two developed a close personal relationship during that assignment. Then followed a two year tour as captain and commander of Troop D, Middleboro. Following that assignment, Captain Luciano in late 1964 was reassigned to General Headquarters.

When John A. Volpe re-entered the governor's office in January, 1965, he appointed Captain Luciano his executive assistant with broad oversight for criminal justice policy. That post enabled the former trooper to help shape policy and legislation beneficial to the state force. Later that year Volpe again turned to his trusted policy aide to fill a key post, that of Superintendent of the Bureau of State Buildings. With the development of the state's government center complex just getting underway, the position was central to major capital outlay decisions then impending. In addi-

tion, as superintendent, Luciano became administrative head of the Capitol Police Force.

Thirteen years followed in the superintendent's office, climaxed by Governor King's offer of the state's top law enforcement post. Criminal justice experience first gained as a trooper, had coincided with King's perception of the skills required to manage the public safety secretariat. The result brought one who had worn the state police uniform for over twelve years to a critical leadership responsibility. That 1979 outcome could not have been prophesied when George A. Luciano accepted his trooper's badge in October, 1953.

TROOPER DONALD E. SHEA

The governor's announcement of the Luciano and Condon appointments was only hours old when disbelief, then sadness, enveloped personnel of the state force. Trooper Donald E. Shea was killed in the early morning hours of December 16 in a cruiser accident on route 9 in Natick. Shea, enroute to a Newton accident, had swerved to avoid a pedestrian in the roadway. The cruiser skidded out of control, hitting a pole. The 28 year old enforcement officer died of massive injuries a short time later at Leonard Morse Hospital.

Commissioner Condon, Colonel Trabucco and Shea's commanding officer, Captain Robert E. Hunt, joined Mrs. Kathryn S. Shea at her young husband's side. Just weeks before, they had watched him honored at the July 8 graduation of the Sixtieth Recruit Troop. Trooper Shea that day had received the State Police Medal for Meritorious Service. He had won the coveted honor for his successful investigation of a major felony case in Framingham.

Trooper Donald E. Shea had enlisted in the uniformed branch on February 28, 1975. He ranked high in academy performance, followed that with superior enforcement work in barracks' assignments. His career, when measured by its length, had been relatively short. But that yardstick falls short. A more accurate assessment is the esteem felt for him by his brother officers as a husband and father of two young children, and as one who had, with the supreme sacrifice, honored the uniform he had worn so proudly.

Trooper Shea's untimely death came at particularly difficult time for the uniformed force. Just days before the Natick tragedy, Trooper Paul J. Darmery of the Andover Barracks had survived a close call on route 93 near the New Hampshire border. As Darmery had responded to an emergency call, thread stripped from a rear tire. His cruiser struck a guard rail, flipped over, and exploded. The young trooper, despite his painful injuries, kicked open a door and escaped.

On that same December 8 morning, Trooper Brian R. Kynock was transporting a prisoner to the Northampton Barracks. Without warning, the prisoner lunged at Kynock with a knife, slashing at his throat. The injured trooper freed his service revolver and fired. The wounded assailant was rushed to the hospital. He died several hours later.

These tragic events in the final month of 1978 underlined the personal dangers inherent in the state enforcement role. While the organization's duties had evolved steadily through six decades, one constant remained. The individual officer was *the* organization, the essential ingredient no matter the advances in technology and procedure. That, it seemed, would never change. It had always been true. It would remain so in the time ahead.

Nineteen Seventy-Nine began for the state force on a bright

note. The inaugural activities of the King Administration featured a strong state police presence. The distinctive uniforms added to the color of the numerous official and social events which mark the early days of an incoming administration.

In the first month of 1979, moreover, there was an additional accomplishment to celebrate. The pay dispute that had triggered the acrimony between the Dukakis Administration and the state police Association of Massachusetts had been settled in December. Months of negotiations had finally brought the long overdue salary package increase for the uniformed rank and file.

The contract was signed on December 6, 1978. A comprehensive document, it contained agreements on a full range of policy and procedural questions essential to the effective performance of the uniformed force. The central issue, however, was salary. Inflation had eroded dramatically pay checks that had not been increased since 1973. The agreement sought to mitigate the cumulative effect of the inadequate salary structure in the presence of the nation's unremitting inflationary spiral. The contract document contained the following pay specifications:

Rank:	Trooper	
Effective Date	Minimum	Maximum
June 30, 1976		
(in effect since 1973)	$10,228.40	$12,755.60
July 1, 1976	10,882.04	13,446.68
July 1, 1977	12,404.08	15,034.24
October 1, 1978	12,929.28	15,559.44
September 30, 1979	13,529.36	16,159.52

Similarly, the negotiated agreement contained retroactive provisions for all ranks in the SPAM bargaining unit, those through the grade of staff sergeant. The effect was to create the following salary scale:

	Corporal	
Effective Date	Minimum	Maximum
June 30, 1976		
(in effect since 1973)	$10,888.80	$13,650.00
July 1, 1976	11,552.32	14,354.08
July 1, 1977	13,091.00	15,964.52
October 1, 1978	13,616.20	16,489.72
September 30, 1979	14,216.28	17,089.80

	Sergeant	
June 30, 1976		
(in effect since 1973)	$11,570.00	$14,658.80
July 1, 1976	12,243.92	15,379.52
July 1, 1977	13,800.28	17,013.88
October 1, 1978	14,325.48	17,539.08
September 30, 1979	14,925.56	18,139.16

	Staff Sergeant	
June 30, 1976		
(in effect since 1973)	$12,373.40	$15,602.60
July 1, 1976	13,059.28	16,338.40
July 1, 1977	14,635.92	17,996.16
October 1, 1978	15,161.12	18,521.35
September 30, 1979	15,761.20	19,121.44

SIX DECADES CLOSE

Governor Edward J. King on March 22, 1979 administered the oath of office to Dennis M. Condon in the State Capitol. The governor's reappointment of Condon as public safety commissioner established state police leadership responsibilities for the King Administration. The ceremonies also witnessed the swearing in of George H. Tully and Michael F. Farrington as assistant secretaries in the executive office of public safety. Tully and Farrington thus joined Secretary George A. Luciano in the cabinet secretariat, charged with the management of the state's comprehensive public safety services.

A week later, 339 troopers reported to Boston's Commonwealth Armory. The March 31 assemblage, however, was unlike state police activities that had transpired there during the state force's earlier decades. These personnel were vying for promotion to two corporal's vacancies! The candidates, however, could anticipate that another 50 or so promotions to corporal would open up during the two year life of the final eligibility list.

That same morning news media struggled to inform the nation what had happened on a small island in Pennsylvania's Susquehanna River. It was not easy. The atomic age's seemingly remote hypothetical imperatives overnight had become an alarming reality. The March 31 editions of the Washington Post with a Middletown, Pa., dateline attempted a description: "The day that no one wanted and few believed possible — the day nuclear power would drive people from their homes — arrived here today. As the crippled Three Mile Island atomic power plant near here continued to leak radiation, Middletown and sister communities began small-scale evacuations of preschool children and pregnant women . . . . Emergency vehicles toured, warning residents to take cover. Workers scurried about with bright yellow Geiger counters checking for radiation . . . Banks were shut down. Some families hurriedly tossed suitcases into car trunks. Others stayed. Police reported several accidents along main routes. Tonight's Middletown High senior prom was cancelled . . . Extra police were brought into Middletown, a borough of 11,000, where the mayor said he would order his 13 man force to shoot looters." Experts sought to calm fears. But their credibility overnight had been seriously damaged, eroded even further as deadly radiation seeped through the four foot thick walls surrounding the reactor's 36,000 uranium fuel rods.

In that ill-defined contemporary setting, the state's force faced the future's unknowns with the rest of humanity. In spite of the ominous portents inherent in the nuclear accident, life in the Atomic Age would go on. And, as before, the delicate balance between individual liberties and majority rights would remain the bedrock of the Federal Republic and its enforcement agencies.

As the Commonwealth's premier criminal justice agency, the Massachusetts State Police in 1979 was, by any standard, a superior enforcement organization. Review of the state force's structure and staffing seems appropriate in a work which has sought to illuminate the salient junctures in its history.

That history has been authored by individuals. The 1921 cadre that encamped at Framingham's "Poor Farm," had, in 1979, grown to 1,016 uniformed officers. In addition, 63 officers staffed the Office of Investigations and Intelligence Operations, formerly the detective branch of the Division of State Police. The rank structure was staffed as follows:

Rank	Number
• Colonel	1
• Lieutenant Colonel	3
• Major	5
• Captain	14
• Detective Captain	3
• Lieutenant	35
• Detective Lieutenant	58
• Staff Sergeant	58
• Sergeant	61
• Corporal	67
• Troopers	773

The ranks as well as the total complement included uniformed personnel assigned to the Massachusetts Turnpike and Port Authorities. The Commonwealth annually was reimbursed for those police services. Earlier pages contain a summary of pay scales through the staff sergeant's rank. The following schedule presents the salary structure for the commissioned ranks:

Rank	Minimum	Maximum
• Lieutenant	$15,172.00	18,753.00
• Detective Lieutenant	15,955.00	19,808.00
• Captain	16,811.00	20,792.00
• Detective Captain	17,592.00	21,879.00
• Major	18,466.00	23,040.00
• Lieutenant Colonel	20,286.00	25,243.00
• Colonel	21,944.00	27,444.00

In addition, salary increments were earned in accordance with specific levels of educational achievements. Moreover, SPAM's newly signed contract for officers through the rank of staff sergeant contained specific provisions for court appearances and overtime pay. The same document contained agreements on special details, paid assignments worked on one's regular time off.

General Headquarters in 1979 was at 1010 Commonwealth Avenue in Boston. There, the state force's administrative structure was staffed as follows:

- Commissioner, Superintendent — Dennis M. Condon
- Deputy Commissioner — Fred I. Lamson
- Colonel, Deputy Superintendent, Executive Officer — Frank J. Trabucco
- Lieutenant Colonel
  Office of Field Operations — James T. Canty
- Lieutenant Colonel
  Office of Investigations and
  Intelligence Operations — John R. O'Donovan
- Lieutenant Colonel
  Office of Staff Operations — Robert R. Wills
- Major
  Bureau of Eastern Field Operations — George H. Hall
- Major
  Bureau of Western Field Operations — Richard N. Loynd
- Major
  Bureau of Investigative Services — John F. Regan
- Major
  Bureau of Administrative Services — John F. Kennedy
- Major
  Bureau of Technical Services — James E. Halloran
- Major
  Headquarters Section — Robert C. Woodward

The field troops since September, 1921, had been the backbone, the essential component of the state police organization. In the beginning, there had been but two: Troop A, Framingham, and Troop B, Northampton. Troop C in 1923 was established in Paxton, and Troop D in Middleboro. Those four line organizations were the state police visible presence for almost four decades. Then, Troop E was opened in May, 1957, on the Massachusetts Turnpike. The final field troop, F, was established at Logan International Airport in the early 1960's.

"Troop Commander" for half a century was the most prestigious rank one could hold in the uniformed force. That designation connoted a precise mandate; authority and accountability for a specific, carefully defined section of the state. The field "CO" and his personnel *were* the state police. They were the visible presence, the ever available, uniformed symbol of a much admired statewide enforcement agency.

Recent years had brought several reorganizations. Additional ranks had been authorized. New administrative structures had been created. The "chain of command" had lengthened between the troop commander and the state force's top administrative posts. Nevertheless, the field commander and his personnel remained the one indispensable strength in state enforcement operations. Everything else, all the modern technologies, existed for one principal purpose: to ensure that the troop commander and the field trooper discharge the accountability inherent in the state force's statutory mandates. As the seventies ended, the following provided field leadership much as their predecessors had done for six decades:

- Captain Robert E. Hunt — Troop A, Framingham
- Captain Leonard F. VonFlatern — Troop B, Northampton
- Captain Raymond G. Ethier — Troop C, Holden
- Captain George A. Kimball — Troop D, Middleboro
- Captain John J. Cronin — Troop E, Mass. Turnpike
- Captain Michael J. Noone — Troop F, Logan International Airport

These commanders supervised a system of 29 strategically located barracks:

Troop A, Framingham
- Andover
- Topsfield
- Concord
- Foxboro
- Lynnfield

Troop B, Northampton
- Lee
- Shelburne Falls
- Monson
- Pittsfield
- Russell

Troop C, Holden
- Athol
- Grafton
- Brookfield
- Leominster
- Sturbridge

Troop D, Middleboro
- Norwell
- Yarmouth
- North Dartmouth
- Oak Bluffs
- Nantucket
- Bourne

Troop E, Turnpike
- Headquarters Weston
- Charlton
- Westfield

Troop F, Port Authority
- Headquarters Logan International Airport

Troops A, B, C and D had operational substations within the troop headquarters facilities. The Troop D barracks at Rehoboth, formerly D-4, was phased out in the early 1970's. Troop F, headquartered at Logan Airport, patroled the Port Authority's piers, Tobin Memorial Bridge and Hanscomb Field in Bedford.

Backing the field troops was a broad spectrum of administrative and technical capabilities. Some, like the forensic sciences, pre-dated the uniformed force. Others, for example, photography, accident analyses and similar staff functions, dated from the mid-1920's. Finally, there were the advanced technologies, an expanding feature of the contemporary criminal justice agency. The best example seemed the Law Enforcement Agencies Processing System (LEAPS). A highly technical computer based system, LEAPS in 1970 had replaced the traditional teletype machines as the organization's vital communications network. By 1979, LEAPS had evolved substantially toward a state criminal justice information system (CJIS). It was contemplated that CJIS's esoteric technology would make possible a comprehensive repository of data responsive to the information needs of the state's enforcement, judicial and penal agencies.

The state police fleet also reflected the organization's structure and enforcement systems. Mobility remained essential. But the mode, like the state force itself, had changed dramatically in sixty years. Where horses and motorcycles had once backboned field operations, the former, as the 1980's impended, were only a memory, while the latter had been reduced to ten two wheelers. Thus, in 1979, the fleet was composed of the following:

• Two-tone blue cruisers	520
• Unmarked cruisers	350
• Motorcycles	10
• Snowmobiles	4
• Snow-Cat Tractor	1
• Helicopter	1

Additionally, there was a support fleet of some thirty vehicles; trucks, vans, buses, and the like. The fleet in 1979 would log approximately 20,000,000 miles, use some 1,700,000 gallons of gasoline a commodity on the leading edge of the nation's unnerving inflationary spiral.

The budget required to support the total state police operation had expanded inexorably through the years. Like the force itself, increases had been marginal through the Great Depression, World War II and the immediate post-war years. But with accelerating responsibilities, fiscal appropriations had escalated dramatically.

The result in 1979 was a state police budget of $21,800,000. Of that amount, $16,862,250. was earmarked for personal services, principally salaries. The state force's budget request submitted for the first year of the 1980's was $25,030,770. The personal services request totaled some $18,675,890. Such figures are abstract. They convey no insights, no specific, comprehensible information. But they confirm even the casual observer's intuitive sense that 1921 and 1980 represented two different eras in the department's history.

• • •

The following officers were killed in the line of duty during the nineteen seventies:

Robert J. MacDougall: Died August 6, 1971 as the result of a motor vehicle accident on Route 20 in Worcester.

Edward A. Mahoney: Died November 21, 1976 as the result of a motor vehicle accident on the Massachusetts Turnpike.

Donald E. Shea: Died December 16, 1978 as the result of a motor vehicle accident on Route 9 in Natick.

• • •

The following were among those appointed to the Detective Branch during the 1970's:

Walsh, David F.	Denehy, Joseph F.	Bider, Robert J.
Ellsworth, Charles L.	Dwyer, John P.	Thorpe, Frank P.
Hamilton, James F.	McGarity, George E.	Sibley, Roy F.
Amirault, John A.	Boyajian, Alfred P.	Spartichino, Thomas E.
DeFuria, Ralph F.	Penta, Vincent G.	O'Halloran, Thomas F. Jr.
Smith, Edward J.	Fuller, Alton J.	Horgan, William P.
Cummings, Robert J.	Mowles, John A.	McDonnell, Joseph T.
Miller, William A.	Boike, Samuel J.	DeStefano, Peter L.
Sharkey, James S.	Riley, William J.	

• • •

The following were appointed to the Massachusetts State Police Academy during the 1970's:

FIFTY-FOURTH RECRUIT TROOP
April 21, 1970

Young, James E.	Winters, John	Jordan, Barry D.
Greaney, Paul M.	Daigle, Joseph B.	Stoddard, Larry H.
Turner, Stephen J.	Tavares, Ernest J.	Vandal, Wayne R.
Lynch, James J.	Hamilton, Raymond G., Jr.	Ferrick, Michael E.
St. Jean, Robert J.	Abraham, Robert M.	Comeau, Ronald M.
DeCiero, Robert J.	Belhumeur, Robert T.	Gregoire, Ronald J.
Bellevue, Steven T.	Cucinelli, Donald A.	Sjoberg, Carl E.
Hayes, John J.	Desmond, Edward A.	Mott, George
Holloway, Richard E.	Shannon, John I.	Cratty, Frederick T.
Gabriel, Michael J.	Livingston, William R.	Glynn, John A., Jr.
Pelletier, Ronald G.	Dellorfano, Michael II.	Budd, Frank H., Jr.
Lavers, Charles W. III	Gradowski, Stanley J., Jr.	Larsen, Reginald W.
Brangan, Douglas C.	Souza, Joseph	Dumas, Francis A.
Allen, John J.	Wykes, Douglas W.	Donovan, James C.
Lamoly, Ronald	Palermo, Matthew A. Jr.	Keating, James J.
Hennesey, Michael G.	McLaughlin, Thomas L.	Coleman, Peter F., III
Ursini, Joseph W.	O'Brien, Thomas J., Jr.	Podlovits, Edward F.
LaRossa, Richard	O'Connell, John T. Jr.	Fogarty, Edward F.
Fasulo, James P.	Doherty, Joseph F. Jr.	

FIFTY-FIFTH RECRUIT TROOP
September 18, 1971

Murphy, John E.	O'Donnell, James T.	Handlin, Denehy J.
Shanahan, Michael B.	Hackett, Walter F.	Lacasse, Roland Jr.
Bird, Robert J.	Dushame, John J.	Hopper, Bruce W.
MacDougall, George D.	Cedrone, Steven M.	Liebel, Francis J.
Riley, Francis D.	Comerford, James D.	Meier, Robert C.

Pinkham, John D
Bradley, Robert J.
Bumpus, Michael C .
Gordon, Bruce P.
Shattuck, Edwin W.
Gosselin, Robert C.
Kavanaugh, Daniel J.
Powers, Richard
Redfearn, James G.
Burkhard, Charles P.
Fallon, Kevin J.
Ray, Joseph L.
Baima, Donald E.
Bogosian, Bruce A.
Lynch, Philip E.
Gillespie, Michael F.
Spellacy, John M.
Noyes, Peter M.
Stefani, Michael T.
Boyd, Richard W.
McKinnon, Charles J.
Conwell, John E.
Douthwright, David H.
Martin, Randall J.
Scofield, Robert W.
Dalbec, Leo P.
Samuelson, Richard P.
Fitzgerald, Daniel M.
Donovan, Daniel J.
Kelley, Frederick J., Jr.
Morrison, Charles E.
Bowlby, Charles L.
Rand, Richard P.
Tourigny, Clement G.
Burnickas, Thomas F.
Fitzgerald, James M.
Gonsalves, Jose C.
Poehler, Peter K.
Hubbard, Edward J.
Porche, Arthur J.
Nulty, John W.
McHugh, Paul F.
Shea, John B.
Wehr, Dale L.
Bourque, Arthur J., III
Flynn, William F.
Nowak, Paul E.
Sibley, Brian W.

FIFTY-SIXTH RECRUIT TROOP
April 29, 1972

Seguin, Richard W.
Zepf, Robert G.
Kelley, John J. Jr.
Ranieri, David A.
Hepworth, Richard A.
St. Andre, Richard A.
Dion, Thomas M.
Soutier, Thomas E.
Kelly, Richard E.
Lauria, Richard D.
Delmolino, John E.
Wilson, George B. Jr.
Kenney, David B.
Toomey, James M.
Maile, Robert P.
Cerra, Robert L.
Flaherty, John F.
Johanson, Gilbert A.
Jubinville, Robert L., Jr.
Burns, Gary J.
Fogarty, William F.
Nicosia, Thomas F.
Gelnett, Larry B.
Pogodinski, David T.
Ford, Roger A.
McCarthy, Joseph F.
Marcotte, Henry N.
Petrucci, William P.
Keller, James J.
Godfrey, William E.
McDonald, Paul H.
Norton, Francis A.
O'Connor, James A.
Roy, James E.
Keane, Patrick J.
Murphy, Kevin M.
Colson, Lawrence M.
Martin, Andrew R.
Brown, William M.
Johnson, Edward F., Jr.
Murphy, Gerard D.
Doody, Richard L.
Sterling, Earle S. Jr.
Scott, Robert G.
DeLesDernier, Richard F., Jr.
Cattabriga, Wayne E.
Walsh, James F.
Blanchard, Kenneth R., Jr.
Souza, Russell V.
Elms, William J., III
Humphrey, Paul R..
O'Neil, Charles J.
Palombo, Andrew C.
McDermott, Francis J.
Maloney, John F., Jr.
Rober, John W.
Dorn, Michael P.
McNally, Thomas M.
Wainwright, Richard S., Jr.
Hackett, Timothy G.
Dusoe, Michael E.
Brock, Thomas P.
Yancey, Carl S.
Boudrea, John F.

FIFTY-SEVENTH RECRUIT TROOP
June 30, 1973

Mullen, Bradley J.
MacDonald, Bruce D.
Kennedy, Daniel J.
Andrews, Ronald R.
Malone, John J., III
Sheehan, Daniel J.
Noyes, Charles E.
Holmes, Pehr B.
Robichaud, Martin E.
McKeon, Robert J.
McCue, Thomas K.
Charpentier, Donald E.
Cox, Cyrus E.
Taliaferro, Frederick D.
Tavares, Antonio A.
Walsh, John J.
Tarsook, Charles E.
Okraska, Richard S.
Casassa, Robert C.
Credit, George E.
Spriggs, James
Scott, Ronald R.
Bulgar, Stephan C.
Toney, Albert M. Jr.
Nicosia, Jeffrey A.
Siebert, Richard Sr.
Mitchell, Albert C.
Manuel, Kenneth L.
Cardoza, Richard P.
LaPage, John D.
Howley, Joseph F, III
Woodson, Donald F.
Dwyer, Neal D.

FIFTY-EIGHTH RECRUIT TROOP
October 19, 1974

Saltzman, Michael J.
Parmakian, Joseph E.
Jacobs, Robert D.
Papineau, Thomas L.
Sousa, Stephen J.
Howe, Brian L.
Quigley, Thomas J.
Venezia, Gerald
Spirlet, Raymond J.
Constantine, Tom T.
Fraelick, Richard L.
Ozyzewski, Boleslaw A., Jr.
Riopel, Joseph T.
Sullivan, Brian A.
Lindberg, John W.
Mucci, Michael C.
Corry, Robert A.
Snow, David A.
Driscoll, Francis S.
Murphy, Peter A.
Mooza, Robert J.
White, Walter C.
Hanlon, Richard P.
Kenney, Wayne J.
Garvin, John E.
Pennini, Robert A.
Bernard, Gilbert M.

Smith, George P.
Creighton, Thomas E. II
Koumanelis, Frank T.
McLaughlin, Arthur W. Jr.
Landry, Paul R.
Jamroz, Daniel E.
Regan, Paul J.
Dreaney, Mark F.
Connolly, Edward P.
Higgins, Peter J.
Hillman, Reed V.
Catellier, Richard G.
Benoit, Robert E.
Grabowski, Daniel A.
Caulfield, John F.
Sprague, John R.
Hendrigan, Roderick A.
Ilg, Reynold A., Jr.
Pease, Gary B.
Hanna, George L.
Leary, William F., Jr.
Owens, Lawrence M.
Powers, William J.
Krainski, James J.
Israel, James E.
Byron, Stephen F.
Kelly, John D.
Puller, Alfred
Crowley, Peter D.
O'Brien, Francis M.
Yagodzinski, Charles J.
Gravelle, Stephen L.
Cunningham, John A.
Moulaison, Thomas G.
Fitzgibbon, James J., Jr.
Kozaczka, Francis S.
Leccese, Thomas R.
Colby, John F.
Barboza, Kenneth G.
Jackson, Eugene M.
Lynch, Stephen G.

FIFTY-NINTH RECRUIT TROOP
February 28, 1975

Hollenkamp, Gregory T.
Pucinno, Albert W.
Bennett, Dean R.
Coulter, William J.
DiFava, John
Hult, Dana R.
Bennett, Stephen L.
Duffy, Thomas B.
Simpson, John W.
Hibbard, Bradley G.
Crowley, Joseph L.
Melia, Michael P.
Murphy, Paul J.
Shea, Donald E.
White, Richard F.
Consigli, John E.
Gorman, William E.
Brady, Richard T.
Calderwood, Roger L.
Cronin, Jerome J. Jr.
Mason, Gary N.
Downey, Peter J.
Koenig, Christopher F.
Fogarty, James P.
Cherven, Michael F.
Healy, John F. Jr.
Galvin, Dennis J.
Leveille, Charles F.
Bowman, Jay A.
Melia, Robert J.
Thompson, Eino A, Jr.
Carney, John A.
Creati, James P.
Martin, Arthur E.
Regan, Kevin W.
*First female troopers
Rea, David F.
Malenfant, Bruce A.
Brown, Herbert E.
Winsor, Brian J.
Greeley, Thomas F., Jr.
Richards, Neal H.
Jillson, Bruce A.
Lee, Michael W.
Burson, James H.
O'Brien, Stephen J.
LaPointe, Michael A.
O'Malley, John J.
Farrel, Joan M.*
Gillespie, John F.
Flaherty, Joseph F.
Gagne, Gerard J.
Helberg, David E.
LaPrade, William N.
Laprel, Robert C.
Friend, Robert H., Jr.
MacLean, John D.
Dunn, John V.
Anger, Norman O.
Fleming, James F.
Mackin, James F.
McCabe, John F.
Whelden, Robert L., Jr.
Kennedy, Brian M.
Fell, James M.
Bishop, Chester
Cummings, James M.
Roy, Lorraine R.*
Harbour, Ronald C.
Bolduc, Richard R.
McGreal, William G.
Hickey, William R., Jr.
Walsh, John J.
Carroll, William A.
Freeman, William J.
Nee, John A.
Gonsalves, George C.
Barrett, Richard J.
Brien, John W.
Jaworek, James M.
Foley, Gregory J.
Cox, Robert A.
Wilbur, Alfred C.
Duffy, Daniel J.
Costa, Daniel
Fisher, William D.
Reopell, Earl J. Jr.
Sinkevich, Joseph A.
Eastman, Charles E., Jr.
Souza, Gerald A.
Johnson, William A. Jr.
Yanchun, Timothy J.
Howe, Edwin C.
Fitzgerald, Robert E.
Balzano, Paul L.
Caramiello, Giovanni
Whittier, Robert H.
Kokocinski, William J.
Ashman, Edwards S.
Balestra, Albert A.
Farias, Michael W.
Summers, Thomas W.
Silva, Peter N.
Greene, Warren G.
Crosby, Michael A.
O'Hare, Joseph M.

SIXTIETH RECRUIT TROOP
July 8, 1978

Alliette, Steven J.
Apgar, William R.
Auld, Raymond J.
Baker, William J., Jr.
Beith, Eric P.
Belanger, Richard P.
Berghaus, Lawrence C.
Blatch, William E.
Blazuk, Robert P.
Bradbury, James J.
Burke, Edmund V., Jr.
Burns, Richard J.
Godfrey, John L.
Godin, Ronald G.
Govoni, Mark A.
Grady, James F.
Greeley, Brian G.
Henley, John C.
Higginbotham, Thomas A.
Horton, Kevin M.
Joyce, Justin
Keeler, Dennis P.
Kelleher, Kenneth C.
Kelliher, Robert T.
Maziarz, Robert J.
McDougall, Philip E.
Miller, Richard P.
Moore, Francis E. Jr.
Mulhern, Brian W.
Mullen, Richard G.
Murphy, Robert A.
Muto, Robert S.
Neff, Thomas W. Jr.
O'Hara, Brian M.
O'Keefe, Robert F.
Pagliarulo, Nicholas A.

Carlisle, James P.	Kynock, Brian R.	Peck, Thomas M.	Damery, Paul J.	Lussier, Alfred L. Jr.	Stephens, Martin K.
Cawley, Richard T.	Lahan, Richard G.	Popko, Edward S., III	Erickson, Timothy	Mackiewicz, Wayne L.	Sullivan, Kenneth E.
Chapdelaine, Raymond G.	Langford, Oscar J., III	Remkus, Dennis M.	Fletcher, Paul E.	Magner, Craig P.	Sullivan, Paul D.
Charbonnier, Thomas J.	Lazarz, Walter J.	Richer, Donald L.	Galeazzi, Richard L.	Maher, Paul J.	Tobin, Michael F.
Cisternelli, William S.	Lemay, Gary P.	Ross, John P.	Gallagher, Thomas N.	Manzi, Albert P. Jr.	VanLandingham, Paul G.
Coletta, Kathleen M.*	Lilly, Brian X.	Salerno, Anthony M.	Gilardi, Monte M.	Marinick, Richard J.	Walsh, Gary R.
Conley, James E.	Lokitis, Michael P.	Sheehan, Robert L.	Giulino, John T.	Marks, Dennis J.	Walsh, Thomas M.
Costa, Joseph J.	Long, Stephen F.	Skerry, Michael P.	Glasheen, Francis J.	Martin, Harry J. Jr.	Welby, Richard J.

First female academy staffer

Boston, State Capitol, September, 1970. Governor Francis W. Sargent signs legislation abolishing "live-in" barracks' system, reducing duty week from 84 to 40 hours. L to R. Trooper Kevin W. Peabody, Commissioner William F. Powers, Trooper G. William Dunderdale, Sergeant James V. Oteri, Trooper John W. Giardino. Within days of the September 9, 1998, publication of Odyssey, *Governor Seargent died in his Dover home following a lingering illness. His 1969-1975 gubernatorial tenure was marked by some of the most significant personnel and organizational improvements in the history of the state force. An impressive contingent of uniformed officers brightened a November 4 "Celebration of His Life" that was conducted in Wellesley's Saint Andrew's Episcopal Church. It was a poignant good-bye from an enforcement organization whose history will always reflect the imprint of a remarkable life.*

State Police Academy, Framingham, 1974. Left to Right: Major Stanley W. Wisnioski, Jr., James A. Malger, Lieutenant Robert J. Fitzgerald, academy commandant. Malger had just received the state police meritorious service award for his long years of support services to the uniformed branch. His career-long commitment to the statewide force was typical of the critical skills provided by "civilians," especially during the 1921-1971 era of the "live-in" barracks' system.

Troop B, Northampton, September, 1970. S/Sergeant Robert J. Gustavis examines marijuana cache seized in raid. Illegal drug use skyrocketed during the Viet Nam War and the emergence of the "counter culture" and its disdain for governmental authority. It was only the beginning, as major crime cartels turned to violence to settle drug turf issues. Gustavis in 1970 was rounding out nearly two decades in the state force, a member of 1952's 36th Recruit Training Troop.

State Police Boxing Team, 1977. Left to Right: (kneeling) J. Sprague, L. Gerstel, R. Benoit, S. Bennett, J. Cunningham, (standing) J. Flaherty, J. LePage, D. Grabowski, B. Mann, M. Delaney, R. Ilg, J. Dunn, J. Redfearn, J. Cronin. First organized in 1976 by Trooper Bob Benoit, the boxing team has earned countless thousands for worthy charities, created much camaraderie in the state force, in October, 1996, celebrated the 20th anniversary of its founding.

State Capitol, Boston, 1970. Left to Right: First Lady Jessie Sargent, Governor Francis W. Sargent, Commissioner William F. Powers, Lt. Colonel Robert D. Murgia, Detective Captain Daniel I. Murphy. This was the annual "hand shaking" day wherein the commonwealth's governor on Washington's birthday greeted thousands of citizens in the capitol's ornate Hall of Flags. Murphy in 1934 joined the uniformed force, from 1950-1953 was state commissioner of public safety, served until 1971 as captain of detectives.

Academy, Framingham, 1978. Left to Right: (front) Sergeant Frank E. McGovern, Major John F. Kennedy, academy commandant, (second row) Secretary of Public Safety Charles V. Barry, State Police Commissioner John F. Kehoe, Jr. (behind Kehoe), Colonel Frank J. Trabucco. This was the July 8, 1978 graduation of the 60th Recruit Troop. Barry was a career Boston police officer, twice served as head of the executive office of public safety, the state's ranking law enforcement official.

State Capitol, Boston, mid-1970's. With the "Golden Dome" as backdrop, state police families picketed the Dukakis Administration demanding increases in trooper salaries and upgrading of enforcement equipment. This photo illustrates, more than a thousand words, the impact of the evolving social and cultural forces that, by the mid-70's, were increasingly affecting the organizational odyssey of the state force.

State Police Academy, Memorial Service, Framingham, 1976. (placing wreath) Former Troopers' Secretary Theodore J. Stavredes and President Joseph J. Regan, (standing rear) Lt. Colonel Frank J. Trabucco, Lt. Colonel George B. Hacking, Lt. Colonel John R. O'Donovan, Jr., Lt. Colonel Wintrop E. Doty, Jr., Former Captain Charles W. Eager, (standing right) Colonel Americo J. Sousa, Commissioner John F. Kehoe, Jr., (behind Sousa). Stavredes enlisted in 1934, was first president of Former Troopers, preserved many of the historical documents used to write this volume, lived out his retirement years at his long-time Winthrop residence.

State Police Academy, Framingham, 1978. Captain John F. Kennedy was academy commandant, had trained at the academy in 1956, rose through the ranks and retired at the major's grade. Since the 1921 founding, the state force has seen the best of its personnel drawn to the academy staff. They, in turn, have ensured that training and education remain the central strength of one of the nation's premiere law enforcement agencies. Kennedy went on to a federal career, is a senior official in the National Highway Traffic Safety Administration.

State Capitol, Boston, 1979. Left to Right: Commissioner Dennis M. Condon, Governor Edward J. King, Public Safety Secretary George A. Luciano. Condon in August, 1978, had been appointed to the commissioner's post by Governor Michael S. Dukakis. Governor King in March, 1979, reappointed the Boston College graduate, capping a career begun in 1951 with the Federal Bureau of Investigation.

General Headquarters, Boston, 1971. Sergeant John F. Kennedy and Commissioner William F. Powers. Kennedy in 1956 graduated from the academy with the 39th Recruit Troop, served in several troops in field and staff assignments, was major and commanding officer of state police academy prior to late 1970's retirement. Since retirement, he has authored a second professional career as a law enforcement specialist in the federal National Highway Traffic Safety Administration.

Governor's Office, State Capitol, 1979. Left to Right: Colonel Frank J. Trabucco, Governor Edward J. King, Commissioner Dennis M. Condon, Public Safety Secretary George A. Luciano. Governor King had signed contract agreement with the State Police Association of Massachusetts, the trooper's union, one of many rank and file improvements implemented during his 1979-1983 gubernatorial tenure.

State Capitol, Boston, 1979. Left to Right: Assistant Secretary of Public Safety George Tully, Governor Edward J. King, Secretary of Public Safety George A. Luciano. Tully managed state police resource allocation for the King Administration. His efforts resulted in several academy recruit classes, new field installations and support facilities, and a dramatically upgraded cruiser fleet.

Academy Graduation, Commonwealth Armory, Boston, late 1970's. Left to Right: (front) Lt. Colonel Edward F. Kelly, Lt. Colonel Frank J. Trabucco, Lt. Colonel George B. Hacking, Lt. Colonel Edward J. Teahan, Colonel Americo J. Sousa, (rear) Major Wintrop E. Doty, Jr., Major James E. Halloran, Jr., Corporal Robert E. Dunn at lectern. The historic armory long served as an academy graduation site, including 1933's 25th Recruit Troop, the first class to wear French and electric blue for their graduation ceremony.

State Capitol, Boston, Mid-1970's. These state police wives were picketing the Dukakis Administration, protesting stagnation of troopers' salaries and aging of the cruiser fleet. The troopers' union, the state Police Association of Mass., led the salary fight, openly campaigned against Dukakis and was instrumental in the governor's startling defeat in the 1978 Democratic primary.

State Police Academy, Framingham, 1979. Left to Right: Chaplain Frank J. Bauer, Captain George R. Dolan, Chaplain John E. Hartigan. Reverend Bauer and Father Hartigan long served the spiritual needs of state police personnel and their families. Hartigan during World War II saw extended combat service in the Asiatic-Pacific Campaign, was both curate and pastor of several Framingham parishes, died in the rectory of his Sudbury parish in 1987. A native of Boston's Charlestown neighborhood, he was a 1943 graduate of Boston College.

Troop C, Sturbridge Barracks, 1971. Left to Right: Captain Robert E. Herzog '48, Captain Stanley W. Wisnioski, Jr., '49, Captain John F. Downey, '47, Captain Americo J. Sousa, '51, Captain Edward J. Teahan, '51, Major Melville R. Anderson, '47, Major John R. Moriarty, '47, Lieutenant Frank J. Trabucco, '56, Major Francis T. Burke, '48, Major Edward P. Tonelli, '51. The occasion was a retirement luncheon for "Roy" Anderson. Trabucco on July 1, 1980, was named state commissioner of public safety by Governor Edward J. King. He thus became the first superintendent of the Massachusetts State Police who had held every rank in the uniformed branch from corporal through colonel and deputy superintendent. He retired in 1987.

LEFT: General Headquarters, Boston, 1970. Left to Right: Trooper Robert A. Long, Commissioner William F. Powers, Sergeant Thomas H. Peterson. Peterson and Long won the State Police Medal of Honor for their gunpoint capture of William M. "Lefty" Gilday. Boston Patrolman Walter A. Schroeder was gunned down during a Boston bank holdup by Gilday, Robert Valeri, Stanley Bond, Susan E. Saxe and Katherine Power. Saxe and Power, 1960's "Weathermen," years later surfaced from underground lives and were sentenced for the ruthless murder of the Boston officer.

State Capitol, Boston, 1971. Left to Right: State Representative James F. O'Brien, Commissioner William F. Powers, Governor Francis W. Sargent, Major John F. Downey, Former Trooper James J. Murphy. Murphy in 1952 graduated from the State Police Academy with the 36th Recruit Troop, suffered a heart attack, in uniform, working an Andover Barracks' patrol, was summarily discharged because he had not completed six months' service. Sargent in 1971 signed state police sponsored annuity legislation to lessen the unjust impact of the arbitrary termination of Murphy's state police career many years before. Former Trooper James J. Murphy died in Fall River on August 26, 1996.

Troop C, Sturbridge Barracks, 1971. Left to Right: Major John R. Moriarty, Major Melville R. Anderson, Commissioner William F. Powers, Major Edward P. Tonelli, Major Francis T. Burke, Major John F. Downey, Mr. Robert Roth, Captain Stanley W. Wisnioski, Jr. Occasion was a retirement luncheon for Anderson, a World War II "ETSPO," who had served in key field and staff posts during a distinguished law enforcement career. Wisnioski was captain and Troop C commander, and in later decades authored a remarkable criminal justice career in Florida.

General Headquarters, Boston, 1971. Deputy Public Safety Commissioner Walter P. Parker and Commissioner William F. Powers. Parker in 1969-1971 led the political and administrative coalitions that ended the live-in barracks' system, reduced from 84 to 40 a trooper's duty week, launched the "cruiser per man" patrol concept and incentive pay for post-secondary educational achievement. A World War II combat veteran of the European Campaign, he later served for many years in key federal leadership posts.

162

State Police Academy, Framingham, May 29, 1971. Commissioner William F. Powers and Lieutenant Governor Donald D. Dwight have just cut the dedication ribbon on the new state police academy. The first permanent academy facility constructed in the 50 years since the 1921 founding, the modern complex ended an era, now a nostalgic mosaic, when tents and Quonset Huts sheltered hundreds of recruits as they earned public service careers in the French and electric blue by successfully completing the defining academy experience.

State Police Academy, Framingham, 1971. Built on the site where scores of recruit troops had trained, the new academy cost $3.5 million and was dedicated in 1971 on the 50th anniversary of the 1921 founding of the "State Police Patrol." In 1994, the Framingham academy was converted into a modern general headquarters complex. A new academy had been opened in New Braintree in 1992.

Promotion Ceremony, General Headquarters, Boston, 1972. Left to Right: Lt. Colonel John R. Moriarty, Major Americo J. Sousa, Commissioner John F. Kehoe, Jr., Captain James L. Killoran, Lieutenant Edward R. MacCormack, S/ Sergeant Joseph M. Desilets. Moriarty that day earned top career rank as executive officer, Sousa became adjutant of state force. Killoran trained with 1949's 35th Recruit Troop, the last of five academy classes immediately following World War II.

South Boston, 1979. Trooper Edward L. Sullivan at the ready during the Boston school integration crisis. Such duty, an extremely sensitive law enforcement assignment, went on for months as officials and families alike sought solutions to one of the nation's most intractable social problems. The state force earned much praise for the way personnel responded to one of the most difficult assignments since the 1921 founding.

Chelsea, June, 1979. Left to Right: Trooper Bradley J. Mullen, (center) protesting truck driver, (right, dark glasses), Lt. Colonel James T. Canty. Truckers had blockaded New England Produce Center in Chelsea to protest law restricting Sunday truck hauling. Eight truckers were arrested, a large crowd was dispersed and produce center and surrounding roadways were opened to traffic.

South Boston High School, November, 1975. Left to Right: Lieutenant James T. Canty, Federal District Court Judge W. Arthur Garrity, with U. S. Marshals. The federal court had ordered cross-city busing to achieve racial balance in the South Boston High School. Canty in 1957 graduated from the state police academy with the 41st Recruit Troop, in 1980-1985 served as colonel and deputy superintendent, the top career rank. He was the first officer to win each promotion following implementation of the landmark competitive promotional statute in 1966.

Leominster Barracks, December, 1977. Left to Right: Trooper Edward Sullivan, (rear) Trooper Brian Andrews, Rhode Island State Police (right) Trooper William Mann. Troopers had just arrested suspect in a multimillion-dollar bonded vault robbery that had occurred in Providence, Rhode Island, months earlier. Such multi-state investigations have escalated in the highly mobile modern era as law enforcement has worked hard to keep pace with high tech operations of crime cartels.

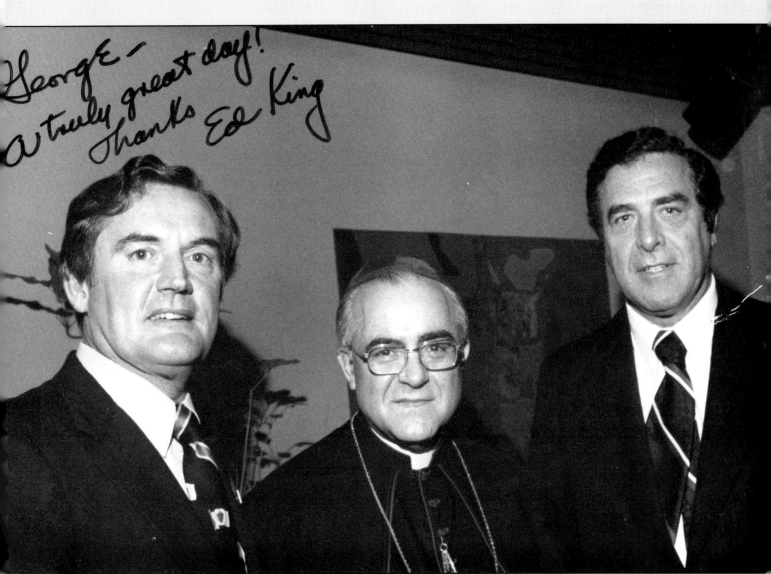

Boston, 1980, Left to Right: Governor Edward J. King, Humberto Cardinal Medeiros, Public Safety Secretary George A. Luciano. Cardinal Medeiros was born in the Azore Islands of Portugal, spoke no English at 15 when he arrived in the United States, was valedictorian of his Durfee High School 1937 graduating class, became Boston's Cardinal Archbishop in a quintessential American story, chose burial with his immigrant parents in Fall River's St. Patrick's Cemetery. The King Administration was strongly supportive of state police policy and legislative initiatives including several recruit troops, salary increases, and the construction and upgrading of key operational facilities.

Chapter Eight

Author's Chapter Note

Producing Odyssey required a close review of 1979's French and Electric Blue. It was a revelation. The level of detail in that earlier volume is amazing. In retrospect, with almost two decades of hindsight, one can see that it is pretty much a king-sized oral history, composed of many such first person accounts. The stories, the detailed specifics, were handed down in a classical oral tradition. Many were preserved by the late Sergeant (Ret.) Theodore J. Stavredes. Ted for more than three decades authored the Newsletter of the Former Troopers' Association. There, month by month, he chronicled stories that he had heard from the "old timers," all of whom had served in the decade of the 1920's.

Added to that storehouse of historical vignettes, was Stavredes' own prodigious memory. He was a keen observer. He saw much. He never forgot what he saw and heard, unless it was a negative. Those, and they were there, he put aside where time's passage has completed their obscurity.

Finally, many of my own "mind's eye images" were woven into French's pages. Enlisting in the state police in the aftermath of World War II, I came to know many of the early veterans. I remembered their "yarns", embellished them a bit, then shared them. Later, I participated in, or knew about, several major incidents or historical junctures. Examples would be 1956 guard duty at the Charles Street Jail for the Brink's Gang, the 1959 Coyle Brothers' manhunt in Middleboro, and the 1970-1971 abolition of the live-in barracks' system. These, and many more, found their way into the text of the earlier volume. In a word, French was a mosaic, a tapestry, created by scores of oral histories melded with personal recollections of times and events long since past.

That's where the details came from. And it took 300 pages and some 250 photographs to share them. Now, here in Odyssey, we have arrived at the modern era, the last two decades of the Twentieth Century. How does one provide the same level of detail, the "inside" stories, the hundreds of oral histories? For two decades that have witnessed organizational and societal changes that take one's breath away?

The answer is, simply, it can't be done. A balanced presentation of the past twenty years would necessitate a new volume in and of itself. That's what would be required to describe the accelerating change ongoing in the state force even while these words are being written. Compared to earlier decades in the long enforcement journey, the current pace of change is, again, breathtaking. And the end is not yet in sight.

One is left then with the task of selecting the major happenings of the 1980's and 1990's. It is hoped that this will provide a historical snapshot of a truly remarkable time in the enforcement odyssey, now almost eight decades removed from the 1921 founding of the "State Police Patrol." Others, in another time, will be challenged to provide the details of an era marked by an information overkill that shows no signs of subsiding anytime soon. That will be a formidable challenge. But the results, a precise, detailed account of a remarkable era in the state force, will be well worth the effort.

W. F. P.

ONE ORAL HISTORY

This book's predecessor volume, French and Electric Blue, was published in June, 1979. Several hundred attended a publication program at the state police academy in Framingham. Among the attendees was Lieutenant (Ret.) John A. Carroll. Carroll in 1923 had enlisted in the state force, serving in field and staff posts until 1947. More especially, it was Carroll in 1933 who had modeled the French and electric blue uniform colors for Governor Joseph B. Ely. The governor's response was, in a word, enthusiastic. The rest is history, as the two-tone blue for the past 65 years immediately has identified a Massachusetts state trooper.

John A. Carroll preserved an oral remembrance of the historic uniform change. And well that he did. He died within days of attending the Framingham ceremony, leaving an account of a historical juncture whose importance has been validated by time's passage. Now, more clearly, we appreciate the value of his departing memoir.

Shortly after the Framingham publication program, the 61st Recruit Troop on September 4 began the arduous academy challenge. They, like their predecessors, faced one of the nation's most comprehensive training and educational programs. For many of them the discipline was a rude awakening, its sting even more biting than the pressures they had been warned to expect.

Yet, they persevered. They had to. They wanted to be troopers. Their reward came on Friday evening, January 18, 1980, in Boston's Commonwealth Armory. That night, in the presence of several thousand, the 57 recruits became state police officers. It was a proud moment, a mind's eye image that would endure for each of them.

To that point of time, only three females had graduated from the academy as troopers. Yet, nine women took their oaths that evening. Moreover, Trooper Kathleen M. Coletta had reviewed the recruit troop as a member of the academy staff, the first woman to do so in the department's history. In retrospect, one perceives that these were portents of accelerating organizational change, energized by evolving values in the larger society.

A Leadership Change

Commissioner Dennis M. Condon had officiated at the January graduation ceremonies of the 61st Recruit Troop. First appointed in 1978 by Governor Michael S. Dukakis, he had been reappointed the next year by Governor Edward J. King. With that vote of confidence, Condon excelled in the taxing post. Now, in spring, 1980, he announced his intention to leave the commissioner's office. Subsequently, the Boston College grad saw a son, James, and a daughter, Elaine, graduate from the state police academy and don the French and electric blue. Moreover, he would later continue his public service with an extended tour as a senior official in the state's executive office of public safety.

Following Commissioner Condon's departure, the King Administration carefully reviewed the professional qualifications of a score of applicants for the state's top public safety post. The prestige of being state police superintendent made that office one of the nation's most sought after law enforcement assignments. Governor King, a hands-on chief executive, enjoyed unique insights about state police operations and the organizational culture that shaped its personnel. These advantages stemmed principally from his tenure as executive director of the Massachusetts Port Authority. That agency was responsible for Logan International Airport, where law enforcement and security services were provided by state police personnel. From that vantage point, King, a perceptive executive if ever there was one, had dealt with both field troopers and the department's leadership. He was, in a word, remarkably familiar with the agency's operational prowess and its leadership requirements.

As noted in this volume's earlier pages, the governor in late 1978 had selected former Trooper George A. Luciano as secretary of the Executive Office of Public Safety, a key cabinet post. Luciano since his 1953 academy graduation had maintained an active interest in both operational and administrative issues affecting the state force, its personnel and their families. Clearly, the King Administration was uniquely qualified to select a state police superintendent with the professional credentials and personal temperament to discharge the exacting responsibilities of that office in superior fashion. Their choice would not disappoint.

Governor King on July 1, 1980, administered the oath of office to former Trooper Frank J. Trabucco as the Commonwealth's new state police superintendent. By any measure, and from any perspective, the state police veteran was a popular choice. Trabucco in 1956 had graduated from the state police academy with the 39th Recruit Troop. For the next two decades, he was posted to a variety of field and staff assignments. With a first promotion to corporal, the Korean War veteran rose through the ranks, winning promotions to every grade in the uniformed branch from corporal's stripes to colonel and deputy superintendent. That had never been done before. Clearly, the state's new public safety chief was uniquely qualified for the daily burdens of that high office.

While Trabucco would enjoy an extended tour in the superintendent's post, his prescient views emerged early. In a 1980 interview with Trooper, the editor, Trooper Jim Lane, asked him about the possibility of a consolidation of state enforcement agencies, the creation of a mega-state police agency. Lane wrote: "As for the merger of the three departments, the Commissioner responded saying that 'down stream it's the idea that has to be given serious consideration.' He said that the state can't afford duplication of effort and warned that if the administration of the other agencies didn't stay away from duplicating police services it could well serve as a catalyst for the legislature to move toward a merger." Trabucco's prescience on the controversial consolidation issue was validated twelve years later. On July 1, 1992, enforcement personnel from the Metropolitan District Commission, Registry of Motor Vehicles and Capitol Police were merged into a new Department of State Police. Because of its historical importance, "consolidation," as it came to be called, receives expanded examination in this volume's following chapter on the 1990's decade.

Commissioner Trabucco soon was immersed in the more rewarding administrative activities of his demanding office. Thus, on November 21, 1980, 3,000 spectators joined him at Boston's Commonwealth Armory for the graduation exercises of the 62nd Recruit Troop. As always, it was a sober yet festive occasion for the recruit troopers and their admiring families and friends.

Governor Edward J. King and Public Safety Secretary George A. Luciano joined Trabucco in a review of the graduating troop, later congratulating the 63 men and women sworn to law enforcement careers in the state force. The badge pinning ceremony was especially noteworthy. First, Former Commissioner Dennis M. Condon pinned a new shield on his son, James. Next, Lt. Colonel John R. O'Donovan did the honors for his son, James. Finally, Trooper Kenneth Kelleher affixed the hard earned badge of office to the dress uniform blouse of his wife, Recruit Trooper Anne Kelleher. That was a state police first. Fifty-nine years after the November, 1921, graduation of the First Recruit Troop, the uniformed force had the first husband and wife team in its ranks. It was a portent of things to come. And it would continue. A traditional enforcement organization was responding to the changing values of its social environment. Slowly, at times imperceptibly, it had always done that.

PAUL G. KIRK

One who had adhered to enduring values while responding to the inevitability of changes was Paul G. Kirk. Kirk was 29 in 1934 when Governor Joseph B. Ely appointed him as the state's public safety commissioner and head of the Massachusetts State Police. The media immediately dubbed him the "boy commissioner."

By 1981, Kirk was no longer a boy. He was 76. And, in July, 1981, he died. His passing must be noted in these pages, because Paul G. Kirk gave the best years of his life to public service, and to the citizens of his native Commonwealth. It was said that in addition to his family, he had two loves, the military and the state police.

Kirk in 1935 was reappointed commissioner by Governor James Michael Curley. There, at the nadir of the Great Depression, he initiated legislative and policy actions that led to historical personnel reforms in the late 1930's. At the same time, he got Curley's backing for a transfer of general headquarters from the obscure recesses of the Capitol's basement to Commonwealth Pier in South Boston. In short, Commissioner Kirk was a mover and a shaker, always with the goal of improving the status of state police personnel, their families and their organization.

Paul Kirk in World War II was a colonel in the 26th Yankee Division, with overseas service in Africa, Italy, France and Germany. Following a long tenure as an associate justice of the state's Superior Court, Governor Foster Furcolo in 1960 named him to the Supreme Judicial Court where he served until his retirement in 1970.

In his later years, he often attended state police functions and activities, including the June, 1979, publication of this book's predecessor volume. He lived out his retirement on his beloved Cape Cod, observing from a distance an enforcement odyssey that he had affected in so many ways during a long public service career.

General Otis M. Whitney

"General," that was the title he preferred even when, in 1953, Governor Christian A. Herter appointed him state public safety commissioner and head of the Massachusetts State Police. Whitney went on to several prestigious posts, but his 1953-1959 state police tenure was what he did best, and what he enjoyed most. When, in July, 1982, he died, the state police detail at Concord's Trinity Episcopal Church was one of the most impressive in memory. Clearly, his old organization remembered what he had done for the state force, its uniformed personnel and their families. They remembered well. He had done much.

On the broadest level, one remembers the Whitney tenure as the years when the state force "opened," operationally, administratively, and "politically." On the political front, the general knew how legislative initiatives lived or died on Beacon Hill. He had earned that knowledge the hard way, as a member of the House of Representatives and as an elected member of the Governor's Council.

As commissioner, Whitney used his political savvy to launch legislative initiatives to raise trooper salaries, increase substantially the department's authorized complement, and broaden promotional opportunities with an expanded rank structure. But he didn't act alone. In a departure from long standing traditions, he opened the legislative process to uniformed personnel. In short, he broke from a traditional, authoritarian ethic by cooperating with rank and file representatives in the pursuit of mutual legislative goals. That was a first. And it began an era of cooperative achievements that yet evolves even as these words are written.

On the administrative and operational levels, Commissioner Whitney did it his way. While traditionalists would gasp, the general would mount a motorcycle in full dress uniform, drop in on unsuspecting troopers in remote barracks, informally discuss with them issues they cared about. He was different. They had no doubt about that. But his genuine concern for the welfare of the field trooper came through. The result was a feeling that Whitney's style, his instinct for cooperation and coalitions, would energize operational and personnel improvements in the state force. He didn't disappoint.

His six-year tenure was marked by a steady stream of improvements, some large and some small, but all important to uniformed personnel. Changes that now seem trivial were welcomed with relief. For example, those were the years when troopers were first allowed to take summer vacations. For almost four decades, uniformed personnel were not allowed vacations during the summer season. It was a tradition. And by the mid-fifties, it chafed. Summer uniforms would have to wait, but Whitney had created the opening. More accurately, he created a direction, one wherein a score of similar administrative improvements energized a liberalizing impulse that foreshadowed the major reforms of the following decades.

A number of those advances are described in some detail in this volume's earlier pages. They are noted as well in the historic photographs that document the general's fondness for the state police uniform, and his enthusiasm for the leadership post he held during most of the 1950's. Leaving the commissioner's office in 1959, he was appointed by Governor Foster Furcolo as the state's commissioner of insurance. Later, he was appointed a trial judge in the Commonwealth's district court system. A number of

uniformed officers attended the latter event, even though his state police years were, by then, some years past.

The general's July 10, 1982 funeral in Concord's Trinity Episcopal Church was a military service, impressive in its time-honored, poignant rituals. State police colors were everywhere. Though a quarter of a century had passed, the state force he had once led remembered with much appreciation the operational achievements and personnel improvements wrought by his leadership.

One realizes in retrospect that the Whitney tenure was a bridge, a passage from slowly yielding authoritarian traditions to the openings that yet unfold at century's end. For that reason, his 1982 passing is recorded in these pages to preserve an account of an important historical juncture in the enforcement odyssey. At least that much is due to one who, in his time, contributed much to that organizational journey.

Trooper George L. Hanna

It is not likely that Commissioner Otis M. Whitney had ever met Trooper George L. Hanna. Had that happened, however, Whitney quickly would have sensed what many others did, that here was an officer proud of the uniform he wore, faithful to the values of the state force he strengthened with his public service.

Hanna on October 19, 1974 had graduated from the state police academy with the 58th Recruit Training Troop. He had handled the academy's challenges superbly, growing in knowledge, professional skill and maturity during the defining transformation from civilian to state police officer. He actually had enjoyed the Framingham experience, aware that its personal trials were portents of the realities confronted daily by a field trooper.

Predictably, George Hanna excelled in a variety of field assignments. As the years passed, he earned a reputation as a solid professional, a guy you could count on when the going got tough or when the extra effort would make the difference. In a word, he was a team player in a profession where teamwork is essential. That was his reputation, that's the way his peers felt about him. He had worked hard to become a respected professional. He had succeeded. It meant he could take care of himself, while, at the same time, being there for others.

And that is what Trooper George L. Hanna was doing in the early evening of February 26, 1983. Being there for others. That meant enforcing the law, firmly but fairly. Patrolling in state police cruiser 668, he stopped a car for a motor vehicle violation near the intersection of Routes 12 and 20 in Auburn. The young trooper had stopped thousands of motor vehicles. But this one was different. Something went terribly wrong. As Hanna questioned three of the vehicle's occupants, gunfire erupted. Six shots found their mark. Trooper Hanna fell, mortally wounded. Rushed to a Worcester hospital, he died several hours later. At age 33, he left his widow and three children.

Trooper George L. Hanna's murder left the state force in profound shock and sadness. Hundreds of uniformed officers strengthened his loved ones at his funeral mass in Natick's St. Patrick's Church. It was a poignant goodby for a man who had honored the French and electric blue each day he wore the colors of the enforcement organization he served for nearly a decade.

The three felons who took George Hanna's life were convicted of his murder and sentenced to life imprisonment. Many believed that they deserved the death penalty, a state's ultimate criminal sanction. But the Massachusetts legislature years earlier had abolished that final penalty. Ironically, as one wrote these words, the Massachusetts House on November 6, 1997 defeated a bill to reinstate the death penalty with a tie vote. Governor Paul Cellucci had vowed to sign it. He would have to wait.

Feelings remain strong about the use of the death penalty, especially among law enforcement officers. That came through strongly at the 1996 presentation of the Trooper George L. Hanna memorial award. The award honors the public service and memory of the fallen trooper, and is given each year to an officer for an act of heroic enforcement action.

Colonel Reed V. Hillman in 1996 made the Hanna award presentation. A 1974 academy classmate of the slain trooper, he harkened back to those early years in his presentation remarks: "Twenty two years ago today, George L. Hanna and I awoke after our very first night in the state police academy, members of the 58th Recruit Training Troop. Unable to sleep in those strange beds, we were awakened before 6:00 a.m. for an hour of vigorous exercise followed by a five mile run.

George and I trained together for 17 weeks, and then served as troopers together for years in Troop C, for *part* of my career,-and for *all* of George's career. How many times did I hear George call his barracks on the radio: '668 to C, 668 to C'? I couldn't go to Worcester Court without seeing George there, ready to testify in a myriad of cases he was involved in. George was a trooper's trooper, a friend, a classmate, a brother.

I'll never ever forget the phone call I got from Trooper Tryon when he said to me, 'Reed, George Hanna was *murdered* last night.' And what of George's three killers? They continue to live, inmates,-hoping for the day they escape, or their sentences are commuted, or their convictions overturned, or maybe even for a pardon from some future governor. *They* have hope. They laugh,- they love,-they live."

After discussing the inmate culture in correctional institutions, Hillman focused on the personal issues, the feelings: "Those of us who loved George know that nothing will ever heal the holes in each of our hearts. We can hope for *no* relief from the never ending anguish of knowing we will never again see Trooper Hanna on this earth. Without the deaths of the murderers of Trooper Hanna, those of us on the state police who miss George so terribly will never have closure. The continued existence of these cold blooded killers grates like a hot knife on an open sore." Comparing Trooper Hanna's assailants with the convicted killer of Trooper Mark S. Charbonnier in 1994, Superintendent Hillman zeroed in: "Criminals are as thinking and calculating as any one of us. They can make reasoned decisions based on the options in front of them.

It's time to put in the mind of every criminal contemplating the murder of a cop, that *his* life is in the balance, that one of the possibilities is his own demise. That the worst case scenario won't simply be to go back to a warm prison bed, but rather to face a rendezvous with an executioner, and a quick trip to hell.

We owe a death penalty to those who killed George, Charbo, and many other murdered officers. But mostly, we owe this to all of the men and women who sally forth every day to protect our lives and property. A criminal with a gun must know that killing a cop is no longer a viable option because in this state, we have a death penalty."

Colonel Hillman's heartfelt remarks at the 1996 Hanna Awards ceremony resonated with citizen and legislator alike. As noted earlier, Governor Paul Cellucci is committed to a death penalty bill. The November, 1997, tie vote in the Massachusetts house on the death penalty demonstrates that it is an emerging public policy issue with the state's electorate. That focus likely will continue during an era when violent acts against law officers is of a magnitude unknown in this nation before the drug culture descended several decades ago.

REAPPOINTMENT

Michael S. Dukakis in January, 1983, was sworn as governor of Massachusetts. Dukakis, the state's chief executive from 1975 to 1979, in November, 1982, had defeated Governor Edward J. King in the democratic primary. That outcome had reversed the results of the state's 1978 gubernatorial primary when King had ousted Dukakis.

In any event, one of Governor Dukakis' early public events was the May, 1983, graduation of the 65th Recruit Training Troop. The colorful ceremony, held on the academy grounds in Framingham, was witnessed by several thousand. "Witnessed" is the correct word in this context, because those in attendance witnessed a state police first.

Following traditional graduation drills and skill exercises, the recruits formed an impressive troop front. The program's highpoint was at hand; announcement of the honor graduate of the 65th Recruit Troop. The academy's most prestigious award would be made in the presence of family and friends, state police leadership, and the Commonwealth's chief executive officers, including its governor. It was not an insignificant moment.

It is reasonable now to speculate that the recruits knew the identity of the best and brightest in their midst. After all, hadn't they survived Framingham's challenges together? Certainly, academy staff must have known. They, after all, had made the selection, a choice made objectively based on academic and performance criteria.

Nevertheless, when Commissioner Frank J. Trabucco made the honor graduate announcement the audience response was enthusiastic, to put it mildly. Trooper Elizabeth A. Murphy had won the academy's top prize, the first woman to graduate at the top of a recruit training class. Accentuating Murphy's remarkable achievement was the fact that only eight years had passed since the 1975 academy graduation of the department's first two female troopers. That was a lot of history in eight short years. Female troopers. A female honor graduate of the state police academy. Those historical firsts would have been beyond the comprehension of the rugged cadres that had served in the early decades. Theirs had been a different world, with starkly different cultural norms. But things had changed in the organizational environment, and the state force, wisely, was responding to those cultural dynamics.

Trooper Elizabeth Murphy led the recruits in the "pass in review," a final tribute from the new troopers. Governor Michael S. Dukakis and Commissioner Frank J. Trabucco accepted the parting salute. Then Dukakis, saving the best for the last, confirmed officially what had been rumored; he would reappoint Trabucco as public safety commissioner and head of the Massachusetts State Police. The governor's announcement could not have been more timely, or more popular. Trabucco had done a superior job with the taxing responsibilities of his office since his appointment in 1980. He had led the state force through a period of accelerating change. His reappointment provided the opportunity to pursue and consolidate the legislative and policy initiatives launched during his first term. As noted, it was a universally popular appointment, one that capped almost three decades of service in the state force.

Charles V. Barry was an enforcement veteran with long years of service in the Boston Police Department. With wide experience in field and staff posts, he had risen through the ranks to that department's senior leadership offices. When Michael S. Dukakis in 1975 first won the governorship, he quickly had selected Barry as secretary of the Executive Office of Public Safety, the state's senior public safety official. After a four-year hiatus, Dukakis in 1983 was returned to the governor's office. He again turned to Barry, once again naming him to the top public safety post.

Thus it was Secretary Barry who joined Governor Dukakis in the State Capitol on September 24, 1985, for the award of the Trooper George L. Hanna Medal of Honor. Dukakis in 1983 had established the award in memory of the deceased trooper. The recipient that first year had been Hanna's widow Marilyn, and their three children, Debbie, Kim and Michael.

Secretary Barry and Commissioner Frank J. Trabucco co-chaired the selection committee for the 1985 Hanna award. The committee, adhering to award selection criteria, chose state police Sergeant James P. Jajuga. Jajuga was a unanimous choice, and rightly so. At the risk of his own life, the state police veteran had disarmed and captured an armed felon who was threatening to kill several of Jajuga's fellow officers. Mrs. Hanna joined Governor Dukakis, Secretary Barry and Commissioner Trabucco in awarding the coveted honor to Sergeant Jajuga. For her and her family it was a poignant moment. Moreover, it reminded everyone present of the supreme sacrifice memorialized by the award itself in the presence of the deceased trooper's loved ones.

The 1985 Hanna Award ceremony brought home the fact that the state police organization is a family. The officer is out front. He or she is the visible symbol. Every trooper, however, knows that it is the home front that really counts. That's where the really difficult challengers lie in life's journey. It is where joy comes alive, the place where achievement gladdens all. But it is also the hearth where great sorrow is shouldered, and shared, and survived. Where life will go on, because faith and hope never die.

And it was just those enduring values that on April 5, 1986, sustained the family of state police Corporal Robert Schofield. That day, without warning, the Schofield family needed those strengths as never before. Stephen Schofield, age 11, had been killed in a tragic accident. He left his mother, dad and sister. Time's passage does not provide words to respond to such heartbreak. But someone has to try. Someone, somewhere, has to say something.

And that is what Trooper Tom Neff did when Stephen was killed. Neff, writing in the journal of the State Police Association, tried to make sense of the Schofield family's loss. Dedicating the annual publication to Stephen's memory, Trooper Neff struggled to share his feelings. "You have a boy like him on your street. He's the kind of kid who's up every Saturday morning riding his bike before you roll out of bed. He waves and smiles at you as you go to the garage to get the lawn mower. Maybe he'll even offer to cut the grass for you. But most of the time, he's busy with those things that keep all kids occupied on a Saturday, things that we've long since forgotten, or at least pretend we have forgotten.

He's the kind of kid of whom you say, 'If I had a son, I'd want him to be just like that.' And if you have a son, this is the boy you want him to hang around with. He's not an angel, not a model child, he's just a good kid, a diamond in the rough, a combination of tousled hair and grass-stained trousers...at night, he lies with his dad in front of the television, as gentle and fragile and vulnerable as the day he was born." Neff described how he was affected by notes written by Stephen's classmates. One, written by a girl in Stephen's class, was particularly appealing in its simplicity. She said she had admired Stephen for a long time, but always from a distance. Finally, one day he had walked her home while carrying her books. "That," she wrote, "was the happiest day of my life."

The memory of Stephen Schofields' tragically shortened life endures as a poignant reminder of how fragile one's existence really is. It is not always in some violent enforcement tragedy that the state police family must encounter seemingly unbearable grief. But tragedy's different faces do not lessen the sorrow that it imparts on family, friends and colleagues. Nor, fortunately, can it long delay the renewal that emerges inexorably from the faith and hope of those it touches.

One who believed in renewal, indeed practiced it, was state police Chaplain John E. Hartigan. Raised in Boston's Charlestown neighborhoods, he early learned from his immigrant parents that education and knowledge were the underpinnings of a life well lived. A 1943 graduate of Boston College, he left The Heights for extended combat service in World War II's Asiatic-Pacific Campaign. It was there, thousands of miles from home, that he received the call to the priesthood. He knew then what his life's work would be. He would serve others. That was the commitment he made.

At war's end, a decorated combat veteran, he entered the seminary. For the next forty years he served congregations throughout the Boston Archdiocese, several in the greater Framingham area. There, he befriended scores of troopers. These were easy relationships. Father Hartigan was easy to like. He was a man's man. That, more than anything else, came through.

Needless to say, his appointment in the 1960's as a state police chaplain was a popular choice. He plunged into his new duties with enthusiasm, actively participating in the myriad public activities of the state force. More importantly, he was always there for those who were hurting. No one knows how many troopers he helped when help was really needed. He never talked about those personal encounters. It was not his way.

Father Hartigan in 1977 was instrumental in the establishment of the state police stress unit. His wide experience with personal counseling had convinced him that enforcement personnel needed such support. Once established, the unit's staff often turned to him for the spiritual guidance that would help lift the difficulties encountered by uniformed officers. He also accomplished this for years in the "Chaplain's Corner," a feature of the widely read *Trooper* newspaper. Writing as "Smokey's Sky Pilot," Father Hartigan used disarming wit and practiced intuition to make generalized points that targeted the individual. He rarely missed his mark. His readers always got the idea.

Reverend John E. Hartigan's state police service came to an end on July 18, 1987. The beloved chaplain that day died in the rectory of Our Lady of Fatima Church in Sudbury. Needless to say, his passing saddened the state force. He, too, had worn the French and electric blue, earning appointments to the commissioned ranks. For some two decades troopers had felt the quiet strengths of this intensely human priest. Now he was gone. Time has since softened the memory of his passing, focusing instead on the good works that mark his lifetime. It is hoped that a few of those will endure for a time in these pages, a remembrance from the enforcement organization he honored with his service.

Because Father Hartigan had always participated in the annual memorial services of the state force, he would have known James H. Hayes. Hayes in 1933 had graduated from the academy with the 25th Recruit Training Troop, the first class to wear the newly authorized French and electric blue for their graduation ceremonies. That had been a first, and for Trooper Hayes the beginning of a distinguished public service career.

More than five decades later, James H. Hayes in 1987 was the honored guest at public ceremonies marking the fiftieth anniversary of the founding of the New Hampshire State Police. Newspaper accounts told how Hayes in 1937 had been asked by the Granite State's governor to organize a state force similar to that in Massachusetts. The news story heralded the outcome: "Hayes' Vision Molded New Department." The story went on to describe how Hayes and his colleagues modeled the new enforcement agency on the Massachusetts experience to ensure uniform, statewide coverage.

Predictably, James H. Hayes became the new department's first director. He served with distinction in that post, and subsequently won election to several key offices. His public service was such that the state's safety complex in Concord is the "James H. Hayes Public Safety Center."

Clearly, Jim Hayes authored a unique and remarkable career. He was often recognized for those achievements, and he appreciated the honors. Yet, as the years lengthened, he always returned for the public functions of the state force where in 1933 he had begun his enforcement career. One witnessed this fidelity particularly in 1971 at a unique presentation in the New Hampshire governor's office. There, in the presence of family, friends and dignitaries, Hayes received the trooper's badge he had earned when he graduated from the Massachusetts State Police Academy at the nadir of the Great Depression. It was easy to see that the former trooper was deeply moved. Years had gone by. Much had happened. Life had moved on. But all that did not lessen the pride he still felt for having earned the privilege of wearing the distinctive colors of the Commonwealth's statewide enforcement agency.

A CAREER CLOSES

Commissioner Frank J. Trabucco on May 16, 1983, had been reappointed state police superintendent by Governor Michael S. Dukakis. That vote of confidence had been widely popular. Trabucco was "one of our own" as uniformed personnel often put it, with a thorough grasp of the organization's operations and culture. Thus, he was able to forge effective coalitions among the

department's interest groups, especially with the union that represented the rank and file. In other words, he was an effective leader because he understood the need to establish policy goals with others, and possessed the personal skills and temperament to share credit for their achievement.

Trabucco, too, had built a solid leadership team. It was anchored by Colonel James T. Canty, a member of 1957's 41st Recruit Training Troop. Canty's professional credentials were impeccable. His first promotion, to corporal, had resulted from a statutory, competitive examination in 1967, the first required tests since the 1921 founding. From that start, he had earned each promotion competitively through the commissioned ranks. When on July 1, 1980, he was appointed colonel and deputy superintendent by Commissioner Trabucco, Canty became the first officer in history to go from trooper to the department's top career rank through the competitive system first established by the 1965 promotional statute. It had taken fifteen years, but the reform program had produced its first bottom to top leader. That remains an important organizational change.

The Trabucco-Canty leadership team was particularly effective in merging the agency's multiple centers of interest. Such a requirement in the early years was unknown. The military model was ascendant, and with it the iron discipline and arbitrary edicts that ensured its effectiveness in that era. But much had changed, especially during the social upheavals that marked the 1960's. New leadership skills were required, particularly in enforcement organizations. The old ways were right for their times. But times clearly had changed.

In that climate, the Trabucco administration in 1981 had implemented the "cruiser per man" patrol concept. Originally a key provision of the 1970 barracks abolition statute, its full implementation had been delayed for a decade by a variety of setbacks. Thus, the 1981 program completed the historic change from far flung barracks' outposts, to a new system of deployment based on substantially increased mobility and enhanced communications technology. The 1981 cruiser program, in retrospect, completed a major juncture in the historical journey of the state force.

The early eighties also had witnessed the dedication of new "streamlined" barracks in Peabody and Cheshire. Unlike earlier patrol outposts, the new facilities were geared to enforcement activities without the living accommodations of prior decades. If anyone doubted that the state force was, of necessity, constantly evolving, the modern buildings confirmed that ongoing change.

The foregoing reflect the modernizing impulses that had energized Commissioner Trabucco's tenure when in late 1986 he announced his intention to leave office. It had been a long time, three decades, since his 1956 enlistment in the uniformed branch. The first state police superintendent to have served in every rank, he had brought superb preparation to the top leadership post. That broad-based experience had shown. In many ways. Thus, on January 17, 1987, a remarkable enforcement career closed, an important biography in the historical mosaic of the state force.

Governor Michael S. Dukakis shortly announced the appointment of William McCabe as the state's new public safety commissioner and head of the Massachusetts State Police. McCabe, a career state police officer, in 1962 had graduated from the state police academy with the 43rd Recruit Training Troop. He was destined to be involved in the policy and legislative initiatives leading to the 1992 consolidation of the state's enforcement agencies.

But that major historical merger was yet over the horizon. More prosaic activities impended as he took office. These are the everyday problems, the pressures that compete for the time and attention of each individual accorded the prestige of a leadership office.

Some of these, of course, are pleasurable. One thinks especially of academy graduations. These have always been showcase events for the state force, a public opportunity for the department to display the superior quality of its training requirements and the fitness of the young officers who successfully respond to those exacting standards.

The academy and its disciplined training staffs since 1921 have been a central strength of the Massachusetts State Police. Superior personnel have always aspired to academy staff assignments. There, they have used that select opportunity to strengthen their organization by ensuring the integrity of the transforming process wherein a raw recruit becomes a law enforcement officer. Especially in the modern era, that has become a complex challenge and a major, public responsibility. Yet, the rewards are great. Teachers, it has been said, touch the future. When the future is centered on the timely and equitable enforcement of the law and the balance between individual rights and social order, the stakes are much higher.

Several hundred recruits during the 1980's had successfully completed Framingham's defining passage. As the decade drew to a close, 159 carefully chosen applicants on June 13, 1988 assembled on the academy grounds. Excitement was in the air. They had made it. Almost. There were a lot of unknowns ahead, unspecified barriers to the goal, a state trooper's badge and uniform. They had heard the rumors. That didn't help. It was day one. Graduation from the famed academy suddenly seemed a long way off.

This was the 69th Recruit Troop. The anxious recruits could not have known that they would be the last to train at the Framingham site, the last academy class for four years. A state budget crisis was just around the corner. It would impact the state force severely. But that was yet over the horizon. Their job was in the here and now. And the challenge couldn't have been clearer. Get through the academy. Survive. That was their reality.

Most did survive. But, as always, it was a memorable experience. Years later, a seasoned trooper remembered how it was. Robert H. Leverone that day had made the short trip from his Norwood home to the Framingham academy. He knew it would be tough. But he badly wanted the two-tone blue and its prestige. This is how he remembered that quest: "June 13th, 1988 broke hazy, hot and humid. The sun was up. And bright red. 'Red sky in morning, sailor take warning.' That saying kept going through my head as I, along with 159 other state police recruits, waited nervously on the front lawn of the State Police Academy in Framingham.

We were the 69th Recruit Training Troop of the Massachusetts State Police. Little did we know we would be the last to endure the rigors of state police training at that historic site. Framingham's last recruits. The end of an era.

At precisely 0800 hours, a half-dozen square jawed troopers strode single file out the front door of the academy in our direction. They were an impressive sight, crisp French and electric blue uniforms, spit shined boots. A collective nervous hush swept over us as they approached.

We were politely ordered into a single-file and guided onto the rear company street where we deposited our luggage in neat rows. We were then guided into the lecture hall where we each took a seat. 'Sit down and relax. How's everyone doing?', one of the troopers said. After a short welcome we were told to relax until the program started. The troopers left the room.

Lost in the haze was the exact duration of time we sat alone in the room. After five minutes or so, we were beginning to feel comfortable. Small talk ensued and it seemed that this was not going to be as bad as we heard. Little did we realize we were about to embark on an odyssey that would shake us to our collective core. In the end, some of us would be standing tall. Others would fade into the dusty recesses of our memories. A moment later, our lives changed forever.

The four heavy wooden doors in each corner of the room unexpectedly opened and in poured a dozen troopers shouting at the top of their lungs. 'On your feet! Get out of those chairs!'. Up and down the aisles they stormed. Some of them strode menacingly along three foot high heaters looking for anyone who dared glance anywhere but straight ahead. The sound of campaign hats bouncing off the faces of the now numb recruits could be heard throughout the room as the instructors interrogated each newcomer.

We were then marched to the company street to get our suitcases. With bags overhead, we hurried into the gymnasium, where we were arranged in rows and told to open our suitcases. The vision of Staff Sergeant Roger Ford, swagger stick held high overhead, reminded me of Moses parting the Red Sea as he bellowed, 'Eyes front! Don't be looking around! I can hear an eyeball click a half mile away.'

While all this went on, our suitcases were emptied into large piles. We were told to find our gear and pack it up in sixty seconds. Nobody was able to do it. We all paid the price. Many were seen leaving, never to come back. Such was the beginning of twenty weeks of stress training.

As days became weeks, there was constant stress. Rigorous calisthenics, demanding academics, endless drilling, and the constant in your face drill instructors, began to weed out those who were mentally and physically unprepared for the rigors of this last academy class at Framingham's historic site.

As the weeks turned into months, intensive day and night class sessions made for academics as tough as any college courses I had taken. Criminal law, motor vehicle law, first responder (advanced first aid) and much more were drilled into us. Combative firearms, water safety and driver training were some of the courses outside the lecture hall.

Finally, after twenty weeks, the 140 surviving recruits, with the motto 'Old Breed, New Tradition' marched into Worcester's Veterans Memorial Hall to the spirited sounds of the Marine Corps Band. Speaking for Governor Dukakis, Massachusetts Secretary of Public Safety Charles V. Barry emphasized the fight against crime that these new troopers were joining. Then, as video tape cameras whirred, Secretary Barry pinned shiny silver badges on each new trooper. Some were able to have their badges pinned by relatives. In my case, my father, a retired thirty year police veteran, pinned my badge to my new uniform. It was a proud moment. I tendered a snappy salute, received my diploma, and found myself a changed man, a state trooper.

The 69th Recruit Training Troop in 1988 would be the last state police class to train at Framingham. A private school in pastoral New Braintree would become the site of future training. Framingham now serves as general headquarters. Still, if you stand in the still night air and listen carefully, you can hear the muffled sounds of marching feet and the haunting cadence of drill instructors molding young men and women into some of the nation's finest law enforcement officers."

Trooper Bob Leverone got it right. Those sounds on the old muster field will endure. They are at the center of historic traditions that young men and women will carry well into the 21st Century. That will not be an inconsequential legacy to uphold by continuing adherence to long established public service ideals. That will be their challenge in their time.

Trooper Leverone had noted Governor Dukakis' absence from the Worcester graduation. That was understandable. Dukakis then was in the middle of his quest for the U. S. presidency. One may assume that his managers had decided that the governor that day could make a more effective impact elsewhere on the campaign trail. No matter. The state's chief executive missed impressive graduation ceremonies in Worcester's beautiful Memorial Auditorium. The 69th Recruit Training Troop had been superbly prepared for the statewide enforcement responsibilities they would shortly face. They demonstrated that fitness with disciplined displays of the skills they had internalized while successfully meeting Framingham's daily trials. No question, they were ready. Their time had come.

Standing stiffly at attention, the 140 academy graduates repeated Secretary of State Michael J. Connolly's oath of office. Pledging fidelity to the state's constitutional safeguards, they, at that moment, became state police officers. Moreover, they had earned the privilege of wearing the French and electric blue. Like the hundreds who had gone before them, they could feel the professional stature that uniform imparted. They sensed also the responsibilities each accepted in earning the opportunity to wear the widely admired two-tone blue colors. Each day in the field would bring ample opportunity to respond to that ever-present accountability.

That began almost immediately as Commissioner William McCabe and Colonel Thomas J. Fitzgerald presented badges to the fledgling troopers and made troop assignments. As always, the latter ritual induced some anxiety. Where would a new trooper be assigned? Where was that barracks? How many miles from home? Time honored inquiries. Somewhat humorous to enforcement veterans. But not so funny in the first hour of state police duties fraught with similar unknowns.

The 69th Recruit Troop, though, had been well prepared. In fact, they had been superbly trained by a first rate, professional staff. For academy staff, graduation is bitter sweet. They are proud of the men and women they have equipped for an enforcement career. But graduation is a poignant time as well. The recruit troop is gone. The academy is silent. Only the images remain. It is, to repeat, a bitter sweet time. Academy staffs, uniquely, have always known that feeling.

It is important in this pages, then, to recognize those who guided the 69th Recruit Troop through the Framingham experience. Their skills were essential. Their personal commitments ensured success. These were the academy professionals as the 1980's closed:

Captain Thomas R. White
Commandant

Sergeant Roger A. Ford
Assistant Commandant

Sergeant Thomas E. Creighton III
Director of Recruit Training

Corporal William J. Coulture
Director of Health Maintenance

Corporal Brian G. Greeley
Director of Operations

Trooper John M. Spellacy   Trooper John M. Richardson
Trooper David A. Snow   Trooper C. Blake Gilmore
Trooper Daniel J. Duffy   Trooper Dagoberto M. Driggs
Trooper Christine M. Bernard   Trooper Julia A. Nau
Trooper William F. Murphy   Trooper Kevin J. Kelly

As the new graduates departed Worcester for their far flung duty posts, they joined a state enforcement organization far removed from its 1921 founding, but firmly rooted in its historic traditions. As the 1990's loomed, those strengths would be essential. A state budget crisis impended. As one consequence, there would not be a new recruit troop until 1992. Fiscal constraints would delay other administrative initiatives. It was not the best of times for the department's leadership. But that is what leadership is all about. And, as the 1980's closed, the state force was administered by a veteran leadership team. Each had long since established strong professional credentials. As a command staff, they would lead the department into the early stages of the accelerating change that would mark the 1990's decade:

William McCabe
Commissioner

Edward F. Kelly
Deputy Commissioner

Colonel Thomas J. Fitzgerald
Director

Lieutenant Colonel Paul E. Lambalot
Office of Field Operations

Lieutenant Colonel William P. McAuliffe
Office of Staff Operations

Lieutenant Colonel John R. O'Donovan
Office of Investigations and Intelligence Operations

Lieutenant Colonel Peter W. Agnes
State Office of Investigations

BUREAU COMMANDERS
Major Edward J. Cronin
Bureau of Eastern Field Operations

Major John J. Hanlon
Bureau of Western Field Operations

Major William C. Nally
Bureau of Investigating Services

Major Peter M. Rickheit
Bureau of Technical Services

Major David J. Brosnan
Headquarters Section

In the final chapter, one reviews the historic changes that are challenging the department and its leadership in the closing months of the Twentieth Century. While change has been the enduring constant in the enforcement odyssey, the 1990s have energized organizational dynamics unlike anything experienced since the 1921 founding.

That fascinating story emerges in the pages that follow.

Former Troopers' Dinner, Braintree, 1980. Corporal James J. Battcock and Trooper Peter F. Quinn. The officers had just received their "Trooper of the Year" awards at the Former Troopers annual dinner. Battcock and Quinn on August 9, 1979, with emergency action saved the lives of several people trapped in a Chelsea apartment house engulfed in flames. Also honored that night on the 50th anniversary of their 1930 enlistment in the state police were former troopers Arnold W. Olsson and Anthony J. Golden. Golden in October, 1996, at age 88, traveled from Parsippiny, N. J., to attend the state police 75th Anniversary Gala at Boston's World Trade Center.

State Police Boxing Team, Warwick Prison Camp, 1980. Left to Right: Troopers Mike Lee, Bob Benoit, Leo Gerstel and Phil McDougall. State troopers that evening demonstrated their prowess at handling inmates inside the squared circle as well as on the state's highways. The boxing team for two decades has raised thousands of dollars for worthy charities across the Commonwealth.

Freeport Hall Boston, 1980. State Police Boxing Team. Left to Right: (front) B. Farrell (trainer), J. Flaherty, J. Sprague, D. Galvin, R. Benoit, D. Grabowski, (rear) L. Kerr (coach), J. Redfern, L. Gerstel, J. George, A. Toney, K. Regan, J. Dunn, T. Burnickas. In a night of boxing at Dorchester's Freeport Hall, the Bay Stater's defeated the police boxing team from Bermuda. Trooper Benoit in 1976 was the team's founder and remained its ace warrior for years. The Boxing Team on October 4, 1996, staged a 20th anniversary program in Sturbridge honoring the team's original members, and raising several thousand dollars for area charities.

61st Recruit Troop
JANUARY 18, 1980

BACK, Frederick T.
BEAUDOIN, Stephen D.
BENANTI, Stephen R.
BERNSON, Gabriel S.
BEURMAN, Laura A.
BLANCHETTE, Wayne A.
BOIKE, Samuel J.
BONES, Marcial, Jr.
BROWN, Richard R.
CARLSON, Walter T.
CARNEY, William D.
CATALANO, Martha A.
CELLUCCI, Michael J.
CLIFFORD, Elizabeth
CONNELLY, Richard P.
CRONIN, Michael F.
CRONIN, Susan M.
DERN, Gregory C.
DILL, Maryann
DONOGHUE, Thomas B.
DRUMMY, Michael W.
DUFFY, Brian G.
ELIAS, Thomas M.
FARNAM, John J.
FISHER, Gary A.
FOSS, Stephen R.
FRIES, Craig W.
GIBBONS, John
HANAFIN, Charles G.
HORTON, Edward W.
KELLEY, Richard J., Jr.
KELLEY, Stephen M.
KENNEFICK, Donald P.
KINDSCHI, Denise R.
LANGTON, Philip E.
LINDNER, Bernard E.
LIVRAMENTO, Joseph A.
MacGREGOR, Kenneth L.
MacLEAN, Marian J.
McCRAVY, George W.
McNEIL, Arnold O.
MOYNIHAN, Joseph F., Jr.
O'CONNOR, John B.
O'DOWD, Russell J.
O'REILLY, Stephen M.
PRISCO, Carlo F.
QUIN, Thomas G.
ROBBINS, Thomas G.
SANIUK, Rosemarie E.
SHANNON, Thomas A.
SMITH, Richard M.
SOLANA, Leonardo, Jr.
STUART, John J.
TONEY, Alvin D.
TRYON, Robert W.
WALSH, Marianne T.
YEE, William A.

62nd Recruit Troop
NOVEMBER 21, 1980

LYONS, William M.
CHEVALIER, Randall H.
MARTIN, Kenneth F.
SZALA, Scott E.
WASKIEWICZ, Ronald F.
CURRAN, Thomas E., Jr.
GARRITY, Shirley J.
GALLIGAN, Thomas A.
LAWLESS, Joseph M.
O'DONOVAN, James H.
GALIZIO, Gerard F.

BUTLER, Kevin J.
DUBINSKI, Kenneth P.
LOWELL, Stephen J.
CONDON, James F.
ELLIS, James P.
RIZOS, Byron L.
ALEXANDER, Gordon W.
HENNIGAN, Paul J.
PUGSLEY, Stephen M.
McGLYNN, Paul D.
GALLAGHER, John P.
DeCRISTOFARO, Jerry J.
FOLEY, Thomas J.
GONZALES, Dennis M.
HART, Robert W.
DEVIN, Charles R.
TURNER, Robert S., Jr.
O'GRADY, John F., Jr.
WHITE, Scott A.
STEVENS, Robert C.
PELLEGRINO, Joseph F.
SCOTT, Robert C., Jr.
EUBANKS, Richard W.
KELLEHER, Anne E.
REGAN, Gerard P.
EISEMAN, Robert J.
McMAHON, Kevin J.
PALLADINO, Veronica C.
SULLIVAN, John W.
ANDRADE, Robert A., Jr.
BONES, Edwin R.
FURFARI, Kenneth P.
ANDERSON, Gordon W.
MacPHEE, Donald R.
DICHIO, Anthony
DONLON, Joseph M., Jr.
CROCKER, Robert H.
GARRETT, Mark E.
CALNAN, Neil R.
SYLVIA, Paul G.
DEYERMOND, James M.
CROSSMAN, Leonard G.
COREY, Richard L.
ROSE, Dennis J.
HANNA, Mary T.
COTUGNO, Matthew J.
MOYE, Donald
BERNARD, Christine M.
FLYNN, Julie A.
BARRETT, Kathleen M.
ALVINO, Stephen C.
BLAKELY, Paula J.

63rd Recruit Troop
JUNE 27, 1981

CRISP, Michael J.
COLETTA, Gerard A., III
GRASSIA, Michael J.
TUTUNGIAN, John, Jr.
MARONI, Cary M.
McDYER, Joseph P.
McGILVRAY, Thomas R.
LITTLEFIELD, Peter L.
HEBB, Arthur W.
GLYNN, Thomas P.
PERRY, Paul A.
SMITH, Robert D.
MATTHEWS, Stephen G.
PARE, Scott S.
RUSSELL, Paul M.
BROOKS, James F.
GONSALVES, Jeffrey J.
D'ANGELO, Aldo D.
KERLE, Thomas M.
WEBBER, David A.
SIEBERG, Ronald J.

FERRARO, Robert J.
DOMINGOS, Barry J.
KONDERWICZ, Michael D.
SOUZA, Richard A.
PLATH, James W., Jr.
SULLIVAN, Thomas J., III
NOWAK, Philip B.
COFLESKY, John P.
MOORE, Robert W.
SPLAINE, Kenneth C.
MIHALEK, Stephen T.
KALIL, Thomas M., Jr.
STONE, Jeffery M.
NAGLE, Richard L.
BILLIE, Anthony F.
LYNCH, Mark S.
GILHOOLEY, James S.
POTTER, Harvey G., Jr.
GREENE, Thomas G.
GRANDFIELD, Leonard M.
MURPHY, William F., Jr.
LOWNEY, Dennis
LAWLOR, Paul P.
McPHAIL, Charles E., Jr.
POITRAST, Francis G., Jr.
PARE, Dennis L.
DESMOND, David J.
HOWARD, Stephen F.
DRISCOLL, Patricia A.
McGILLVRAY, John H.
McHUGH, Kerry P.
JOACHIM, Jeffrey C.
BLOMGREN, Robert C.
NICOLOSI, Donna L.
AHERN, Jeffrey T.
LANZA, Michelle J.
BUCKLEY, Jude T.
LOCKHART, Edwin E.
TEDEMAN, Ellen E.

64th Recruit Troop
DECEMBER 3, 1982

SHEA, Kevin P.
VOLPE, Michael L.
SMITH, Steven A.
LAWRENCE, John F.
BAKER, Thomas A.
KROM, Robert P.
BARBIERI, Paul S.
RAYMOND, Neil H.
KEENAN, Walter A.
JOHNSON, Stephen D.
COOPER, Timothy G.
BRODETTE, Barry A.
BURKE, William J.
McNULTY, Mark S.
MENTON, Brian D.
WHITE, James R.
DEVLIN, James T.
ST. SILVA, Augusto R.
GILL, Kenneth J.
KASABIAN, Edward S.
FLADGER, David F.
CANTY, William C.
PINTO, Bruce P.
CANDEIAS, Kenneth M.
DIETRICH, Alan W.
REARDON, Timothy P.
CHARETTE, Stephen D.
BIGELOW, Harvey D.
GARCIA, Alan D.
BROOKS, Dennis L.
MATTHEWS, Francis J.
CEDERQUIST, William A.
SULLIVAN, Michael J.
MORRILL, David F.

KEENAN, JOHN F., Jr.
CAPONETTE, Mark A.
BROOKS, John M.
RICHARDSON, John M.
FORSTER, Edward L.
GILMORE, Charles B.
LINT, Bruce H.
ZUK, Norman C.
DRIGGS, Dagoberto M.
PATNODE, David M.
MAHONEY, Denis C.
SULLIVAN, Michael P.
PERREAULT, David J.
CIPOLETTA, Randy J.
DiPADUA, Debra F.
CONDON, Elaine M.
McKEON, Richard D.
WHITE, Paul J.
CONNOLLY, James M.
GARBACIK, Lawrence J.
McGINN, James C.
EATON, Howard K.
NAU, Julia A.
BARBARO, Michael M.
GILLESPIE, Timothy M.
JOHNSON, Bruce T.
CARROLL, Roger V.
MATOS, Elliot J.
BEAL, Alyce B.
ROTTENBERG, Susan R.
GONSALVES, William, Jr.
ZEVESKA, Christine E.
NESTOR, James T., Jr.
COLLARD, Deborah L.
STEVENS, Marc A.
ROSE, Peter J.
HARDING, Carol
VARKAS, Mark P.
MacAULAY, Gale A.
BYRNE, Dwyn
COGGINS, Cheryl A.
JEMMOTT, Richard D.
ADAMS, Denise E.
SHAW, Rosemarie
DiPIETRANTONIO, Diana L.

65th Recruit Troop
MAY 7, 1983

MURPHY, Elizabeth A.*
HANAFIN, James M.
VON FLATERN, Leonard F., III
RYAN, James M.
KRASCO, Peter N.
COATS, Cleveland M., Jr.
AMBROSE, Gregory P.
FITZPATRICK, William R., Jr.
VRONA, Steve E.
KALMBACH, Michael J.
CHRISTIANSEN, William N.
KELLY, Kevin J.
PLACE, Donald L., Jr.
POWERS, Edward F.
BOIKE, Joseph J.
BOUNDY, Paul F.
HINES, Steven D.
CEPERO, Jaime, Jr.
O'CONNOR, Michael P.
FIORE, Michael S.
CONLEY, Martin P.
HOLMES, Frederick C.
STEVENS, Raymond M.
WOLANSKI, Richard D.
MILOS, John E.
MITCHELL, Joseph F.
First female honor graduate

RIZOS, David L.
MORIARTY, Dermot P.
DEL NEGRO, Steven J.
MARRON, Mark S.
McMANUS, Martin S., Jr.
CADRAN, Richard C.
PANACOPOULOS, Ross J.
CONDON, Joseph A.
VIEL, Daniel J.
ALBEN, Timothy P.
SAWYER, David J.
BAXTER, Sean M.
FOLEY, Martin T.
MURPHY, James F.
MATTALIANO, Gerard R., Jr.
HUDSON, Kenneth J., Jr.
SICARD, Timothy P.
WEDDLETON, Douglas A.
CARON, Mark J.
BUSA, John P.
McCARTHY, Robert E.
HORGAN, Mark D.
FINACOM, Robert P.
DRISCOLL, Kevin J.
CROFTON, Eric R.
COFFEY, Thomas J., III
HART, Francis E.
MATTALIANO, James
JAKOBOWSKI, John P.
JENNINGS, Scott C.
O'GRADY, Kevin F.
MICHEL, John T.
DEWBERRY, Stanley E.
DELANEY, William F., Jr.
COURTOIS, Mark T.
PULIAFICO, Kenneth
MOAKLEY, Donna M.
MARSELL, William L., Jr.
STAPLES, John C.
HARDING, Michael T.
NICHOLSON, Wayne T.
COLEMAN, Michael F.
PETTORUTO, Richard J.
SCANLAN, Michael J.
MACEDO, Michael J.
WEST, Mark K.
McCARTHY, Robert M.
WELCH, James M.
FREEMAN, James J., Jr.
MacKNIGHT, Carl G.
PARKER, Susan J.
FRENIERE, Robert K., Jr.
ROTKIEWICZ, William F., Jr.
RODRIGUES, Robert
GROVER, Robert R.
YIANACOPOLUS, Glenn L.
BACHELDER, Robert L.
CILA, Vincent P.
DeCOLA, Paul A.
MINIHAN, Mary M.
THOMAS, Anthony E., Jr.
HARRIS, Timothy A.
McCARTHY, Thomas G.
MATTE, David E.
SNOW, Donna M.
CROWLEY, Heather A.
WHITNEY, Robin A.
BEARD, Walter T., Jr.
SCHIAVINA, Maura L.
FIMIANI, Gerald J.
PAPPAS, Louis C.
KEARNEY, Maureen
BENNETT, Barbara J.
O'HALLORAN, Brian M.
REILLY, Barbara C.

66th Recruit Troop

DECEMBER 6, 1985

MURPHY, Thomas J.
CORTESE, David
CLARK, Daniel M.
NOONE, Richard J.
PRIOR, Richard P.
POWELL, Paul A.
DOMNARSKI, Michael J.
CAPPS, Paul M.
MONTAGANO, Peter J.
SUGRUE, Arthur W.
DUNN, Brian F.
HANKO, Charles S.
BERNA, Scott A.
FOLEY, David B.
DESY, Mark O.
HORMAN, Robert
O'BRIEN, James P.
HANSON, Terry G.
FOX, Richard D.
KNOTT, Robert J., Jr.
BLACKMER, William C., Jr.
KILEY, Devin T.
DALEY, Thomas J.
O'NEILL, Kevin B.
LEWIS, William K.
REILLY, John F.
LANE, Richard G.
LANNON, John M.
PAGLEY, Dana J.
MINNEHAN, Roy E.
SMITH, Stephen N.
BOUTILETTE, Robert J.
CRAVEN, Michael
WHITE, John J.
BARRETT, Michael C.
NANOF, James S.
DOTY, Cindy A.
HUNTE, Alan D.
DACOSTA, Edmund
MURRAY, Charles D.
PALAZZO, Paul S.
ZANI, Alan C.
RIVERA, Ramon
CONCANNON, Michael P.
JOUBERT, Alan P.
VALAIR, Michael J.
COWIN, Michael F.
OTTE, David H.
CAPILLO, Joseph C., Jr.
IRWIN, Robert M.
GRIFFIN, Stephen J.
CONNORS, Timothy
HOPE, Kevin H.
MOORE, Brian F.
MONAHAN, Robert J.
MILLS, Stephen E.
O'NEIL, Raymond C.
HUGHES, Steven C.
AHEARN, Robert J.
DUGGAN, Joseph P.
MEDEIROS, Thomas S.
WOODS, Gary
MAGEE, Paul E.
Gregory, Gilbert V., Jr.
REBEIRO, Deborah A.
DeVELLIS, Francis J.
BOYLE, Owen J.
EARLE, Stephen D.
COSGROVE, Charles E.
KONDELL, Kenneth
GAWRON, Stephen W.
WORDELL, David C.
D'AMORE, Paul F.
PAPA, Joseph M.
REGAN, Daniel P.
RILEY, Wayne H.
TETREAULT, Roger A.

HOLLERAN, Michael S.
GIAMMARCO, John M.
FISHER, David B.
PAULO, John, Jr.
McCULLOUGH, John H.
PINA, Daniel N.
MALONEY, Jon J.
DEVLIN, Thomas W.
RENEY, Thomas M.
BURKE, Elizabeth A.
CHMIELINSKI, Denis F.
HAZELRIG, John P.
KENNEY, William P.
LEVIS, Lisa B.
DANCE, Charles M.
PATTERSON, Melissa A.
RICCI, Susan M.
HANNA, Kevin W.
FLEMING, Daniel T.
MURPHY, Janet M.

67th Recruit Troop
DECEMBER 12, 1986

WHEATON, T.P.
DeJONG, D.S.
MURPHY, J.G.
COPPENRATH, L.G.
ADAMS, T.H.
CUNNINGHAM, S.J.
O'BRIEN, B.J.
LYNCH, B.W.
COLLURA, J.M.
JOINER, M.C.
O'CONNELL, W.H.
SHIELDS, C.P.
CURRIER, M.D.
LAWLOR, J.M.
LAVOICE, D.C.
ZONA, T.R.
WARAWAKA, C.S.
DEVEREAUX, W.J.
O'HARE, B.W.
COLEMAN, P.F.
MASON, J.V.
CHIARETTA, J.M.
TAMARKIN, J.R.
DOWNER, R.F.
YE, E.
HUGHES, F.P.
SULLIVAN, E.J.
RISTEEN, D.F.
CONDON, T.B.
CONTI, M.E.
GURA, J.E.
BARRY, M.J.
TROY, E.H.
SENNOTT, P.J.
WARE, C.D.
SANSOUCY, L.P.
COONEY, M.J.
WILSON, D.W.
WILLIAMS, G.J.
MULLONEY, R.K.
MARTIN, J.W.
NELSON, J.C.
NARTOWICZ, T.V.
COWHIG, J.A.
BENNETT, S.C.
GRIFFIN, D.J.
DeBUCCIA, D.G.
O'BRIEN, J.E.
DeYOUNG, A.J.
REID, B.L.
MAZZA, M.S.
PETRINO, P.E.
ROLLINS, R.C.

FOGWILL, K.A.
MAGUIRE, J.E.
HARRINGTON, R.A.
ACKERMAN, R.C.
BRYDEN, D.J.
McDONALD, S.M.
CHASSEY, P.
POPOVICS, M.
PRINCIPE, E.
KILEY, D.R.
GOULD, D.A.
RUSSELL, W.N.
MURPHY, D.F.
HACKETT, J.E.
BARRETT, W.A.
TEVES, R.E.
BOHNENBERGER, J.F.
THIBODEAU, A.D.
NOLAN, W.J.
PAINE, D.R.
GILLEN, P.A.
PUOPOLO, F.M.
DOCKREY, P.G.
MONTEIRO, E.P.
SCHEPIS, G.M.
LETSCHE, P.S.
MORRIS, S.A.
BURKE, K.M.
MURRAY, S.A.
CHAN, C.H.
DOUCETTE, J.J.
GARVIN, J.L.
ZIPPER, P.T.
MacDONALD, N.P.
McCARTHY, S.M.
NEILLY, P.J.
LUCE, T.J.
LEE, J.M.
HILTON, J.J.
ENOS, R.F.
BEEHAN, P.A.
SZETO, C.
LILLY, D.M.
McGOWAN, P.F.
THOMAS, E.
PEHOVIAK, J.D.
FIORE, R.A.
CAMBRIA, L.M.
CAHILL, M.A.

68th Recruit Troop
JUNE 27, 1987

DONNELLY, Timothy S.
AMODEO, Edward
FORD, Kevin F.
PENNIMAN, James R.
CUMMINGS, John H.
IMELIO, Michael J.
DOMINGOS, David P.
FINN, Dennis P.
LEAHY, Francis D.
FRANZELLA, Robert P.
ARSENAULT, Michael

FLAHERTY, Gerard F.
GOZALEZ, Richard C.
MEIKLEJOHN, Christopher J.
DUFFY, Jeffrey A.
MAHONEY, Richard
PULLMAN, Dana A.
FINNEGAN, Joseph P.
MITJANS, Lazaro
MONTEIRO, Robert
BYRNE, John F.
McGRATH, Robert P.
FITZGERALD, Thomas I.
THOMPSON, Deborah L.
HARRISON, Kim L.
WESINGER, Maureen M.
STEWART, Jeanne M.
ALEJANDRO, Jose O.
MALEK, Toni J.
FILGERLESKI, Darlene K.
WILMOT, Michael G.
FORREST, Lorraine A.
JOHNSON, Gerard D.
DERBA, Suzanne C.
KIM, Hyo-Suk
HARRINGTON, Sarah A.
SULLIVAN, Erin K.
PINA, John Jr.

69th Recruit Troop*
OCTOBER 28, 1988

LEYDET, Richard P.
MAJENSKI, Thomas J.
MARTINEAU,Elizabeth T.
BEDARD, Stephen T.
GODFREY, Steven P.
MAHAN, David C.
WHEATON, Michael T.
VASCONCELOS, Arthur N.
SKELLY, David S.

LOMBARD, Kerry A.
LOMBARD, Brian H., Jr.
BOTT, Fred J.
SULLIVAN, Sean P.
DOMNARSKI, Matthew J.
MCKENNA, JAMES M., II
KLANE, Andrew S.
TOVAR, Mario, Jr.
BODOR, Leslie M.
PACKARD, Kevin W.
ATCHISON, Charles W., III
RAY, Christopher M.
LEE, Brian
LOMBARD, Michael J.
SCOTT, William J.
HABEL, Michael W.
DALTON, James P.
LEVERONE, Robert H.
COUGHLIN, James F.
O'NEILL, Eugene
CUMMINGS, Peter C.
PERCY, David B.
BUNKER, Steven F
MURPHY, Matthew D.
LAMBERT, David E.
ROY, Matthew R.
KOTFILA, John R.
PATTOW, Jeffrey D.
KEEFE, David J.
BURKE, David J.
BAZZINOTTI, James A.
FLEURY, Roger W., Jr.
CORMIER, Donald J.
HAMILTON, George M., III
WILDER, Jennifer M.
MARQUIS, James J.
HIORNS, Bruce F.
BERGERON, John E.
RICHARDSON, James M.
BROJAN, Jacqueline A.
STANFORD, Joseph
MATTIOLI, Deborah A.
KANSANNIVA, Jennifer A.
GAMARI, James N.

MCGINN, Francis M.
TASKER, John J.
CROUSE, David W.
CHARBONNIER, Mark S.
RUDOLPH, Kenneth W.
BARRY, Sheila M.
CANTY, James M.
TOBEY, Dana
MULKERN, Daniel E.
KILEY, Mark W.
SANFORD, David C.
BALLANTINE, Mark C.
LYNCH, Michael T.
CHAVIS, Michael J.
FRIGON, Richard H.
BIGELOW, James P.
CAHILL, John F.
GILL, James M.
ROTA, John J.
WASHINGTON, Aaron V.
O'LEARY, John F.
L'ITALIEN, Paul J.
PECEVICH, Christine O.
O'MALLEY, Scott M.
O'SULLIVAN, Daniel C.
MCDONALD, Jeffrey P.
KENNY, Marie T.
MAGEE, Gary E.
PEIRCE, Jeffrey
MIRON, Caryl W.
SPRAGUE, David E.
GETCHELL, Bryce L.
SYLVESTER, Robert J.
HATTEN, Edward E.
TORTI, Kurt M.
ENOS, Randall S.
MENG, John J.
LEVANGIE, Dean A.
DUGGAN, Jeanne E.
O'NEIL, Brian
HOGAN, Michael F.
PINA, Edward R.
POIRIER, Thomas J.

NANGLE, Barry P.
DIXON, Tracy A.
FRITZ, Thomas R.
DUGGAN, John P.
MOLET, Jerry J.
EMMETT, Kevin D.
JONES, James A.
CARBONE, Peter J.
ELLIS, James B.
ALBERT, Joseph A.
BLAKE, Audrey J.
MURPHY, Timothy
LEEMAN, Timothy F.
ARCHER, Mark E.
RUEF, Gary P.
POWERS, Martha F.
SABOTA, Julie A.
DEMASI, Karen E.
CAMERON, Regina G.
RENAUD, Todd M.
PATNODE, Diane
SANCHEZ, Christopher N.
BROWN, Christopher M.
HASELTON, Richard A.
GORTON, Linda C.
RITCHIE, Mary E.
GILHOOLEY, Sharon S.
HALLORAN, Kenneth P.
LONG, Dana M.
MURPHY, Sean P.
O'NEIL, Shawn P.
ROBIN, Joette E.
MAGILL, Pamela J.
HESTER, Thomas J.
GAUGHAN, Martin J.
HARTSELL, Kimberely A.
MONZON, Mario R.
FORTES, John
CROSSEN, Brenda M.
MEDINA, Orlando
ANDREWS, Michael A.
COLON, Juan
ROACH, Randall D.
SPENCER, Anthony

*Last recruit troop to graduate from the Framingham Academy.

State Capitol, Boston, July, 1980. Left to Right: Governor Edward J. King swears in State Police Commissioner Frank J. Trabucco. Trabucco trained in 1956 with the 39th Recruit Troop, during more than two decades in uniform served in key field and staff posts, in 1980 was the first person appointed to the commissioner's office who had held every rank in the uniformed force before being sworn in as State Commissioner of Public Safety and head of the Massachusetts State Police.

Massachusetts State Policewomen (retired), First Annual Dinner, 1981. Left to Right: (seated) Mora E. (Terry) Schomer '49, Beverly R. Ellis '55, Mary P. Kirkpatrick '43, Kathryn G. Mead '49, (standing) Grayce V. (O'Dell) Johnson '56, Evelyn S. Kenney '54, Trooper Kathleen M. Coletta, Mary E. (Sullivan) Coveney '49, Elinor P. (Coleman) Desmond '49.   Mary S. Ramsdell and Lotta H. Caldwell in 1930 were the nation's first state policewomen, Kirkpatrick was the first commissioned officer, Coletta in 1978 was the third woman to graduate from the state police academy as a trooper, was the academy's first female staff member for 1980's 61st Recruit Troop.

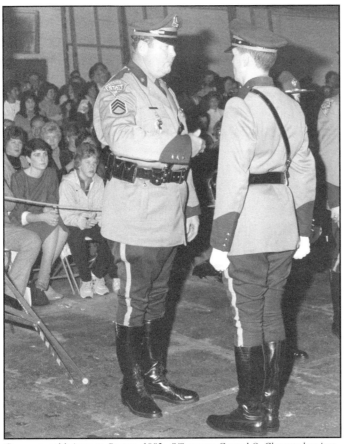

Commonwealth Armory, Boston, 1982. S/Sergeant Gerard O. Charette has just pinned the state police badge on his son, Trooper Stephen D. Charette at the December 3, 1982, graduation of the 64th Recruit Training Troop. The senior Charette had just completed twenty years service, graduating from the academy in December, 1962, with the 45th Recruit Training Troop.

Troop C, Worcester, 1985. Left to Right: Sergeant Fred MacDonald, Trooper Bob Benoit, Marvelous Marvin Hagler and Sugar Ray Leonard. Hagler, a Brockton boy, was middleweight champion of the world. Leonard held the welterweight crown. Both were solid supporters of the state police boxing team, and active in its many charitable programs. Hagler authored one of boxing's most memorable fights in a spectacular knockout of Detroit's Terrible Tommy Hearns.

Sheraton Hotel, Boston, 1981. Left to Right: Lt. Colonel John R. O'Donovan, Jr., Joe Hamel. Hamel presented O'Donovan with the Boston Press Photographers' Good Fellowship award for 1981. O'Donovan enlisted with the 40th Recruit Troop in 1956, narrowly survived a 1966 Boston shootout, as lieutenant colonel commanded state police investigative services, in 1997 continued 40 years in law enforcement as chief of police for the Massachusetts Bay Transportation Authority.

State House, Boston, 1983. Left to Right: House Speaker, Thomas McGee, Major William McCabe, Governor Michael S. Dukakis, Public Safety Commissioner Frank J. Trabucco. Trabucco on May 16, 1983, was reappointed by Governor Dukakis as state police superintendent, capping a career first begun in 1956 in the uniformed, statewide force. McCabe in 1987 succeeded Trabucco as the state's public safety commissioner and superintendent of state police.

New York City, March 17, 1988. Left to Right: (with colors) Troopers W. Murphy, D. Cortese, D. Risteen, C. Shields, M. Cherven, Sergeant F. Morse, (rear) Trooper W. Powers, Sergeant E. Johnson, Corporal J. Howley. The Massachusetts State Police Drill Team lit up Fifth Avenue for Gotham's annual St. Patrick's Day parade.

New York City, March 17, 1988. Trooper Robert P. Krom carries colors at head of the state police contingent in New York's famed tribute to Ireland's patron saint, Patrick. "New York's Finest," themselves, long have been notable for the heavy concentration in their ranks of sons and daughters of the Emerald Isle. To be a police officer in New York for years was the fulfillment of the American dream for the teeming immigrants from Erin.

New York City, March 17, 1988. Left to Right: Trooper W. Powers, Sergeant E. Johnson, Corporal J. Howley, (rear) Trooper R. Krom with colors. Howley directed the state force's public relations, was a committed Irishman, traveled many times to his ancestral home, died in 1995 while in state police service.

Concord Reformatory, 1988. Deputy Commissioner Edward F. Kelly and Commissioner William McCabe with Mother Teresa. A native of Albania, the renowned humanitarian in 1979 was awarded the Nobel Peace Prize. She was visiting Concord's prisoners, characteristic of her lifelong commitment to the world's less fortunate, a ministry she led until her September, 1997, death in Calcutta, India. Kelly and McCabe were career state police officers prior to appointment to the top administrative posts in the state force.

Boston, Cathedral of the Holy Cross, 1989. Commissioner William McCabe with Bernard Cardinal Law. Cardinal Law, Archbishop of Boston, that morning celebrated the annual Public Safety Mass. McCabe, a career state police officer, served as commissioner and state police superintendent from 1987 until 1992, became an executive in the private security field.

BELOW: *Governor's Office, State Capitol, Boston, 1980. Left to Right: Daniel Twoomey, president of the State Police Association, Lt. Colonel R. Woodward, Colonel F. Trabucco, Lt. Colonel J. Canty, Lt. Colonel J. O'Donovan, Commissioner Dennis M. Condon, Major R. Ethier, Major L. VonFlatern, Public Safety Secretary George A. Luciano, (seated) Governor Edward J. King. Governor King signed contract negotiated with the state police association containing a package of benefits for state police personnel.*

ABOVE: *Commonwealth Armory, Boston, 1982. Left to Right: Lt. Colonel George Dolan, Major William McCabe, Lt. Colonel Anthony J. Grillo, Public Safety Secretary George A. Luciano, State Police Commissioner Frank J. Trabucco, Colonel James T. Canty, Major Karl Hupfer, Major Robert E. Dunn, Major George Mallet. State police leadership had assembled for a recruit troop graduation in Commonwealth Armory, since the 1921 founding a center of state police training and ceremonial activities.*

Textile Avenue Bridge, Lowell, May 12, 1982. Aboard helicopter, Lieutenant David J. Brosnan rescues woman from raging waters of the Merrimack River. Sergeant Clement G. Tourigny maneuvered the chopper over the surging rapids while Lieutenant Brosnan made the dramatic rescue.

Everett, November, 1985. Left to Right: Troopers William R. J. Fitzpatrick and Roger V. Carroll guard sealed ballots following a disputed election. Troopers through the years have ensured ballot integrity and security when the results of local elections have been disputed.

Boston, June 23, 1980. Officer Arthur Brown, Registry of Motor Vehicles, Trooper Stephen Benanti, with friend. The officers had roped the porker for jaywalking on an interstate. Brown and his Registry Colleagues on July 1, 1992 became state police officers in the consolidation of state enforcement agencies.

Lawrence, 1988. Left to Right: Troopers Robert P. Krom, Francis J. Devellis, S/Sergeant Theodore E. Harvey, Troopers Robert H. Friend, Joseph M. Papa, Martin T. Foley, David L. Rizos, Richard Maloney and John J. White. Troopers were called in to assist in quelling a riot at the Lawrence jail. Harvey, station commander at the Andover barracks, retired as a staff sergeant in 1989.

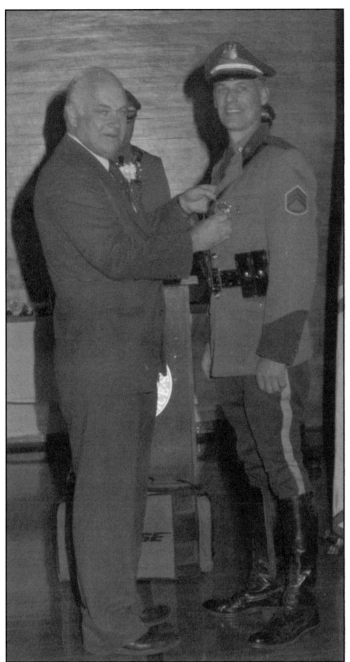

Dedham, 1986. Left to Right: Sergeant Frederick J. Morse and Trooper Francis G. Poitrast, Jr. escort one Myles Conner into Dedham District Court. A dangerous career criminal, Conner on April 27, 1966, shot and severely wounded Corporal John R. O'Donovan in a Boston gunfight. A top state police investigator, O'Donovan earlier had received the Medal for Meritorious Service at 1965's Centennial Banquet, rose to the Lt. Colonel's rank, later was appointed chief of the Massachusetts Bay Transit Police.

State Police Academy, Framingham, 1989. Commissioner William McCabe and S/Sergeant Reed V. Hillman. Hillman in 1974 trained with the 58th Recruit Troop, in 1996 was appointed by Governor William F. Weld as state police superintendent following field service as captain and Troop D commander. The 1992 consolidation of state enforcement agencies abolished the commissioner's post, creating the top rank of colonel and superintendent. Colonel Charles F. Henderson on July 1, 1992 was the first to occupy the top office in the new Department of State Police.

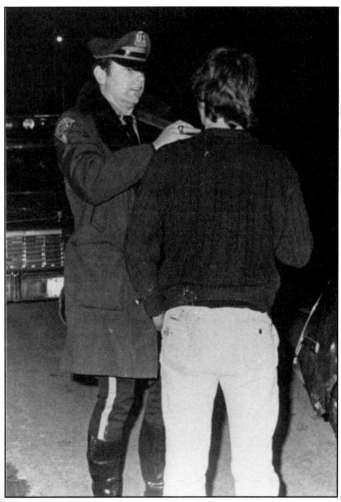

New Year's Eve, Auburn, 1982. Trooper George L. Hanna, who graduated in October of 1974 from the State Police Academy with the 58th Recruit Training Troop, is shown giving field sobriety tests at a roadblock on New Year's Eve. Hanna tragically was gunned down in Auburn on February 26, 1983 after a motor vehicle stop. Three assailants were apprehended and convicted of his murder. He was the first officer murdered since Trooper Alje M. Savela in 1951.

ABOVE: *Westboro, late 1980's. Left to Right: Sergeant Joseph F. Howley and Trooper Barbara J. Bennett. Trooper Bennett was briefing press on a violent incident at a Westboro hotel. After an exchange of gunfire, Troopers Timothy S. Donnelly and Aaron V. Washington captured a heavily armed felon. Sergeant Howley and Trooper Bennett long had lead responsibility for state police public affairs activities. In addition, Bennett, now a sergeant, made key contributions to the publication of Enforcement Odyssey.*

Route 190, Leominster, 1988. Left to Right: Troopers Mark A. Caponette, Martin T. Foley, S/Sergeant Timothy G. Hackett, Trooper Heather Crowley. Troopers examine the aftermath of an accident involving this state police cruiser and two pedestrians. Investigation revealed that the two were playing "chicken" with traffic, and jumped in front of the cruiser. One of the victims lies dead in the front seat.

Worcester Auditorium, October 26, 1988. Left to Right: Trooper Sean M. Baxter, Sergeant Roger A. Ford, Trooper Martin T. Foley. Graduation exercises for the 69th Recruit Training Troop were held at the Worcester Auditorium. The 140 members of the 69th Recruit Troop were the last state police recruits to complete training at the Framingham academy. Ford, a fixture at the academy for many years, retired as a lieutenant in 1995, became major and executive officer of the Mass Bay Transit Authority.

Worcester Auditorium, October 26, 1988. Left to Right: Troopers David E. Sprague, Caryl W. Miron, Mark E. Archer. Troopers Sprague and Miron, classmates in the 69th Recruit Training Troop, later married and were stationed together at the Springfield Barracks.

Worcester Auditorium, October 26, 1988, 69th Recruit Training Troop graduation. Left to Right: Troopers Linda C. Gorton, Caryl W. Miron, Brenda M. Crossen, David E. Sprague. The three women pictured here were part of the largest contingent of female state police officers to that date graduating from the academy. More than 200 women currently serve in the distinctive two-tone blue.

General Headquarters Boston, July 1, 1980. Left to Right: Commissioner Frank J. Trabucco, Corporal Thomas Walsh, S/Sergeant Charles N. Appleton, Jr., Colonel James T. Canty. Trabucco that day was sworn as public safety commissioner and state police superintendent. Canty stepped up to deputy superintendent, the top career rank, while Appleton and Walsh received merit promotions and new stripes.

LEFT*: Boston, July 13, 1988. Left to Right: Troopers Michael J. Grassia and Paula J. Loud. Grassia, Loud and Trooper Carol Harding carried out an undercover narcotics operation in Boston. Both Grassia and Harding were shot. Their assailant was seriously wounded. Grassia recovered from his wounds and returned to the Narcotics Unit. The suspect also recovered and was sentenced to twenty-six years at Walpole State Prison.*

Rossi's Restaurant, Dedham, 1985. Left to Right: (seated) Sergeant Harold E. Ameral, Lieutenant Peter F. Dolan, Jr., Mr. Sabino "Sam" Lauretano, Lieutenant George D. MacDougall. (Standing, Left to Right): Troopers Dennis J. Galvin, Michael J. Celucci, Kerry P. McHugh, Arthur E. Martin, Thomas W. Neff Jr., Brian J. Winsor, Lieutenant William S. Anderson, Trooper Brian M. O'Hara. Members of the crime Scene Service Unit gathered for Lieutenant Dolan's retirement after 25 years of service. MacDougall later retired as captain and head of the unit. Laurentino, one of the department's many loyal civilian employees, served for many years as custodian at General Headquarters in Boston. Tom Neff for years has been a positive force in the activities of the State Police Association. A gifted communicator, his professional skills and professional ethics have energized his work as editor of "Trooper," the union's monthly publication.

Logan International Airport, 1980. Trooper Michael L. Doyle, Captain William McCabe, President Ronald W. Reagan. McCabe and Doyle welcomed President Reagan to the Bay State during his successful campaign for the presidency. Trooper Doyle graduated in 1968 with the 51st Recruit Training Troop, served for many years in Troop F. McCabe trained with the 43rd Recruit Training Troop in 1960, rose through the ranks, served as commissioner from 1987 until 1992.

Troop B Headquarters, Northampton, 1984. Left to Right: (standing), Troopers Edwin C. Howe, Thomas J. Burnickas, Wayne J. Kenney, David G. Pogodinski, Walter J. Lazarz, Francis S. Kozaczka, William A. Carroll, William J. Peterson, William D. Fisher, Jeffrey T. Ahearn, John M. Richardson. (Kneeling), Troopers Michael M. Barbaro, John T. O'Connell, Jr., Roland Lacasse, Francis T. Duke, Francis Johnson, Richard G. Catellier, Arthur W. Hebb, Albert J. DiCarlo. These troopers were preparing to leave Troop B Headquarters for the National Troopers Coalition (NTC) picnic in Wilkes-Barre, PA. The group chartered two motor homes for the trip, arrived safely in Wilkes-Barre, participated actively in NTC activities.

General Headquarters, Boston, January 3, 1987. Left to Right: Mr. William F. Fitzgerald, Ms. Sui Lee, Governor Michael S. Dukakis, Mrs. Deborah Hottleman. The department had just instituted an advanced fingerprint system. Fitzgerald served over four decades in key state police administrative posts. His daughter, Mrs. Hottleman, continues the family tradition in the department's crime laboratory in Sudbury.

Troop C, Host Hotel, Sturbridge, 1996. Members of original State Police Boxing Team. Left to Right: Lieutenant Jack Dunn, Captain John Cunningham, Sergeant Dan Grabowski, Trooper John Lepage, Lieutenant Jim Redfearn (Ret.), Trooper Bob Benoit, Lieutenant Steve Bennett, Lieutenant Leo Gerstel, Lieutenant Mark Delaney. All were fledgling troopers when they began the boxing team in 1976. The photo was taken at the October, 1996, 20th anniversary boxing show in Sturbridge, a benefit program that enabled a $14,000.00 donation to Springfield's Crippled Children's Hospital.

Chapter Nine

CENTURY'S END—THE 1990s

Author's Chapter Note

The pace and magnitude of change in the Massachusetts State Police during the 1990's is difficult to comprehend, much less write about. So many things have been going on simultaneously. Legislative initiatives. Policy formulations. Operational planning. The three branches of state government have been actively involved. There has not been a time quite like these years in the history of the state force. It is not likely there will be another such era anytime in the foreseeable future. The central focus of the dynamics has been consolidation, the merger of state level enforcement agencies into a single department of state police. In reality, it is not a new issue. The portents had been there for years. There were other issues as well. A new training and educational complex was needed. The general headquarters facility in Boston for years had lacked the basic infrastructure of a modern state police operation.

These major initiatives were moving in tandem as the decade of the 1990's began. Scores of committees were meeting, legislative, policy and operational planning groups were at work. Over time, hundreds of people were involved. Some were active, up front and participating. Many more were just as active, but behind the scenes. Long standing vested interests were at stake. It was an unsettled time in the enforcement odyssey.

It is far beyond the scope of this work to attempt a detailed account of this era. Such an effort would necessarily bog down in a quagmire of legislative, policy and operational reports. That is not the purpose of this volume, certainly not the objective of its closing pages. In this context, the best one can offer is a snapshot, a summary of the historical changes that were wrought. The details, the esoterics and their accompanying tensions, must be left for another time and a different chronicler.

W. F. P.

HISTORY REVISITED

The *Washington Post*'s lead story did not mince words: "Uncertainty about whether the three-week dispute really had been resolved hung over the U.N. tonight as world leaders tried to absorb the previous 24 hours of fast-moving events, in which Iraq, responding to a Russian initiative, seemingly blinked in the face of a major buildup of U. S. forces in the Persian Gulf." The *Post* also noted that "...Iraqi President Saddam Hussein (has) apparently ended his defiance of the world body and averted a possible military confrontation with the United States..." Nineteen ninety and Desert Shield? Nineteen ninety one and Desert Storm? Hardly. The *Post*'s editions of November 21, 1997 were reporting Saddam Hussein's latest threat to world order even as these words were being written.

The Iraqi dictator in 1990 had misjudged America's will when he occupied neighboring Kuwait. Shortly, the United States and its Allies in 1991 unleashed Desert Storm. Saddam's vaunted Republican Guards were quickly crushed by history's most devastating air attacks. The Persian Gulf War ended in mere days, but Saddam survived in his Baghdad bunker, saved by a United Nation's resolution that prohibited a ground attack on the Iraqi capital. Predictably, in late 1997 he was defying U. N. weapons inspection teams, still intent on destabilizing neighboring regimes in the volatile Gulf region.

When in late 1990 Desert Shield moved several hundred thousand American troops to the Gulf Region, a number of state force personnel were called up for active military service. Like their predecessors in French and electric blue who had served in World War II, Korea and Vietnam, they answered their country's call no matter the sudden hardships imposed on them and their loved ones. Among those swapping the two-tone blue for military garb were the following:

Trooper Timothy S. Donnelly 68th Recruit Troop - 1987	Trooper Kevin N. Hope 66th Recruit Troop - 1985
Sergeant Ronald Lamoly 54th Recruit Troop - 1970	Trooper Paul J. L'Italien 69th Recruit Troop - 1988
Trooper Frank M. Puopolo 67th Recruit Troop - 1987	Trooper Christopher M. Sanchez 69th Recruit Troop - 1988
S/Sergeant Clement G. Tourigney 55th Recruit Troop - 1971	S/Sergeant John J. Allen, III 54th Recruit Troop - 1970
Trooper James A. Bazzinotti 69th Recruit Troop - 1988	Trooper James P. Bigelow 69th Recruit Troop - 1988
Trooper William A. Carroll 59th Recruit Troop - 1975	Trooper Tom T. Constantine 58th Recruit Troop - 1974
Trooper Paul F. D'Amore 66 Recruit Troop - 1985	

There were undoubtedly others who were called up for military service during the Gulf War. In addition, quite a number of veterans of that conflict later enlisted in the state force, graduated from the New Braintee academy, and are now posted throughout the state. Wherever they are stationed, they have participated in a dynamic era of pervasive organizational evolution. Nothing quite like it has ever happened before in the state force's enforcement journey.

THE DYNAMIC NINETIES

One observes three principal historical junctures of the 1990's decade: a new academy and a new department of state police in 1992, and in 1994 a new general headquarters.

With "consolidation," the complement of the state force in 1992 doubled to some 2,400 officers. It seemed sudden. Events, once triggered, had moved rapidly. But consolidation of state enforcement officers, the idea itself, had been around for a long time.

Newly sworn Commissioner Frank J. Trabucco in 1980 had predicted that such a merger would one day occur. But the field trooper knew it long before that. One remembers the "duplication of services" issue accelerating with the late 1950's construction of the Defense Highway System. The "Interstate," as it was soon called, was a magnet for all manner of enforcement agencies that sensed its value for organizational expansion. That's when the jockeying began to get serious.

The mind's eye image remains vivid, even after some four decades. A state trooper and a registry of motor vehicle officer are on the interstate. Each has a motorist stopped for a violation. The officers are not a quarter of a mile apart. They are both state enforcement officials, representing different state agencies, performing the same function in the same location. In full view of the motorist-tax payer. That scene recurred with regularity. Only the location changed. Even casual observers knew something was wrong. They sensed the solution as well. In retrospect, the real surprise is that the resolution of such a visible public policy issue was so long in coming.

But, inevitably, it did come. A new Massachusetts Department of State Police was created on July 1, 1992. On that day, enforcement officers from the Metropolitan District Commission, the Registry of Motor Vehicles and the Capitol Police became state police officers. As noted, almost overnight, the Massachusetts State Police doubled to a complement of some 2,400 personnel.

Without question, consolidation emerges as the single most important historical juncture since the 1921 founding of the State Police Patrol. As discussed in the chapter's introductory note, the research, planning, policy and legislative initiatives that were required boggle the mind. Another chronicler will need another volume fairly to report on the circumstances, people and merging of interests that in 1992 made state enforcement consolidation a reality.

The aftermath is equally complex,-and challenging. It is as though four different cultures were merged. Different languages, different antecedents, different folkways,-all must be reconciled. It will not be easy. But it must be done. An enforcement odyssey does not stop. But its direction changes. Change has always been the constant in the history of the state force. More than ever, that is the central challenge as the Twentieth Century's final months impend.

Before moving on, it is important briefly to observe the long and distinguished histories of the three enforcement agencies merged with the state police in the historic consolidation. For example, the Capitol Police long had provided security and enforcement services on Beacon Hill and throughout the State House. While the origin of the department is somewhat obscure, its personnel for years were participants in the state's major ceremonial and political happenings.

The Registry of Motor Vehicles enforcement authority dates to April 27, 1902, when automobiles made their appearance on city streets. Inspectors first wore uniforms in 1929, and in 1960 the agency adopted its distinctive dark blue coat and light blue trousers. At about the same time, a select few inspectors were authorized to carry firearms. Subsequently, on January 1, 1971, the agency's enforcement officers were granted full police powers. When Governor William F. Weld on December 27, 1991 signed Chapter 412 of the Acts of 1991, some 250 Registry enforcement officers were included in the pending merger of state level police organizations.

The Metropolitan District Commission Police Department, the "Mets," on July 1, 1992, were about to complete ten decades of public service when they became part of the new Department of State Police. First authorized in 1893, the agency initially had separate police operations for its decentralized jurisdictions. The police command was unified in 1895, an earlier "consolidation," and activities were merged into a single enforcement agency.

The "Mets" during the next ten decades evolved into a modern, statewide law enforcement organization. Because of the uniqueness of its urban-rural responsibilities, the agency through the years developed a full range of operational activities supported by an array of modern technical support services. The Metropolitan Police Department, in a word, was a premiere enforcement organization as its personnel in 1992 became an integral part of the Massachusetts Department of State Police.

David C. Benoit, a career "Met's" officer, in 1995 published a history of his former department. Now a state police sergeant, Benoit closed the book's introduction on a personal note: "I was very proud to be a Met. I'm just as proud to be a State Trooper. I wasn't born with pride. I earned it, then and now. There is an individual pride and a departmental pride. I was very proud of the majority of Mets as I am very proud of the majority on the new State Police. The Metropolitan Police Department exists in history, our minds and forever in our hearts. That can never be erased."

Sergeant David C. Benoit on July 1, 1992, was one of more that 1,000 "Mets" who became state police officers. He did not ask for that change. More than likely, he did not wish for it. It happened because human institutions are dynamic. Organizations change because their environments change. They either adapt and prosper, or resist and dissolve. The enforcement odyssey for almost eight decades has confirmed that observation. It is an important lesson validated by the Past even as the unknowns of a new century become the Present.

A NEW GENERAL HEADQUARTERS

As noted earlier, the 69th Recruit Training Troop in 1988 was the last recruit troop to train at the Framingham academy site. When the 70th Recruit Troop in June, 1992, reported for training at New Braintree, efforts intensified to convert the Framingham training complex to a modern state police general headquarters facility.

"G.H.Q.," as it is popularly known, had been at 1010 Commonwealth Avenue in Boston since early in World War II. An industrial building with huge freight elevators, "1010" had frustrated every effort to transform its structure and atmosphere into an acceptable administrative and technical environment. No matter, the old building for five decades had housed the command and control functions of the state force, together with key investigative, technical and support activities. In a word, "1010" had been synonymous with the enforcement odyssey for fifty years. Like an old soldier, it had served well in its time. But, by 1994, its time had long since passed. A new era was about to begin.

Governor William F. Weld, Public Safety Secretary Kathleen M. O'Toole and Colonel Charles F. Henderson on October 25, 1994, officially opened the new general headquarters complex in Framingham. The modern facility resulted from a $2.7 million dollar transformation of the Framingham academy on the site of a World War I muster ground. The modernizing construction program had taken some eighteen months, about the same time required for the 1969-1971 construction of the training academy.

Actually, state police headquarters operations had been phasing into Framingham even while facility modernization proceeded. Secretary O'Toole commented on the difficulties during the dedication ceremony: "Having worked here during the construction (as a state police lieutenant colonel), I can appreciate the difficulties which were overcome by the state police command staff in providing top notch service despite the disruption this project entailed." Colonel Henderson focused on the upgrading of statewide enforcement services: "This ceremony is yet another way the state police is delivering on its commitment to a partnership with the community and local police for more efficient and effective services."

With the October 25, 1994, dedication of the modern Framingham General Headquarters, the enforcement odyssey had reached yet another historical juncture. Since 1921, that locale had been the focus of training and operational activities. But "G.H.Q." had always been elsewhere: the State Capitol, Commonwealth Pier, 1010 Commonwealth Avenue,-the long vilified "1010." Now, the historical roots and the administrative and operational nerve center had become one and the same. It was a defining moment in the historical evolution of one of the nation's most admired statewide law enforcement agencies.

CHANGE AT THE TOP

While the major organizational changes had been transpiring, the leadership structure continued to evolve as well. Commissioner William McCabe beginning in January, 1987, had been intimately involved with the legislative and policy initiatives that resulted ultimately in the consolidation of state enforcement agencies, a new academy, and the new general headquarters complex. Ironically, McCabe's post as commissioner of public safety was abolished in the consolidation law. Accordingly, the highly respected enforcement veteran in February, 1992, completed his 32 - year state police career. McCabe had seen it all in his long service in the uniformed ranks, and especially in the commissioner's post while unprecedented historical changes were ongoing. His leadership during a unique passage in the enforcement odyssey will endure as a remarkable contribution to that organizational journey.

With McCabe's departure, Deputy Commissioner Edward F. Kelly temporarily assumed the responsibilities of the top office. Kelly in 1949 had graduated from the academy with the 35th Recruit Troop, served in all manner of field and staff assignments, and had risen to the top commissioned ranks. While the impending consolidation law made his appointment a temporary one, Kelly's wide experience and political acumen were major assets during a sensitive transition. In one of his final administrative actions, the

43 - year enforcement veteran in June, 1992, appointed members of the 70th Recruit Troop to the new academy at New Braintree. They were the first recruits to train in the Berkshire's foothills, and the last class appointed in the Department of Public Safety. When later that year they completed academy requirements, the new troopers were assigned to field posts in the Massachusetts Department of State Police. Uniquely, the 70th Recruit Troop had bridged the historical transition from the old and understood to the new and uncharted. No matter, it is not likely they had been distracted from the daily challenge to survive New Braintree's transforming experience. Everything, after all, is relative. The immediate challenge was survival. Organizational esoterics would have to wait.

When first McCabe and then Kelly departed the commissioner's office, an era ended. Governor Calvin Cooledge on December 1, 1919, had appointed General Alfred E. Foote as the state's first commissioner of public safety and head of its division of state police. When on May 27, 1921, the "State Police Patrol" was founded, the rural force was placed in the existing state police division under the commissioner's immediate authority. Sixteen commissioners followed Foote in one of the nation's most prestigious public safety posts. Seven decades imposed their influences on the ever-evolving state police organization. Suddenly, in mid - 1992, the office and its administrative structure were gone. Such is the fate of the institutions men create, and, inevitably, of those who serve in them. At such junctures, it is useful to remember with Santayana that "We must welcome the Future, remembering that soon it will be the past; and we must respect the Past, knowing that once it was all that was humanly possible."

A NEW OFFICE

Charles F. Henderson on July 1, 1992, became the first superintendent of the Massachusetts Department of State Police which came into being on that day as well. Appointed to the legislatively created post by Governor William F. Weld, Colonel Henderson brought strong professional credentials to his new office. A graduate of the state police academy in 1968 with the 50th Recruit Training Troop, the enforcement veteran's career had begun astride two earlier organizational transitions. First, the department's competitive promotional system had been implemented in 1967. That meant that Henderson subsequently would earn each of his promotions competitively through the senior commissioned ranks. Secondly, his first field assignment in 1968 had been into the barracks' system. That meant travel to and from a remote post at one's own expense, required living in the barracks, and an 84 - hour duty week. That is the kind of background that sharpens one's appreciation for modernization initiatives that strengthen an organization and improve its personnel policies.

Henderson as deputy superintendent had been centrally involved in the modernization activities of the early 1990's. Coupled with his long field and staff experience, he was thus prepared for the exacting responsibilities of the newly structured superintendent's office. It was a complex period of time, and it created organizational tensions. Statewide enforcement standards had to be maintained even while a new department emerged from four agencies with unique histories. A modern headquarters complex would be created while, at the same time, dedicated personnel worked inside the structure itself. One senses the complexity of the leadership challenge in just writing about it. It was not one of the easier assignments in the long enforcement odyssey. But Colonel Henderson had a lot of help. There are not enough pages in this volume to list the dedicated professionals who made the commitments and accepted the sacrifices that brought their enforcement organization through the most complex and challenging era in its lengthening history. Their satisfaction rises from the knowledge that they helped prepare the state force for the yet undefined public service opportunities that will materialize in a new century.

One among the many was Kathleen M. O'Toole. A member of the Boston Police force for seven years, O'Toole from 1986 to 1990 served in the Metropolitan District Commission Police Department, the "Mets." In that agency she rose to the civil service rank of captain and, as deputy superintendent, was responsible for patrol operations, the police academy, special events planning and technical units. Subsequently appointed to superintendent, she was the commanding officer of 680 enforcement personnel and one of the nation's law enforcement leaders.

From that vantage point, Superintendent O'Toole was an active participant in all aspects of the planning leading up to the 1992 consolidation of state enforcement agencies. In that critical role, she acquired solid knowledge of the history and operations of the state police, as well as the other agencies involved in the impending merger. When on July 1, 1992, the consolidation legislation became effective, Attorney Kathleen M. O'Toole became a lieutenant colonel in the new Department of State Police. As commanding officer of the special operations division, O'Toole was responsible for all tactical field and traffic personnel and their statewide activities. More importantly, Colonel O'Toole chaired the implementation team responsible for the merger of some 2,400 officers into the new state police organization, while integrating policy, personnel and pension systems years in the making. There may have been more complex leadership assignments in the long history of the state force, but they do not come readily to mind.

It was not especially a surprise, then, when Governor William F. Weld on July 5, 1994, named O'Toole the Secretary of the Executive Office of Public Safety, the state's senior public safety official. In retrospect, one marvels at Secretary O'Toole's historic achievement in earning the state's highest law enforcement office. It had only been 19 years since Joan M. Farrel and Lorraine R. Roy in 1975 graduated from the academy with the 59th Recruit Troop as the first female troopers since the 1921 founding. Needless to say, the new secretary had bridged a series of historical firsts in the enforcement journey of the state force.

"SPECKY"

Not long after Secretary O'Toole's appointment, a state police legend passed away and, with his death, a nostalgic era in the long journey of the state force receded more deeply into the lengthening past. Francis J. "Specky" McVeigh, Sr., on December 16, 1994, died in Milford after a lingering illness. McVeigh in the 1930's arrived at his first barracks assignment as a "Mess Boy." Mess Boys from the 1921 founding until 1971's barracks abolition were the all purpose support system of the state force. They cooked, served the food, washed the dishes. They did it all. Most came and went after short stays. Some stayed on for years. A select few became legends in their own time. "Specky" was among the elite.

Just a boy when he saw his first barracks, an innate toughness matched a savvy of one beyond his years. He was a hard worker. Aa quick learner. Those admirable traits led subsequently to a state job as a barracks' cook. From there, "Speck" moved on to his lifetime calling, - head chef at the Framingham academy. It was at the academy that McVeigh befriended hundreds of recruits during the four decades following World War II. One of them was his son, Francis J. McVeigh, Jr. When on September 10, 1966, "Specky" pinned the state police badge on his son's uniform blouse, it was the culmination of his own long held aspirations.

"Specky" McVeigh in 1971 was awarded the State Police Medal for Meritorious Service. The award was richly deserved recognition for his lifetime commitment to the public service ideals of the state force. His death at 81 in 1994 was the symbolic close of a nostalgic era in the enforcement odyssey.

A CAREER CLOSES

Colonel Charles F. Henderson had first met "Specky" McVeigh in 1968 at the state police academy in Framingham. In that setting, McVeigh was the seasoned veteran, the head chef. Henderson was the raw recruit, giving his all for an enforcement career. Time's passage imparted its inexorable changes, however, and by 1996 the state force's superintendent was himself a 30-year veteran, with almost four years in the department's top post. When in spring 1996 Colonel Henderson announced his retirement, he had witnessed one of the more organizationally active periods in the lengthening enforcement journey.

Henderson's July 1, 1992 appointment as superintendent had marked the culmination of the most dramatic change in the department's history, consolidation of state enforcement agencies. Simultaneously, the state police academy, the organizational heartbeat, was relocated to New Braintree. In October, 1994, a modern general headquarters complex had been dedicated in Framingham, the ancestral "home" for the legions who had worn French and electric blue. A state of the art crime laboratory in September, 1995, had begun operations in Sudbury. Clearly, the pace and scope of change had been unprecedented. Nothing even approaching such organizational evolution had occurred since the 1921 founding.

In a word, and with retrospective perception, it was breathtaking. Hundreds had committed their skills to the scores of requisite administrative and operational initiatives that made it all happen. Colonel Henderson was just one among the many who ensured organizational integrity during the most trying passage in the state force's history. But as superintendent, he had borne the lion's share of the accountability. Today's enforcement organization and its professional stature is validation of the administrative achievements that will always be identified with his tenure in the 1990's decade.

NEW LEADERSHIP

Governor William F. Weld on May 1, 1996, appointed Captain Reed V. Hillman superintendent of the Massachusetts State Police. Hillman in 1974 had graduated from the state police academy with the 58th Recruit Troop. First posted to Troop C, he subsequently served in field and staff assignments in Troops D, E and general headquarters. Having earned his law degree from Suffolk University, he was admitted to the Massachusetts Bar in the same year that he graduated from the academy, - a remarkable feat.

The new superintendent rose through the ranks via the department's competitive promotional system, attaining the highest or second-highest test score on each examination he took. Promoted to captain in 1994, he was assigned to headquarters' operations, and in July, 1995, became Troop D commander, with enforcement responsibilities throughout Southeastern Massachusetts, Cape Cod and the islands. He was serving in that key post when Governor Weld selected him for the top leadership office of the Department of State Police.

Colonel Hillman's appointment coincided with activities planned to celebrate the 75th anniversary of the 1921 founding of the "State Police Patrol." During the autumn of 1996, "state police nights" were held both at Fenway Park and Foxboro Stadium where the Boston Red Sox and New England Patriots sponsored public tributes to the state force and its remarkable 75-year enforcement odyssey. The celebratory activities culminated on October 5th with a 75th anniversary banquet at Boston's World Trade Center. Several hundred guests joined Colonel Hillman and Governor Weld at the vast waterfront location. History was present as well. The site for decades had been known as Commonwealth Pier. And, in the 1930's, Governor James Michael Curley and Commissioner Paul G. Kirk had moved general headquarters from the Capitol's basement to the sprawling complex on Boston Harbor, a major coup in that depression-plagued era.

The 75th anniversary gala was a memorable evening marking a significant juncture in the enforcement odyssey. Jointly sponsored by the Former Massachusetts State Troopers and the current state force, the event was co-chaired by President Richard J. Barry of the Former Troopers and Lt. Colonel Ronald J. Guilmette. The high point of the anniversary program was the presentation of the Trooper of the Year award to Troopers Mark F. Blanchard and Eugene O'Neill. The prestigious award is named for Trooper Alje M. Savella who was killed in the line of duty in a 1951 tragedy. Blanchard and O'Neill won the coveted honor for the gunpoint capture of three armed felons wanted for attempted murder and armed robbery in the Essex County area.

The 75th anniversary activities comprised a fitting public observance of a historical juncture in the enforcement journey. Looking back, time's passage had been swift. It is always that way. Years lengthen, and seemingly momentous events recede in the institutional memory and become mere moments in the historical mosaic that is an organization's legacy.

THE 73RD RECRUIT TRAINING TROOP

Over 100 strong, members of the 73rd Recruit Troop arrived at New Braintree in the spring of 1996. It is highly unlikely that they were aware that they were the focus of history in the making. Much else occupied their crowed thoughts; things like survival and, just maybe, the coveted state police shield. That was their agenda. Nevertheless, each slowly would sense that theirs was a unique juncture in the enforcement odyssey. They were the 75th anniversary academy class. That honor always would remain theirs alone.

Seventy-five years had fled since the First Recruit Troop in 1921 had departed Framingham to police the state's rural hinterland. Seven and a half decades. A long time. That first cadre of enforcement pioneers were to succeed or fail with a new enforcement concept, an untested idea. The presence in New Braintree of the 73rd Recruit Troop during the spring, summer and

autumn of 1996 confirmed that the First Recruit Troop, and all those that had followed, had succeeded with their daunting mission beyond the expectations of even their most ardent supporters.

As the 75th anniversary class advanced toward its November 1 graduation from New Braintree, one was given the singular opportunity to provide an essay for inclusion in the graduation yearbook. Needless to say, acceptance was both swift and genuinely appreciative. After tracing the historical legacy the fledgling troopers were about to embrace, thoughts turned to the future: "The 73rd Recruit Troop is the future. You will serve into the 21st Century, the Third Millennium. Your focus, then, must necessarily be energized by the future and its possibilities. The future, moreover, is where both your challenges and opportunities lie. No academy class before you has been better prepared for that formidable public task. None, it is certain, has been more eager to prove its merit with its public service contributions.

You are the beneficiaries of one of the premiere educational experiences in law enforcement. You understand now the professional depth and integrity of the academy staff. The best and the brightest have always sought the challenge of molding new troopers. And the academy experience, transforming aspirations into the reality of public service, has consistently rewarded academy staffs with a full measure of professional pride.

The 73rd Recruit Troop will strengthen that tradition. Your academy class of 1996 will, with its public service achievements, richly reward those who have guided you through New Braintree's defining transformation.

You owe that much to them. More, you owe it to yourselves, your loved ones, and the citizens you will be sworn to serve. There is no higher calling. You will face no greater challenge. The rest is up to you."

GRADUATION

The 73rd Recruit Training Troop on November 1, 1996, assembled for graduation on the campus of the University of Massachusetts at Amherst. It was 75 years to the month from the distant time when the First Recruit Troop had graduated in Framingham's less auspicious surroundings. Seventy-five years. A long time. Yet, in some ways, a short time too.

Governor William F. Weld, Secretary of Public Safety Kathleen M. O'Toole and State Police Superintendent Reed V. Hillman led a notable group of dignitaries to the dais. But the hour belonged to the 98 graduates of the recruit troop. It was their day. Theirs alone.

The recruits went through a series of time-honored demonstrations, each focused by the skills acquired during the months at New Braintree. Governor Weld, Secretary O'Toole and Colonel Hillman then addressed the academy graduates, reminding them that they would carry into the 21st Century a tradition of public safety achievements the equal of any in the American police service. Following the traditional "pass in review" and colonel's dress inspection, the recruit troop, collectively, received its oath of office. As members promised to uphold the United States Constitution and that of their Commonwealth, they became troopers in the Department of State Police. It was a defining moment. Their pride was palpable. They had earned the French and electric blue, colors that would energize their enforcement careers well into the 21st Century.

The graduation ceremonies complete, the 75th Recruit

Troop paraded for a final time under the watchful eyes of the state police command staff. These were their leaders, the senior officers who would guide them through the early stages of their enforcement careers:

COMMAND STAFF

November 1, 1996

Colonel Reed V. Hillman	Superintendent
Lt. Colonel Glenn B. Anderson	Deputy Superintendent
Lt. Colonel Ronald J. Guilmette	Assistant Superintendent
Lt. Colonel Nelson N. Ostiguy	Div. of Investigations & Intell.
Major Donald C. Cody	Div. of Administrative Services
Major Bradley G. Hibbard	Div. of Administrative Services
Major Robert J. Mullen	Bur. of Professional Standards
Major John A. Burns	Office of Affirmative Action
Major Paul G. Regan	Troop A Commander
Major Charles N. Appleton	Troop B Commander
Major John J. Kelley, Jr.	Troop C Commander
Major Albert A. Simon	Troop D Commander
Major William F. Cronin, Jr.	Troop F Commander
Major John DiFava	Troop H Commander
Captain Frank P. Baran	Troop E Commander

MAJOR FRANCIS T. BURKE

As the youthful troopers reported to their first field posts across the state, Major (Ret.) Francis T. Burke died following a lingering illness. There was much irony in his passing. Fran Burke was a trooper's trooper, an officer and a gentleman. He had always been there when help was needed. Now, as 98 young men and women set out to follow in his footsteps, he was gone.

A young Francis T. Burke in 1942 had enlisted in the U. S. Marine Corps. At war's end he returned to his Walpole home, having survived the bloody assault landings at Iwo Jima and Tarawa. Achieving a longtime goal in 1948, he graduated from the state police academy with the 33rd Recruit Troop. The marine veteran served in a variety of field and staff posts during the next two decades, rising to the major's rank in 1970. When in 1973 he retired from the uniformed force, Burke began a second criminal justice career as a senior official in the U. S. Justice Department. After more than two decades of federal service, he was a ranking administrative officer in the U. S. Marshal's Service when he died on November 5, 1996, mere hours after the 73rd Recruit Troop had departed New Braintree.

Major (Ret.) Francis T. Burke's passing belongs in these pages because he embodied the kind of values and attributes that merit emulation. Certain words come to mind when one reflects on his lifetime of public service: integrity, faithfulness, commitment, sensitivity, enthusiasm, competence. In short, he was a role model for public service aspirants and practitioners alike. As these words are written, one remains thankful for having been touched by his life.

THE LAST TROOPER

Leo F. Stankard in 1921 graduated from the state police academy with the First Recruit Troop. Stankard had planned to attend both the October 75th anniversary gala and the November 1 graduation of the 73rd Recruit Troop. A worsening illness had prevented both appearances.

With an irony that recurs in the long enforcement odyssey, former Trooper Leo F. Stankard died on November 17, 1996, almost 75 years to the day after his state police enlistment. He was 100, the last survivor of the enforcement pioneers who, in November, 1921, departed Framingham to prove their mettle and the value of a new policing concept they would carry to the Commonwealth's rural hinterland.

Stankard was also the last survivor of Company F of the 26th Infantry Division, the Bay State's famed World War I "Yankee" Division. He had received a battlefield promotion in France, while earning the Purple Heart, Silver Star and Victory Medals. Lt. Colonel Ronald J. Guilmette led a uniformed detail at the former troopers's November 20th funeral service in St. Bernard's Church in Newton, joining Former Troopers' President Richard J. Barry and his delegation in a final tribute to the old soldier and state police pioneer. An era had closed. All those who had begun the enforcement odyssey in 1921 now had completed their personal journeys.

STATE POLICE ASSOCIATION

OF MASSACHUSETTS

Trooper Leo F. Stankard and his colleagues in the 1920's never dreamed of an organization like "SPAM," the State Police Association of Massachusetts. SPAM was founded in 1968, the first union in the history of the state force. A detailed account of SPAM's origin and early development is told elsewhere in this volume. But it is important briefly to note the union's central role in the major organizational developments of the past three decades.

SPAM in 1970-1971 was a significant force in the abolition of the "live in" barracks' system and the reduction of a trooper's duty week from 84 to 40 hours. In that major effort, President James V. Oteri and his union colleagues coordinated closely with state police leadership in forging the legislative and executive coalitions that brought swift passage of the historic reforms. In retrospect, one perceives more clearly how SPAM's 1968 founding came at a critical juncture in the department's enforcement journey. Reform of the barracks' system was needed. In fact, it had been long overdue. The timing was right. SPAM's emergence at that moment completed the fortuitous convergence of organizational and political interests that earlier had been lacking.

Needless to say, SPAM has been centrally involved in every significant agency and personnel issue of the 1980's and 1990's. These have run the gamut from minor operational disputes to the defining historical changes wrought by the 1992 consolidation of state enforcement agencies. SPAM seems to have been everywhere, pursuing the interests of its members while ensuring an openness of state police administrative practices unknown to earlier generations of state police officers.

The union since its 1968 founding has prospered from clear articulation of its legislative and policy goals, as well as the administrative leadership of its elected officers. Even while these words were written, the union's membership elected a new slate of officers to ensure focused leadership at century's end:

Dean R. Bennett	President
Richard R. Brown	Vice President
John P. Coflesky	Treasurer
Thomas Neff	Secretary

Bennett's predecessors in the president's office since 1968 made timely and significant contributions to the substantial improvements in operational and personnel practices of the past three decades. It is important in this context, then, to list those who have led SPAM during an era marked by ongoing organizational dynamics:

John D. MacLean	1992-1997
Kevin W. Regan	1991
William J. Powers, Jr.	1990
Francis W. Riley	1984 - 1989
Ronald J. Bellanti	1981 - 1983
Daniel J. Twomey	1979 - 1980
Frederick T. Guerreiro	1978
Richard L. Whelan	1974 - 1978
Robert C. Woodward	1973
James V. Oteri	1968 - 1972

Each tenure has left its unique imprint on SPAM, indeed on the state police organization itself. In that way, each will endure as part of the historical mosaic that is the fascinating story of the Commonwealth's statewide enforcement agency.

THE CONTEMPORARY ORGANIZATION

As the final months of the Twentieth Century impend, the Massachusetts Department of State Police is staffed by 2,245 officers. Of that total complement, 2,023 are men, and 222 are women.

The Department is organized in three principal divisions: the Division of Administrative Services, the Division of Investigative Services, and the Division of Field Services. Administrative Services handles a myriad of technical and support responsibilities in close support of the department's field enforcement operations. Needless to say, the division's highly skilled professionals are crucial to the timely and effective discharge of the department's public mandate.

The Division of Investigative Services is accountable for the statewide investigation and prosecution of criminal activities subject to its broad jurisdictional authority. Personnel in this division are heirs to a remarkable enforcement legacy that dates to the 1865 founding of the Massaachusetts State Constabulary, as well as the 1919 Constitutional Convention which structured a state police division in the new Department of Public Safety. The latter,moreover, was the readily available locale for the uniformed "State Police Patrol" at its 1921 founding.

That "uniformed branch" has evolved to today's Division of Field Services. More than 1,600 officers are deployed throughout the state in a time-honored "barracks" system. While military lifestyles and 100 hour duty weeks are now but quaint artifacts, strategic field operations are remarkably similar to the enforcement techniques developed in the early decades.

These are focused by seven field troops, headquartered in the following key locations:

TROOP A—Danvers. Area: north and northwest of Boston.
TROOP B—Northhamptom. Area: the four western counties.
TROOP C—Holden. Area: central part of the state.
TROOP D—Middleboro. Area: southeastern part of the state, Cape Cod, Martha's Vineyard, and Nantucket.
TROOP E—Weston. Area: Massachusetts Turnpike.

TROOP F—Logan International Airport. Area: Logan Airport, Tobin Bridge, World Trade Center, Boston waterfront.
TROOP H—South Boston. Area: Eastern part of the state; key sections of metropolitan Boston area.

Thirty-four strategically located substations blanket the state in support of the seven troop headquarters. Field services has also launched a member of *community policing* initiatives, especially in the greater metropolitan Boston area. Some of these are jurisdictions assigned to the department in the July 1, 1992, consolidation of state enforcement agencies.

PERSONNEL POLICIES

When in November 1921, members of the First Recruit Troop graduated from the state police academy, they received $75.00 per month. After six months, salaries for these enforcement pioneers were raised to $1,200.00 annually. For that, they had 48 hours off *per month*. It was a system and a lifestyle for the times. And times were spare.

Today's enforcement professionals bring superior personal skills to their exacting responsibilities. Things may not be as spare as they were decades ago, but the weakening of normative social constraints has made a law enforcement career a challenge of the highest order. Fortunately, the citizens of Massachusetts have ensured that these and other contemporary considerations are reflected adequately in the department's personnel policies.

SALARY

Rank	Minimum	Maximum
Trooper	$31,140	$40,960
Sergeant	$42,116	$47,636
Lieutenant	$52,399	$55,019
Det./Lieutenant	$56,145	$58,953
Captain	$60,233	$63,245
Det./Captain	$64,684	$67,919
Major	$69,535	$73,013
Lt. Colonel	$74,827	$78,569
Lt. Colonel	$80,559	$84,588
Dep. Superintendent		
Colonel	$86,770	$91,110

In addition to the foregoing salary scale, the department's enforcement personnel are eligible for the following educational incentives:

Associate's degree 10 percent of base salary
in Criminal Justice
Bachelor's degree 20 percent of base salary
in Criminal Justice
Master's degree 25 percent of base salary
in Criminal Justice
or Law Degree

Personnel may retire after 20 years of service at 60 percent of salary. An additional 3 percent of salary is earned for each year over 20, with a cap at 75 percent of salary. State law currently imposes mandatory retirement at age 55, but the department has waived this requirement until a pending lawsuit is settled.

DUTY WEEK

Field personnel adhere to a "4 and 2" schedule in staffing the statewide barracks systems. Officers work four 8 1/2 hour duty tours, and then have two days off. The cycle is then repeated. Uniformed personnel commute in state police cruisers between their duty stations and residences. This "cruiser per man" (and now woman) was a key enforcement concept in the 1971 abolition of the "live in" barracks system which overnight reduced the duty week from over 84 hours to 40. In the contemporary organization, it is an essential strength in the department's provision of public safety services to the state's citizens.

Enforcement officers assigned to key administarive posts, many in gneral headqaurters, work a regular Monday-Friday duty week with an extra day off each third week. Historically a "G.H.Q." posting was a prized assignment, a 40-hour duty week while personnel in the "troops" (and their families) chafed at the constraints imposed by a duty week that hovered around 100 into the 1960s decade. Moreever, staff promotions were easier to come by at a time when field operations were rigidly structured. These contrasts for decades were a source of consdierable organizational tension, and occasional personal animosity. Preditably, time's passage has softened such rough edges as they have melded into the historic mosaic that yet evolves in the ongoing odyssey.

IN MEMORIAM

Trooper Llewllyn A. Lowther on September 24, 1924 was killed in a motorcycle accident in Adams. A 1922 graduate of the state police academy with the 4th Recruit Training Troop, he was the first Massachusetts trooper to die in the line of duty. Tragically, since then, twenty state police officers have been killed while wearing the French and electric blue. Five of these tragic deaths have occurred thus far in the decade of the 1990's, four within six months in 1994 - 1995.

Words fail adequately to convey the profound sorrow borne by each of the bereaved families, or the shock and dismay inflicted on the state force. Such a passage is profoundly personal. It must be experienced. There is no other way to know how deeply affected are the most sensitive of human emotions.

The following state police officers have been killed in the line of duty thus far in the decade of the 1990's:

TROOPER JOSEPH F. MOYNIHAN, JR.

Trooper Moynihan on January 18, 1980 graduated from the state police academy with the 61st Recruit Training Troop. He was killed in the line of duty on June 19, 1990, in a light plane crash in Maine enroute to a Federal Bureau of Investigation training exercise in that state.

TROOPER DAVIDSON G. WHITING

Trooper Whiting on October 16, 1992 graduated from the state police academy with the 70th Recruit Training Troop. He was killed in the line of duty on August 18, 1994 in Lexington when a vehicle traveling in the opposite direction crossed the median divider and hit his cruiser head on. Davidson's recruit troop was the first to train at the New Braintree academy, and the first to enter the ranks of the newly created Department of State Police.

TROOPER MARK S. CHARBONNIER

Trooper Mark S. Charbonnier on October 28, 1988, graduated from the state police academy with the 69th Recruit Training Troop. He was shot and killed on September 2, 1994, in an exchange of gunfire with a fleeing felon on Route 3 in Kingston. A native of Dorchester, the son and brother of police officers, Trooper Charbonnier in May, 1995, would have completed studies for his law degree.

TROOPER JAMES MATTALIANO

Trooper James Mattaliano on May 7, 1983 graduated from the state police academy with the 65th Recruit Training. He was killed in the line of duty on February 22, 1995, in a helicopter crash in Cambridge. A pilot in the State Police Air Wing since 1989, Mattaliano was survived by his widow, Trooper Jennifer M. Mattaliano, and his brother, Trooper Gerard R. Mattaliano.

TROOPER PAUL A. PERRY

Trooper Paul A. Perry on June 27, 1981, graduated from the state police academy with the 63rd Recruit Training Troop. He was killed in the line of duty on February 22, 1995, in a helicopter crash in Cambridge. A pilot in the State Police Air Wing since March, 1994, Perry shortly before his death had established a law practice with his wife, Attorney Carol Perry.

AUTHOR'S AFTERNOTE
A MEMOIR

On February 7, 1998, I traveled some 500 miles from my home in Leesburg, Virginia, to my hometown of Fall River, Massachusetts. There, at Durfee High School, I watched with fascination, and much nostalgia, as more than 500 young men and women took the entrance examination for the Massachusetts State Police. Simultaneously, more than 16,000 additional applicants were taking the same test across the state.

As I watched these earnest, intense hopefuls, I was distracted by thoughts of an earlier time, not long after the close of World War II. Then, some fifty years past, I stood in the gravel yard of my dad's gasoline station (he was the "manager" _not_ the owner) and dreamed of becoming a "state trooper". One did not in those days see a uniformed trooper often. It was still the era when the public's perception was that of a solitary figure astride a motorcycle in the state's rural Hinterland. No matter, an occasional glimpse of a uniformed trooper was enough for me. Those colors created a mind's eye picture that fired my imagination. I was twenty one. From where I stood in that gasoline station yard there was no higher calling, no greater aspiration.

When in 1949, I passed the entrance examination and was appointed to the State Police Academy, my joy was unbounded. While time's passage has weakened the focus of much that has happened in a lengthening lifetime, I recall that moment with yesterday's clarity. I could not believe it. I had made it. I was going to become a "state trooper". Let the scholars try to describe upward social mobility. I felt it. It was a feeling that inspires these words after five decades.

I had it right in 1949. My career in the Massachusetts State Police brought me much personal satisfaction and many professional opportunities. It was good for me. It was good for our family. I hope it was good as well for the law enforcement organization that made it all possible.

These were a few of the thoughts that distracted me on February 7 in my native city as I watched several hundred young people aspire to a public service career in French and Electric Blue. They are right where I was fifty years ago. I hope some of them want it as badly as I did. If they do, I hope they make it. I know their personal commitments will be rewarded with professional career opportunities as they make their contributions to the enforcement odyssey in their time.

I have written on an earlier page that having once worn the French and Electric Blue remains the most closely held of personal remembrances. That is a paraphrase of an enduring sentiment I first shared some twenty years ago. The past two decades have fixed that feeling even more firmly. It "is" the most closely held of personal remembrances. I hope "Enforcement Odyssey" helps others to understand why.

W.F.P. Winter 1998

70th Recruit Troop*
OCTOBER 16, 1992

DAUTEUIL, Paul J.
CONDON, Kevin M.
DOLAN, John P.
RICHARDS, Michael E.
McCARTHY, Paul D.
JOHNSON, Robert A.
YOUNG, Keith E.
WARMINGTON, Richard S.
LAPOINTE, Dana J.
HORGAN, Paul A.
LAVOIE, Edward J.
MORAN, John T.
MISKELL, Michael J.
ROSS, Joseph F.
WILDGRUBE, Danial J.
KATZ, Damon A.
FOX, Andrew T.
SOJKA, Robert E.
NOLAN, Charles W.
BOUSQUET, Robert M.
FLAVIN, Douglas R.
MURPHY, Thomas J.
BOHNENBERGER, Kris J.
BAKER, Gene A.
PINKES, William M.
PINTO, Robert M.
FRENZO, Mark R.
ZACCONE, Laura
RYLEY, Dan
WILCOX, Christopher T.
CONNORS, Brian P.
PETERS, Michael J.
LOISELLE, William C.
SAMPSON, Michael J.
KELLY, Stephen E.
McCARTHY, Travas T.
TARBOKAS, William H.
FOLEY, Patrick R.
SPECHT, Darren R.
CARDOZA, Scott J.
McGARY, Craig J.
LYONS, James F.
FITZGERALD, Daniel P.
MURRAY, Matthew J.
FOLEY, Timothy E.
FRAIOLI, John A.
BARRY, Michelle L.
DOWNSBROUGH, PI
CANNING, Thomas D.
MANNY, Roger M.
MASSARI, James M.
BIBEAU, John M.
SMITH, Michael P.
HANAFIN, John J.
COOK, Michael J.
MACKENZIE, Scott E.
FALLON, John P.
BOMBARD, Timothy P.
GARRANT, Brian B.
RODRIGUEZ, Melvin N.
CULLEN, William J.
FARRELL, James F.
WHELAN, Timothy R.

KENNEDY, Jane E.
LEGROS, Ronald V.
McCABE, Scott E.
LIBERTY, Joseph N.
HENNIGAN, Steven P.
ELWOOD, John F.
BAKER, Ronald F.
PEASLEE, Michael L.
BRETTA, James G.
MARTIN, Allan J.
SAMPSON, Kathleen M.
PERWAK, Gerald D.
SOTO, Daniel
FLAHERTY, Stephen V.
WALSH, Timothy J.
FINN, Timothy E.
COYNE, Michael E.
DEAMBROSE, Kellie L.
FOSTER, John F.
HOPPER, Michael S.
FITZHUGH, Stanley P.
KERVICK, David W.
DEAMBROSE, Keith P.
WARD, John T.
ROSE, Daniel C.
COAKLEY, Paul L.
KONSTANTAKOS, Peter J.
CONNOLLY, Michael J.
BERLO, Gary L.
MCCARTHY, Thomas
LOPES, Steven M.
AUMAIS, Matthew A.
BROOKE, Lisa J.
JOYCE, Thomas J.
MARSH, Stephen
McAULIFF, Keith A.
NOTHELFER, Brenda J.
OLEY, Carl F.
HALLE, Kevin P.
TALIAFERRO, Dennis M.
BATES, Michael B.
McKEARNEY, David G.
CONNOLLY, Michael T.
HASLIP, Cheryl A.
ANALETTO, John M.
McNEIL, John R.
MAILLET, Paulette D.
REGAN, Craig A.
MULVEY, John J.
JAKUBOWSKY, John C.
FERGUSON, Donald R.
PADOVANI, Roger
McNEIL, William F.
HILLIARD, Erik R.
DEVLIN, James P.
BABBIN, Timothy G.
LAROSE, Pamela J.
SBROGNA, Andrew V.
McCABE, Deborah A.
CARY, Laura L.
HANLEY, Walter J.
O'NEIL, James E.
O'NEIL, Kevin P.
CABRERA, Hector
BOSSI, Donald R.
BOUDREAU, Craig
PIMENTAL, Joseph S.
GIBBONS, Ronald

*First recruit troop to graduate from New Braintree Academy, and to enter new department of state police.

MacKENZI, Charles E.
CORLISS, Michael J.
ARROYO, James J.
RODRIGUE, Arlindo
MCGUNIGLE, Steven J.
FLETCHER, Marion B.
MAPLE, Kevin M.
SOMERVILLE, Arthur E.
SULLIVAN, Stephen J.
CRUZ, James M.
WHITING, Davidson G.
FRASER, Marque R.
CONNELL, John W.
CABRERA, Jose A.
LARRIU, Angel T.
BLANCHARD, Mark F.
LAWRENCE, Eugene F.
O'NEILL, Kristine M.
KING, Karen A.
FONSECA, Casille E.
SOMERVILLE, James R.
HEALEY, Sharon M.
EATON, Daniel J.
JACKSON, Carlton L.
MUZZI, Leonard A.
LEDUC, Peter E.
SCHUBERT, Scott M.
SHANKS, Brian C.
LONG, Richard F.
GOLENSKI, Michael J.
OXNER, David M.
O'BRIEN, Kevin M.
CORDERO, Angel L.
KOSSAK, Phyllis M.
THORPE, Michael F.
HODGDON, Sean M.
REID, Mark L.
SMITH, Michael J.
PENA, Jose F.
DIAS, Catherine J.
GALVIN, Catherine T.
VASQUEZ, John M.
RAMOS, Ronald D.
YEE, Frederick FC.
SCIGLIANO, Edward A.
MORELAND, Terry
ANTOINE, Romere D.

71st Recruit Troop
OCTOBER 14, 1993

HILL, Michael J.
REIS, David A.
CAMBRA, Todd P.
FARLEY, Michael E.
GALE, Daniel R.
GAWRON, Richard S.
BALL, Richard M.
NADEAU, Greg A.
WATSON, Brian J.
LEBLANC, Jeffrey A.
SERPA, William R.
MAWN, John E.
FITZGERALD, James M.
PROVOST, Jon E.
RANGE, Richard S.
VACCARI, James E.
COSGROVE, Richard W.
KASPERZAK, Heather A.
BALLOU, Joseph F.
WOSNY, Paul M.
O'NEIL, Robert A.
SEMENTELLI, Richard J.
MURRAY, TIMOTHY R.
SCAPLEN, Kevin P.
RAMSLAND, Erik F.
KELLEY, Thomas F.

CRANE, John F.
LAVOIE, Marc A.
McGINN, Daniel C.
HAKKARAINEN, Adam J.
MASON, CHRIS S.
SULLO, Paul J.
JOYCE, Bryan
RENZI, Anne
BEAUPRE, George A.
GULLAGE, Lee A.
FRUSTACI, Karen J.
SUYEMOTO, John L.
LYVER, Michael J.
RILEY, Timothy J.
NAPOLITANO, David
MICHNO, Michael J.
MULKERRIN, Lynn F.
CAPPS, Michael A.
FERRARI, Michael L.
WONG, Kenneth H.
O'RIORDAN, Brian C.
MORAN, Brian J.
WEINSCHENK, Paul R.
CRUMP, James K.
GLADU, Brian G.
BRUCE, James R.
GERHARDT, Wayne J.
DOWD, Philip R.
MALONEY, Sean P.
STERNFIELD, Jason H.
BAKEY, Thomas F.
MAGUIRE, Scott C.
HEPPLESTON, Douglas E.
DOYLE, Michael J.
HUME, Jean M.
MURPHY, Matthew G.
BERNSTEIN, Eric S.
McKENZIE, Albert E.
SCHRIJN, John S.
O'LEARY, James D.
RUSSOLILLIO, Pasquale
FITZGERALD, James A.
CASSILLE, Marianne
WALSH, Kevin K.
LETHIN, Gerard T.
GAVIOLI, Brian C.
SMITH, Robert G.
DONOGHUE, William
MULLANEY, Stephen C.
TRIPP, Loriann
HANLON, James A.
CARNEY, Kathleen T.
GALLAGHER, David M.
WILLIAMS, Kevin P.
WELLS, Daniel P.
WALSH, Stephen J.
TENNEY, Kevin J.
LOMBARDI, Mark J.
WESOLOSKI, Kevin R.
RYAN, Kimberly F.
RYAN, Thomas R.
SWENSON, Eric A.
BEDARD, Steven H.
MURPHY, Robert E.
CHOQUETTE, Robert
WALLS, Francis M.
CONCANNON, James J.
STONE, Joseph A.
DEMORANVILLE, Richard
MORRIS, John J.
WALSH, Shawn J.
ORLANDO, Nunzio
McDONALD, Edward T.
BZDEL, Andrew P.
STANLEY, Edward W.
BARRETT, John
BUTLER, Michael P.
DZIADOSZ, Patricia
CHICOINE, Shawn T.
BRALEY, Kenneth E.

FENNESSY, Steven P.
BARNES, Stephen J.
MOONEY, Neil C.
DEAS, James M.
MacDOUGALL, Timothy F.
BAXTER, Michael L.
QUALLS, William
FRIES, Robert F.
O'HARA, Edward
BRENNER, Karl P.
FROTHINGHAM, Peter M.
ZULLO, Carol A.
BAKER, Ross R.
RUYFFELAERT, John E.
CASEY, Mary T.
NUNES, John B.
KOCH, Stephen J.
DOHERTY, Ernest G.
PUCCIA, John A.
FAHEY, Scott F.
ROSS, Daralyn A.
FOGARTY, Laura
BLAIR, Mark S.
KASTRINAKIS, Paul J.
PAULO, Joseph G.
McLEOD, Thomas C.
KEOHANE. Edward
REINE, Karen
PACIFICO, Steven M.
DEAR, Anthony
PITTS, Robert P.
McSWEENEY, David
QUELLETTE, Margaret
ATKINSON, Dana R.
NORRIS, Grace E.
NOONAN, David M.
O'CONNOR, Stephen J.
GAHAGAN, Eric J.
BRITO, Kevin A.
DUGGAN, James
ENG, Brian T.
LOSARDO, Donna M.
DeMARCO, Dante J.
BAKER, Michael H.
DORAN, Francis W.
BURCHFIEL, David W.
NIGHTINGALE, Kara L.
DAY, Karen M.
FERRAZZANI, Kurt M.
COTE, Lisa
RIDLON, Richard M.
MORAN, John M.
MARTINO, Tony D.
DOUGHERTY, Chris
CUNNINGHAM, James M.
RYAN, Daniel P.
SHUGRUE, Bredhan S.
CARD, Paula J.
KENNEDY, Rachel C.
JONES, William B.
CESAN, Paul E.
KUDLAY, Christopher M.
ELICHALT, Etienne G.
REILLY, Jody A.
BAKER, Joseph T.
BOHN, Robert A.
SECREST, Kelly L.
DOTOLO, Jodi M.
QUINN, Matthew K.
FOLEY, Deborah J.
WILSON, Winifred J.
McCLURE, Elizabeth
HOLLAND, Scott M.
McANALLY, Brian T.
NAVAS, Robert W.
HOWELL, Shawn K.
HARVEY, Michael D.
GOULD, Kathleen M.
ARRENDONDO, Elkin O.
HALFKENNY, Damian

BROOKS, Robert F.
SUTHERLAND, Michelle
BRITT, Tracy A.
WAKEFIELD, Wendy A.
GARABEDIAN, Gail

72nd Recruit Troop
OCTOBER 7, 1994

DILORENZO, Americo C.
RICHARD, Daniel G.
TALBOT, James R.
GOSLIN, John J.
GRAY, Donald C., II
MILL, John A.
COOKE, Peter A.
O'ROURKE, Bruce E.
CANAVAN, Brian J.
DELHOME, Gina M.
VITALE, Jamie P.
KANE, Peter J.
KATSARAKES, George N.
BATES, Jonathan J.
CALLAHAN, Robert J.
HALBACH, Terrance J.
VALENTINI, Angelo
RICHARD, Thomas F.
FOREST, Thomas
ROGERS, Mark
GUARINO, Matthew J.
ENGLISH, Peter A.
PROVOST, Michael E.
IGIELSKI, Marian J.
ROCHEFORD, George E.
PILLSBURY, Donald S.
PALMER, David C.
DAIGE, Andrew M.
KING, Joseph F.
WAKEHAM, Mary A.
HIGGINS, James F., Jr.
AHERN, Michael A.
BOULOS, Richard A.
GRAVINI, Matthew C.
ROBINSON, Patrick J.
SHEA, Barry M.
KILNAPP, Robert J.
PRUSSMAN, David P.
O'DONNELL, James
FORTIN, Stephen P.
AUGUSTA, Mark D.
RODERICK, Jeffrey G.
CORDER, Lawrence A., Jr.
STOKES, Geoffrey
CLEMENT, Dean F.
WEINER, Mark A.
GILPIN, Kerry A.
CHAN, Bobby Y.
CAVANAUGH, Daniel E.
ROBBINS, Mark D.
DUCHINI, James D.
DOYLE, Paul J., III
HUGHES, Michael G.
BELANGER, Paul E.
GALLANT, Steven J.
SILVA, Patrick R.
BULMAN, Paul E.
BIBEAU, Kevin P.
HODGDON, Heather Q.
FERNANDES, Derrick M.
SILVIA, Joseph J., Jr.
BIGELOW, James L.
DOWD, Timothy E.

BRIGGS, James M.
COLON, Ruben D.
KIELY, Lawrence W.
CONROY, John H.
LISIEN, Christine T.
CURTIN, Timothy J.
VANN, John A.
MACKIN, David R.
HEBERT, Gary R.
MORRILL, Jeffrey P.
SAWICKI, Scott A.
LANGTON, Derek L.
COSTA, Mark
WALSH, Katherine E.
GRASSO, Jimi
SYLVA, John F.
DOWNING, Michael S.
WENTRUP, Heidelore K.
MILLETT, Mario J.
BROWN, Donald R.
GALLANT, Robert W.
REESE, Edward D., Jr.
O'HARA, Christine M.
FISHER, Denise E.
MARTIN, Christopher J.
TOBIN, Bruce J.
LLOYD, Thomas D., Jr.
BRAY, Jonathan R.
GOMES, Melissa A.
SANDERS, Carla B.
DOHERTY, Denise M.
MURRAY, Kevin E.
PARK, Jay Y.
SOUCY, Jean A.
GAGNON, Erik P.
SUAREZ, Shayne A.
D'AMATO, Shawn
WHITE, Carolyn N.
ROMANO, Sheryl A.
BROOKES, Anna C.
SIMMONS, Christine
OWENS, Lisa M.
SICARD, John N.
HICKS, Tanya

73rd Recruit Troop*
NOVEMBER 1, 1996

JOHNSON, Richard
LENNON, William P.
COLLETTI, Robert S.
COSTA, Derrick A.
BULIS, Jeffrey A.
ANDRADE, David A.
CONNOLLY, Kevin M.
CAMPINHA, Shawn D.
BERKEL, Brian D.
DESFOSSES, Gregg A.
BAKER, Paul F., Jr.
DATEO, Robert W.
AHERN, Timothy M.
CLEMENT, John N.
FITZGERALD, Thomas E.
EUGIN, Dennis M.
FREDETTE, Kevin J.
LaBARGE, Robert C., Jr.
JORGE, Lucas
KENNEDY, Christopher G.
HATHAWAY, David C.
LAVELLE, Louise C.
GILLIS, Laurie A.
LOPILATO, Anthony S., Jr.
GALLANT, David
MORGAN, Lisa
MASTERSON, Joseph W.
LUGAS, James D.
PARSONS, David F.

LEONARD, William S.
McCANN, David P.
McGREAL, Gerard
MANISCALCHI, Charles J., Jr.
NIEVES, David
O'MALLEY, Dean
FERRERA, John, Jr.
NEWMAN, Seth B.
SONIA, Michael M.
POWERS, Michael F.
SULLIVAN, Brian S.
SARROUF, Thomas K.
SMITH, Lawrence P., III
TIBBETTS, Stephen L.
WOLFE, Paul A.
WEST, Matthew G.
YOUNG, Kevin C.
SICARD, Stephen T., Jr.
TEVES, Irma D.
ROBLES, Francis V., Jr.
SHANAHAN, Michelle J.
BREAULT, Paul C.
STORRS, May E.
HAYES, Laura M.
CROWTHER, David A.
CARROLL, Sean F.
COPPONI, Paul J.
BROOKS, Brian P.
COHEN, Mark D.
CONGDON, Jeffrey E.
ARAKELIAN, Brandon R.
CHEVREN, Michael F., Jr.
ALESTOCK, Anthony A.
WHITE, Nicole R.
FROIO, Katrina L.
LEHTINEN, Lisa M.
JONES, Raymond, III
KILEY, John A., Jr.
GIOSSI, Daniel M.
GORDON, Jeffrey S.
EDWARDS, Bruce H.
FERNANDES, Paul A., Jr.
KELLY, John J.
FITZGERALD, Kevin W.
FITZGERALD, Michael J.
NUGENT, Terry J.
NICOLORO, Daniel J.
PATTERSON, David A.
PECJO, Eric C.
McCARTHY, Robert B., Jr.
McMAHON, Edward P., III
MARTIN, Michael P.
PAQUETTE, Brian C.
LENTI, Jeffrey M.
MURPHY, Kevin R.
MALLOY, Robert W., Jr.
MATHURIN, Edward O., Jr.
WONG, Michael S.
ROUTHIER, Rachael A.
PITTS, George E., Jr.
SHEA, Gerald T.
RAFERTY, Gregory
TOTO, John M.
SPENCER, Mark S.
SLATTERY, John P.
TANGUAY, Craig M.
SCHENA, Anthony III
SMITH, Robert A.
THOM, Daniel H.
75th Anniversary recruit troop

Consolidation

On July 1, 1992, state level enforcement agencies were consolidated into the Massachusetts Department of State Police. The following personnel on that date became state police officers:

Metropolitan District Commission Police

Adams, Bruce E.
Adell, Wanza
Ahern, Robert
Ahlstedt, Stephen R.
Albonetty, Victor R.
Altieri, Stephen M.
Anderson, Eric A.
Ashe, Gerald R.
Austin, Paul G.
Avola, Alexander
Ayer, Charles R.
Ayuso, Carmelo
Ayuso, Ulises

Babcock, Robert L.
Bailey, James E.
Baird, William A.
Bakey, John J.
Balboni, Harold E.
Banik, John F.
Banks, Stuart A.
Bannister, Robert
Barrows, Robert J.
Barry, Charles T.
Barry, Thomas R.
Batchelor, Steven P.
Beach, Leonard H.
Bearfield, Gary R.
Beckwith, Robert B.
Bedford, James J.
Belanger, Stephen C.
Belden, Vernon L.
Bell, Lemuel S.
Bender, Laurie A.
Benoit, David C.
Bernard, Ronald S.
Bianchi, John E.
Bishop, Robert J.
Blaney, Keith B.
Boehme, Richard L.
Boisvert, Bernard E.
Bolas, Edwin P.
Borey, George
Borgomastro, Joseph J.
Boudreau, Joseph R.
Boyle, Robert E.
Brady, Roy M.
Brandos, Steven K.
Brant, John M.
Briand, David G.
Brien, Joseph L.
Brighton, Christopher R.
Briody, Thomas J.
Brown, David E.
Brown, David W.
Brown, Donearl W.
Bruce, James R.
Brush, Ronald R.
Buckley, Christopher J.
Buckley, Kevin G.
Buell, David L.
Burke, Gerald F.
Burke, Mark E.
Burns, John A.
Butler, Stanley L.
Butner, Calvin B.
Butner, Ernest E.
Butner, Lisa

Cahill, David M.
Cahill, William R.
Callender, Donald E.
Calnan, Kevin J.
Calnan, Kevin T.
Campbell, Robert W.
Capece, Charles A.

Caron, Brian A.
Carroll, John E.
Carter, Robert J.
Casagrande, Carl J.
Cashin, Richard J.
Castadoro, Edward A.
Cataldo, Richard R.
Catanese, Joseph M.
Celino, James A.
Chaisson, David E.
Chaisson-Grenham, Rosemary
Chambers, Sidney J.
Chambers, Zina J.
Chandler, Drew C.
Chase, Richard
Chiasson, Edward F.
Cloonan, Thomas R.
Coalter, John B.
Collins, Nancy M.
Collins, Scott T.
Combs, Walter
Condon, John L.
Connell, William D.
Connolly, Coleman F.
Connor, Janes W.
Conrad, Donald
Conrad, Paul
Considine, James J.
Coogan, James A.
Cooney, William A.
Corbett, Joseph F.
Courage, Bruce W.
Cournoyer, Arthur W.
Crehan, Eileen T.
Cresta, Dana M.
Cronin, Mark
Crosby, Richard J.
Crowley, Paul
Crowley, Paul C.
Cullinane, James J.
Culliney, Thomas F.
Cummings, Paul F.
Cunniff, James R.
Cuoco, Kathleen M.
Curcio, William J.
Cyr, Stephen H.

Dacyczyn, Walter J.
Dahill, Richard J.
D'Aiuto, Gregory P.
Daley, David J.
Darian, Edward S.
David, Philip K.
Davis, Patrick L.
Dean, Ray C.
Deary, William E.
Delucca, William A.
Demaio, Paul M.
Dentremont, Donald I.
Devereaux, Robert T.
Dhionis, Daniel C.
DiSalvo, Alfread T.
Dixon, Marilyn A.
Dixon, Ronald
Doane, Lawrence D.
Doherty, John J.
Dolan, Charles F.
Dolan, Christopher J.
Dolan, Thomas E.
Donahue, Richard A.
Donovan, Richard A.
Dooling, Jeffery M.
Doucette, Philip P.
Downey, John F.
Drane, Joseph J.
Drawec, John W.
Duane, Thomas J.
Duff, James T.
Dugan, Thomas S.

Doucette, Philip P.
Downey, John F.
Drane, Joseph J.
Drawec, John W.
Duane, Thomas J.
Duff, James T.
Dugan, Thomas S.
Durden, Sammy L.

Edgerly, Richard J.
Evans, Mark C.
Evers, Noel T.

Fanning, Francis P.
Favale, Matthew J.
Favuzza, Robert J.
Fay, Kevin B.
Febles, Dennis
Federico, Michael A.
Fera, Anthony F.
Finneran, Lawrence W.
Fitzmaurice, William J.
Fitzpatrick, Lawrence J.
Flaherty, John N.
Flaherty, Kevin P.
Flaherty, Richard E.
Flynn, Charles W.
Flynn, John P.
Flynn, John T.
Foley, John T.
Foley, Kenneth W.
Foley, Ronald
Foley, Thomas F.
Follett, Robert L.
Ford, David E.
Ford, David F.
Ford, Joseph A.
Ford, Mark S.
Frazier, Gerald F.

Gagliardi, Samuel E.
Gagner, Steven H.
Galante, Joseph R.
Gallant, Barry R.
Galvin, Robert J.
Gately, Daniel J.
Gately, Jerome F.
Gately, Sean P.
Gaudet, Richard L.
Gay, Edward T.
Gentile, John J.
Gesualdo, John E.
Gesualdo, Paul R.
Gibbons, Raymond A.
Gibson, Walter F.
Gillis, Laurence A.
Gilmore, James F.
Gilroy, Paul T.
Gioia, Andrew J.
Giso, Michael A.
Glass, John R.
Glassford, Francis L.
Glennan, Gerald A.
Glover, Kenneth
Good, Robert P.
Grady, Thomas F.
Grant, Daniel J.
Grant, Timothy F.
Grassia, Anthony S.
Gray, Ronald S.
Grealish, John J.
Grealy, Thomas F.
Green, David L.
Green, Robert P.
Grenham, Thomas D.
Griffin, Michael J.
Grushey, William O.
Gullage, John

Hadley, Robert A.

Hagman, Frederick
Hall, Frank C., III
Halpin, Paul F.
Hamill, Richard A.
Hanley, Joseph T.
Hanley, Michael F.
Harrington, James J.
Harrington, Robert E.
Hartley, Paul J.
Hayes, Paul M.
Healy, John
Hennessey, Deborah A.
Herbert, John D.
Hermes, Brian D.
Hickey, Paul S.
Hicks, Rosemarie
Hodgdon, Gary M.
Hogaboom, Kevin C.
Hogan, Daniel G.
Holub, Richard
Hoskin, Gary W.
Howard, Joseph E.
Hubbard, John L.
Huber, Richard P.
Huffam, Richard R.
Hunter, Edward F.
Hunter, Howard J.
Hunter, Richard C.
Huntley, Arthur L.
Hymon, Ross W.

Internicola, Nicholas P.
Ioven, John L.

Jackson, Daniel P.
Jalbert, Roger R.
Jefferson, Daniel
Jenkins, Kenneth R.
Johnson, Anthony
Johnson, Cornelius
Johnson, Ronald
Jones, Robert M.
Joyce, James C.
Julian, Joseph W.

Kalton, Drew H.
Kane, Carolyn A.
Kane, Charles F.
Karsh, Richard N.
Kee, Eugene A.
Keith, Alan R.
Kelley, Gerald J.
Kelley, William E.
Kelliher, Jeremiah
Kelliher, Michael J.
Kelly, Michael J.
Kelly, Robert P.
Keys, Leroy
King, Daniel S.
Kipetz, Alan D.
Knight, Joseph H.
Kondratiuk, Rostislaw
Kurciviez, Bradford

Lapan, John F.
Lavargna, Lawrence J.
Laverde, Richard G.
Layden, Kevin E.
Leavey, Thomas H.
Lee, Edward J.
Lemar, David J.
Lemieux, Mark V.
LeMoine, Arnold D.
Leon, Baldwin
Leurini, Steven M.
Linquata, John T.
Loconte, Anthony F.
Loring, Douglas W.
Lugas, Jeffrey J.
Lydon, Shawn W.

Lydon, Thomas P.

MacDonald, Francis G.
MacDonald, John J.
MacDonald, Robert A.
Mack, Donald E.
Mackiewicz, Michael T.
MacLean, Daniel M.
Maglio, Dominic D.
Mahoney, James M.
Mahoney, John F.
Mainieri, Shirley J.
Malloy, James B.
Maloney, Paul C.
Manning, Robert L.
Mannke, Robert F.
Marag, Theodore G.
Marchand, Paul R.
Marino, Walter J.
Martin, John A.
Martinez, Hemenegildo M.
Martucelli, Robert L.
Mason, Megan R.
McCarron, John D.
McCarthy, Charles R.
McCarthy, Dermont F.
McCarthy, George R.
McCarthy, Michael F.
McCarthy, Michael J.
McCarthy, Paul
McCoy, Joseph P.
McDermott, William A.
McDonough, Kevin
McHale, John B.
McKay, William L.
McKinnon, Marvin L.
McLean, William J.
McNamara, John M.
McPhee, William G.
McQuade, David P.
McQueeney, David J.
Meech, Francis X.
Melendez, Hernan A.
Melia, John N.
Melvin, Sean K.
Mendes, Douglas A.
Merrill, Michael J.
Mills, Carolann
Mills, Frederick A.
Mills, James D.
Minghella, Thomas M.
Miranda, Joaquin P.
Moister, Gregory R.
Montagano, Pardo A.
Montanez, Efrain
Moore, Robert J.
Moquin, John T.
Morales, Elvin
Morgan, Michael P.
Morgan, Robert M.
Morris, John S.
Moseley, Eric D.
Mosely, Jonathan A.
Mosely, Julia C.
Mozuch, Gary E.
Mullen, Kevin J.
Munroe, Robert M.
Muolo, Francis L.
Murphy, Michael W.
Murray, Christopher A.
Murray, Lawrence C.

Narris, Robert J.
Nasuti, William J.
Nee, William J.
Noel, George E.
Noseworthy, Kenneth W.
Nugent, Robert B.

O'Blenes, Richard A.

O'Brien, Francis X.
O'Brien, John L.
O'Brien, John T.
O'Brien, Joseph K.
O'Connell, Richard B.
O'Connell, William F.
O'Leary, David
Oliver, Charles R.
O'Loughlin, Thomas J.
O'Neill, Edward J.
Orlando, Linda P.
O'Rourke, Francis X.
O'Rourke, Susan M.
O'Toole, Kathleen M.*
Ouellette, Armand G.
Outerbridge, Derek L.
Owen, Dana C.

Pagliccia, John L.
Pagliuca, Joseph F.
Palmer, Robert W.
Parker, Albert P.
Parker, Frank H.
Pavone, Michael F.
Peachey, Kristan A.
Pellissier, Joseph E.
Pembroke, Denis J.
Penn, Lamont W.
Perez, Peter J.
Perry, John F.
Perullo, John J.
Picardi, John F.
Pierce, Albert F.
Pierce, Paul T.
Poor, Kevin A.
Power, Willard D.
Powers, James J.
Powers, James R.
Powers, Ronald J.
Preczewski, Robert J.
Prendergast, Stephen D.
Pultar, William H., Jr.

Quinn, Dermot J.
Quirk, Thomas M.

Rafferty, Michael F.
Rafferty, Robert T.
Rafferty, Robert T., Jr.
Regan, John M.
Renzullo, John C.
Ricci, James G.
Richardson, Ralph E.
Richman, Andrea F.
Rideout, Reid L.
Riordan, Dennis P.
Rivard, Sharon A.
Robdau, Peter K.
Roberts, Kevin E.
Robertson, William W.
Roche, John E.
Roche, Robert E.
Rock, John J.
Roode, James E.
Rooney, James H.
Ross, Allan L.
Ross, John L.
Rourke, Thomas F.
Roy, Robert P.
Rubino, Michael A.
Ruiz, Teotiste
Ryan, Allan J.
Ryan, Robert M.
Ryan, Thomas F.

Salvaggio, Richard J.
Santiago, Luis A.
Santoro, Carmen
Savage, James E.

Savino, Richard A.
Scalese, Michael R.
Scannell, Robert J.
Scarpaci, Philip F.
Schifone, Frank M.
Schone, Donald R.
Schroth, Philippe C.
Schulze, William
Scully, Henry F.
Scunziano, Joseph
Seabury, Edward J.
Serrano, Carmelo
Setalsingh, Karrol G.
Shackelford, Talt G.
Shanley, William H.
Shaw, Frank D.
Shields, William R.
Shorey, Robert D.
Simenson, Donald O.
Simon, Albert A.
Simon, Debra A.
Simons, Susan G.
Smith, Charles S.
Smith, Francis J.
Smith, Gary R.
Smith, George M.
Smith, Lloyd F.
Smith, Robert G.
Soto, Jose M.
Spartichino, Raymond J.
Sparuk, Peter M.
Spinney, Pauline M.
Spring, Francis G.
Springer, Robert J.
Staco, John R.
Stewart, Thomas W.
Stolgitis, Kenneth J.
Stone, Paul A.
Strain, Marcell S.
Stratman, Gregory L.
Sullivan, Arthur F.
Sullivan, Daniel E.
Sullivan, Dennis J.
Sullivan, James L.
Sullivan, John D.
Sullivan, Lawrence E.
Sullivan, Richard J.
Sullivan, Robert E.
Sullivan, Sean P.
Sweeney, Edward E.
Swift, Jonathan D.
Swift, Robert T.

Tamuleviz, Colette M.
Taylor, Lynne K.
Thompson, David J.
Thompson, Delores
Thompson, William A.
Thornton, Paul R.
Tierney, Robert F.
Timmons, Basil L., Jr.
Torname, Louis J.
Torres, Rudy J.
Tourkantonis, Charles N.
Treseler, Edward G.
Trudell, William

Valardi, Salvatore G.
Vinci, William S.
Vines, James
Viola, Stephen L.
Vitiello, Joseph T.

Wahlefield, Julia C.
Waite, Bradford A.
Walker, Stephen V.
Wall, Lawrence C.
Walsh, David J.
Walsh, James G.
Walsh, John M.

Walsh, Richard M.
Walsh, Stephen J.
Wanagel, Wesley A.
Weaver, Ralph S.
Wedge, Walter T.
West, Curtis L.
Wetteland, David F.
White, Richard J.
White, Timothy C.
Whitney, Daniel H.
Whittier, Eugene P.
Whittier, Paul G.
Wicks, Daniel C.
Wilmoth, Leonard E.
Wilson, Antone
Wilson, Scott D.
Workman, Robert L.
Worthley, Roger W.
Wright, John R.

Yee, Warren

Zielinski, Thomas M.

Registry of Motor Vehicles Police

Abbondanzio, Louis, Jr.
Adduci, Carolyn J.
Agcaoili, Durval A.
Aiello, Jeanne B.
Allen, James
Andrews, Malcolm
Archibald, Robert T.
Ardizzoni, Charles A.
Atlas, John K.
Azzari, Edward E.

Baggetta, Nicholas R.
Bambrick, Henry G.
Beaulieu, Louis C.
Benton, John J.
Bianco, John F.
Blais, Ronald O.
Bond, William
Bono, Daniel J.
Boswell, Ronald J.
Botellio, John A.
Boudreau, Richard J.
Bower, Jeffrey B.
Brugman, Michael H.
Butler, Brian M.

Cameron, Wayne V.
Cancella, Donald H.
Capozzi, James M.
Casamassima, Michael P.
Casella, Joseph
Cederquist, Gary
Chambers, Wainright J.
Chan, Loming
Chase, Thomas C.
Chicco, Antonio M.
Chicoine, Leon D.
Clancy, Francis J.
Clay, Hanford
Clifford, John P., Jr.
Coakley, James F.
Cochrane, Richard J.
Collazo, Jaime
Connors, Richard W.
Costa, Jeffrey J.
Cote, John F., Sr.
Cote, Thomas P.
Cronin, Richard A., Jr.

Daddabbo, Kenneth R.

Daly, Richard F.
Delaney, James T., Jr.
Denault, Ronald J.
Dennen, David J.
DesRosiers, Leon F.
Devlin, Robert J.
Didomenica, Peter J.
Doherty, Peter D.
Donnelly, William J., Jr.
Downs, Thomas A., III
Doyle, Louise D.
Doyle, Michael C.
Drolette, Joseph F.
Ducharme, Francis K.
Dwight, Randy L.

Edwards, James F.
Esposito, Gerald J.
Eures, David

Fabry, Robin L.
Falcone, Robert E.
Fall, Michael P.
Felton, Richard L.
Fiorini, Joseph R.
Fisher, Donald L.
Fitzgerald, Rory J.
Flynn, Maynard S.
Forcum, Steven J.
Forrest, Robert A.
Freeman, Kathleen M.
Fries, Wesley P.
Frydryk, Thomas W.
Fulmine, Eugene B.

Gadreault, Gary M.
Gaffney, Paul F.
Galvin, James M.
Gardyna, Peter G.
Gayle, David P.E.
Giffen, James O., Jr.
Gile, Kevin F.
Giovannacci, David P.
Glynn, Charles V.
Grano, John A.
Grant, Joseph A., II
Greaney, Paul G.
Griffin, Donald M.
Gurney, Craig A.

Hanna, John J.
Hart, Harold
Harzmovitch, John J.
Heller, Laurence D.
Hickey, Arthur G.
Hogan, James J.
Hoynoski, Lester G.
Huegel, Erik O.
Hull, Bruce E.

Jackson, Ray M.
Jackson, Robert F.
Jamieson, George D.
Jankowski, Steven J.
Johnson, Alan C.
Johnson, Anthony T.
Johnson, Donald S.
Johnson, Peter F.
Johnson, Vinton-Ann C.
Joslyn, Michael W.
Jung, David G.T.

Keeler, Harley E., III
Kelley, Brian R.
Kelly, James W.
Kennedy, Robert S., Jr.
King, Michael V.
Kingsley, Frederick A., Jr.
Kirby, Robert L.
Krikorian, John M.

Kumiega, Annette M.
Kuszay, Joseph M.

LaBonte, Richard D.
LaFlamme, Paul J.
LaFleche, Laurence R.
Lambert, David E.
Lamonica, Salvatore
LaMonuntain, Kirk C.
Langer, Thomas A.
Lapomardo, Rocky J.
Larnard, Richard G.
LaRosa, Peter
Lavigne, Eugene L.
Leatherwood, James S.
LeBlanc, Joseph E.
Lee, Daniel B.
Lessa, Lorna L.
Lewandowski, Lynn A.
Lockwood, Howard R.
Loud, Paul L.
Lupi, Robert M.

MacDonald, Carol L.
Machado, Joseph
Maciel, Neal J.
Macklin, Eddie W., Jr.
MacLeod, George E., III
MacQueen, F. William
Macrina, Samuel
Mahoney, Francis J.
Makros, Kathleen J.
Malloy, David F.
Mannix, Robert J.
Marcucci, James
Marculitis, Edward W.
Martin, Gary W.
Massone, Lawrence
Maynard, Don R.
McAnulty, Thomas A.
McCarthy, Earl F.
McCarthy, Paul T.
McCarty, Thomas J.
McCormack, John J., II
McDonough, Shane G.
McDonough, Stephen F.
McElhiney, William D.
McGhee, Todd E.
McGillivray, Thomas R.
McGrath, Jay P.
McGrath, John F.
McInnis, Robert D.
McLaren, John S.
McLaughlin, Gerard P.
McMillan, Edward F.
McNair, James L., Jr.
Mendes, Perry R.
Merrill, Steven L.
Micale, Vincent
Middleton, Joseph A.
Miller, Michael G.
Mirabello, Joseph D.
Montague, Edward J.
Moszynski, Mary C.
Mott, Richard I.
Mullay, John J.
Murphy, Gail A.
Murphy, William F.
Murray, James M.
Mustafa, Ahmed A.

Naja, Alexander
Nason, John A., Jr.
Nelson, Charles D.
Niles, Paul W.
Nutter, John R.

Palli, Thomas A.
Parker, Johnny L.

Peabody, Ann T.
Perry, Charles F.
Pierce, David W.
Pinto, Paul D.
Platt, Edith
Poore, Richard A.
Proulx, Gerard R.
Puchalski, David F.

Quealy, Alan G.
Quinn, James M.

Ralph, William J.
Rathbun-Ryan, Susan
Raymond, Daniel
Raymond, David A.
Riggieri, William A.
Ring, Robert J., Jr.
Rivera, Henot
Rizzotto, Santo S.
Robinson, Arthur E.
Rogers, Charles P.
Rolak, Richard M.
Rolli, Anthony A.
Rose, Arthur D., Jr.
Rose, Leonard D., Jr.
Rowe, Robert R.
Rufo, Bova J.
Ryan, James A.

Sahovey, William J.
Saraiva, David A.
Sateriale, George R.
Sattler, Arthur
Scanzani, Ronald C.
Schaefer, William F.
Scully, Marcia L.
Sedares, George T.
Sgarzi, William A.
Sheldon, Arthur M.
Shepard, Henry E.

Short, Michael J.
Silva, Charlotte M.
Silva, Joseph L.
Singletary, Willie, Jr.
Sisson, William H.
Skutt, Kenneth W.
Smallwood, Mark S.
Smith, Richard A.
Smith, Robert A.
Soojian, Robert K.
Stevens, Homer L.
Stone, Norris W., Jr.
Strang, Steven
Streeter, Theodore E.
Strother, Vincent C.
Swenson, William E.
Szynal, David C.

Tavares, David A.
Tetrault, Joseph A.
Torres, Maria M.
Trecartin, Joan E.
Tremblay, Robert E.
Turco, Daniel J.
Turner, Robert E.
Twist, Craig A.
Tzitzon, James

Ulm, Robert M.

Vachon, Ronald A.
Valler, Irving G., Jr.
Villa, Joseph T.

Washington, Lisa M.
Watson, Richard W.
Wihtelin, Ronald L.
Wiley, Harold O.
Woodson, Edward L.

Youngclaus, Robert F.

Zewinski, Eugene R.
Zucco, Richard F.

Capitol Police

Ahern, James M.

Balvin, Thomas F.
Burgess, Michael G.
Burgo, Elario
Bushfan, Henry G.

Cahill, James, Jr.
Chace, Raymond R.
Concannon, Robert C.
Conley, Joan E.
Croxton, Howard

Davis, Lionel L.
Dolan, Charles J., Jr.
Dunn, William F., Jr.

Fedorchak, Darryl A.
Fontes, Joseph L.

Geary, Joseph W.

Harrington, Daniel J.
Hayes, Daniel J.
Heaton, Charles D.
Hogan, Phillip R.
Horgan, James J.
Hubbard, Vernon B.
Hurley, Eugene J.

Kelly, John J.
Keohane, Sylvester S.
Kingsbury, David A.
Koons, Michael W.
Kurland, Richard

LaFreniere, Robert E.
Logan, Thomas M.
Los, Thomas T.
Lowre, David C.
Lynch, Paul W.

Mahoney, Paul L.
McCarey, Robert A.
McDonald, Paul F.
McLaughlin, Herbert
Mula, Lisa A.
Mullins, Helena M.

Nutter, William V.

O'Brien, Stephen

Parker, Thomas L.
Pisani, Catherine D.

Ripley, Kevin M.

Saccone, Vincent J.
Saunders, Francis L.
Shaw, Alfred R., Jr.
Short, Robert E.
Smith, Paul R., Jr.
Stapleton, Kathleen J.
Sullivan, Dennis L.
Sweeney, Harry F.
Szufnarowski, Stanley K.

Vanschaick, Paul
Vasquez, Rafael L.
Ventura, Donald J.

Webb, Albert C.
Wheeler, James R.
Winston, Tawanna D.

State Police Academy, New Braintree, 1996. Nestled in the Berkshire's foothills, New Braintree on June 15, 1992, opened for the 70th Recruit Troop. Since then, more than 500 young men and women have successfully completed the defining transition from eager applicant to professional state police officer. The 73rd Recruit Troop graduated from the modern educational complex on November 1, 1996, 75 years to the month after the 1st Recruit Troop departed the academy at Framingham's "Poor Farm" to establish B Troop Headquarters in the Northampton Armory.

Washington, D. C., National Law Enforcement Memorial Program, May, 1995. Left to Right: Lieutenant J. H. Crawford, Troopers E. J. Gahagen, D. L. Langston, B. B. Garrant, E. F. Ramsland, Colonel C. F. Henderson. Photo taken on Capitol's West Front prior to annual memorial service for nation's law officers killed in the line of duty.

Blue Hills Cemetery, April, 1995. Left to Right: Lieutenant J. H. Crawford, Troopers D. L. Rizos, W. P. Qualls, R. P. Ridlon, L. F. Mulkerrin, J. J. Doucette, Lieutenant D. Baima. Color Guard had just attended graveside services for Sergeant Joseph F. Howley, paid respects to gravesite (memorial stone, front) of Trooper Mark S. Charbonnier, killed in the line of duty on September 2, 1994.

General Headquarters, Framingham, October 23, 1996. Colonel Reed V. Hillman presents the department's lifesaving award and medal to Trooper Frank P. Hughes. Two days later, Trooper Hughes was stabbed by several assailants in a Haverhill undercover drug operation. Following a dramatic manhunt, all the felons were arrested and charged with the vicious attack on Hughes. The young trooper later received the department's medal of honor for his heroic actions in the Haverhill operation.

General Headquarters, Framingham, 1994. The new headquarters building was dedicated on October 25, 1994. The modern administrative complex resulted from a multi-million dollar modernization of the state police academy. The academy first opened on May 29, 1971, was moved in June, 1992, to the sprawling training and educational complex in New Braintree, sited in the rolling foothills of the Berkshires.

Taipei, Republic of China, May 27, 1994. Left to Right: Major R. Guilmette, Trooper R. Larsen, Massport Public Safety Director J. Lawless, Sergeant M. Mucci, Lieutenanat J. Marshall. Major Guilmette led delegation to Taipei to receive professional accredidation from International Association of Airport and Seaport Police, as lieutenant colonel in 1996 co-chaired state police 75th anniversary celebration at Boston's World Trade Center.

National Law Enforcement Memorial, Washington, D. C., May, 1991. (Seated) Lieutenant P. A. Cahill, Captain J. C. Saccardo. (Standing) Left to Right: Sergeant D. J. Donovan, Trooper F. M. McGinn, S/ Sergeant J. H. Crawford, Corporal R. J. Welby, Troopers D. W. Lynch, J. J. Rota, E. A. Murphy, J. M. Stone, R. A. Harrington, A. Vasconcelos, D. L. Rizos, R. P. Franzella, B. L. Rizos, Sergeant D. L. Bennett. This was the state police honor guard at the May, 1991 dedication of the nation's memorial to its fallen officers. Trooper Elizabeth A. Murphy was the honor graduate of 1982's 65th Recruit Troop, the first female to earn that prestigious award.

ABOVE: *St. Mark's Church, Dorchester, September 6, 1994. This was the impressive yet poignant assembly of state police officers for the funeral services for Trooper Mark S. Charbonnier killed in the line of duty by a fleeing felon's gunfire in Kingston.*

South Boston, June 28, 1992. Left to Right: Metropolitan Officer John Gullage with Trooper William P. Kenney. Gullage and Kenney no doubt were discussing pending legislation that on July 1, 1992 merged the two agencies into a new Department of State Police. The two officers were standing in front of the South Boston station of the Metropolitan Police. Three days later it became a state police installation.

75th Anniversary Banquet, World Trade Center, Boston, October 5, 1996. Left to Right: (seated) Lt. Colonel Ronald J. Guilmette, Lt. Colonel Glenn Anderson, (standing) Former Troopers' President Richard J. Barry, Former Troopers' Secretary James J. Foley, Trooper Eugene O'Neill, Former Troopers' Board Member Nicholas L. DeCola, Trooper Mark F. Blanchard. Troopers O'Neill and Blanchard were honored by the Former Troopers' Association for superior law enforcement achievements during 75th anniversary festivities commemorating the 1921 founding of the rural, uniformed force first called the "State Police Patrol."

State Police Academy, New Braintree, June 7, 1993. Left to Right: Academy instructor Richard F. Zucco, unidentified trainee, Academy instructor Trooper Jacqueline A. Brojan. The 71st Recruit Troop had only been at New Braintree several hours when this trainee was introduced to the realities of state police training. The facial expressions tell it all.

State House, Boston, 1991. Left to Right: Patrolman Howard G. Croxton, Capitol Police, Trooper William A. Cederquist, State Police, Inspector Gary Cederquist, Registry of Motor Vehicles, Officer Joseph Scunziano, Metropolitan District Commissioner Police. These officers were from the four state enforcement agencies that on July 1, 1992, became the new Department of State Police. Consolidation was a major historical juncture, joining the 1921 founding and 1971 barracks' abolition in the fascinating mosaic that is the history of the Commonwealth's statewide enforcement agency.

State Police Academy, Framingham, January 12, 1992. Trooper Leonard G. Coppenrath and his son Ethan L. Coppenrath admire the award the senior Coppenrath received at a ceremony held at the Framingham academy. Coppenrath, assigned to the Plymouth County District Attorney's office, received the award for his work in solving the 1991 murder of a Bridgewater State College student.

Route 1, Saugus, May 30, 1994. Trooper Timothy F. MacDougall examines a beer can found in the wreckage of a fatal crash on Route 1 in Saugus. MacDougall's father, Trooper Robert J. MacDougall, was a member of 1968's 50th Recruit Training Troop. The senior MacDougall was killed by a tractor trailer unit on Route 20 in Worcester on August 6, 1971.

State Police Academy, New Braintree, October 16, 1992. Governor William F. Weld and Colonel Charles F. Henderson review the troops at the graduation ceremonies of the 70th Recruit Training Troop. The 70th was the largest recruit class to that date, with 177 graduating troopers. The class had entered New Braintree in June under the "old" state police, and, with the July 1, 1992, consolidation, graduated in October for assignment to the new Department of State Police.

Saxonville, June 1990. Left to Right: Trooper Donald R. MacPhee, Mrs. Genevere Moynihan, Sergeant William J. Coulter. MacPhee and Coulter assist Mrs. Moynihan at the funeral service for her son Trooper Joseph F. Moynihan, who died in a tragic plane crash on June 19, 1990. Moynihan died enroute to an F.B.I. training exercise in Maine.

General Headquarters, Framingham, 1995. Colonel Charles F. Henderson, Mr. Mark C. Ide, Mrs. Cynthia L. Ide. Colonel Henderson presented Mr. Ide with a certificate of appreciation for his many years of service to the state police. Ide, a photo-journalist, has long committed his professional skills to state police projects, including many photographs in this volume.

Sturbridge Host Hotel, November, 1993. Left to Right: (standing) Lieutenant John H. Crawford, Trainer William Smith, Trainer, Trooper John M. Richardson, Officer Edward Peitrowski, Amherst Police Department Troopers Ross R. Baker, Robert E. Benoit, Robert P. Krom, Charles D. Murray, Sean M. Baxter, James M. Jaworek, Mr. Thomas Collette, Trooper Martin S. McManus. (Left to Right, kneeling) Troopers Daniel Ryley, Paul M. Capps, Kevin H. Hope, Officer Brian Guyney and Officer Thomas Toomey, Barnstable Police Department, Troopers James P. Devlin, Sean P. Sullivan, Lonny Kerr (head trainer). The occasion was the 100th fight of the Massachusetts State Police Boxing Team. Benoit began the team in 1976, and continues his active involvement as a referee. The team thus far has raised thousands for various charities across the Commonwealth.

New Braintree Academy, October, 1992. Sergeant Dean R. Bennett, Trooper Robert D. Smith. Bennett and Smith, members of the State Police Airwing, display the American Eurocopter helicopter at the graduation exercises of the 70th Recruit Training Troop. Tragically, this same helicopter would crash in Cambridge in 1995 taking the lives of Trooper James Mattaliano, Trooper Paul A. Perry, and two corporate employees. Bennett in late 1997 was elected president of the State Police Association of Massachusetts.

State Police Academy, New Braintree, October, 1993. Left to Right: Lt. Colonel William E. Kelley, Lt. Colonel Kathleen M. O'Toole, Lieutenant Bradley G. Hibbard (at lectern), Sergeant Daniel T. Donovan, Trooper Kevin H. Hope, Lt. Colonel Thomas J. Kennedy, Colonel Charles F. Henderson. This was the graduation of the 71st Recruit Training Troop, with 191 members the largest class to date. Colonel O'Toole came to the state police in the 1992 consolidation following a distinguished career in the Boston and Metropolitan District Commission police departments.

Salem State College, Fall, 1995, Left to Right: (standing) Troopers Martin P. Conley, James A. Cowhig, Michael J. Currier, Former President George W. Bush, Troopers Mark J. Caron, Michael J. Chavis, Sergeant Dennis M. Bertulli and Charles E. Noyes. (Kneeling): Troopers Thomas W. Devlin, Daniel P. Regan, Jr. The uniformed detail provided tight security for President Bush, a critical duty since the 1921 founding.

State Police Academy, New Braintree, 1996. Colonel Reed V. Hillman arrives for the ground breaking ceremonies of the new, state-of-the-art range facility. Hillman on May 1, 1996 became superintendent succeeding Colonel Charles F. Henderson who had held the post since its creation on July 1, 1992, with the consolidation of state law enforcement agencies.

Blue Hill Cemetery, September 6, 1994. Trooper Gerard R. Mattaliano pays last respects at gravesite of Trooper Mark S. Charbonnier. Trooper Charbonnier on September 2, 1994 was killed in a violent gunfight with a fleeing felon on Route 3 in Kingston. His murderer is serving a life sentence. Tragically, Trooper Mattaliano's brother, Trooper James Mattaliano, and Trooper Paul A. Perry on February 22, 1995 were killed in a helicopter crash in Cambridge.

General Headquarters, Framingham, October 25, 1994. Left to Right: Major Michael J. Roche, Colonel Charles F. Henderson, Governor William F. Weld, Secretary of Public Safety Kathleen M. O'Toole. Secretary O'Toole spoke at the dedication of the new general headquarters facility. After serving as the state police academy since its May 29, 1971, dedication, the sprawling facility was transformed into a modern headquarters in a multi-million dollar renovation.

State Police, Grafton, 1995. Trooper William J. Donoghue counts cash seized in a large narcotics arrest. Donoghue's father, Corporal Dennis J. Donoghue, was a long-time member of the state force prior to his death on November 10, 1980. The younger Donoghue trained with the 71st Recruit Training Troop, has served in field posts and the Attorney General's Office since his academy graduation.

Paxton, February, 1994. Front, Trooper Aaron V. Washington, Left Rear: Left to Right: Lieutenant Joseph E. Parmakian, Sergeant Philip E. Langton, Captain Francis T. Duke, Lieutenant Joseph T. Bruneau, Colonel Charles F. Henderson. Washington and other members of the STOP Team prepare to search the woods in Paxton for the killers of Police Chief Robert Mortell, who was murdered following a foot pursuit of two suspects in a home invasion. Both were captured by state police troopers and later convicted of Mortell's killing.

Roxbury, 1995. Trooper James M. Fitzgerald with Boston officers following a fight after Fitzgerald stopped a motorist in the Roxbury section of Boston. Fitzgerald was not seriously injured in the incident, and would leave the state police in 1996 to pursue a career with the Federal Bureau of Investigation.

Paxton, February, 1994. Troopers James F. Murphy, Timothy R. Whelan, John E. Maguire and Mark S. Charbonnier form color guard at the funeral of Paxton Police Chief Robert Mortell. Charbonnier, member of the 69th Recruit Training Troop, was fatally shot on September 2, 1994 in a gun battle with a convicted felon on Route 3 in Kingston. The assailant, David Clark, was convicted of the young trooper's murder.

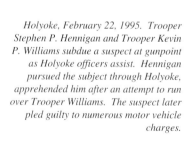

Holyoke, February 22, 1995. Trooper Stephen P. Hennigan and Trooper Kevin P. Williams subdue a suspect at gunpoint as Holyoke officers assist. Hennigan pursued the subject through Holyoke, apprehended him after an attempt to run over Trooper Williams. The suspect later pled guilty to numerous motor vehicle charges.

Paxton, February, 1994. Trooper Michael P. Butler plays taps at the funeral of slain Paxton Police Chief Robert Mortell. Butler, a member of 1993's 71st Recruit Training Troop, had the poignant duty of departmental bugler at four state police funerals in 1994 and 1995. He began this sensitive task while in the academy, playing taps each night before lights-out.

Sandwich , February, 1995. Left to Right: Troopers Gerard R. Mattaliano, John M. Spellacy, Jacqueline A. Brojan (back to camera) and Trooper Jennifer Mattaliano at the funeral of Mattaliano's husband, Trooper James Mattaliano. Mattaliano and Trooper Paul A. Perry were killed on February 22, 1995, in the crash of a state police helicopter in Cambridge.

Sandwich , February, 1995. Trooper Gerard R. Mattaliano and Trooper Jennifer Mattaliano held flag at funeral services for Trooper James Mattaliano. The helicopter crash which killed Mattaliano and Trooper Paul A. Perry was one of the most tragic accidents in the history of the state force.

Westover Air Reserve Base, Chicopee, 1996. Trooper John L. Godfrey and Sergeant Francis S. Kozaczka at the 1996 Westover Air Show in Chicopee. Godfrey and Kozaczka were assigned to the motorcycle unit's west team. The motorcycle, not as widely used as in previous years, continues to play a key role in state police assignments across the Commonwealth.

Salisbury, Connecticut, 1991. Left to Right: (back) Troopers John M. Spellacy (coach), Thomas Poirier, John M. Richardson, Michael W. Habel, David J. Perreault, Thomas J. Daly, Michael J. Sullivan, Thomas J. Murphy, Timothy Murphy, Michael D. Konderwicz. (Front) Troopers Roger A. Tetreault, John G. Murphy, Asst. District Attorney Scott LaMountain, Troopers Stoddard H. Mason, Steven W. Gawron, John L. Godfrey, Michael J. Imelio. The Troop B hockey team traveled to Salisbury for the annual Connecticut State Police Hockey Tournament. Hockey remains a popular sport with troopers. Both Troops B and C field teams each year to compete in various regional tournaments.

Fenway Park, State Police Night, 1996. Trooper Daniel Clark sings the National Anthem at State Police Night at Fenway Park. Clark was promoted to sergeant in 1997, and served as the de-facto chief of police in Spencer. Spencer officials relieved most of the town's police force in early 1997, requested state police assistance with policing duties until a replacement force could be hired.

Spencer, May 9, 1997. Trooper William M. Pinkes walks past idle Spencer police cruiser. State police personnel took over responsibilities in the town for several months in 1997 at the request of officials after the town had dismissed its police force. Pinkes trained with the 1992's 70th Recruit Training Troop, the first class to graduate from the new academy in New Braintree.

General Headquarters, Framingham, January 28, 1997. Colonel Reed V. Hillman pins a sergeant's badge on Sergeant Kevin H. Hope. Hillman served on the Implementation Team which oversaw the 1992 consolidation of the state police with the law enforcement branches of the Registry of Motor Vehicles, the Metropolitan District Commission and the Capitol Police. He later served as captain and Troop D commander prior to becoming superintendent. Hope, a member of the academy staff during the 1990's, served with distinction in the US Army during the Gulf War.

State Police, Russell, June 12, 1997. Left to Right: Troopers Seth B. Newman, John L. Suyemoto, Michael H. Baker, John F. Crane, Stephen H. Bedard, Lieutenant Roland LaCasse, Jr., Troopers Daniel R. Gale, George A. Beaupre, Scott A. Sawicki, David Nieves, Angel T. Larriu. State Police Russell's troopers, representing the four classes that have graduated from the New Braintree Academy in the 1990's are arrayed in front of two 1995 Chevrolet Caprice cruisers. Lacasse, a member of the 55th Recruit Training Troop, had served as the station commander at State Police Russell since 1992.

RIGHT: New Braintree Academy, June, 1993. Trainee John J. Morris and Sergeant Thomas R. McGilvary. The 71st Recruit Training Troop found Morris singing "Going to the Chapel" under the watchful eye of McGilvary, then serving as academy executive officer. Morris was married after the first week of training and was required to wear the "ball and chain," in reality, a bowling ball attached to a chain and handcuff.

BELOW: Route 91, Springfield, 1995. Troopers Daniel J. Wildgrube and Stephen Kelly confer after an arrest on Route 91 in Springfield. Wildgrube in 1997 received the State Police Metal of Valor for his actions in October, 1996 at a melee in the Nubian Athletic Club in downtown Springfield where he apprehended four subjects at gunpoint following the shooting of a fifteen year old girl.

Newton, 1996. Former Trooper Leo F. Stankard and Lieutenant Colonel Ronald V. Guilmette met at Stankard's home in Newton. Colonel Guilmette presented Stankard with a certificate from the Department recognizing him as the oldest former trooper. When the photo was taken, Stankard was the sole survivor of 1921's First Recruit Troop. He died at 100 in 1996, just after the 75th Anniversary celebration of the state force.

State Police Academy, New Braintree, October, 1993. Left to Right: (front) Lieutenant Bradley G. Hibbard, Lieutenant Phillip A. Trapasso, Mr. John Kelly, Sergeant Daniel T. Donovan. (Behind Trapasso and Kelly): Trainees David A. Reis, Michael J. Hill, Jon E. Provost. Kelly, a famed marathoner, came to New Braintree on the day before graduation of the 71st Recruit Training Troop for a troop run. Hill, the honor graduate of the class, received the William V. Shimkus award. Shimkus enlisted in 1923 and served as captain and executive officer from 1942 until 1947. Hibbard would be promoted to Major and Troop C Commander in 1996. Donovan, a long-time academy staffer, retired in 1995. Trapasso served as academy commandant at New Braintree for the 70th and 71st Recruit Training Troops.

State Police Academy, New Braintree, June, 1993. Left to Right: (standing) Trainees Brian J. Moran, Brian C. O'Riordan, Matthew G. Murphy, Kevin A. Brito, Francis W. Doran, Lieutenant Reed V. Hillman, Trainee Timothy J. Riley. (Seated) Trainees Stephen J. Walsh, Robert G. Smith, Robert W. Navas (behind Walsh). Lieutenant Hillman taught a criminal law class to the 71th Recruit Training Troop. Hillman had passed the Massachusetts Bar in 1974 while still a recruit at the Framingham Academy, in 1996 became colonel and superintendent of the state police.

State Police Academy, New Braintree, June 7, 1993. Trooper Michael J. Domnarski, Second Platoon Leader, welcomed Trainee Mark S. Blair to the New Braintree training facility for day one of training for the 71st Recruit Training Troop. Domnarski, a member of the STOP Team was promoted to sergeant in 1997. He has been a key member of the academy staff since 1988.

State Police Academy, New Braintree, October 14, 1993. Left to Right: (standing) Trainees Kevin P. Scaplen, Jon E. Provost, Richard S. Gawron, Pasquale Russolillo, Daniel P. Wells, Brendhan S. Shugrue. Left to Right: (kneeling) Trainees James E. Vaccari, Shawn J. Walsh, David A. Reis, Douglas E. Heppleston. Members of the 71st Recruit Training Troop prepare for graduation exercises on the final day of their training. They were assigned across the state, including the newly-formed Troops H and I, consisting of elements of the former Metropolitan District Commission Police and Capitol Police stations in and around Boston.

Firing Range, Amherst, August, 1993. Sergeant Gerard J. Gagne, Trainee Daniel R. Gale. Sergeant Gagne instructs Gale in the proper use of the Sig Sauer 9mm pistol, in use by the department since 1988. Range practice, an integral part of recruit training, has been greatly enhanced with the opening of the new range facility at the New Braintree academy.

State Police Academy, New Braintree, October 14, 1993. Sergeant Brian G. Greeley, Lieutenant Bradley G. Hibbard, Governor William F. Weld. Governor Weld addressed graduates of the 71st Recruit Training Troop. The Weld Administration strongly supported the 1992 consolidation of state enforcement agencies, the new educational complex in New Braintree and the graduation of four recruit training troops, together with Framingham's new general headquarters facilities.

Brockton, July 30, 1992. Trooper Steven F. Bunker and canine companion stop for a drink during a search for subjects wanted for armed robbery and kidnaping. The K9 Unit is an important part of the state police mission across the Commonwealth. The unit is trained in all aspects of K9 work including cadaver recovery, accelerant detection, narcotics and attack work

Dorchester, September, 1994. Trooper Paul J. L'Italien stands at parade rest next to cruiser 953, the car assigned to Trooper Mark S. Charbonnier. Charbonnier on September 2, 1994 was gunned down by a convicted felon on Route 3 in Kingston. He was the fourth trooper murdered since the 1921 founding of the state force.

General Headquarters, Framingham, October, 1996. Lieutenant Leonard F. VonFlatern, II and Leonard F. VonFlatern, Jr. The elder Vonflatern pins the lieutenant's badge on his son at a promotional ceremony at General Headquarters. The senior VonFlatern trained in 1956 with the 40th Recruit Training Troop, retired as a lieutenant colonel.

Washington, D. C., May 1996. Left to Right: William F. Powers, Attorney Carol Perry, Ms. Sue Lange, Attorney General Janet Reno, Trooper Jennifer M. Mattaliano, Trooper Gerard R. Mattaliano. Ms. Lange was president of Concerns of Police Survivors, sponsor of annual seminar for police survivor families. Attorney Perry's husband, Trooper Paul A. Perry, and Trooper Mattaliano's husband, Trooper James Mattaliano, in 1995 were killed in a Cambridge helicopter crash. Mattaliano was also survived by his brother, Trooper Gerard R. Mattaliano.

Gino's Barber Shop, Georgetown, July 12, 1996. Mr. Christoper Ryan and Mr. Gino Marchese. Marchese has been a fixture in the Troop A area for many years, a legend in his own time. His small shop is festooned with police patches, photographs and memorabilia, including many photos and mementos of fallen troopers. Ryan works as a civilian technician at the Sudbury headquarters of the State Police Crime Scene Services section.

Middleton Jail, February 13, 1997. Lieutenant Robert F. Monahan, Cardinal Bernard Law. Lieutenant Monahan greets the Boston Archbishop during his 1997 visit to the Middleton jail.

State House, Boston, June 25, 1996. Trooper Joseph E. Gura, Governor William F. Weld. The governor presented Gura with the Trooper George L. Hanna memorial award. Gura earned the honor for his actions in a 1995 armed standoff in Wilbraham. The trooper shot and killed an assailant who had previously shot his own mother, holding police at bay for several hours. The award honors the memory of Trooper George L. Hanna, murdered in 1983 by four felons in Auburn.

BELOW: State Police Springfield, July, 1992. Left to Right: (rear) Troopers Thomas J. Daly, Michael D. Konderwicz, Lieutenant Richard G. Catellier, Troopers Edward Ye, David E. Sprague, David C. Sanford, Jr., Alan W. Dietrich, William A. Carroll, Gary Woods, Joseph R. Tamarkin, William E. Blatch. Left to Right: (front) Troopers Michael J. Domnarski, Maura L. Schiavina, Jacqueline A. Brojan, Caryl W. Miron. This photograph was taken on July 1, 1992, the effective date of the consolidation legislation and the day when the ranks of corporal and staff sergeant were eliminated. All staff sergeants were promoted to lieutenant, including Catellier, the Springfield station commander.

Westover Air Reserve Base, Chicopee, 1991. Left to Right: Troopers Donald Moye, Edward F. Podlovits, Sergeant Daniel E. Jamroz, Troopers Edwin E. Lockhart, William D. Fisher and Edward S. Ashman. The Troop B 55 Team poses in front of a giant American flag at the reception center at Westover Field during the Gulf War. Troopers often greeted soldiers on their way home from the Gulf, as Westover served as a major hub of activity during the war. Jamroz, later became captain and academy commandant.

State Police Academy, March 31, 1990. Left to Right: Lieutenant Colonel Thomas Spartichino, Lieutenant Colonel Edward J. Cronin, Deputy Commissioner Edward F. Kelly, Commissioner William McCabe, Lieutenant Colonel Thomas J. Kennedy, Major Charles N. Appleton, Jr., Colonel Charles F. Henderson. Members of the command staff gather for a promotional ceremony at the Framingham Academy, long the site of state police training and administrative activities. The Framingham complex in October, 1994, was dedicated as the department's new general headquarters.

BELOW: *Massachusetts State Police Pipes and Drums. Formed in 1995, the group is in increasing demand at both state police and civilian events throughout the region. Left to Right: Pipe Major Iain Massie, Piper Trooper William Wee, Piper Trooper Joseph Liberty, Snare Drummer Trooper James Galvin, Bass Drummer Trooper Thomas McCarthy, Tenor Drummer S/Sergeant (Ret.) Gerald Tully, Piper Richard Cronin, Piper Michael Wilmont.*

General Headquarters, Framingham, July 1, 1992. Left to Right: S/Sergeant Leo R. Gerstel, S/Sergeant Harry F. Craig, Captain Stephen C. Leary, Major Charles N. Appleton, Jr., Captain Nelson N. Ostiguy, Captain Robert J. Mullen, S/Sergeant John H. Crawford. These officers participated in ceremonies marking the July 1, 1992 consolidation of state enforcement agencies into the new Department of State Police. They were all classmates in 1969's 53rd Recruit Troop, the last academy class to experience their training challenges while sheltered by World War II "Quonset Huts." A modern academy was opened on May 29, 1971 at the Framingham site.

Annual Awards Ceremony, General Headquarters, Framingham, October 21, 1997. Left to Right: Colonel Reed V. Hillman, Trooper John F. Crane, State Representative Daniel F. Keenan. Crane won the State Police Metal of Lifesaving in a dramatic rescue of a youngster from an icy cliff in Blandford. A member of 1993's 71st Recruit Training Troop, the young officer is a resident of Blandford. Keenan represents that bucolic Berkshire town in the state legislature. Crane's professional skills and personal commitment helped make this volume a reality.

Annual Awards Ceremony, General Headquarters, Framingham, October 21, 1997. Left to Right: Trooper David A. Gould, Colonel Reed V. Hillman, Sergeant Daniel M. Clark, Troopers Arthur W. Cournoyer and Steven H. Bedard. These officers were awarded the Superintendent's Unit Citation for providing professional law enforcement services in Spencer after town officials discharged the local police department. Sergeant Clark, noted for a fine singing voice, functioned as chief of police during the unique, challenging assignment.

Annual Awards Ceremony, General Headquarters, Framingham, October 21, 1997. Left to Right: Troopers John L. Suyemoto, Daniel R. Gale, Michael H. Baker, Lieutenant Roland Lacasse, State Representative Daniel F. Keenan, Colonel Reed V. Hillman, Troopers Paul E. Cesan, George A. Beaupre, John F. Crane, Sergeant James F. Murphy. These officers from the Russell Barracks received the Superintendent's Unit Citation for sustained, superior performance of law enforcement duties throughout their patrol jurisdiction. Keenan represents that area in the state legislature.

General Headquarters, Framingham, March 5, 1998. Sergeant Robert H. Leverone had just received the badge and chevrons of the sergeant's rank during a headquarters' promotional ceremony. Leverone from the beginning made key contributions to the development and publication of Enforcement Odyssey. Graduating from the academy in 1988 with the 69th Recruit Troop, the last training class at the historic Framingham site. His essay in the 1980s chapter is a memoir of a recruit's passage through the Framingham transformation from aspiring civilian to professional state police officer.

Division Commanders Awards Ceremony, General Headquarters, Framingham, October 8, 1997. Left to Right: Lt. Colonel Ronald J. Guilmette, Trooper James E. O'Neil. O'Neil was one of 75 troopers recognized for their key contributions to the field indoctrination and training of the members of 1996's 73 Recruit Troop. Guilmette was the commander of the Division of Field Services.

Division Commanders Awards Ceremony, General Headquarters, Framingham, October 8, 1997. Left to Right: Majors Stephen C. Leary, Troop A, Charles N. Appleton, Jr., Troop B, and William F. Cronin, Jr., Troop F. The troop commander's's rank in 1996 was elevated to major from captain. Captains now serve as troop executive officers. Lt. Colonel Ronald J. Guilmette had arranged for display of famed "Mount Rushmore Flag" in background.

EPILOGUE

Hemingway was right. There remains at the end of this work the nagging sense that much has been left out. This seems especially true of certain activities, or themes, that long have been essential to the statewide force. One thinks, for example of training, a crucial strength in the uniformed branch since its founding. Others also come to mind. While accounts of these activities appear in the volume itself, it seems appropriate to conclude this work with brief overviews of some enduring contributions.

THE ACADEMY

Training has been the central strength of the uniformed branch throughout its history. No other function has made a comparable imprint on the state force. From the beginning, the training school, as it was first called, ensured a disciplined cadre of personnel equipped to deal with the responsibilities of a law enforcement career. Those responsibilities have changed dramatically. But the training program has always responded with the relevant instruction that provided essential knowledge and skills.

The first march down Southboro Road to the "Poor Farm" is documented early in this work. There, training took place under the discerning eye of Captain George A. Parker. Training troops in early years went through their paces on that site. In the mid-twenties, the training school moved to the World War I muster field on state route 9, the Boston-Worcester Turnpike.

Lieutenant James E. Hughes took over the training school in 1926. He would remain in that post for a number of years. Meantime, training was shifted to Boston's Commonwealth Armory. Portable buildings were constructed to house personnel. The vastness of the armory, and its dirt floor, made it an excellent location for that era's rigid horsemanship requirements. The 1933 training class graduated in that building, the first recruit troop to wear the new French and electric blue uniforms.

In 1934 the recruits trained in West Bridgewater. This was the "Golden Class," the only group to go through the rugged recruit program at that Troop D location. Like those before them, these fledglings benefitted from the excellence of the school staff. Lieutenant Hughes was commandant, ably assisted by Corporal Joseph E. Phillips and Patrolman John W. Collins. Sergeant James P. Ryan presented special lectures, and Detective Lieutenant Michael J. Barrett handled the criminal law.

By the mid-thirties, the training school had returned to Framingham. There, the 1938 class lost its tents to the Great New England Hurricane. The 1941 class was the last group to train at the Framingham site until after World War II. Then, from 1947 to 1949, five training troops provided well over 200 new officers for ranks depleted during the long war years. The Thirty-Fourth Recruit Troop graduated at Framingham in late summer, 1948. They were the last to go through the rugged training requirements while living in tents. Canvas had provided the shelter since 1921. That era closed when Quonset Huts were erected in 1948.

The training school always drew to its staff the best of state police personnel. The late forties exemplified that fact. Lieutenant Arthur T. O'Leary was commanding officer. His staff, seasoned veterans all, was composed of Sergeant John W. Collins, Sergeant John C. Blake and Patrolman Joseph M. Lynch. Collins left the staff after the 1948 training classes. His able replacement was Patrolman Walter F. "Tiny" Bowen, a survivor himself of the 1938 "hurricane" training troop.

By late 1951, Blake had succeeded O'Leary as commandant. Lynch remained at the training school, having been promoted to sergeant. Rounding out the staff were Sergeant James A. Cretecos, Corporal William R. Finch and Corporal Stanley W. Jackson. Although not on the staff itself, Lieutenant Thomas P. Davy of General Headquarters had presented lectures to so many recruit classes as to be considered a fixture at the Framingham training site.

Nineteen fifty-one also brought a new statute establishing a formal training program for municipal police officers. The first of these local classes were conducted at the State Police Training School. Until that time, the school had been operated on a temporary basis. It was activated for recruit troops and in-service courses, but closed the remainder of the time. With the advent of municipal police training, the staff was increased and the program was redesigned as a full-time operation.

Lieutenant James A. Cretecos was appointed commandant in the early 1950s. There was also a name change. From the beginning, the training function had been known simply as the "training school" or the "recruit school." Its formal title for many years had been the Massachusetts State Police Training School. That was changed in the early fifties to the "Massachusetts State Police Academy," the official title it has borne to this day.

Ranks at the academy were upgraded during this period as the scope of training responsibilities continued to expand. Cretecos was subsequently promoted to captain. His staff was bolstered by the assignment of William J. Owen, Raymond T. Alzapiedi, Robert F. Lynch and Robert E. Herzog. Each shortly was promoted to special officer sergeant. This period marked the early expansion of the academy's structure and rank.

As the fifties closed, academy staff were instrumental in the development of the first law enforcement education programs in the state. Professor Robert Sheehan of Northeastern University chaired meetings at the academy attended by representatives of each of the New England states. Those first efforts were launched under the aegis of the New England State Police Administrators Conference (NESPAC). This initiative led to the establishment in the early 1960s of the first police education courses at Northeastern. The dramatic increase in college enforcement curricula since then has profoundly affected all police organizations, and the concept of law enforcement itself.

The academy throughout the fifties and sixties remained at Framingham. The Quonset Huts first erected in 1948 provided both shelter and classrooms during those decades. By the mid-1960s the facilities were woefully inadequate and concerted efforts got underway to obtain funding for a modern training facility. That work culminated in the September 26, 1969 groundbreaking for a new academy on the Framingham site. Construction went smoothly, and a modern training/education complex was dedicated on May 29, 1971. Because these historic events are covered fully elsewhere in this volume, their importance need not be repeated here.

When Captain Cretecos left the academy for a troop command, he was succeeded by Captain Stanley W. Wisnioski, Jr. Earlier pages contain accounts of Wisnioski's tenure, and the identification of the academy staff members that helped him impart essential knowledge and skills to several recruit troops, as well as a number of municipal training classes. Since Wisnioski's departure in 1966, a number of officers have served as academy commandants, clearly one of the most responsible leadership posts in the state force. They are:

- Captain William J. Owen
- Captain Charles W. Gilligan
- Captain Edward F. Kelley
- Captain Robert J. Fitzgerald
- Captain James T. Canty
- Captain John F. Kennedy
- Captain George R. Dolan

Each has left an imprint upon the academy, and upon the state force as well. They, and their predecessors, shaped the attitudes and skills of hundreds of recruits making the difficult transition from civilian to state police office. They discharged that important accountability faithfully, under all manner of circumstances.

The State Police Academy has always attracted to its staff the best of the organization's personnel. The opportunity to work with recruits, to help mold their values and enforcement techniques, has always challenged those with superior motivation and a well developed understanding of the state police mission. Service on the academy staff for such personnel has been a rewarding experience. Without exception, each has retained throughout his own career a strong sense of pride in having helped recruit troops earn the privilege of wearing the distinctive French and electric blue colors.

THE MODERN ERA

Thirteen recruit troops have completed academy requirements since the foregoing paragraphs were written in 1979. The academy in 1992 moved to New Braintree, and in 1994 the Framingham site became the new general headquarters. The details of these historic changes are discussed in the 1990's chapter. For example, since 1992 more than 500 recruits have become troopers by successfully completing New Braintree's defining transformation.

The Berkshire training site since 1992 has been a beehive of activity. Trooper Robert S. Muto, a senior staffer, has noted his academy experiences:

"The recent graduation of the 73rd Recruit Training Troop on November 1, 1996 sent 98 more French and Electric Blue officers into the ranks of what now total almost 2400. Their

Academy stay is history; now part of the tradition of training which has been shaped and re-tooled for seventy-five years. New equipment, methods, techniques and skills continue to foster changes in Academy development, teaching, and learning.

"Many changes affected Academy operations during the 1980's and 1990's. Following graduation of the 60th Recruit Training Troop in July of 1978, eight classes were trained in six years. The last class to be trained at Framingham, the 69th Recruit Training Troop graduated in October of 1988. These recruits had waited four years for appointment. Like other classes with firsts in training, (the 25th Recruit Training Troop first wore the French and electric blue uniform at graduation in 1933), the 69th would be the first to carry 9mm pistols.

"The Weld administration's leadership on consolidation nearly doubled the existing complement of state police overnight. Then, keeping a campaign promise to the residents of New Braintree, Governor Weld halted construction of a medium security prison on the grounds of the old Pioneer Valley Academy. Phase 1 of some old state police plans was now ready to be realized. The pristine countryside and rolling farmland of rural New Braintree would now become the backdrop for the new home of state police training. Nine classrooms and two dormitories capable of housing over 250 students were among the features surrounded by 750 acres of real estate. Phase II would bring state police general headquarters from Boston's 1010 Commonwealth Avenue to the old academy at Framingham. Both facilities received extensive renovation.

"What was commonplace at Framingham: the gymnasium, indoor training tank, skid pan, and the short ride to the Southborough firing range, would have to be constructed at New Braintree. In the meantime, during June of 1992, recruits from the 70th Recruit Training Troop would fall out on the rear company street for muster and exercise. The existing building in need of refurbishing, their 'gymnasium' would be the large patch of lawn located between the mess hall and the administration building. This exercise yard would also be utilized the following year by the 71st Recruit Training Troop and careful observers may still notice the vanishing grooves their calisthenics bore into the soil.

"When the 72nd Recruit Training Troop entered the academy in the spring of 1995, a rejuvenated gym was ready for use. Its modern rubberized floor was large enough for two basketball courts and electrically expanding bleachers that sat up to 700. A flight of stairs led into the adjacent "higher fitness level" of barbells, treadmills, stair masters and electronic bicycles.

"The move from Framingham to New Braintree was an in-house operation. The staff, as always, answered the call. Academy Commandant Lieutenant Philip Trapasso, Executive Officer Lieutenant Bradley Hibbard, and Director of Training Sergeant Daniel Donovan welcomed the new recruits of the 70th Recruit Training Troop, New Braintree's first on June 15, 1992. One hundred and seventy seven recruits would graduate on October 16, 1992, to then, the state's largest class. But one year later, the 71st Recruit Training Troop with 191 graduating, would set the record for size. Two more classes in 1994 and 1996, respectively, would bring the total of New Braintree trained to 573. Graduations were held rain or shine on the picturesque front lawn of the Academy until the 73rd Recruit Training Troop on November 1, 1996, graduated at the Mullins Center on the grounds of the University of Massachusetts at Amherst.

"Changes in training were commensurate with the transforming educational community. Lieutenant Trapasso assumed

STATE POLICE ACADEMY STAFF
New Braintree, November 1, 1996

Captain Daniel E. Jamroz
Commandant

Lieutenant Thomas R. McGilvray
Executive Officer

Sergeant Ronald F. Waskiewicz
Director of Operations

Sergeant Kevin J. Kelly
Director of Training

Sergeant Richard R. Brown
Health Fitness Director

Trooper Robert Bannister
Drill Instructor

Trooper Lorraine M. Cambria
Compulsory Training Coordinator

Trooper Stephen D. Charette
Driver Training Coordinator

Trooper Cheryl A. Coggins
Medical Records Coordinator

Trooper Paul J. D'Auteuil
Platoon Leader / Second Platoon

Trooper Michael J. Domnarski
Senior Drill Instructor

Trooper John W. Drawec
Director of Specialized Training

Trooper William D. Fisher
Duty Officer

Trooper C. Blake Gilmore
Director of Medical Unit

Trooper Joseph E. Gura
Defensive Tactics

Trooper John E. Hackett, Jr.
Physical Training

Trooper Peter F. Johnson
Motor Vehicle Law Training

Trooper Donna M. Losardo
Drill Instructor

231

Trooper Philip E. McDougall
Director of Computer Operations

Trooper William D. McElhiney
Medical Officer

Trooper Todd E. McGhee
Drill Instuctor

Trooper Robert S. Muto
Director of Curriculum

Trooper John Paulo, Jr.
Physical Training

Trooper James Tzitzon
Medical Officer

Trooper Richard F. Zucco
Platoon Leader / First Platoon

command in the spring of 1989 and was academy commandant until spring of 1996. His seven years of service were notable for the competence of staff members who furthered the educational interests of law enforcement.

"What New Braintree may lack in location, it more than makes up for in potential. The 750 acre site has much to offer in future training plans for all law enforcement agencies. For example, a new 24-lane firing range was opened in late 1997. Plans continue to be made for a defensive driving track, and a training tank in a separate building in front of the gymnasium. The firing range features state of the art targetry such as pop-ups and running man.

"On July 31, 1994, academy staff said farewell to a very dear friend, Sergeant Daniel J. Donovan. Donovan retired from a most fitting assignment, the Massachusetts State Police Academy in New Braintree. He had served twice at the State Police Academy. The first tour was 1974-1983, and the most recent 1992-1994. During the interim years he also saw academy duty for the Criminal Justice Training Council at Foxborough, Plymouth, and Hanscom Air Force Base from 1985-1990. Donovan was greatly admired by recruits of all ages as he poured his energies, skills, and compassion into the love of his life: training.

"Midway through their training, the 73rd Recruit Training Troop assembled on the rear company street for a special ceremony. Commandant Bradley Hibbard, newly promoted to major, would command Troop "C" Headquarters at Holden. Captain Daniel Jamroz assumed the duties of commandant and the supervision of the 73rd Recruit Training Troop. When on November 1, 1996, these 98 young officers took their oath of office and received the coveted state police shield, they were superbly prepared for the public service opportunities they had earned by successfully completing New Braintree's defining transformation."

Trooper Muto noted that Captain Daniel E. Jamroz had been academy commandant for the 1996 graduation of the 73rd Recruit Troop. He currently remains in that post. Jamroz's predecessors since the 1979 tenure of Captain George R. Dolan have been the following:

• Lieutenant Paul F. Matthews
• Lieutenant Robert E. Dunn
• Captain Clifford J. Taylor
• Captain Frederick J. Bohnenberger
• Captain Thomas R. White
• Lieutenant Philip A. Trapasso
• Captain Bradley G. Hibbard

One had written in 1979's French and Electric Blue that the state police academy had always attracted to its staff the best of the organization's personnel. If anything, that observation has been validated by the two decades since it was made. Training and education, now more than ever, are the central strengths of the state force. That is not likely to change in the presence of the social and technological imperatives that will energize the early decades of a new century.

THE CHAPLAINCY

A close bond had always existed between men of the cloth and the Massachusetts State Police. It could not have been otherwise. Inexorably they were drawn together from the earliest years of the uniformed branch, through each of the decades, and now into the closing years of the twentieth century.

As soon as the barracks system was established, the first troopers made contact with clergy throughout the Commonwealth. Each barracks area had a police "buff," an individual who, although in the clergy, had a special interest in law enforcement. Friendships developed easily, especially since the men of the "State Police Patrol" were away from their own homes for such prolonged periods of time.

An important factor in the easy relationship was the semi-military structure of the uniformed branch. Almost all of the early enlistees were veterans of the First World War. Many of them, as noted in these pages, had served in Europe and on the high seas during that conflict. They learned there the strength of men doing God's work in the presence of grave personal danger. It was natural, then, for strong bonds quickly to develop between clergy and troopers as the enforcement organization developed and matured between the two world wars.

It appears that the Chaplaincy continued on an informal basis into the post World War II period. Again, personnel entering the state force in that era, almost without exception, had served in the second world conflict. American Chaplains had seen service during those four years in every theatre of the global fighting. A number of them were lost in battle action as they moved with their comrades through history's most devastating armed conflict.

In retrospect, it seemed natural for the long and mutually satisfying relationship between clergy and state police personnel to be formalized in the early 1950s. It appears that a longtime state police friend and admirer, Father James E. Dunford was the first officially designated State Police Chaplain. The designation was entirely appropriate. He, for twenty years, had befriended uniformed personnel at the Framingham barracks, as well as many of the recruits who had passed through the Framingham training site.

Father Dunford had been ordained in 1931. His first parish assignment was at St. Bridget's, just a mile down route 9 from Troop A Headquarters and the Supply Depot. The proximity of St. Bridget's to the enforcement installations ensured that his admiration for the men in the state force would result in timely visits with them, and later, in his designation officially as the first State Police Chaplain.

Meantime, as noted elsewhere in these pages, Ernest A. Thorsell, an ordained minister, had graduated in 1933 from the State Police Academy. Reverend Thorsell had served in the uniformed branch until the 1940s, leaving to return to his ministry. He would join Father Dunford in the 1950s as a State Police Chaplain, serving at many of the official functions throughout that decade and in the early 1960s. The two were assisted during that period by a third chaplain, Reverend Nikos Georges.

Following a lingering illness, Father Dunford died in 1963. His replacement as Catholic Chaplain was Father John E. Hartigan of Framingham's St. Stephen's Parish. Where Father Dunford had served in World War II as a chaplain, Father Hartigan had seen extended service as a combat soldier. Thus, the strong ties developed in the military ensured continuity in the State Police Chaplaincy.

While Reverend Thorsell maintained a closeness to his old organization, he was, at the same time, fully engaged with his ministerial duties at Theodore Parker Church in West Roxbury. For that reason, Father Hartigan was shortly joined in the Chaplaincy by Reverend Frank J. Bauer. From that time on, the two would serve the State Police faithfully, participating in all major public activities of the state force.

Reverend Thorsell had been first to wear the French and

electric blue uniform. In fact, his 1933 academy class was *the* first recruit troop to wear the distinctive colors for its graduation ceremonies. Father Dunford frequently wore the uniform also. He especially enjoyed joining the state police marching unit for ceremonial appearances in the 1950s. His death in 1963 had saddened his many friends in the state force. Later, a memorial carillon was dedicated in his memory at St. Celilia's Church in Ashland. Members of the uniformed branch contributed to the beautiful memorial under the coordination of Staff Sergeant Martin A. Murphy.

Father Hartigan and Reverend Bauer have grown close to state police personnel these past fifteen years. They have served selflessly at numerous public functions involving the state force. In reviewing recruit graduation programs, one finds their names listed each time, adding to the ceremony a moral dimension essential to acceptance of a public trust as profound as that of law enforcement. For a long time, neither wore the state police uniform, even though both have strong military backgrounds. Of late, however, they have been persuaded to wear the distinctive colors that Reverend Thorsell first donned in 1933, and Father Dunford wore throughout his tenure in the Chaplaincy. Thus, in uniform, they are a visible reminder of an essential resource that has strengthened the statewide enforcement agency since its founding.

The Chaplaincy in recent years has taken on a more personalized dimension. Father Hartigan and Reverend Bauer have provided counselling for individual members in need of a caring relationship in an era seemingly controlled by impersonal forces. In addition, each authors a column in the monthly publication, "Trooper." Through that medium they provide a positive value, an upbeat dimension, for the hundreds serving in the state force throughout the Commonwealth.

The Chaplaincy has been an important positive force in the uniformed branch. Only meager commentary has been provided here. No one, no matter his background, could assess accurately the positive influence exerted by scores of clergy through their close contacts with enforcement personnel through the years. Those efforts are merely sensed by this brief review of what the Chaplaincy has meant to the state force. More satisfying is to have known those who have served. That personalized experience has deeply imprinted an understanding of the essential values imparted to an admired enforcement organization by those select few chosen to serve in its Chaplaincy.

At Century's End

The foregoing paragraphs are but a snapshot of the Chaplaincy. Written in 1979, they still provide an accurate portrayal of the essence and importance of the Chaplaincy's evolving role in ministering to the personnel of the contemporary state force on the cusp of a new century.

For those who wonder: "What does a State Police Chaplain do?", Reverend Gerard P. Walsh has provided some answers. The senior state police chaplain with the rank of major, Father Walsh's essay on the Chaplaincy brightened the pages of the October, 1997, issue of Trooper:

"People, whenever they find out that I am a Massachusetts State Police chaplain, ask, with a strange look on their faces, what I do as a chaplain, do I get paid, and am I entitled to retirement benefits? I will say very quickly, in response to the inquiring minds, that I do not receive a salary, or any other benefits from the Massachusetts State Police. Even after getting promoted last July, I would tell people that I received a large pay raise-a fifteen percent increase, fifteen percent of nothing is still nothing.

"To answer the often repeated question of what I do as a Massachusetts State Police chaplain, permit me to ramble for a few minutes. After all it is difficult to put in writing so many events of the past eighteen years. A few weeks ago I traveled to the end of Route 128-North to officiate at a wedding of a member of the Department who was married in Gloucester in a beautiful quaint New England style church. A good number of members of the Department were present for the ceremony to participate in the event, as well as, to make sure the wedding took place. At this ceremony, there were present a number of troopers who I was privileged to have performed their weddings a number of years ago and later baptized their children. It is all in the family, as I always say.

"In a few weeks, I have been asked to officiate at a wedding of a member of the Department that will take place in Harwichport on the Cape and, having had the great privilege of performing so many weddings for members of the Department through the years, I know that this will be such a joyful and happy occasion to spend quality time with great people, those who make up the rank and file of the organization we call the Massachusetts State Police.

"A few weeks ago, I was very happy to respond to an invitation to go to Leominister to baptize a baby boy, a future member of the Department. This was the first child of a wonderful couple, he is a sergeant, who have waited seven years for this very happy event to occur. Again, it was a great moment to spend quality and special time with this family and invited members of the Department for such a happy time. We need more happy occasions like this so we can enjoy one another's company.

"In the past weeks, I had the opportunity to attend, as well as participate, in the Departmental Award Ceremony. These awards given by the Department are bestowed upon members who go beyond the call of duty and who personify the "best" of what it is to be a Massachusetts State Trooper. Those who received the awards that Tuesday evening at headquarters in Framingham deserve our applause and recognition for their outstanding work as police officers. The recipients of the awards continue to inspire all the members of the Department to serve and protect and place the interest of the public of the Commonwealth ahead of their own and be the best police officer possible.

"As we continue on the road, a month ago or more, I had a call from a member of the Department who wanted to see me and talk about a problem. He came and spent a number of hours talking about his recent breakup of a long term relationship and what were his options. After the initial meeting, I met with both members of the relationship to determine the best path for both concerned. After spending a few hours with the couple, it was mutually agreed that the lines of communication were to be kept open and the future would determine the best course of action.

"On the road again, some weeks ago, I was blessed, and I say that sincerely, with the presence of a group of troopers who came to my rectory for a noontime meal. I have mentioned this before, these occasions when this can happen is always a time of great joy and happiness for me. Just to sit for a few minutes, enjoy one another's company, and be able to discuss matters of state and "job" are always great times. These opportunities over the years are not one of the chaplain preaching to the trooper or even the Major pulling rank, but we all meet as friends and co-workers around the table.

"What do I do as a Massachusetts State Police chaplain? The other day I received a call from the officer in charge of a unit, he wanted to come to see me to talk about a member of his unit who was experiencing difficulty in performing his duties. After spending a number of hours listening to the officer, it was decided that he would go back and once again redefine his expectations for this particular member of the unit with the hope that he would then understand his expected role.

"What do I do as a Massachusetts State Police chaplain? Please follow me for a couple of weeks and see for yourself. My only regret in these eighteen years - I did not keep a journal of all the happy events, yes and the many sad events, that I have been extremely privileged to have been part of. To all of you that I have been singularly privileged to have served, I am eternally grateful for the memories."

Father Walsh's insightful perspective provides a snapshot of the importance and complexity of the timely contributions of a state police chaplain. One who earlier had inspired much admiration was Father Donald J. Rebokus. A sensitive and caring man, in the early 1980's he was chaplain for Western Field Operations. In early 1983, he had presided at the funeral service for Trooper George L. Hanna, Jr., who had been gunned down in the line of duty, carrying out that poignant responsibility despite growing awareness of his own illness. When Father Rebokus died within weeks of Trooper Hanna's interment, personnel of the state force mourned for two of their own. Like George L. Hanna, Jr., State Police Chaplain Donald J. Rebokus was a "trooper's trooper." There are no more heartfelt words of affection, and they will long honor the memory of this gentle man of God.

The state force at century's end is an enforcement organization strengthened by its Chaplaincy. More than ever, the men and women who wear French and electric blue feel that quiet presence as they confront the complex public service challenges of

General Headquarters, Framingham, 1996. Colonel Reed V. Hillman pins the major's badge on Rev. Gerard P. Walsh, the senior chaplain of the Massachusetts State Police. The chaplaincy was first formalized in the early 1950s when father James E. Dunford began its ministry of the statewide force.

Former Trooper's Annual Dinner, Marlboro, October 25, 1997. Left to right, James J. Foley, Jean Bauer, Rev. Frank J. Bauer, Stanley W. Jackson. A state police chaplain since the early 1960s, Rev. Bauer is now chaplain for the Former Troopers' Association. Foley is secretary, and Jackson, treasurer of the Former Troopers.

Former Trooper's Annual Dinner, Marlboro, October 17, 1992. Left to right, Commissioner William McCabe, Rev. Gerard P. Walsh. First appointed in 1980, Father Walsh is senior chaplain of the state force with the rank of major in the uniformed branch.

their era. These are the select few who are always there, no matter the difficulty of the mission:

Reverend Gerard P. Walsh, Senior Chaplain
Reverend David P. Mahn
Rabbi Bernard Stefansky
Reverend Joseph L. Baggetta
Reverend Frank J. Bauer

They give much and ask only for the opportunity to share the inevitable personal burdens imposed by the enforcement odyssey.

CIVILIANS

There could not have been a State Police Patrol without civilians. Without them, the experiment with a uniformed, statewide enforcement agency could not have succeeded. In short, there would not be a state police history to write about had there not been a dedicated civilian to match the commitment made by each enforcement officer.

The early pages of this volume sought to communicate how it was in the first months on the state force. Right from the start, beginning with the night march down Southboro Road to the "Poor Farm," civilians stood tall in their commitment to the uniformed state agency. When the first troopers rode into Northampton in November, 1921, civilian specialists were with them. It was the "farrier" who kept the horses fit for those first winter patrols. His value was such that his salary was greater than that paid a trooper.

There was an immediate need for cooks. If upgraded salary and equipment would take time, even years, the quality of the food, right from the start, made the fledgling organization go. The first cooks were men. It appears that Tom Murphy of Springfield was among that cadre. He satisfied the discerning palates of the original B Troopers when they quartered in the Northampton Armory. Later, when Troop B headquarters moved to Leeds, Mrs. Della Hilliker became the first woman cook in western Massachusetts.

About that same time, across the state, substations were established in Norwell, and in Barnstable on Cape Cod. The early arrangements at Norwell found enforcement personnel taking their meals at Mrs. Phipps' "Tea Room." Shortly, she became part of the state police family, the first regular cook in that area. Meantime, on

the other side of Cape Cod Bay, Mrs. Nickerson prepared her gastronomic delights for uniformed personnel quartered at the Barnstable Court House. Many remembered her cooking long after time had dimmed accounts of law enforcement accomplishments.

By 1923, troop headquarters had been established in Framingham, Northampton, Holden and Middleboro. Critical to headquarters staffing was the troop "clerk." That was an unfortunate description. In actuality, the position was essential to management of the enforcement effort. All administrative requirements were lodged in that single post. It was not a place, in the mid-1920s, for someone short on specialized skills, stamina or a highly developed sense of adventure.

There were, fortunately, from the beginning, a few people who met that test. They became the first cadre of civilians to staff the field troops. One was Harold S. Craig, destined to become a legend in his own time. Craig became on June 1, 1925, the troop clerk at Northampton headquarters. He would remain a "B Trooper" for 51 *years and 9 months,* not retiring until March 31, 1977. Craig and his peers handled a troop's administration alone in the early years. For example, he did not get help at Northampton until joined in 1928 by Daniel P. Carty.

Mess boys came from all types of backgrounds, all manner of circumstances. But they soon had one thing in common. They truly became valued members of the barracks family. One cannot imagine how it might have been without them. The meals they served, the leather they polished, the floors they scrubbed, all these things, and much more, ensured the success of an enforcement experiment not likely again to be duplicated in the American Police Service.

Every trooper has fond memories of a particular civilian specialist; a cook, perhaps a mess boy, maybe a favorite janitor. That is related to one's own experiences. It is not to diminish those remembrances to note that several individuals, like Harold Craig, became state police legends in their own right. Two others come quickly to mind; Alexander "Albie" Woick and Francis "Specky' McVeigh. Each came to the uniformed branch as a mess boy, hardly into his teens. Each served meals and cooked in almost every barracks at one time or another. They did it all, under all circumstances, and for nothing much more than a chance to serve in the State Police. Each received in 1971 the State Police Medal for Meritorious Service, the first to win that coveted honor in the department's history.

Honored that same day were Louis Berube and Clarence Ferrari. They too had spent their entire adult lives, some four decades, in the service of the statewide force. Ferrari for years had held forth at the supply depot, his voice the last word on the quality of uniforms and equipment one was likely to draw. The Ferrari name, beginning with the famous detective team of "Stokes and Ferrari," had appeared on official rosters from the 1921 founding. He and McVeigh, in addition, had seen their sons sworn to enforcement careers in the uniformed branch.

There were many, many others. Some are mentioned elsewhere in this volume. A few appear in photographs that are included. But justice could never be done here to the cooks, mess boys, clerks, teletype operators, janitors, mechanics, tailors, laborers and others, who have supported state police operations in the far flung barracks systems.

There has been another important dimension to civilian service, one not readily appreciated by most uniformed personnel. These have been the specialists with the skills necessary to manage the principal administrative functions of the department. As the field organization grew, so did the requirements for payrolls, personnel administration, and the myriad of related activities essential to competent management of the state force.

The professionals who provided these essential skills have always been in the background. Uniformed personnel were out front, basking in the glow of an approving public perception of their law enforcement achievements. That is understandable. But the enforcement officers could never have done it alone. They were backed up every step of the long and successful journey by skilled, dedicated civilians.

These people have always been there, in the background, making the state police organization go. Names are selective. They leave out the scores of people who contributed a lifetime of service to the Commonwealth's citizens. Yet certain personalities, because of their extended tenures, seem representative of their colleagues:

	Service Dates	*Years*
• Charles E. Wilson	1924-1975	51
• Edmund L. Reardon	1929-	50
• Joseph J. Burke	1931-	48
• Chester E. Wright	1927-1975	48
• Mitchell Hambro	1919-1964	45
• Etta F. Reynolds	1911-1953	42
• Sadie J. Graham	1920-1961	41
• Charles Colontuoni	1927-1967	40

These are but a few of the skilled professionals who, behind the scenes, have had much to do with maintaining the state force's public safety capabilities. They but represent many others who have done the same thing in times past, and, even as this is written, ensure those same organizational strengths today. Theirs has always been a background role. More than likely it will remain so. By now, they are used to that. That fact will not diminish the essential contributions the department's civilians make to public safety services throughout the Commonwealth.

Today, civilian managers, supervisors, specialists and support staff are posted in the general headquarters building at 1010 Commonwealth Avenue in Boston, in each barracks, and in eight public safety offices in the following communities: Salem, Lowell, Springfield, Shelburne Falls, Worcester, Fall River, Pittsfield and South Boston.

These people are key to state police operations. Some perform administrative functions, while others are more directly involved with technical support duties. For that reason, the following is merely a representative example of the scope and substance of responsibilities discharged by the department's civilians:

• **COMMISSIONER'S OFFICE**

William F. Fitzgerald, Executive Assistant to Commissioner

Ann M. McDermott, Head Administrative Assistant
Louise L. Garrity, Secretary
Pauline A. Murphy, Grant Coordinator

• **STATE POLICE EXECUTIVE OFFICE:**

Frances J. Mahoney, Executive Secretary
Gertrude Kingston, Executive Secretary

• **BUREAU OF PERSONNEL AND ACCOUNTS:**

Andrew M. O'Brien, Director of Administrative Services
Harriet A. Swett, Administrative Assistant
Ann M. O'Malley, Senior Accountant

• **STATE POLICE PHOTO DUPLICATING**

John N. Tarrant, State Police Photo Duplicating Clerk

•**FIREARMS RECORDS:**

Roy F. Dewing, Firearms Specialist

•**CHEMISTRY LABORATORY:**

John J. McHugh, Chief of Laboratory
Frank R. Hankard, Assistant Chief of Laboratory

•**BUREAU OF IDENTIFICATION:**

Rita M. Mills, Supervisor of Policy and Procedures
Edmund L. Reardon, Supervising Identification Agent

•**COMPUTER CENTER:**

Emile F. Thibault, Director of Teleprocessing Communication

Donald F. Kuzia, Assistant Manager of Computer Operations

Finally, there is another civilian who must be acknowledged in these pages. He represents all those who have befriended uniformed personnel since their organization was founded. This civilian, for example, was in that small group that welcomed the first troopers into Northampton on Thanksgiving Day in 1921. He really is *Everyman,* in the sense that each barracks area has always had staunch local supporters, faithful friends, people who stuck with the troopers in bad times as well as in good.

Every trooper has known him. He may have been a barber, the local garage mechanic, or, in many cases, the solitary figure in a rural police department. This civilian has been there from the beginning doing countless numbers of things to help out, just being a friend when one was really needed.

It is difficult to describe what these relationships have meant. One must have lived the state police life fully to appreciate what words may here fail to communicate. In that special sense, these civilians will be immediately recognized by the hundreds of uniformed personnel who remember how important those friendships were during the years they wore the French and electric blue colors of the Commonwealth's statewide law enforcement agency.

THE AGE OF TECHNOLOGY

Writing these paragraphs some years in the past, one would not have dared dream of the number and skills of "civilians" professionals in today's Massachusetts State Police. It is truly a "high tech" world. And it may be just the beginning. Wendell Willkie in the 1940 presidential campaign was right when he proclaimed that the once incomprehensible globe had become "One World." And what a small world it has become. Small indeed. And getting smaller with each tick of the high tech clock.

The state force has always depended on dedicated, skilled

professionals. But never like now, as the organization engages the ubiquitous unknowns of the 21st century. Now, as never before, the timely and equitable provision of public safety services will depend on the career professionals who will provide the essential human insights in a world of esoteric technological advances.

Those unsung professionals will be there. They will deliver. They always have, and they always will. It is the only way they know. And it will be their essential skills and professional ethos that will ensure the integrity of the statewide force as the *Enforcement Odyssey* confronts the dynamic influences of a new century.

STATE POLICE ASSOCIATION
OF MASSACHUSETTS

The State Police Association of Massachusetts (SPAM) was founded October 13, 1968. That date marks the official beginning of the organization that has become an influential force in the shaping of policies and legislation which directly affect state police personnel. It seems important, however briefly to review the historical threads to an earlier time, a different era. Links to the past become clearer when the time frame is expanded.

The 1921 statewide force was based on the military model. Discipline was rigid. Internal communication was limited, tightly controlled. The *organization* was paramount. Individual needs and aspirations gave way to the state force's *modus operandi*. It was a system for its times. And it succeeded far beyond expectations. That fact is confirmed by the distinguished public record authored during that now distant era.

Through the middle years of the 1930s decade, state police personnel remained essentially without any personal protection. More precisely, state police *families* faced enormous difficulties when, as happened too frequently, the breadwinner suddenly was seriously injured or killed. By the late thirties the individual's problem had evolved to an organizational policy issue.

Commissioner Paul G. Kirk during that period had pushed hard for policies to protect personnel and their families. Legislative initiatives to reform the pension system, however, were defeated in the 1937 and 1938 legislatures. Kirk, meantime, left the commissioner's post for appointment to the Superior Court Bench. He was succeeded by Eugene M. McSweeney.

In 1938 Leverett Saltonstall won the governorship. His support of the uniformed branch proved crucial as the 1939 General Court enacted mandatory retirement at age fifty, with one half the last year's salary. Disability provisions were also made law, substantially improving personnel policies. These important achievements are discussed fully in earlier pages, especially in the chapter on the 1930s.

Commissioner McSweeney, meanwhile, had appointed a committee to examine the insurance protection of uniformed personnel. A survey revealed the startling fact that 75 percent carried *no* insurance. That poignant situation was resolved in 1939 with development of a group insurance plan. Members could purchase one thousand dollars of insurance, payable at death for any cause. Dues initially were 85 cents monthly. Approximately ninety percent of eligible personnel joined.

The group insurance program was organized as the Associates of the Division of State Police. By-laws were approved. Officers were elected. Those actions represented the first *formally organized* unit of rank and file personnel structured within the state

force. The events of 1939, it can be seen in retrospect, set in motion three decades of slowly evolving actions that resulted ultimately in the 1968 founding of SPAM. How that link grew stronger merits review.

The Associates of the Division of State Police (The Associates) was not an especially active fraternal unit in the early years. World War II had intervened. The state force experienced serious personnel shortages. The era was not conducive to rapid development of a new, tentative organizational entity. Moreover, the rigid traditions of the uniformed branch constrained the growth of any movement that threatened the authoritarian leadership style rooted in the 1921 founding.

Thus, it was not until the 1950s that The Associates began seriously to consider matters affecting the general welfare of the uniformed force. The annual meeting of the group, for example, began to develop more structure. While substantive policy issues did not reach the agenda, the mere coming together of a representative group of personnel, for other than an enforcement detail, was itself a significant departure from traditional practices.

The annual meetings were unique to say the least, a bit humorous. The Commonwealth's governor each year held a reception in the State Capitol's beautiful Hall of Flags. The traditional ceremony was held in February, usually on Washington's birthday. Personnel were assigned from throughout the state. It was a formal detail, troopers in their dress blues, officers with high boots and spurs. One group could count on getting the assignment each year; the elected officers of The Associates.

There was a reason. The annual meeting of The Associates was held following the Hall of Flags detail. But not at the state capitol. Instead, a line of two-tone blue cruisers would roll up Commonwealth Avenue to General Headquarters. The meeting would be called to order. A quorum would be certified. A slate of officers would be elected. The election provided the only real discussion. If one were elevated to office in The Associates it meant, *with certainty,* an assignment the next year to the Hall of Flags detail on Washington's birthday. That imperative dampened enthusiasm in all but the activists in the state force.

Nevertheless, The Associates continued slowly to evolve. The early focus on insurance protection inexorably expanded to broader social welfare concerns. While personnel who gave leadership to the early movement deserve recognition, their numbers are too great to risk naming some and missing others. Let it be recorded here, however, that those who led The Associates of the Division of State Police in the formative years are due lasting appreciation from current and future personnel of the state force.

While The Associates organization continued to evolve, a parallel initiative developed. An increasing number of uniformed personnel had joined the Massachusetts State Employees Association (MSEA), the comprehensive bargaining unit for state employees. The MSEA assigned a seat on its executive committee when a constituent group, like the state force, reached a specific number of memberships in the parent structure. The uniformed force in the early 1950s reached the requisite plateau. A seat on the MSEA executive committee was officially allocated to the State Police.

It appears that Alfred J. Sanders was the first elected representative to the MSEA executive committee from the uniformed force. Sanders had enlisted in 1936, served throughout the state, was a sergeant (junior grade) while in the representative's post. A physically powerful man, he later completed his career as a captain in Troop D, and, poignantly, died in California not long after retirement.

An organizational event then occurred that requires mention in this context. It did not happen in direct relationship to the evolving MSEA initiative, but it spurred the direction and speed of that movement. Time's passage makes the perception clearer now than it was when the event transpired.

Mass transfers, or "shakeups," as they were known to those affected, were part and parcel of state police life. They were accepted. They had always been there. Mobility was a principal strength for over three decades. As a consequence, individual needs had never drawn a priority focus in the policy councils of the state force.

Even that tradition, however, failed to minimize the sense of shock and dismay that permeated the uniformed ranks when the dimensions of a December, 1952, "shakeup" became clear. Scores of uniformed personnel had been transferred. There seemed no pattern. Except one. Men were moved long distances, many miles from their homes. Press inquiries brought a muffled administrative response, one that said something about the need for personnel to be familiar with all sections of the state. In a barracks system that required 105 duty hours per week, the arbitrary, insensitive use of management prerogatives in that long ago December was, in retrospect, the catalyst for contemporary outcomes which mark today's statewide enforcement agency.

The organizational trauma engendered by the infamous "shakeup" did not pass quickly. It was the fulcrum of endless conversations in the far flung barracks system, the butt of a generation of bittersweet humor. In that setting, Trooper James J. Foley was elected to the executive committee of the MSEA. That juncture of biography and history, marked a turning point in management/employee relations in the uniformed force.

Foley had been an Emergency Temporary State Police Officer (ETSPO), one of many appointed immediately after World War II. Following academy graduation in 1947, he was assigned to barracks in his native Worcester County, Troop C. The December, 1952, mass transfers had brought him to Troop D, Norwell. Foley's corporal there was Theodore E. "Ted" Fitzgerald, already a 25 year veteran. In something of a paradox, Fitzgerald, out of the "old" school, had proposed Foley as the Troop D nominee for the MSEA executive committee seat. His election followed.

For the next twelve years "Senator" Foley labored in a no man's land of blurred perceptions, conflicting instructions and thinly disguised imperatives for his own career. It is not possible here, with mere words, to communicate the reality of that period. Such reports would seem an exaggeration. For example, Foley would take cover in a State House ante-room while senior commissioned officers opposed legislation designed to modify traditional organizational constraints. Once assured of their departure, he would emerge to generate support for the proposals among friendly forces in the General Court.

Meantime, Otis M. Whitney had become public safety commissioner. General Whitney's policy goals melded substantially with those of Foley and his colleagues. Although from a military background, Whitney perceived the need to adapt the state force's personnel policies to the acceleration changes then taking hold in the larger society. A series of meetings produced agreement on several legislative goals.

During this period, a Troop Representative Committee was organized. This provided a statewide structure for Foley's efforts, and brought personnel into the mainstream of policy and legislative initiatives. The following were among the early troop representatives elected by uniformed personnel: Sergeant John D. Butler, Sergeant Timothy F. Moran, Corporal James F. Cummings, Corporal Joseph J. Cooney, Trooper Raymond F. DePaola and Trooper Noel E. Henault.

One of the early rewards of the newly developed legislative capability was a reduction on the uniformed branch's duty week. This was the so called "two in eight" statute that reduced the work week from 105 to 94 hours. The welcomed change signalled the end of the traditional "night pass," a 24 hour respite scheduled between regular days off.

As an executive committee member in the MSEA, James J. Foley labored in the policy and legislative minefields during several state police administrations. Often caught in crossfires between uniformed traditionalists and commissioners sympathetic to needed change, he succeeded consistently with high risk initiatives. He and his colleagues were out front, ahead of their time. Those select few established right of entrance into the legislative debates and policy dialogues that held profound implication for uniformed personnel and their families. Their achievements ensured the continuing development of a statewide enforcement agency responsive to the public safety needs of the Commonwealth's citizens.

Lieutenant James J. Foley closed his state police career in 1966. At the time, he was lieutenant and executive officer of Troop E, the Massachusetts Turnpike. A year earlier, Foley had been succeeded in the MSEA elective post by Daniel J. O'Brien. O'Brien had joined the uniformed branch in 1956, and, for the most part, had been stationed in Troop B, Northampton.

Trooper O'Brien's tenure was marked by an increased public dialogue on policy and procedural issues. Several long standing problems were coming to a head. Chief among them was the "time off" question. While administrative actions had brought modest reductions in the work week, *structural* constraints remained. Thus, as late as 1968, the uniformed branch's duty week was 84 hours. Organizational tensions were especially fueled by the issue. It was in that setting that state police wives and children picketed General Headquarters, urging an end to the barracks system.

Behind the scenes, a more substantive initiative was taking form. The 1968 annual meeting of the Division of State Police Associates (The Associates) was chaired by President Sanford I. Brodsky. These, now, were the same *Associates* organized under the aegis of the 1939 group insurance plan. But the 1968 meeting focused on far more than insurance. The time had come, it was said, to organize a *collective bargaining unit.* That kind of talk was heady stuff. More, it was provocative. But its hour had come.

The legislature in 1965 had enacted a statute authorizing such bargaining units. Three principal imperatives operated to push the 1968 Associate's meeting toward a political course of action. First, there was discontent with the state police role in the umbrella state employees association. The MSEA responded to major concerns of its membership, those issues which cut across the broad spectrum of state employees. The narrowly defined problems of the state force did not meet those criteria. Hence, there was no political action focus for the uniformed branch within the MSEA.

The second consideration was a natural outgrowth of the

state force's history. The *organization* was largely apolitical. There was deeply rooted, classical perception of public administration. The legislature enacted laws and appropriated funds. The executive, and that included the State Police, carried out the legislative intent. That had been the traditional administrative posture. One of the results was that rank and file *legislators* did not *really* understand the uniformed branch's issues. As late as 1968 there was only vague awareness among legislators that the state force was one of just two such enforcement agencies with personnel living in a barracks system.

Finally, the most compelling of the forces at work was that of change itself, dynamics imposed by the constantly evolving "outside" world. There, in that larger environment, the police *union* movement was mushrooming across the nation. It was a fact of life. No amount of rhetoric could blunt it. While the movement first flourished in large urban departments, its thrust inevitably began to reach the total law enforcement community.

In that context, The Associates organized a committee at the 1968 annual meeting to explore the founding of a state police bargaining unit. There was tension. Uncertainty was in the air. The hypothetical imperatives for those involved in such a bold precedent stunted the natural enthusiasm that might have attended such an historical enterprise.

In retrospect, a towering paradox merits brief review. It seems clear that those who initiated the 1968 actions would not have done so, *at that time,* but for the 1965 statute which mandated competitive promotions in the uniformed force. The historical impact of the law is reviewed fully in earlier pages. In this context, however, the statute's effect was to seriously weaken administrative leverage anchored in a highly subjective promotional system. Put another way, promotions could no longer be *withheld* from individuals deemed to have merited such a severe penalty.

The promotional law had become effective in March, 1966, following a protracted legislative struggle. Many within the uniformed branch had opposed the bill. But two legislators made it a public issue, generating broad support for the historic measure. The then young representatives were Michael S. Dukakis and Paul J. Cavanaugh. Without that law, the collective bargaining movement would have been delayed several years. Ironically, it was the same bargaining unit which spearheaded the public confrontations with Dukakis when he occupied the governor's office in the late 1970s.

The committee authorized by The Associates moved quickly. Much ground was saved through consultations with the Boston Police Patrolman's Association and its counsel. Among those involved in those early strategy sessions were Sergeant James V. Oteri, G. William Dunderdale, Thomas L. Byrne and Thomas J. Cain. From that process emerged the knowledge of procedural requirements necessary to establish a bargaining unit in accordance with statutory criteria.

The stage was set for formalizing the bargaining unit. That action followed quickly. An October 13, 1968 meeting was held at the headquarters of the Boston Police Patrolman's Association. Following procedural discussions, SPAM's first officers were elected. They were:

- President James V. Oteri
- Vice President Richard J. Powers
- Secretary G. William Dunderdale
- Treasurer Thomas J. Cain

A vote confirmed the following as Troop Representatives:

- Troop A: Thomas L. Byrne
- Troop B: Daniel G. O'Brien
- Troop C: Francis R. Mahoney
- Troop D: Michael J. Norton
- Troop E: Stanley E. Paine
- Troop F: Alexander J. Campbell
- GHQ: William E. Crosby

The leadership of the fledgling organization was thus established. Members were next. Broad based support was an essential ingredient. By the end of October the movement had taken hold. It was grasped by many as natural, overdue outlet for blunted personal aspirations. The outcome of the membership drive was never in doubt. A November 23 meeting confirmed that 616 uniformed personnel had already joined the SPAM ranks.

Four decades had passed since the 1939 founding of the insurance group, the Division of State Police Associates. The thread of continuity had, at times, been seriously strained. But it had never broken. It is doubtful that SPAM's organizers perceived that link. Yet it seems clear that their 1968 actions completed the halting journey first begun in the Great Depression's final stages.

SPAM's first weeks were marked by a variety of administrative pressures designed to slow, if not halt, planned initiatives. There was conflict. It could not have been avoided. An organization steeped in military traditions was entering upon a new and uncertain relationship with its personnel. There were many unknowns, a period marked by organizational tensions. It was an inevitable condition in the historical transition marked by SPAM's entrance into the policy and legislative councils once reserved solely to the uniformed branch's leadership.

There is not need here to describe in detail how that entrance proceeded. One need only examine the events of the early 1970s to observe how the SPAM leadership quickly added critical strengths to state police initiatives in the General Court. A brief review seems merited.

As SPAM organized in late 1968 and early 1969, several parallel events occurred. Lieutenant Governor Francis W. Sargent in January, 1969, became governor when John A. Volpe was named Secretary of Transportation by President Richard M. Nixon. Volpe had been a strong state police supporter throughout two separate tenures as chief executive. He had especially wanted an end to the uniformed branch's long duty week. But requisite support had never jelled. Planning efforts had never focused. In short, a *cohesive* program to accomplish a substantially shortened work week had never come forward.

Later, during the summer of 1969, Commissioner Leo L. Laughlin was appointed executive director of the prestigious Hundred Club of Massachusetts. Composed of leaders from the Bay State's business and professional communities, the "100 Club" provided financial assistance to families of public safety officers killed in the line of duty. Following Laughlin's departure, Governor Sargent named Captain William F. Powers commissioner of public safety.

The Powers appointment introduced an additional factor in the initiatives to reduce the duty week of the uniformed force. He had lived in the barracks system: understood the strengths; was conscious of its profound, historical contributions; knew, too, of the personal constraints the system imposed, pressures steadily increasing in the presence of expanding enforcement responsibilities.

The usual grace period granted a new administration was not this time applicable. The immediate policy and legislative agenda had been years in the making. The *goals* were clear. Construction of the process was the task.

In that setting, several major initiatives merged in one organizational program. SPAM throughout the 1969 legislative year had done yeoman work in focusing attention on state police bills, especially reduction of the duty week. Although their proposals had failed of passage, SPAM had solidified relationships with legislative leaders. Those friendships later delivered essential support at critical legislative junctures.

Meantime, Deputy Commissioner Walter P. Parker was assigned responsibility for expanding the state force's research and planning capabilities. The function was restructured. Select uniformed and civilian personnel were appointed. Captain Charles W. Eager was assigned the key post of supervisor, with command of day to day operation. Finally, professional quarters were obtained in the new Saltonstall Building in Government Center.

SPAM was asked to nominate one of its members to the select planning cadre. The association responded quickly with Robert C. Woodward. The group immersed itself in its work. Their mandate was clear. Reduce the duty week. Maintain statewide coverage. SPAM and the department's administration worked in tandem to gain political support. Governor Sargent and legislative leaders were kept closely informed. In short, there existed a broad coalition of influential support for reduction of the uniformed force's duty week, while, at the same time, creating new enforcement systems to ensure traditional capabilities.

In that setting, SPAM was a positive force, essential to a successful outcome. President James V. Oteri spent uncounted hours on Beacon Hill. His presence at each stage of the esoteric legislative process was a constant reminder of the hundreds he represented. The contacts he and his colleagues developed were key factors whenever an issue was in doubt. There were many such junctures. SPAM's leadership presence ensured a steady, positive influence that had much to do with the comprehensive state police program enacted by the legislature that year.

In September, a SPAM *Newsletter* summarized the 1970 accomplishments. It spoke for itself. While it was set out in an earlier chapter, it merits review in this context:
• Abolishment of the "live in" barracks system, effective May 1, 1971.
• Reduction of the duty week from 84 to 40 hours.
• $800,000.00 for 270 cruisers to implement the "cruiser per man" system. $270,000.00 was obtained for additional cruises through a federal grant.
• Salary increments for officers working toward educational degrees.
•Payment for court appearances. Formerly, neither money nor compensatory time was received, even for court appearances on a day off.
• $100,000.00 for special equipment to respond to the expanding urban civil disorders.
• An appropriation to support an administrative reorganization. Included were funds for four new majors, and a supervisor of policewoman.

Governor Francis W. Sargent signed the authorizing legislation in a symbolic ceremony held in his office. The department's leadership was present, as were key legislators. Their support had been essential throughout. A photograph taken that day

is in chapter seven of this volume. But, in this context, it is important to note the SPAM officers whose leadership and dogged determination helped make that picture possible:
• President James V. Oteri
• Vice President Richard J. Powers
• Secretary G. William Dunderdale
• Treasurer Thomas R. Mulloney

The 1970-1971 achievements established SPAM's credentials as a force in administrative and legislative matters affecting the state force. Oteri remained in the president's post through 1973. Powers, Dundale and Mulloney continued in their elective positions also, with one exception. Robert C. Woodward in 1972 succeeded Powers in the vice-president's office.

SPAM President Oteri in 1973 earned promotion to the lieutenant's rank. Because commissioned officers were not eligible for membership in the bargaining unit, Oteri relinquished the top post. Woodward moved up to the president's office. His colleagues in SPAM's administrative structure were: Vice President Richard L. Whelan, Secretary William J. Brooks and Treasurer Richard E. Downey.

Whelan in 1974 was elected president. He retained the leadership post through the annual elections of 1975, 1976 and 1977. During those four years, the association's administrative positions were filled by a number of uniformed branch personnel. Following the 1977 election, President Whelan was joined in office by Vice President David M. Moran, Secretary Paul J. Driscoll and Treasurer James D. Comerford.

That period marked SPAM's continuing evolution as a strong advocate for its membership. The association involved itself in every issue with implications for uniformed personnel. While those specific accomplishments are documented in the association's journal, it is noted here that the SPAM officers and membership exerted a profound public influence on that period's protracted salary struggle with the Dukakis Administration. The 1977 "Christmas March" at the State Capitol, for example, ushered in a new era in the dynamic relationship between the Commonwealth and its statewide enforcement agency.

The Whelan tenure had also brought the first negotiated contract between the Department of Public Safety and its uniformed force. That historic document became effective on May 14, 1974 when signed by the following:

For The Department	*For SPAM*
• Commissioner John F. Kehoe, Jr.	• President Richard L. Whelan
•Lt. Colonel Americo J. Sousa	• Treasurer Richard E. Downey
• Major Frank J. Trabucco	• Secretary William J. Brooks
• Major Charles W. Gilligan	• Association Bargaining Committee David W. Moran
	• Attorney for Association Robert L. Wise

The contract covered a broad spectrum of relevant issues. SPAM, however, was not authorized to bargain collectively on salary. Thus, the pay issue remained unsettled for several more years. Salaries were eroded as the nation's inflationary spiral accelerated with alarming speed. By the late seventies, pay scales last adjusted in 1973 were woefully inadequate. SPAM hardened its public stance. The 1977 "Christmas March" brought into the open the association's feud with the Dukakis Administration. The gauntlet had been thrown down. It would not, in that Administration, be recovered.

Chapter seven describes in more detail the SPAM role in the 1978 contests for the governor's office. It was said there that the association in those campaigns established its credentials as a major factor in such statewide political contests. There seems no reason to alter that perception. Pundits were near unanimous in their political postmortens. SPAM *had* made a difference. Some said *the* difference. On one point there was unanimity. The yet fledgling organization quickly had come to full maturity. Only time's passage would provide answers as to what degree that new found influence would be exerted in the pursuit of productive goals.

December 6, 1978 was a red letter date for SPAM. President Frederick T. Guerreiro on that day signed a new contract on behalf of the association's membership. Present among others at the benchmark ceremony were Vice President David W. Moran, Treasurer James D. Comerford and Secretary Paul J. Driscoll. The comprehensive pact covered 28 pages, and several attached memoranda.

The new contract's salient provisions settled SPAM's long standing salary dispute with the state's administration. Because the basic feature are highlighted in Chapter Seven, they require no repetition here. Thus, as 1978 ended, the association capped with the pay settlement a remarkable year. The accomplishments had not come easily. Such gains never do. But the tensions produced by past difficulties seemed to have eased as the association entered the century's final two decades with increased stature.

* * *

TOWARD NEW PUBLIC SERVICE HORIZONS

Those who organized the Division of State Police Associates in 1939 could not have imaged an organization like the current State Police Association of Massachusetts. Not, in any event, in the statewide enforcement agency *they* knew, with its strict military traditions and rigid personal disciplines. Yet, everything is relative. Everyone, every institution, must change. Time's passage ensures that constant in human affairs.

The narrowly focused insurance protection issue decades ago thus has evolved to the broad spectrum of activities which mark SPAM's contemporary agenda. In that way, the association's historical journey has not been so different from that of 1921s rural, enforcement cadre that has become one of the most respected of the nation's state police organizations.

The historical journey paused momentarily on May 2, 1979 in Framingham, on the grounds of the state police academy. That weekend marked the 58th anniversary of the founding in 1921 of the State Police Patrol. The return to Framingham was symbolic, appropriate to the occasion. Nearby in that community was the location in 1921 of the "Poor Farm," the training site in September of that year for the First Recruit Troop.

The state police organization, in that sense, returned in 1979 to the locale of its origin. There, the Annual Memorial Services were conducted. Later in the day, a program was held in conjunction with this volume's predecessor work *French and Electric Blue*. Within hours, the evening's darkness closed one day in the organizational life of the Massachusetts State Police.

The academy then stood silent. But commands shortly would echo in its halls, measured cadence would impart a disciplined step on the parade field. And, to that place would come again young men and women eager to earn the privilege of wearing the *French and electric blue.*

S.P.A.M. IN THE MODERN ERA

While most of those words were written two decades ago, nothing since then has changed the essential accuracy of what they predicted. Young men and women eager to earn the privilege of wearing the French and electric blue did continue to come to Framingham to prove their mettle. Several hundred during the 1980's survived the rigorous requirements and earned the coveted diploma of the Massachusetts State Police Academy. Trooper Bob Leverone earlier in these pages shared his remembrances of a recruit's life at the Framingham academy. A bit humorous now, it was deadly serious when everything was on the line. With academy operations in 1992 moving to the modern educational complex in New Braintree, over 500 men and women have been sworn to public service careers in the 1990's alone.

Most of these career officers have become members of the State Police Association of Massachusetts (SPAM). Thus, SPAM's elected officers in the modern era must strive to respond to the aspirations of their members. That is a major accountability. It will become more so as the new century unfolds.

As discussed more fully in the 1990's chapter, SPAM has been a central force in the shaping and implementation of the historical changes of the last two decades. Coming of age with 1971's barracks' abolition issue, the union's influence has been evident in each of the major organizational initiatives that yet are energizing the direction and contours of the enforcement odyssey.

Needless to say, SPAM's leadership has played a strong advocacy role in the countless initiatives, large and small, that have directly affected its membership. On occasion it has been a personal problem affecting an individual. More often, and more visibly, SPAM's concerted actions have been focused by compensation issues with profound implications for the entire uniformed complement of the state force. No matter the size or the complexity of the issue, SPAM has been there for its members.

A lot of people since SPAM's 1968 founding have committed their skills and energies to the union's causes. Their contributions, large and small, have made the difference. It is not possible here to pay tribute to each, even if one knew who they were. They will have to settle for the self satisfaction of knowing that their efforts helped to create, nurture and solidify the positive strengths that SPAM is poised to contribute as the enforcement odyssey confronts the unknowns of a new century.

As discussed earlier in this volume, James V. Oteri in 1968 was SPAM's first president. The following career enforcement officers have succeeded him in that prestigious office:

Robert C. Woodward	1973
Richard L. Whelan	1974 - 1978
Frederick T. Guerreiro	1978
Daniel J. Twomey	1979 - 1980
Ronald J. Bellanti	1981 - 1983
Francis W. Riley	1984 - 1989
William J. Powers, Jr.	1990
Kevin W. Regan	1991
John D. MacLean	1992 - 1997

Sergeant John D. MacLean in September, 1997, resigned

from the union's presidency, completing his long state police career shortly thereafter. Within weeks, elections were held for SPAM's constitutional offices and the following new leadership team was officially installed even as these words were written:

President: Dean R. Bennett
Vice President: Richard R. Brown
Treasurer: John P. Coflesky
Secretary: Thomas W. Neff

Newly elected Secretary Tom Neff for many years has been the editor of Trooper, the union's monthly newspaper. Trooper Neff deserves much credit for Trooper's emergence as a preeminent unifying force for SPAM's policy and legislative initiatives. A gifted communicator, the career enforcement officer consistently has made a steady commitment of his personal energies and professional skills in support of the union's causes. Alternatively, his evenhandedness and professional ethics equally have ensured superior contributions to the state force he has served these past two decades.

Needless to say, Neff during his long tenure as Trooper's editor has had strong support from a score of talented correspondents, almost always career enforcement officers. Their pithy commentaries have built the paper's reputation for cogent, insightful reports on issues of critical import to uniformed personnel. Chief among these have been Sergeant Brian O'Hare and Sergeant Bob Leverone. Each is an associate editor, and their professional skills have added much relevance to Trooper's timely communications and focused commentaries on topical issues.

SPAM has come a long way these past three decades, having been actively engaged in the enforcement odyssey's most historic changes. That journey continues apace on the cusp of a new century. New opportunities surely lie ahead. SPAM's constructive, cooperative engagement of those issues will be essential to the strength and integrity of the statewide enforcement organization that has provided all uniformed personnel with their professional status and career opportunities.

73rd R.T.T.
GUEST INSTRUCTORS

Tpr. Robert C. Ackerman - Defensive Driving
Sgt. Norman O. Anger - CDL
Major Michael Backry - Essex County Sheriff
Sgt. Sean M. Baxter - Patrol Procedures
Tpr. Gilbert M. Bernard - Stress Awareness
Atty.Karen Betournay - Civil Liability/Const. Law
Tpr. Kevin P. Bibeau - Medical
Mr. Bill Blane - LEAPS
Tpr. Donald R. Bossi - Medical
Capt. Robert J. Bradley - Incident Command
Tpr. Jacqueline A. Brojan - Defensive Tactics
Major John A. Burns - Affirmative Action
Mr. John Byron - Radio Communications
Capt. John F. Caulfield - Controlled Substances
Tpr. John M. Collura - Report Writing
Tpr. Michael E. Conti - Firearms
D/Lt. Robert A. Corry - Interview & Interrogation
Tpr. Lisa T. Cote - Medical
Sgt. Paul J. Damery - Firearms
Tpr. Peter J. DiDomenica - Altered Documents
Ret. Capt. Raymond Eugenio - Dom. Violence
Tpr. Dennis P. Finn - Medical
Tpr. Richard H. Frigon - MV Law / Breathalyzer
Lt.. Robert C. Gosselin - Search & Seizure
Tpr. Joseph E. Gura - Defensive Tactics / OC
Major Bradley G. Hibbard - Ethics
Tpr. James F. Higgins, Jr. - Medical
Tpr. Kevin H. Hope - Riot Training / Firearms
Special Agent John Huyler - F.B.I.
Tpr. John P. Jakobowski - Breathalyzer
Dr. Richard Jarelewitz - TQM
Atty. Michael Kass - Civil Liability
Tpr. Marie T. Kenny - Domestic Violence
Tpr. David E. Lambert - Community Policing
Tpr. Richard G. Lane - Defensive Driving
Lt. Oscar J. Langford III - Community Policing
Mr. Howard Liebowitz - N.C.J.T.C.

Ms. Patricia Lawrence - Special Needs
Sgt. Edward J. Lee - Stress Awareness
Ms. Maureen Maher - Radio Communications
Lt. Kenneth F. Martin - Crime Scene
Tpr. Jeffrey P. McDonald - Patrol Procedures
Ms. Jane McLaughlin - Narcotics
Tpr. William McNeil - Firearms
Tpr. Jerry J. Molet & K-9 "Aldo" -
    Patrol Procedures
Mrs. Ruth Moore - Community Access
Tpr. Julia C. Mosely - Dom. Viol. / Cult. Diversity
Tpr. John G. Murphy - Patrol Procedures
Tpr. Matthew J. Murray - Defensive Tactics
Tpr. Dana J. Pagley - Defensive Driving
Tpr. Ross J. Panacopoulos - Acc. Invest / OPUE
Tpr. Jay Y. Park - Firearms
Lt. Edith Platt - Cultural Diversity
Atty. John Pucci - Ethics
Sgt. Stephen M. Pugsley - Criminal Law
Tpr. Steve O'Connor - Interview & Interrogation
Tpr. Erik Ramsland - Land Navigation
Tpr. John M. Richardson - Defensive Driving
Tpr. Richard M. Ridlon - Medical
Tpr. Alyce B. Risteen - Stress Awareness
Tpr. Mary E. Ritchie - Medical
Tpr. John J. Rota - Firearms / Medical
Tpr. Stephen N. Smith & K-9 "Brackett" -
    Patrol Procedures
Tpr. Robert K. Soojian - Breathalyzer
Sgt. Thomas Schnare - Dept. of Env. Protection
D/Lt. Paul A. Stone - Narcotics
Tpr. Paul J. Sullo - Medical
Tpr. Eno Thompson - Accident Investigation
Capt. Philip A. Trapasso - Counseling
Tpr. Richard M. Walsh - Stress Awareness
Tpr. Timothy R. Whelan - Land Navigation
Tpr. David W. Wilson - Accident Invest / OPUE

PICTORIAL APPENDIX

The photos preserved in this pictorial appendix were first published in 1979's *French and Electric Blue*.

1949...STARTING OUT

1959...WITH T/SERGEANT GEORGE A. LUCIANO

RIGHT, 1969...WITH GOVERNOR
FRANCIS W. SARGENT

BELOW, 1979...WITH GOVERNOR
EDWARD J. KING

THE AUTHOR,
THROUGH THE YEARS

GENERAL HEADQUARTERS, BOSTON, JULY 1957

From left: Captain of Detectives Joseph C. Crescio '23, Commissioner Otis M. Whitney, Detective Lieutenant Theodore W. Johnson '26. Whitney accepted the Lieutenant James E. Hughes Memorial Pistol Trophy donated by the Former Troopers Association. Hughes trained with 1922s Third Recruit Troop, was a long time commander of the training academy, led the pistol team to scores of victories against the best law enforcement squads in the East.

GEORGE A. LUCIANO
*Secretary
Executive Office of
Public Safety*

EDWARD J. KING
*Governor
Commonwealth of
Massachusetts*

DENNIS J. CONDON
*Commissioner
Department of Public
Safety*

STATE CAPITOL, 1979

ANNUAL MEMORIAL SERVICES, FRAMINGHAM, MAY 25, 1963

From left: Major Julian Zuk, Governor Endicott Peabody, Commissioner Frank S. Giles, the late Herbert J. Stingel, president that year of the Former Massachusetts State Troopers. Stingel in 1922 had enlisted in the "State Police Patrol." Former Troopers donated the granite memorial in the early 60s.

STATE CAPITOL, BOSTON, DECEMBER 1963

From left: Howard H. Dacey '31, Theodore J. Stavredes '34, Governor Endicott Peabody, Former Troopers' President Herbert J. Stingel '22, Commissioner Frank S. Giles. Governor Peabody accepted membership in the Former Troopers Association. Stavredes in 1949 was one of the founders, served as first president of the Former Massachusetts State Troopers.

ANNUAL MEMORIAL SERVICES, FRAMINGHAM, MAY 30, 1974

From left: George A. Pollard '28, James P. Green '27, Daniel L. Jacobs '29, Joseph P. McEnaney '38, John F. Lally '27, Ernest J. Ryan '25, Joseph W. Doyle '28, Herbert J. Stingel '22, Hollis C. "Sam" Beattie '26, Henry F. Myers '36, Timothy F. Moran '41, Thomas P. Davy '36, Theodore J. Stavredes '34, William F. Powers '49, Clarence J. Ferrari. All but Ferrari served in the uniformed branch. He handled key support and supply functions for over four decades, received in 1970 the State Police Medal for Meritorious Service.

"We must welcome the Future, remembering that it soon will be past; and we must respect the Past, knowing that once it was all that was humanly possible."

Santayana

September 1, 1921. The "First Class" being sworn in on steps of the State Capitol. Governor Channing H. Cox, center, straw hat in hand. Commissioner Alfred E. Foote next to governor. Captain George A. Parker behind Foote. William F. Fitzmaurice, uniformed man on left. Thomas J. McConnell, uniformed man on right. Secretary of State Frederick Cook, extreme right. By nightfall, they had marched down Framingham's Southboro Road to encamp at the "Poor Farm" and begin the State Police Patrol.

September 1921. Picking up the first Indian motorcycles at the Springfield factory. From left: Thomas J. McConnell, Charles Armstrong (instructor), William F. Fitzmaurice, Richard H. Mooney, Charles T. Beaupre, Joseph A. Fouche. Motorcycles took a heavy toll in the early years. Beaupre in 1925 became the second captain and executive officer, succeeding George A. Parker.

WINTER 1923

From left: Axel A. Manning, Edwin W. Streeter, Arthur A. Keefe, Edward J. Majesky, John J. McConologue. The first Troop C Headquarters in Paxton.

WESTMINSTER BARRACKS, 1923

Richard F. terpstra on left, with John J. McConologue, Westminster was an early troop C substation.

NOVEMBER 1921. THE FIRST "B" TROOPERS

From left: Duncan MacMillan, William J. Sullivan, Nicholas Glarus, John J. O'Donnell, Eugene E. Stowell, Howard M. Whittemore, Leo F. Stankard, Axel A. Manning. They rode five days to establish Troop B Headquarters in the Northampton Armory.

TROOP B, HEADQUARTERS AT LEEDS, 1924

From left: Julius W. Toelkin, John J. O'Donnell, Martin J. Beattie, Lt. William J. Sheerin. Known as "B Troop Day," this was the first in-service training course.

AGAWAM, 1924

Patrolman Llewelyn A. Lowther. He was killed in September of that year in a motorcycle accident in Adams, the first line of duty death in the State Police Patrol.

248

SPRINGFIELD FAIR, 1923

From left: Lieutenant Charles T. Beaupre, Corporal John J. O'Donnell, Corporal James P. Ryan, Thomas H. Mitchell, Francis Manning, William J. Colleran, William H. Martin, Kenneth G. Annis, William H. Cotter, Joseph A. Burke. Massachusetts Building in background. Ryan enlisted in 1922, served until September, 1950, completed his 28 year career as Troop C commanding officer.

TROOP C HEADQUARTERS, HOLDEN, 1924

This was replaced in 1930 by the first building constructed specifically as a state police headquarters facility.

TROOP A, SUBSTATION IN WRENTHAM, 1924

Located on Route 1, it was followed by several other Wrentham locations. A permanent barracks building was opened in the late 1950s on Route 1 in Foxboro.

SPRINGFIELD FAIR, 1925

From left: John J. Donahue, Herbert J. Stingel, Richard F. Terpstra, Thomas J. McGuinness. Real horses and "iron" horses were the principal transportation.

BROCKTON FAIR, 1926

From left: Thomas P. Norton, George A. Dodge, Desmond A. Fitzgerald, John P. Regan, Patrick A. Whalen, Harold J. McGinnis, Hollis E. "Sam" Beattie, Sergeant Albert W. Dasey. Dasey, a member of the 1921 First Training Troop, supervised the trick riding team.

FRAMINGHAM, 1926

From left: Sergeant Charles A. Jobert, George A. Smith, Albert W. Dasey, Lieutenant Harold B. Williams, Sergeant Charles B. Cooley. New cruisers at Troop A headquarters. Williams enlisted on September 1, 1921 with the "First Class."

READING BARRACKS, 1925

From left: Frank D. McGarry, George T. Knox, Corporal Charles A. Jobert, William V. Shimkus, Joseph J. Krukowski. Reading was a Troop A substation. Shimkus became captain and executive officer in 1942.

THE "AUTO SQUAD," 1925

From left: Detective Lieutenant Silas Smith, Jeremiah J. Dacey, Everett I. Flanders, Joseph C. Crescio, John F. Dempsey. They put a lot of pressure on 1920s style auto thiefs. Crescio, in the late 40s, became a captain of state police detectives

BARNSTABLE BARRACKS, TROOP D, 1928

From left: Mechanic Carey, Leo V. Storme, Charles J. McCarthy, Herbert S. Berglund, Corporal John F. Dempsey, Myron H. Hayden, James P. Green. "Jerry" in front. Dempsey became a legend in his own time, covering the Cape Cod area until his early 1970's retirement from the detective branch.

SACCO-VANZETTI ELECTROCUTION DETAIL

Charleston State Prison, August, 1927. From left: Daniel A. Murphy, John E. Higgins, Roland H. Chamberlain, Thomas M. Norton, Michael Manning, Lieutenant James E. Hughes, William H. Delay, Homides Carpenter, Thomas E. Burke, George J. Conn, Theodore W. Johnson, Sergeant William V. Shimkus, Antonio N. Altieri, Myron H. Hayden, Francis J. McGady. The crucial testimony of state police ballistician Charles J. Van Amburgh remains uncontroverted more than a half century after the Sacco-Vanzetti trial and execution.

TROOP B, SHELBURNE FALLS, 1928

From left: Joseph A. Keating, Frank W. Geist, Abner F. O'Brien, Michael D. Scannell, Charles J. O'Connor, Nicholas Glaris. Glaris trained with the First Recruit Troop in the Autumn of 1921.

SHELBURNE FALLS, 1928

Frank W. Geist on left with Abner F. O'Brien. Note O'Brien's leather jacket, a great favorite with personnel in that era.

TROOP C, HEADQUARTERS, HOLDEN, 1928

From left: Sergeant John F. McLaughlin, Sergeant Richard F. Terpstra, Lieutenant William V. Shimkus, Sergeant Melville S. Riley, Sergeant Edward J. Canavan. Lieutenant was the troop commander's rank until 1951.

PISTOL TEAM, WAKEFIELD, 1929

From left: Joseph C. Crescio, Theodore W. Johnson, Norman S. Sidney, Lieutenant James E. Hughes, Stanley B. Skillings, Arthur J. Shea, Thomas E. Burke. Johnson later served for many years as a lieutenant in the detective branch.

"The only thing we have to fear is fear itself."
Franklin Delano Roosevelt

STATE CAPITOL, BOSTON, JULY 1930

Reception for President Herbert C. Hoover during the Bay State's tercentenary celebration. In front: Detective Captain Thomas E. Bligh. First row, from left: Frank G. Hale, David J. Manning, Silas Smith (behind Manning), Joseph L. Ferrari, William F. Murray, Edward J. McCarthy, Albert L. Brouillard, John F. Stokes. Middle, from left: Edward J. Sherlock, Michael F. Fleming, Ernest S. Bradford, Edward P. O'Neil, Theodore W. Johnson, Harry L. Avery. Rear row, from left: Francis W. Clemmey, Edward J. Canavan, John A. Carroll, Harold A. Delaney, Harold B. Williams, Richard K. Townsend, Joseph C. Crescio. Johnson, Avery, Canavan, Carroll, Delaney, Williams, Townsend and Crescio were from the uniformed branch. The others were detective lieutenants under Captain Bligh.

1930. Patrolman Martin W. Joyce with one of the first radio equipped cruisers.

EASTERN STATES EXPOSITION, SPRINGFIELD, SEPTEMBER 1930

From left, front: Thomas E. Hazelton, Hollis E. "Sam" Beattie, Thomas M. "Red" Norton. Standing, from left: John W. Collins, Karle T. Howe, Theodore E. Fitzgerald, Richard A. Hiller. Collins, Fitzgerald and Beattie served well into 1950s, saw dramatic changes from their trick riding days.

SPRINGFIELD FAIR, 1930

Patrolman Joseph P. Fraser on Captain Charles T. Beaupre's horse, "Friend." Long a mainstay of the state force, horses were phased out by the end of 1933.

FRAMINGHAM, 1931

From left: Sergeant John F. Dempsey, Sergeant George H. Thompson, Lieutenant James P. Mahoney, Sergeant John F. Horgan, Sergeant Herbert J. Stingel. Horgan in the winter of 1928 won the Carnegie Medal for Heroism for his actions when the steamer Robert E. Lee, with 263 passengers aboard, ran aground on Manomet's treacherous shoals.

ABOVE, PATROLMAN CHARLES A. BETTER

Better enlisted in the State Police Patrol on February 3, 1930. He was killed later that year in Topsfield as the result of a tragic motorcycle accident. The two wheelers took a heavy toll in death and injuries during the first five decades.

LEFT, TROOP C, HEADQUARTERS, HOLDEN

Opened on December 20, 1930, it was the first building constructed specifically as a state police barracks and troop headquarters facility.

COMMONWEALTH ARMORY, BOSTON, NOVEMBER 4, 1933

Graduation of the 25th Recruit Troop. From left: Captain and executive officer James P. Mahoney, Lieutenant James E. Hughes academy commandant, Commissioner Daniel E. Needham, Patrolman James H. Hayes. This was the first training class to wear the French and electric blue issued in June of that year. Note blue braid on officer's blouse, later replaced by gold.

TROOP B, MONSON, 1933

Patrolman Karle T. Howe astride "Duke." Patrolman Richard A. Hiller in late 1933 rode the last B Troop patrol from Shelburne Falls to Northampton where he turned "Ginger" over to officials of the Belchertown State School.

TROOP B, MONSON, 1934

From left: Bernard D. Horan, Leo H. Walden, Michael W. McCarthy, Cook - Mrs. King, Theodore W. Peters, Karle T. Howe, Theodore J. Stavredes. This was the first fall and winter for the new, two-tone blue uniforms. The winter reefer replaced a long leather overcoat that had seen yeoman service throughout the 1920s.

CONCORD BARRACKS, LAKE WALDEN, 1933

From left: Charles F. Furze, Donat A. LaCasse, Stanley B. Skillings, Corporal Robert S.F. "Dusty" Rhodes, George J. Conn. Conn is holding "Teddy," the last of Troop A's once formidable stable of trusty steeds.

MILLEN-FABER TRIAL, DEDHAM SUPERIOR COURTHOUSE, 1934

From left: John Powers, Joseph M. Noone, Victor Nelson, Lorance P. Salmonsen, Michael D. Scannell, Michael J. Shea. The Millen Brothers and Abraham Faber paid with their lives for the gunshot killings of two Needham policemen.

TRAINING ACADEMY, WEST BRIDGEWATER, 1934

From left: Detective "Captain" Michael J. Barrett, Corporal Everett I. Flanders, Sergeant James P. Ryan, Lieutenant James E. Hughes, Corporal John W. Collins. Barrett, from the folding chair, held a generation of recruits spellbound with his lectures on criminal law, buttressed by accounts from his own storehouse of state police experiences.

SALISBURY BEACH, SUMMER 1935

From left, front: Arthur E. McCabe, Senior Patrolman Charles F. Furze, Arthur F. Chaisson. From left, rear: John C. Blake, Alexander Woick, William B. Killen. Woick began service as a "Mess Boy," became a legend in his own time, received the State Police Medal for Meritorious Service in 1971.

SUPPLY DEPOT, FRAMINGHAM, 1935

From left: Lieutenant John A. Carroll, Lieutenant Martin W. Joyce, Father James E. Dunford, Lieutenant Edward J. Gully. Gully was in the 1921 First Training Troop. Father Dunford was first State Police Chaplain. Lieutenant Carroll in early 1933 modeled the proposed French and electric blue uniform for Governor Joseph B. Ely. Captain Charles T. Beaupre was the principal advocate of the new, two-tone blue breeches and blouses.

JOHN BEY CAPTURE, NORTHAMPTON, SEPTEMBER 1935

From left: Sergeant Francis J. O'Connell, Patrolman Walter A. Burke, Bey, Patrolmen Francis S. Regan and D. Francis Murphy. Bey died in prison in the early 1970s, convicted of the murder of a Connecticut law enforcement officer. Patrolman George E. Grady and a Connecticut trooper took Bey at gunpoint in a Northampton milk shed.

TROOP C, LUNENBURG BARRACKS, 1935

From left: Corporal George A. Pollard, Patrolmen Augustine L. Murphy, Stephen S. Wersoski, Edward E. Kukkula, Leonard J. King, Thomas P. Norton, Arthur H. Bruno, Arnold W. Olsson. Olsson in 1942 topped the statewide examination for state police detective lieutenant, a test taken by more than 1,000 state and municipal police officers.

BOSTON ATHLETIC ASSOCIATION MARATHON, HOPKINTON, APRIL 19, 1936

From left: Patrolman Charles J. Collins, Donat A. LaCasse, Carl H. Thomas, Sumner D. Matthes, Lieutenant John F. McLaughlin. Collins died in a tragic gunfight in Byfield in May 1942.

PISTOL TEAM, 1936

From left: Corporal Wilfred Sirois, Patrolman Hollis E. Beattie, Theodore W. Johnson, Commissioner Paul G. Kirk, Lieutenant James E. Hughes, Sergeant Joseph C. Crescio, Patrolman George E. Grady. Kirk convinced Governor James Michael Curley of the need to move State Police Headquarters from the basement of the State Capitol to Commonwealth Pier in South Boston.

TROOP A, ANDOVER, 1937

From left: Patrolmen William Blustine, Bernard D. Horan, Carl H. "Old Soldier" Thomas, James F. Moran, George C. Edwards, Robert J. Mitchell. Note heavy leather gauntlets, essential equipment when motorcycles were heavily used throughout the year.

GENERAL HEADQUARTERS, COMMONWEALTH PIER, 1937

Corporal Wilfred Sirois with Commissioner Paul G. Kirk. Kirk in December 1937 was appointed to the Superior Court Bench, served as a colonel in World War II, was elevated in 1960 to the Supreme Judicial Court by Governor Foster Furcolo. Sirois for two decades was one of the best shots in New England.

TROOP D, REHOBOTH, 1938

From left: Corporal John W. Collins, Patrolmen Theodore J. Shimkus, Michael F. Treacy, Joseph P. Hannon, Arthur H. Bruno. Rehoboth was phased out in early 1971. The original barracks in that area was on Milford Road in Swansea.

Recruit Frank P. Sweeney gets shot from Dr. Donald Currier. Next in line, Edward F. Brosnahan. The 1938 recruit class was assigned guard duty in devastated Buzzard's Bay shore communities in the aftermath of the 1938 hurricane.

TRAINING ACADEMY, FRAMINGHAM, 1938

From left: John F. Lally, Walter F. Bowen (in front), Peter A. McCauley (behind Bowen), William J. Sienkiewicz, Joseph P. McEnaney, Joseph M. Lane, Stephen S. Wersoski, Francis D. Egan. The 28th Recruit Troop lost some of its tents and equipment to the Great New England Hurricane of 1938.

OCTOBER 1938, TRAINING ACADEMY, FRAMINGHAM

From left: William R. Boakes, Winston J. Lawrence, John H. Buckley. "K.P." was rotated among the squads within the training troop. For many, the experience came in handy during World War II service.

TROOP D, NORWELL, 1938

From left: Joseph M. Lynch, James F. Dailey, Marshall T. Burpee, Corporal Henry W. Eliason, Donald L. Hornby, Herbert Hamilton, James V. Grant, Albert E. Goslin. Grant saw lengthy service throughout Troop D, later was commanding officer at Norwell, completed his career as a captain at D Troop Headquarters in Middleboro. He and Goslin were members of the 1934 "Golden Class" that trained at West Bridgewater.

"Never...was so much owed by so many to so few."

Sir Winston Churchill

AUTUMN 1940

From left: William J. Mack, Sergeant Thomas E. Burke, Sergeant James P. Ryan, John Powers, Wendell L. Willkie, Republican nominee for U.S. Presidency, Martin J. Daley, Lieutenant George H. Thompson, Albert E. Goslin, Norman A. Peltier, Harold J. Peloquin. Willkie failed to stop Franklin D. Roosevelt's bid for a third term in the White House.

GENERAL HEADQUARTERS, COMMONWEALTH PIER, SOUTH BOSTON, 1940

From left: Theodore W. Johnson, Richard Tonis, Wilfred Sirois, Oliver F. Nichols, Lieutenant James E. Hughes, Hollis E. Beattie, George E. Grady. Headquarters was moved to 1010 Commonwealth Avenue, Boston, shortly after the outbreak of World War II.

TROOP B, NORTHAMPTON, 1940
Cruiser colors were patterned on the French and electric blue uniforms first used in 1933.

PITTSFIELD BARRACKS, 1941
William J. Sienkiewicz on left, with Charles R. Boakes. Boakes by 1941 was a 16 year veteran, having enlisted in 1925. Sienkiewicz and his classmates in the 1938 training troop did patrol duty in the aftermath of the Great New England Hurricane just days after reporting to Framingham.

PITTSFIELD BAR-RACKS, 1941
From left: Kenneth T. Brown, John E. McGrail, James P. Ashe, Timothy F. Moran, Francis F. Griffith. Following World War II service, Moran became captain and public relations officer in the early 1960s.

PISTOL TEAM, 1941
From left: Theodore J. Stavredes, Walter C. O'Brien, Julian Zuk, Lieutenant James E. Hughes, Alfred J. Sanders, Commissioner Eugene M. McSweeney, Theodore H. Stronach, Hollis E. Beattie, Martin J. Daley, Wilfred Sirois, George F. Alexander, Donat A. LaCasse. "Sam" Beattie enlisted in 1926, served almost three decades, helped organize a modern state police mounted unit in the 1970s.

TROOP B, HEADQUARTERS, NORTHAMPTON, 1942

Patrolman Francis D. O'Keefe. A member of the 1938 recruit troop, O'Keefe served many years in Troop C, Worcester County, was noted for a fine singing voice as well as his law enforcement accomplishments.

TRAINING ACADEMY, FRAMINGHAM, FEBRUARY 1942

From left: Harold Ellis, Wendell LaFreniere, Edward Nolan, James J. Stavredes, Thomas P. Costello, Francis J. McCarthy, Peter Yankunas, Walter H. Hobbs and Robert F. Tabaroni. There were 10 others appointed to this, the 30th Recruit Troop. Because of World War II's disruptions, they actually did not receive their training academy diplomas until 1948!

MYOPIA HUNT CLUB, HAMILTON, WINTER 1943

From left: Gardner F. Bayley, Francis W. Hennigan, John Powers, Augustine L. Murphy, Corporal Michael J. Shea, Sergeant John A. Maturo, Lieutenant Williamm T. Armstrong, Captain and executive officer William V. Shimkus, John C. Blake, Alfred J. Sanders, Frank W. Geist, Charles J. McCarthy, Escort detail for United Nations Building Committee. Bayley in 1938 began long civilian service, became radio maintenance supervisor, served until 1971, received the State Police Medal for Meritorious Service.

TROOP D, HEADQUARTERS AT BRIDGEWATER, 1940'S

This was the operations center, part of the Corrections Department's sprawling "State Farm." Uniformed personnel slept in the nearby "Villa."

TROOP B, FLOODS, HADLEY, 1936

From left: Charles J. Collins, Donat A. LaCasse, Burton D. Hunt. Collins and Hunt were members of the 1934 recruit troop that trained in West Bridgewater.

TROOP B, HEADQUARTERS, NORTHAMPTON, JANUARY 1944

From left: Lieutenant Michael J. Noonan, Sergeants Edward J. Majesky, George F. Alexander, Theodore H. Stronach and George H. Carter. Lieutenant was the troop commander's rank until 1951.

SALISBURY BEACH, SUMMER 1946

From left, front: Patrolman Daniel F. Driscoll, John C. Blake, Julian Zuk. Rear: George F. Houghton, Carl M. Larson, Walter D. LaShoto. Blake was in charge. Houghton and LaShoto were "ETSPO's." Note heavy winter uniforms.

PATROLMAN BYRON E. BLAKE, TROOP A, FRAMINGHAM, 1947

Blake was sworn following World War II as an Emergency Temporary State Police Officer (ETSPO), trained with the second 1947 recruit class, completed his service in Troop D, Middleboro, as a commissioned officer in the late 1960s.

TRAINING ACADEMY, FRAMINGHAM, 1947

From left: Lieutenant Francis J. O'Connell, Lieutenant George F. Alexander, Captain William V. Shimkus, Lieutenant Michael J. Noonan, Sergeant John F. Barnicle, Lieutenant Timothy L. Flynn. Tents were replaced by Quonset Huts in 1949.

Patrolmen Harold W. Brewster, left, and Paul F. Kane, Troop C Holden, 1949. Brewster and Kane were cited for outstanding law enforcement work in Troop C in the late 40s.

TRAINING ACADEMY, FRAMINGHAM, AUTUMN 1949

Patrolman Joseph M. Lynch and Recruit John N. Shea. Lynch in 1957 became the first troop commander on the Massachusetts Turnpike, organized round-the-clock coverage, helped to develop new high speed pursuit tactics.

DECEMBER 7, 1949, GRADUATION OF THE 35TH RECRUIT TROOP

From left: Recruit Walter R. White Jr., Lieutenant Arthur T. O'Leary, Commissioner John F. Stokes, Lieutenant Michael J. Noonan (seated). Patrolman Walter F. Bowen. The December 1949 recruit class was the first to be issued the then newly designed shoulder insignia. It is still in use.

CAPTAIN AND EXECUTIVE OFFICER JOHN P. SULLIVAN CONGRATULATES MEMBERS OF DECEMBER 1949 RECRUIT TROOP

From left: Martin A. Murphy, Walter R. White, Thomas Hibbert, John N. Shea, Lawrence J. Thompson, Joseph A. Ryan. Behind Captain Sullivan is academy staffer Walter F. Bowen. Immediately to Bowen's left is Leo J. Carney. Next to Carney is Daniel Furtado, later to die in a motorcycle accident in West Boylston in October, 1950.

ACADEMY STAFF, 1949

From left: Lieutenant Arthur T. O'Leary, Patrolmen Walter F. Bowen and Joseph M. Lynch, Sergeant John C. Blake. Later, Blake became the first to hold the rank of lieutenant colonel and executive officer.

DECEMBER 7, 1949, MEMBERS OF 35TH RECRUIT TROOP ABOUT TO TAKE OATH OF OFFICE

From left, front row: Joseph R. Herbst, Edward F. Shea, Winthrop E. Doty Jr., William F. Ready Jr., Daniel F. Sullivan, Walter R. White Jr., Cornelius J. Duggan, Richard C. Spofford. Doty retired as a lieutenant colonel in the Spring of 1978. He was the last to leave the uniformed branch of the several hundred who enlisted in the years immediately following World War II.

TROOP C, HEADQUARTERS, HOLDEN, 1949

From left: N. Allen, D. Callahan, M. Flaherty, J. Martin, J. Sidney, D. O'Keefe, A. Bergeron, W. LaShoto, W. Powers, H. Brewster, Lieutenant James P. Ryan, P. Kane, K. Meade, not identified, A. Rizzo, T. Shimkus, G. Cederlund, E. Doukszewicz, L. Hodgeney, G. Lubin, R. Ackerman. The photograph was actually taken in August 1950, but is representative of a troop headquarters' uniformed/civilian staffing as the 1940s closed.

FRAMINGHAM, DECEMBER 1949

From left: Lieutenant Timothy L. Flynn, Lieutenant James P. Ryan, Captain John P. Sullivan, Lieutenant George E. Grady, Commissioner John F. Stokes, Lieutenant Arthur T. O'Leary, Lieutenant Michael J. Noonan, Lieutenant Francis J. O'Connell. Double gold braid on uniform blouse signified the lieutenant's rank until troop commanders were elevated to the captain's rank in March 1951.

STATE POLICE ACADEMY, 1949

From left: motorcycle shack, mess hall (rear), staff quarters (front with chimney), recruit quarters, classroom. These buildings replaced tents in 1949. They were used until the September 1969 groundbreaking for the Framingham academy. During that construction, the 1970 recruit class trained at a military installation in Sudbury. The new academy was dedicated on May 29, 1971. It is now State Police General Headquarters.

"There is nothing more difficult to take in hand, more perilous to conduct, or more uncertain in its success, than to take the lead in the introduction of a new order of things."

Nicolo Machiavelli

**GOVERNOR PAUL A. DEVER AND
COMMISSIONER DANIEL I. MURPHY
STATE CAPITOL, BOSTON, JULY 20, 1950**

Murphy's 1934 enlistment in the uniformed force was followed by service in the detective branch during the 1940s. Leaving the commissioner's post in 1953, he served as captain of state police detectives until his June 1971 retirement.

GENERAL HEADQUARTERS, BOSTON, 1951

From left: Major George F. Alexander, Commissioner Daniel I. Murphy, Captain Timothy L. Flynn. Alexander in 1951 was first to hold the major's rank as executive officer; Flynn was the first to hold the captain's rank as adjutant.

WIANNO, CAPE COD, JULY 26, 1951

From left: Captain John W. Collins, Sergeant John J. Kelly, Patrolmen William J. Harvey, Robert H. Rammel, John D. Butler, John F. Downey and Henry D. Gates. Patrolman Charles W. Eager was also on this detail, an assignment for the New England Governor's Conference hosted by Massachusetts Governor Paul A. Dever.

STATE HOUSE BOSTON, WASHINGTON'S BIRTHDAY, 1952

From left, front: Captain Arthur T. O'Leary, Major George F. Alexander, Commissioner Daniel I. Murphy, Captain and adjutant Timothy L. Flynn. Rear: Captains John W. Collins, Michael J. Noonan, Edward L. McGinley and George E. Grady. Flynn succeeded Alexander as executive officer. McGinley later held that post.

TRAINING ACADEMY, AUTUMN 1952

From left: Patrolman William J. Owen, Lieutenant James A. Cretecos, Patrolman Raymond T. Alzapiedi. Cretecos later commanded Troop D, Middleboro.

TROOP D, HEADQUARTERS, BRIDGEWATER, 1953

From left: T/Sergeant John D. Sadler, Patrolmen Francis Abbate, Robert F. Tabaroni, Henry C. Cordery and Lieutenant Charles F. Furze. Sadler later commanded the general headquarters photography bureau. Furze in 1953 had completed 25 years of service.

TROOP D, BRIDGEWATER, 1953

Patrolman Charles M. Harrington with Bloodhound pups. Harrington trained the famous trackers when a kennel was constructed at the Rehoboth Barracks in the early 1950s. He commanded Troop D in early 1970s.

TROOP A, ANDOVER, 1953

"Sadie" with part of her litter of 11 sired by "Lieutenant Sid." Bloodhounds did yeoman work in all of the famous manhunts and searches involving the state force.

NORMAN S. SIDNEY, EARLY 1950'S

Sidney enlisted in the uniformed branch in 1928, commanded Troop D, Bridgewater, in the early 1950s, helped plan the opening of the new Middleboro Barracks in 1956. He closed almost three decades of service as captain and division inspector in the late 1950s.

SENIOR LEADERSHIP, GENERAL HEADQUARTERS, BOSTON, 1952

From left: Theodore H. Stronach, Michael J. Noonan, John C. Blake, John A. Maturo, Edward L. McGinley, Commissioner Daniel I. Murphy, Major Timothy L. Flynn, Arthur T. O'Leary, John W. Collins, Robert L. Ferrari. Flynn was retiring. McGinley succeeded him as major and executive officer. Ferrari earlier commanded Troop D, Bridgewater; he was the son of Detective Captain Joseph L. Ferrari of "Stokes and Ferrari" fame.

ACADEMY STAFF, SPRING 1952

From left: Corporal William R. Finch, Sergeant (Sen. Grade) Joseph M. Lynch, Captain John C. Blake, Lieutenant Thomas P. Davy, Sergeant James A. Cretecos, Corporal Stanley W. Jackson. Lieutenant Davy, assigned to General Headquarters, long presented specialized traffic subjects at the academy.

GOVERNOR'S OFFICE, STATE CAPITOL, 1954

From left: Walter C. O'Brien, Captain Theodore H. Stronach, Julian Zuk, Hollis E. "Sam" Beattie (behind governor). Governor Christian A. Herter, Richard A. Sherburne, Donald L. Bowles, Commissioner Otis M. Whitney, William J. Owen (behind Whitney), Captain John C. Blake. The Pistol Team yearly won honors throughout New England. Zuk closed his career in 1964 as lieutenant colonel and executive officer.

TROOP D, HEADQUARTERS, MIDDLEBORO, 1956

From left: Troopers Joseph P. Pastuch, Henry D. Gates and John D. Mahoney, Staff Sergeant Thomas P. Costello, Troopers Samuel M. Range and Donald D. Callahan. Range was the first black to serve in the uniformed branch. Pastuch and Gates were classmates in 1948's Thirty-Fourth Recruit Troop. Each served until the end of the 1960s.

AUGUST 1954, GENERAL HEADQUARTERS, BOSTON

From left: Commissioner Otis M. Whitney, Martin P. Luthy, Vice President, Lumbermens Mutual Casualty Company, Trooper Arthur G. Fralin, Major Edward L. McGinley. Fralin had won a fellowship for a year's study at the Traffic Institute, Northwestern University, Evanston, Illinois. Luthy made presentation on behalf of Lumbermens, sponsor of the $1,650 educational stipend. Lieutenant Edward J. Gully of the 1921 First Recruit Troop was the first to attend Northwestern, graduating from the famed school in 1938. Many uniformed personnel have attended since Fralin's selection.

TROOP A, FRAMINGHAM, OCTOBER 1955

From left: Edward T. Aucoin, Thomas J. Leccese, Edward G. Byron, Robert D. Murgia, Stanley W. Wisnioski, Walter S. Matowitz. This detail was leaving for Miami, FL, to participate in the American Legion parade, Motorcycles and equipment were transported in trucks. Murgia in February 1967 became lieutenant colonel and executive officer.

SAINT PATRICK'S DAY PARADE, SOUTH BOSTON, MARCH 17, 1957

From left, front: Commissioner Otis M. Whitney, Captain James A. Cretecos, Chaplain James E. Dunford, T/ Sergeant William J. Owen. Second row, from left: Troopers John F. Kennedy, George A. Kimball, Joseph H. White and Robert J. Russo. The marching unit annually added color to the South Boston festivities.

ACADEMY STAFF, APRIL 1958

From left: Sergeant Robert E. Herzog, T/Sergeant Robert F. Lynch, Lieutenant William J. Owen, Sergeant Martin A. Murphy. Murphy later became captain and chief of state police detectives. Herzog commanded Troop F, Logan International Airport in late 1960s and early 1970s.

SUMMER 1957, SALISBURY BEACH

"The Beach" was a Troop A summer season substation. From left, front: Trooper Charles W. Gilligan, Sergeant Robert D. Murgia, Corporal Peter J. Murphy. Rear, from left: Troopers Robert J. Birmingham, Dominic J. Arena, Donald H. MacDonald. Gilligan later commanded the training academy, played a key role in street protests in the early 1970s, commanded state police units during the Boston school crises, retired as a lieutenant colonel in 1976.

SUMMER 1958, FRAMINGHAM

From left: Special Officers Grayce O'Dell, Alice Bragdon and Mary T. Connolly with T/Sergeant William J. Owen. State Policewomen Mary B. Ramsdell and Lotta H. Caldwell in 1930 were the nation's first. Mary P. Kirkpatrick in 1954 became the first commissioned officer in the country. Gloria Kennedy's Spring 1978 retirement closed almost five decades of service by state policewomen. Women are now enlisted as troopers with regular field assignments.

FRAMINGHAM–ACADEMY, 1958

From left: Captains Francis T. Halloran, Frederick F. Sullivan, Cyril P. McQueen, John J. Kelly, William F. Leary, Lieutenant John F. Sadler, Captain William T. Knightly, Chaplain James E. Dunford, Captains Carl M. Larson and William J. Mack. With the exception of Larson and Sadler, members of the 1941 training class, all had enlisted in the 1930s and were nearing completion of their careers.

COYLE BROTHERS: SEARCH COMMAND POST, JUNE 1959

From left: Troopers Basil B. Walsh and Robert J. Cummings, Lieutenant William J. Owen, Captain Robert F. Bourbeau, Trooper James P. Dunne. Owen's academy staff spearheaded round-the-clock action at the field command post throughout the celebrated manhunt.

CAPTURE OF JOHN COYLE, MIDDLEBORO, JUNE 1959

From left: Trooper Donald H. Gould, Trooper Paul V. Conway, Coyle, Sergeant Martin A. Murphy, Trooper John J. White (behind Sgt. Murphy), Trooper John J. Powers Jr., Trooper Leonard F. VonFlatern (behind Powers). John and William Coyle, fugitives from their Philadelphia murder of a police officer who surprised them stealing a bottle of milk, held out for three days and nights in Middleboro's swamps. The younger Coyle, William, was killed by state police bullets in a violent exchange of gunfire. VonFlatern, in Spring 1979, was captain and troop commander of Troop B, Northampton.

TROOP D, HEADQUARTERS, MIDDLEBORO, 1956

Trooper George B. Hacking on left, with Trooper Earle N. Logan. The new headquarters building on Route 28 in Middleboro opened early that year. Hacking enlisted in 1949, retired in mid-1970s as a major.

PRESS CONFERENCE: COYLE BROTHERS MANHUNT, JUNE 1959

From left: Colonel John C. Blake, Commissioner J. Henri Goguen, Sergeant Martin A. Murphy, Trooper Paul E. Keating, Trooper Edmund J. Souza (behind Keating), Captain Joseph P. McEnaney, Trooper Paul V. Conway, Trooper William E. Warner. McEnaney and his public information staff handled superbly one of the state force's most spectacular enforcement actions. Warner later became police chief in Middleboro.

WALPOLE STATE PRISON RIOT, SPRING 1959

Leading assault team, from right: Trooper John N. Shea, Corporal George E. Wall, Trooper Robert C. Woodward, Trooper Robert N. Harlow. Riots at Walpole and Concord, and the Coyle Brothers Manhunt, made the early months of 1959 a violent springtime. Woodward in 1979, two decades after Walpole, was a major posted at General Headquarters, Boston.

COMMONWEALTH ARMORY, BOSTON, OCTOBER 7, 1960

The 43rd Recruit Troop stepping out in traditional "Pass In Review." In front with colors, Trooper Walter L. Drewniak Jr. First row, from left: Troopers John T. Riordan, William E. Balcom, Richard D. Lewis and Richard H. O'Shea Jr. On right: Academy instructor Eugene H. Dzikiewicz. Dzikiewicz was instrumental in development of the 1966 promotional system enacted by the legislature, became an instructor at Northwestern University's famed Traffic Institute, joined the U.S. Department of Justice in the early 1970s.

NOVEMBER 1960, HYANNIS, CAPE COD

President-elect John F. Kennedy with state police escort. From top, clockwise: T/Sergeant George A. Luciano, Trooper Karl W. Hupfer, Trooper Donald D. Callahan, Trooper Richard N. Loynd, Sergeant Raymond M. McGuire. Walking with President-elect Kennedy, Lt. Colonel John C. Blake and Trooper John L. Grinham. These were hectic, heady days for the state force as the Hyannis area overnight became the focus of the frenetic activities which surround the presidency.

BELOW, PRESIDENT JOHN F. KENNEDY AND DETECTIVE LIEUTENANT JOHN F. DEMPSEY, HYANNIS AIRPORT, 1961

Dempsey had been stationed on Cape Cod since the late 1920s, was close to the entire Kennedy family, became a legend in his own right prior to his 1972 retirement.

GENERAL HEADQUARTERS BOSTON, MAY 1961

From left, Sergeant Charles W. Gilligan, Colonel Lem D. Gladding USA, Lieutenant Stanley W. Wisnioski, Trooper Eugene H. Dzikiewicz. Colonel Gladding accepted an expression of appreciation for the military's assistance to the uniformed branch, especially to Wisnioski's academy staff.

ANNUAL MEMORIAL SERVICE, FRAMINGHAM, MAY 1961

From left: Lt. Colonel John C. Blake, Commissioner J. Henri Goguen, Chaplain James E. Dunford, Major Carl M. Larson. The granite memorial was donated by the Former State Troopers Association.

STATE CAPITOL BOSTON, OCTOBER 1961

Governor John A. Volpe signs proclamation memorializing the 40th anniversary of the uniformed branch. From left: Lieutenant George A. Luciano, Commissioner Frank S. Giles, Trooper Richard N. Loynd, Major John J. Kelly, Former Governor Channing H. Cox, Lt. Colonel Carl M. Larson, Trooper William J. Stewart. Governor Cox on May 27, 1921, had signed the legislation that created the "State Police Patrol."

NOVEMBER 1961, SHERATON PLAZA HOTEL, BOSTON

The occasion was a 40th anniversary banquet celebrating the 1921 founding of the uniformed branch, the "State Police Patrol." From left: Former Commissioners Daniel I. Murphy, Daniel A. Needham and Alfred E. Foote, Former Governor Channing H. Cox who, on May 27, 1921, signed the authorizing legislation, Governor John A. Volpe, Commissioner Frank S. Giles, Former Commissioners Paul G. Kirk, John F. Stokes and Otis M. Whitney.

STATE CAPITOL, JANUARY 1962

State Policewoman Sally H. Raynes takes oath from Deputy Secretary of State Edward Sullivan. Gloria T. Kennedy enlisted with Raynes, served until May 5, 1978. Her separation closed an era begun in 1930 with Mary S. Ramsdell and Lotta H. Caldwell, the nation's first state policewomen.

FAR RIGHT, MEMORIAL SERVICES FRAMINGHAM, MAY 1963

Lieutenant William J. Owen escorts Governor Endicott Peabody. Trooper William M. Cloran is behind the governor, Trooper Francis E. Boutiette on right. The Commonwealth's governors long have attended the uniformed branch's recruit graduations and annual memorial service held on the academy grounds.

STATE CAPITOL, BOSTON, HALL OF FLAGS, FEBRUARY 22, 1962

From left, first row: Captain Joseph M. Lane, Captain Thomas D. Murphy, Captain Julian Zuk, Major John J. Kelly, Commissioner Frank S. Giles, Mrs. John A. Volpe, Governor Volpe, Lieutenant Colonel Carl M. Larson, Captain William F. Leary, Captain Francis T. Burke, Captain William F. Grady.

From left, second row: Lieutenant Joseph P. O'Neill, Lieutenant William J. Sienkiewicz, Lieutenant Melville R. Anderson, Lieutenant George A. Luciano, Lieutenant Byron E. Blake, Lieutenant John R. Moriarty, Lieutenant Harold Ellis, Lieutenant Robert D. Murgia, Sergeant William H. Forbush, T/Sergeant Raymond T. Alzapiedi.

NORTHBORO, JUNE 1963

Troper Harvey W. Trefrey with Corporal Eugene H. Dzikiewicz. Trefrey and Dzikiewicz joined a score of other troopers in the June 12-13 Slocum-Manley manhunt which ended with the fugitives' capture.

STATE CAPITOL, BOSTON, 1963

From left: Lieutenant Edward J. Teahan, Governor Endicott Peabody, Trooper Walter L. Drewniak Jr., Sergeant Edwin F. Kelley. Teahan later was first commander of Troop F, Logan International Airport, retired as lieutenant colonel in mid-1970s.

STATE CAPITOL, HALL OF FLAGS, FEBRUARY 22, 1964

First Row, from left: Lieutenant William F. Powers, Lieutenant Stanley W. Wisnioski, Sergeant Edwin F. Kelley, Lieutenant Edward J. Teahan, Lt. Colonel Julian Zuk, Governor Endicott Peabody, Lieutenant Governor Francis X. Bellotti, Dep. Commissioner Clayton L. Havey, Major Thomas D. Murphy, Captain Robert D. Murgia, Lieutenant Arthur W. O'Leary, Lieutenant James P. Herrick, Sergeant Robert J. Cummings.

Second row, from left: Lieutenant Byron E. Blake, Captain Francis T. Burke (behind Kelley), Lieutenant Melville R. Anderson, Lieutenant John M. Keeley, Lieutenant Edward M. Prendergast, Trooper Leonard F. VonFlatern, Sergeant Henry W. Bienkowski, Sergeant William F. Gross, Sergeant Raymond W. Kret.

STATE CAPITOL, HALL OF FLAGS, FEBRUARY 22, 1964

GOVERNOR'S OFFICE, STATE CAPITOL, BOSTON, APRIL 1964

Governor Endicott Peabody administers oath to Commissioner of Public Safety Robert W. MacDonald. MacDonald had served as an assistant district attorney, and earlier had run for the U.S. Congress.

BOSTON, APRIL 1965

Planning committee for centennial anniversary of the 1865 founding of the State Constabulary. From left, seated: Captain Melville R. Anderson, Captain Peter Zuk, Commissioner Richard R. Caples, Captain George F. Houghton, Captain Harold Ellis. From left, standing: Captain Michael E. Faherty, Lt. Colonel Thomas D. Murphy, Detective Captain Daniel I. Murphy, Captain Francis T. Burke, Captain Edward J. Teahan.

CENTENNIAL BANQUET, BOSTON SHERATON HOTEL, OCTOBER 31, 1965

From left: Commissioner Leo L. Laughlin, Lieutenant William F. Powers, Sergeant Edward R. MacCormack, Trooper Thomas L. Byrne. Seated at right, J. Gordon "Buck" MacKinnon. At podium, Mary S. Ramsdell, in 1930 the first state policewoman in the country. MacKinnon for years spearheaded public state police functions.

274

AUGUST 11, 1965, STATE POLICE NIGHT AT FENWAY PARK

From left: Trooper Thomas R. Mulloney, Sergeant Joseph H. White, Red Sox Announcer Curt Gowdy, Commissioner Richard R. Caples. Corporal Lawrence J. Thompson and Trooper Mario E. Indorato are directly behind Caples. The Red Sox held "State Police Night" in conjunction with the 100th anniversary of the State Constabulary's 1865 founding.

CENTENNIAL BANQUET, BOSTON SHERATON HOTEL, OCTOBER 31, 1965

From left: Commissioner Leo L. Laughlin, Detective Lieutenant John F. Dempsey, J. Gordon "Buck" MacKinnon, Trooper Kenneth J. Carew (behind MacKinnon). Dempsey enlisted in the State Police Patrol in 1923, was honored that night with William J. Puzzo who had joined the state force in 1922.

FRAMINGHAM, SEPTEMBER 10, 1966

Trooper Francis J. McVey Jr., receives badge from his dad, Francis J. McVey Sr. Looking on, from left: Merrill W. Wright, Frank "Dutch" Holland (behind McVey Jr.) Lieutenant Governor Elliot L. Richardson, Commissioner Leo L. Laughlin, Lt. Colonel Thomas D. Murphy. McVey Sr., "Specky" to hundreds of troopers, served over four decades as a "mess boy," cook and chief cook, received in 1971 the State Police Medal for Meritorious Service.

STATE CAPITOL, HALL OF FLAGS, FEBRUARY 22, 1967

From left, front row: Staff Captain Francis T. Burke, Captain Edward J. Teahan, Major Robert D. Murgia, Mrs. John A. Volpe, Governor John A. Volpe, Commissioner Leo L. Laughlin, Captain of Detectives Daniel I. Murphy, Detective Lt. Edward B. Kelley, Captain Arthur W. O'Leary.
From left, second row: Captain William F. Powers, Captain Arthur G. Fralin, Captain Stanley W. Wisnioski Jr. (behind Teahan), Captain Melville R. Anderson, Captain John M. Keeley, Captain Raymond T. Alzapeidi, Lieutenant Raymond W. Kret, Captain John R. Moriarty, Captain Edward F. Murphy, Detective Lt. John D. Butler, Senior Explosives Technician Joseph Sainato, Detective Lt. James F. DeFuria, Detective Lt. John J. Carney.

FRAMINGHAM, NOVEMBER 1, 1967

Nancy Ellen Kennedy admires her dad's new sergeant badge. Sergeant John F. Kennedy that day was one of 124 officers promoted. The promotions resulted from examinations held in May 1967, the first conducted under the landmark promotional statute which became effective in March 1966. Kennedy later commanded the academy, held the major's rank in 1979, went on to Federal service.

ARLINGTON NATIONAL CEMETERY, WASHINGTON, D.C.

Captain James L. Wilt of the Fairfax County Virginia Police Department pays respects at President John F. Kennedy's Eternal Flame. The memorial wreaths from the Massachusetts State Police and the Barnstable Police are placed each year at the Kennedy grave on May 29, the President's birthday anniversary. The poignant ceremony was begun by Detective Lieutenant John F. Dempsey and Barnstable Chief Albert L. Hinckley, and continues years after the Dallas tragedy.

STATE CAPITOL BOSTON, JANUARY 1969

Captain George A. Luciano bids farewell to Governor John A. Volpe. Volpe in 1966 had won the state's first four year term as governor, was leaving to accept appointment in the U.S. Cabinet as Secretary of the Department of Transportation.

NORWOOD AIRPORT, OCTOBER 1969, NEW STATE POLICE HELICOPTER

From left: Trooper Bruce V.M. Whittier, Trooper George R. Shea, Trooper Thomas J. Flaherty, Governor Francis W. Sargent, Commissioner William F. Powers. Behind Whittier, Trooper Edward R. Ardini, Captain Stanley W. Wisnioski, Captain John F. Downey. The Bell Jet Ranger established the Air Wing. Corporal Donald C. Cody and Trooper Clement G. Tourigny later joined the Wing. Captain Charles W. Eager teamed with Director James Stratford of the Governor's Office for Highway Safety in getting federal funding for the helicopter. Commissioner Leo L. Laughlin had pushed for the chopper, a 1966 recommendation in the Massachusetts Taxpayers Foundation report in the state force.

FRAMINGHAM, SEPTEMBER 26, 1969

Ground breaking for new State Police Academy. From left: Staff Captain Francis T. Burke, David E. and Irving P. Rocheford, General Contractors, Deputy Public Safety Commissioner Walter P. Parker, Commissioner William F. Powers, Walter J. Poitrast, Director of the State Bureau of Building Construction, Lieutenant Colonel Robert D. Murgia, Major John R. Moriarty. The modern academy complex cost just over three million to construct, was dedicated May 29, 1971. In 1994 it was converted to General Headquarters.

*"God gives all men all earth to love,
But, since our hearts are small,
Ordained for each one spot should prove
Beloved over all."*

Rudyard Kipling

DECEMBER 1969, HARRISBURG, PENNSYLVANIA

From left: Captain Charles W. Eager, James E. Ellis, Lieutenant Sidney C. Deyo, Pennsylvania State Police, Lieutenant John F. Duignan, Pennsylvania State Police, Deputy Commissioner Walter P. Parker, Detective Lieutenant Martin A. Murphy, George K. Campbell. Parker, Eager, Murphy, Ellis and Campbell were visiting the Pennsylvania State Police research and development unit. Later, this leadership cadre spearheaded the planning effort that resulted in historical changes in the barracks system and enforcement procedures in the early 1970s.

TROOP B, NORTHAMPTON, MAY 1970

From left: Corporal Albert C. Alben, Captain Americo J. Sousa, Trooper John H. Driscoll, Corporal Edward H. Jurczyk. Sousa in 1974 became the first lieutenant colonel and executive officer to post his son to his first barracks assignment. Trooper Stephen J. Sousa graduated from the academy in October of that year with the 58th Recruit Troop.

SEPTEMBER 1970, GOVERNOR'S OFFICE, STATE CAPITOL

From left: Trooper Kevin W. Peabody, Commissioner William F. Powers, House Speaker David M. Bartley, James V. Oteri, Richard J. Powers, G. William Dunderdale, Major John R. Moriarty, Dep. Commissioner Walter P. Parker, Senate Minority Leader John F. Parker, Trooper John W. Giardino. Governor Francis W. Sargent seated at desk. Sargent signed legislation which phased out the barracks system, reducing the duty week from 84 to 40 hours. Oteri was president; Powers, vice-president; and Dunerdale, secretary, of the State Police Association of Massachusetts (SPAM). SPAM played a key role in the pasage of the historic legislation.

SEPTEMBER 1970, GENERAL HEADQUARTERS, BOSTON

From left: Commissioner William F. Powers, Trooper Robert A. Long, Turnpike Chairman John T. Driscoll, Boston Police Commissioner Edmund L. McNamara, Major Melville R. Anderson, Sergeant Thomas H. Peterson. Peterson and Long had just received the State Police Medal of Honor for their capture of William M. "Lefty" Gilday. Gilday, Robert Valeri, Stanley Bond, Susan E. Saxe and Katherine Power had gunned down Boston Patrolman Walter A. Schroeder in a September 23 holdup of a Boston bank.

REHOBOTH BARRACKS, ROUTE 44

Between Taunton, MA, and Providence, RI, Rehoboth was a Troop D substation for four decades, was phased out in 1971.

APRIL 1970, STATE POLICE ACADEMY, SUDBURY

From left: Staff instructors, Troopers Robert E. Hunt, Dennis Donoghue, Robert E. Dunn. One recruit class, the 54th Troop, trained at Sudbury while the new Framingham academy was being constructed. Hunt was captain and troop commander of Troop A, Framingham.

FALL 1971, GENERAL HEADQUARTERS, BOSTON

Detective Captain Martin A. Murphy receives badge from Commissioner John F. Kehoe Jr. Murphy enlisted in the uniformed branch in 1949, was on the academy staff for several years, became a detective lieutenant inspector, was captain and chief of state police detectives until his 1974 retirement.

AUGUST 31, 1971, STATE CAPITOL, BOSTON

From left: Commissioner William F. Powers, Governor Francis W. Sargent, Commissioner John F. Kehoe Jr., Secretary Richard E. McLaughlin. Kehoe was sworn in that day, succeeding Powers in the commissioner's office. Governor Sargent in July had named McLaughlin to the public safety cabinet secretariat.

ACADEMY STAFF, FRAMINGHAM, SEPTEMBER 18, 1971, GRADUATION OF THE 55TH RECRUIT TROOP

From left: Troopers L.P. Fay, R.J. Walsh, R.E. Hiller, J.B. Sorbera, Corporal R.E. Hunt, S/Sergeant R.J. Fitzgerald, Captain C.W. Gilligan, S/Sergeant J.V. Oteri, Troopers W.F. Grant, J.W. Gilman, R.E. Dunn. Gilligan played key roles in the urban confrontations, prison unrest and Boston school desegregation duties of the early 1970s. He retired as a lieutenant colonel in 1976.

MAY 16, 1972, TROOP B, NORTHAMPTON

From left: Herbert M. Spafford Jr., Burton G. Perch, Rodney Wallace, William D. Garvey, Noel E. Henault, Ralph R. Nasuti, Winthrop E. Doty Jr., Leonard F. VanFlatern Jr., John D. Ashe, Walter M. Sullivan, Ralph Olszewski. The occasion was Nasuti's retirement from the uniformed branch. Doty retired in the Spring of 1978 as a lieutenant colonel, the last officer separated from the state force of the several hundred who enlisted in the decade of the 1940s.

SOUTH BOSTON HIGH SCHOOL, 1975

From left: Major Charles W. Gilligan, S/Sergeant Arthur Jowett, Lieutenant Thomas E. Carr. The State Police involvement in the Boston School crisis is recounted in this chapter. It was the most extended, complex, sensitive assignment in the state force's history.

DECEMBER 28, 1974, STATE CAPITOL, BOSTON

From left: Commissioner John F. Kehoe Jr., Governor Francis W. Sargent, Colonel Americo J. Sousa, Major Stanley W. Wisnioski Jr., Major Frank J. Trabucco, Major George B. Hacking. Sousa that day became colonel and deputy superintendent, the first to hold that new post. Wisnioski and Hacking were classmates in 1949's Thirty-Fifth Recruit Troop. Trabucco in the Spring of 1979 was himself serving as colonel and deputy superintendent. Sargent left office the next month after six years as the state's chief executive.

SOUTH BOSTON HIGH SCHOOL 1975

From left: Major Charles W. Gilligan, Lieutenant Harold J. Reddish, Captain Bohdan W. Boluch (behind Reddish), Lieutenant Robert C. Woodward (behind Boluch), Staff Sergeant Walter J. Kane Jr. Reddish made a presentation to the women who manned the cafeteria. State police personnel received cordial treatment from school personnel throughout the long stay in the capital city during the early 1970s.

MAY 19, 1975, GENERAL HEADQUARTERS, BOSTON

From left: Colonel Americo J. Sousa, Lieutenant Colonel John R. O'Donovan Jr., Major John F. Regan Jr., Commissioner John F. Kehoe Jr. O'Donovan that day was promoted to the new rank of lieutenant colonel, commanding the Office of Investigation and Intelligence Operations (formerly the detective branch of the Division of State Police). Major Regan was named second-in-command, supervising the Bureau of Investigative

DECEMBER 1975, SPECIAL TACTICAL OPERATIONS TEAM (STOP)

Front, from left: Troopers J.B. Sorbera, J.W. Ursini, G.P. Stevens, Captain R.E. Hunt. Rear, from left: Troopers S.M. Petrie, F.G. Bohenberger, J.E. Machado, S/Sergeant J.A. Stone, Trooper R.J. Spirlet, Helicopter Pilot Corporal D.C. Cody, Troopers N.S. Ostiguy and P.D. Rembiszewski, Lieutenant R.E. Dunn, Trooper B.J. Mullen. Hunt organized the STOP team in 1972, trained the first members, saw it develop into a skilled, cohesive tactical unit.

OCTOBER 1976, STATE POLICE STRIDERS

From left: Daniel J. Donovan, Alfred Puller, Bruce A. Malenfant, Kenneth R. Blanchard, Natale L. Lapriore, Donald E. Shea, Nelson T. Brace, William J. Coulter, Dennis B. Moschella, Bruce A. Jillson, James G. Redfern, John F. Good, Robert E. Dunn, Dunn's sons Brian and Bobby, Redfern's son Michael. This was the first big race for the Striders, the 5.5 mile test sponsored by the Quincy-Morrisette Legion Post. Donovan organized the Striders, has seen it grow to 120 members. The team has aided a number of charities.

TROOPER ROGER L. CALDERWOOD

A member of 1975's Fifty-Ninth Training Troop. This photograph has won much acclaim. It was taken by Don Finn, staff photographer for Trooper, *the publication of the State Police Association of Massachusetts. A number of other photos in these pages were used courtesy of Mr. Finn.*

JUNE 21, 1977, GOVERNOR'S OFFICE, STATE CAPITOL, BOSTON

From left: Lieutenant Colonel Thomas R. Mulloney, Colonel Frank J. Trabucco, Representative Paul J. Cavanaugh, Major George H. Hall, Major John A. Neilson, Major Robert R. Wills, Secretary Charles V. Barry, Commissioner John F. Kehoe Jr. Governor Michael S. Dukakis officiated at the promotional ceremony for the veteran officers. Dukakis and Cavanaugh spearheaded legislation in 1965 establishing the uniformed branch's competitive promotional system.

JULY 8, 1978, FRAMINGHAM

Academy Staff Instructor Donald F. Woodson on right, readies Recruit Trooper Robert J. Maziarz for graduation ceremonies of the 60th Recruit Troop. Maziarz was one of the 84 officers sworn that day, following completion of the rugged 20 week recruit training program.

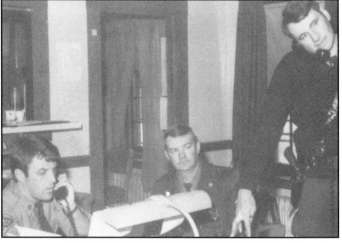

FEBRUARY 1978, FRAMINGHAM

Round-the-clock duty during the "Great Blizzard of '78." From left: Trooper Gerard D. Britt, Sergeant Gerald F. Tully, Trooper William E. Gorman. It was the week "the state stood still." The state force spearheaded emergency public safety measures. Uniformed personnel reached hundreds stranded in their cars by the killer blizzard.

JULY 8, 1978, FRAMINGHAM

Trooper Donald E. Shea receives the State Police Medal for Meritorious Service from Lieutenant Colonel James T. Canty. Trooper Shea was killed in December of that year in a tragic cruiser accident on Route 9 in Natick. The young trooper was driving at high speed to an accident scene, swerved suddenly to save the life of a pedestrian running across Route 9. The heroic action resulted in his untimely death.

JULY 8, 1978, FRAMINGHAM, GRADUATION OF THE 60TH RECRUIT TROOP

On left, Trooper S. Muto the honor graduate receives the William V. Shimkus memorial trophy from Staff Sergeant Michael J. Shimkus. Looking on, from left: Major John F. Kennedy, Albina H. (Shimkus) Sochin, Detective Lieutenant (Ret.) Daniel A. Shimkus. William V. Shimkus enlisted in 1923, served as captain and executive officer from 1942 until 1947. Muto, in 1997, was director of curriculum development at the State Police Academy in New Braintree.

JULY 1978, TROOPER KATHLEEN M. COLETTA

Trooper Coletta graduated from the academy on July 8, 1978, with the 60th Recruit Troop. She was the third woman to complete academy requirements, following Lorraine R. Roy and Joan M. Farrell who enlisted in 1975, and the first female academy instructor.

SEPTEMBER 1978, STATE CAPITOL, BOSTON

Commissioner Dennis M. Condon takes oath of office from Governor Michael S. Dukakis. Behind governor, James F. Condon, next to him, Dennis M. Condon Jr. and Condon Jr.'s wife, Joyce. Behind the commissioner, Senate President William Bulger. Condon thus became the fifteenth commissioner since the December 1, 1919, founding of the Department of Public Safety.

JULY 8, 1978, FRAMINGHAM, INSPECTION OF 60TH RECRUIT TROOP

Reviewing party, from left: Sergeant Frank E. McGovern, Commissioner John F. Kehoe Jr. (behind McGovern), Major John F. Kennedy, Colonel Frank J. Trabucco (behind Kennedy). On extreme right, from right to left: Recruits (they had not yet been sworn) Ronald G. Godin, John C. Henley, Brian X. Lilly, Paul E. Fletcher, Kevin M. Horton, Edmund V. Burke, Richard P. Belanger, Michael P. Skerry, Thomas M. Walsh. Staff instructor in front of recruits is Trooper Daniel J. Donovan.

NOVEMBER 1978, RANDOLPH

From left: Lieutenant Colonel James T. Canty, Lieutenant Colonel John R. O'Donovan Jr., Deputy Commissioner Fred I. Lamson, Former Commissioner John F. Kehoe Jr., Colonel Frank J. Trabucco, Lieutenant Colonel Robert R. Wills. The occasion was Kehoe's testimonial banquet, capping seven years in the commissioner's post, and 37 years in law enforcement.

TRAINING ACADEMY, FRAMINGHAM 1978

Staff Sergeant James J. Martin. Martin enlisted with 1959's Forty-Second Recruit Troop. His father, James J. Martin, joined the uniformed branch 25 years earlier, training in West Bridgewater with 1934's "Golden Class." The Martin family commissioned the James J. Martin memorial award, presented at each recruit graduation for special achievement. Martin, in the Spring of 1979, was commanding officer of the Sturbridge barracks.

THANKSGIVING DAY, 1956, TROOP D, REHOBOTH

From left: Trooper Paul F. O'Brien, Mrs. Florence Rogers, Trooper George A. Luciano, Corporal Edward F. Murphy. Close examination of Mrs. Roger's table gives some hint of the amount and quality of food served during the era of the "live in" barracks system. Murphy in the late 1960s was captain and commanding officer of Troop D, covering all of southeastern Massachusetts, Martha's Vineyard and Nantucket.

JULY 1978, ACADEMY STAFF, FRAMINGHAM

From left: Troopers, Alexander J. Exarhopoulos, John W. Nulty, Francis R. Ardita, Donald A. Cucinelli, John E. Murphy, Corporal Thomas J. McNulty, Major John F. Kennedy, Sergeant Frank E. McGovern, Troopers Alan H. Thompson, Donald F. Woodson, Daniel J. Donovan, Gerald Venezia, John DiFava. Trooper James G. Redfern was also a member of the 1978 academy staff that trained the 60th Recruit Troop.

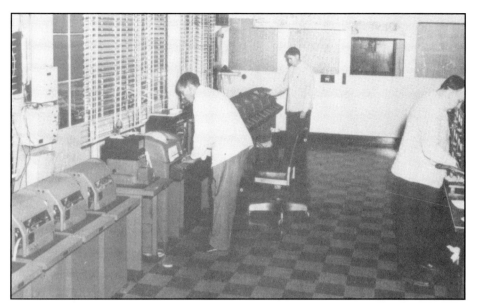

GENERAL HEADQUARTERS 1954, TELETYPE OPERATIONS

From left: Communications Dispatchers Chester L. Arnold, William F. Fitzgerald, Joseph L. Gilooly. This was the command and control center for statewide enforcement operations from the early 1940s until the Spring of 1970. The Law Enforcement Agencies Processing System (LEAPS), a computer based system in 1970, replaced the teletype or "TT" system that performed so well during that generation of communications' technology.

TROOP D, SOUTH YARMOUTH, LATE 1950'S

From left: Captain James V. Grant, Commissioner Otis M. Whitney, Mrs. Ann S. Chapman. The occasion was an appreciation dinner for Mrs. Chapman, a great favorite of the uniformed personnel who were stationed at South Yarmouth during her long years of service at the Cape Cod enforcement installation.

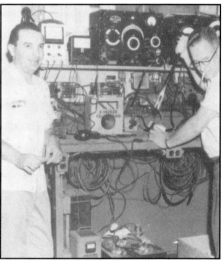

SUMMER 1957, TROOP A, FRAMINGHAM

Raymond J. Sestini on left, with Gardner F. Bayley. Bayley in the late 30s began as a radioman, supervised the critical support function for many years prior to his retirement in the early 1970s. Sestini began in 1955, was now in charge of radio operations in the state's largest enforcement troop.

SPRING 1964, GENERAL HEAD-QUARTERS, BOSTON

From left: Helen Knag, Mary A. Langford, Grace P. Dyett, Trooper Francis R. Long, T/Sergeant William J. Hansbury, Sergeant James F. Cummings, Victoria Lerardi, Trooper William M. Cloran (behind Cloran) Sergeant Edward R. MacCormack and Trooper Kenneth J. Carew. The occasion was Hansbury's retirement from the uniformed branch. He had first enlisted in 1942, saw World War II service, returned to uniform at the end of the world conflict.

SEPTEMBER 1966, TROOP B, HEADQUARTERS, NORTHAMPTON

Captain Melville R. Anderson on left, with Harold S. Craig. Craig began Troop B service in 1925, ensured professional administrative services for over 50 years for a score of B Troop commanders like Captain Anderson. "Roy" Anderson in 1971 completed 25 years in the uniformed branch, retiring at the major's rank.

APRIL 1960, GENERAL HEADQUARTERS, BOSTON

Mary A. (Fischer) Watkins with Major Arthur T. O'Leary. Mrs. Watkins was one among scores of civilian specialists who have provided essential support services to the uniformed state force throughout its 60 year history.

TROOP D, MIDDLEBORO, 1970

Mrs. Nellie C. Grimshaw began as a cook in December 1942. She served countless numbers of personnel at the old troop headquarters on Bridgewater's "State Farm," completed her career on the day the barracks system phased out, April 30, 1971. Mrs. Grimshaw and her colleagues kept the uniformed branch going with home style meals for almost five decades.

OCTOBER 27, 1967, WESTFIELD

From left: Harold S. Craig, Troop B Radio Supervisor Thomas E. Murphy, Troop B. Truck Driver John W. McNeish. Murphy was killed in a cruiser accident in July 1977, following three decades of service in the state force. McNeish began service in 1942, died in 1977 after retirement. The occasion for the photo was the retirement party for long time B Trooper Richard A. Gosselin. Craig's extraordinary career, spanning over 50 years, is recounted in several places in this volume.

OCTOBER 1975, BOSTON

Chester E. Wright on left, with Senior Identification Operator Joseph E. Crowley. Wright joined the Department of Safety on June 20, 1927. He served in key administrative posts for almost five decades, capping his long career as executive assistant to the commissioner of public safety. The occasion was Wright's October 31, 1975, retirement from the department.

OCTOBER 1953, FRAMINGHAM

Father James E. Dunford with Commissioner Otis M. Whitney. Father Dunford appears to have been the first official State Police Chaplain. He was close to the state force for over three decades, befriended hundreds of troopers during their trying days as academy recruits in Framingham.

MAY 1963, MEMORIAL SERVICE, FRAMINGHAM

State Police Chaplain, Father John E. Hartigan. Behind Father Hartigan, Lieutenant James Evangelos with members of the State Police Auxiliary, composed of former members of the uniformed branch.

GENERAL HEADQUARTERS, AUGUST 31, 1971

From left, seated: Louise L. Garrity, Commissioner William F. Powers, Ann M. McDermott. Raymond J. Lord standing left, with Sergeant John F. Kennedy. Louise Garrity and Ann McDermott have provided top flight administrative support for several occupants of the commissioner's office. Lord was the department's legislative liaison for many years prior to his early 1970s death. Kennedy completed more than 23 years service in May 1979, rising to the major's rank.

MAY 1974, FRAMINGHAM, ANNUAL MEMORIAL SERVICE

From left: Sergeant Martin E. Fay, Commissioner John F. Kehoe Jr., Former Commissioner William F. Powers, Chaplain John E. Hartigan, Chaplain Frank J. Bauer. Father Hartigan and Reverend Bauer have ensured a strong Chaplaincy for the state force since the early 1960s. Their unique understanding of the strains imposed upon the individual officer in an era seemingly dominated by impersonal forces provided an essential strength for the enforcement organization.

STATE POLICE ACADEMY, FRAMINGHAM, APRIL 1979

From left: Chaplain Frank J. Bauer, Captain George R. Dolan, academy commandant, Chaplain John E. Hartigan. Father James E. Dunford in the 1950s first wore the state police chaplain's uniform. Reverend Bauer and Father Hartigan wore the French and electric blue for appropriate public functions of the uniformed branch.

APRIL 1979, FRAMINGHAM

From left: Chaplain John E. Hartigan, Chaplain Frank J. Bauer, Trooper John W. Nulty (standing), Trooper Alan H. Thompson. Father Hartigan and Reverend Bauer handled countless duties for the uniformed branch, provided counseling services for personnel, each authors a column in the Trooper, *the monthly newspaper of the State Police Association of Massachusetts.*

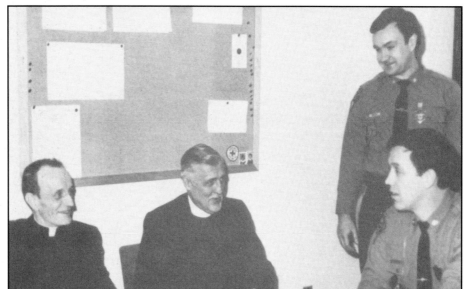

TROOP D, MIDDLEBORO, 1956, LIEUTENANT ALFRED J. SANDERS

Sanders in the early 1950s was elected to the executive committee of the Massachusetts State Employees Association (MSEA). His tenure in that post represents an essential link in the historical development of 1979's State Police Association in Massachusetts. Sanders graduated with 1936's Twenty-Seventh Recruit Troop, died in California in the mid-60s.

JULY 1957, BOSTON

From left, front: T/Sergeant Timothy F. Moran, Commissioner Otis M. Whitney, Sergeant James J. Foley. From left, rear: Trooper Noel E. Henault, Trooper Raymond F. DePaola, Sergeant John D. Butler, Corporal Joseph J. Cooney, Corporal James F. Cummings. Foley was the elected state police member of the executive board of the Massachusetts State Employees Association. The other men comprised the troop representatives committee of the uniformed branch. Whitney met with them to develop policy and legislative initiative.

SENATE CHAMBERS, STATE CAPITOL, BOSTON, SEPTEMBER 25, 1969

From left: Thomas R. Mulloney, Commissioner William F. Powers, Governor Francis W. Sargent, James V. Oteri. Mulloney was Treasurer of the State Police Association of Massachusetts (SPAM), Oteri was SPAM's first president. Sargent, a year later, signed one of the most comprehensive legislative programs in the state force's history. Oteri in the mid-1970s retired as a major, Mulloney as a lieutenant colonel.

MAY 14, 1974, GENERAL HEADQUARTERS, BOSTON

Signing of the first negotiated contract between the department's administration and the State Police Association of Massachusetts (SPAM). From left, seated: SPAM President Richard L. Whelan, Commissioner John F. Kehoe Jr. From left, standing: Attorney Robert L. Wise, Trooper William J. Brooks, Trooper David W. Moran, Trooper Richard E. Downey. The 1974 contract did not cover salary. Following protracted, difficult negotiations, such a pact was consummated in December, 1978.

STATE CAPITOL, HALL OF FLAGS, JANUARY 1979

Governor Edward J. King greets Frederick T. Guerriero Jr., president of the State Police Association of Massachusetts. Trooper Michael C. Mucci in center, Public Safety Secretary George A. Luciano on right.

FEBRUARY 1979, HUDSON

Trooper Robert E. Benoit on left, squares off with Trooper Albert M. Toney Jr. Benoit is founder and captain of the state police boxing team. The team presents boxing shows throughout the state. This bout and several others, held in Hudson's National Guard Armory, raised $1,000 for the local boy scout troop.

MARCH 20, 1977, SAINT PATRICK'S DAY PARADE, LAWRENCE

From left: Trooper Gale P. Stevens, Lieutenant Richard B. Olson, Sergeant John W. Gilman, Sergeant Eugene J. Kelley. Horses backboned the field troops from 1921 until 1933. A ceremonial unit was organized for a time in 1971. The mounted cadre trained under the practiced eye of Hollis E. "Sam" Beattie of the 1926 Training Troop, and a long time member of that era's championship trick riding teams.

READING BARRACKS, 1928

From left, front: Ernest J. Ryan, Corporal Joseph G. Crowley, Howard C. "Slim" Reed. From left, rear: Edward J. Canavan, Timothy J. Mahoney, Hollis E. "Sam" Beattie. Reading was an A Troop, substation during the 20s. The forest green uniforms were phased out in June 1933. Earlier, shirts had been white with red/ties.

TOPSFIELD BARRACKS, 1935

From left: John C. Blake Jr., Robert F. Bourbeau, John J. Carney. The Topsfield substation was "Nangels House" until the barracks was constructed. Blake, Bourbeau and Carney were classmates in 1934's Twenty-Sixth Recruit Troop.

JUNE 1977, ROUTE 27, SHARON

From left: Lieutenant Philip J. Reilly, Trooper Alfred Puller (behind Reilly), Troopers Kenneth R. Blanchard and Joseph C. Crowley. Members of the State Police Striders, these men were running a leg on a 163 mile relay from Provincetown to Framingham.

GENERAL ALFRED E. FOOTE

Foote on December 1, 1919, was the first commissioner of public safety. He co-chaired the commission in 1920 that recommended the uniformed branch, and in 1921 was the first commanding officer of the State Police Patrol and served until 1933.

COMMISSIONER PAUL G. KIRK

Kirk was commissioner from 1934 until 1937. Governor Charles F. Hurley in December of 1937 appointed him to the Superior Court Bench. In 1960 he was elevated to the Supreme Judicial Court by Governor Foster Furcolo. Justice Kirk served on the Commonwealth's highest court until Decemer 31, 1970. In 1979 he was residing on Cape Cod, still in occasional contact with the state force he led almost 50 years ago.

B TROOP, FLOODS, HADLEY, 1936

From left: Troopers John J. Carney, Donat A. LaCasse, Burton D. Hunt, and Charles J. Collins. Carney, Hunt and Collins in 1934 trained in West Bridgewater with the "Golden" Class. Carney in 1949 joined the detective branch, and completed over four decades of service in the late 1970s. Collins died in a tragic 1942 shooting in Byfield.

WESTFIELD, SEPTEMBER 1937

Pistol Team: From left: George E. Grady, Joseph C. Crescio, Lieutenant James E. Hughes, Wilfred Sirois, Theodore W. Johnson. They were all expert shots, and, while members of the uniformed branch, occasionally wore their "Sunday best" to a pistol competition.

MARSHFIELD FAIR, SUMMER 1946

From left: James A. Cretecos, James McGarry, Robert Loker, James V. Grant, Joseph J. Regan. Fair details were a primary duty of the uniformed branch from its 1921 founding. Troopers would be assigned from throughout the state, live at the closest barracks, work the "fair week" straight through without time off. Regan was a World War II "ETSPO." Many personnel were first enlisted as "ETSPOs."

TRAINING ACADEMY, SUMMER 1953

From left: Sergeant Hollis E. "Sam" Beattie, Recruits Edward A. Haraden, Robert J. Birmingham, John F. Regan Jr., James E. Halloran Jr. In 1979 Haraden was chief of police in Wenham. Regan and Halloran later held the major's rank.

GENERAL HEADQUARTERS, BOSTON

Photography Bureau, 1950. From left: Sergeant Arthur W. O'Leary, Sergeant Daniel F. Driscoll Jr., Sergeant Joseph P. McEnaney. O'Leary later commanded the photography bureau as a captain. Driscoll rose to captain and commanding officer of the Bureau of Criminal Information. McEnaney as a lieutenant and captain was long time head of state police public relations bureau.

HYANNIS, NOVEMBER 9, 1960

President-elect John F. Kennedy leaves National Guard Armory after making victory statement, escorted by Lieutenant Colonel John C. Blake. Trooper Karl W. Hupfer in background. A state police detail was posted at the "Kennedy Compound" in Hyannisport throughout the 1,000 days of the Kennedy Presidency.

GENERAL HEADQUARTERS, BOSTON, AUGUST 1956

From left: Arthur J. Austin, Lumbermens Mutual Casualty Co., Commissioner Otis M. Whitney, Trooper William F. Powers, Martin P. Luthy, Lumbermens' Vice President, Henry F. Myers, Assistant to Mr. Luthy, Captain and Adjutant Arthur T. O'Leary. Powers received Kemper Foundation Fellowship for year's study at Northwestern University, Evanstown, IL. Myers trained with 1936's Twenty-Seventh Recruit Troop, served with State Police auxiliary after leaving state force, is a member of Former Massachusetts State Troopers.

**TROOP B, NORTHAMPTON, WIN-
TER 1962**

*Trooper Robert O. Heck with Bloodhounds King
(sitting) and Princess. Heck enlisted in 1957, was a
leading proponent of the value of Bloodhounds in
law enforcement work.*

**TROOP B, NORTHAMPTON,
FEBRUARY, 1963**

*Trooper Robert I. Heck with Bloodhounds, from left:
Tracie 18 months, Princess 10 years. King and
Princess were from the same litter, in 1954 were the
original B Troop Bloodhounds. Tracie was from a
litter sired by King.*

**COMMONWEALTH ARMORY,
BOSTON, 1968**

*Academy Staff. From left: Sergeant James V. Oteri,
Sergeant Frederick A. Henley, Staff Sergeant William
H. Irving Jr., Trooper John P. Tobin, Captain
William J. Owen, Staff Sergeant Robert J. Fitzgerald,
Corporal Thomas R. Mulloney, Trooper Robert E.
Hunt.*

**SEPTEMBER 1970,
STATE CAPITOL, BOSTON**

*From left: Governor Francis W. Sargent, Commis-
sioner William F. Powers, Major Edward P. Tonelli,
Major Francis T. Burke, Major Melville R. Anderson.
Tonelli, Burke and Anderson were promoted to major
as the result of legislation signed by Governor
Sargent on the day the photograph was taken. John J.
Hyde, not present for the picture taking, was also
promoted to major that day.*

ACADEMY, FRAMINGHAM, SEPTEMBER 1971

From left: Trooper William J. Grant, Commissioner John F. Kehoe Jr., Major John R. Moriarty, Honor Graduate John F. Murphy. Murphy represented his classmates in the 55th Recruit Troop.

GENERAL HEADQUARTERS, BOSTON, JUNE 1972

From left: Lieutenant Colonel Robert D. Murgia, Detective Captain Martin A. Murphy, Lieutenant Detective John F. Dempsey, Commissioner John F. Kehoe Jr., Major John M. Keeley. Dempsey in 1923 enlisted in the State Police Patrol, joined the detective branch in the 1930s, was receiving the State Police Medal for Meritorious Service upon completion of five decades in the state force. Keeley enlisted in 1947, supervised the early 1970s transition to computer based communications, retired with the major's rank in 1973.

TROOP A, FRAMINGHAM, 1978

Trooper Robert F. Monahan and "Schultz." The K9 corps was quartered at A-H, provided a wide variety of law enforcement services.

LOGAN INTERNATIONAL AIRPORT, TROOP F, MID-1970'S

Staff Sergeant Armand J. Longval Jr. "Sam" Longval graduated from the academy with the 36th Recruit Troop in February 1952, served more than two decades throughout Troop A Framingham, brought long field experience to Troop F's expanding duties in the 1970s.

SOUTH BOSTON, OCTOBER 1974

Commissioner John F. Kehoe Jr. with Trooper G. William Dunderdale. State police personnel like Dunderdale, during the long school crisis, added an exemplary chapter on public service to the annals of the nation's first statewide law enforcement organization.

SOUTH BOSTON, OCTOBER 10, 1974
Lieutenant Colonel Americo J. Sousa on left, with Commissioner John F. Kehoe Jr. The Boston school busing crisis of the early 1970s was one of the most difficult, emotionally charged assignments in the history of the uniformed force.

TROOP F, LOGAN INTERNATIONAL AIRPORT, 1978
Trooper Norman G. Baron. State police duties include patrol of the airport, all port facilities, the Tobin Bridge and Hanscomb Field in Bedford. Logan was formerly an A Troop substation, became Troop F in early 1960s. Baron trained with 1966's Forty-Seventh Recruit Troop.

"SWAT" - 1970'S
Team members Frederick G. Bohnenberger and Raymond J. Spirlet. The SWAT operation provides the state force with a key technical capability in responding to barricaded fugitives. The photograph is courtesy of Don Finn of the Trooper *newspaper.*

STATE CAPITOL, BOSTON, SEPTEMBER 1978
Commissioner Dennis M. Condon on left, with Colonel Frank J. Trabucco. Condon was sworn by Governor Michael S. Dukakis as the 15th commissioner since the 1921 founding of the uniformed branch of the State Police. Trabucco was only the second officer, following Colonel Americo J. Sousa, to hold the newly created position of deputy superintendent of the State Police.

CLINTON, MARCH 17, 1977
From left: Troopers Mathew A. Palermo, Joseph A. Barber, David W. Moran, Robert T. Tocchio, Corporal Richard C. Whelan, Trooper James C. Lane. The occasion was President Jimmy Carter's "Town Meeting" in Clinton. The presidential limousine is in background. Whalen was president of the State Police Association of Massachusetts (SPAM), the state force's official bargaining unit.

GENERAL HEADQUARTERS, BOSTON, 1978

From left: Colonel Frank J. Trabucco, Commissioner John F. Kehoe Jr., Trooper Robert E. Benoit, Trooper Frederick T. Guerriero Jr. Benoit accepted citation for having organized and captained the state police boxing team in conjunction with the State Police Association of Massachusetts (SPAM). Guerriero was SPAMs president. The boxing team has raised substantial sums for a variety of charitable causes.

SPRING 1979, TROOPER JAMES C. LANE

Lane was editor of Trooper, *the monthly newspaper published by the State Police Association of Massachusetts.* Trooper *was developing as an influential communications vehicle for state police personnel, their families, and a growing number of readers throughout the state and beyond.*

STATE POLICE ACADEMY, FRAMINGHAM, DECEMBER 7, 1949.

Left to right, Troopers John Cooney, Joseph Ryan, Donald Walsh, and Winthrop Doty. Members of 1949's 35th Recruit Troop, they had just been sworn as state police officers. Doty in 1978 retired as a lieutenant colonel, the last of several hundred World War II veterans who trained at Framingham during the years immediately following the global conflict. The wall in the background is that of a "Quonset Hut," a WWII innovation that housed academy recruits from 1949 until the May 29, 1971 dedication of a modern training and educational complex.

Note To Third Printing

General Headquarters, Framingham, September 9, 1998, Publication Program. L to R: Former state police commissioners Frank J. Trabucco, Dennis M. Condon, John F. Kehoe, Jr., state police superintendent Colonel Reed V. Hillman, former commissioner William F. Powers, former deputy commissioner Edward F. Kelly. Attending the September 9 Publication Program of Enforcement Odyssey, this group represented the nineteen administrators honored with the top state police leadership post since the 1921 founding of the uniformed state force.

Odyssey's publication program on September 9, 1998, was held at General Headquarters in Framingham. No one present imagined that the book's first two printings would be exhausted in little more than a year. That, however, is exactly what has happened. *Odyssey's* enthusiastic reception is a tribute to all those who made a commitment to preserving the historical journey of the Massachusetts State Police.

Odyssey's colors and tones, its physical beauty, for years will enhance living room coffee tables. Turner Publishing's skilled artisans deserve much credit for a beautifully crafted volume. Their professional commitment has ensured the continuity of the department's historical mosaic.

With this new printing, the story of a fascinating enforcement odyssey breaches the Third Millenium. Current and future personnel will wisely consider Santayana's enduring reminder to "...welcome the Future, remembering that soon it will be the Past; and to respect the Past, knowing that once it was all that was humanly possible."

W.F.P.
Leesburg, Virginia
January, 2000

(Left) General headquarters, Framingham, September 9, 1998, Publication Program. L to R: William F. Powers, Colonel Reed V. Hillman, Richard J. Barry. The author and Former Trooper's President Barry presented Superintendent Hillman with the first volume of Enforcement Odyssey. (Right) General Headquarters, Framingham, September 9, 1998, Publication Program. L to R: Richard J. Barry, President, Former Troopers Association, Keith Steele, Turner Publishing, James J. Foley, Secretary, Former Troopers Association. The Former Troopers Association presented its outstanding public service award to Turner Publishing for the company's professional skills and commitment in producing Enforcement Odyssey.

Index

73rd Recruit Training T

Massachusetts State Police Academy. (All left to right.) Row 1: Tpr. J. Drawec, Tpr. W. McElhiney, Sgt. P. Damery, Sgt. R. Waskiewicz, Lt. T. McGilvray, Lt. Col. G. Anderson, Col. R. Hillman, Maj. B. Hibbard, Capt. D. Jamroz, Lt. R. Gosselin, Sgt. R. Brown, Sgt. K. Kelly, Tpr. J. Hackett. Row 2: (standing) Tpr. M. Domnarski, (seated) T T. McGhee, T R. Zucco, T P. McDougall, T L. Cambria, T P. Johnson, T R. Muto, T C. Gilmore, T J. Paulo, T J. Tzitzon, T C. Coggins, T R. D'Auteuil, T. R. Bannister, (standing) T D. Losardo. Row 3: M. Wong, B. Berkel, L. Lavelle, A. Lopilato, D. Crowther, M. Shananhan, L. Mogan, G. Pitts, S. Newman, M. Storrs, R. Routhier, D. Gallant, P. Breault, J. Clement, N. White, T. Ahern, L. Gillis, L. Hayes, J. Lugas, J. Slattery. (Note: Row 3 begins in staggered formation. Standing behind T M. Domnarski and to the right of M. Wong are J. Masterson, D. Parsons.) Row 4: (holding guidon) R. Johnson, C. Tanguay, P. Copponi, J. Toto, S.